Martin F. Feist
501 S. 11th St.
Bismarck, N. Dak.
58501

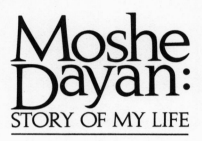

Moshe Dayan:
STORY OF MY LIFE

By MOSHE DAYAN

MOSHE DAYAN: STORY OF MY LIFE
DIARY OF THE SINAI CAMPAIGN

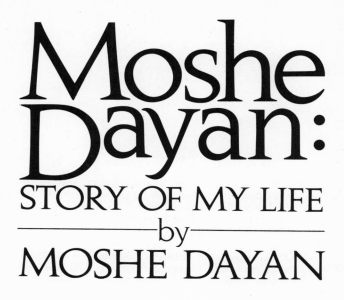

Moshe Dayan:
STORY OF MY LIFE
by
MOSHE DAYAN

WILLIAM MORROW AND COMPANY, INC.
NEW YORK   1976

Portions of Chapter 15, "The Sinai Campaign," previously
appeared in *Diary of the Sinai Campaign*, copyright © 1965
by Moshe Dayan. Copyright © 1966 in the English translation by George Weidenfeld & Nicolson Ltd., by permission
of Harper & Row, publishers.

Grateful acknowledgment is hereby made to *The Washington Post* for permission to reprint reports from Vietnam by
Moshe Dayan which originally appeared in that newspaper,
copyright © 1966 by *The Washington Post*.

The letter from Winston Churchill to General Eisenhower
on pages 450–451 is reproduced by kind permission of C
and T Publications Limited and Mr. Winston Churchill, MP.

Printed in the United States of America.

1   2   3   4   5   6   7   8   9   10

Library of Congress Cataloging in Publication Data

Dayan, Moshe, 1915-
    Moshe Dayan: story of my life.

    Includes index.
    1. Dayan, Moshe, 1915-   2. Israel—History,
Military.
DS126.6.D3A35   956.94′05′0924   [B]   76-18144
ISBN 0-688-03076-9

BOOK DESIGN   CARL WEISS

CONTENTS

LIST OF MAPS

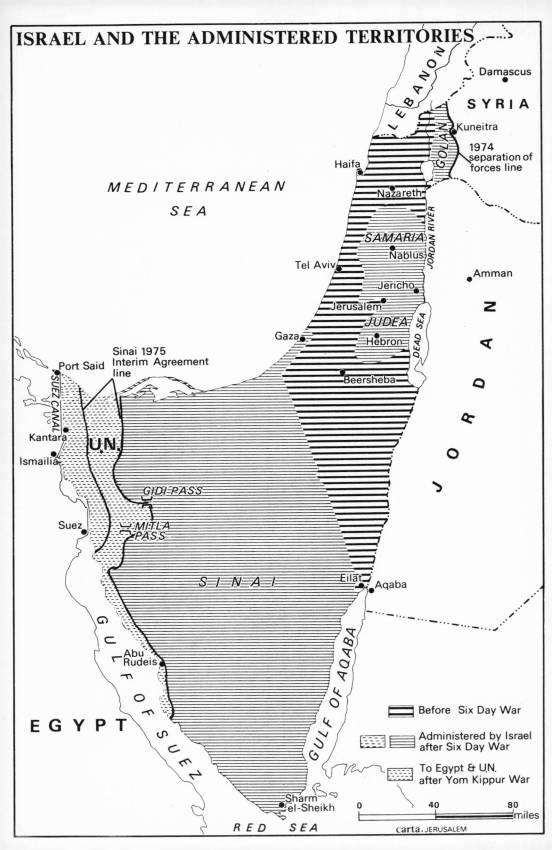

ISRAEL AND THE ADMINISTERED TERRITORIES

SYRIA

Damascus

LEBANON

Kuneitra

1974
separation of
forces line

GOLAN

Haifa

MEDITERRANEAN
SEA

Nazareth

SAMARIA

JORDAN RIVER

Nablus

Tel Aviv

Amman

Jericho

Jerusalem

JUDEA

DEAD SEA

Gaza

Hebron

JORDAN

Sinai 1975
Interim Agreement
line

Beersheba

Port Said

SUEZ CANAL

Kantara

U.N.

Ismailia

GIDI PASS

Suez

MITLA
PASS

SINAI

Eilat

Aqaba

Abu
Rudeis

GULF OF SUEZ

GULF OF AQABA

EGYPT

Before Six Day War

Administered by Israel
after Six Day War

To Egypt & U.N.
after Yom Kippur War

Sharm
el-Sheikh

0   40   80

miles

RED SEA

carta. JERUSALEM

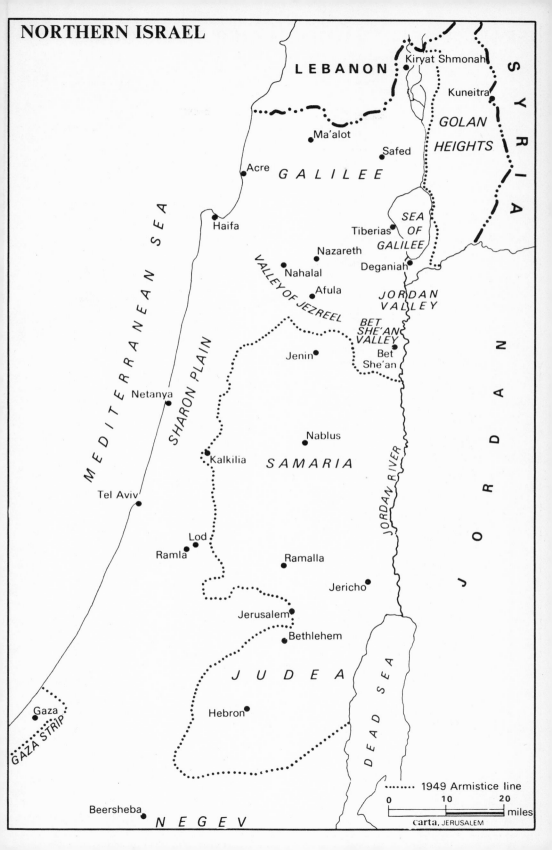

PROLOGUE

IT WAS NOONTIME Tuesday, the second day of the Six Day War. Twenty-four hours earlier Jordanian artillery had pounded the Jewish areas of Jerusalem. Motta Gur's paratroop brigade had gone into action after midnight and following bitter battles throughout the hours of darkness had captured the Arab Legion fortifications on the northern outskirts of the Old City. Uri Ben-Ari had just signaled that his mechanized brigade had captured French Hill. Thus, the road to Mount Scopus was almost open, and Scopus, which had been an Israeli enclave in hostile Jordanian territory for nineteen years, was about to be linked to the Jewish half of Jerusalem. I decided to go there.

My helicopter landed outside the Jerusalem Convention Hall, where Uzi Narkiss had established his Central Command forward headquarters. He said that fighting was still going on and we had not yet linked up with Mount Scopus. But I did not care to wait, and I pressed Uzi to start moving. He led me over to the vehicle park and stopped at a closed armored half-track. Fortunately the driver was unable to start the engine, so we set off in an open command car and jeep. With me were Chief of Operations Ezer Weizman and his deputy Gandi, and my military secretary, Yehoshua

Raviv. Uzi drove and I sat next to him—a familiar pattern, for that is how we had driven from E-Tor on the Suez Gulf to Sharm el-Sheikh some ten years earlier, during the Sinai Campaign. Then, too, the road had not yet been cleared of the enemy.

We proceeded to the Pagi Quarter—the jump-off point for the paratroopers during the night—and from there, along a track which had been cleared of mines, up to the Police Training School below Ammunition Hill. The buildings were shattered and still smoking, but it was possible to get through. We stopped for a few minutes at the newly captured Ambassador Hotel to look around, particularly at the wadi which lies between Jerusalem and Scopus. We saw no Arabs. The civilians had shut themselves in their houses. They had apparently learned the lessons of 1948 and this time did not flee. I saw no reason to wait, and we pushed on to Scopus. On the way up the slope, we spotted occasional clusters of Arab Legion troops on the adjoining hills. They were no doubt survivors of the night's grim battles, and now they stood surprised and hesitant, not knowing what to do with themselves—or, fortunately, to us.

At the entrance gate to the Mount Scopus zone, we met the first Israeli soldiers from this outpost, and they seemed even more surprised than the Arab Legionaries had been. I asked to be taken to the observation post, and the commander, Menahem Sharfman, a Galilean from Yavniel and an old friend, took us to the roof of the National Library building. This was part of the original Hebrew University campus, and access to this center of higher learning, and to the adjoining Hadassah Hospital, had been barred by the Jordanians since 1948. From the roof we had a superb view of the city. From all sides came the sounds of artillery and light-weapons fire. In the north, Uri's 10th Brigade was fighting its way toward us, and battling in the west and south were Motta Gur's paratroopers and Eliezer Amitai's Jerusalem Brigade. Yet the Old City seemed still. Its crenellated stone walls, the Temple Mount, the mosques, the olive trees, the surrounding hills, all gave forth an air of calm, of majestic indifference to the explosive booms resounding all around them. I looked down upon this walled city in all its strength and splendor, wrapped in eternal tranquillity.

I had waited nineteen years for this moment. In 1948, when I was commander of Jerusalem, and later, when I was chief of staff, I had cherished the hope of a liberated Jerusalem and a freed Mount Scopus. Throughout all the generations, during the two thousand years of their exile, the Jewish people had yearned for Jerusalem. It was the object of their pilgrimage, their dreams, their longings. In the previous two decades, this craving of the centuries had found expression in operational plans. Jerusalem and its environs had a place in the General Staff files, on air reconnaissance photographs, and in exercises at the sand table. But Jerusalem's permanent place was in the heart. There are moments which bear within them solace for the sufferings of a nation, consolation for a private loss, reward for the fearless and unremitting pursuit of a noble goal. This was one of them. It was with reluctance that I turned from this view of Jerusalem and clambered down from the roof.

Twenty-four hours later, I was again at Central Command advance headquarters, but this time we drove to the Old City. It had been captured shortly before by Gur's paratroops. They had crashed through the Lions' Gate, and a few minutes later Gur signaled "The Temple Mount is ours. Repeat: The Temple Mount is ours."

As we drove, the sounds of volleys came from the northeast corner of the city, but only of light weapons. Jordanian artillery was now silent.

With me in the car were the chief of staff and the head of Central Command. We reached the arch of the Lions' Gate and entered the Old City together, side by side. This was indeed an historic moment.

In the very early hours of their first day of fighting, the paratroopers had suffered extremely heavy casualties; but on this morning, June 7, 1967, when they had broken into the Old City, no one had been hurt. The situation turned out to be as I had expected. After Jerusalem had been encircled and cut off from Jordan, the enemy troops who had remained laid down their weapons.

From the Lions' Gate we turned left and reached the Temple Mount. On the spire of the Dome of the Rock an Israeli flag fluttered. I ordered it to be taken down at once. If there was one thing we should refrain from doing in Jerusalem, it was putting flags on top of the mosque and the Church of the Holy Sepulcher. We walked the length of the mount, then turned right through the Mograbi Gate and went down to the Western ("Wailing") Wall. The narrow plaza in front of the Wall was crowded with soldiers who had taken part in the grim battle for the liberation of Jerusalem. All were greatly moved, some wept openly, many prayed, all stretched out their hands to touch the hallowed stones.

I stood in silence facing the Wall. Then I took a small notebook out of my pocket, wrote a few words, and, following the Jewish tradition of centuries when pilgrims would press their written pleas and prayers in the crevices of the Wall, I folded the note and thrust it in an opening between the ashlars. Moshe Pearlman, my special assistant, was somewhat surprised and asked what I had written. Without speaking I wrote again: "May peace descend upon the whole House of Israel."

When we left the Temple Mount area, a microphone was put in front of me for a few words on this historic occasion. I said: "We have returned to the holiest of our sites, and will never again be separated from it. To our Arab neighbors, Israel extends the hand of peace, and to the peoples of all faiths we guarantee full freedom of worship and of religious rights. We have come not to conquer the holy places of others, nor to diminish by the slightest measure their religious rights, but to ensure the unity of the city and to live in it with others in harmony."

On leaving the Western Wall, I had noticed some wild cyclamen of a delicate pinkish mauve sprouting between the Wall and the Mograbi Gate. I plucked a few to bring to Rahel. I was sorry she could not have been there that day.

Though I had lived in Jerusalem for several years, I was not a Jerusalemite. Before 1948, when I had visited the Old City, it was as though I had stepped into another world, a world of thick stone walls that enclosed teeming bazaars crowded with shoppers and merchants, tourists and pilgrims from overseas, Arabs in their *kefiehs*, Hassidic Jews in their traditional black garb, and monks and nuns in the robes of their orders. Crooked steps led upward from the narrow market lanes and lost themselves in dark mysterious alleys. It was all very different from the Israel in which I was born and brought up, an Israel open and flooded with light. But now, on this day of its liberation, Jerusalem was unlike the city I had known. Paratroopers, tank-men, and troops of the Jerusalem Infantry Brigade filled the city, their weapons slung over their shoulders, exultation in their eyes. This was the Jerusalem we had yearned and fought for, this was our Jerusalem, Jewish Jerusalem, free and gay with celebration. But there was also sadness, sadness over the lives that had been lost in making this celebration possible, sadness at our first sight of the Jewish Quarter that had been destroyed in 1948.

On this day, Jerusalem belonged to the army that had liberated it. Henceforth, it would again be the Jerusalem it had once been, the Jerusalem of all Israel.

I ordered Uzi to open wide the gates in the Old City wall. We would need to consider and determine the arrangements for the now united city, west and east, and how to introduce a new harmonious pattern of living for the Jewish and Arab communities. This would take time. The walls of the Old City were a magnificent creation, with a grandeur more compelling than any monument in the world. But I did not want them to serve as a divisive barrier between the communities. I wanted their gates opened to the old and the new— in every sense.

I flew back to General Headquarters. Inside the helicopter I wrapped myself in my coat and curled up in a corner. Not that I wished to sleep, but I had no wish to talk. I was loath to dispel the feeling aroused by the vision of the liberated city. Jerusalem was closer to me than it had ever been. Never again would we be parted.

PART I

Underground to Freedom

[1915 ~ 1948]

1

ROOTS

My name Moshe was born in sorrow. It had been inscribed a year before on a solitary tombstone in an olive grove in Deganiah, where the Jordan River flows out of the southern end of the Sea of Galilee. It marked the first grave in this fledgling settlement, which was the initial venture in Zionist collective farming. Deganiah became the cradle of the kibbutz movement. In 1914 it was a tiny and struggling settlement, barely four years old and consisting of fewer than twenty young pioneers, men and women. One of them was nineteen-year-old Moshe Barsky. Like his companions, he had come from a village in Russia to revive the Land of Israel. Unlike them, he knew something about farming and had quickly adapted himself to the kind of agricultural pioneering called for in the marshy, undeveloped Jordan Valley. His amiability and good nature had endeared him to the group.

Late one Sabbath afternoon, my father had taken ill, and Moshe had volunteered to ride over to a village a few miles away to get some medicine. It was no ordinary errand in those days. Arab marauding was rife, and wandering alone beyond the fenced perimeter of an isolated Jewish settlement after dark could be dangerous. Nevertheless, Barsky rode off. Just after sunset his frightened mule returned without him. The men of the kibbutz promptly formed small search parties, locked the iron gates behind them, and went off to find their friend. Riders with torches in hand lit the way through the fields. They searched for hours, impeded by the strong east wind that swept across the Sea of Galilee and stilled the voices of the teams calling to each other. Finally they came upon Barsky's body lying on the bank of the Jordan, a shoe, a staff, and part of an Arab headdress at his side. It turned out later that he had been attacked by six Arabs who had tried to steal his mule. They had shot him in the back, after he put up a struggle, and the frightened mule had taken off during the scuffle.

My father sent the saddest letter of his life to Barsky's parents in Russia. The father of his dead comrade wrote back: "We neither wail nor weep. The dear sons of our people must strive hard to revive and strengthen our nation. We are sending you our second son, Shalom, to take the place of his brother who has fallen. Moshe's death brings us all to the Land of Israel."

Shalom arrived shortly thereafter. He was followed by his sister, then his mother with the remaining three children, and finally by the father himself.

A year later, on May 4, 1915, I was born in Deganiah and given the name Moshe. The Land of Israel was called Palestine at the time, and it was under Turkish rule, part of the Ottoman Empire. That empire would collapse two and a half years later with the Allied victory in World War One, and Palestine would be governed by a British Mandatory administration. But I grew up in an independent Jewish society that spoke Hebrew and fostered the values of Israeli Jews who had struck roots and were living in their ancient homeland.

My parents had helped to create that society. They had been privileged to be among the first of the redeemed—and the redeemers. It was not their parents but they themselves, individually, who had "made the ascent" to the Land of Israel, experiencing with their whole being, heart and body, the revolutionary transition from the Russian diaspora to the unknown. The unknown was the wasteland of the Jordan Valley and the malarial marshes of the Valley of Jezreel.

Both my father, from the poor household of a horse-and-cart peddler, and my mother, from the well-to-do home of a lumber merchant, came to Palestine as young idealists. They had suffered no personal persecution in Russia, and they had not been driven out. Indeed, their reluctant parents had been unhappy at their departure. But their single-minded purpose—Father with exuberant enthusiasm,

Mother with a quiet but deep inner consciousness of duty—was prompted by the feeling that the place for a Jew was in the Land of Israel. And so they came. The atmosphere in which I was born was that of a Jew in his own land. My children and their children have known no other state or mood. My parents, however, had been faced with the choice and the spiritual struggle. They had made it and had reached the correct decision.

My father, Shmuel, was a forceful person with rugged features and a sturdy physique. He grew up in the Ukrainian village of Zaskow in the district of Kiev. It had a poor Jewish community of some three hundred families who made their living as small merchants, craftsmen, laborers, and horse traders. He came from a Hassidic family. His grandfather and great-grandfather had been rabbinical judges —*dayan* in Hebrew. His father had not followed the family calling but had adopted the name, and what the family name had been before no one remembered.

My grandfather seems to have been rather ineffectual, trying his hand at various occupations to feed seven hungry children and ending up an itinerant peddler traveling around the area with a wagon. He was assisted at first by the eldest boy, Eliyahu, and later by my father, who had left the *heder*, the Jewish religious school, when he was thirteen, just after he had celebrated his *bar mitzvah*.

My grandfather kept a religious home. But among the sacred books were Zionist pamphlets and copies of the journal *Hatzefirah* in modern Hebrew. My father would also get *The Young Worker*, a Labor Zionist publication with descriptions of the Land of Israel, and there he would read about "the land of the Jordan," the "peaks of the Hermon," the "wonders of Jerusalem," the "waters of the Red Sea," and the "slopes of Galilee." The tumbledown dwellings and muddy alleys of Zaskow were a far cry from the gleaming waters of the Jordan and the snowy ridge of Mount Hermon. But the gap was bridged by the Zionist orators who would preach to synagogue congregants and to Zionist groups in Odessa, where my Uncle Eliyahu had gone to live. It was he who had brought into their home the zeal for Zion, which had greatly influenced his younger brother, Shmuel. It was Eliyahu's dream to join the Zionist pioneers in Palestine. By 1908 he had scraped together 600 roubles and had promptly set out for the Holy Land, taking with him Shmuel, then eighteen years old, and one of their sisters, Beilah. Four years later, by then a farmer at Ein Ganim, some ten miles north of Tel Aviv, he went back to Russia to fetch the wife and children he had left behind.

My father sought the challenge of working on the land, and everything about it was a challenge at the time—the heat, the flies, the malarial mosquitoes, the squalor, the poverty, the general decay of the country under Turkish rule, and the physical work itself. But he was undeterred, and he obtained jobs as a hired farm hand in various localities in the coastal plain, Petach Tikvah, Rehovot, Ein Ganim, and Hadera.

It was very hard at first for young Jews like my father who had been unaccustomed to manual labor but who were determined to work with their hands. In Petach Tikvah, he bound wheat sheaves and dug irrigation ditches, and after each work shift he would wander back to rest, with throbbing head, aching back, swollen fingers, and blistered hands. He lunched off flat bread, chick-pea paste, and the tomatoes he loathed, and flung himself on his reed mat. Like his young companions, he soon succumbed to the prevailing malaria. But malaria, they told him, was not a sickness, so he would continue working in the fields or orange groves and lie flat on his back through all the hours between.

He gradually became inured to the hard labor and the harsh conditions. But after a severe bout of malaria, he took a brief spell as a night watchman in the vineyards at Rehovot, armed with a club and a whistle to protect himself from Arab marauders! Then back to the fields at Hadera and Ein Ganim. As the weeks sped by and he grew more accustomed to manual labor, his leisure hours could be used for something other than sleeping. His room in a hut became a kind of clubhouse, where his friends would gather in the evenings and hotly debate the nature of the ideal society, study Hebrew, and avidly read what the young pundits were saying in the journal of the nascent Jewish labor movement. He already showed a taste for organization, and he would later play a role in the development of the movement.

At that time there was plenty of work to be had in Judea and the Sharon coastal plain, but the lure of the open frontier lay with the pioneering efforts in Galilee. The settlements there were in need of more Jewish laborers and watchmen. My father bought himself an old Turkish pistol and cartridge belt in Jaffa, and off he went to the north, where he was hired by a Jewish farmer in the village of Yavniel. Here he was in his element. He plowed and sowed and reaped and threshed and rode horses and drove a team of mules. He soon graduated to sleeping in the stables to feed and guard the animals, and, as he wrote home at the time, he was delighted with the promotion. His work in Yavniel was "real farming," just the kind of work that only the Gentiles did in Zaskow in the Ukraine. He was proud to be "a laborer in Galilee, with a *kefieh* [Arab headdress], riding boots, a pistol at my hip, and mule reins in my hand . . ."

After six wonderful months at Yavniel, he was again laid low with malaria. When he recovered he joined a group of workers on a tract of land at Kinneret, on the Sea of Galilee, and was welcomed as a seasoned farm laborer, strong and hardened despite the occasional malaria relapses. He now spoke fluent Hebrew and was completely at home with the group. They were all conscious of the historical change they were helping to bring about, and this belief gave them the stamina to meet the physical hardship.

Kinneret had been acquired by the Jewish National Fund, the land-owning authority established by the Zionist Organization. At the end of 1909, seven of the workers on the Kinneret farm formed an independent group and arranged to cultivate another tract of National Fund land at nearby Um Juni for a year. That was the beginning of Deganiah, the name derived from the Hebrew word for grain. At the end of the year, the seven left to pioneer elsewhere and were replaced by a larger commune. My father joined it in 1911.

The question mark hanging over the lives of the Deganiah settlers was what kind of communal society they were to fashion. It was the subject of literally endless discussion, not only at formal meetings but also in the fields, at meals, on walks, in the dormitory before they fell asleep. Up to then, these workers had been wandering pioneers who prepared a stubborn tract for cultivation, so that it could be taken over by a settlement group, and then went on to prepare another piece of land in a desolate area for settlement. Yosef Bussel, the central figure of this group, urged that Deganiah should be their own permanent settlement. Here they would create a pattern of life based on the principle of complete cooperation. There would be no private property. All would work and all would receive according to their needs. Children would be brought up in a communal creche, and women would be free to engage in occupations which were normally the province of men. Deganiah would be a settlement subsisting on the labor of its own members. My father, incidentally, favored the itinerant pioneer approach.

If the idea of the kibbutz, which Deganiah pioneered, was their overriding concern, the members had also to struggle with the daily problem of living: the energy-sapping heat at 650 feet below sea level throughout the long summer, the insipid water to slake perpetual thirst, the inadequate food, the dust, the mosquitoes, the flies, the reaping and threshing in the searing wind, and all the other never-ending chores of farm life. Yet with it all, there was always the energy to sing and dance and read and argue in the evenings.

It was this world that my mother, Dvorah, entered in the spring of 1913. She was attractive and slight, with deep-set brown eyes and long dark hair worn in braids around her head. She was the same age as my father and, like him, came from the district of Kiev in the Ukraine. But by family background, upbringing, and temperament they were quite different. Her father was the only Jew in the village of Prochorovka on the Dnieper River. He was the manager of a lumber business that had trees felled and floated downstream on rafts when the ice thawed. He came from a rabbinical family and was an enlightened Hebrew scholar who spent the long winter months, when the river was frozen, studying and writing. He had published a book on Jewish life during the period of the Chmielnicki pogroms in the seventeenth century, and he contributed articles to periodicals devoted to the Hebrew revival. My grandfather had been drawn into the Lovers of Zion movement, and followed with keen interest the early settlement activities in Palestine.

My mother grew up without sharing her father's pursuits either in Hebrew culture or Zionism. She was given a secular Russian education, first in the village parochial school, then in a high school in a larger town, and later enrolled as a student in the Faculty of Education at the University of Kiev. The 1905 Russian Revolution made a deep impression on her. She was greatly moved by the plight of the workers and angered by the oppressiveness of the tzarist regime. She saw her mission as helping the needy and alleviating suffering. She avidly read the great Russian novelists of the time and was deeply influenced by Tolstoi. She joined a student branch of the Social Democratic Party and assisted her professor in a survey of slum children in Kiev. My mother, in short, had the intellectual tastes and social ideals of the intelligent and serious-minded Russian youth of her time. Out of humanitarian motives, she even served as a volunteer nurse on the Bulgarian front in 1911, when Bulgaria was fighting Turkey with Russian support.

At about this time, a change came over her outlook, for reasons that are not clear to me and maybe were not quite clear to her. She started feeling self-doubt, became ill at ease with her fellow students, and felt an urge to explore her Jewish identity. She left the university and returned home, where she spent time in discussions with her father. In his study she read letters sent to her father by the representative of the Lovers of Zion movement in Palestine, Ze'ev Tiomkin, describing the hard but rewarding lives of the dedicated Zionist pioneers there. Filled with a new zeal to throw in her lot with her own people, she decided to go to Palestine. That was in 1913, when my mother was twenty-three years old.

Taking passage in a Russian pilgrim ship from Odessa, she landed in Haifa a week later. Her only contact was a letter of introduction to Yisrael Bloch, one of the original Deganiah settlers. He failed to meet her because he was away in Damascus buying cows for the kibbutz. So she made her way by train to Zemach, at the lower end of the Sea of Galilee, and arrived at Deganiah on foot.

From all accounts, my mother's efforts to integrate into the life of the small group were at first a painful failure. Whatever her romantic expectations had been, the reality was tough. The kitchen and farm-yard chores she undertook were exhausting, especially in the hot and humid summer climate. The living quarters were cramped, the food coarse and unappetizing, and the amenities of life she had taken for granted were lacking. She could not speak Hebrew or Yiddish. The others thought her bourgeois in dress and values and had no interest in the Russian culture she loved. When she applied for membership in the kibbutz, she was turned down, after a long discussion, on the grounds that she did not fit in with the group. There was a kibbutz joke at the time that my father had opposed her membership for he feared rivals for her affections if she stayed.

At all events, my mother went to work and learn Hebrew in another settlement, Sejera, and she and my father kept in touch by corre-spondence. When my father went to Beirut to have treatment for an ear infection caused by a mosquito, she spent the last of her funds on a one-way ticket to see him there, and they came back to Deganiah as an engaged couple. This time Dvorah was received into the group without further reservations.

My parents were married in the kibbutz in the autumn of 1914, soon after World War One broke out. The ceremony was performed by the *shochet* (ritual slaughterer) brought by cart from another set-tlement in the neighborhood. The canopy consisted of a blanket tied to poles used for propping up the orange trees. It was set up on the bank of the Jordan River. Clinging to her own background, my mother wore a white dress she had sewn herself.

I was the first child born in Deganiah, though I was not the first kibbutz child. Gideon, the son of founder-members Yosef and Miriam Baratz, had been born two years earlier, but kibbutz conditions then were such that his mother had to go to Tiberias for the delivery.

Moshe Barsky had not been forgotten, and there had been more

murders later. Yet relations with the neighboring Arab farmers remained friendly. Both Jews and Arabs were tillers of the soil, and
they would learn much from one another, exchange visits, and join
in each other's celebrations. Attacks on Jewish workers were not
prompted by nationalist motives. The Arab peasants were also occasional victims of Arab marauders. Since it was impossible to rely
on the Turkish authorities for protection, the Jewish settlements in
Galilee formed a joint defense group to patrol the roads and villages
and ferret out the attackers in their hiding places.

The first few years of my childhood were the war years, and they
were grim for all of us. Turkey had joined Germany and Austria-
Hungary, and there was general mobilization in Palestine. The Turkish authorities distrusted the loyalty of the Jewish community and
expelled a number of its leaders to Egypt. The members of Deganiah
decided to acquire Ottoman nationality and went through all the
red tape involved. A few of the men were conscripted into the Turkish
army. Heavy payments were extracted from the kibbutz and some of
its property was impounded. The main concern of the settlers was
to remain on the kibbutz and preserve what they could of its hard-
won development.

The first year of the war brought the locust plague to Deganiah.
One sultry day a great swarm of them appeared from the east and
landed on our fields. The members tried everything possible to destroy them or to protect the trees and crops. A sticky paste was
smeared on the tree trunks, and the branches were wrapped in white
sacking. Ditches were dug around the threshing floor and filled with
water. But nothing helped. When the locusts moved on, their eggs
hatched, and there were caterpillars everywhere. Little was salvaged.
I was born in the worst period of the locust invasion.

When I was a year old, I contracted trachoma, the endemic eye
disease of the Middle East, and my mother caught the infection
from me. We spent some time with my father's sister, Beilah Hurwitz,
who lived at Nachlat Yehuda, south of Tel Aviv, where we could
receive treatment. Though our eyes got better, we had not been
cured when we returned to Deganiah.

As the war continued, conditions grew worse. A group of German
pilots arrived at Deganiah and commandeered our houses. The members of the kibbutz had to move into the cowshed and storehouse and
huddle there through a cold and rainy winter. All the children were
ill. I had a bout of pneumonia and my eye disease got worse. It was
only early in 1919, after the British victory in the Palestine campaign
and the end of the war, that Mother was able to take me to Jerusa-

lem, where we were both hospitalized, I for trachoma and Mother for a kidney ailment. I was almost four years old, and Mother used the time to start teaching me to read and write.

With new settlers arriving from Eastern Europe, it was decided to establish a sister kibbutz, Deganiah B, and Father was put in charge of the preparations. It came under attack by Bedouin bands and had to be hurriedly evacuated back to the mother kibbutz. From there Father and the other men would go out in the morning to work in the fields of Deganiah B. At this time there was much discussion about trying a different type of cooperative farming, in which each family would have greater privacy because it could own its own cottage on a separate plot while pooling the main farming and marketing operations. The system was called a moshav. It was distinct from the communal living in a kibbutz, where everything was owned, worked, and shared collectively. The first moshav to be established was Nahalal in the Jezreel Valley, where a large-scale Jewish reclamation project was being launched. My father had become discontented with life in the kibbutz and joined the group that would found Nahalal. The parting from the kibbutz was a sad one. Even I, who was then six years old, can remember tears upon saying goodbye to the children with whom I had played along the river bank or gone to the nearby hamlet of Zemach, where we would wander through the *shuk* (market) or wait for the train to come by.

It took some time for the moshav idea to be approved by the Zionist Congress, a budget allocated, and the land acquired. Meanwhile, we lived in Tel Aviv, where Father worked in the agricultural center of the party, Mother found temporary employment in the Missing Relatives Bureau, and I was sent to kindergarten.

In September 1921 we moved to Nahalal, on the slopes not far from Nazareth. Our new home was still a group of tents. Below, as far as the eye could see, was the Valley of Jezreel, dotted with patches of swamp, the tels of ancient buried towns, clumps of Bedouin goatskin tents, and the mud hovels of a few miserable Arab villages. Because of the rigorous conditions and the fear that Arab riots elsewhere in the country might break out in our locality as well, Mother and I, together with the other women and children, spent the first eight months in two rented houses that were, oddly enough, in the heart of Arab Nazareth. There was no trouble. Regular treatment at a local clinic finally cured us both of the trachoma that had persisted for years.

Having been born at Deganiah, the first kibbutz in the country, I was now to spend the rest of my childhood in the first "workers' moshav" (the word means settlement). Where Deganiah had grown by trial and error, Nahalal was from the beginning a carefully planned model village. Richard Kauffmann, a celebrated architect and planner, had designed the moshav. The layout was like a giant cartwheel, with the communal buildings at the hub, the farmers' cottages forming an inner circle, and their plots of land radiating out to the perimeter like the spokes of the wheel. Ours was one of eighty homesteads, with each family cultivating twenty acres. Some of the farm facilities were jointly owned, while both the marketing of the produce and the purchase of supplies were done through cooperative channels. Some of the basic tenets of the kibbutz were preserved: the ideological importance of tilling the soil, of working with one's own hands, and of complete equality of the members. Nahalal became the prototype for the many hundreds of moshavim that now exist all over Israel, though their design is looser than that of Kauffmann's pure radial one.

The Valley of Jezreel at the time was infested with malaria and typhus and a quagmire of mud in winter. It had to be drained by cutting canals, while the men working on the reclamation shook with fever. In time our tent was replaced by a hut and then by a small cottage with a living room, two bedrooms, a kitchen, and a porch. We walked to an outside privy and bathed in a tub on the kitchen floor. When I was eight and had a baby sister, my mother insisted that Father add a wooden cubicle to the porch for my use. I occupied that room of my own until my marriage.

After school I helped my father with the farm work—milking, plowing, planting, reaping, and riding with the wagon to the grain mill in an Arab village. I also had chores to do for my mother, such as kneading the dough for bread and stirring the tub in which she made fig jam.

My father had always had an urge to play a part in public life. He became active in party and organization work and was sent on missions abroad—at least twice for nearly a year at a time. During these absences, my mother had to carry the full burden of the farm work, with what assistance I could give her. Looking back I realize more clearly than I did at the time with what fortitude and tenacity she carried on, in spite of poor health, chronic debts, and a growing family. When I was seven, my sister, Aviva, was born in Haifa, where my mother's brother lived. Four years later my brother, Zohar (Zorik), was born, also in Haifa. My father was in the United States at the time, and I, then eleven, was left in charge of the farm. The years of drudgery and recurrent illness could not altogether drain Mother of her intellectual curiosity and literary streak. I imbibed from her a love of reading and was enthralled by the Russian tales she told me on winter evenings. I think she also gave me a taste for solitude and reflection. When I was about fourteen, Mother started contributing articles to the women's section of the largest daily newspaper, *Davar*. She was invited to join its editorial board and to be a delegate to the Women's Labor Council. She could only occasionally go to Tel Aviv for these activities as the two younger children had to be taken with her, and she hated to leave me alone.

About a year after Nahalal started, a lean, blue-eyed young man called Meshulam Halevy turned up seeking work as a teacher and was engaged for the fifteen children then in the moshav. He divided us into three age groups, and classes were conducted in the living room of his hut, without school benches and desks, until a schoolhouse with two rooms was provided. Meshulam was a gifted and unorthodox teacher, more concerned with encouraging creative self-expression in us than in sticking to any formal curriculum. Through him we became familiar with both our biblical background and our natural surroundings. Many of the classes were held outdoors, and on long hikes we learned about the animal and plant life of the region. I was good at writing and drawing, and a few of my essays, poems, and sketches were "published" in the single-copy children's newspaper Meshulam helped us produce.

Apart from class outings, I enjoyed going on hiking and camping trips with one or two companions, or alone. I learned to mingle with the boys of the Arab villages and Bedouin encampments and to talk to them in their own language. Wahash, a Bedouin boy my age, attached himself to me in the Nahalal fields, and we became firm friends. Although the Arabs in our neighborhood were rather poor and backward by our standards, I developed a liking and respect for their patient stoicism, their ancient folkways, and a certain innate dignity in even the humblest peasant or tribesman. From my boyhood days, I have found it easy to get along with Arabs.

In 1926 when Nahalal was five years old, Wizo (the Women's International Zionist Organization) opened a farm school for girls there, the first venture of its kind in the Middle East. Its director was the redoubtable Hannah Meisel Shochat. For us young boys, the girls from all over the country studying at the school were a never-failing source of interest. When my age group of Nahalal children had finished with Meshulam's primary school, it was arranged that we could continue at the Wizo school, boys as well as girls. I was one of a few boys who actually did so; the rest dropped out and became absorbed in farm work. Later on, the inaccurate story became current that I was the only boy to be educated at the girls' school!

2

ON GUARD

IN 1929, AT THE AGE of fourteen, I was initiated into the secret organization called the Haganah, the underground self-defense force of the Jews of Palestine. Among the youth in Nahalal who joined, I was the youngest. The Haganah decided to enroll us shortly after the Arab massacre of sixty-seven Jews in Hebron—men, women, and children. Sixty others were wounded in the Arab attack, synagogues were razed, and Torah scrolls burned. The Haganah was determined that isolated Jewish communities in town and country would never again be helpless, unarmed, or at the mercy of Arab extremists who could impose their will on Jews or Arabs friendly to their Jewish neighbors. Each community had to be able to defend itself. Each had to have arms and trained men and women.

But the British declared as illegal the possession of unlicensed weapons and military training for self-defense. The British Mandatory authority, through its police force and troops, maintained order in the country. They were supposed to protect the citizens, but they were comparatively small forces and were unable—and often unwilling—to rush to the defense of Jewish settlements in danger. And when they did come, they frequently arrived too late. The British responded in some measure to the demands of the Jewish authorities and allocated a few weapons to the kibbutzim and moshavim. But for the most part they gave us only shotguns, which were not very effective. The Haganah therefore distributed its own weapons, which were hidden in a cache in each settlement. This was an illegal act, as was membership in the Haganah. Hence the secrecy.

When we joined the Haganah, we received training in the use of firearms, though that was unnecessary in my case. There had always been a weapon in the house, an old German carbine which my father had brought with him from Deganiah. He kept the carbine wrapped up in the cowshed, and I would often take out the gun to clean and oil it and had long ago learned to use it. But only now, with my cherished and secret membership in the Haganah, did I feel I might be using the carbine to good purpose. It would be our task to defend Nahalal and race to the defense of neighboring settlements if they were attacked.

When I was a little older, Yehuda Mor, a member of Nahalal, organized a group of five teenage riders to guard the fields against marauding Arab bands. We had two riding instructors, also men of Nahalal, who had served in a Cossack regiment in Russia, and they put us through our paces in the best traditions of the Russian cavalry. We attacked imaginary foes, brandished sticks, galloped, and let out blood-curdling yells as we charged. This training at least was great fun. I called my horse Tauka, after the Indian steed in a Jules Verne novel.

The Bedouin of the el-Mazarib and other tribes would from time to time bring their goats into the village fields to pasture. It was our job to drive them off. Stealing and exploiting fields belonging to others were part of their life-style. There was no political basis to our quarrels. They were simply arguments over trespassing, as often arise between rural neighbors, and particularly between the nomadic Bedouin and the peasant cultivator.

The political quarrels were mostly among the Jewish parties, and they carried on a sharp debate over the ideal internal organization of the Jewish community in Palestine. By now a number of kibbutzim and moshavim existed in the country, and they belonged to one or the other of the two labor movements of the time, uniting in 1930 to form Mapai, the Labor Party of the Land of Israel. They had a youth wing, but I was not attracted to party work. I had become more interested in the diverse activities that took place in Nahalal's youth hut, where we arranged debates, lectures, community singing, and folk dancing. I remember organizing evenings of poetry readings and literary discussions, to which we would often invite outside

lecturers. My prize catch involved getting the poet Avraham Shlonsky to talk to us about trends in Hebrew poetry and read some of his
poems, which I loved. Our literary club chose me to visit him and
extend our invitation. I did so, traveling to a convalescent home near
Jerusalem, where he was staying, and he accepted. He captured the
hearts of our young people, though the older settlers continued to
stick to the works of Chaim Nachman Bialik, our national poet, and
Rachel, the poetess of the Jordan Valley.

One night in December 1932, a bomb was thrown into the hut of
Yosef Ya'akobi, a neighbor of ours in Nahalal, killing his eight-year-
old son. The father died of his wounds in the morning. This murder
marked a new trend in our relations with the neighboring Arabs. It
had nothing to do with disputes over land or pasture rights. Clearly
political and nationalist considerations motivated the attack, which
had been preceded by a similar attack on members of nearby Kibbutz
Yagur. The British authorities arrested a number of Arabs connected
with the outrage, but the murderous attacks did not cease.

The attackers belonged to a fanatical underground association
called the Bearded Sheikhs, later known as the Kassamiya after its
leader and founder, Sheikh Az-el-Din el-Kassam. The large Arab village of Zippori near Nazareth served as headquarters of the organization. Father believed—and that was the belief on which I had been
brought up—that the Arabs were by nature men of violence, marauders, and a source of disturbances. But here for the first time I realized
that the matter was not so simple. I rode out to Zippori and talked
to some of my Arab acquaintances there and also with the elders of
the el-Mazarib tribe. They all spoke with adulation of the Kassamiya,
saying that they were devoted idealists, humble in their ways, spending much time at prayer, and acting out of deep religious and national
principles.

My own attitude to our Arab neighbors was always positive and
friendly. I liked their way of life and I respected them as hard workers, devoted to the land and to our common natural environment.
I had no doubt that it was possible to live at peace with them, they
in their own villages and according to their traditional patterns, and
we according to ours. The Kassamiya, and above all the esteem in
which they were held by the Arab peasants and the Bedouin who
lived side by side with us, clarified one aspect of the relations between us. This did not involve the personal feelings we had for one
another. The emergence of the Kassamiya shed light on the deep national and religious chasm that separated the Arabs from the Jews
who were fulfilling the ideals of Zionism.

My studies at the Wizo Agricultural School ended, but not my visits there. Judith was the attraction, a beautiful blue-eyed girl who was older and taller than I. On Sabbaths we used to spend much time in the tree nursery at Kfar Hahoresh in the Nazareth hills, and in the evenings we would take long walks through the cornfields.

I was still active in the youth club which met in the hut for our literary and social gatherings, and I now extended our range of interests by organizing what we called an ideological circle. We would read and discuss the writings of the Jewish leaders in the country, notably David Ben-Gurion, who had already made his mark as a man of dynamic leadership; Berl Katznelson, regarded as the theoretician of the labor movement; Chaim Arlozoroff, who headed the Political Department of the Jewish Agency until his murder; and Moshe Sharett, who succeeded him. We soon found ourselves shedding our former aloofness and becoming more and more involved in what was being said and done in the labor movement. We drew closer to it, came to know it, and eventually were absorbed into it.

Life in Nahalal called for long hours of hard work on the farm, in the fields and the cowshed, and on the communal projects. There were added burdens when Father was away on his frequent trips on behalf of the Labor Party and the Zionist movement. Mother managed to find time for public activities and for writing, mostly for the Labor daily, the largest newspaper in the country. And though my world until now had been bounded by Nahalal and its environs, I, too, had begun to develop an overriding interest in what was happening outside our village and was inexorably drawn to our national and political struggle. I thought hard about the prospect of higher studies, but I could not leave Nahalal.

In 1933, when I was eighteen, we began the construction of permanent housing in the village. Our home was among the last to be built. I joined a building team casting concrete in standard molds, which were devised by an ingenious engineer named Papper. The work was difficult, drab, and tiring and it brought little financial reward. But we kept at it, although the engineer offered us more lucrative jobs in Tel Aviv.

By autumn we had completed the construction of the forty houses for which the village had a budget. The building of the remaining houses had to be put off for two years, so eight of us accepted Papper's offer and went to Tel Aviv. We were prompted to do so not only by the wages but in the hope that we could further our education. We worked during the day erecting scaffolding at the building sites, first in Tel Aviv itself and later in the suburb of Ramat Gan, and in the evenings we studied higher mathematics and attended lectures on literature and the Hebrew language at the Popular University run by the cultural department of the Histadrut, the Labor Federation. We would take our evening meal at a cheap restaurant near the school.

I continued to see Judith, who in the meantime had finished the agricultural school in Nahalal and returned to her home in Rishon le-Zion. We would meet at her home or in Tel Aviv. My parents were not very pleased about this, and Judith also had second thoughts about the teenager from Nahalal who had strayed to Tel Aviv to become a building laborer.

We worked in the city only during the slack season on the farm. But in the summer of 1934, we returned to Nahalal. In the autumn, after plowing and before sowing, another lull occurred. This was the time for hiking through the country. That year I went on a walking tour with two friends. Equipped with a little pocket money, water bottles, a few tins of food, and a map, we set off for Bet She'an, walked along the Jordan Valley to Jericho, and from there went on to Beersheba and Gaza. It was an arduous trip in the *khamsin,* the hot desert wind, and through the thick vegetation along the Jordan, which made hiking difficult, while our water bottles were frequently empty. But it was a rewarding experience.

One episode in particular made a deep impression on me—precisely because it was undramatic. The details remain with me to this day. We arrived one night at a wadi near the northern end of the Dead Sea utterly exhausted. It had been hot all day and remained as hot now, after dark, in the rift valley below sea level. We flopped down and were instantly asleep. At dawn an Arab shepherd passed by with his flock. We asked for water, and he took us to a nearby Bedouin encampment. We were brought to the tent of the chief and given not just a drink but hospitality in the best Bedouin tradition. After the meal, the chief said that one of his men was taking a donkey to Jericho, and he suggested that we go with him so that we would come to no harm. We thanked him, accepted, walked to Jericho with the tribesman, and then left him to make our own way to Sodom at the southern end of the Dead Sea.

I was struck by the kindness of these Bedouin, so different from the behavior portrayed in the stories we read and the tales we had heard from the older Jewish settlers. They had not stolen our watches or cameras or money. They had not turned their backs on three dust-covered, unshaven, thirsty young Jews who spoke an ungrammatical Arabic. They had taken us in, been most hospitable, and sent us safely on our way. It was not that I had romantic notions of the desert

Bedouin. Some were kind and some were cruel, like any other people, and I sensed as a boy that they should not be prejudged. Indeed, this episode near Jericho had not been my first experience with Arab kindness. We had often gone into Arab villages—sometimes together, sometimes alone—and had stones thrown at us by young urchins spoiling for a fight. Time and again the older Arabs would come to our aid, take us into their homes, offer us olives and *pitta* (the flat Arab bread), and send us back unharmed.

A few weeks after our return, toward the end of 1934, we had a different kind of encounter with Bedouin. The occasion was a very serious land dispute with the el-Mazarib tribe. Some years earlier, the Jewish National Fund had bought a parcel of land not far from Nahalal from its Arab landowner and had allocated it to our village. But the land had not yet been cultivated. Nahalal now decided to start working the fields, and a group of us went out with our implements and began work in a broad wadi.

A friend of mine led the plowmen and I followed with a sack of seeds to sow. As we worked, a few members of el-Mazarib gathered on the slopes to watch. They were soon joined by others, and a little later by considerable numbers. I noticed my friend Wahash among them, and then I spotted my other young Bedouin friends. They all looked very sullen. Until now, although it was our land, they and other tribes had used the area for grazing, and they resented the fact that it was now being tilled. We went on working, and they went on watching. The silence was menacing. Suddenly, they began throwing stones, and one of the plowmen was hurt. Our people replied in kind. Tempers rose. The Bedouin summoned Arabs from the nearby village of Mahlul, while we were joined by the men of Nahalal and the nearby kibbutzim of Gvat and Ramat David. Stones flew and clubs swung, while I went on sowing along a shoulder of the wadi. When I reached the top of a rise, I was struck on the head by a club. I had the impression that my attacker was my friend Wahash. I lost consciousness for a short while and was then put on a horse and brought back to Nahalal. Since I had lost blood and the doctor feared a concussion, I was bandaged and put to bed. After a few days I was sent to the convalescent home near Jerusalem, where I had first met the poet Shlonsky. Had he still been there, I might have stayed longer.

But I soon got bored and returned to Nahalal with a scar on my head but no enmity in my heart toward Wahash and his el-Mazarib tribe. I could understand their feelings, but I could not assuage them. They had been pasturing their flocks on other people's land, and watering them at other people's springs, for generations. But the land then had been untilled, untended, and misused for grazing because it had fallen into disuse. It was ours now, and we were working it, putting it under cultivation, redeeming its ancient fruitfulness after centuries of neglect. I knew the Bedouin viewed the matter differently, and so I bore them no ill will. Indeed, some six months later I invited Wahash and his tribe to my wedding in Nahalal. They all came and performed the traditional dances done at their own marriage celebrations, while a young Bedouin boy named Abed played the accompaniment on the flute. It was a scene of much shouting and laughter, and we all had a merry time.

One of the girls who arrived in our village in the autumn of 1934 was Ruth Schwartz. She had come from Jerusalem to attend the agricultural school in Nahalal. She was two years younger than I. Her father, Zvi, and her mother, Rachel, had graduated from the prestigious Herzliya Secondary School, the first modern Hebrew-language high school, which turned out men and women who were to become prominent in the public life of the country. Ruth's parents were well established and active in the social and political affairs of the capital. But Ruth, idealistic and romantic, had been a member of a Labor youth movement. She saw her future not in the town but in the kibbutz, and wished to train for a pioneering life in agriculture. And so she had enrolled in the Nahalal school.

We talked and met often. I wished to improve my English, and Ruth had known the language since childhood. We soon became very attached, and shortly thereafter she felt at home in my parents' house, helping my mother with various chores and becoming friendly with Zorik and Aviva.

We were married on July 12, 1935, in the courtyard of our home, beside the walnut tree. From Jerusalem, Ruth's mother brought an abundance of drinks and dainties in her car, and she was followed by a busload of friends of the Schwartz family, among them Dr. Arthur Ruppin, one of the founding fathers of Jewish farm settlement in Palestine; Moshe and Zipporah Sharett; and Dov Hos, one of the top men in the Jewish Agency. Our own contribution to the wedding feast consisted of mounds of grapes, which I had harvested that morning, and tubs of corn on the cob. Nahalal's Rabbi Zechariah, who had been born in Yemen, performed the marriage ceremony. And so, at the age of twenty, dressed in a white shirt, with a cap on my head and sandals on my feet, I embarked upon family life, the first of my age group in the village to do so. After the ceremony, while the el-Mazarib Bedouin were dancing the *debka* to the tune of Abed's flute, Ruth went out to the cowshed to do the milking.

We had no definite plans for the immediate future. I thought I would not remain at Nahalal. I dreamed of starting something new—as my parents and their friends had done at my age—perhaps founding a farm settlement in some stubborn area, like the Huleh marshes to the north of the Sea of Galilee. But I also yearned for a broader education. My Haganah duties at the time did not take up much of my energies, so I was comparatively free. The opportunity to improve my knowledge of English and perhaps take a university entrance examination presented itself when we found tickets for a trip to England among our wedding presents.

Laden with numerous parcels, among them eiderdowns, while I was still wearing those comfortable sandals, we set sail on the S.S. *Marietta Pasha* for Marseille and continued from there by train to Paris and London. Ruth loved London. She had lived there for five years as a child when her parents studied at London University, and she was glad to see it again. To support us, she taught Hebrew. She felt thoroughly at home. For me, life in England was less rosy. I had hoped to study and work part-time. But with my primitive English I could not get a job, and without a secondary school diploma I could not embark on university studies. The London fog did nothing to lighten my mood. It made sunny Palestine seem further away than ever. My father's letters were filled with moralizing about the easy life I had chosen to pursue while the farm needed me so badly.

It seemed purposeless to stay. I was not working and I was not studying. I longed to get back. A few months after our arrival, two events occurred which prompted us to pack and return. One was the outbreak of Arab violence in Palestine in May 1936. Tension had been mounting for some time. Two months earlier Avraham Galutman had been murdered. He was the Nahalal expert on orchards, and he had taught me the art of grafting. He was a wonderful man, and I was saddened by the news that he had been killed. Sporadic Arab attacks on settlements throughout the country now left more victims in their wake. My place was at home.

The second event concerned the decision of a group of my Nahalal friends to found a farm settlement of their own. They would eventually establish a kibbutz on the border so that they could engage in both farming and defense. But now, to make their start in independent communal living, the Nahalal village council had given them, on a provisional basis, 100 acres located on a nearby site called the hill of Shimron. We decided to join them.

It proved not so easy—for me. The group immediately admitted Ruth as a full member. I was accepted only as a candidate, to be admitted to membership after six months if I proved I could fit into this kind of community life, which was doubted. I regarded such reservations as a mark of no-confidence, and indeed it was. My friends knew me, and they did not believe that I could be wholehearted about belonging to a collective group. Emotional partnership, sociability, and absolute egalitarianism were not in keeping with my nature. I did not believe I would change my character in six months, but I accepted their verdict. When the term of my candidacy ended, I was given full membership.

We started off with seventeen members, all from Nahalal. We were then joined by a group of young members from a labor youth movement who had immigrated from Poland and Rumania, and later still by some of the graduates of the Wizo girls' agricultural school at Nahalal. Ruth and I were allotted a small, bare room, and I made our furniture from oak logs. Ruth worked in the sheep pen, while I was put on night guard duty.

The Shimron settlement venture did not prove a success for its founding members. Economically, things turned out well enough. The Jewish National Fund gave us afforestation work on contract in the nearby Nazareth hills and supplied us with huts, animals, and farm implements. But there were strong differences of opinion within the group about the social organization that should govern our lives, and this was the subject of passionate debate throughout the two years that Ruth and I were there. By November 1938, when the Shimron group moved to its permanent settlement site at Hanita on the Lebanese border, most of the Nahalal members of the original group had left, many for other kibbutzim. Their places were taken by new members. Ruth and I had left two months earlier and returned to Nahalal, where we lived in a hut of our own.

My first serious involvement in the military arena occurred during my stay at Shimron and coincided with what the British called the "Arab revolt," a reference to the Arab disturbances which started in May 1936 and harassed the country until May 1939, when Britain issued its new Palestine policy restricting Jewish immigration and land settlement. In those three years, the Jewish community struggled to preserve its security, and the younger generation was called upon to play an active part.

The revolt began with an Arab general strike aimed at paralyzing the economic life of the country. It soon developed into a terror movement by Arab extremists directed against the Jews, the Mandatory government, and the moderate Arabs. Britain rushed additional troops to Palestine to maintain order, and by the end of 1936 the main body of armed extremist groups had been neutralized, though sporadic terror continued and would flare up again later. By then a British Royal Commission headed by Lord Peel had been appointed to inquire into the causes of the conflict and to submit recommendation on future diplomacy.

Since the Jews and the British were both targets of Arab terrorism, the Mandatory government and the Jewish authorities found themselves working together. The first measure of cooperation followed a British army request for Jewish guides who knew the country and who spoke Arabic. It developed into the establishment of a Jewish Settlement Police Force as an auxiliary to the army and regular police. I became a *ghaffir*, a member of the supernumerary police.

The first official military letter of appointment I ever received carried the letterhead of the Palestine Police Force. It was dated March 1937 and was addressed to me at Shimron. My salary came to 8 Palestine pounds a month. I was then twenty-two. I served as a guide to British army units stationed at Afula, the rural center of the Valley of Jezreel, on their patrols along the Iraq Petroleum Company oil pipeline. The pipeline ran through the valley to the port terminal at Haifa. We covered a sector that lay between Tiberias, on the Sea of Galilee, and Ein Dor, the biblical Endor, which figures in the story of King Saul and the witch, located to the south of Mount Tabor. This stretch of IPC pipeline became a frequent target of Arab sabotage, for the area favored the saboteurs. Ordinary cars and trucks could not pass through, and most of the villages there were Arab.

As a *ghaffir* I was given a uniform and a licensed weapon. I lived in a tent in a British army camp and got one night a week off as "home leave" to spend in Shimron. I worked with a Scottish regiment and the Yorkshire Fusiliers, who were not trained in reconnaissance. Their officers assumed that they had fulfilled their task if they simply showed their presence by patrolling the area. The Arabs could and did sabotage the pipeline and set fire to the oil without interference either before or after the patrol had passed by. During the eight months I spent with the units in this sector, I came to realize the ineffectiveness of regular troops, using routine methods with fixed times and routes of patrol, against saboteurs who knew the terrain, moved stealthily on foot, could lose themselves in the local population, and could choose the convenient time and place for their operations. It became clear to me that the only way to fight them was to seize the initiative, attack them in their bases, and surprise them when they were on the move.

The Jewish Settlement Police Force grew, served most of the kibbutzim and other farm villages, and included some 1,300 members of the Haganah by the end of 1936. After my service in Afula, I returned to Shimron as a *ghaffir*, was soon promoted to sergeant, and was appointed commander of a mobile squad. With six *ghaffirs* under my command and a light truck as our vehicle, we were very active, going on daylight patrols along dirt paths and setting ambushes at night on the roads leading from the Arab areas to Jewish settlements.

In December 1937 the Haganah sent me on a Platoon Commanders' Course, and there I got to know Yitzhak Sadeh, the veteran underground officer, who served as one of the instructors. Though he was much older than I, he was a man after my own heart. Bursting with original ideas, he grasped the essence of a problem and demanded of us great daring, bordering at times on recklessness. It was a good course, with realistic battle exercises, and it meant much to me for having studied under Sadeh. I could not say the same about the school I went to next—a British course for sergeants held at a British military camp. I did not care for the highly disciplined inspection parades with the strict insistence on shiny boots and smartness of dress. And the content of the military instruction served no use whatsoever for ensuring the safety of the Nahalal region and the rest of the Jezreel Valley. Yet I found it interesting, and I realized that in order to run an empire, there may have been some virtue in the spit and polish of British army tradition.

The cooperation between the Mandatory government and the Jewish authorities opened up extensive possibilities to improve and broaden our own military training. Licensed weapons for supernumeraries served as a cover for the possession of illegal arms. Furthermore, since I was in uniform and in command of a mobile patrol unit, it became easier for me, as for others, to carry out my clandestine Haganah activities.

The Arab revolt flared up again in the autumn of 1937, when the Peel Inquiry Commission published its proposals. Its principal recommendation called for the partition of Palestine into a Jewish state, an Arab state, and a British mandated area. The Arab countries rejected this partition plan, and the Arab struggle against the Jews and the British administration grew in intensity.

In 1938 I served as a Haganah instructor for Nahalal and the surrounding area and I also taught courses for section commanders at another Haganah base. In these courses, I tried to crystallize a method of training that went beyond the routine teaching of weaponry and drill. I wrote a manual called "Fieldcraft" on the importance of getting to know terrain and the correct tactical exploitation of its features. The manual also contained instructions on guarding, infiltration, and ambush, as well as guidance on such minor items as how to cut gaps in a fence. The manual came into the hands of Ya'akov Dori, the Haganah commander of the northern region, who summoned me to his headquarters and, to my delight and pride, praised me for it.

I spent some time teaching in the Nahalal area, where I emphasized the art of attack, the stealthy approach, and the surprise infiltration of an enemy base. To test all this training and to show up weak spots in our own defenses, I would take my own men to a quartered and fenced kibbutz or other Jewish settlement where we would often get right to the heart of the village without being detected. I cannot say that my superiors commended me for such exercises, and I had no convincing answer for them when they asked me what I would have done if the guards had spotted and shot us. I just knew in my heart that as long as I was crawling at the head of my men to break through a guarded fence, we would not fail. Nevertheless, I obeyed orders and stopped "invading" our own settlements.

I carried out my training duties with the Haganah while continuing as a sergeant *ghaffir* in command of a mobile patrol subordinate to the British police. Having a vehicle at my disposal made it easier to live two lives. Ruth remained at Shimron, and when we met, and in our letters, we now started discussing our plans for the future. We talked of leaving the group, founding our own farm, having our own home, spending our time in the fields and on reading and study. We thought that when the Shimron group was ready to leave for their permanent settlement in Hanita, Ruth and I would return to the parental holding in Nahalal as a first step toward establishing our own homestead.

However, the move of the Shimron group was not to occur until November 1939, and the actual establishment of Hanita would take place eight months before, not by the group but by the Haganah. Early in 1938, when Arab violence again reached its peak, the Jewish national institutions completed their purchase of the lands of Hanita and resolved that it should be occupied immediately. It was a daring but wise decision. Jewish Hanita on the Lebanese border would close the gap in the frontier through which Arab gangs infiltrated into the country. And it would demonstrate both the right of the Jews to settle the land and their capacity to hold and defend it, even though Arab territory surrounded the area and there were no Jewish communities nearby. A Haganah force would occupy Hanita, since the Arabs would attack it at the very outset, and after it was fortified, the fields cleared, and an access road built, Hanita would be given to the Shimron group for permanent settlement.

The Haganah set March 21, 1938 as the date for its Hanita operation. It mobilized a special force of 400 men, including 100 *ghaffirs*, from settlements in Jezreel, Galilee, and other parts of the country. To preserve secrecy, both against the Arabs and the British administration, they assembled in a kibbutz in the coastal plain. Yitzhak Sadeh commanded this force, and Yigal Allon and I served as his deputies. Ya'akov Dori would be overall commander on "settlement day," when we took occupation of the site.

On March 21 we moved out of our assembly point before dawn and headed northward for Hanita. We had to leave the vehicles on the road and laboriously climb the rocky slopes. While one group started hacking out a smooth track, the rest of us carried heavy loads of fortification equipment and materials by hand. On the hilltop site we began erecting a wooden watchtower and the standard perimeter fence, a double wall of wood filled with earth and boulders. We hoped to do all this during the day so that the tented compound within would be defended by nightfall, when we expected the first attack. But night came and we had not completed the fortifications. There had been too much to do, and we were also hampered by a strong wind. We could not even put up the tents.

At midnight we were attacked. The Arabs fired from two nearby hills, and it was impossible to determine their exact location. Yitzhak Sadeh suggested to Dori that he call his men, Yigal Allon's unit and mine, to attack the Arab assault group, but Dori thought the proposal irresponsible and turned it down. We had to make do with more-or-less aimless firing from our positions behind the perimeter fence. After both sides shot at each other for eighty minutes, the attackers retreated across the Lebanese border. Our casualties consisted of two killed and several wounded.

Work proceeded at Hanita for the next three days, and though the situation remained tense, no shooting took place. On the fourth day, while one of our construction teams busily worked on building an access road, the Arabs attacked. This time we went out to engage the enemy. We hoped to cut off their retreat, but they were too quick and took to the hills before we could catch them.

Sadeh's force remained at Hanita while the construction of the settlement continued, and to hasten the process workers arrived from the coastal town of Nahariah. One of my duties was to transport these workers to and from their city in a homemade armored car, an ordinary truck with steel-plated sides. The rest of the time we engaged in patrol and guard duty. A few weeks later, when the huts and the main fortifications, however primitive, had been erected, Sadeh disbanded his force and I returned to the Jezreel Valley and my command of the supernumerary mobile unit. Hanita, however, remained a Haganah defense and training base until its permanent settlement later that year.

One evening a few weeks later, a Haganah man from Haifa turned up at Shimron accompanied by a strange visitor. He was Orde Wingate, a captain in the British army. I had heard of this extraordinary soldier who had come to Palestine upon the outbreak of Arab disturbances in 1936. I knew even then that he had unconventional ideas about how to deal with Arab terrorism and sabotage, and, unlike any of his military colleagues, thought well of the Jews. In fact he had become an ardent supporter of the Zionist idea, strongly recommended British cooperation with the Haganah for the good of both, and had gained the confidence of the Jewish leaders. This was our first meeting.

Wingate was a slender man of medium height, with a strong, pale face. He walked in with a heavy revolver at his side, carrying a small Bible in his hand. His manner was pleasing and sincere, his look intense and piercing. When he spoke, he looked you straight in the eye as someone who seeks to imbue you with his own faith and strength. I recall that he arrived just before sunset, and the fading light lent an air of mystery and drama to his coming. The drama heightened as the evening progressed, right up to the unorthodox climax.

He called for a gathering of the group. He wanted to teach us how to fight. He insisted on speaking Hebrew, which he had started to learn on his arrival in the country, but after a while we asked him to switch to English, since we had difficulty in following his strange Hebrew accent and could understand only the recognizable biblical quotations in our language. He told us of his experiences with guerrilla warfare in the Sudan, where he had been stationed for some years, and described the techniques of the night ambush. He ended his talk with the surprising proposal that we go out with him there and then and set up an ambush. He would show us how to pick a location and where to site the ambush party, illustrating in the field what he had told us in the Shimron dining room.

He called for a map and gave us our first surprise. He picked as the ambush site a crossroads located close to the Arab village of Mahlul, a few miles away. This concept was new to us, for we had always set our ambushes near the approaches to the Jewish settlement to be defended and not near the exit from an Arab village serving as a terrorist base. We gathered our weapons and off we went. Under Wingate's instructions, we moved along the hill ridges and not the paths. He insisted on walking ahead and not, as had been our practice, with two trackers in front. When we reached our objective, he divided us into two groups and positioned us 100 yards apart. His orders were that if and when the terror gang appeared, it should be allowed to get between us, so that it could be attacked from both sides. No hostile Arabs appeared that night, but the lesson had sunk in.

I was greatly impressed by Wingate. Just before we left on the mission, I looked at this slight and, as I thought, inexperienced stranger and wondered whether he would indeed be able to advance in the dark terrain unknown to him. And when we had moved from the beaten path to clamber over rocks and through the bushes, I doubted that he would be able to keep up the brisk pace. He seemed so fragile. And what did he know of the Arabs, or of the slopes and gullies of the Nazareth hills which had been part of our lives since childhood? By dawn, my doubts had evaporated. On my home ground, this unusual British officer knew better than I what to do. It was hard going, and it tired him out, but he was sure-footed, never slipped, and at no time did he ask us to halt and rest.

The seeds of Wingate's novel ideas and tactics had already been implanted in us by Yitzhak Sadeh, the pioneer of the "emerge-from-the-fence" school. But there was a professionalism about Wingate, a positiveness, a stubborn lack of compromise. A dominating personality, he infected us all with his fanaticism and faith.

I met him often thereafter. We would go out after terror gangs in areas far from my beat, from the hills of Galilee to the wilderness of Judea near Bethlehem. Sometimes we were lucky, encountered the enemy, and inflicted casualties. At other times we would go through the night without incident. But even when nothing happened, we learned much from Wingate's instruction. Moreover, the Arab attackers had been forced to realize that no longer would they find any path secure for them. They were likely to be caught in a surprise ambush anywhere.

Wingate was not physically robust. On warm nights he would tire from long marches and the tough climb and scramble between boulder and bush. I saw him stop one night to pull a melon from a field, cut it open with his knife, and suck its moisture to refresh himself. There were times when he reached the edge of exhaustion, and I thought he would collapse. But he would march on, driven by an iron will. He had an unshakeable belief in the Bible. Before going on an action, he would read the passage in the Bible relating to the places where we would be operating and find testimony to our victory —the victory of God and the Jews.

At dawn we would return to Shimron and prepare breakfast. We would enter the wooden structure which served as the communal kitchen and watch the scores of cockroaches scurry away at our approach. There we would fry omelets and potatoes on a primus stove and prepare a tomato salad. While all this was going on, Wingate would sit in a corner, stark naked, reading the Bible and munching raw onions as though they were the most luscious pears. Judged by ordinary standards, he would not be regarded as normal. But his own standards were far from ordinary. He was a military genius and a wonderful man.

His unorthodox ways and pronounced Zionist sympathies proved too much for his British superiors in Palestine, and they had him recalled to London. But in World War Two, thanks to the intervention of Winston Churchill, he was able to put his novel ideas into practice on a far wider scale, in the campaigns in Ethiopia and Burma. He was killed in 1944 in the jungles of Burma, a general leading his famous Chindits.

3

IN JAIL

THE MEMBERS OF THE SHIMRON communal group established Kibbutz Hanita on the Lebanese border as their permanent farm settlement in November 1938. Ruth and I joined them, but only as guests. We wished them luck, and returned to our hut in Nahalal, which we had rented from the village council. We had two rooms and a kitchen, a vegetable garden, and a boxer bitch. In February 1939 our daughter, Yael, was born.

In May of that year, Britain issued what was called a Government White Paper on Palestine, formulating a new policy for that mandated territory. It limited Jewish immigration for the next five years and virtually banned it thereafter; and it restricted Jewish purchase of land in extensive areas of the country. This was a reversal of the spirit of the Balfour Declaration, which had been issued in 1917, and the provisions of the League of Nations Mandate. If carried out, the new policy would doom the Jewish National Home. The Jewish community was up in arms, determined to resist the White Paper, and this reaction inevitably brought to an end the cooperation between the Haganah and the British administration and its security forces. Once again the Haganah went underground.

In mid-August 1939, the Haganah started a Platoon Commanders'

Course to which I was sent as an instructor in field tactics. Because of the suspected heightening of British vigilance, this course was held not in one of the regular Haganah training bases but near the village of Yavniel in Lower Galilee, about four miles west of Deganiah. For purposes of cover, the course was ostensibly an extended physical education program under the auspices of a Jewish sports federation. The outbreak of World War Two shortly after the course opened gave an added urgency and importance to our military exercises. All went smoothly for the first seven weeks.

The alarm bell rang on October 3, just as the trainees had gathered for a lecture. As we had no time to disperse, the lecture continued, with the subject switched from tactics to track running, and a few moments later two British security officers appeared at the entrance to the tent. They stood there listening for a while and then went off to search the other tents and huts. They had no difficulty in finding a few rifles beneath the mattresses and none in seeing through the "sports training" cover. They made a note of the arms they had discovered, recorded the innocuous answers we had given to their questions, and departed. The course commander promptly reported this to Haganah headquarters and was ordered to evacuate the camp. He was to transfer the course to the area of Ein Hashofet, a kibbutz just beyond the western edge of the Valley of Jezreel, about twenty-five miles away as the crow flies—far longer by the devious route we would have to take.

We split up into two groups. Yigal Allon, who was also one of the instructors, was put in charge of the smaller contingent, consisting mostly of supernumerary policemen who had the right to bear arms. They set off via the foot of Mount Tabor and reached Ein Hashofet without incident. The larger group of forty-three was led by the course commander. They were to cut across the hills to the southwest, cross the Arab-populated region of Wadi el-Bira while it was still dark, and continue in daylight through the Jewish-populated area of Jezreel. Mordechai Sukenik and I were to be the guides.

Unfortunately, we were late in departing. We had to assume that the camp was under surveillance, and it took care and time to gather up our main supply of arms, which had been secreted in various caches. It was 2 A.M. before we left. We climbed steep and difficult paths through the remaining hours of darkness, but daybreak found us still miles away from the nearest Jewish settlement. We were near the entrance to Wadi el-Bira, which was traversed by the Iraq Petroleum Company pipeline. Sukenik and I, who were ahead of the others, sat down to rest.

Suddenly a Transjordan Frontier Force patrol appeared and halted beside the two of us. The rest of the group was not in sight. This force made up part of the British security units that operated in the two adjoining mandatory territories of Palestine and Transjordan. In answer to their question, we told the patrol that we were hikers, and Sukenik even produced his firearms license. They seemed satisfied and left. So did we. But not long afterward they appeared again, made straight for the rest of the group, and rounded them up. One of their vehicles came after Sukenik and me and added us to those in custody. After leaving us, they had apparently been stopped by an Arab peasant who drew their attention to the file of armed men walking along the pipeline, and they had come back to investigate. After radioing a report, the patrol was soon joined by a British officer and a mounted squad of the Frontier Force. Our weapons were removed, and we waited several hours while their superiors presumably considered what was to be done with us. We were then put aboard two trucks and taken to the prison in Acre. On the way I scribbled a note to my family, "Arrested. No need to worry," with the address on the back and wrapped it around a stone. I spotted my friend Kalman at the crossroads when the truck stopped and threw it to him. In the truck, we talked ourselves into believing that the matter would soon be cleared up and we would be freed.

Our mood changed after the iron gates clanged behind us and we found ourselves locked within this huge stone fortress. It was the citadel built by the Turks in the eighteenth century, when Palestine was part of the Ottoman Empire, on thirteenth-century crusader foundations. The British Mandatory administration had used it as their central prison, and during the period of active resistance after World War Two, many underground Jewish fighters were confined there. Some went to their death in the execution chamber in this very building.

We were first brought to a dank detention room, where our personal belongings were taken from us, and then led into a dark and narrow vaulted hall. We were given water and directed to the tattered, well-worn, and filthy mattresses that lay scattered on the floor. Too tired by now to think, talk, or plan—beyond agreeing that on interrogation we would simply state our name and age and ask for our lawyer—we dropped off to sleep. We had barely closed our eyes before several policemen came in, switched on the light, and asked who among us spoke English. Zvi Brenner and I were among the few who did, and Zvi was the first to be taken for interrogation.

He was not taken far. It was no doubt by design that the interrogation room was close enough for us to hear something of what was going on. We heard voices, then the sound of blows, followed by the moaning of someone in pain, then more talk and more groaning. After a time, the door of our hall was opened, the lights again switched on, and Zvi was thrust in, staggering. As he fell upon his mattress, I was told it was my turn, and I left, so it was only later that I heard from Zvi that he had been kicked and beaten, revived, and then beaten again because he had refused to answer questions.

My interrogators tried to break my spirit by explaining the grave plight I was in. I had been caught in illegal possession of arms, and this, under the Emergency Regulations at the time, was a capital offense. Unless I told them what they wanted to know, they would exact the full penalty, and I would be executed in this very prison. My daughter would be orphaned and would grow up with the burden of knowing that her father had been hanged as a common criminal.

None of us had ever experienced an interrogation, but I decided on the way to my inquisitors that we would gain nothing by sticking rigidly to silence except in the presence of our lawyer. There was no point in being stubborn for the sake of stubbornness and suffering blows for refusing to answer innocuous questions. I worked out for myself what could and what could not be said and acted accordingly. So in addition to giving my name and age, I told them details about my family, and I also saw no reason to hide the fact that we belonged to the Haganah, even though it was an illegal organization. It was quite evident that we had been engaged in military training, and in any case the British knew what the Haganah really stood for and had even cooperated with it in the recent past. But when I was asked for names and for details, such as the source of our firearms, I remained silent. My interrogators repeated that unless I divulged this information I would not have long to live. I said nothing. Two warders then came toward me with raised truncheons and were about to strike me when I uttered a warning. They stopped. I told them not to dare raise their hands against me or any of us. If they did, our friends on the outside would intervene, and those responsible would be punished. I added that their actions and behavior were atrocious, for, after all, we were partners with the British in the struggle against Hitler. They stopped the interrogation and returned me to the others. I believe I saved those who were questioned after me from a good deal of suffering that night.

The jangle of keys woke us in the morning. We were allowed to go up to the tower for fresh air and were greeted by the happy sight of the sea and the wide sweep of Haifa Bay. Below us was the prison courtyard, bounded by thick stone walls on one side and the crusader moat on the other.

We were given olives and *pitta*, the flat Arab bread, for breakfast, and were allowed to get in touch with a lawyer in Haifa. We spent the first day in prison weighing our prospects, and by evening were full of optimism, having been spared further interrogation and having been allowed to receive food sent in to us from Haifa. We reckoned that the Jewish national institutions would get the matter settled at the highest level. We were not criminals. The British well knew that the weapons we carried were for the defense of our isolated settlements against Arab attacks. We would surely be released before long.

Our status until we appeared for trial was that of detainees. We did no work, wore our own clothing, received food from the outside, and were allowed Sabbath visits from our families. We organized morning exercises to keep fit, played chess on a marked cardboard with pieces kneaded out of bread, and secured occasional permission to use the showers and, after a few days, to get books from the prison library. A lawyer from Haifa came to see us and heard details of the events leading up to our arrest. We empowered him to represent us at the trial.

Further interrogations were now conducted in an orderly fashion at the offices of the British Criminal Investigations Department. We were accused of illegal possession of arms, told again that it was a capital offense, that we would be tried before a military court, and that its sentence was final. There could be no appeal. But we were not daunted. We had faith in the efforts of the Jewish national leaders. At worst, we thought, we might get a token sentence.

All of us looked forward to the first family visit on the forthcoming Sabbath. It turned out to be an exercise in frustration. On the great day we were taken to the showers and then led outside the building, where we were ranged in a line along a shallow ditch. Several yards away, in front of and above us, was a concrete platform where the visitors stood. Between us was a wide roll of barbed wire. There would be no quiet privacy about this or any subsequent prison visit.

We were each allowed only two visitors, so while the rest of the family remained outside the prison compound, my mother and Ruth were allowed in—though Ruth was not stopped when she carried nine-month-old Yael through the gate. I had an aching moment when Yael, festively dressed for the occasion, wriggled out of her mother's arms and started crawling toward the barbed wire.

It was all a miserable letdown. Ruth would hold up the baby and keep shouting "How are you?" while I would ask, and hope she and my mother could hear, about my sister, Aviva, and my brother, Zorik, and about the farm and how the sowing was coming along. What could one manage to say in ten emotion-laden minutes in such absurd conditions and above the shouting of other prisoners and other families to the left and the right, who were also trying to throw a word of love to each other from ditch to platform across a barrier of barbed wire? And almost from the first of the few minutes allotted for these visits, we were heckled by the unceasing "Yalla, yalla"—hurry up, hurry up—of the Arab warders.

Our trial opened on October 25 in an army camp near Acre. We, the accused, were seated on benches which almost filled the military hut while counsel sat at tables to our left and right. On a bench in front of us were the "exhibits," grenades and ammunition found in our possession. On the floor was a neat and impressive collection of our rifles.

The prosecutor was a British major. Defense counsel consisted of three lawyers, one of them my father-in-law, Zvi Schwartz. Three British officers served as the judges. The charge against all of us was illegal possession of arms, but one of our group, Avshalom Tau, was further accused of aiming his rifle at the unit which had arrested us. The prosecution line was straightforward: carrying weapons without authority contravened the Emergency Regulations. Our line of defense was also simple: we were a group of young men training to prepare ourselves for the fight against our common enemy, Nazi Germany, and should receive the understanding and indulgence of the court.

The trial lasted three days. Judgment was handed down on October 30. At 10 A.M. that day we were brought to the courtroom as detainees. We left it as convicted prisoners. We were found guilty, and each of us, with one exception, was sentenced to a ten-year prison term. Avshalom Tau was sent to jail for life.

We were a shocked forty-three who were shoved out of the courtroom, roughly chained together and driven back to Acre prison. The chains and the surliness of our guards had been the immediate indication of our instant change of status. The fact that we were now prisoners was heavily underlined upon our arrival back at the prison gates. We had to give up our clothes and personal belongings and don the prison garb that was thrown in our direction: brown sandals, baggy trousers without belt or buttons, a collarless brown shirt, and a brown cloth cap to cover the head, which had been shaved. We were quite a sight. In fact, seeing each other was the only funny thing that had happened to us since our arrest, and we shook with laughter. But we were sobered by the next sight—that of our future home, a long dark cell with a high vaulted ceiling and two narrow barred windows in the thick stone wall that gave onto the courtyard. We would be sleeping on rag mattresses on the concrete floor with two thin blankets for cover.

The daily prison routine started before dawn. Awakened by a bell, we folded mattress and blankets and stood by for the first roll call. With sunrise came morning exercise—a ten-minute walk in pairs under guard in the inner courtyard. After that we underwent a thorough body search, then breakfast, then work. At 11 A.M. we had the first of the day's two main meals, *pitta*, olives, and an Arab minced-meat patty in a chick-pea paste. We had another ten-minute walk and returned to work until 3 P.M., when there was a second roll call followed by the second meal. We were then locked in our cell for the next fourteen hours, disturbed only for the evening count to ensure that no one was missing.

Somehow we had to get ourselves organized to make the most fruitful use of our idle hours, secure improved conditions, and maintain contact with the Jewish authorities in their efforts to secure our release. The forty-three accordingly chose a committee of three, of which I was one. The other two were to be responsible for arrangements and activities within the cell, and I was to represent the group in dealing with the prison administration and keeping in clandestine touch with our own authorities on the outside. We quickly drew up a list of demands, which I presented to the prison governor, and some of them were met. The most important was the one allowing us to work only half a day and spend the other half studying. Others were permission to use writing materials, receive books, and have lighting in the room until 8 P.M. We were thus able to study English, Arabic, the Bible, and chemistry, the teachers being those among us who were students of these subjects. We also renewed the theoretical studies of our Haganah course which had been interrupted at Yavniel. When it got dark, we would huddle round the torch we had been allowed to bring in and read and write by its dim light until the last roll call and lights out. On the material side, we obtained warm underwear and a third blanket, and we became experts at smuggling food in and letters out—for we were now allowed to write only once a month. Visits were once every two months.

Families were a worry, natural but needless. They worried about the prisoners and the prisoners worried about their worrying. My family was the same. I could sense the suffering in their letters and in their eyes when they came to visit. I remember telling them in an early letter that things were not so bad and that imprisonment was not the end of the world. A spell in prison was just that, nothing more. One had to put up with it, "and when it's over, go out, have a good wash, and start life anew." They, however, looked upon jail as a veritable disaster and went about in mourning. To my parents, prison was what they had read in the writings of Dostoevski and heard from friends who had been jailed by the Turks during World War One, when Palestine was part of the German-allied Ottoman Empire.

I, on the other hand, regarded my stay behind bars as a passing episode—unpleasant for the inmates, difficult for their relatives, but certainly not to be spent huddled in a cocoon of misery. Acre was no rest home, but it was no medieval dungeon, and it was not Siberia. Moreover, imprisonment was part of our struggle for the Jewish National Home. I was sorry only that we were in jail as the result of a luckless error and not of some special operation with a significant impact. What was particularly burdensome for all of us was being cooped up and helpless while a war in which we all so desperately wished to take part was being waged.

At the end of November, the judgment was confirmed but the sentence was reduced from ten to five years. We went on a one-day hunger strike in protest against the failure to set us free, while throughout the country manifestoes were distributed by the Haganah. A month later we were transferred to another wing of the prison and divided into groups in four cells. Fortunately, the corridor was wired for electric lighting, and enough light filtered through to enable us to read till late at night. The windows were also better sited for improved contact with the outside.

On her first visit after the trial, Ruth asked the deputy chief warden, a certain Captain Grant, to allow me a close-up glimpse of Yael, who had just had her first birthday. Grant gruffly turned her down, and the exchange left Ruth in a tearful fury of frustration. I was dead against such requests, which only humiliated the supplicant and gained nothing. I wrote to Ruth: "I am not prepared to give Grant the satisfaction of seeing us hurt. I ask nothing of him for he is a boor who gets a sadistic pleasure out of refusing an appeal. So why make one? We don't kowtow to such people to curry favor, and we expect none. Many Jews are being arrested every day and brought here to Acre, many of them Revisionists [members of the Irgun Zvai Le'ummi]. There are also a lot of Arabs. At the moment there are four prisoners in the condemned cell awaiting execution. And in Poland, in Germany, in Russia! A dreadful world, full of horror. And you? A kiss for our baby, and may she enjoy other days in a different kind of world."

But until the arrival of those other days, the days we were living through slipped into a set routine. I began working in the vegetable garden, a small plot enclosed by a wall. We were not driven like slaves, and when the chief warden came around, our guard would tip us off and we would bend our backs. The garden served as a useful hiding place for the canned food that was smuggled in to us. One day I was careless enough to thrust my spade in the wrong place and the treasure was discovered—three tins of bully beef. I was brought before Grant and he gleefully gave me two days in solitary. My comrades arranged with a sergeant warder for food to be brought to me to supplement the regulation diet for those in solitary confinement— flat bread and water.

The solitary cell was small, dark, and bare. In the evening I was given a mattress and a thin blanket. I wrapped myself in the blanket, stretched out on the cold floor—there was just enough room—and thought how good it would be to doze off when I heard a sweet voice lifted in gentle song. It came from the adjoining solitary cell. In it was an Orthodox Jewish lad from the Galilean city of Safed. I had forgotten that it was Friday night, and he was reciting the Sabbath eve prayers and chanting the biblical Song of Songs with great feeling. The acoustics were excellent in this crusader fortress, and the stout walls added resonance to the voice that floated out of the open embrasure of his cell and into mine. My young neighbor at prayer, his voice filled with emotion, apparently had good reason to pour out his heart in supplication to Heaven. I lay with my eyes closed in the darkness, and Acre, incarceration, the cold, and all mundane thoughts vanished. Solomon's Song of Songs and the young man from Safed had conquered the solitary confinement wing of this jail and imbued it with the spirit of the Jewish Sabbath, the Sabbath queen.

Dov Hos, one of the top men in the Political Department of the Jewish Agency—and also in the Haganah—told us on one of his visits that he hoped we might be transferred to the detention camp at Mazra'a, a few miles north of Acre, where conditions were better and family visits were allowed more frequently. We of course wanted the national institutions to keep pressing for our release, but until that was secured the move to Mazra'a would be welcomed. As I wrote to the family at the time, once we started moving "we might finally end up at home."

Home was a distant concept and belonged to the world of letter writing. Zorik and Aviva bore the brunt of the farm work while Father was away (some of his missions were concerned with attempts to get us freed). Ruth and Yael were often in Jerusalem, staying with Ruth's parents. But home was brought closer by the rains. As I watched the raindrops spattering against the prison walls, I would conjure up the plowed expanse of the Jezreel Valley quietly bursting open as the wheat and barley sprouted, casting in a single night a covering of green over the entire area as far as the eye could see, from the Carmel range to the Kishon River.

Father would write us a weekly review of the political scene, and we learned of the approaching threat of war to the country. We learned more at first hand from new prisoners, for there were additional arrests of Haganah groups for illegal possessions of weapons. It seemed that the British authorities were determined to break the Haganah, even though they knew it was the Jewish community's self-defense force. Indeed, among the new arrivals whom we veterans helped to get accustomed to their new life were a group of eleven members of Kibbutz Ginnosar, at the northern edge of the Sea of Galilee. They had gone to the rescue of their comrades out in the fields, who had suddenly been attacked by an Arab band, and they had beaten off the assailants. Shortly after the clash, a British security unit had arrived and found the defenders with their weapons still in their hands. No explanations were accepted. Possession of arms was illegal, and they were brought to Acre. Also among the new prisoners were thirty-four members of the Irgun Zvai Le'ummi, the right-wing dissident underground organization, who had been sentenced for carrying arms and explosives. We belonged to different organizations and held different views on what underground activities should be pursued, but I met with them and we agreed on joint representation before the prison authorities, and they were granted all the special conditions we had managed to secure.

The human landscape among the Arab prisoners was more varied, ranging from common criminals to dedicated nationalists. The elite were several hundred nationalists who were serving life sentences. They included members of the Kassamiya, the Arab band of zealot-terrorists who had been followers of Az-el-Din el-Kassam. Relations between us were friendly and were marked by mutual respect. After all, there was a common background to our imprisonment. Neither we nor they had been sentenced for acts of common crime, like murder or burglary. We had both been moved by national ideals and had risked our freedom and our lives for our people. On Moslem festivals they invited us to their cells to share their choice Oriental meals, and we returned the hospitality on Jewish festivals.

One of my most touching prison moments was meeting Abed el-Salim, the Bedouin boy from the el-Mazarib tribe who had played the flute at my wedding. He arrived in Acre to serve a brief jail sentence. Shortly before my arrest there had been a feud between one of the Arab marauding bands and the el-Mazarib tribe, and the latter had sought shelter in Nahalal, which they received upon my intervention. They had not forgotten this act and looked upon me as their ally.

During my jail term, several condemned Arab prisoners were executed by hanging. The weeping and the wailing of their relatives was heart-rending. After a hanging the entire prison would be gripped by an atmosphere of tension. The prisoners would go about their work in utter silence, and the warders would avoid looking any prisoner in the eye. The next day life would return to normal.

The Englishmen among the warders were not distinguished for their scrupulous sense of fairness. Some were honest and correct, but others would plague us without cause. The worst offender was Captain Grant, who went out of his way to humiliate and insult us. But he did not always find it easy. He knew that if he went too far, the news would reach the Jewish leaders in Jerusalem, who would complain to the British High Commissioner. Furthermore, we political prisoners were a strong and well-organized group, and when such a group is united it eventually has the upper hand—even in a jail.

We were transferred to the Mazra'a camp at the end of February 1940, after five months in Acre and after lengthy negotiations. The kibbutzniks from Ginnosar and the members of Irgun were transferred with us. The camp also held Arab political prisoners. We were guarded by British and Arab policemen, and the camp commander was a drunken and somewhat demented British army officer named Pike. Compared to Acre, conditions were relatively good. We lived in huts, slept on proper mattresses, had utensils for our food, and worked at the nearby experimental-agriculture station. Inspection by the warders was less strict, and visitors were allowed more often.

Despite this, our patience wore thin. We read and studied, but the content of our lives was empty. We found ourselves reliving the past rather than forging plans for the future, and our daily concerns were with such immediate trivialities as the quality of the food and how much prison work would be expected of us. In such a mood, we were, of course, critical of the efforts being made for our release by the Jewish leaders. As far as we were concerned, they were not doing enough. We ignored the fact that they were preoccupied by the immense problems of "the state in the making," pressing ahead with the Zionist ideal of transforming the Jewish National Home under a British Mandatory administration into an independent Jewish state. They were agonizing over how—whether by peaceful or activist means—to react to the restrictive White Paper ordinances limiting land purchase and immigration.

Meanwhile, we continued our work at the experimental station, thinning out wheat, spreading fertilizer, and doing the special tasks called for by the season. Family visits were now more agreeable, and occasionally we were allowed real meetings, in a room, so that we could converse as human beings—and I could hold my little daughter. We were also able to steal a meeting with relatives and friends at our place of work. Dov Hos came often and brought us up to date on what was happening in the outside world. He was tireless in his efforts to secure our release.

In the spring, we celebrated Passover, the Jewish festival of freedom, understandably with special feeling. A truck arrived laden with food, wine, sweets and *matzah,* the unleavened bread eaten on this festival to recall the hasty Exodus of the Children of Israel from Egypt. Avraham Harzfeld, the ebullient spirit behind Jewish pioneer farm settlement in the country, conducted the traditional Seder, the ritual service on the first night of Passover, when we read the account of the liberation of the Israelite slaves from Egyptian bondage. He was in fine form, led us all in song and dance, and gave us the merriest evening of our prison stay.

Throughout the seven-day festival we received many visits. Eliyahu Golomb, the commander of Haganah, came to see us and told us of the plan that was being pressed to establish a Jewish fighting formation within the framework of the British army. We hoped this would speed up our release, for surely the British would welcome additional volunteers. Their situation was critical. The Allied forces were suffering setbacks in Europe, and one after another, countries were being overrun by the Nazis.

We had great expectations for the 6th of June, the birthday of the king of England. When it had been decided to grant a pardon on grounds of mitigating circumstances, it was customary to save the announcement for the king's birthday. But June 6 passed and we remained in jail. It was hard to understand. By then, France had fallen. The British Expeditionary Force had been defeated and evacuated, heroically, back to England. In Palestine preparations for war and for air defense were proceeding apace. And there we were, in prison, drawing up memoranda to remind our people of our existence. We wrote to the Jewish leaders asking them to explain the ludicrous paradox of negotiating with Britain over the enlistment of Palestinian Jews in the British army while we, so eager to volunteer, were kept behind bars.

It was autumn again. A year had gone by. We were still in prison, helpless and frustrated. My English improved—poor consolation—by reading. I started with O. Henry's short stories and moved on to Shakespeare. I also had to do something with my hands. I fashioned necklaces from fruit pits, made olive-wood picture frames, and decorated a jar with exotic sea shells, hardly an appropriate occupation for a young Jew, a soldier, when Europe was falling to the Nazis, Jews were being massacred, and the battlefront was approaching the borders of my own country.

Unlike our celebration of Passover, we greeted the Hanukkah festival in December with sadness. Hanukkah is the Feast of Lights, when we recall the heroic struggle of the Maccabees who liberated Jerusalem from the Seleucids and regained independence for Israel in the second century B.C. We light candles in a special Hanukkah candelabrum to mark their purification of the Jerusalem Temple from pagan sacrilege. We had lit the candles in Acre the previous year with every expectation of lighting them this year at home. It now seemed as though we would be spending the third Hanukkah in the Mazra'a detention camp. To add to our despondency, Dov Hos was killed in a car crash on his way home after a visit to us. He had been the loyal and devoted guardian of our interests and our hopes, a man of heart and of political understanding. His death cast a pall over all of us.

January 1941 was rife with rumor. Snippets of news and rumor of a change in the attitude of the British authorities toward the Palestinian Jewish community began reaching us. We heard that Jewish Agency and Zionist Organization leaders had succeeded in persuading the military chiefs in London to expand the ranks of Palestinian Jewish volunteers to form additional units in the British army and that the British military command in the Middle East was much in favor of using the fighting services of the Jews of Palestine. We also heard that the army authorities were pressing the Ministry for Colonial Affairs, which was responsible for the Mandatory administration, to set us free. Rumors, news, we did not know what to believe. Logic dictated that all such reports, talk, or gossip be discounted. We had had too many letdowns to pin renewed expectations on anything but hard fact and deed. Yet we secretly prized every scrap of information which could add fuel to our hopes.

To buttress the efforts being made on our behalf on the outside, we decided to draw added attention to our case by declaring a hunger strike. We set March 1 as the date. It turned out that we would not have to fast on that day after all. On February 16, 1941, we were informed that we would be released the following morning. With doubt struggling with hope, we hardly slept that night. But at dawn, to our delight, we were given back our civilian clothing and told to pack. We assembled near the entrance to have our palms stamped with a release symbol. The gates were opened and we walked through. Prison was behind us.

4

RELEASE TO THE BATTLEFIELD

I WAS FREE, enjoying freedom with an added dimension that only a spell behind bars can induce. Not that I recommend a prison term. But release endows with a quality of wonder the simple, everyday acts and habits one had always taken for granted, like the drawing of breath after swimming underwater. Freedom is the oxygen of the soul.

Acre is only twenty miles from Nahalal. It had taken me almost a year and a half, from October 1939 to mid-February 1941, to make the trip. Back on my parents' farm, I immediately plunged into the familiar tasks in the cowshed and poultry run and out in the fields at the plow. When pressure on the farm eased, I worked as a hired hand on village projects, mixing concrete, laying floors, and building troughs. At night I did my stint of guard duty. I spent the leisure hours playing with Yael. She was indeed the most lovable of infants.

The bliss of freedom lasted. My stay in Nahalal did not. Beyond the village came the gathering threats of invasion. In the Western Desert, Rommel's Axis forces had launched their second offensive and throughout March and April were advancing toward the Egyptian frontier. To our north, French-mandated Syria, which included Lebanon, was under the control of the Nazi-collaborationist Vichy government, and an attack on northern Palestine, coordinated with Rommel's drive in the southwest, was indeed a possibility. In this situation, the British administration in Palestine agreed to renew their acceptance of the help proferred by the Jewish Agency. More Jewish volunteers were accepted into Palestinian units of the British army, and cooperation was renewed between the British authorities and the Haganah.

The result was the establishment by the Haganah of a country-wide force with the dual purpose of defending the Jewish community from Arab attack and assisting British units on special operations. Yitzhak Sadeh, one of the most colorful of the Haganah's top officers, was put in command of this force, and Yigal Allon and I were made company commanders. We were given the immediate task of enlisting select volunteers from the Valley of Jezreel and Galilee.

Early in May Yitzhak Sadeh had called on me in Nahalal, together with Zvi Spector, one of the Haganah's young veterans. Sadeh had given me the general outline of the plan for mobilizing and training our men but no clear notion of the kind of operations in which we would be used. The only thing that was clear when he left was that my three months' vacation on the farm with my family had come to an end. I would be returning to military duties with the Haganah.

We soon learned that our special units would be serving with Allied formations in the invasion of Syria, an operation designed to neutralize the threat from the north. Our men were expected to be familiar with the area of the northern frontier and would guide the advance of the Allied invasion force.

My unit was not the first to go into action within the framework of British-Jewish Agency cooperation. The first was a special operation to blow up the oil refineries at the Syrian port city of Tripoli, in order to deny fuel for German warplanes which had begun to operate from Syrian bases. A unit of twenty-three Haganah volunteers, commanded by Zvi Spector, set out from Haifa during the night of May 18 aboard the motor vessel *Sea Lion*, which carried three light landing craft. With them, as an observer, was Major Anthony Palmer, of the British army's Special Operations Branch. Among the twenty-three were a few of the men who had been with me in the Acre jail. The objective was not gained. The men did not reach Tripoli, and they never returned. Exactly what happened to them is a mystery to this day, though subsequent investigations shed a slight glimmer on the event. Unknown to the men, shortly after they set forth, British aircraft had bombed Tripoli and the defenses of the refineries had immediately been reinforced. It appears that some of the twenty-three managed to land but must have been overcome by an enemy on double alert. It is assumed that the *Sea Lion* itself was sunk by enemy air action.

I remember sitting on the roof of the tallest building in Haifa with a clear view to the north two days after the twenty-three had left and were already overdue. We were all very anxious, and we kept scanning the water with our field glasses for a hopeful sign of their return. The loss depressed us all. I was particularly pained in the light of what Zvi Spector had told me the evening before he sailed. Though we had not been intimate friends, we knew each other well, and I was fond of him. I happened to run into him that evening and we talked about the operation. He was in poor spirits. He had had a motorbike accident some time before, which had left him with a game leg and rendered him helpless in the water. If anything happened to the boat, he would sink like a stone. I also had gathered that he had hesitations about the likely success of the mission. Another man had in fact been scheduled to command the operation but had dropped out, and Sadeh had asked Zvi to take over. Zvi said he could not refuse a request from Yitzhak Sadeh.

A few days after the mishap, I was summoned by the force commander and given the assignment of my unit, which I still had to form. We would constitute part of an Australian force which would spearhead the Allied invasion. Our task would be to undertake preliminary reconnaissance patrols to check the strength and locations of the enemy defenses and to find subsidiary tracks of advance passable by motor vehicles—since the main arteries were likely to be cut by the Vichy French. On the eve of the invasion, our mission would be to make an advance crossing of the border, proceed to the area of the village of Iskenderun, some six miles north of the present Israeli-Lebanese frontier, and seize and guard the nearby bridges that carried the main coastal highway to Beirut. The Australians feared the French would blow them up and thus delay the Allied advance. Sadeh told me that D-day for the invasion was only about a week and a half away.

In that time I had to find men for the unit, brief, train and equip them, carry out patrols, and then go into action. Sadeh gave me the names of likely volunteers whom I could enlist, most of them from kibbutzim and moshavim in the Jezreel Valley. I sent a message to Kibbutz Hanita on the Lebanese border, which would be my base, and asked its members to make preparations for the arrival of thirty men. I then made a hurried reconnaissance of the frontier. That done, and armed with the names given me by Sadeh, I drove from kibbutz to kibbutz to find the men on his list, informing them of the mission and telling them to report to Hanita within twenty-four hours. Rounding up the men took all night, but by the following evening all thirty were at the base. They were young and ready for action, but they were inexperienced and insufficiently trained. Only one knew Arabic, yet reconnoitering in Syria called for both a familiarity with the language and an idea of how to appear as an Arab. And only one knew how to drive, though one of our tasks was to find passable routes for vehicles. Few could use a machine gun, and only a handful had ever fired a rifle with live ammunition.

It was important for us to succeed in our assignment, both for its contribution, however slight, toward the success of the overall operation and for the wider opportunities it might open up for increased participation by the Jews of Palestine in the war against Hitler. The British administration in Palestine had largely spurned Jewish volunteers who had sought to join the British army upon the outbreak of war. They were afraid this would drive the Arabs even further into the Nazi camp. They had eventually relented somewhat and allowed a restricted number of our men to join Palestinian units. (Only in 1944 did they agree to the establishment of a fighting Jewish Brigade.) It was largely the British military authorities who perceived the value of our aid in the invasion of Syria. But even they probably considered our participation as a one-time effort. For our part, we hoped that if we did well in this action, we would be used for further special operations. We therefore tried to enlarge our force. Even with my unit, for example, the Allies expected us to provide only a handful of guides. We had recruited thirty but had been furnished by the British with only ten military guide certificates and only nine revolvers—with ammunition of the wrong caliber. We obtained four more with fifteen rounds each after much haggling.

We overcame the weapons problem by securing arms from the Haganah's illegal arsenal. We overcame the training problem by getting two experienced Haganah officers who put the men through a concentrated crash course. But our main problem remained: not one of us knew Syria and not one was familiar with the terrain over which we were expected to guide the lead invasion unit! And before that we had to carry out our reconnaissance patrols, yet we had no detailed maps.

Yosef Fein, the father of future Air Force Commander Mottie Hod, came to our rescue. A member of Kibbutz Deganiah, he had spent some years in the northern frontier village of Metulla and had many Arab friends in the area. Some of them knew every track and wadi in the region in which we would be operating and through Yosef's mediation agreed, for a suitable fee, to accompany our reconnaissance units across the border. I split my men up into small groups, each with an Arab guide. They were to operate only at night, leaving at dusk and returning at dawn, dressed as Arabs and avoiding clashes with enemy guards.

I myself preferred to do my own reconnoitering accompanied only by a guide, and the one Yosef found to attach to me was a Circassian. To make sure, as Yosef put it, that the Circassian would not give me away once we were across the border, he installed the guide's wife and children in a Haifa hotel, so that if anything befell me, they would suffer. I thought the precaution absurd. The Circassian knew as well as I that no matter what happened to me, no harm would come to his family.

On our patrols, my guide and I would try to avoid encountering anyone, but we would occasionally come across smugglers and watch-men who were probably as interested in chatting as we were. We would greet each other on the move with a welcome in Arabic and go our respective ways. The nights were cool, and walking across the mountain tracks was pleasant. We would drive to a short distance from our side of the border and I would hide my car against a hedge. On our return in the morning, we would drive to Hanita, where I would mark the possible routes negotiable by vehicles and the places where one would have to clear an obstruction, like breaching a stone fence, to break open a passage.

We carried out these intelligence patrols for a week. There were some narrow escapes, but all ended well and we gave the enemy little cause for suspicion. Our men got used to walking long distances over rough ground in the dark and became acquainted with the terrain on the Syrian side of the border.

The invasion date was fixed for Saturday night, June 7. The day before, I had to visit Haganah headquarters in Haifa to make some last-minute arrangements, so I drove first to Nahalal to pick up Ruth, who wanted to wait in Hanita for my return from the Syrian action. In Nahalal I also picked up Zalman Mart, who happened to be pass-ing through the settlement. Mart was an able and experienced Haga-nah officer who was also doubling as a sergeant in the British-run supernumerary police. The British, of course, had not known of his Haganah connection. I asked him to join me on the Syrian mission and he readily agreed. We drove off to Haifa, arranged matters at headquarters, and then stocked up with food and drink for the party we would be having the next evening with our Australian comrades before setting out on our assignment.

We then sped north to Hanita, but in Nahariah we were stopped by a Haganah liaison officer with British headquarters who had information for me. He said the British had just had a detailed report of a new and better invasion route, more easily negotiable by vehicles than the ones we had found, but it had to be confirmed by an additional night reconnaissance. I promptly left Ruth and the supplies in Nahariah and returned with Mart to Haifa to find Yitzhak the Druze, the finest guide in the business, to accompany us. After collecting him, we set out again northward to the border. On the way we chanced upon the driver of a bread van and promptly enlisted him for the job of waiting for us near the frontier. If we failed to return from our patrol by morning, he was to drive to Hanita and tell my men to carry out the assignment without me.

When darkness fell, Yitzhak the Druze, Mart, and I crept to the border, crossed it, and for the next few hours covered the area of the potential new route. It was worth the effort. We walked through plantations and tobacco fields and judged that it was possible, without much difficulty, to open a dirt track firm and wide enough to take vehicles. We also kept our eyes and ears open to gather intelligence on the strength and frequency of enemy road patrols and the state of alert at military bases in the region. We got back before dawn, much to the disappointment of the waiting bread-van driver, who had spent the night framing the dramatic announcement he had expected to make in Hanita upon our failure to return.

I immediately contacted Haganah headquarters in Haifa to deliver my enthusiastic report. Yitzhak Sadeh listened patiently and then calmly explained that it was now Saturday morning, H-hour was that night, and it was simply too late to change the invasion route. He doubted whether there was even any responsible officer at Allied headquarters to whom the report could be usefully transmitted or time enough to coordinate with all the various units that would be engaged in feverish last-minute preparations. He told me to do what I thought fit and arrange matters directly with the commander of the Australian unit to which I would be attached.

The Australians arrived in Hanita that Saturday afternoon, a young, enthusiastic, and friendly bunch. I sat with two of their officers and we went over the final plans—how we would get to the Iskenderun bridges, silence the sentries, gain control, check for explosives and neutralize them if necessary, and defend the causeway until the arrival of the invasion force.

For this mission we would be a tiny unit, only five of our men, ten Australians—including three officers—and Rashid Taher, an Arab guide. Our weaponry was meager, but it would prove sufficient. The

Australians carried one machine gun, one sub-machine gun, and a few rifles and revolvers. We had a Tommy gun, semi-automatic pistols, a couple of rifles, and a few hand grenades.

Ya'akov Dori, who would be Israel's first chief of staff and who was now in effect chief of staff of the Haganah, arrived together with Yitzhak Sadeh for our pre-departure meal. Though they did not refer to the misadventure of the *Sea Lion* operation, the incident was clearly very much on their minds, and one could sense from their manner and expression a concern for our fate and the desperate wish that we succeed. Our participation with the British in future special operations depended on our success.

We set out at 9:30 P.M. in high spirits, feeling somehow that we were the entire Allied invasion force, instead of a puny handful of commandos, and glad at last to be on the job itself after the days and nights preparing for it. The moon was full, which made it easier to see where we were going but also easier to be spotted. We made a wide sweep across the mountains so as to reach our objective from an unexpected direction, marking our own steep and tortuous trails across the trackless slopes. After some four hours of stiff walking and climbing, we reached the ridge above our objective. Here we rested, munched on chocolate bars, and turned our field glasses onto the coastline, the village of Iskenderun, and the bridges. It was not light enough to see details, and we could not detect the French squads guarding the bridges, but we had to assume they were there.

We split the unit into two groups, one to tackle each bridge, and my group proceeded stealthily toward the northern bridge. We stopped a short distance away and waited. All was silent. Three of us then crawled to the bridge, Rashid in the lead, myself just behind him, and one of the Australian officers, Kyffin, behind me. We found it unguarded, and it had not been prepared for demolition. This was also true of the other bridge.

It was an anti-climax, but a great relief. After a week of patrolling, with little sleep, and after the tiring climb that night under the tension before an expected action, it was good to breathe freely. Formally, our job was done, without firing a shot. The bridges were secure and all we needed to do was hold them until the arrival of the lead unit of the invasion force, which was due at 4 A.M. It was just about 2 then, so we deployed for the defense of the bridges, and I then stretched out in the roadside ditch and went to sleep.

I awoke to daylight. The sun had already risen, and there was a sound of firing in the distance. I looked around me and was uneasy. The invasion vanguard, which should have reached us before dawn, was nowhere to be seen. But we were very visible indeed—and likely to be attacked any moment. We were in an indefensible position, near the bridge in a deep valley, easy prey to anyone in the hills above.

Rashid mentioned to me that there was a police station about a mile or so away, manned, he believed, by a few policemen. I thought we should try to seize the station before we ourselves were attacked. I put the suggestion to the Australians and they agreed. So we left a guard at the bridge, and the rest of us moved off to the police station. When we got close to it, we saw not policemen but troops in French uniform, and we promptly took shelter in an orange grove across the road from the two-story stone police station. The Frenchmen spotted us and opened fire. At the sound of shooting, other troops came out to the entrance to the station and joined their comrades in the sharp exchange of fire which ensued. Rashid, our Arab guide, turned out to be a courageous soldier and a first-class marksman. Taking accurate aim, he shot the Frenchmen who were trying to approach us under cover of the trees. We found some protection behind the low stone fence at the edge of the grove and kept up our shooting. But we were being pinned down by machine-gun fire directed from the terrace of the building. Our ammunition was getting low, and the situation was desperate. Continuing to exchange shot for shot while we remained where we were would prove purposeless, indeed fatal. It would only exhaust our ammunition supply and render us unable to fight. The alternative was to storm the building.

I asked the men to provide covering fire for Mart and me, and we dashed out of the grove and into the ditch across the road from the police station. From there I tossed a hand grenade toward an open window through which we were being fired on. But I missed and the grenade exploded outside. However, the noise must have disturbed the machine gunner, for he stopped firing for a few moments. In those moments we raced across the road, got close to the building, and from there I tossed my second and last grenade. This time it went through the window, and when it burst in the room, firing from the building ceased. Our unit rushed to the assault and seized the station. The French surrendered.

Their machine gun had not been damaged, and we quickly brought it up to the roof, as we were likely to be attacked by French reinforcements. It was not an ideal tactical position and there was little cover, but it served as an excellent observation point, and this was important. We also took over the rest of the French weapons and ammunition. These now included a mortar which had been located in the grove. Near it was a French soldier who joined the other prisoners under guard on the ground floor of the building. We now had arms and ammunition in abundance.

It transpired that this police post had served as the headquarters of the Vichy French forces in this region. We learned that their main units were now deployed close to the Palestinian border to resist the Allied invasion. They had put up roadblocks on the main highway and set ambush positions to cover them.

It was evident that we would soon be attacked by other French detachments in the Iskenderun area, and it would be useful if contact could be made with the invasion force, which presumably had not yet crossed the frontier. There was a motorcycle outside the building, and Mart took it and rode off toward the border, hoping somehow to get through the French roadblocks. But after his tires were shot up, he returned. He was lucky to get back alive. There was no choice but to organize ourselves for defense and await the arrival of the Allied advance unit. I took up a position behind the machine gun on the roof.

French reinforcements drew near and began to surround the building. I opened up with the machine gun and drew heavy fire in response. I took up my field glasses to try and locate the source of the shooting. I had hardly got them into focus when a rifle bullet smashed into them, splintering a lens and the metal casing, which became embedded in the socket of my left eye. I immediately lost consciousness, but only for a moment. I came to and lay stretched on my back. I was also wounded in the hand.

Mart soon came up to the roof, bandaged my eye and the damaged fingers with field dressings, and wrapped my face in a *kefieh*. I was then lowered in a makeshift stretcher of blankets to the ground floor, and there I lay, conscious all the time. Mart took my place on the machine gun but came down every so often to find out how I was doing and to report on what was happening. From then on, sightless, I followed the progress of the battle through my ears, from Mart's reports, though I must say it required a considerable effort to concentrate. We had no pain killers with us, and my head felt as if it were being pounded with sledge hammers without stop. Fearing that I might not survive the loss of blood, one of the Australian officers suggested that I be handed over to the French so that I could receive medical treatment before it was too late. I refused.

Our unit was doing well. The machine gun was trained on the orange grove, and the very effective captured mortar covered the highway. We even managed to stop and seize several French military trucks and their occupants, part of a convoy traveling south from the direction of Beirut to resist the invasion. We were stuck, surrounded, with no way of escape. But we had weapons, ammunition, stout walls, and courageous fighters, and they kept the enemy at bay. We held out.

Hours later, the lead Australian detachment of the invasion force reached us, having broken through or bypassed blocked or blasted stretches of the route. Together with two wounded Australian soldiers, I was put aboard one of the captured French trucks and driven south. With me were Mart and Rashid. It was an inordinately slow drive on a battered road and dirt-track bypasses, made even slower by having to contend with the invasion convoys moving in the opposite direction. At long last we reached Rosh Hanikra on the border, where the field medical unit and assembly point for wounded was located. The British doctor who saw me thought it unwise to remove the bandages and ordered me off to hospital by ambulance. Still accompanied by Mart and Rashid, I was driven to Haifa and reached the hospital just before nightfall, twelve hours after I had been wounded.

We had carried out our assignment. Though the bridges we had been sent to secure had not been sabotaged when we reached them, there was no chance of subsequent damage once we had got there. They remained intact. True, the French had blown up another stretch of the coastal road which was outside our area of operations, but it had not proved a crucial barrier, and though it had held up the invasion force, a new path had soon been cleared.

In the operating theater in the Haifa hospital, the surgeon examined the wounds and praised Mart for not having removed the splinters of glass and metal that had lodged in the eye socket. They had in fact served as a stopple and stanched the bleeding. I asked the doctor about my condition. "Two things are certain," he said. "You've lost an eye and you'll live. What is not clear is the condition of your head, with so many bits of glass and metal embedded in it."

5

RECOVERY

I THOUGHT AT FIRST I would be well enough to resume an active role in the war. But the treatment of my wounds was very protracted. We moved to Jerusalem, staying with Ruth's parents, so that I could attend the hospital's out-patients' department each day. The trickling pus from the eye socket, the innumerable bits of shrapnel in my body, the severe headaches, and the paralyzed fingers of my wounded hand did nothing to lighten my mood. Nor was my remaining eye yet accustomed to doing its double job. My vision was out of focus. Reading was blurred, and when I poured water from a kettle, I inevitably missed the glass and drenched the tablecloth. I found it difficult to adjust to the dark. I almost gave up hope of ever recovering my fitness to fight, and I reflected with considerable misgivings on my future as a cripple without a skill, trade, or profession to provide for my family. This problem was given added urgency, for when I was wounded Ruth was pregnant with our second child, Ehud.

Fortunately Reuven Shiloah lived on the ground floor of the house where we were residing. He was in charge of Special Services in the Political Department of the Jewish Agency, the supreme body responsible for Jewish affairs in Palestine, and he would often drop in to "visit the sick soldier." On one such visit, he suggested that I work in his section. I readily accepted. That was one problem solved—how to support my family. It also gave me a psychological lift. I had a job, a salary, and the prospect of making my way in the political field, which was new to me. My spirits soared, and my body, too, began gradually to accustom itself to its new state. I started reading again without too much trouble and without the use of glasses. I learned to estimate distances with a single eye, well enough to drive a car. And in order to get used to the change from light to dark, I walked a lot at night. I wandered for hours around the environs of Jerusalem, over rocks and into bushes, often falling, but learning to speed up my reactions and keep my balance.

The Special Services Section was concerned at the time with the ways in which it might continue to serve the Allies in the event that the Germans invaded Palestine. The threat of an invasion was very real, with German successes on the eastern front and Rommel's victories in the Western Desert. One of the proposed projects was the transmission of intelligence information from Palestine to the Allied forces in the event that the Germans occupied the country. At the time, the British Intelligence Service in the Middle East was cooperating with the Jewish authorities and the Haganah, in view of the Nazi threat. The British approached Shiloah with the proposal that we set up an underground network which could gather military information on the enemy and radio it to their headquarters. British Intelligence would give us technical help. The task of organizing and running the intelligence-gathering communications network was given to me, and I presented a detailed plan in August 1941.

The plan called for the establishment of a central exchange in Jerusalem and sub-stations in Tel Aviv, Haifa, Hadera (midway between the two) and at Kibbutz Maoz Chaim in the Bet She'an Valley, just south of the Jordan Valley. Manning each sub-station, or cell, would be a commander, radio operator, and the intelligence squad, which would secure information.

The British approved the plan, and in September a professional course was held for twenty radio operators. Commanding the course was one of our own boys, Rehoboam Amir, who later parachuted behind the German lines in Europe. The subjects taught were reception, transmission, use of codes, and technical instruction on the radio sets. I went from cell to cell deciding the location of each station, briefing the squad commanders, arranging the "safe" hiding places in case of emergency, and laying the ground for future sources of information. Financial support for the cells—wages for the squads and the cost of equipment—was authorized and borne by the British, and they also paid my salary—£20 a month plus £5 for the rent of a small apartment, which also served as the central exchange in Jerusalem.

The official name given to the network by the British was P.S.—the Palestine Scheme—but it was commonly known as "Moshe Dayan's network." While it operated directly under the British, it maintained close contact with the Haganah, and all the men in my network were Haganah members. The British officer responsible for the network was a Col. Reid, from Middle East Command Intelligence, and an officer named Hooper served as his liaison with me. He told me that he had been born in Egypt, where his father had been a police chief. He spoke fluent Arabic and was very familiar with the region. Living with us in the apartment-station in Jerusalem were two pleasant young Englishmen. One was the radio instructor and the other the Jerusalem operator.

My open wounds had dried up, the shrapnel in my body ceased to trouble me, the assignment was of absorbing interest, and I was again on my feet. During the week I would be on the road, traveling from place to place, organizing, meeting, and directing the cell-squads. I would always return home on the Sabbath. I loved to wander around the Old City, especially to walk the narrow path along the top of its encircling walls. The New City, West Jerusalem, with its suburbs, was somewhat strange to me. But the Old City, with its magnificent walls and lively bazaars, its holy sites and mundane profanity, was an enchantment. I could never get enough of it.

In the course of my work, I proposed that in the event of invasion and occupation, we should extend our intelligence activities and, in addition to our communications network, should also train special "Arabized" and "Germanized" groups among our people. I thought that the best way to gather information in case of a German conquest would be through the help of Jews who could appear, speak, and behave as Arabs or Germans. Part of this plan began to be carried out, though in a different form. We recruited candidates for missions into Nazi-occupied Europe, mainly the Balkans, and the British Intelligence Service sent an officer to select and instruct them. He had been T. E. Lawrence's pilot during the Arab revolt in World War One. Among the first to go behind enemy lines were four of our radio operators. One was Rehoboam Amir. Another was Peretz Rosenberg, who was married to a girl from Nahalal and who had also been an instructor on our course. (He parachuted into Yugoslavia in May 1943 and served as the radio operator to the British mission with Tito.) Another batch of volunteers was sent to Cairo for training, half of them from Palmach, the most active combat units of Haganah. The twin aim of the parachutists was to join the partisans, help rescue and find escape routes for Jewish survivors, and do the same for Allied pilots who had been forced to bail out over Nazi-occupied territory.

Many fulfilled their missions and survived. A number were caught and executed. Among them was Hannah Szenes, a young poetess and kibbutznik who had been dropped in Yugoslavia, worked with Tito's partisans, but was captured when she crossed into Hungary to help the Jewish community there. Another was Enzo Sereni, a highly educated idealist and member of a distinguished Italian-Jewish family who had left Rome to settle in Palestine and had been a founder of Kibbutz Givat Brenner, south of Tel Aviv. Captured by the Nazis, he was taken from one camp to another as the Germans retreated throughout 1944 and was finally shot in the Dachau death camp in November of that year. Tragically enough, an ironic fate awaited some of those parachutists who had come through the war unscathed. They were killed in 1954 while attending a memorial ceremony for their dead comrades at Kibbutz Ma'agan on the eastern shore of the Sea of Galilee. A light plane circling overhead to parachute a scroll bearing a presidential message for the occasion suddenly stalled and crashed among the assembled gathering. One of Sereni's children was among those killed.

In the summer of 1943, the Palmach took over the parachute drops into Nazi Europe, as well as the plan to establish "Arabized" and "Germanized" groups. But the threat of a German conquest of the Middle East passed with the rout of the Germans in the Western Desert. The Palestine Scheme was discontinued, and at the end of August 1942 I returned to Nahalal.

Before doing so I "hitched" a ride to Baghdad. I had heard that a convoy of buses belonging to a Jewish transport cooperative had been chartered by the British army to take an Indian battalion to Iraq and bring back to Palestine the English unit that was being replaced. I approached one of the drivers, and he agreed to "adopt" me as "driver's mate" for the journey. As soon as my Haganah supervisors heard of this arrangement, they asked me to take three suitcases of small-arms weapons to deliver to the Haganah cell in Baghdad.

British forces were stationed in Iraq at the time because there had been a *coup d'état* in that country and the pro-British government had been replaced by a pro-German regime, headed by Rashid Ali, who declared war on Britain in May 1941. Britain had reacted swiftly, rushing troops from India to Basra and sending a British column from Palestine to Baghdad. Within a few weeks the revolt was quelled. But before this happened, the Arabs attacked the Jewish Quarter of

Baghdad and in two days, June 1 and 2, they massacred some four hundred Jews, destroyed their homes, and looted their possessions. No matter what new regime would emerge, the Jewish community would always be vulnerable to further action by violent elements among the Arab population. Haganah cells were therefore established in Iraq both to organize self-defense against future attacks and to overcome Iraqi impediments to the departure of Jews from Iraq and the British ban on their entry into Palestine by establishing clandestine routes.

We traveled for three days through the almost trackless desert, some of the buses occasionally losing the rest of the convoy and finding themselves alone in the wilderness. But we finally made it and reached a British military camp some twenty miles outside Baghdad. The British ordered the drivers not to leave the camp, fearing possible anti-British reprisals by the Arabs if the arrival of Jews from Palestine became known. We were instructed to remain in the transit camp until the Indian troops had relieved their English counterparts. We were then to transport the English unit straight back to Palestine. We were not to set foot inside Baghdad. I resolved to smuggle myself out and somehow get to the Iraqi capital.

I left before dawn. Carrying my clothes rolled in a bundle, my eye patch left behind, wearing only my undershirt and shorts, and barefoot, I stole silently through the camp fence, crawled until I was out of range of the camp, crossed ditches filled with water and mud, and reached the highway. Shortly afterward, a long line of donkeys laden with farm produce came by on their way to the Baghdad markets. I broke off a branch from a bush, attached myself to this bedraggled convoy, and passed through the police checkpoints on the bridge before the entrance to the city, prodding a reluctant donkey with my branch as I walked.

Once inside Baghdad I left my "saviors" and put on my clothes. But in my muddy and disheveled state, I found it difficult to gain entrance to the swank Hotel Umayyad, where the Haganah emissary was staying. He was Enzo Sereni, who a few months later would parachute behind the enemy lines into Nazi-occupied Europe. I had had no problem in passing myself off as a wretched Iraqi peasant boy. My problem now, at the hotel, was to convince the hall porter that I was not really a miserable serf. After further entreaty—plus an appropriate quantity of *baksheesh*—he deigned to telephone Sereni's room and ask him to meet me in the street. Sereni came down and, after a little more *baksheesh*, took me up to his room. I showered, got a change of clothing, and out we went to explore the city. It was well to wait until dark, he said, before we visited the Jewish Quarter.

We toured the museum and Sereni waxed enthusiastic as he explained to me the background of the ancient Mesopotamian swords and the inscriptions of the eighteenth-century B.C. Babylonian king Hammurabi. At that time, unfortunately, I had little interest in archaeology. The Baghdad I saw was a great disappointment. I expected, if not the formidable palaces of the caliph Harun al-Rashid, at least the exciting bazaars of Damascus. But this Baghdad, with no greenery to relieve the drabness of its low, dun-colored, dusty brick buildings, was bare and depressing.

In the evening we went into the Jewish Quarter and met the people who were active in the community and anxious to leave for Palestine. They asked me to smuggle into Palestine two young Jewish refugees from Poland who had managed to escape from the Nazis and to make their way to Iran. From there they had arrived in Baghdad, another step en route to Palestine. I agreed, and we organized an "exchange operation." I returned to the camp that night and crept out again the following evening with the suitcases of weapons. I gave them to the Haganah cell and took in exchange the two refugees, whom we dressed in British army uniforms.

I had to make the return journey to Palestine in another bus. The drivers were reluctant to take the risk of transporting "illegal immigrants" in their vehicles. But one driver finally agreed. A *sabra* from Petach Tikvah, a suburb near Tel Aviv, he was the son of Avraham Shapiro, the famed "watchman" of the early pioneering days, when a colorful band of mounted Jewish guards would roam the area of isolated Jewish farm settlements challenging Arab marauders and helping to maintain security. We got back without incident. I left the refugees at Kibbutz Maoz Chaim in the competent hands of Nessia, the wife of Uri Brenner, who had been in charge of the kibbutz substation near the Jordan in the Palestine Scheme network. Then I returned to Nahalal.

Back on the farm I spent the next two years with my family living in a prefab hut on my parents' farmstead. We were anxious to get our own farm, and I again saw my future as a member of the Nahalal cooperative settlement. In 1944, a farm in Nahalal became available, but just as we were negotiating its acquisition, Eliyahu Golomb, head of the Haganah, urged me to come to Tel Aviv and serve as a full-time officer in the underground defense establishment. I agreed.

We lived for a year in Tel Aviv. I was engaged mostly in intelligence duties, which were connected with my former activities. But I also took part in what became known as "the season," and what to me and to many of us was then a very "unhappy season." This was the period during World War Two when the Jewish Agency and its underground arm, the Haganah, were cooperating with the British in the fight against Nazi Germany. They were therefore anxious to stop the independent actions of the dissident paramilitary organizations, the Irgun Zvai Le'ummi and the Lehi (Stern Group), which would undertake terror reprisals after anti-Jewish acts by Arabs or by the British and refused to respond to the Haganah's call for "restraint." The Haganah tried persuasion, and I had several most interesting talks with the leaders of Lehi and with members of the High Command of the Irgun. I understood their motivations and respected the self-sacrificial devotion of their men. I also had a long talk with Menahem Begin, the commander of Irgun. But in spite of our conversations and the common language, I remained a "Haganah man" in the eyes of these men of the dissident underground. I was completely at one in my thinking and my actions with the path marked out by Ben-Gurion, who was firmly opposed to the dissidents and called for an end to their terror activities. His—and the Haganah's—policy was to search out and hit back against the Arab attackers, not engage in indiscriminate reprisals which might result in the death of innocent Arabs.

When we returned to Nahalal a year later, it was not to my parents' home but to our own farmstead. It consisted only of citrus groves and had no livestock. We bought some cows, and I built a chicken run. The heavy farm work from dawn to dusk was something I knew and loved. I planted vegetables—tomatoes in summer, Japanese cauliflower in the autumn—and to my egg-laying poultry I added turkeys for meat. Curiously enough, I was the only member of my family at the time who was doing any farming. My sister, Aviva, and my brother, Zorik, had joined the British army. Zorik was in the Jewish Brigade, where he served in Italy and Belgium, and Aviva was a nurse and later an army driver serving in Egypt.

In 1945 our third child, Assaf (Assi), was born in Nahalal. I was now spending almost all my time at home and on the farm. The first time I was away for more than a day or two was late in 1946. It also marked my first active participation in political party affairs. I joined the Labor Party (Mapai) delegation as an observer to the Twenty-second World Zionist Congress in Basle. One thing which seemed important to me was the activist line urged by Ben-Gurion, in contrast to Chaim Weizmann's policy of moderation toward the British administration. The world war had ended, Hitler had been defeated, and there was no point in continuing to cooperate with the British, who harshly restricted Jewish immigration into Palestine and Jewish settlement and development in the country.

Ben-Gurion called for an active struggle against the British, who were trying to stop Zionist activity. I was an enthusiastic "Ben-Gurionist" and "activist." In my view, this approach included not only defense matters but all Zionist aims, particularly land settlement and immigration. At an internal meeting of the party delegation in Basle, I expressed my view, and I was young enough to be very pleased when Ben-Gurion made specific mention of my wide definition of "activism," with which, he said, he fully agreed.

At the end of the Congress, and on the urging of my family, I stopped off at a hospital in Paris for an operation. The intention of the surgeon was to plant a bone in my eye socket so that it would hold an artificial eye. I was ready to make any effort and stand any suffering if I could only get rid of my black eye patch. The attention it drew was intolerable to me. I preferred to shut myself up at home, doing anything, rather than encounter the reactions of people wherever I went. It is difficult for a normal-eyed person to understand how unpleasant it is to be the constant object of curious stares and whispers. I wanted to be able to walk in the street, sit in a café, or go to a movie without rousing any special interest.

The operation was unsuccessful. My body rejected the bone transplant, producing a fever with a high temperature. I lay for a month in a miserable hospital room, nursed by French-speaking nuns. Ruth and her sister, Reuma, took turns at my bedside, and when we had scraped together enough money for the fare we flew home.

The British Mandate would soon be terminating, and we heightened our efforts to prepare militarily for the possibility of an invasion by the neighboring Arab states. Ya'akov Dori, whom Ben-Gurion had appointed as national commander of the Haganah, called me, and I again found myself on full-time defense service dealing with Arab intelligence.

On November 29, 1947, when news came through of the United Nations Partition Resolution, I was in Nahalal. It was nighttime. I took the children from their beds and we joined the rest of the village in festive dancing in the community hall.

The U.N. decision recognizing Israel's right to statehood was an historic event. The successful passage of the resolution represented an enormous political achievement, in which Ben-Gurion had played the major role. However, underlying our expression of joy was a far deeper emotion, one that I felt as a Jew—indeed, more as a Jew than

I had ever known before. I felt in my bones the victory of Judaism, which for two thousand years of exile from the Land of Israel had withstood persecutions, the Spanish Inquisition, pogroms, anti-Jewish decrees, restrictions, and the mass slaughter by the Nazis in our own generation, and had reached the fulfillment of its age-old yearning— the return to a free and independent Zion. We were happy that night, and we danced, and our hearts went out to every nation whose U.N. representative had voted in favor of the resolution. We had heard them utter the magic word "yes" as we followed their voices over the airwaves from thousands of miles away. We danced—but we knew that ahead of us lay the battlefield.

The Arab states refused to accept the U.N. decision and announced that they would make war on the Jewish state. But many Arabs did not wait for the formal act of statehood. Palestinian Arabs, aided by government-backed irregulars from neighboring lands, started their attacks immediately in the hope of nullifying the Partition Resolution. For the next five and a half months, the country was ravaged by violence. Arab attacks on Jewish rural settlements, towns, and inter-urban transport mounted daily. The British government, announcing that it would relinquish the Mandate on May 15, did little to stop them. Order gave way to anarchy. As a consequence, several countries which had voted at the United Nations for partition were having second thoughts, and there was heavy international pressure upon Jewish leaders to forgo independence. It was their fear that a Jewish state would be wiped out at birth, for the local Arabs would be joined by the armies of the surrounding states. The Jewish leaders resisted the pressure and ignored the advice of their worried friends. Determined to go ahead with their proclamation of independence, they would fight off the attackers. They knew, as did every Jew in the land, that from now on, and for as long as the war would last, fighting it would be our sole concern. Unless we did fight, and won, there would be no fulfillment of the Zionist dream—no independence, no immigration, no land settlement.

My function on the General Staff of the Haganah as officer for Arab affairs was the recruitment of agents who would supply us with intelligence on what was happening among the irregular Arab forces in Palestine. I was helped in this work by Giora Zeid and Oded Yanai, the sons of pioneer families, who had excellent contacts with Arabs and Druze in Haifa and the north.

Among those fighting us before the full-scale invasion in May was a battalion of Druze mercenaries commanded by Shabib Wahab. The Druze mercenaries were responsible for operations in the Haifa region and had their base at Shfaram in Lower Galilee. The battalion was under the overall command of Fawzi al-Kaukji, leader of the semi-regular Arab Rescue Army, which was aiding the Syrian forces. Giora Zeid, with the help of his friend the Arab mayor of Shfaram, Sheikh Salah Hanifas, sought to neutralize Wahab and his Druze battalion. In the meantime, however, in March 1948, Kaukji suffered a grave defeat in his assault on Mishmar Ha'emek, a strategic kibbutz south-west of Nahalal, and to ease the pressure on his forces, he ordered Wahab to attack Kfar Ata and Kibbutz Ramat Yohanan, two settlements east of Haifa.

My younger brother, Zorik, was one of the officers in the northern front's Carmeli Brigade fighting to defend Kibbutz Ramat Yohanan against the Druze battalion. The battle went on for four days in mid-April. Our units suffered heavy casualties, particularly among the young officers. On the second day of the battle, April 14, Zorik went out on an assault and did not return. I rushed up from Nahalal to look for him on the battlefield, but with fighting going on my search could only be cursory. Only when combat ceased, with our victory and the advance of the Carmeli Brigade, was my brother's body found, by others. He had stormed an enemy position at the head of his men and had fallen with a bullet in his forehead. He was twenty-two. He left a wife, Mimi, and a baby boy, Uzi, who was never to know his father.

With my brother-in-law, Yisrael Gefen (my sister Aviva's husband), I entered the kibbutz dining room, where the bodies of the fallen were laid out. Among them I identified my brother. My mother had told me: "It won't be difficult to identify him after all the scrapes he's been in. His body is covered with scars."

The house was in mourning. The war that was going on and the many sons who were being killed daily blurred the individual sorrows, but not at home, within each bereaved family. Mother was more attached to Zorik than she was to me or Aviva, partly because he was the youngest but largely because of his character. I had not been particularly close to him, for when he was growing up I was away from home a good deal. But I was conscious of his extraordinary vitality, his bubbling good humor, and the seriousness beneath his gaiety. From childhood on he broke through into life as though it held no restraints. When he decided to join the Jewish Brigade of the British army, the world war was in its final stages. With his departure there would be no one left to share the burdens of the farm with my parents. It would be very difficult for them. Father tried to talk him out of volunteering, arguing that the farm would be ruined. Mother did nothing to stop him. "But he really wants to join up," she said, and for her this was what counted. Everyone, she explained, had his own life to live, and no one had the right to ask Zorik to live it in accordance with the needs and wishes of his parents.

After he was killed, I would drop by my parents' home and sit with them for a while, mostly with Mother, and I knew that this was a wound that would never heal. Mother was regarded as a tough woman. Actually, she was rather frail and suffered ill health most of her life. Extremely sensitive, though not given to sharing her thoughts with others, she was deeply responsive to the experiences of life. She was a woman of independent mind, uncompromising but not stubborn. And she could be scathing about those who demanded of others only what was desirable to themselves. When she spoke to me about my children (mostly Yael) or about myself, she would ask not what we were doing but whether we were doing it wholeheartedly.

For Zorik she had a special love because of the completeness of his character. He was different from the rest of the family. With us, whichever path we chose, whatever we believed in, there was always a "but," a "perhaps," a reservation, the other side of the coin. Mother was like that too. Yet here she had given birth to and brought up a boy who was all faith and confidence. High-spirited, fond of sports, he also had a passion for poetry. After his death, Mother, very dear to me, would say little whenever we met. She was a broken woman. The light had gone out.

A few days after this battle, Giora Zeid renewed his contact with the Druze and informed me that he thought it might be possible to neutralize them. A rendezvous was arranged for us with several officers of the Druze battalion at Tivon, in Lower Galilee. When I was presented to them as one whose brother had been killed in the Ramat Yohanan action, they went pale. They suspected a trap, that the meeting had been a stratagem to avenge the blood of Zorik. They were Arabs, and the blood feud was part of their custom and tradition. They assumed it was part of mine too. But I was a Jew and followed Jewish custom and tradition, in which the blood feud has no place. Moreover, Zorik's death was my private grief, and I kept it strictly apart from the purpose in which I was engaged. I had come on a political and military mission, to turn an enemy into a neutral or a friend. The Druze officers were soon reassured. At the end of our negotiations, they agreed to take no further part in the war. Some even came over to our side and fought with us.

I was anxious to leave intelligence work and take an active part in the battles. The lack of one eye did not bother me. By now, I was no longer worried by the thought of what might happen if the other eye was hit. When Yitzhak Sadeh of the Haganah High Command turned to me with the proposal that I form a commando battalion, I eagerly accepted the assignment. I immediately began to plan its establishment.

I had barely started when the State of Israel came into existence— and was promptly invaded by six Arab states. I was called away to deal with a hazardous situation.

PART II

Independence

[1948~1952]

6

DANGER ON THE JORDAN

THE SETTING WAS MODEST, the occasion momentous. At 4:30 in the afternoon of May 14, 1948, David Ben-Gurion formally opened a special session of the Jewish National Council of Palestine. Meetings of the Jewish leadership usually took place in Jerusalem. But Jerusalem was now under siege, and most of the leaders were headquartered temporarily in Tel Aviv. The session was therefore held in the only large hall in the city, an exhibition gallery in the museum.

Ben-Gurion rose—and made history with his opening words. Nineteen turbulent centuries after the Roman destruction of Jerusalem and the Jewish state, he announced the rebirth of Jewish freedom in its ancient land, proclaiming the re-establishment of the State of Israel. The state would come into existence at midnight, the hour when the British Mandate would terminate. The advent of the Jewish Sabbath had made it necessary to advance the hour of this unique and historic ceremony. In an atmosphere of deep emotion, Ben-Gurion then read to the hushed assembly the Declaration of Israel's Independence.

A few hours later, the new state came under attack. From the north, the east, and the south rolled the expeditionary armies of Lebanon, Syria, Iraq, Transjordan (later known as Jordan), and Egypt. Saudi Arabia sent a formation that fought under Egyptian command. They crossed the frontiers and invaded Israel.

We faced a precarious situation. These enemy armies were all equipped with the standard heavy weapons of the regular forces of sovereign states. They had had no difficulty in acquiring armaments openly through normal channels. The Jews possessed no matching arsenal in the opening days of their War of Independence, for throughout the Mandatory period, the only weapons the Haganah underground defense force could secure were little more than small arms, some homemade armored cars, and a few light training planes.

The Syrian army moved into Israel shortly after midnight. For the next two days they shelled and bombed the Jordan Valley villages and stood posed to storm and overrun them. On the third day, May 18, I was summoned from my commando preparations and sent north to take command of the Jordan Valley sector. The headquarters were at Kvutzat Kinneret, on the southwestern edge of the Sea of Galilee, the neighboring kibbutz to Deganiah.

Despite my being from Nahalal and thus no longer a kibbutznik, but a moshavnik, Deganiah, after all, was my first home, and I was always conscious of this bond. The tree-lined lane from the kibbutz dining room to the Jordan River, the large open court, the indestructible Miriam Baratz, the Deganiah veteran who knew me as a baby, the dusty road to Zemach, the basalt-covered hills, the burning summer wind had never been forgotten—nor changed. And they remained a part of me. What I had encountered later were layers added to the Deganiah base. They had not replaced it. I never just "came" to Deganiah. It was always a return home.

The forces deployed for the defense of the Jordan Valley were weak indeed. The Barak Battalion of the Golani Brigade had been holding the line with two companies. When I reached the sector's command headquarters at Kinneret, I was told that in the early hours of that very morning, the Syrians had mounted an attack on the company in Zemach, at the eastern approaches to Deganiah. This unit of local recruits had retreated, leaving behind killed and wounded; members of the nearby kibbutzim of Sha'ar Hagolan and Massada (not to be confused with Masada in the south) had abandoned their settlements; and the Syrians were now all set to attack Deganiah and its sister kibbutz, known as Deganiah B. The only hope lay in reinforcements from outside. Fortunately, en route to the sector, I had run into my friend Uri Bar-On with a unit of volunteers who were also on their way to the Jordan Valley. So was a company of Gadna, senior schoolboys who had been on a pre-army NCO's Course and who arrived at the Deganiahs via Tiberias. I myself had also brought in my car a rare and handsome contribution—three PIATs (anti-tank bazookas).

The commander of the Golani Brigade, Moshe Montag, received me courteously but with little enthusiasm. True, I had been sent by the General Staff, but it was not clear for what. I had been told to carry out special operations behind enemy lines and to give support to the Jordan Valley but that the local troops did not come under my command. At first I was annoyed. However, after I had gone on an inspection tour of our positions at the front, in the Deganiahs and in the adjoining no-man's land, I ceased to be bothered by who was subordinate to whom. The situation appeared to be so desperate that the problem was not who was to give orders but what was to be done.

The Syrian force, now headquartered nearby in occupied Zemach, consisted of an infantry brigade reinforced by tanks, armored cars, and artillery. It also had occasional air support. All we had were Molotov cocktails (homemade bombs—explosives in bottles), a few anti-tank bazookas, some small arms, and lots of spirit and dedication. Other volunteers also began coming in—some singly, some in small groups—from the Valley of Jezreel, from the ancient town of Tiberias, and from the village of Yavniel, to help the Deganiah kibbutzim. Montag, the brigade commander, told me that four 65 mm. guns were on their way.

On this third day of the fighting, with Zemach lost and two settlements abandoned, the area was plunged into gloom. Children and non-combatant women were evacuated. In the evening the Palmach, the most active combat units of the Haganah, still hoped it could restore the situation. A company from its Yiftach Brigade went off to recapture the fort-like police station of Zemach, but it returned after midnight having failed to take it. There was nothing left to do but prepare ourselves for defense, and we did that all the next day, May 19.

The settlements that had relied on the Zemach defense line had not dug in properly, and it was now necessary to do so quickly. The man responsible for the defense of Deganiah was Giora, from nearby Kibbutz Afikim, but I had to find an outside man to take over the defense of Deganiah B. I asked a Haganah veteran and a neighbor of mine in Nahalal if he would do so and was pleased when he agreed. I also found a gap in the defense of the northern flank; Bet Yerach, just north of Deganiah, was unoccupied. True, it was an archaeological mound, not a settlement, but it controlled the road from Zemach to Deganiah and the bridge over the Jordan. I asked the

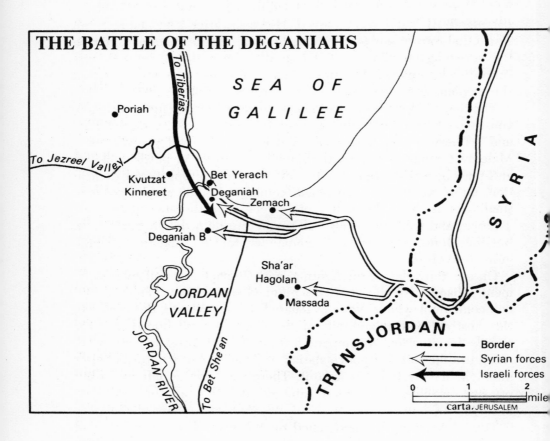

THE BATTLE OF THE DEGANIAHS

To Tiberias

SEA OF GALILEE

Poriah

To Jezreel Valley

Kvutzat Kinneret

Bet Yerach

Deganiah

Zemach

Deganiah B

Sha'ar Hagolan

Massada

JORDAN VALLEY

JORDAN RIVER

To Bet She'an

SYRIA

TRANSJORDAN

Border
Syrian forces
Israeli forces

0   1   2
                              mile

carta, JERUSALEM

volunteers from Yavniel to deploy at Bet Yerach and entrench themselves on its eastern slopes, so that they would be on the flank of the Syrian force that might move from Zemach to Deganiah. I could do no more in that one day. I assumed that the Syrians would concentrate their assault on the northern corner of the Jordan Valley and would try and capture the two Deganiahs and the corridor between the Jordan River and the Sea of Galilee. This was the key to an advance northward, to Tiberias, or westward, to the village of Poriah on the heights of Galilee. I knew very few of the men in the Barak Battalion, but among the volunteer reinforcements were many friends from Nahalal and Yavniel.

Early the next morning, Thursday, the Syrians attacked. They opened up with artillery shelling and mortar bombing at 4:15 A.M. and half an hour later their tank forces, accompanied by infantry, began to advance upon us. With only very brief intervals, the attack lasted nine hours. The Syrians directed their assault at Deganiah and Deganiah B. During the fighting, Syrian planes carried out bombing raids, but they were very inaccurate and had no impact on the situation.

The Syrians advanced according to the book, tanks flanked by infantry. When they came within range of our men, the infantry halted and took cover in the fields of barley, and the armor continued. The Syrian tanks reached the fences of the Deganiahs. In Deganiah, one tank even managed to break through the fence and penetrate the court, but it was knocked out by an anti-tank bazooka and Molotov cocktails. Several tanks were hit by the men of Yavniel at Bet Yerach, and others were wiped out from a range of only a few yards by the men defending the kibbutz outposts. From Poriah, on the heights of Galilee, I received word that the expected 65 mm. guns had arrived and would be ready for action toward noon. Radio connections were not working, so I sent my deputy to Deganiah B to find out how they stood, and I sent a note to my friend Uri to say that if he needed artillery support I would give the necessary instructions; if not, we would not use the guns that day. Both Uri and my deputy reported that the situation in Deganiah B was very grave, and I therefore asked Poriah to fire off the guns as quickly as possible.

The Syrian attack was broken, and the Syrian force retired. This was brought about by two factors. The assault was repulsed by the defenders of the Deganiahs and Bet Yerach, and the Syrian order to withdraw came after our guns had hit the police station and the groves in Zemach. To be more precise, it was the Syrian tanks that got the order to withdraw as soon as our guns opened fire. The Syrian troops, who heard the shriek of the shells over their heads, did not wait for the order. They just took to their heels.

By evening, the Syrians appeared to have evacuated Zemach and withdrawn to the eastern hills. But I could not trust them. Glueing my eye to the field glasses trained on Zemach, I could see neither light nor movement. I decided to go there and examine the situation on the spot. Yitzhak Broshi, commander of the Barak Battalion, and a few friends from Nahalal came with me, and the reconnaissance detachment gave us cover. The moon was not full, but it provided enough light to see. Zemach was empty, silent, abandoned. The bodies of our men who had been killed in the battle there two days earlier still lay in a ditch at the side of a road.

It was evident that the Syrians had fled in panic, leaving weapons and vehicles scattered in street and outpost. We took a Syrian radio car and returned to headquarters at Kinneret. The battle was over— a tough, tragic, and depressing battle. Much young blood had been shed, the blood not of trained and experienced veteran warriors but of youngsters meeting death wide-eyed. Wounded had been left groaning at the side of the road, their untrained comrades pursued by fire and unable to tend them. Against Syrian tanks, armored cars, and artillery, the defenders could put up only limited quantities of meager weapons (except for the four guns that arrived at the last minute), and even many of those were defective. The flame thrower, for example, failed to work; Molotov cocktails exploded prematurely; a settlement had dug no protective trenches; another had not been armed for war. Yet despite misadventure, unpreparedness, and inexperience in combat, the danger had been faced and overcome in fighting which had been desperate at times. All knew in this opening round of our War of Independence that there could be no retreat and no surrender.

7

THE 89TH COMMANDO BATTALION

WHEN I GOT BACK from the Jordan Valley, I set about raising the "mechanized assault battalion," as it was formally called, which Yitzhak Sadeh asked me to form before I had left for Deganiah. It was given the number 89 and was to be a unit of Sadeh's armored brigade. This brigade, however, during my time at least, never fought as a single formation, and the 89th Battalion, when I was its commander, always operated independently.

I was happy with this appointment. It was exactly what I wanted. Yitzhak explained that the battalion was to serve as a special commando unit, rather like such British assault units as the Long Range Desert Patrols and Popski's Private Army in World War Two. Ours, of course, would be smaller in scale, without either their resources or the distances they had to cover, but with the same spirit of daring and unorthodoxy. At first I was told that the battalion would be mounted entirely on jeeps and would be lightly equipped, without support weapons and without armor. Its function would be to penetrate deep into enemy territory and operate behind the lines. Later it was decided to include a support company and give the battalion half-tracks as its principal vehicle.

I confess that though table of organization and weaponry were important and would determine the unit's fighting capacity, I con-cerned myself little with these matters. I left them to my deputy, Yohanan Peltz, an experienced combat officer who had served in the Jewish Brigade of the British army in the world war and who was more of an "organization man," more familiar with administration and logistics. I concentrated on the selection and recruitment of the men. Before long we had four distinctive groups, and each became the nucleus of a company. Young men from kibbutz or moshav farm settlements formed one company; another comprised Tel Avivians; a third numbered members of Lehi, the Hebrew acronym for the Stern Group, one of the dissident former underground movements; and the fourth was composed of overseas volunteers, mostly Jewish veterans from South Africa. Each of these groups attracted to itself further volunteers, largely through personal friendships. The men of Nahalal drew others from the moshav, and were joined by friends from Yavniel in Galilee and from Gvat and other kibbutzim in the Valley of Jezreel. The group from Tel Aviv, headed by Akiva Sa'ar, recruited their city companions. And the commander of the Lehi company, Dov Granek, known as Blondie, called on his old comrades from all parts of the country. Many of these volunteers already be-longed to other units, and they needed permission from their com-manding officers to join us. This was not always granted. Yet they came, with or without permission.

One of the men in the overseas group was an unusual volunteer, a somewhat flamboyant Frenchman whom we knew as Teddy Eitan. He had apparently served in a French armored formation in the world war, and he joined us as a training officer. He was quite popu-lar, but the area of his teaching was limited. He was helpful mainly in technical instruction in various types of weapons, signals equip-ment, and vehicle maintenance. But when it came to exploitation of terrain or such elementary combat skills as cover, support, and "move-ment and fire," most of our men, particularly the officers, were more knowledgeable. All, of course, were more familiar with the country. And tactics anyway had to be suited to the individual conditions of each battle.

The battalion base was located at the former British army camp of Tel Litvinsky (now Tel Hashomer), situated midway between Tel Aviv and the Arab villages of Yehudiya and Ono, which at the time were occupied by Jordanian troops. We were given tents and a few prefabricated huts to serve as offices and mess, but mostly to store equipment.

Vehicles, weapons, and men reached the base in dribs and drabs.

But the most important element was present in full measure—confidence and fighting spirit, the will to get into action and strike at the enemy. This was the very quality I was looking for, and I did everything to encourage it. I truly believed that we could emerge victorious from every battle. There was always some fold in the ground along which we could advance, some rock which afforded cover, and a surprise and judicious military tactic which could give us the advantage over the enemy.

It was summer. The nights were warm, the air was soft, the land spread out before us. Our uniform consisted of khaki pants and shirt, with no badges of rank. Our weapons were a jeep and a machine gun. Our men were first rate.

By now, the lack of one eye was no handicap for me. Even in the dark I did not stumble; my legs found their own way. At the sound of shot or shell, I felt no instinctive recoil, and when I thought about this later I found it was not courage but simply a physical indifference to the noise of incoming fire and the climactic burst. Even when hits were close, kicking up dirt which sprinkled my face, I felt little danger. Rather the reverse: once you could see where the shells were falling, you could avoid them.

On June 20, 1948, shortly before we had completed the organization and training of the battalion, I was hurriedly called to the headquarters of Yitzhak Sadeh, the commander of the armored brigade. Sadeh told me that an arms ship called the *Altalena* had been brought to our shores by the Irgun, the larger of the pre-state dissident underground movements. During the Mandatory period, the Jewish Agency for Palestine had been responsible for administering Jewish affairs. The Irgun, however, had refused to accept its authority. The underground resistance arm of the Jewish Agency had been the Haganah, but the Irgun and the Stern Group (Lehi) had pressed for more extreme measures against the Arab terrorists, as well as the British administration, and took independent action. The moment the state came into being, it was assumed that the Irgun would submit to the jurisdiction of the Israeli government. When the first U.N. cease-fire went into effect on June 11, 1948, Israel and the Arab states agreed not to introduce new arms into their territories. Both sides, of course, violated this agreement, but covertly. However, the Irgun resolved to bring in an arms shipment openly on the *Altalena*. This act could only be viewed as an irresponsible and wanton defiance of government authority, and it had to be vigorously and speedily dealt with.

While I was being briefed by Yitzhak Sadeh, the *Altalena* was anchored off Kfar Vitkin, twenty-three miles north of Tel Aviv, discharging its cargo of arms in order to equip the members of the Irgun, which had not yet been disbanded. The Alexandroni Brigade of Central Command had been ordered to seize the arms, but some of its troops were reluctant to attack the Irgun men. This task had therefore been assigned to my battalion. I was not very certain about the complex internal relations between the Irgun and the government, but I did not question my duty to carry out this order. However, I decided not to involve ex-members of the Stern Group, to whom armed confrontation with former fellow-dissidents in the Irgun would have been particularly distasteful, but to use only the company drawn from the farm settlements.

This company, commanded by Uri Bar-On, went off to Kfar Vitkin, and I got there later, toward dusk. Our men called on the Irgun to give themselves up. Their reply was a volley of fire in which eight of our men were hit, two of them fatally. We set up our mortars and began shelling the beach. The Irgun promptly stopped firing. The engagement was over, and negotiations were started between their commander and Uri Bar-On. The vessel by then had weighed anchor and was on its way to Tel Aviv, leaving small heaps of weapons on the beach.

The quarrel between the Irgun and the government was political, and the clash on the Kfar Vitkin beach had muffled our true military purpose. This was not the war we were engaged in, and these were not our enemies. This was the thought in my mind when I was suddenly summoned to General Headquarters and told to get ready to accompany the body of Col. David Marcus for burial in the United States. I would be joined by Yossie Harel, another young Haganah veteran.

I had had only a few chance meetings with Marcus and did not know him well, but I had heard much about him. He was an American Jewish army officer, a West Point graduate, with an excellent record in World War Two. Though not a paratrooper, he had asked to participate in the airborne assault on D-day and had parachuted into Normandy despite his lack of previous training. Early in 1948, he had volunteered to come to Israel and fight in our ranks, and his character and professional background had been valuable in helping the new Israeli army take shape while emerging from the Haganah underground. He had been appointed commander of the Jerusalem front at the end of May. Eleven days later he was dead, accidentally shot by an Israeli sentry when he left his tent during the night and was walking near the perimeter fence of the encampment.

I had no idea of the burial protocol at West Point, where I would be representing Israel, but I was promised the necessary guidance when I got there. In the meantime, a uniform and badges of rank had to be improvised. I was taken to a men's outfitters in Tel Aviv and after a general consultation, in which the salesmen drew on their recollection of the color and cut of the dress uniform in the armies of the countries from which they had come, they chose a dark-green jacket, added epaulettes, and produced a suitable beret and belt.

We flew in a KLM chartered plane which had been used to transport race horses. The iron rings were still fixed to the floor, and we attached to them the ropes that bound Col. Marcus' coffin. At the side were two mattresses and blankets for Yossie and myself.

We stopped in Paris to refuel, and there I was handed a cable from Prime Minister Ben-Gurion ordering me to return as soon as possible for a meeting with him. I accordingly stayed in the United States only a few days, and apart from West Point and New York saw nothing of America, though this was my first visit.

In New York I met with the Marcus family and with a number of other Jews who were interested in what was happening in Israel. One was a young man named Abraham Baum, who had distinguished himself in the European fighting during the world war while serving with the American 4th Armored Division in a tough combat unit under Col. Creighton Abrams, later the commanding general in Vietnam. One of his exploits had been to lead a small task force and penetrate deeply behind the German lines to rescue American prisoners. This particular mission, undertaken shortly before the end of the war, had failed. Baum's force had indeed crossed the enemy lines and then a river and had broken into the POW camp. But it was decimated by the Germans on the way back, and Baum, wounded, had been taken prisoner. However, after a few minutes of conversation at our New York meeting, I recognized in him a soldier who knew what he was talking about. What interested me in particular was that we in the Haganah, because we were an underground movement, necessarily had to operate in small units, while now, as the legal army of the independent State of Israel, we had to wield larger formations. I was glad to hear from Baum's combat experience as part of a large army that there was still room for, and indeed great value in, a commando unit like the one I had just organized.

Baum's words well fitted my own ideas, and I still remember our conversation. He preached the supreme importance of speed and mobility in battle. According to him, it was best not to undertake preliminary reconnaissance patrols to the projected target of attack, for the information thus received was usually meager, and by tipping off the enemy, the element of surprise was lost. It was best to go straight to the assault positions, with the reconnaissance unit moving ahead, observing, sensing, feeling out the situation, reporting back, and guiding the main force. Baum's experience was born of a different kind of war, but several of his points seemed to me to be applicable to us, too. One was the need to maintain continuous movement. Another was to have the commander direct the action from the front line so that he could see what was happening with his own eyes, rather than rely on second-hand reports.

I returned to Israel in the same plane, and again I slept on a mattress on the floor, for the aircraft was now carrying boxes containing the first Israeli bank notes, which had just been printed in the United States. As we began landing at the airfield of Ein Shemer, midway between Tel Aviv and Haifa, we were fired on from nearby Arab positions; but it was amateur shooting, nothing serious. I was glad that this somewhat unusual trip was over and I was back home. I lost no time in returning to the 89th Battalion, driving there straight from the airfield with the sound of the motors on the long flight still buzzing in my ears. The first cease-fire of the war had not yet ended, and I planned to get into bed the moment I reached Tel Hashomer, where the battalion was stationed. I would start work with the battalion in the morning.

I never got to bed. As I entered the gates of the base, I met the battalion column. It was on its way to Kfar Syrkin, some ten miles slightly northeast of Tel Aviv. From there the unit would be jumping off at dawn on "Operation Danny," the major action on the central front, aimed at thrusting the Arabs back from the positions they held only a few miles to the east of Tel Aviv. I quickly changed clothes and joined my men.

The main battalion objectives were the capture of the enemy posts around the Arab villages of Kula and Tira, which formed part of the advance enemy line in this central sector. Tira, the southernmost of the two, was less than three miles to the northeast of the Lod international airport, which was in our hands but under the enemy's guns. The town of Lod itself, which was wholly in Arab hands, was just over two miles south of the airport. I did not much care for the operational plan worked out by my deputy, Peltz. It called for a long softening-up preparation by our 81 mm. mortars. I favored the quick dash.

We moved off at dawn in the direction of the Arab village of Kula. It was the first time we would be fighting as a battalion. As we approached the target, we came under heavy fire. The half-tracks, which were to have broken into the village, halted, set up their mortars, and got off a few rounds. Instead of giving full expression to its fighting capacity, flinging its entire weight against the target, using all its firepower, and storming the enemy positions, the battalion merely fired off half a dozen mortars. This was not the real thing. Something had to be done, but talk on the radio network would have gotten me nowhere. So I went over to Akiva Sa'ar and told him to stop using kid gloves. He should break into Kula without delay, and I would take the second company and storm the neighboring village of Tira. We did just that, and both positions were captured. Our casualties were five wounded.

The next target we were given was Deir Tarif, a strong Arab position some two miles south of Tira and about the same distance due east of the airport. Our attack here was to be coordinated with brigade headquarters, so I told my deputy to work out the arrangements while I drove to Tel Aviv to meet Ben-Gurion. During the night, shortly after my return from the United States and a few hours before we had gone into action, I had been given a further, rather sharper message reminding me of the cable I had received in Paris and ordering me to come at once. I had made my excuses and gone off with the battalion. Now that there was a brief respite, I proceeded to the Prime Minister's Office.

I found Ben-Gurion rather worried. We were being attacked by the Arabs, and he was having trouble with the Jews. The Irgun and the Stern Group were not accepting government authority. Nor was everything to his liking in the Israel Defense Forces. He had called me, he said, because he wished me to take over the Jerusalem Command from Col. David Shaltiel. It was evident that, to Ben-Gurion, Jerusalem posed one of the central problems of the war, and he did not think the current commander was sufficiently vigorous and aggressive. I appreciated the importance of the proposed assignment, but I turned it down flat. I reminded him that I had just taken over command of the new commando battalion, and we had begun our first battle only that morning. Under no circumstances would I wish to leave it, relinquishing command of a combat unit with the responsibility of personally leading it into action. In the Jerusalem Command I would be ordering others to fight. Here I would be fighting together with my men.

Ben-Gurion asked how the battle had gone that morning, and I told him. He then agreed that I could return to my unit for the time being. The question of my Jerusalem posting would be postponed until the completion of "Operation Danny."

While I was with the prime minister, my battalion had been on the move, and I set out to join them. I learned that they were now near Deir Tarif. I drove slightly northeast toward Petach Tikvah, swung southeast before reaching it, and was moving on toward Deir Tarif when it began getting dark. I was on a track which seemed not to have been used recently, and I presumed that it had been mined, for it was unlikely that the Arabs had failed to block the routes running from our front line to theirs. I therefore decided to wait until first light before continuing, and I stretched out for a nap in an adjacent field of millet, my first chance to nap in some forty-eight hours. Now, too, as a member of the mechanized "cavalry," fighting the war from the back of a vehicle and in constant movement, nothing was more restful, relaxing, comforting than the good earth.

I woke at dawn, spotted the tracks of vehicles, and took care to keep my wheels in their ruts. After about an hour I caught up with one of my detachments. I asked for my deputy, Peltz, and found him wrapped in an old blanket in an olive grove, snatching a few hours' sleep after a tough and wearying day and night. I prodded him awake to get an account of what had happened in my absence. From his mumbled reply I gathered that the battalion had been split up and dispersed from Tira to Deir Tarif. Our men had been battling the Arab Legion at Deir Tarif, and Uri Bar-On and Arik Nehemkin, my company commanders, had been wounded and evacuated. The 82nd Tank Battalion, which had maintained a holding operation at that position, had decided to withdraw the previous afternoon, and our jeep company had taken its place.

I was boiling with anger. I wished Peltz pleasant dreams and promptly ordered all the other battalion units to move immediately toward Deir Tarif—and not to forget that immediately meant immediately! I failed to understand why the 82nd Tank Battalion had retired and how a jeep unit was expected to fight armor without any armor of its own. But none of this was important at that moment. What angered me was that instead of using our battalion as a concentrated iron fist, spitting fire and storming the enemy, it had been broken up and used piecemeal, some detachments being assigned to what was tantamount to guard duty in Arab villages that had already been captured.

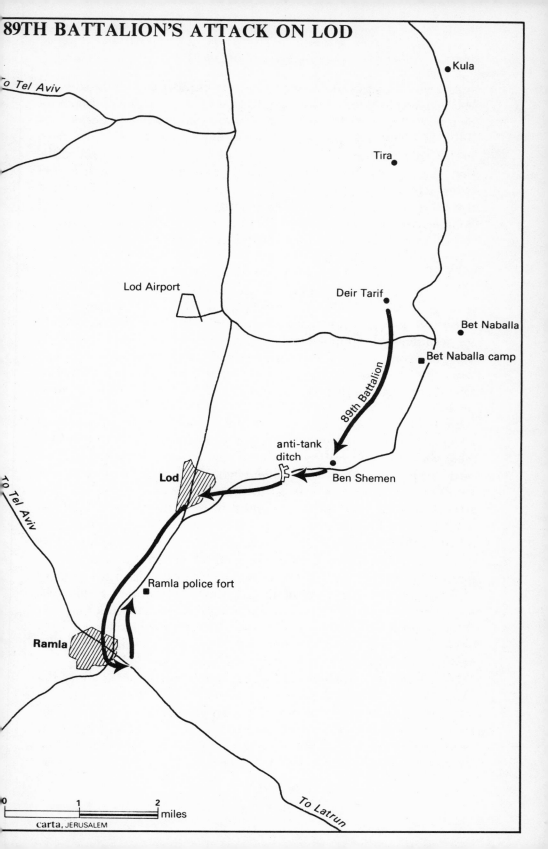

89TH BATTALION'S ATTACK ON LOD

To Tel Aviv

Kula

Tira

Lod Airport

Deir Tarif

Bet Naballa

Bet Naballa camp

89th Battalion

anti-tank
ditch

Lod

Ben Shemen

To Tel Aviv

Ramla police fort

Ramla

To Latrun

0   1   2
miles

carta, JERUSALEM

At Deir Tarif I found Akiva Sa'ar with his half-track company. He had arrived the previous evening to give support to Uri, and now his men were dug in and holding the western and northern slopes of the hill, while the Arab Legion dominated the eastern slope. Akiva tried to dissuade me from going to the top of the hill to survey the situation, since it was under continuous artillery fire and Jordanian snipers were fast on the trigger when they glimpsed a raised head. I ordered my driver to race to the hilltop and park his jeep behind a pile of boulders which I had spotted. The jeep made a wild zigzag dash up the slope, and between the twists and turns I noticed that Akiva was right behind me, as I had expected.

I looked down and saw several of our disabled vehicles stuck on the side of the hill. But I also saw an abandoned Jordanian armored car lying on its side, with its side wheels in a ditch. I could hardly believe so beautiful a sight—a real armored car, with thick plating, apparently serviceable, and equipped with a 2-pounder gun! All we had to do was pull it out, get it over to our lines, and use it. True, the Jordanians were shelling and sniping at anyone attempting to get near the armored car, but with ingenuity, a bit of luck, and a tow cable, it could be done.

In the meantime the rest of the battalion had arrived, refueled, and restocked with ammunition. I began to feel slightly uneasy. What were we waiting for? Why weren't we in action? And what was the next target? The Deir Tarif salient would soon be entirely in our hands. What next? Opposite us to the east, in the next valley, was Bet Naballa. On the hill just beyond it were fortified positions of the Arab Legion. To capture them by frontal attack meant going down into the valley and climbing up to them. Such an action held no chance of success. Nor could we repeat the method whereby in a day and a night we had stormed and taken the enemy positions in the villages of Tira and Kula and most of Deir Tarif. Local indirect actions climaxed by a sudden dash and breakthrough would not work here, for there could be no surprise and no lightning strike. Against our half-tracks were ranged Arab Legion artillery, armored cars with thick protection, anti-tank weapons, and possibly tanks.

I pondered this problem as I looked around me. Showing above the orange groves, about three-and-a-half miles away to the southwest, was the important Arab town of Lod. The land between us was flat. It struck me that our wisest course would be to tie down the local Arab Legion units here and let them scuffle with a small holding force, while the rest of the battalion moved on Lod. We would be reaching it from an unexpected direction—from the east, from the Arab lines, along the very corridor which linked it with the main Legion forces to the east—and it was unlikely that the town would be fortified and properly defended in that sector. A breakthrough here seemed to be the most logical move, and it would be best to do it quickly, now, when Lod least expected it.

Could the battalion do it? When we had gone into action two nights earlier, none of the companies—half-track, jeep, or support weapons—was up to full strength. All were short of men and equipment. Since then, after our casualties in troops and vehicles, we were an even smaller force. At the same time, we were better coordinated and more assured. The men were confident of victory. There was a pervasive feeling that all was going well. The first signs of hesitation which were evident when the battalion had got the order to storm Kula had vanished, and there was a new respect for the mobility of the half-track and the accurate fire from the jeep-mounted machine guns. It had been two of these machine guns which had caused the Arab Legion armored car to overturn, scoring direct hits at short range through the driver's slits.

I called the company commanders and told them half jokingly, half seriously, but in a voice loud enough for some of the troops to hear: "Let's finish up here and make for Lod." It was evident from their response that they thought I was joking. Lod, after all, was no small out-of-the-way village with a paltry number of inhabitants. How, then, could we, with our few vehicles, hope to capture a town, with its stout stone buildings, its large population, and the well-armed military forces stationed there?

Whatever we might do, what had to be done now was to finish off the capture of Deir Tarif, so I went off to visit the platoons across the road and get them to advance eastward and push the enemy further back. I had almost reached the first platoon when a runner came up with a message summoning me to the signals center. The commander of the Yiftach Brigade, Mulla Cohen, had contacted us and wanted to speak to "the battalion commander." I knew that this brigade was operating opposite us—it was one arm of the pincers and we were the other—but I did not know exactly where it was at that moment. I recognized Mulla's voice as he came straight to the point. One of his units had approached Lod but had come under heavy fire, and it was now stuck in the orange groves southeast of the city. Could we give it support? (When we saw each other later, I discovered that he had taken us for the better equipped and larger 82nd Armored Battalion, and not the commando battalion.) I told him we could. We would settle things here and then we'd come. I reckoned it would take us till noon to complete the current job, and by about 2 P.M. we should be on our way to Lod.

We were now committed to our next action, so we had to hurry. Our mortars renewed their fire to push back the Legion from the Bet Naballa area, and the Lehi company sent more men down toward the Kula-Lod road. But I was also determined to make every effort to retrieve the Legion's overturned armored car from the area of fire. With its 2-pounder gun in service with us, we would be kings!

Though I had emphasized the high value of this vehicle and its weapon, it still lay where it had been knocked out, with two wheels in the ditch and the other two in the air. The men had had too serious a respect for enemy shells to move it. I jumped onto a half-track and called out to one of the mechanics, asking whether he was prepared to risk it and join me in salvaging the car. "Sure," he said, "with you there's no risk." I had long had my eye on this boy. He was a lean, courteous, baby-faced youth from a farm settlement in the Sharon Plain. For wild driving there was no one like him, and in no time we reached the armored car, hitched it to our vehicle, jerked it out of the ditch and onto its wheels, and towed it back to the bottom of the hill.

The signalmen set to work repairing its radio and the mechanics its engine and, with special reverence, its gun. But we needed training to operate it, so a jeep was dispatched to a nearby artillery unit for an instructor. He promptly put some of our men through the fastest gunnery course ever, and within an hour I was informed that the armored car was ready for action. We selected a crew and they dubbed their vehicle "The Terrible Tiger," just the sort of name a Galilean farmer from Yavniel would choose. Deir Tarif grew less noisy. Enemy fire abated. The battalion seemed suddenly less fatigued. All thoughts were on the next move—to Lod.

I went to inspect the "Tiger." The radio set had been replaced, and the engine was in order. One of the wheels was a bit flat, but there was no spare wheel, and it could not be changed. In the turret stood the new "gunner," a private from the jeep company. I told him to aim and fire at a tree about 500 yards away. He did so—and whipped off its main branch.

Blond Dov Granek and his company were left behind as a holding and harassing unit, while the rest of the battalion got ready for the Lod action. We set off at 2 P.M. The vehicles were not in ideal shape, but the men were. Heading the column was the armored car. Someone had chalked an arrow on its gun barrel and the words "Straight to the point." Just looking at it gladdened everyone's heart. Following the "Tiger" was a reconnaissance detachment of jeeps, and after them came the half-tracks. Another jeep detachment brought up the rear.

We got onto a short stretch of road just southeast of Deir Tarif, advanced along a wadi into Bet Naballa, and intended to continue on the paved road. But just as we reached the point a few hundred yards from Bet Naballa where the road forks—one branch going southwest to Lod and the other running off to the southeast—we came under anti-tank fire. I got out and went to the head of the column, and there I saw that the fire was coming at us from a nearby olive grove. There was no point in wasting time, so we turned back and found another route, leaving the road and moving across the fields. At one point we encountered a group of Arabs who opened fire, but a few bursts from the jeep machine guns drove them back into the millet fields. En route we lost one jeep to a mine.

We arrived at Ben Shemen, the Jewish settlement midway between Bet Naballa and Lod. Surrounded by hostile Arabs, Ben Shemen had been cut off from the rest of the Jewish community in the country for months. Its people now stood at the gates and watched us with pent-up excitement, but as we entered they could restrain themselves no longer. They rushed to greet us, touching us to see if we were real, running their hands along the weapons and the vehicles. After their long and dangerous isolation, they had welcomed a unit of Yiftach Brigade, which had reached them from the south only a short time earlier, and now they were welcoming from the north an "armored column" of the Israel Defense Forces, complete with steel helmets, a covering of dust, radio antennae, and the "Terrible Tiger." We certainly made an impression!

The battalion arrayed itself along the road in column formation headed toward Lod, two miles to the west. Yiftach Brigade's commander, Mulla Cohen, told me where his units were located, and I pointed out the sector where we would be moving and requested him to keep his men clear of this area. My plan was based on the assumption that the enemy in Lod would have made no special defense provision for an attack from this direction, and we would therefore be able to penetrate through this Bet Naballa-Lod corridor.

We had no field intelligence about the enemy, his strength, dispositions, or armament. With only a general picture of the situation, the one decision to be made was whether to attack or not. I had a clear idea of the one way our battalion had to proceed. I assembled the unit commanders and issued my orders: The "Tiger" would lead, followed by the first half-track company, then the second half-track company, and finally the unprotected jeeps. I would be with the first half-tracks. If the "Tiger" or any of the half-tracks were hit, or stopped en route for any other reason, the rest of the force was to break column, spread, find some way of getting round the halted vehicles, and continue to advance. Once we got past the enemy outposts and entered the city, the battalion was to split up, keep firing left and right, sow panic, and thereby perhaps bring about the enemy's surrender. On reaching the town's main street, the first company was to turn north and the second company south. The jeeps were to find cover behind the stone fences or the courtyards of buildings and take up positions. They were not to race around the streets, for they would be hit. When the companies had completed their tasks, they were to rendezvous at the main crossroads. If one company got into difficulties, the second was to go to its aid.

I told, the officers that I attached the highest importance to the method of attack. If the battalion in column formation was stopped head-on, in effect, the only active elements coming up against the enemy were the first vehicles. The rest were not only passive but they also represented a static, compact target to the enemy. Therefore, if that happened, they were to deploy promptly to the flanks and storm the enemy positions from all sides. We would thus be exploiting our fire power to the full. We would also be less vulnerable, particularly if we moved fast. Indeed, speed was essential. It would certainly lessen the chances of being hit, and it would also increase the shock impact on the enemy. We had to bear down on our adversary, "run him over," crush him in spirit and body. There were no questions. The briefing took only a few minutes. The day was passing. We had to get on.

The sappers cleared the defensive minefield and removed the barriers which protected the sector of Ben Shemen facing Lod. The local inhabitants, who had shown us the location of the mines, watched us with evident reservations. Removing their safety barricade left them exposed and vulnerable, and who knew whether we would succeed in our operation? The radio network was opened, radiator shields were closed, helmets pushed down on foreheads, and the post-preparation and pre-action calmness descended upon the unit.

We advanced 100 yards and were spotted. We came under fire but continued to advance without replying. After a few minutes the

"Tiger" stopped, fired, and destroyed two enemy positions. We went on but stopped again after a few hundred yards. This time we had come within range of the main line of enemy posts, and their machine-gun fire rattled like hail against the sides of the half-tracks. The entire battalion opened up. The jeeps deployed to either side of the road and directed accurate flanking fire, and the half-tracks found suitable firing positions and added their weight. But they were all static. None moved. The stretch of road immediately ahead of us was impassable. It was cut by an anti-tank ditch.

I left my half-track and walked up to the "Tiger," which was busy pounding the main defensive positions of Lod. The ground ahead was assuredly unfavorable, but that was not the main reason why the half-tracks had stopped. They had halted because, armed only with machine guns, they wanted the "Tiger," the sole vehicle carrying an anti-tank weapon, to be the first to enter the town. They preferred to follow the "Tiger" rather than the reverse.

The shells of the "Tiger" had split the sandbags at the enemy positions and waves of dust and sand clouded the air. Through the haze we saw Arab soldiers taking flight. This, then, was the moment to push ahead. Fortunately, there was a side track nearby which ran off the road through the fields and looked as though it would take us around and beyond the anti-tank ditch. I ordered the commander of the "Tiger" to stop firing at the sandbagged targets and advance along the track. It might have been mined, but there was no time to investigate.

The battalion moved. The track was not mined. I returned to my half-track. Movement was slow, for the track was narrow, cut by frequent shallow ditches, and strewn with light barriers. The jeeps, whose sole "armor" were their machine guns, fired almost without a stop, cutting the thick cactus hedges as with a scythe. We soon picked up speed, crossed the line of enemy posts, and entered Lod. From the police station came heavy fire. The "Tiger" responded on the move, and the rest of the battalion followed. We reached the crossroads. The "Tiger" turned right, as planned, but the first half-track company, which should have done the same, went on traveling south, and the second company and the jeeps followed it. Thus, the battalion had not split up. All were now together, except for the "Tiger," which was on its own inside Lod.

The suburbs near the entrance to the town were full of Arab troops who had fled to Lod after their nearby positions and villages had been captured. They now fired and flung grenades at us from all directions, running and shouting as they did so. We pushed steadily on, and as we reached the center of town the firing lessened. Most of the people in the streets were civilians.

The "Tiger" had turned north, got separated from us—or we from it—and carried on a lone war. The rest of us crossed the city of Lod and continued in the direction of Ramla, until we reached the fortress-like police station on the Lod-Ramla road, occupied by an Arab Legion company. Our arrival here was clearly unexpected. Standing outside and watching us as we approached was a smart-looking bare-headed man in khaki. He was apparently the commander of this military post, had heard the shooting, and had come out to see what it was all about. When he got a closer look, he bounded into the courtyard and disappeared. The first half-track company had managed to pass the building almost without drawing a shot and went dashing ahead. But when the second company and the jeeps came up, they drew very strong fire, mostly from the heavy machine guns on the tower of the police station and through embrasures on the top floor. In the short, sharp engagement that followed, a grenade flung from above exploded inside one of the half-tracks, wounding all who were in it. Firing on the move, the rest of the battalion passed the building and drove on. I had tried to halt the vehicles of the first company ahead of me, but the radio set was no longer operating, and they did not see my hand signals. Nor did they hear my shouts—my voice was already hoarse. At the exit of the town, near the Ramla railway station on the Jerusalem road, I managed somehow to stop them. We got off the vehicles.

There was silence all around. The jeeps took up positions at the nearby road junction. I inspected the units. The jeep detachments had sustained four killed. Some of the wounded in the half-tracks were in serious condition. Several men were missing—wounded who had fallen off their jeeps near the police station—and a jeep from the reconnaissance unit had also been left there in flames. Most of the vehicles had punctured tires and leaking radiators. On one jeep, the barrel of the machine gun had been hit and the gun itself blown clear off its mounting. In another, bullets had sliced the brakes. We set about bandaging the wounded and changing those tires for which there were spares. Before we had finished, word came through from the lookout jeeps that enemy armored cars were moving toward us from the nearby Arab Legion camp. Mortar fire was also coming at us from the police station. The situation was becoming unpleasant, and the men were getting edgy. We put on a little distance until we reached a turn in the Ramla-Latrun road and got ourselves organized to fight our way back. But we were still within enemy range, and the bullets still flew. The lookouts reported that the armored cars were getting closer. I hurried the men, got the column in order, decided which detachments would give cover, had the wounded placed in a half-track, and we moved off.

My own vehicle limped along on two flat tires, its engine coughing and spluttering, the water in the radiator boiling away. We could drive only in first gear, and before long the other vehicles passed us, so that we were on our own when an Arab Legion armored car suddenly appeared near the corner of a side turning on the Ramla road and opened up with its 2-pounder. A direct hit would have finished us, for the thin skin of our half-track was useful only against light ammunition. Fortunately, the Arab gunner fired short, and there was enough time to tell my radioman—whose father was the Yemenite Rabbi Zechariah of Nahalal who had performed my marriage ceremony—to reply with his machine gun. There was also enough time for him to do so, even though it was now working only on single-shot. The armored car turned tail.

The radio network was again in operation, and I was surprised to hear the voice of Dov Granek, whom we had left behind with his unit at Deir Tarif. He said that the Legion troops had attacked and recaptured the salient. Several of his men were missing. He requested help. I told him that I could not send him reinforcements at the moment, but when we finished here we would get to him. In the meantime he was to call brigade headquarters. Perhaps they could give him aid. He said he had no link with the brigade and asked what he should do.

What advice could I give him, while we here were battling our way through the streets of Lod? I told him that if he could not hold his position, he should fall back on Tira, and we would deal with Deir Tarif the next day and retake the salient. Dov did not seem pleased with my answer. It also seemed that he wanted to go on talking. With a certain hesitancy, he asked: "Perhaps I could organize the rest of my men and try and retake it myself now?" And then I understood that he was not asking for an order but for encouragement. I shouted into the microphone, "Commandos or not commandos?" He did not get it at first. "What? What?" he asked. I repeated: "Are we a commando battalion or not?" This time he caught on, and shouted back: "Commandos. Commandos. We attack." "Take the salient from the east," I told him. "Right," he said.

We were now back at the police fort between Ramla and Lod. At the side of the road stood the burned-out jeep, and in the adjoining ditch lay the wounded. Our only hope lay in the accuracy of our fire. We deployed and emerged from our half-tracks. There was no need to spur anyone. All held on like bulldogs and did what had to be done, oblivious of the blows they were absorbing. One had only to direct and coordinate the action.

Enemy troops in the police fort opened fire and flung grenades. To stop them, or clear them from positions where they could do most damage, our machine gunners directed concentrated fire at the embrasures, windows, tower, and roof, while one company commander moved his half-track close to the building and flung a grenade over the parapet. Under cover of this fire, our dead and wounded were collected, and we moved on.

But it was heavy going. The half-track whose men had been hit by the grenade earlier on was driven by Akiva, who had himself been wounded in both hands, and he pushed a second half-track. A jeep pushed another vehicle whose engine had been smashed. And my own vehicle, which had drawn its last breath and moved on three riddled tires, was propelled by a half-track.

After passing the police building we stopped and reorganized. The jeeps were now in the lead and the half-tracks in the rear. We still had to pass the second police station inside the town, and there we got cover from the "Tiger," which had held its own all this time. Waiting till we had passed, it fell in at the end of the column. Only the "Tiger" and two half-tracks could move freely. All the other undamaged vehicles propelled vehicles that had been hit. Our casualties were 9 killed and 17 wounded. All had been collected and were now with us. We had left behind only one destroyed jeep.

We moved slowly. The jeeps now provided our main fire power, and they used it to the full. Indeed, the ceaseless rattle of their machine guns almost deadened the groans of our half-tracks grinding along in low gear. As we proceeded further into Lod, we sensed that apart from the noise of our own movement, and the continued shooting from the police building, the streets were quiet. We stopped firing for a moment and experienced an eerie stillness. Lod was silent.

We reached the exit from the city, the one leading to Ben Shemen, without further incident. There we were met by men of the Yiftach Brigade waiting to mop up and occupy the town.

While we had been moving, an undamaged half-track had driven up to mine, and the platoon commander, Charlie, asked permission to return and check whether one of his wounded men had not been left behind near the police station after all. I was inclined to refuse, but the eyes of the other men in the detachment were fixed on mine. It was as though each imagined himself lying wounded in a ditch and abandoned by his comrades. "Very well," I told him, "but don't get into any trouble." The detachment did not waste a moment. The vehicle screeched a U-turn and raced back into Lod.

8

BREAKTHROUGH TO THE NEGEV

WE REACHED OUR TEL HASHOMER base the next morning after spending the night moving through fields and searching for a safe track.

Back at the base, stories of the exploits of the battalion—the capture of Kula, Tira, Deir Tarif, capped by the breakthrough into Lod—may have sounded impressive. The battalion itself, or what was left of it, was in a sorry state. Most of its vehicles had been hit, and many of the men, particularly the officers, had been wounded.

I slept for a few hours, and when I awoke I was given a message from the chief of operations at General Headquarters. I was to present myself at his office the next day, July 13. The chief of operations was Maj. Gen. Yigael Yadin, and when I appeared before him he instructed me to take my battalion down south. We were to join the Givati Brigade in breaking through to the Negev. At the time, the Egyptians held a line running from the coast eastward, based on the Majdal-Faluja road, which cut the country in two, the Negev in the south from the population centers in the north. The plan was to breach this line by capturing three Egyptian bases. Hatta and Bet Affa, which were close to our own forces, were the targets assigned to infantry units of the Givati Brigade. Our battalion target was Karatiya, which was further away, and to reach it we would have to cross the line of Egyptian military posts. When we had captured it, we would return to base and the site would be held by a Givati company, which would be following us. The success of the entire breakthrough operation to link up with the Negev clearly depended on our capture of Karatiya, the most difficult and complicated of the three targets.

I knew that Yadin was familiar with our action in Lod, and he had some good words to say about it. But I was not certain that he knew the present state of the battalion, so I told him. Some of our half-tracks had been badly hit, and even the serviceable ones needed attention. Casualties had thinned our manpower, particularly the officers. Among the wounded were Peltz, my deputy, and the two senior company commanders, Akiva Sa'ar and Uri Bar-On. The battalion was, of course, ready for further action, but if it set out now, with its depleted forces, on a tough assault which would certainly cost us heavily in killed, wounded, and vehicles, the commando unit would emerge a battered husk.

Yadin reflected for a moment, then said he would have to discuss the situation with Ben-Gurion. He asked me to wait, and left for the Defense Minister's Office nearby. He returned after a few minutes and said they had one question: was the battalion in its present state capable of breaking through to the Negev? I said it was. "In that case," said Yadin, "break through, and after the next cease-fire we'll organize a new battalion."

We discussed the operational plan, and I then raised the problem of vehicle replacements. I was promised an additional six half-tracks and four scout cars. I left with the operational order in my pocket for the battalion to move south immediately and went in to see Ben-Gurion, at his request.

He returned to the subject of my appointment to the Jerusalem Command, but again agreed to postpone it until after the imminent action in the Negev. He then asked me about the Lod operation, but in the course of my account I noticed that he did not share my enthusiasm. To his mind, this was not "war" but a "prank." He did not agree with my implied thesis that the way to get past the first line of enemy positions was through the fast and daring dash. To him, an attack should be planned and carried out methodically and steadily, like the movement of a steamroller. We ended our brief exchange with his regarding me as a bold enough commander but somewhat of a partisan, and my regarding him a wise and inspiring political leader who had learned and heard much of the Arabs and of war, but who had no close, personal, first-hand knowledge of either. He knew *about* them, but he did not know them.

I returned to base. With the addition of the promised 6 half-tracks, the battalion strength was now 12 jeeps, 8 half-tracks, 4 open scout cars, the "Terrible Tiger," and 2 "tin cans"—ordinary trucks with thin metal casing. The battalion comprised 5 "companies"—I use the term even though each was hardly larger than a platoon: 1 jeep company of 25 men, composed of 3 detachments, each with 3 jeeps armed with machine guns (only 1 was equipped with a medium type); 2 companies of mechanized infantry, one of 35 men and the other of 25; a support company of 4 scout cars; and the command company, which included the reconnaissance unit (2 jeeps), intelligence unit (1 jeep), signals unit ("tin can"), and the workshop and maintenance unit ("tin can"). The number of actual fighting men totaled 130. The pride of the unit was the "Terrible Tiger," with its turret and 2-pounder, and it was the only vehicle with real protective armor.

On July 15 we left Tel Hashomer and drove to the Masmiya crossroads, midway between Tel Aviv and the Negev, where we established our forward base and got ourselves organized in an orange grove near the road. I was not familiar with the Negev. I had hiked through it several times, but it had always remained strange to me. It was bare, exposed, without orchard or garden, without water, without even the soft sand of the desert dunes; a bleak, flat, gray, dusty expanse, marked here and there by clusters of mud huts, the drab, pleasureless villages of the area.

In the evening I received the operational warning order from Givati Brigade, to whom we were attached. The operation's aims, as stated in the order, were to drive the enemy from the positions which he had seized north of the Majdal-Faluja road (Bet Affa and Hatta) and on which he had established his line; and to drive a wedge by capturing and holding Karatiya.

Our battalion was to capture Karatiya on the night of July 17. In the operational consultations held at brigade headquarters for this particular action, I said that it would be very difficult for us to operate at night with our armored cars, and I suggested that we carry out the attack in daylight. But my suggestion was turned down, for the other units taking part in the action favored night fighting. The order to fight at night would make it very hard for us.

On the night of July 15, we sent out a reconnaissance patrol to find an access route to Karatiya. It reached the edge of the Faluja airstrip, which was not far from our target, came under heavy fire, and returned without having reached the objective. We would have to find the most suitable approach path during the action. But if we were out of luck on the reconnaissance, we were definitely in luck with another item. After the engagement at Lod, the "Tiger" was left with only six shells. Headquarters, of course, had no such ammunition. By a happy chance, on the day before we were to go into action, we came across twenty 2-pounder shells which had been left behind in a grove not far from our Masmiya encampment.

H-hour was 22:00. In the afternoon I assembled the battalion for a briefing. It turned out, in fact, to be a lesson-learning post-mortem of our Lod action, for we had had no time to hold this discussion earlier. The general lines of our operational plans were to break into the Faluja airstrip, held by Egyptian forces, by driving through and firing on the move; to cross the main Majdal-Faluja road and go on until we reached a wadi south of the Karatiya mound; to cross the wadi and capture the mound on our vehicles. A road to the top of the mound was marked on the map as negotiable by vehicles. I gave orders that if it were to prove impassable, we were to capture the mound on foot. I emphasized that the most dangerous stretch would be crossing the Egyptian lines, namely, the airstrip and the road. This stretch had to be traversed at maximum possible speed, with constant fire at the flanks, and, for the men in the armored cars, with heads down.

The departure point was the abandoned village of Juseir, and there we arranged the last-minute coordination with the Givati units. I cannot claim that we and Givati were psychologically in tune with each other. They appeared to us to be tired and worried, and we seemed to them to be light hearted and cocky. They had named this operation "Death to the Invaders," which I though pompous, like the headline of an ideological tract. That was not what we needed to break through to the Negev, and the term "Invaders," while true, conjured up visions of the Nazi invasion of Europe in World War Two and seemed to me to be bombastic when applied to the scale of our war. The general behavior in the Givati units that would be fighting with us that night also seemed strange. The battalion commander stayed at the rear base and "directed" the battle from there. When the Givati officers learned that I would be driving with the lead unit of my battalion, they said I would be unable to control the operation. I did not argue, but I wondered privately how it was possible to "control the operation" without being on the spot with one's

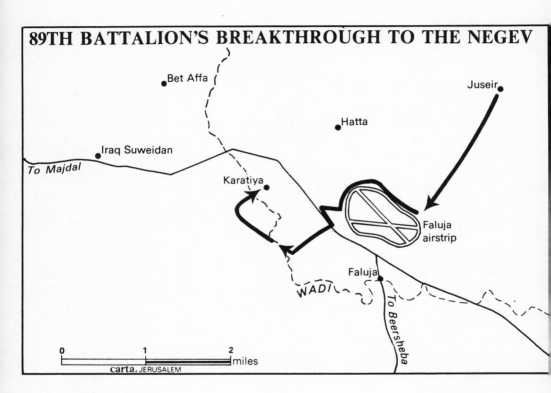

89TH BATTALION'S BREAKTHROUGH TO THE NEGEV

Bet Affa

Juseir

Hatta

Iraq Suweidan

To Majdal

Karatiya

Faluja
airstrip

Faluja

WADI

To Beersheba

0   1   2 miles

carta, JERUSALEM

own battalion. It was possible to receive reports and transmit orders by radio, but a commander could lead a unit into battle only by fighting with them, not by remote control, and not by sitting safely in the rear and ordering one's men to storm the enemy.

At H-hour, 10 P.M. on July 17, we moved forward. One of the half-tracks went off the path and hit a mine—one of our own. It was abandoned and its crew climbed aboard the other vehicles. The immutable principle was not to stop for any reason. The column drove toward the Faluja airstrip, with the reconnaissance unit on two jeeps in the lead, followed by the "Tiger," the two companies of mechanized infantry and the jeep company, with the support company bringing up the rear. I traveled in the second half-track of the first mechanized company, so that in front of me were a half-track, the "Tiger" and the two advance jeeps. If anything happened to these reconnaissance jeeps, the soft-skinned vehicles were to deploy to the sides while maintaining their fire and enable the others to deal with the enemy. Any vehicle hit was to be abandoned, so as not to hold up the rest of the column.

The moon was full, but even in total darkness we would have had no chance of remaining undetected. The noise of the moving column, particularly of the half-tracks, could be heard from afar, and, indeed, as the first vehicles reached the airstrip, at about 10:30 P.M., the enemy opened up with mortars and machine guns. We continued moving without replying until we got within a 150-yard range of the enemy positions, and then, at an order, every weapon in the battalion opened fire. Several of the enemy fled their posts, but it seemed that we had entered the target area of fire from the main Egyptian stronghold at Faluja. I popped my head out of the half-track to examine the situation. I saw that the fire was concentrated but not accurate. We crossed the airstrip without casualty.

Now came the hardest part—covering the stretch from the airstrip to the Majdal-Faluja road. Spotlighted by enemy rocket flares and stirring up clouds of billowing sand, we were a perfect target, and we were subjected throughout to powerful Egyptian artillery, mortar, and machine-gun fire. Yosef Bentowitz, a neighbor of mine in Nahalal, who was the gunner on the "Tiger," rose in his turret to direct his fire and was killed instantly. Six men were seriously wounded, when shells burst in their half-tracks. The jeeps, using the other vehicles as a protective shield and maneuvering along the edges, emerged unscathed.

There was still no letup from the enemy as we reached the main road, so after a short distance we turned off and cut across the fields to the south. To get off the road we had to negotiate a steep embankment, and one of our homemade armored cars overturned. The column went around the damaged vehicle and continued south until it reached the dirt track which should have taken us straight to Karatiya.

Enemy fire was still heavy, and the moonlit sky was made brighter by exploding shells and tracer bullets. But we were now further away, although still within range, and we could safely raise our heads and breathe. We drove on south along the dirt track until we reached the wadi which had been marked on the map as passable to vehicles. The map showed a track which crossed it. The map was wrong. There was no track, and the wadi was too deep for vehicles to get out by climbing its bank, as they would have to do to reach Karatiya, only a third of a mile away on top of a mound. We could, of course, go back the way we had come, but that would have meant abandoning our mission. Yet there seemed no way to advance. We were stuck.

The hour was late. The men were becoming restless. Teddy Eitan, the Frenchman who had asked to come with us on this action, lost his composure completely. He cursed and swore and went around telling everyone in not very elegant language what *his* commander would have done to *him* if he had got his battalion stuck in such a spot.

The wounded were transferred to the first-aid half-track and bandaged. The drivers attended to the vehicles that had been hit. Others went looking for an exit—in vain. Guard detachments were posted above, on both banks of the wadi, and occupied themselves with the casual interrogation of "prisoners"—a couple of fleeing Arabs they had caught—and taking occasional potshots at enemy troops—or their shadows, or perhaps just cows which were seen to be escaping from Karatiya.

The Egyptians had had no difficulty in following our movements, and they kept up their mortar and machine-gun fire. The company commanders asked me with some concern what was to be done. If we were to return, it would be best to do so immediately.

I felt drained. In my briefing I had categorically insisted that "no man is to stop for anyone—except by order—and no time is to be spent tending the wounded until we reach the wadi. If a vehicle cannot move it is to be abandoned. Until we get to the wadi there is only one rule: Break through and move, fire and move."

Well, here we were in the wadi, and, of course, stuck—as we had been in our earlier action. Nor was it the first time this night. We had been delayed on leaving Juseir, our departure point, when a vehicle hit a mine. We had been forced to stop for a while by enemy fire on the Faluja airstrip. We had been held up when the homemade "tin can" overturned on the steep embankment. On each occasion we had had to find some means of overcoming the obstacle and to keep going, and we had found it. Now, too, though our situation was far more grave, I felt there must be some way by which we could extricate ourselves. And as I took in the problem presented by the wadi, I saw there was a way out, the only way.

I ordered the men to start digging into the bank of the wadi so as to hack out a path of shallower gradient which would offer the vehicles an exit. It seemed a herculean task—and it had to be done under mortar and machine-gun harassment. There was no alternative.

Near the digging site stood a platoon commander, Amos Abramson from Yavniel in Galilee, who had come on this operation straight from an Officers' Training Course. He was fresher, more sprightly than the others, and he showed no sign of anxiety or dejection. His whiskers curled at just the right angle. He was the man for me. I told him to take matters in hand—to see to it that the diggers dug, the guards guarded, and the rest of the men kept quiet. I then took myself back to the opposite side of the wadi, lay down, wrapped my head in my Arab *kefieh*, and went to sleep.

We were still being assailed by sporadic enemy fire when I woke up about an hour later. I was pleased that I had rested, pleased that I had delegated the preparation of the exit path to the most suitable person, and above all that I had not taken hurried decisions in a state of exhaustion. It was now easier to think straight and make correct judgments. I decided that we would go on preparing our exit for another half an hour and then move. Vehicles which could then take the gradient would be driven out, and those unable to do so would be abandoned and their crews carried aboard the others. And then—on to Karatiya.

I rubbed the sleep from my eyes and stood up to stretch. I was about to turn, join the men, and issue my orders when I was grabbed from behind. A voice shouted in my ear, "What, you still on this side of the wadi?" and I promptly found myself pulled to the side which now had an exit. It was the platoon commander from Yavniel. He later claimed, with only the faintest quiver of his mustache, that he had failed to recognize me.

The battalion came to life when I notified the commanders: "At 04:00 we advance on Karatiya with whichever vehicles manage to get out by then."

The reconnaissance unit led off, followed by the "Tiger," the jeeps, and five half-tracks. In addition to their normal complements, they now carried the men, weapons, and ammunition of the vehicles left behind. Following the column was the Givati infantry company, which in the meantime had caught up with us in the wadi, as previously arranged. Their task would begin when we had captured Karatiya.

The vehicles proceeded to a crossroads (or, rather, a crosspaths) and got onto the track leading up to Karatiya. When they were about 200 yards from the village, the half-tracks fanned right and left, and, still on the move, laid down concentrated fire from mortars and machine guns. The enemy response was feeble, just some scattered shots. The "Tiger" advanced toward the mound and shelled the summit. The jeeps moved off to the flanks, and the half-tracks entered the village, taking it without casualty.

The Givati infantrymen now followed. They were to hold this village and enemy base, and they began clearing Egyptian emplacements, neutralizing possible points of opposition, and securing their own defenses. In this phase of the operation they encountered no opposition, though later they were to suffer casualties when they came under heavy Egyptian artillery and mortar bombardment.

Our commando battalion began rounding up their vehicles, which were dispersed throughout the village, and concentrated them at the foot of the mound. Reconnaissance men were sent off to find the exit from Karatiya which led to Hatta, one of the two targets of the Givati Brigade just north of the Majdal-Faluja road, which they had captured during the night. They had failed to capture their second target, Bet Affa, sustaining heavy casualties in their attack, and this position remained in Egyptian hands. With Hatta and Karatiya now in our possession, a wedge had been driven into the main Egyptian line and the Negev was no longer cut off from the north.

It was 6 A.M. on July 18 when we left Karatiya and returned to base via Hatta without further incident. I did not know it then, but this was to be my last day with the 89th Commando Battalion.

A few hours later I drove to the hospital to visit the men who had been wounded in this action. Among them were Arik Nehemkin and Micha Ben-Barak, who had suffered eye wounds. I found the two of them in the same ward, lying in adjoining beds, eyes bandaged, pain and misery in their faces. I recalled my own feelings when I had lost an eye and thought I might share with them some of the experience I had acquired since then. "Boys," I said to them, "for all that's worth seeing in this wretched world, one eye is enough."

9

MY FRIEND THE ENEMY

FIVE DAYS AFTER THE BREAKTHROUGH in the Negev, on July 23, 1948,
I was appointed commander of Jerusalem. A delegation from the
89th, headed by Dov Granek of the Stern Group or Lehi, tried to
prevent my posting from the battalion, but without success. The
delegation met with Prime Minister Ben-Gurion, explained to him
the importance of my remaining with the commando unit, and even
threatened to follow me to Jerusalem—with the entire battalion. Ben-
Gurion heard them out and then asked them how it was that I had
gained the trust of dissidents like the men of the Stern Group. Dov
said it was because I had always personally led the battalion in battle
and had been absolutely straight with the men. At the end of the
meeting, Ben-Gurion told them that Jerusalem needed a good fighting commander, and Jerusalem took priority over every other place.

When Ben-Gurion said this, two months after the Arab invasion
and one month after the siege of Jerusalem had been lifted, he may
well have thought that there would be a renewal of fighting in the
city. In fact, by then the decision in the battle for Jerusalem had
already been cast. Shortly before I assumed my new post, two agreements had been signed by my predecessor, Col. David Shaltiel, on
behalf of the government of Israel. One, called the "Mount Scopus

Agreement," had been reached two weeks earlier, on July 7. By its terms, Mount Scopus was to be demilitarized and come under the supervision of the United Nations. The second agreement was signed two weeks later. The signatory for Jordan this time was the Jordanian commander of the Arab part of Jerusalem, Lt. Col. Abdulla el-Tel. This agreement formally established the cease-fire and fixed the *status quo* in no-man's land between the lines of the two parties.

During the next five months, up to the end of the war on January 7, 1949, we were permitted only two very limited military actions, both of which failed. One of the reasons was the standard of combat of the Etzioni Brigade, which fell below that of crack units like the 89th Commando and even the average of other combat formations. Some of its troops were recent immigrants—new to the language, conditions, climate, and terrain of the country and with insufficient army training. And the brigade as a whole had been through a bad time. Its men had held the Jerusalem city lines for a long period and were split up into small detachments manning isolated posts under constant harassment by Arab Legion snipers. The fall of the Etzion bloc of settlements between Jerusalem and Hebron, the surrender of the Jewish Quarter of the Old City, the unsuccessful attempts to break through and return to it, and the sense of dejection among senior officers of the brigade had all left their mark on the fighting capacity and spirit of the men. When I had assumed the Jerusalem Command, I had inspected the front lines round the city and visited all the posts, having to reach each one along communications trenches, between ruined walls, and up and down ladders. Inside, the posts were dark, with old sacking covering the narrow firing slits. This kind of static fighting—holed up in such places in this kind of atmosphere, in the bitter cold of a Jerusalem winter, and without sufficient food—was hardly calculated to fire the men with a burning spirit of combat and self-confidence. Nor—and this was of utmost importance—did it give them the required training and experience in open battle, fighting as a combat unit at company or battalion strength.

I tried to raise morale by talks with the officers and men, and to show self-confidence in my personal behavior on inspection tours. I ordered an intensive training program, improved the equipment, and brought in additional officers. The standard of the brigade rose, but the fighting was not renewed. The line dividing Jerusalem between Israel and Jordan remained the one determined by the fighting at the beginning of the war, with the Old City in Arab hands; Mount Scopus in our hands, but as an enclave within Arab-held territory and cut off from the rest of Jewish Jerusalem; our road to Ramat

Rahel exposed to enemy fire from Zur Bahar; and Jewish Jerusalem linked to the coastal plain only by a narrow corridor. Jerusalem was a focal point of unsolved problems, military, political and Jewish.

I had come to Jerusalem with a military appointment, and had indeed been selected for this post because of my combat qualifications. But my main activity turned out to be political—negotiating local arrangements with the commanders of Arab Jerusalem and national agreements with King Abdulla of Jordan himself.

At first I had ascribed little importance to the idea of negotiations with the Arabs. I planned for and expected military decisions. I viewed the problems through fortified posts and trenches and their solution through fire and assault. But when the cease-fire had put an end to the fighting, the struggle passed from the battlefield to the council table, and I soon became deeply involved. This political work brought me in direct contact with Prime Minister Ben-Gurion. I was, of course, personally acquainted with him, as I was with the other political leaders. But I now saw for the first time and at first hand how superior he was to his colleagues in his basic approach to problems, and I was impressed by his political wisdom, powers of leadership, and vision.

When I was posted to Jerusalem, I brought my family, and we were given an apartment in a large, handsome, and empty stone house that was fully exposed to the Jordanian positions on the Old City wall. When the Jordanians opened fire, as they did from time to time, the east side of the house was spattered with machine-gun bullets and shrapnel from the enemy's 6-pounder guns. We lived in the more sheltered western side and were able to go down to the cellar during artillery shelling.

When the sniping became less frequent and the city more or less quiet, additional tenants moved in. Finance Minister Eliezer Kaplan and his family lived on the floor above, and we had officers and students in the other rooms who gave the place a friendly social atmosphere. So did the press correspondents, Foreign Office personnel, and friends and acquaintances who would drop in for tea and a "what's new" chat, for some of my duties involved me in sensitive and newsworthy affairs. I had to discuss arrangements arising out of the cease-fire with the head of the U.N. observer teams, U.S. Marine Corps Gen. William Riley, and with the three-man Consular Truce Commission—Jean Nieuwenhuys of Belgium, who was chairman; René Neuville of France; and William Burdett of the United States. The results of such meetings usually made news. It was headline news when I met with the commander of Arab Jerusalem, Lt. Col. Abdulla el-Tel.

Ruth started to work for the Jewish Agency in developing home industries and crafts among the new immigrant villages in the Jerusalem corridor. She would visit them, encourage them in their local weaving and other crafts, provide them with the required raw materials, and market their products. Out of this grew the Maskit Home Crafts stores, which developed into a broad, nationwide project. With Ruth away from home for much of the day, most of the household duties were done by Simcha, who soon became part of the family. She was a widow of about fifty when she came to live with us. Her people belonged to the ancient Jewish community of Kurdistan. Simcha had had no formal education, but she was full of wisdom, kindness, and common sense. The children were very attached to her, loved her cooking, and were entranced by her folk tales, full of wondrous adventures in which the hero emerges victorious and the villain is vanquished at the last moment.

Yael and Ehud went to the Rehavia school and Assaf to the kindergarten. I do not know how much of the new education they picked up, but they certainly had not forgotten what they had learned before coming to Jerusalem. On one occasion, the brother of Reuven Shiloah of the Foreign Ministry sent us a mournful note about his cherished dovecote: Udi had apparently opened it and the birds had flown. Another time, Mrs. Kaplan telephoned the police in near hysterics to report that "Dayan's children" were burying a corpse in her back garden. Apparently Udi and Assi had discovered a skeleton that had been thrown up by a Jordanian shell in the small cemetery in Mamilla Road and had decided to bury their treasure in Mrs. Kaplan's flowerbed. These were just the normal pranks of headstrong youngsters. But when U.N. observers brought Assi home one day—he was four at the time—having found him wandering alone in no-man's land at the bottom of Mamilla Road, we began to sit up. It seemed that the children could not get used to the difference between Nahalal, with its cows, and birds, and open fields, and Jerusalem, with its hovering dangers—sniping and mining and light-trigger-fingered Arab Legionnaires manning the Old City walls.

Truth to tell, the change was odd not only for the children. I, too, found the move from Nahalal to Jerusalem more than geographic. There were endless meetings, discussions, hair-splitting arguments over formulas, cocktail parties and fattening dinners. This was certainly a new pattern of life.

In one area there was no change: I continued my visits to the men in the line with the same frequency and the same concern. The frequency, of course, may have been prompted by my never-ending wish to get out of the office and spend my time out of doors. When I could leave the office for several hours, I would climb near the strategic height known as Miss Carey, after the lady who had run a charming tearoom there during the British administration, drive to the top of the Castel, and inspect our other posts on the high ground dominating the road to Tel Aviv. But even when I had a crowded office schedule of meetings and consultations, I always got away, even for an hour, to visit the positions nearby, each of them only yards from the Arab lines. It took only a few minutes to reach them from my office, get into the trenches, climb the ladders, meet our soldiers, and watch the Arab Legionaries in the posts across the way. Though there was a cease-fire, I felt more secure—like parents taking a peep at their sleeping children before going to bed—when I could see for myself that the front was peaceful and all was well.

I would often have to go directly from these visits to a formal meeting with dignitaries, still in my muddy boots and dusty clothes, having had no time to change. But no one seemed to mind. And neither did I—though I would not have wanted to appear with grease spots or the stains of spilled coffee. I found nothing scruffy about the mud or dust that clung to me after crawling through a communications trench or having to hit the dirt when someone opened fire.

On August 10, a fortnight after I had assumed my post in Jerusalem, Count Folke Bernadotte, the U.N. mediator, arrived on his second visit. He had apparently decided to solve "the Palestine problem" personally and had formulated a plan which ran counter to the U.N. Partition Resolution of November 1947. Among other proposals, it assigned Jerusalem to the Arabs and would surely have had the effect of prolonging the fighting rather than bringing about peace.

Bernadotte met with Dr. Dov Yosef, who had headed the Jerusalem Emergency Committee during the siege and was now the government representative responsible for the administration of Jerusalem. With Dov Yosef were Yitzhak Ben-Zvi, who was to become Israel's second president, and Daniel Auster, Jerusalem's first mayor. The meeting took place in the Belgian Consulate, and when Bernadotte arrived, a group of young men and women sitting in jeeps in front of the building whipped out banners bearing such slogans as "Stockholm is yours, Jerusalem is ours" and signed "Fighters for the Freedom of Israel," the full name in English of the dissident Lehi group. I heard about this only when Dov Yosef telephoned me and asked me to disperse the demonstrators. I went to the spot at once and told the protesters to go home. They did so without argument.

Just over a month later, on Friday, September 17, Bernadotte again came to Jerusalem. Before meeting with Dov Yosef, he went to Government House, which had been handed over by the British to the Red Cross, with the idea that it might serve as the headquarters of the U.N. Truce Supervision Organization (UNTSO). He then left for Dov Yosef's home, traveling in a convoy of three U.N. cars. Midway along the route, the cars were blocked by a jeep carrying three men, apart from the driver, all dressed in nondescript army uniforms. The three jumped out, rushed to Bernadotte, shot him and his French chief of staff, Col. André Pierre Serot, who was sitting next to him, and made off. It later transpired that the hold-up vehicle was a U.N. jeep which had been stolen some time before.

The assailants were not found. Leaflets discovered outside several consular buildings bore the unfamiliar signature "Homeland Front," which claimed responsibility for the action. Suspicion was directed against Lehi, but its leaders denied it. At all events, this outrage brought matters to a head, and the government decided to take immediate steps to disband the dissident organization. The next day, at 2 P.M., Israeli army units surrounded the Lehi camp in Jerusalem and the forty young men who were there handed over their arms without opposition.

Until then Lehi had operated openly in Jerusalem and enjoyed an independent status. Indeed, on occasion it had carried out joint army operations with some of our squads, and personal relations between the two were often most friendly. But we clearly had to put a stop to this abnormal situation (which was true only of Jerusalem) in which a paramilitary unit could exist and operate independently and refuse to accept government authority. The larger Irgun had proclaimed its wish to be absorbed into the defense forces of the state. Lehi in Jerusalem had not, and there was considerable speculation as to how it might react to an order for its disbandment.

When Lehi handed its arms to regular Israeli units, the pre-state situation which had continued to exist in Jerusalem was brought to an end. That the dissidents had offered no opposition gave me particular satisfaction, for I had come from the command of a battalion in which one of the companies had been made up of Lehi men, and its commander, Dov Granek, and I were bound by ties of mutual friendship and respect.

The political implications of the murder of Bernadotte were not known to me at the time, for this was outside my sphere of activity.

I was also less familiar and less concerned with politics than I was to become a few weeks later. But I was directly affected by one consequence of the unfortunate episode: military authority in Jerusalem was no longer split between the army and the dissidents. I was now commander of all Jewish troops in the area. It made my task easier.

The political affairs into which I was suddenly plunged began with negotiations over local agreements in Jerusalem with Jordan. It continued with meetings between King Abdulla and Israeli representatives, negotiations toward Armistice Agreements in Rhodes, and my supervision of the execution of these agreements with the four main Arab states that had taken part in the 1948 war: Egypt, Jordan, Syria, and Lebanon.

The lines held by the opposing forces in the Jerusalem area when the fighting stopped left the city cut in half. Roughly, the west of the dividing line came under Israeli control, with the addition of Mount Scopus, which remained an Israeli enclave. The Old City, including the Western Wall of the Temple compound, the most sacred Jewish site, as well as the destroyed Jewish Quarter, fell within Jordan. The Latrun salient, midway between Jerusalem and Tel Aviv, was held by Jordan, so that we had to build a six-mile diversionary stretch of road to get around it. Israel controlled part of the main Jerusalem-Bethlehem road, so the Jordanians had to use a longer secondary route.

While there was to be no more fighting along the Jordanian front, there would be serious action on the other fronts. In the south, the Egyptians were driven out of Beersheba in mid-October, and at the end of that month a lightning two-day campaign in the north drove Kaukji's irregular forces entirely out of the Galilee. The final major battles of the War of Independence would be fought against the Egyptians in the last week of December 1948 and the first week of January 1949, with Egypt's expeditionary army completely driven from our borders and pursued by our forces into Sinai.

On November 30, 1949, I signed an "absolute and sincere cease-fire" agreement in the Jerusalem area on behalf of Israel. Signing in the name of the Jordanian forces "and all other Arab forces in the Jerusalem area," namely, the Egyptian and the irregular troops, was Abdulla el-Tel. Attached to the agreement was a map marking the cease-fire lines of the two parties and the no-man's land between them. The agreement allowed for a fortnightly convoy through the Arab lines to the Israeli enclave on Mount Scopus for food supplies and the changing of personnel.

In the negotiations that led up to the agreement, I got to know my

Arab counterpart rather well. Abdulla el-Tel was a tall young man, sinewy, handsome, light skinned, with a directness about him—he looked you straight in the eye—and an open and friendly smile. He came from a prosperous family in Irbid, in the hill region of northern Jordan, and had received his secondary school education in Egypt. He joined the Arab Legion at the beginning of World War Two and in 1942 completed a British Officers' Training Course in the Suez Canal area.

In the invasion of Israel in 1948, he served as a company commander with the rank of major. In one of the early battles, King Abdulla visited Jerusalem, met el-Tel, liked what he saw, and promptly promoted the young officer to the rank of lieutenant colonel, even though he had held his majority for only two months. A month later he was appointed commander of the 6th Battalion and was later given the Jerusalem Command.

When I met him, el-Tel impressed me as being far superior to the other Arab officers and political functionaries I had encountered in that period. Incidentally, he hated the British officials who were the real rulers in Amman, and was contemptuous of his friends who toadied to them.

During the negotiations which preceded the "sincere" cease-fire agreement, I got fed up with the "mediation" of the U.N. representative, a Col. Carlson of the United States, who, instead of cutting through to the simple basic issues, complicated them with heavy-handed nitpicking, and instead of smoothing the path toward an accord, kept raising obstacles. At one of the meetings, I found Carlson's contribution just too much, and I turned to Abdulla el-Tel and suggested that the two of us adjourn to another room. He agreed, and to the surprise of all the parties present—four officers on each delegation and some half a dozen U.N. observers—we upped and left. At our private consultation, the two of us settled our differences very quickly. We returned to the meeting and reported our agreement, which was read into the protocol. Carlson's face had turned red, but he said nothing. What awaited him was an even bigger surprise: el-Tel had agreed to my proposal that we establish a direct telephone line between us without having to go through the U.N. exchange. Even General Riley, chief of staff of the U.N. Truce Supervision Organization, was somewhat embarrassed when he heard of it. He was without doubt a distinguished general in the Marines, but a knowledge of the Middle East was not his forte. I mollified him by explaining that surprises were the most delightful things in life, and this was also true of the direct Dayan-el-Tel telephone link.

This field telephone from my house to el-Tel was the first and, to date, the only hot line in the Middle East, and it proved very useful. When there was an exchange of fire in one of the sectors, I would telephone him and the incident would be disposed of quickly. But the link was particularly helpful for arranging secret meetings, at first between the two of us and in the course of time also with King Abdulla, in his winter palace at Shuneh. If we had had to depend on the apparatus and mediation of the U.N. for such matters we would have failed utterly.

Col. el-Tel showed himself at his best, and faced his stiffest tests, over arrangements for our secret meetings with King Abdulla in the heart of Jordan and over the release of our prisoners of war. To get us to the king, he had to take us in his car through the Arab lines without the Arab Legion guards being aware of his cargo. True, we wore red checkered *kefiehs* of the Legion on our heads and wrapped round our faces, and when we were caught by daylight we lay on the floor of the car, but his personal risk was considerable. On one occasion, when a Jordanian soldier poked his head through the window and it seemed to el-Tel that I had been recognized, he went white as a sheet. "They would have shot us both, and asked questions later," el-Tel said as we sped off from the checkpost without further incident.

I raised the prisoner of war problem shortly after we had established mutual trust. At that time—unlike any other post-battle period, when we usually had anything from ten to one hundred times more POWs in our hands than the Arabs had—the position was reversed vis-à-vis Jordan. We had about a dozen Legionaries, while there were 670 Israelis in the Jordan POW camp at Mafrak. Almost half, 320, were captives from the Etzion bloc of kibbutzim, of whom 85 were women, and the rest had been captured in the Jewish Quarter of the Old City, mostly old men who had been engaged in talmudic study, their wives, and children. I asked el-Tel that they be released.

He said he would think it over. His answer came a few days later, acceding to my request. El-Tel said he knew that Jordan was losing a trump card in the forthcoming negotiations—the prisoners were freed a month before the armistice talks began at Rhodes—but he was swayed by humanitarian considerations. He had raised the matter before King Abdulla and had received the king's consent. According to el-Tel, he had told Abdulla that it was dangerous to leave Jewish prisoners at the mercy of Arab guards for too long, and if anything happened to stir Arab anger and the Jordanian troops guarding the POW camp went wild, the king would be unable to lift his head before the world.

When we were reviewing the technical arrangements for the return of the POWs, I asked el-Tel if there were any financial expenses involved. We would be prepared to pay any sum that was asked. He frowned and said he would send me a bill when it was all over. And he did. He gave me a bit of paper on which was marked an insignificant amount, and attached were receipts signed by the bus drivers who had brought the POWs from Mafrak to Jerusalem. I extended to el-Tel my heartfelt thanks. Before we parted, he said he had a personal request: could I perhaps persuade the editor of the *Palestine Post* (which became the *Jerusalem Post*) to attack him from time to time for his stubborn hostility to Israel? He said he needed that sort of thing to preserve his good name in Jordan.

I continued to follow the fortunes of el-Tel long after I had left the Jerusalem Command. His military-political career ended suddenly when he broke with King Abdulla over his attitude toward the British. El-Tel wanted them kicked out of Jordan. The king neither wished nor was able to agree. In June 1949 el-Tel resigned. The king tried to appease him and even promised him a promotion, but el-Tel refused. He left for Syria, where he met Husni ez-Zaim, who had led a *coup d'état* a few months before, in March, and was now head of a military junta. El-Tel was greatly impressed by him and by the idea of leading a similar revolution in his native Jordan. Zaim himself was the victim of a *coup* shortly afterward; he was shot on August 14, 1949. From Damascus, el-Tel moved to Cairo.

I heard from him twice thereafter. The first time was through an Egyptian army officer at a party in London in 1951. He gave me el-Tel's regards and said he now headed a guerrilla battalion that was harassing British troops stationed in the Canal area. The second el-Tel goodwill greeting came through an American clergyman who visited me in Jerusalem. He added that el-Tel would like to see me to discuss "a certain matter," and the Catholic prelate volunteered to arrange the clandestine rendezvous. It never took place, and I never discovered what was on el-Tel's mind, but it was of no political import. His messages were simply human signals of greeting. And that, from an Arab officer to an Israeli, was in itself something.

10

TALKS WITH AN ARAB KING

IMMEDIATELY AFTER THE signing of the "sincere cease-fire agreement" with Jordan, Abdulla el-Tel informed me that he had been empowered by King Abdulla to enter into negotiations with us on all subjects concerned with the Jerusalem area, including Bethlehem, Ramalla, and Latrun. El-Tel's proposals were based on an exchange of territory and joint control. Ben-Gurion very much wanted a full, final, and formal peace treaty and was ready to agree to certain territorial exchanges, but he did not believe that joint control was feasible.

On November 29, 1948, el-Tel proposed that Jordan return the Jewish Quarter in the Old City to Israel in exchange for the Arab Katamon Quarter in the New City. Concerning the Latrun road, which was midway between Jerusalem and Tel Aviv and which had become a no-man's land lying between the Israeli-Jordanian cease-fire lines, he proposed that it be opened to the free movement of both parties. Ben-Gurion turned down both proposals. "Latrun," he said, "was not a question of traffic arrangements but of division of territory" (we had suggested that the no-man's land be divided between Jordan and Israel), and he was not prepared to give up the Katamon Quarter.

At a further meeting on December 5, el-Tel put forward additional proposals in the name of the king. One again related to Latrun: Jordan would relinquish part of Latrun and the area would be controlled by a mixed Arab-Jewish police force. In exchange, Abdulla asked that a number of Arab refugees be allowed to return to Lod and Ramla. The second proposal was a response to my suggested reopening of the Tel Aviv-Jerusalem railway line, which passed through a small section of Arab territory. Jordan agreed, but wanted in return permission to use the road from Bethlehem to Jerusalem up to the Jaffa Gate. Ben-Gurion was basically opposed to partial arrangements, and the reply he gave me to transmit to the king via el-Tel was that we would not continue discussions merely on the basis of the truce. We were ready, indeed anxious, to negotiate the conditions for a real peace with a political representative, and it was in such peace negotiations that we would solve all the problems—electricity supply to Jerusalem, opening the railway line, the road to Bethlehem, and so on.

At a meeting with the prime minister on December 18, 1948, Ben-Gurion stressed that "our primary aim now is peace," and he warned against our being "flushed with victory." He added: "Immigration demands that there be an end to war. Our future need is peace and friendship with the Arabs. Therefore I am in favor of talks with King Abdulla, although I doubt whether the British will let him make peace with us."

A week after I had given el-Tel Ben-Gurion's categorical answer that we would be prepared to enter into discussions only for an overall peace settlement, el-Tel telephoned, on December 29, to say that he had seen the king and had been appointed the royal representative to draft a peace plan with us. In his talks with us, el-Tel would be joined by the king's physician. When the draft proposals were completed, the king would bring them before his Cabinet for approval. If they were rejected, he would change the composition of the Cabinet, for the king was all-powerful. El-Tel suggested that we begin our talks that very evening, and that we should conduct them in a Jerusalem building close to the no-man's land between the Jewish and Arab lines. If the sessions continued, they would be held alternately in a Jordanian and an Israeli building. He decided that the first meeting would take place the following evening at 6:30 P.M. on the Jordanian side. El-Tel asked us to come dressed in civilian clothes and to bring maps and appropriate documents.

Ben-Gurion decided that Israel would be represented at these "peace talks" by Reuven Shiloah of the Foreign Ministry and myself. He briefed us and gave us the following directives. One, to continue the talks, even if they did not seem to be productive, for as long as the fighting with the Egyptians continued in the Negev—the truce with Egypt had been broken—so as to preserve the truce in the Jordanian sector. Two, to make no commitment on a Jordanian annexation of the West Bank, but neither to express opposition to it. We should explain the difficulties—the objections of the other Arab states, as well as of Britain and Russia—express our sympathetic approach, and point out that our government had not yet made a decision on the subject. Three, to insist that the border along the Arava Valley, the eastern border of the Negev, should remain as it was during the Mandatory period, namely, up to and including Eilat in the south. Four, to mention the possibility of offering Jordan rights in Gaza with an access corridor through Israeli territory. Five, to deny Jordanian requests with regard to Ramla and Jaffa and to leave open the question of an Arab return to Lod, but not to enter into any discussion concerning the Negev.

The first meeting with el-Tel and the doctor was very general, and only at the second did we get down to substantive talks. We met at 7 P.M. on January 5, 1949, in a building at the edge of the Mandelbaum Gate. There were three in our party, Shiloah from the Foreign Ministry, my aide, and myself. On the Jordanian side, only Abdulla el-Tel was present. The doctor, for some reason, did not appear.

We exchanged our letters of credence. Ours was written in Hebrew, Arabic, and English and signed by Prime Minister David Ben-Gurion and Foreign Minister Moshe Sharett. El-Tel brought a letter written in King Abdulla's own hand. It is doubtful whether the formula and phrasing in the letters would have stood up in a court of law, but sitting where we were, at the edge of no-man's land, they were perfectly acceptable. As an old proverb has it, "the charm of a place imbues its occupants."

When el-Tel had outlined Jordan's proposals, it was evident that there was a veritable chasm between our respective concepts of a settlement. In the Negev the king wanted a corridor linking his country with Egypt. In Jerusalem he wanted the whole of the Old City, except for the Jewish Quarter. He also asked for the Katamon, German Colony, and Talpiot suburbs of Jewish Jerusalem. He also sought Kibbutz Ramat Rahel on the southern outskirts of the city. In return, he would give us the Lifta and Romema suburbs, which were already in our possession. El-Tel said that while the British knew and approved of the negotiations, they were not the ones who had put forward these conditions.

We reported back to Ben-Gurion and said that there was obviously no point in going on with the talks, but he directed us to continue them. "We must probe every possibility of achieving peace," he said. "We need it probably more than the Jordanians—though no doubt they are losing more than a little, becoming more and more subservient to the British."

I followed Ben-Gurion's orders, though without much enthusiasm, and telephoned el-Tel to arrange another meeting. It was set for January 14 at the same place, adjoining the Mandelbaum Gate in no-man's land. However, while on the phone I decided to tell him what I thought of his proposals, airing my personal view that if there were no change in Jordan's approach, they would bring about war, not peace.

It transpired that not only I but el-Tel, too, realized that nothing good would come of continued talks at the Mandelbaum Gate, and a day before our scheduled meeting he called to say that the king was inviting us to come and talk with him at his Shuneh Palace so that he could personally demonstrate his sincere desire for peace. I called Ben-Gurion and received his approval.

We had two meetings with King Abdulla, the first on January 16, 1949, and the second two weeks later. Israel was represented by Elias Sasson, of the Foreign Ministry, and myself. At the first meeting the king had with him el-Tel and his physician. At the second, they were joined by Jordan's prime minister, Taufiq Abu al-Huda. We had been brought to the palace by Col. el-Tel, driving his own car, and though he drove fast the journey took more than an hour.

These meetings took place while on the island of Rhodes we were negotiating an Armistice Agreement with Egypt under the chairmanship of U.N. Acting Mediator Dr. Ralph Bunche. The negotiations had begun on January 13, six days after we had routed the Egyptians in the last major battle fought in our War of Independence, and eight months after they and the other neighboring Arab states had invaded Israel. The fighting had not been continuous during those eight months. Truce had put a stop to battle, and breaches of the truce had brought renewed battle. After each round of combat, one or another of the invading Arab states had been pushed out of further chunks of our territory which they had seized and had been forced to retreat closer and closer to their own borders. The final battle, in the last week of December 1948 and the first week of January 1949, had been against Egypt alone, and it ended with the last vestiges of Egypt's invasion force thrust from our soil and in headlong retreat into eastern Sinai, with our troops in hot pursuit. The Egyptians had also left behind an entire brigade that was trapped in a pocket surrounded by our units. It was this defeat which prompted the Egyptians to agree to negotiate an armistice with us under U.N. auspices in Rhodes, and these talks were going on while we were meeting with King Abdulla. The negotiations with Egypt would end in an agreement signed on February 24. After Egypt had paved the way, the other Arab states would follow suit. Lebanon would be next, with an Armistice Agreement signed on March 23; then Jordan, on April 3; and finally Syria, on July 20.

For the moment, however, the talks with Jordan's king on January 16 and 30 were still exploratory and unofficial, and there were no tangible results—in the sense that they did not bring about an immediate change in the situation. That would occur, said the king, despite the wide gap between us, when Jordan, like the other three Arab states which had fought us, would conclude an Armistice Agreement with us under U.N. auspices. He was hopeful that such an agreement would be reached, and he said that immediately thereafter he would like to begin negotiations toward a peace treaty. This would be done publicly, not in secret, in Jerusalem and without the involvement of the United Nations. There would be a ceremonious opening session, with the king as host, in his palace at Shuneh. He even proposed the composition of our negotiating team, recommending that it be Foreign Minister Moshe Sharett, Sasson, and myself.

The British, he said, knew of his intentions and did not object. He had to consult them, of course, for although Jordan had ceased to be a British-mandated territory and had become independent in 1946, she was still virtually under British protection by virtue of the Anglo-Jordanian treaty of mutual defense. The king added that he was able to tell us all this because we were "like family," and to us he could "speak the truth." And the truth was that in the eyes of his people he was king, but the British treated him as though they were his masters.

There was passing mention of our current talks with the Egyptians in Rhodes, and the king suddenly grew rather anxious and urged us in the strongest possible terms not to give Gaza to Egypt. He himself needed it as an outlet to the Mediterranean. He had no doubt that we could come to terms on this point. The essential thing was not to allow Gaza to go to the Egyptians. "Take it yourselves," he said, "give it to the devil, but don't let Egypt have it!"

Among his ministers, the king made no secret of his relations with us. In our contacts before, during, and after the Rhodes negotiations, the prime minister, other members of the Cabinet, and distinguished Jordanians would occasionally be present for the ceremonial and dining part of the meetings. But they did not participate in the discussions. While they were present, they would be seated on a dais to the right of the king while we Israelis sat on his left. Facing the king, and below him, were some of his advisers of lesser rank. The meeting hall itself was a large oblong room decorated in Oriental fashion, though one wall held an incongruous oil painting of the Battle of Trafalgar, depicting Admiral Nelson's classic maritime victory over the Napoleonic fleet in 1805. It had been a gift to Abdulla from King George V of England.

Although Abdulla was a "son of the desert," the royal court at Shuneh was not without its own formal protocol. His physician was my "guide to the perplexed" in these matters and saw that I did the right thing. Our meetings would open with a series of salutations and expressions of goodwill, and the king would request that we transmit his respects to our leaders—first our president, Dr. Chaim Weizmann, then our prime minister, Ben-Gurion, then our foreign minister, Moshe Sharett, and others. But he had no love for Golda Meir. He had met her on the eve of the war when she tried to persuade him not to take part in it, and he bore her a grudge ever since. According to him, she had placed him in an impossible position, giving him the alternative of submitting to an ultimatum through the lips of a woman or going to war. This, "of course," obliged him to take the second option and join the other Arab states in their invasion of Israel. When he was told at one of the talks that Golda was serving as our minister in Moscow, his immediate response was, "Leave her there, leave her there!" (In Arabic: "Halooha Hoonak, Halooha Hoonak!")

Toward Moshe Sharett he was well disposed—at first. Sharett spoke a polished Arabic and was meticulously well mannered and appropriately reverent in the presence of royalty. But at one of our meetings, a rather unsuccessful one—it was a hot night, we dripped sweat, and there were many mosquitoes on the wing—Sharett corrected the king when he mentioned in passing that China had not been a member of the League of Nations. A king never errs, and Abdulla stood by his statement. Sharett, like a demonstratively patient kindergarten teacher with a backward child, kept saying, "But Your Majesty, you are wrong. China did belong to the League." Of course, that was the end of that meeting—and of the royal regard for Sharett. In the car on our drive back, I asked Sharett what the devil it mattered what the king thought about China and the League. Sharett turned on me with some heat: "But China was a member of the League of Nations!"

We would dine with the king prior to getting down to business, and for an hour or so before the meal there would be political gossip of what was happening in the capitals of the world, an occasional game of chess, and poetry readings. In chess, it was obligatory not only to lose to the king but also to show surprise at his unexpected moves. And when he read his poems, in epigrammatic Arabic, one had to express wonder by sighing from the depth of one's soul.

With all that, I never underrated Abdulla. He was a wise man and a leader who could make critical decisions. When a tough problem came up, he never sent us to his ministers. He asked that the question be brought to him, and he would assume full responsibility for the decision. Nor had he lost the colorfulness of the Bedouin. Every dish brought before him was accompanied by yoghurt, to which he would add an exotic herb, and he would sprinkle our discussions with parables and proverbs. He did not always get what he asked for, but he always knew what he wanted—as we would learn from our continuous secret talks with him at his palace while the formal negotiations would be conducted with his delegates on the island of Rhodes.

These formal negotiations opened on March 1, 1949, and lasted for a month. Jordan had been designated plenipotentiary by Iraq for that sector of the Jordanian front held by the Iraqi army. Heading our team at Rhodes was Reuven Shiloah, and I was his deputy. The Jordanian delegation was led by Col. Ahmed Sudki el-Jundi. The negotiations were held in the Yellow Room of the Hotel des Roses, again under the mediation of Dr. Ralph Bunche, who had presided over the signing of the Israeli-Egyptian Armistice Agreement only a week before. Thus when we arrived in Rhodes, there was not only the precedent of an Arab state which had reached an agreement with us ending the war, but we had before us a textual model whose general articles could be copied, with the simple substitution of "Jordan" for "Egypt."

The opening session at Rhodes began at 4:30 P.M. and was marked by a minor crisis—characteristic and rather pathetic. Before the meeting, it had been agreed with Bunche that when the delegations entered the council chamber, the leaders would be formally presented to one another. When we came in, we found the Jordanian delegation already seated. Bunche went over to the leader of the Jordanian delegation, Col. Jundi, and asked him to rise so that he could be introduced to Reuven Shiloah, the head of the Israeli team. Jundi refused. Shiloah went white and did not know exactly what to do. After the session, he told Bunche that if the Jordanians carried on in this way, he could not continue talks with them. Bunche called Amman and New York, and Shiloah reported to Sharett in Jerusalem. Sharett sent back a pompous and somewhat hysterical cable: "Notify Bunche that if the Jordanians continue to behave in this boorish manner, we shall stop the negotiations and announce that they will be renewed only after we are satisfied that they have learned the elementary lessons in civilized deportment."

It transpired later that the Jordanians had acted without malicious intent. There had been a misunderstanding. Jundi apologized and explained that he had thought the ceremony of formal introductions would take place at the close and not the beginning of the session. I had no doubt whatsoever that he spoke the truth. He was a veteran army officer, correct, smartly turned out—and with an utterly closed mind. He and the other members of his delegation had been sent to fulfill orders they would be receiving from Amman—and not to move a single step outside those orders. If there was a garbled word in a cabled instruction, they would ask for an adjournment so that they could clarify it. These army officers may well have been experts at maintaining order in Jordan and pursuing robber bands in the southern desert, but it was sheer tragi-comedy to plant them in the Hotel des Roses to negotiate with the astute and highly sophisticated Dr. Bunche over juridical and political formulas. They were ready to do anything required of them, but they just did not know what that was. The last thing in the world for which they were suited was conducting armistice negotiations. In fact, they were to prove merely part of the official façade. The hard and basic negotiations were to be conducted unofficially and secretly by their king, Abdulla himself.

After the opening session, our relations with the Jordanian delegation became excellent. Far from being averse to shaking hands, they were most anxious to meet with us in informal sessions, without the presence of U.N. officials. At these informal meetings, they could talk in Arabic and ask us to repeat what we had said over and over again, so they could grasp it, or explain to them the complicated formulas in simple terms.

The first ten days of the negotiations passed without any progress having been made. All the rest was most pleasant—good food, spring weather, enchanting scenery, and interesting company. I spent much of my free time walking along the beach, inspecting the old Turkish fort, and wandering in the woods. Hundreds of butterflies of all sizes and colors flitted between the bushes, giving a fairy-tale air to the site.

It was difficult not to be impressed by Dr. Ralph Bunche's handling of the sessions. He was a broad-shouldered black man of medium height, bright-eyed, with a friendly smile, and never without a cigarette in his mouth. He spoke little and listened to others with intense concentration. It seemed as though he were trying not only to hear what was being said but also to penetrate the mind of the speaker to discover what lay behind his words. He displayed a great deal of charm. Within minutes of meeting someone for the first time, he could establish a rapport and create a mood of amiability and trust.

Bunche was a very adroit draftsman. When both parties had reached a mutual understanding, he could formulate it in clear and incisive phrasing. When the parties failed to agree, he could draft a formula so that each could interpret it in his own way. When I questioned him on this approach, he said the basic aim at the time was to bring about an end to the fighting. Later, when the parties would discover that on certain items they did not get what they had expected, they would not renew the war on that account, but the realities of life would shape the appropriate arrangements. Nicely said. But regarding Article 8 of the Israeli-Jordanian agreement, which dealt with our access to the Jewish holy places, the "appropriate arrangements" turned out to be that Jordan denied us access for the next nineteen years, until the Six Day War. That clause and Article 5 of our agreement with Syria, which dealt with the demilitarized zones, became a source of constant friction. Nonetheless, Dr. Bunche was a man in whose cleverness one could take delight, even when one was ranged against him and he got the better of an argument.

When Israel captured Um Rash Rash, the biblical Eilat, across the way from Jordanian-controlled Aqaba at the head of the gulf of the same name, King Abdulla feared additional Israeli conquests, for we were still at war and Armistice Agreements had not yet been reached. On March 14, 1949, in the midst of the Rhodes negotiations, he sent an urgent message to Foreign Minister Sharett: "It is reported that you have declared that an Israeli army unit has reached the shore of the Gulf of Aqaba in territory considered to be included in Palestine. That, I know, is correct. It is further reported that in your declaration you went on to say that any part of Palestine which is evacuated by the Iraqi army will be captured by Israeli forces to ensure defense stability. Is this true?"

On the next day, Walter Eytan, director-general of the Israeli Foreign Ministry, sent a reply in the name of the Israeli government: "Foreign Minister Sharett is abroad and I am acting in his place. I have the honor to thank you in his name for your kind letter, which was received yesterday. As to the evacuation of Iraqi forces from the areas they now hold (and your taking them over), we have already notified the Acting U.N. Mediator [Bunche] that we regard this step as a flagrant violation of the truce and we shall not recognize it so long as our agreement has not been secured. However, we have no intention of capturing this territory nor threatening its Arab inhabitants, since it is our wish to reach a peace arrangement in this area too. It is our view that a discussion of this matter falls outside the purview of the armistice talks at Rhodes, but we are prepared to recall Col. Moshe Dayan from Rhodes for a talk with the king's representative in Jerusalem on the arrangements acceptable to both parties for the territory to be evacuated by the Iraqi forces. We shall be grateful to Your Majesty if you would let us know if it is your wish that we invite Col. Dayan for such a talk in Jerusalem. We are convinced that this will be agreeable to you, for you, no less than we, would prefer a solution by peaceful means."

Immediately afterward I received a cable in Rhodes directing me to return to Jerusalem at once. I said goodbye to the Hotel des Roses and to the butterflies in the woods and came back to the dark-of-night talks in the no-man's land of Mandelbaum, the gentleman whose name and battle-ruined house between the Jordanian and Israeli lines had entered history as a unique "gate" of Jerusalem.

On March 18 at 6:30 P.M., I met with Abdulla el-Tel. I felt no need for lengthy preliminaries, or for gentle treading around the subject. I told him directly that we wanted the Wadi Ara defile, south of Haifa, and the hills which controlled both the wadi and the narrow coastal plain, where we were being harassed by Iraqi troops. El-Tel replied that this concession was not possible because of both Jordanian public opinion and the stand taken by the Iraqis. Jordan could not withdraw from the line currently held by the Iraqi expeditionary force. I said that if that was the case, it was better for the Jordanians not to take over the Iraqi sector of the front, since fighting there would be renewed. It was then agreed that el-Tel would proceed to the Shuneh Palace to consult with King Abdulla and we would meet again on the next day. He would bring Abdulla's response, and I would bring along a detailed map of the area we wanted to be handed over to us.

On the following day, we received an urgent message from the king addressed to Eytan, of the Israeli Foreign Ministry: "I know you will agree with me on the question of our taking over the Iraqi sector of the front, since this arises out of the talks I have had with Mr. Sasson and Col. Dayan. I myself talked to the Iraqis when I met them at the border and persuaded them that I would take over the entire front. If you and Dayan could meet me, I hope that the results will be what we all desire. 19.3.49. El Shuneh."

I asked the General Staff for a map and promised that in talking to the king we would not "ask for a mountain in order to settle for a mouse" but would tell him what we wanted and would stand by it, rather than indulge in Oriental haggling. We accepted the king's invitation and set off for his palace, this time without civilians—just Capt. Yehoshafat Harkavi, a staff officer, and I. The meeting did not last long. We greeted, dined, explained, and departed at 10 P.M., leaving the king to digest our proposals—which were just, though by no means modest—and to consult with his ministers.

What followed thereafter inside Jordan was a good deal of rushing around and hastily convened sessions of ministers and top officials. The king even sent el-Tel to talk to the prime minister, who was in Beirut at the time. They finally decided that a Jordanian Ministerial Committee should conduct negotiations with us, and our meeting took place at the Mandelbaum Gate on the night of March 22.

Jordan was represented by the minister of justice, Felah Pasha Medadha, and the director-general of the Foreign Ministry, Hussein Seraj. El-Tel was also present. Our team consisted of Eytan; Yigael Yadin, our chief of operations; Harkavi and myself. Yadin opened by putting the map on the table, and the Jordanians received a shock. Yadin explained. They replied, suggesting changes, and backed them with argument. There was discussion and debate, and in the end we all grew tired. In the absence of the king, no one would take upon himself the responsibility of a decision. At that point, I suggested half-jokingly to el-Tel that he exploit the moment of weakness and sign our map in the name of Jordan. El-Tel was in no bantering mood. He pointed to the minister of justice, Felah Pasha, who had fallen asleep with his head on the table surrounded by half-empty tins of bully beef, and spat out contemptuously: "Wake him up. He'll sign anything so long as he doesn't lose his job." We rolled up our maps and went home to bed.

We met the king the next day. Our delegation was the same, but Abdulla had assembled a larger team—all very distinguished men—which suggested to me that this would be the night of decision. The civilian component comprised the acting prime minister, the justice minister, the education minister, and the director-general of the Foreign Ministry. The Jordanian army was represented by a British major, chief of operations, and the head of the Survey Department. After a dinner of five huge courses, which reflected a special effort, we adjourned to the council chamber.

At three in the morning the negotiations ended and the maps were signed. The king had left at eleven in the evening, but after an hour he had to return to get us off the shoals. The Jordanians had a number of demands in exchange for their concessions. At a certain moment in the talks, when the king explained how heavy were the sacrifices he was making, I did not restrain myself but told him that the three military members of our delegation, Yadin, Harkavi, and myself, had each lost a younger brother in this war—a war which we had not wanted and which would not have broken out if the Arab states, including Jordan, had not attacked us. The time to have talked about concessions and compromise was before the war, in order to prevent it. Now one had to bear the consequences and finish with it.

Before we parted, Eytan handed the king a gift from Ben-Gurion—a silver-bound Bible. The king responded with presents for each of us. I got a revolver—without bullets and without an inscription. Everyone was weary, and no one looked happy. The king noticed the expressions on our faces, asked us to wait a few moments, and then gave an order to one of his servants. The man went off and soon returned with a bunch of roses. The king, with a tired but sincere smile, gave each of us a rose as he blessed us on our journey homeward, saying, "Tonight we have ended the war and brought peace."

A few hours later I flew back to Rhodes, and on April 3 Shiloah cabled Sharett: "Signed." We returned to Israel carrying with us the Israeli-Transjordanian Armistice Agreement and its attached map. The signature on the map in the name of Jordan was that of the Englishman Glubb Pasha (General John Bagot Glubb), commander of the Arab Legion. The signature in the name of Israel was mine.

I met King Abdulla again several times at Shuneh and in Amman. The visits to Shuneh had become almost routine, but the trip to more distant Amman was complicated. The drive there and back had to be undertaken during the hours of darkness, and it was just not possible to reach Amman, hold a meeting, and return to Jerusalem in a single night. I had perforce to remain in Amman after the meeting and return to Jerusalem the following evening.

Even after the Armistice Agreement was signed, various difficulties arose, and whenever we came up against a blank wall we would go to the king to straighten out matters. We also tried to advance together with him toward something beyond an armistice. Ben-Gurion had heard from a foreign correspondent who had met King Abdulla, together with Samir Rifai, in London that Abdulla had said he wanted peace. (Samir Rifai was soon to replace Taufiq Abu al-Huda as Jordanian prime minister.) The king had added that Sharett was a moderate but Ben-Gurion was an extremist. Samir had later told the correspondent privately that the king would give up his demand to obtain Lod and Ramla, but within the framework of a peace treaty he wanted Gaza and an access corridor to it. If Israel agreed, Abdulla would secure Egypt's consent.

We pursued this idea, and at one of our last meetings in Shuneh,

on December 17, 1949, when I saw the king together with Reuven
Shiloah, we reached the stage of drafting the terms of a peace treaty.
The king was wary of the explicit term "peace treaty," but agreed to
call it a "paper" on which were inscribed "Principles of a Territorial
Arrangement (Final)." This "paper" was initialed by the king and
Reuven Shiloah. I do not know whether the Israeli government would
have ratified this agreement. Ben-Gurion did not reject it, but he
wrinkled his nose when he read it. At all events, when we returned
to the king to continue the negotiations, he informed us that his
friend Sir Alec Kirkbride, Britain's minister to Transjordan, did not
agree that Jordan should enter into such a treaty with Israel while
other Arab states, mainly Egypt, had not done so. The king therefore
asked us to regard the "paper" as cancelled.

Its principal provisions were Israel's grant to Jordan of an outlet to
the Mediterranean, with a corridor running through Israeli territory
linking Jordan with the coast at Gaza; the transfer to Israel by Jordan
of part of a road on the western shore of the Dead Sea to link the
Israeli-held southern stretch with the Jordanian-held northern end
of the Dead Sea; the inclusion of the Jewish Quarter of the Old City
within the Israeli part of Jerusalem, in return for the inclusion in the
Jordanian part of Jerusalem of a road linking Bethlehem with Jerusalem; access by Israel to the Israeli enclave on Mount Scopus; and
negotiations on mutual compensation and rectification of the borders.

In accordance with what was agreed at Shuneh and signed in
Rhodes, it was necessary for Jordan to hand over to Israel areas which
were in the hands of the Iraqi expeditionary force. In addition, we
wished to divide the no-man's land between the Jordanians and ourselves. This applied particularly to the southern part of Jerusalem,
through which the Tel Aviv-Jerusalem railway line passed. Three
meetings to negotiate this matter were held in April 1949. The Jordanian representatives were the same officers who had been in
Rhodes and were therefore familiar with the signed decisions and
maps. There were three items to be dealt with: the removal of Jordanian military forces and civilians who, contrary to the agreement,
were situated beyond the Jordanian lines, mostly in no-man's land;
the division of no-man's land between Israel and Jordan; and the
physical demarcation of the new lines by a barbed-wire fence. Many
difficulties arose. One was that two Arab villages were in the no-man's
land and a third was in Israel.

The most sensitive item was dividing up no-man's land. There were
two particularly touchy areas, the Government House compound and
the railway line. The railway line itself, plus an additional 200-yard

strip to the south, was to go to Israel; in exchange, several Arab villages in northern Jerusalem in the region of Bet Iksa were to go to Jordan. The two parties also agreed to an equal division of the no-man's land round Government House, but after the Big Powers raised the strongest possible protest against such a move and put heavy pressure on Jordan, the decision we had reached was cancelled. The Government House compound remained under the flag of the United Nations.

When it came to putting the agreement into effect, on May 1, 1949, with the demarcation and fencing of the lines, the old difficulties recurred, this time involving the affected inhabitants. The suburb of Bet Safafa in southern Jerusalem was to be divided, its northern houses close to the railway line going to Israel and the southern houses remaining in Jordan and cut off from Jerusalem. This was also the case with a number of houses in the village of Betar. The mixed group of Israeli and Jordanian soldiers who had gone out to demarcate the border and put up the wire fence encountered opposition from the unfortunate villagers. At first they only held a rather voluble demonstration, but they were soon joined by the troops manning nearby Jordanian military positions, who opened fire. The demarcation work stopped. In the shooting, one of our soldiers was killed and another wounded.

There was nothing for it but to carry out the division quickly and with determination. We notified the Jordanians that if they did not cooperate, we would enforce the division ourselves, even if it meant using force. But the king preferred to assume responsibility and to have his men share in the execution of the agreement. At 9 A.M. on the next day, May 2, a new Jordanian delegation appeared, together with disciplined officers prepared to carry out their orders without reserve. The area was measured and divided. The line was worked out and the fence erected. The dominating military positions of Zur Bahar south of Jerusalem passed into our hands. They, of course, would be of considerable importance if there were a renewal of fighting. But it was precisely because we were entering a period of peace, or at least of no fighting, that there was supreme significance to the arrangement we had made over the railway line. The entire length of the Tel Aviv rail link was now within Israel.

Ben-Gurion was very pleased, and he talked of the railway line and me as a pair, as though I had discovered it. But this was not how the citizens of Jordan received news of the Rhodes agreement and the railway arrangement. The government of Jordan resigned, and the king ordered a new Cabinet to be formed. In an attempt to soften the Palestinians, allay their anger, and get them to share responsibility for his policy, the king brought three Palestinian ministers into his government. This step was to open a new chapter in the history of the Kingdom of Jordan. That history would have been more fruitful both for Jordan and the Middle East if the king's life had been spared. But Abdulla was assassinated by a Palestinian Arab on July 20, 1951, on the steps of the El Aksa Mosque in the Temple compound of Jerusalem as he was leaving after Friday prayers.

From the time of the signing of the Armistice Agreement with Jordan until my appointment as general officer commanding Southern Command on October 25, 1949, I dealt with armistice affairs touching upon all our borders with the neighboring Arab states. Under each of the agreements—with Egypt, Jordan, Lebanon and Syria—a Mixed Armistice Commission was established to supervise the armistice, ensure that the agreements were properly implemented, and settle any differences that arose. Each commission consisted of representatives of Israel and its Arab counterpart and was chaired by a U.N. observer. On June 9, 1949, I was assigned by the General Staff to head the Israeli delegations to all four Mixed Armistice Commissions.

On the whole, it could be said that the agreements were carried out, if not in spirit, at least in accordance with the written text. The Armistice Agreements were to have been a stepping stone toward the achievement of permanent peace. But the Arabs refused to continue negotiations toward peace with Israel. However, with two exceptions, they stood by what had been decided in the signed agreements. The armistice lines were demarcated according to the Rhodes maps and were recognized as the borders of the State of Israel. The military forces were thinned out and deployed further away from the frontiers and the shooting stopped.

The exceptions were the article in the agreement with Jordan which called for free Israeli access to the Jewish holy places and to the Mount Scopus enclave in Jerusalem, and the article in the Syrian agreement which defined the status of the demilitarized zones on the Syrian border.

I did not go into mourning over the non-fulfillment of the agreements on demilitarized zones. I had not favored these arrangements in the first place and did not believe they would work, for they restricted not only the military presence, which was a sound measure, but also civilian development, which was unrealistic. The demilitarized zones included the districts of Kibbutz Ein Gev, on the eastern shore, and Dardara just north of the Sea of Galilee. These areas were an inseparable part of Israel, and there was no point in subjecting them to limitations of settlement and size of population, and certainly not to placing them under the authority of a "governor" on behalf of the United Nations. Sooner or later, the pattern of these zones would be the same as in the rest of Israel—and the sooner the better.

This was not the case with the article concerning Jerusalem, which specifically stipulated that Israelis would have access to the Jewish holy places in the Old City, notably the Western ("Wailing") Wall, and to the Hebrew University and the Hadassah Hospital on Mount Scopus. It also recorded that there was to be free movement along the Latrun road and the Bethlehem-Jerusalem road.

What was promised was not fulfilled. The Armistice Agreement called for a special committee to work out the practical arrangements. The Jordanians turned their backs on this provision, and the situation remained as it was during the fighting, with the Old City of Jerusalem closed to Jews.

I had definite ideas on what we should do, and I spoke to Ben-Gurion about them whenever we met and followed up these thoughts with memoranda. But there was little response. This was characteristic of Ben-Gurion. He would simply avoid discussion of any problem, however urgent it may have seemed to others, until he considered the time was ripe to give it priority. That time, on this issue, came one day late in September 1949, when the prime minister was to visit a training base in the north. It had been arranged that I should drive back with him to Tel Aviv so that we could talk in the car without office pressures.

The result of this review was the order from Ben-Gurion not to fortify the demilitarized zones but to continue with farm settlement, which was what I had asked for. On Jerusalem, however, we remained divided in our views. I proposed that we take action to enforce the Armistice Agreement, using the army to open the roads to Mount Scopus, the Western Wall, and through Latrun. Unless this was done, the joint decision reached at Rhodes would be worthless, an empty promise. After all, it was not up to the Arabs but to us to give tangible expression to our rights, and our failure to do so was tantamount to surrendering those rights.

Ben-Gurion asked me if such military action would not bring about a renewal of the war. I told him I did not think so. I judged that even if it came to an open military clash and the use of force to break open a corridor to the Western Wall and Mount Scopus, it would remain an isolated episode and not touch off general hostilities. Moreover, it was possible that when the Jordanians saw that we were ready to take determined measures, they would themselves fulfill the terms of the agreement, as they had done with the division of no-man's land in southern Jerusalem.

Ben-Gurion did not accept my proposal. His main reason was that we now had to concentrate on the targets of peace—the care and rehabilitation of our immigrants, the settlement of the land, above all the injection of life into the desert regions—and the overall development of the country. At the time of our talk, we were engaged in rescuing, among many others, the entire Jewish community of Yemen, setting up a huge camp in Aden, to which the Jews of Yemen had trekked, and bringing them over in chartered aircraft at the rate of nearly a thousand a day. Many of these immigrants were weak, undernourished, and often suffering from tropical diseases. Those waiting in the Aden camp, together with the ones who were on their weary and dangerous way on foot through Yemen, amounted to tens of thousands. And they were only a part of the huge numbers being brought in from many lands, including the survivors of the Nazi death camps. As Ben-Gurion said, to feed and house these immigrants and put them on their feet promised immense difficulties and demanded a tremendous national effort. So did the creation of the new farm villages and urban centers in the empty areas of the country and the strengthening of existing settlements. These were the burning urgencies. The land of Israel, Ben-Gurion said, would not remain ours solely through war and the power of the army.

In Ben-Gurion's mind, the book of war was closed—for the time being, at least. His eyes were now turned to the realization of the Zionist dream, the essence of which was immigration—the return of the Jewish exiles—and the revival of the land.

11

A NEW WORLD

ONE MONTH LATER, in October 1949, I was promoted to major-general and appointed general officer commanding Southern Command. The area the command covered included the entire Negev desert, the arid and sparsely populated triangle of southern Israel with its apex in the south, at Eilat, on the Gulf of Aqaba. The right arm of the triangle was the border with Jordan, running along the Arava Valley from the gulf to the Dead Sea, its left arm the border with Egyptian-held Sinai, which ran northwest from the gulf to the Mediterranean. This western boundary of the territory under Southern Command then continued further north to skirt the Egyptian-administered Gaza Strip, a finger thrusting up from the northern Negev into the coastal plain.

My predecessor in this command was Yigal Allon, a former commander of the Palmach, the active combat units of the Haganah in the years immediately before the establishment of the state, and he had chosen his staff officers from among the Palmach officers who were very close to him. Though the Palmach's formations had been merged with the Israel Defense Forces upon the establishment of the state in May 1948, it had retained separate headquarters, which Ben-Gurion disbanded in November of that year, much to the resentment of the Palmach members. When I arrived at Southern Command headquarters to take up my duties, I had brought none of my own officers with me, and I asked none of the staff officers who had served with Allon to leave. But most of them did. Their general resentment had not been lessened by Ben-Gurion's announcement of my appointment at a time when Allon happened to be on a visit outside the country.

My functions as front commander were new to me. So was the territory now under my command. I was a "northerner" unfamiliar with the south. I now set about learning my duties, getting to know my units, and familiarizing myself with the new terrain. I started with a trip through the Negev to its southern point, Eilat. I had been there before, but I had then gone by plane. I now took a jeep and, together with Amos Horev, my operations officer, and an accompanying jeep, left command headquarters at dawn and reached Eilat close to midnight. It was a hot, tiring, dust-covered drive over an unpaved rutted road strewn with boulders, and to make any speed at all meant being tossed about and having to cling to the side of the jeep to avoid being flung out.

Our main military position for the defense of the area was at Nakeb, a promontory on the Sinai border a few miles northwest of Eilat. A small unit held it. The hour was very late, and I was dropping with fatigue after the long hours in the bumpy jeep under the burning sun and against the choking *khamsin,* the hot desert wind. Instead of meeting with the local commander, I drove straight to the Eilat beach, took a dip in the waters of the gulf, and stretched out on the sand to sleep. The gentle lapping of the waves kept me awake long enough to reflect on the strange world I had driven through that day, the world of my new command. It was a wide-open expanse, bare, parched, craggy, primeval, yielding only the tropical acacia and tamarisk and a bush with long hard thorns, sharp as spears. It was quite unlike the northern Israel I knew, which seemed to me now to be a soft garden in delicate flower. There was also a strength about the features of the Negev unmatched by those in the north. The Jordan River, the Kishon River near Haifa, the Yarkon River near Tel Aviv were slight depressions compared with the rift of the Arava, the monumental Ramon crater, or the Jirafi ravine in the biblical wilderness of Paran—impressive to me as it must have been to the Children of Israel after their Exodus from Egypt. And the mountains in the north seemed to diminish in my mind to humble mounds compared with the lofty peaks of the central Negev range, or even against the vision of the Scorpions' Ascent, or the cliffs round King Solomon's mines, perhaps because their gaunt mass rose sheer and sudden out of the flat desert. This was a hot, wild world, void of rain and apparently of dew.

At the break of day we drove up a tortuous canyon to reach the unit at Nakeb, with its commanding view of a huge stretch of the Sinai Peninsula. The troops stationed there had no special problems. Enemy movements could be spotted with ease for quite a distance, but the Egyptians caused no trouble in this sector. All was quiet. But a good deal of noise could be heard at another military base I visited. There a unit of the Engineering Corps had begun to tackle the gigantic task of blasting a 150-mile road through cheerless country from Eilat to Beersheba, hacking away parts of mountains to widen passes and carving ledges out of the slopes. Their main problem, they told me, was laying a firm base in the sandy terrain to carry the road. They had overcome it, they said, by mixing salt with the earth. They brought the salt from Sodom at the southern end of the Dead Sea, where it was found in abundance—with the added increment in biblical times of Lot's unfortunate wife. This solution seemed strange to me, but I assumed the army engineers knew what they were doing. After driving along the seashore from the Egyptian to the Jordanian border, we returned to Beersheba by plane.

There were a number of kibbutzim in the Negev which had taken encouraging steps in cultivating the desert. But a lot more could and had to be done to develop this region, and I thought the army could provide considerable help. There existed a Negev Development Authority, but from what I had seen on my exploratory trips in the field, it was not doing very much. I therefore decided to talk to Ben-Gurion about it, and a fortnight after my appointment, I called on the prime minister while I was in Tel Aviv for meetings at General Headquarters. It was rather late at night, and the house was dark. The guards told me that Ben-Gurion's wife, Paula, had gone to sleep but they thought that he was still up. I tried my luck. The front door was locked, but I found the kitchen door at the back open, so I went in, carefully mounted the stairs in the dark, and reached the study. There sat Ben-Gurion at his desk intently covering small sheets of notepaper with large handwriting. He was preparing the speech he planned to deliver the next day at the inauguration of the Weizmann Institute of Science.

Ben-Gurion looked up and seemed pleased to see me, brushing aside my apologies for disturbing him. I wasted no time, telling him

I wished to clarify one matter and would then leave: did he wish me to concern myself with civilian matters relating to the development of the Negev?

His reply was prompt and positive. He said I very definitely should deal with development. The head of the Negev Authority had already been told that he would be subordinate to me. Ben-Gurion then said that in the meantime he wanted three programs established immediately: the building of a large military training base in the Negev; the construction of a highway from the Dead Sea to Beersheba and the Mediterranean just north of Ashkelon—and also possibly a railway; and the development of fishing at Eilat. In the middle of giving me these details, he suddenly stopped and said, "Bevin [Britain's foreign secretary] wants to get the Negev taken from Israel. With all his sweet talk of late, these British plans have not changed. They seem determined to secure the handing over of the Negev to Egypt or Jordan so that there can be an unbroken land bridge between the two Arab countries. We must be prepared for such moves." I began telling him of the military measures I was taking to strengthen security in the south when he interrupted: "Security does not mean military positions. Security means establishing Jewish towns and farm settlements in the Negev and making the desert blossom."

This was the first of many sessions I had with Ben-Gurion on civilian affairs in the area under my command. They were not always to the satisfaction of some of the government ministries and other civilian bodies involved, or, for chain-of-command reasons, of the General Staff. But I was less interested in formal protocol than in settling affairs in the quickest and most beneficial way. Going straight to the top may have ruffled feathers, but it saved time.

A case in point was the arrangement I made to help the Arabs of Majdal, for which I received Ben-Gurion's backing. The coastal town of Majdal adjoined Ashkelon just outside the Gaza Strip. At the end of the War of Independence, Majdal found itself inside the boundaries of Israel and cut off from its Arab hinterland in the strip. Its Arab population of some 2,700 lived in depressed isolation. Most of them had been employed as farm laborers or textile workers in and around Gaza and were now out of work. They came under Military Government administration. After talking to them, I found that the majority wished to move to the Gaza Strip, if this could be arranged, while some wanted to go to other Arab towns inside Israel. I thought this an admirable solution, and I approached Col. Mahmud Riad, for his cooperation. He was the Egyptian representative on the Egyptian-Israeli Mixed Armistice Commission, and I had met him when I had been responsible for armistice affairs. He readily agreed, and I promptly presented the proposal to the General Staff. They were sluggish in their response, so I went to see Ben-Gurion, and he gave his approval. The condition he set—one which I, too, had in mind—was that we would make the transfer only if the Majdal Arabs themselves agreed to it. I notified the deputy chief of staff that Ben-Gurion had approved and received confirmation from General Headquarters.

I was in Majdal preparing the final arrangements with the *mukhtar* when I received an urgent telephone call from the deputy chief of staff telling me to suspend activities and await new instructions. It turned out that Pinhas Lavon, secretary-general of the Histadrut, the Jewish Labor Federation (who would later succeed Ben-Gurion for a brief term as minister of defense when I was chief of staff), had demanded that the defense minister scrap the plan. The Histadrut had its own proposal, which offered the promise of employment for the Majdal textile workers but not to the others. My proposal would provide the opportunity of immediate employment for all the workers of Majdal and would also meet the social and cultural needs of the entire community. Lavon and I were then summoned to Ben-Gurion, who heard both sides and decided in my favor. Egypt's Col. Mahmud Riad proved true to his word. He had trucks waiting at the border roadblock to transfer the Arabs of Majdal to Gaza.

There was a piquant epilogue. When the operation was completed, I notified the senior officers in my command that military rule in Majdal had been annulled. I immediately received a message from the General Staff that I was not authorized to abolish Military Government, which had been instituted by the chief of staff with the approval of the minister of defense. The procedure was for me to make a recommendation to the Operations Branch. The General Staff was quite right, so I exhumed the body from its grave, restored Military Government to an empty Majdal, and reburied it next day with General Staff approval, thereby meeting the meticulous standards of army protocol.

I also had the backing of Ben-Gurion in another area of civilian affairs, encouraging the members of the Negev kibbutzim and moshavim to cultivate state lands right up to the borders and helping them with equipment and vehicles. I thought this was good for the farmers and good for security, since open, neglected areas were an invitation to infiltrators. And infiltration was a problem, with frequent incursions across the borders both for sabotage and for simple stealing or cattle rustling. Indeed, during the quiet year of 1950, the main operational activities of Southern Command consisted of reconnaissance patrols and ambushes to prevent border crossings.

Some of the Bedouin posed a complicated problem. This was particularly so with the hostile Azazme tribe, which claimed the right—as Bedouin—to cross our borders and roam freely between Egypt and Jordan. These Bedouin constituted a grave security risk, and from time to time we had to drive them off. But the Israeli Bedouin gave us little trouble and appreciated the aid they received from us. It was the first time, they said, that any government had provided them with help and services. They received not only social benefits and medical attention, but also land on which they could settle and build homes—often alongside their black tents—and the opportunity to send their children to a real school. We even provided them with arms so that they could defend themselves against hostile marauding tribes.

We also undertook reconnaissance patrols across the borders, mostly into Sinai, and I joined them whenever possible, both to get to know the area more thoroughly and also, I confess, to escape from desk work. I enjoyed seeking out unbeaten paths and sleeping in the open in a sandy wadi. At times we would be shot at, mostly by smugglers who would be wide of the mark and opened fire mainly to delay us while they fled with their contraband. Occasionally the source of fire would be an Azazme Bedouin who wanted to settle accounts with us. We also had to take care near the border to avoid an abandoned enemy minefield left over from the war.

My delight in the desert—the colors, the air, the wild scenery, the vegetation so strange to me, the space, the freedom—grew with each passing week. Sometimes I would take my daughter, Yael, with me on a trip. She was a thin dark-haired child of eleven when she first came with me. Wrapped in a wind-jacket with an Arab *kefieh* around her head and face, and huddled between the soldiers and the jerry cans that filled the command car, she would sit entranced by the desert scenery—as new to her as it had been to me—and by the adventurous tales told by the trackers. And it was a joy to watch her excitement at the sight of a herd of deer rushing past, their feet barely skimming the ground. On our return, I would give her a note for her teacher explaining that Yael had missed school "for special reasons"—which was no less than the truth.

On one of the border-crossing reconnaissance patrols I joined, with the aim of finding a route to biblical Kadesh-barnea in eastern Sinai, we came close to the Egyptian outpost at Kusseima, just beyond the Negev-Sinai border, where the Egyptian officers spotted us. We managed to retire without incident, but the matter came to the attention of our chief of staff. He apparently considered this was going a bit too far, for across the border I might easily be captured, and since I was a front commander this could have grave consequences. He therefore sent a message, which I found on my desk upon my return to command headquarters: "Irrespective of operational orders concerning frontier crossings by reconnaissance and fighting patrols, I forbid you personally from crossing the armistice lines without permission from the deputy chief of staff or from me. Yigael Yadin."

On one winter Sabbath I took my nine-year-old son, Udi, out with me on a wild-pigeon shoot. He could already use a .22-caliber rifle, and though he was not yet an expert marksman, he had the right idea. It was a bright, sunny day following a week of torrential rains, and the atmosphere was limpid. We could hear the braying of donkeys thirty miles away. We drove south from Tel Aviv, turned east on an old stone road near the southern end of the coastal plain, and reached Tell es-Safi, an archaeological mound midway between biblical Gezer and Lachish. We got out of the jeep and began flushing the birds from the ruins when I suddenly spotted a row of jars sticking out of a mud wall in a nearby wadi. On inspection, I found that each one was whole, and all looked as though they had just come off the potter's wheel. It was evident that the heavy rains which had flooded the wadi had washed away whatever had hidden the jars and had exposed them.

I thought at first that these were common Arab jars. But I noticed that the pottery was not black but an unusual polished red. I took one of them home and in the evening showed it to a friend who knew a great deal about archaeology. It turned out to be a vessel fashioned in the period of the Hebrew kings, dating back to the ninth century B.C.

I returned to Tell es-Safi the following Sabbath and this time I carefully examined the wadi. The jars lay in a stratum of dark soil mixed with ashes, clearly the archaeological level of the ancient city, which had been destroyed by fire. Near the jars were reddish and gray potsherds, broken bricks of loam, spouts of ancient oil lamps coated with soot, handles of large jars (which I learned later had been used to store grain), and bits of delicately wrought small flasks. This was my first intimate and tangible meeting with ancient Israel. A new world had suddenly been opened to me, giving me a glimpse of the life that had existed here three thousand years ago. Hidden beneath the roads, houses, fields and trees of the twentieth century were the remains of cities, villages, and artifacts created by the people who had lived in this land, the ancient Land of Israel. It was this experience which excited my passion for archaeology. It is a passion which has never left me.

Over the years, I have built up a collection of antiquities, and I enjoy looking at them. But they are not my principal archaeological attraction. What captured my heart were the potsherds embedded in the different archaeological levels which I would discover during excavations. It was like glimpsing a wild cyclamen peeping out in surprise from the cleft of a rock, or a young deer bounding between the boulders of Ein Gedi above the Dead Sea. These pottery vessels, often soot laden or entangled in roots, lie as they were left thousands of years ago. They might be prosaic domestic utensils used in ordinary homes in some town or village that was destroyed in battle, or perhaps a cruse with its final offering of oil, and a lamp to light the way of the departed in a family tomb. It is these ordinary articles that provide the bond, intimate, personal, with the wonderful world of antiquity, a world that had fallen silent but has not vanished.

The vessels of ancient glass among my antiquities are aesthetic delights, exquisite in color. But they lack one quality possessed by the primitive shard—the personal stamp of creation. On a pitcher, particularly at the point where handle joins body, it is often possible to detect the thumbprint of the potter and sometimes even the print of his fingernail. The finest jars are those belonging to the age of the Patriarchs, almost four thousand years ago. Their successors never quite learned to master the material as they did, to create jugs, lamps, and bowls as thin as glass yet hard and sturdy. They also had a very sophisticated artistic sense, decorating the neck of a jug with delicately engraved lines and adding a small embossment. This served no functional purpose. It was apparently there to ward off the evil eye and may have been a fertility charm. If so, then it had not been fashioned for nought. It had indeed faithfully discharged its mission, keeping watch over the household who sipped from the jug and multiplying their seed and their flocks.

When I discover potsherds from a shattered vessel that have remained in place, I gather them with great care, and bring them to the workshop I built at the back of the garden of my house in Zahala. There I keep glue and plaster of Paris to stick the shards together, and acid to clean away the layers of stone that have clung to them for thousands of years. At the weekend, and late at night, I open the paper packages containing the potsherds, wash them, and start the restoration. I have no other hobby or sport. Most free hours are spent on these antiquities. I love to work with my hands—and I need much time to be alone.

Putting the broken vessels together, fashioning them anew and returning them to the shape given them by the potters and housewives three, four or five thousand years ago, gives me something of the feeling of creation; it is the sense of satisfaction I recall from my youth at Nahalal, when I myself sowed and planted, and helped the cows to bring their delicate young to birth.

I soon familiarized myself with the functions of a regional command and the special functions of Southern Command. They were wider and more onerous and independent than any I had fulfilled before. The area was in its development stage, and it covered almost half the territory of the entire country. Responsibility for its overall defense was considerable. Its western boundary constituted Israel's front against Egypt, the most formidable of the Arab states. There were also two other fronts, the border with Jordan, and the Armistice Line round the Gaza Strip. There were 100,000 Palestinian refugees in the strip, apart from the permanent residents, and it had become a center for the *fedayeen,* Palestinian terrorist and sabotage units which operated against Israel.

The Israeli army concentrated its main armored force in this southern region, and there were also two large air bases. Other regular units of the army came under my command, as did the mobilization and training of the reserve forces.

On the civilian administrative side, in addition to the Bedouin, the border kibbutzim, and other established farm villages, I was concerned with the siting and creation of rural and urban centers for new immigrants. Indeed, this was the region which most demonstrably held the twin civilian challenges of the young state, bringing life to the desolate lands and settling the new immigrants. Thousands arrived every month during this period, many from the Arab countries, where living had become harsh and dangerous for Jews. A large number of them settled in the southern region, and they created new farm villages. Many also came to live in and help build up the towns of Beersheba, Ashkelon, and Eilat.

My activities were thus quite varied. I would review tank maneuvers, call on new immigrants from Yemen who had just settled in, visit a border kibbutz which had become the target of infiltrators, follow the construction of a road through the Arava, inspect the training of reservists, check on the development of Eilat, and give constant thought both to hastening civilian growth and to strengthening our defenses by the more effective utilization of the small forces at our disposal.

During my period as GOC Southern Command, there was only one incident with Jordan which might have escalated into a full-scale battle. It occurred at the end of 1950 at the Kilometer 78 marker on the road to Eilat. Jordan claimed that the road we had built crossed into her territory at this spot and had taken the issue to the Mixed Armistice Commission, but without waiting for its decision, she had blocked the road. At the barrier the Jordanians had put up a notice in Arabic and Hebrew reading "Hashemite Kingdom of Jordan. Road closed," and they posted troops and several armored cars on the hills opposite.

The fact is that it is not easy to determine the exact course of the Israeli-Jordanian frontier in the Arava rift. The armistice map delineates it as lying along the "lowest depression of the Arava rift," but the level changes from time to time as a result of erosion and flash floods, and what was once a ravine had become a broad, flat, winding belt of sand. Israel had no option but to break through the barrier, and Southern Command received orders from the General Staff to drive the enemy off and open the Arava road.

I happened to be in Turkey at the time, on holiday with my family. Israel had been quiet, and I resolved to fill a long-standing desire to wander round the Turkish interior, particularly the desolate plateau between Ankara and Konya. For whatever reason, whether Southern Command was slow in going into action or because the chief of staff feared possible complications, he summoned me home. I arrived back in the evening, went straight from the airport to command headquarters, and the next morning drove to Kilometer 78. Jordanian troops looked down upon the blocked road from the nearby hills, while our own troops, a mechanized battalion from an armored brigade, were busy planning, reconnoitering, maneuvering, and outflanking—doing everything, in fact, except breaking through the barrier.

A Piper Cub was handy, and I asked the pilot to fly me over the Jordanian lines. We decided to fly as low as possible so that we could slip between the hills without being detected prematurely. We did so, and as we passed over—or rather between—the armored vehicles of the Arab Legion, I saw that there were only a few of them. And I could not find any tanks or artillery in the area. It was a useful reconnaissance, and not unpleasant, except for one moment when the pilot took his eye off the altimeter to stare at the Legionnaires. The wheels of the Piper hit the ground, bumped, and sent the plane up again where it belonged. We got back safely with the intelligence I wanted.

The whole affair seemed like a comic opera. I sent a note in the name of the "commander of the Israeli armored column" to the

British officer commanding the Jordanian troops. It requested him to remove the barrier, as we proposed to use the road, and noted that if fired on we would fire back. I added that the Jordanian complaint was under consideration by the Mixed Armistice Commission, and we would abide by its decision. Until then, there was no call to impede Israeli traffic.

The officer who had taken the note, flying a white flag on his jeep, returned with the Jordanian rejection of our demand. I accordingly ordered our unit to proceed to the roadblock, remove it, and continue driving. It was not to open fire unless the Jordanians started shooting. Our troops on half-tracks moved off, cleared the barrier, and went through without any reaction from the Arab Legion.

I thought that was the end of the episode, but the next morning we again found the road blocked. Once more our mechanized column cleared the barrier and drove back and forth along the disputed stretch of road. This time the Jordanians opened fire and hit one of our vehicles in its tracks, though it could still move. The column then went off the road and our mortars went into action, hitting first one Jordanian armored car and then a second with the opening rounds. The Arab Legion retired. The fighting was over.

The Mixed Armistice Commission later found that we had indeed erred and laid the section of the road from Kilometer 78 to Kilometer 74 just inside Jordanian territory. The General Staff issued instructions for the offending stretch to be handed over to Jordan, and we laid a parallel section immediately to the west.

Apart from the incident itself—foolish of the Jordanians, unnecessary for us—I was not at all pleased by the dithering, indecisive way in which the armored brigade had behaved, and I said so in a report to the deputy chief of staff. It was clearly not up to the expected standard, and radical changes were essential if it was to meet the challenge of real battle.

Ensuring the overall defense of the region, guarding the frontiers, and taking action against infiltrators were not ends in themselves. Israel had three basic concerns in this southern area: to settle it, populate it, and make it fruitful. But this civilian purpose could not be achieved, at least in the initial stages, without the assistance of the army. The border kibbutzim, the pre-settlement temporary camps for the new immigrants, and those in charge of the public development projects all looked upon the military command as both the instrument of defense and the broad-shouldered body to whom they could turn for everything, from educational and medical services to plowing and paving access roads.

I regularly attended meetings of the Negev Authority to push forward development and ordered my army staff to provide it with all possible assistance. However, the two civilian areas to which I gave most of my attention and for which we felt a special responsibility were the border kibbutzim and the temporary compounds for new immigrants. The frontier settlements most in need of help sat close to the Gaza Strip. Isolated, the kibbutzniks had to live under difficult social and economic conditions. Young people from the cities had settled in these kibbutzim, and a number of them had left because they found life too difficult. The farms were poor, and they had limited water for irrigation. To reach the settlements one had to travel for hours on end over sandy or muddy tracks, and vehicles and tractors would occasionally hit mines laid by infiltrators from the Gaza Strip. We wanted these settlements to cultivate their lands right up to the border, and not to leave a no-man's land between us and the Arabs. However, they lacked both the manpower and the equipment. I saw no alternative but to place army vehicles, troops, and even a budget at their disposal to help them carry out their tasks.

This decision provoked strong protests from some members of my staff at Southern Command. Our own army units also lacked equipment, they said, above all transport. As for giving the settlements a budgetary allocation, it was for lack of funds that we were unable to provide our own troops with such elementary services as adequate barracks, showers, and lockers. Nor were our priority defense needs fully met. Roads of high operational importance could not be paved because we lacked the money. Nonetheless, I went ahead and gave the necessary orders for equipment, money, and men to go to the settlements I decided were most in need. And, indeed, with this army help, the fields in considerable areas within Southern Command, including all those along the Gaza Strip and some round Mount Hebron, were plowed, sown, and harvested.

The winter of 1950 was harsh. It was evident that something had to be done to ease the living conditions of the new immigrants in their temporary compounds, most of which had been put up during the dry season. No other branch of government, and certainly not the newcomers themselves, had the organization and manpower to deal with the problem. There were fifteen such compounds scattered throughout Southern Command, housing some six thousand families, most of them with many children and aged relatives. The army launched a special operation, and the warning order issued on November 16, 1950, outlined the army's tasks: ensuring shelter, medical attention, supply, and distribution of food; construction of access roads to the compounds; and the installation of telephone and radio communications with the nearest towns.

Care for the new immigrants had become not only a task of great importance, difficult though it was, but also a source of inspiration, human, Jewish, and pioneering, to all the troops who took part. This was what Zionism and brotherhood were all about. Even the most hardened soldiers were moved as they watched women soldiers tending the immigrant children, washing them, feeding them, administering the medicines that the army doctor had ordered, pacifying a crying baby, soothing an aged grandmother. The troops themselves, digging ditches to drain off the rainwater, resiting tents, and laying roads, worked with a will and with a deep sense of satisfaction at being able to help their brothers who had come to join them. Women soldiers with a secondary school education became the teachers in the compounds; army sappers built the access roads; ordnance men who normally handled ammunition supplies brought the daily supply of bread and sacks of rice; and the Medical Corps moved their clinics from army bases to the immigrant centers. In any case, their main work now was with the newcomers, not the army units.

I could not help smiling inwardly when I noticed on my visits that the immigrants themselves seemed to take for granted the treatment they were being accorded. They were right, of course. What was the Israeli army for if not to be with them and care for them?

On one of my drives from the south to the General Staff, I stopped the car to give a lift to a family of new immigrants from Yemen who were sitting by the roadside with their bundles. They were on their way to visit some relatives. The head of the family sat in the front beside me while his wife, brood, and bundles tumbled into the back. He looked like a shriveled old man with a scraggly white beard, but his eyes were young and his manner confident. The thought went through my mind that he must be quite stunned by the exciting change he had experienced in so short a period, catapulted from one world to another. Only a few months before, in Yemen, he had handled no more advanced technology than a primus stove and had known no more progressive means of transport than the back of a donkey—and even that only at second hand, for Jews were often not allowed to ride lest they pass an Arab pedestrian who would then have to look up to a Jew! And here he was in a car flying a general's pennant being driven by a regional commander. I thought he was trying to tell me something of this kind, for he spoke and seemed to be repeating the same phrase, but I had difficulty in understanding his Hebrew accent. Only after a few minutes did I grasp what he was saying, and

I got my chastening come-uppance. He was asking me, with astonishment, "What, no radio in the car?" I begged his pardon and switched it on.

I was dissatisfied by the slow pace of development in the Negev and particularly by the delay in establishing new farm villages. There had been a reluctance to settle new immigrants near the border, but the young settlement groups wishing to establish kibbutzim were not yet ready to do so. Meanwhile, Jewish farmers had cultivated the fields along the western frontier, but not all those in the Mount Hebron area, despite the initiatives Southern Command had taken and the money we had allocated. In the autumn of 1950, I told the chief of staff that unless these fields were plowed immediately, before the rains, there would be no sowing that year. I added the information I had received from the Public Works Department that the western road through the Negev would not be completed before the following spring, which meant that the kibbutzim along the western border would be isolated in the winter.

I therefore recommended to the chief of staff that we should start settling the immigrants in these areas in moshavim, cooperative smallholding settlements. I insisted that these immigrants be located close to existing kibbutzim, so that they could be given guidance, a helping hand, and general supervision in their early stages by the veteran and experienced kibbutz neighbors. Each settlement should be planned with an eye to its special security needs, and the settlers should be given at least one month's military training before going onto the land. The chief of staff accepted my proposal, and after further deliberations both with the General Staff and the civilian authorities concerned, the way was opened for a renewed burst of settlement in the Negev—the establishment of immigrant farm villages.

After the turbulence of the previous years, 1950 was a comparatively quiet period for Israel, and the army undertook a wide and intensive training program for its field officers of all ranks, from majors to major generals. Most of them had a good deal of battle experience but no training in the command positions they held. Most, indeed, had served in the Haganah, which, as an underground force, necessarily had to operate in small units. Only in the War of Independence had former platoon commanders found themselves commanding a company, and company commanders a battalion and even a brigade and more. In the future they would have to wield even larger formations, and this would require more meticulous and professional planning and handling than they had been used to in the old days. A start had been made in 1949 with a Battalion Commanders' Course. Now, in 1950, the General Staff felt that all higher ranking officers should also take this course and then proceed to an extension course for senior officers. I took these courses, which lasted altogether six months, and followed them in 1952 with a three-month spell at the Senior Officers' School at Devizes in England.

At the Battalion Commanders' Course, we generals were the trainees and our instructors were a specially selected team who certainly knew their job. The majority had more individual combat experience than some of the generals, and though we outranked them, we could learn something from them.

I gained a good deal of technical knowledge, even though I had not always felt the lack of it. In the tactical field, however, I occasionally had serious doubts about the correctness of the "school solution." It was not enough to be able to take advantage of terrain, noting the wadis, the hills, the paths, and tracks. We also had to take account of the conditions of warfare which were specific to us, confronted as we were by Arab armies. We had to bear in mind our responsibility for the border settlements and the immigrant villages, the character of the Arab soldier, and the fighting qualities of the Israeli. Discussion and debate were allowed in this course, indeed encouraged, and this, too, interested me. It was not that I relished argument per se, but it prompted me to think things out, weigh the issues, reach a conclusion, and formulate it clearly.

Apart from the practical value of my studies, the course afforded me a kind of home leave, freed from command responsibility, relaxed in a period of lowered tensions. We held tactical exercises in every type of terrain, from the extreme north near the Syrian and Lebanese borders to the southernmost parts of the Negev, and the countryside was always a delight to heart and eye. I attached importance, of course, to working out the proper solution to whatever exercise I was engaged in, and it was useful, for example, to discover all the qualities of the command car—its high mobility and its capacity for crossing sand dunes as well as climbing the rocky slopes of the Galilee. But I confess that I derived most pleasure when I would rest my field glasses on a boulder while scanning a distant hill featured on the exercise and find that the shadow which occasionally crossed the lens was cast not by the hill but by a chameleon hiding behind the boulder that raised its head from time to time to stare back at me with curiosity.

The course in England at the Senior Officers' School took place in the first three months of 1952. Most of those attending were of course from the British army, but there were several places for foreigners.

I was given what the British call a "batman," who woke me with morning tea and polished my shoes—not the kind of service anyone would dream of expecting in the Israeli army. After a prosaic but filling English breakfast, we would have lectures or exercises in the field. We worked in teams, and I, like the other foreigners, left the initiatives largely to the British members. I did not push myself. I had not come to teach the English how to conduct warfare. I had come to listen, to observe, and to widen my military horizons.

The teaching was methodical, with the accent on how to think and plan. The instructor would examine my work and ask by what criteria I had proposed the particular size of a force and the strength of artillery and air support required for an operation. He was not especially concerned about whether my conclusions matched the school solution.

The attitude toward me was correct but cold. Most of the students and instructors had seen service in the Middle East and had no particular liking for Israel and the Jews. One day the newspapers carried long reports of the trial of a British officer who was accused of accepting bribes from Israel during our War of Independence. During the noon recess, I was thoroughly cross-examined, like a criminal in the dock, by my British companions, who asked whether I did not feel a sense of shame. They brushed aside my argument that the one who should feel ashamed was the person who had received money for selling arms belonging to his army, not the one who had bought the weapons to defend his life and his country. They explained to me that Jewish money could turn the head of any upright British officer who was in difficult straits.

I had read about the English winter and now I felt it, with the rain, the snow, and the sleet. But it offered a certain satisfaction to me, a slight requital for the attitude of my fellow students. I, a native of sunny Deganiah, would return from an exercise frozen stiff but with a dry nose. My hosts, natives of this island, would go around muffled in their long woolen scarves, alternately coughing and blowing their red noses.

The course was not exacting. We would depart each Thursday for the long weekend, the other officers in their cars to spend their leave at home, I in the train to join Ruth in London. This weekend practice led to a slight embarrassment. King George VI died in February, on a Wednesday, I believe. A notice was put up in the general dining room of the army base that a black mourning band would be worn on the left arm and a black tie in the evening. Having neither band nor black tie, I hurried off to the nearby village and bought them, wearing them for dinner that evening as instructed. To my surprise, I found when I entered the dining hall that I was the only mourner of the dead monarch. My neighbors at dinner then explained that participants in the course had been given special dispensation for that week and would wear the crepe only the following week. It was recognized that all had the band and tie at home, left over from a previous occasion of national mourning, and they would pick them up on the weekend.

Relations improved toward the end of the course. The British members of my team had apparently told their friends that I had shown more perception than one could have expected of a foreigner, and even a sense of humor, which was not to be expected at all. We exchanged addresses, and on my return to Israel I received a number of cards. I cannot claim that my three months at Devizes turned me into a British type, but it gave me a close look at a bit of England, the English, and their military approach.

Reaching home after my stay in England, I was summoned by Chief of Staff Yigael Yadin, who offered me the appointment of deputy chief of staff and chief of operations. I was to replace Maj. Gen. Mordechai Makleff, who was to go on study leave. I declined. I explained to Yadin that I was unsuited by character to fill the post of deputy, having to echo the voice of my superior. I had no reservations about Yadin's higher authority and would carry out his orders even if I disagreed with them. But I could not hide my own views, and I would find it difficult to represent him if I thought he was wrong. Being his deputy was one thing; being subordinate to him was another.

Yadin listened, understood, regretted my refusal but did not try to change my mind, and appointed me instead general officer commanding Northern Command. I served in this post for the next six months, until my appointment as chief of the Operations Branch of the General Staff in December 1952.

I moved my family to the north, renting a small house in a quiet street in Tivon, midway between Haifa and Nahalal, within reasonable driving distance from command headquarters. I have a lively memory of my venture into carpentry at Tivon. The nearby hills were covered with old oaks, and some were cut down to make way for a new housing estate. With the help of the Nahalal carpentry shop, I made three small garden tables out of their trunks. They were by no means comfortable, but they were very impressive, particularly their twisted legs!

Yael studied at the Reali High School in Haifa, while Udi and Assi went to school in Nahalal. I had no need for a "running-in" period in the new command. I had known the northern region from childhood. The problems on the Syrian frontier were familiar to me from my experience on the Mixed Armistice Commissions. I assembled the staff officers, as I had done at Southern Command, and told them that if any wished to transfer to another unit, they had only to say so, and I would recommend it. I wanted to work with officers who wanted to stay. I do not recall that anyone left. I do know that the senior staff officers who served with me in the succeeding months were first class, two in particular, Col. Chaim Bar-Lev, the command chief of staff, and Maj. Ariel (Arik) Sharon, the Intelligence officer.

In the north I did not encounter the problems which had engaged my concern in the south—infiltration of Arabs from across the border, and the establishment of settlements in the desolate wastes. However, Military Government occupied an important place in the work of the command. The Arabs of Israel are largely concentrated in this northern region. They live in about one hundred villages, most of them in Galilee. There are also Arabs in Nazareth and in villages along Wadi Ara, running from the coast near Hadera almost to the Valley of Jezreel. The Arab community is an integral part of Israel, but not because it chose to be. No Arab wanted to be an Israeli. Belonging to the state had been forced upon them by the outcome of the War of Independence, which their people had forced upon us. When both sides signed the Armistice Agreements, they were faced with the choice of becoming Israeli citizens or leaving their homes and moving to one of the Arab countries. With few exceptions, they chose to stay and accept Israeli citizenship.

In such circumstances, there was deep mistrust between the reluctant Israeli Arabs and the Israeli Jews. The Jews had vanquished the Arab armies but not their hatred. In its administration of the Arab areas, the Military Government had therefore to find the golden mean between an attitude of correctness toward the Arabs as citizens of Israel and an alert awareness that they might serve as a fifth column and their villages might become bases for hostile acts against the state.

The borders of the Northern Command area contained our frontiers with three Arab states, Lebanon, Syria, and Jordan. These frontiers had been quiet since the signing of the Armistice Agreements, but certain issues with Syria still required settlement. The principal problems had to do with the future of the demilitarized zone, the right of Syrians to fish in the Sea of Galilee, and the status of the Huleh area after the drainage of the swamps. We had begun a formidable project of reclamation to clear the Huleh swamps and bring a considerable stretch of land under cultivation, with a portion of it left untouched as a bird sanctuary. To try to reach agreement on these problems, I renewed my contact with the Israeli-Syrian Mixed Armistice Commission.

The U.N. chairman of the commission was an American officer named Texas. He was a pleasant enough man but not too well informed. He told us one day that he had learned about a Syrian movement toward rapprochement. He arranged a special meeting of the commission on October 9, 1952, at the Hotel Shulamit in Rosh Pinah, to the north of the Sea of Galilee, where similar meetings with the Syrians had been held in the past. A team of four permanent members, headed by Col. Jadid, represented Syria, and I headed the Israeli delegation.

It soon became apparent that there was no substance to the chairman's optimism. After detailed deliberation, Jadid announced categorically that he was neither prepared nor authorized to discuss any new agreement which might portend an advance toward peace. I suggested that in that case, we should end the meeting and go to lunch. Jadid, who well remembered the accomplished cooking of the mother and daughters who ran the Shulamit Hotel, quickly agreed. For the first time that morning, he accepted an Israeli proposal.

After the meal, I took Jadid aside for a private talk. I asked him first about Col. Bizri, who had been on the Syrian team during the armistice negotiations. On one occasion during those talks, I had been chatting with Bizri when Jadid had come up and reprimanded him: "What are you two Jews concocting in the corner?" Jadid told me that Bizri was now a member of the Syrian delegation to the United Nations. His mother had apparently been a Jewess who had converted to Islam and married an Arab.

On the topics I had raised at the formal meeting of the commission, Jadid said that if the demilitarized zone were divided, Syria would want all the areas east of the Huleh and the Sea of Galilee, including the Jewish settlements at Dardara, Susita, and Tel Katzir. The only exception they would be prepared to consider was to leave Kibbutz Ein Gev, the first Jewish settlement on the eastern shore of the Sea of Galilee, in Israel's hands. He said he knew this was not a practical proposal, but Damascus preferred the present situation with all its unresolved problems to the signing of an additional agreement with Israel. Syria would continue to hold to this position and express it in increasingly extremist form with each passing year.

PART III

Chief of Staff

[1953~1957]

12

FORGING AN ARMY

ON DECEMBER 7, 1952, I was appointed head of the Operations Branch of the General Staff, and I held this post for one year until my appointment as chief of staff on December 6, 1953. During that year I applied myself to developing the operational capability of the army —the sole purpose.of an army's existence—and sharpening the tools for doing that job—organizing the appropriate combat units and raising the standards of the individual fighting man.

My predecessor in Operations was Lt. Gen. Mordechai Makleff, who moved up to become chief of staff upon the resignation of Lt. Gen. Yigael Yadin. Our appointments came during a difficult financial period for the army. The War of Independence was behind us, and the country's priorities were the reception, absorption, and settlement of the several hundred thousand new immigrants who had reached our shores in the few years since statehood. The treasury coffers had to be channeled to essential immigrant services and civilian development projects, and the budgets of other ministries, including defense, had to be drastically cut.

Makleff and I agreed in principle that the fighting units of the army had to be strengthened at the expense of the service units, and this principle was indeed reflected in the three-year program decided upon by the General Staff at sessions devoted to the reorganization of the army within the framework of our restricted budget. It was generally agreed that we had to change the character of the combat units. They were not what they had been in the War of Independence. Many officers had left. The best of the recruits doing their national service elected to join the Air Force or the Navy. Many of the new immigrants, without experiencing the life and temper of beleaguered Israel, required longer training. Units were understrength and ill equipped.

We had seen the effects of lowered fighting standards in our infantry units reflected in the minor border actions that had taken place in the period since the War of Independence. At the beginning of 1953, the incidence of infiltration for sabotage and murder had increased, and several small-scale reprisal raids had been undertaken against terrorist bases in or near Arab villages just across the border. The results were unsatisfactory. In some cases our detachments returned after one or two men were killed and a few wounded without having fulfilled their mission.

I considered it my job to change all this and to fashion fighting units that could always be relied upon to attain their objectives. This, I felt, should be the sole concern of the head of Operations. I was aware of the great importance of effecting the necessary organizational changes in the structure of the army. Abolishing military laundries, using civilian hospital services for army personnel, or reducing the number of field kitchens would make more funds available for armaments. But these changes could be made without anyone having to crawl on his belly through an enemy fence and risk getting a bullet in his back. It was the fighting man I was concerned with, for he was the cutting edge of the army's tool, and a soldier in the army of Israel, under constant threat from its neighbors, had always to be ready for war. If we failed in minor border actions, as we had in the previous year, how would we stand up to the Arab armies on the battlefield? No amount of reorganization would alter the basic function of the Israel Defense Forces—to be fit for battle at all times.

It seemed to me that the recent failures were due to altered attitudes since the War of Independence in three spheres: the degree of the soldier's readiness to risk his life in fulfillment of his mission; the place and duties of the officer in battle; and the basic approach of the General Staff to casualty rates in a period of restricted hostilities.

It was not difficult to change the approach of the General Staff, and I accordingly met with the Operations officers of all the commands. I told them that in the future, if any unit commander reported that he failed to carry out his mission because he could not overcome the enemy force, his explanation would not be accepted unless he had suffered 50 percent casualties. The term "could not" was relative, and the question was how much effort was put into meeting enemy resistance in order to complete the mission. As long as the unit had not lost its combat power, it had to go on attacking. What I left unsaid when I spoke to the officers was transmitted by the expression on my face. They were left in no doubt that if they failed to carry out their assignment, they would have to face a detailed debriefing, and if their explanations did not satisfy me, there would be little future for them in the army.

The factors that helped to bring about a practical change in combat standards during the year when Makleff was chief of staff and I was head of Operations were the channeling of the better-educated national service recruits to the fighting units and, above all, the establishment of a special unit known as Force 101. This was a volunteer unit which undertook special operations across the border. The commander was the daring and combat-wise Maj. Ariel Sharon, whom I had admired and had known well since he had been my Intelligence officer at Northern Command. Arik, as everyone called him, gathered to his unit picked men, most of them reservists. I confess that when the proposal to establish this unit was brought before the General Staff in May 1953, I did not support it. I felt that our primary problem was not what to do to the Arab terrorists in reprisal, but how to improve the fighting capacity of our army. In fact, however, it was the practical influence of this unit which brought about the very aim I sought—raising combat standards. Force 101 operated with such brilliance that its achievements set an example to all the other formations in the army. It proved the feasibility of successfully carrying out the kind of mission at which other units had failed.

In January 1954, a few weeks after I became chief of staff, Force 101 was merged with the paratroops, and Arik became commander of the Paratroop Battalion. For some time thereafter, this unit alone undertook all the reprisal actions against Arab terrorists and raids across the border. Later, there was a growing recognition that such assignments should also be given to other units. The paratroops ceased to be solely an army formation and became a concept and a symbol—the symbol of courageous combat—that other formations in the army tried to live up to. Through the paratroops, the army recovered its self-confidence, and it was now rare indeed that a unit commander returned from action having to explain the failure of his mission.

My appointment as chief of staff placed me at the top of the army pyramid, and I knew that I had to safeguard the image of the Israel Defense Forces. But I also knew that I had to carry out those changes I thought essential and to mold the army into the shape I wanted. I recognized that I would now have to deal with matters which I had managed to steer clear of up to now. A chief of staff, particularly in times of comparative quiet, is occupied with administrative and technical problems—manpower, budget, armament, equipment, maintenance—and he is further removed from the combat units in the field. As I rose in the military hierarchy, the gap between battle and me widened. Instead of fighting, I would tell others what to do. I would issue directives, give oral and written orders, but in the field, in battle, matters would be decided by the combatants. Sitting at General Staff headquarters, it would be difficult for me to determine, and at times even influence, the character of the fighting by our units in the distant Negev or on the Jordan border. I would have to live through them and their reports. It would be the commanders in the field who would tell me what could and could not be done.

I felt an understandable pride in becoming the number one soldier in the Israel Defense Forces. But even at the height of the ceremony, when Ben-Gurion pinned on my badges of rank and I received the standard of the chief of staff, I had no sense of elation. I realized the weight of the responsibility, and I was ready to shoulder it faithfully and with devotion.

At the end of the ceremony, the secretary of the Cabinet came over to me and casually observed that I would now have to change my partisan character, be circumspect in my ways, become more respectable. I would have to "fashion a new Moshe Dayan," he said. I told him he was wide of the mark. It was not I who would change; the image of the chief of staff would change. It was not I who had made myself a new suit of clothes; it was the army that had acquired a new chief. I intended to change the style and content of the army, abolish the gap between the chief of staff and the private soldier, cut down on the ceremonial, introduce more simplicity in the work habits of the army brass, and fill the higher-echelon posts with talented and battle-hardened young officers who had fought in the War of Independence.

I started the change of style in my own office. I abolished the post of aide-de-camp to the chief of staff and I took over his room. I brought in the field table which I had used when I was head of Operations. The table was covered by a khaki blanket and a glass top. I turned the large, well-furnished office once belonging to the chief of staff into a conference room. I wanted the field commanders who came to see me to feel that they had come to the headquarters of a higher command which was not very different and not cut off from their own. When I inspected units in the field, I wore fatigues, sat on the ground with the troops, got dirty and dusty together with them.

I paid a lot of surprise visits at night, mostly driving alone. I wanted to check whether units were in a constant state of readiness, ensure that there was always a responsible senior officer in every command headquarters, and talk to the soldiers returning from a night exercise or from guard duty at an outpost. Whenever there was an operational problem, I would see the head of the Operations Branch, the unit commander, and his junior platoon commanders. I wanted to learn what had happened, if it was after an action, or what special problems were envisaged, if it was before an operation. I wanted to hear things from them at first hand, without intermediaries, and I believed that the young officers should hear what I had to say directly from me, in my own words and in my own style.

My immediate office staff, my secretary and the head of my bureau, thought I showed too little respect for the chain-of-command principle. They felt this way because of my direct contact with lower-echelon units through unexpected visits without prior notification to the intervening commands. They were probably right, but I was unable and unwilling to behave differently. I understood, demanded, appreciated, and approved of ordered and systematic staff work—on condition that it did not erect a barrier between me and the troops and did not prevent me from keeping in direct touch with all ranks of the army. When any matter aroused my interest, I wanted to discuss it with the person immediately responsible. From time to time I would direct all the army's spotlights upon some inadequacy in an important area, such as combat standards or the state of our armor. I did this whenever I felt special efforts were required to overcome mediocrity or difficulty or to shake units out of lethargic routine.

Ben-Gurion's appointment of me as chief of staff was his last official act as prime minister and minister of defense before he resigned in December 1953 and retired to the Negev kibbutz Sdeh Boker. (He would remain there until his recall to government in

February 1955.) Foreign Minister Moshe Sharett succeeded him as prime minister and Pinhas Lavon became the new defense minister. It was the first time that the Defense portfolio and the premiership were held by two different people. There should have been close cooperation and coordination between the two. Instead there was friction from the very start. It was based on political and personal differences. Each had his own approach to Israel's political and security needs at that time. Nineteen fifty-four was a very difficult year. With Britain's evacuation of her forces from the Suez Canal, America sought to establish her influence in the Middle East. She did so by wooing the Arab states, and there was a danger that the military balance would be tilted even more sharply against Israel. Egypt had tightened her blockade against Israeli ships and cargoes through the Canal and the Gulf of Aqaba. A Security Council resolution in November 1951 had called on Egypt to abolish her limitations on freedom of Israeli shipping through the Canal. Egypt had spurned the resolution. No Israeli ships passed through the Canal, but what Egypt decided were non-strategic cargoes, carried in non-Israeli vessels, were allowed through from time to time. At the end of 1953, Egypt imposed a total ban on all cargoes to and from Israel. Inside Israel, the incidence of murder and sabotage by terrorist infiltrators was on the increase. Israel felt isolated, friendless, cut off.

Prime Minister Sharett saw the solution in diplomatic terms: efforts to get America to change its Middle East policy and give us military aid and security guarantees; efforts to get the U.N. Security Council to force Egypt to lift the blockade—even though friendly powers were reluctant to get involved and when a favorable resolution was eventually presented, in March 1954, Russia vetoed it. This diplomatic exercise, intended to demonstrate Israel's international rights, ended as a demonstration of Israel's international weakness. Lavon saw the solution to Israel's security and political problems in military action that would deter the Arab states from attacking us.

Ben-Gurion had also found little to commend itself in Sharett's approach. But while he had always been correct in his dealings with Sharett, Lavon refused to accept Sharett's authority as prime minister. He regarded him solely as foreign minister, and limited his intervention in defense policy. He did not keep him informed of army action on the borders, and when he did transmit reports, they were partial and not always accurate. Sharett complained that he often got to know of an operation only when he read about it in the newspapers.

My own relations with my ministerial chief cooled after a few months, and led me in mid-June 1954 to submit my resignation. Lavon not only wanted to run the army, he wanted to do so independently of the General Staff. He was making decisions on purely military matters, based on the advice of outsiders and against the recommendations of my senior colleagues and myself. The break was sparked by Lavon's rejection of our recommended acquisition of a particular tank, which would have strengthened our attack capability. Instead, without telling me, he sought to divert the funds to securing heavy mortars, a defense weapon. He refused to talk about the matter with me or even present arguments justifying his proposed decision. It was enough for him that as the minister he was the superior authority over the chief of staff. When I told him I was sorry that he was deciding on a technical military matter without discussing it with me, he simply said, "That's right." Obviously this state of affairs could not continue. Either I had to go or Lavon would have to change his pattern of work. My letter of resignation was designed to force an immediate choice.

Lavon's reaction was to invite me to lunch and blame someone else in his ministry for the "misunderstandings" between us. It was evident from his opening remarks that he had decided against sharpening the crisis and shelved my letter of resignation. At the end of the meal we shook hands. The crisis was over—but its ingredients remained.

In Lavon's rejection of Sharett's political activism, I was closer to the defense minister. But this was not the case with Lavon's exaggerated security activism. On more than one occasion, I had to restrain him from ordering military action which seemed unwise to me. One of our important differences was over a Special Services unit which had been established during the 1948 War of Independence by a department attached to the Foreign Ministry for specified activity in enemy countries. It later came under a branch of the army, and Lavon was anxious to use it. I thought it should be used only in time of war and remain dormant in peacetime. Since he was the minister and insisted on the right to meet with senior officers without my participation, and at times even without my knowledge, I warned one of the responsible officers in the unit to be wary of Lavon's eagerness to activate it.

In the latter half of July 1954, while I was on a three-and-a-half week visit to army bases in the United States, the unit initiated an operation which thereafter would always be referred to as "the security mishap." A detachment carried out a few small-scale sabotage actions in Cairo and Alexandria. The result was the arrest and trial of eleven of its members. Some were sentenced to long terms of imprisonment. The tragic climax was the suicide of one member and the execution of two others on January 1, 1955.

The Israeli public was aghast. Who had ordered such acts to be undertaken, the senior army officer responsible for the unit or the defense minister? The officer insisted that he received the order from the minister orally at a meeting with no one else present. Lavon claimed that the officer had acted on his own. A two-man committee of inquiry appointed by the prime minister and consisting of a former president of the Supreme Court and the first chief of staff concluded that they were unable to determine beyond a shadow of doubt who, in fact, gave the order to activate the unit. This left both Lavon and the officer under a cloud. His colleagues in the government and in the leadership of Mapai, the ruling party in the government, decided that Lavon had to go. He had submitted his resignation on February 2, 1955, and the government approved it on February 20. On that day Ben-Gurion once again became the minister of defense. He had been induced to ease the crisis by leaving his Negev kibbutz, returning to the government, and serving under the premiership of Sharett until the parliamentary elections later that year. In November, he was again prime minister as well as minister of defense. Incidentally, the senior officer in the "mishap" was also removed from his post.

Since it was through the young officers that we could shape the kind of army we wanted, I would use the occasion of a graduation parade at an Officers' course whenever I had something special to say. I remember one such occasion at the end of May 1955, and also what I said when I addressed the cadets on whom I had just pinned officers' insignia. A few days earlier, I had had the unpleasant duty of terminating the service of a young career officer who had ordered a soldier to proceed on a dangerous action while he himself sat in safety. A vehicle of ours was stuck close to the border of the Gaza Strip and was under heavy fire from the Egyptians. The officer in charge sent a driver to retrieve it, while he himself lay behind cover and issued directions from there. I told the cadets: "I would not have dismissed this officer if he had decided that the danger was too great and it was better to abandon the vehicle rather than endanger lives. But if he decided to take daring action and save the vehicle, he should have advanced with his troops and laid his own life on the line together with theirs. Officers of the Israeli army do not send their men into battle. They lead them into battle."

Forging an army, however, requires more than talk, and officers require more than courage and moral leadership. They should also be well educated and of rounded intellect. Most of our officers at that time had fought in the War of Independence and stayed on, having had no opportunity before that war or since to attend the university. I thought that situation should be corrected, and we introduced a system of sending officers to the university at the army's expense. They could take a degree in any subject that interested them, from economics and Middle Eastern studies, to history and literature. One officer who later became commander of the Armored Corps studied philosophy. At the same time, we also started sending officers in the technical services, such as ordnance and engineering, to the Haifa Technion (Institute of Technology) to study subjects directly related to their work.

In mid-1955 we sent a detachment of volunteers on a daring reconnaissance mission through Sinai to find a land route to Sharm el-Sheikh, at the southern tip of the peninsula. Sharm el-Sheikh commanded the narrow Straits of Tiran at the entrance to the Gulf of Aqaba. The Egyptians had blockaded this waterway to Israeli shipping, thereby closing our sea lane to East Africa and the Far East and stifling Eilat port, as well as the development of its hinterland, the Negev. Egypt also closed the direct air route over the gulf for our civilian planes. The reconnaissance was part of our planning preparation for the capture of Sharm el-Sheikh if the Egyptians failed to lift the blockade. The results of the survey would make possible the extraordinary trek of one of our brigades in the Sinai Campaign a year and a half later.

On September 27, 1955, Gamal Abdel Nasser of Egypt opened a military exhibition in Cairo and announced that the week before, "we signed a commercial agreement with Czechoslovakia whereby that country will supply us with arms in exchange for cotton and rice." This was Nasser's innocent-sounding announcement of what was to mark a turning point in Middle Eastern affairs, for his "commercial agreement," which would soon be known as the Czech arms deal, revolutionized the scale and quality of arms supplies to the region, planted a Soviet foot firmly in an area which had been closed to her, opened a second front for the United States in the Cold War, and seriously threatened Israel's existence.

Under this arms agreement, Egypt would be receiving from the Soviet bloc some 300 medium and heavy tanks of the latest Soviet type, 200 armored personnel carriers, 100 armored self-propelled guns, several hundred field howitzers, medium guns, and anti-tank guns, 134 anti-aircraft guns, and 200 MiG-15 jet fighters and 50 Ilyu-shin bombers, in addition to transport planes, radar systems, 2 destroyers, 4 minesweepers, 12 torpedo boats, ammunition, spare parts, ground equipment for aircraft, and hundreds of battle vehicles of various types. All small arms and light weapons were to be replaced by huge quantities of the Russian semi-automatic rifle.

These arms, types and quantities may not seem startling by today's standards. But at that time, they represented a stunning acceleration of the pace of rearmament in the Middle East. In quantity alone, they tipped the arms balance drastically against Israel; in quality, the tilt was even more drastic. We had never imagined that we could ever match the size of the arsenals possessed by the Arab states. But we believed we could bridge the gap by the superior fighting capacity of our troops, as long as we could match the quality of their weaponry. In modern warfare, however, the elements of range, speed, and fire power in technologically advanced aircraft, naval vessels, and armor can be so superior that inferior weapons are simply unable to stand up to them. For every rise in standards of an enemy's arms, there must be a minimum means of reply. Without it, no amount of courage can get the better of objective technical superiority. A brilliant pilot in a propeller aircraft has no chance against mediocrity in a jet. A daring tank gunner in an obsolete Sherman, which is the tank we had, would find his shells bouncing off the armor of a Stalin-3 tank, which was what the Egyptians were about to receive. The Czech arms deal placed in doubt the capability of the Israeli army to give expression to its qualitative human advantages.

It was clear to us in Israel that the primary purpose of this massive Egyptian rearmament was to prepare Egypt for a decisive confrontation with Israel in the near future. The Egyptian blockade, her planning and direction of mounting Palestinian guerrilla activity against Israel, Nasser's own declarations, and now the Czech arms deal left no doubt in our minds that Egypt's purpose was to wipe us out, or at least win a decisive military victory which would leave us in helpless subjugation.

The Soviet arms began flowing into Egypt at the beginning of November 1955, and at meetings of the General Staff we considered that it would take the Egyptian army from 6 to 8 months to absorb and digest most of its new weapons and equipment. We therefore had to expect an attack at any time from late spring to late summer. In that time, we had to acquire at least some planes and tanks which could match their Russian counterparts. The problem for us was that our sources were limited. The United States and Britain produced quality planes and tanks, but they were refusing to sell us arms. There was talk that America might change her policy and consider letting us have defensive weapons, but even that eventually seemed dubious. The one possible source for new tanks was France, but she produced only the light AMX tank. We would try to get the AMX tank and make do with it, and also recondition some obsolete American tanks which we had acquired from World War Two surplus stores in Europe. As for planes, the only European manufacturers, apart from Britain, were Sweden and France. We would try to obtain them quickly from France.

There were other things we could do to confound Egyptian plans, and I suggested them to Ben-Gurion in a memorandum I sent him on November 10. My main recommendations were sharp reprisal actions against Egyptian or Egyptian-directed acts of hostility; the immediate capture of the Gaza Strip, which was a base of terror operations and would be a springboard for an Egyptian invasion; and preparations for the capture of Sharm el-Sheikh to break the blockade of the Gulf of Aqaba.

I followed up this memorandum with a talk with Ben-Gurion three days later, urging military action as soon as possible. I added practical proposals for strengthening the organization of the army in the face of imminent war: to recall Yigael Yadin as chief of staff, Mordechai Makleff as chief of operations, and Yigal Allon as GOC Northern Command. I would step down as chief of staff and would wish to take over Southern Command, which would conduct the war in Sinai, but I would take any other field command—Northern, Central, or the Armored Corps.

Ben-Gurion said he would give me an on-the-spot reply to one of my recommendations: even if war broke out, he did not propose to replace me as chief of staff.

In a meeting with him later in the day, I was told to hold up action on Sharm el-Sheikh until the end of January 1956. I gathered that he wanted to watch developments and had not yet made up his mind on policy, but that he tended to favor a political rather than a military solution. (In the event, action was taken not in January but in October 1956.)

The months that followed the Czech arms deal were not easy. We had to prepare the army and the nation for the probable outbreak of war and do so without impairing our ability to meet the day-to-day problems of border security. To prepare ourselves for the Egyptian military challenge, I set the order of our priorities as the acquisition of suitable arms from whatever source that could be tapped; regional defense and fortification of our border settlements; civil defense throughout the country; and the organization of emergency services and supplies for the civilian population. On border security, in addition to dealing with infiltration, we had serious military clashes with Syrian units entrenched on the northeast bank of the Sea of Galilee that were firing on our fishermen and with units of the Egyptian army that had entered and crossed the demilitarized zone on the Negev-Sinai border and seized one of our outposts. Our actions against both the Syrians and the Egyptians were successful.

The month of April 1956 brought some relief in the form of the first few Mystère warplanes from France and the promise of more. These planes could match in quality and were probably superior to the MiGs that were being supplied to Egypt in large quantities by the Soviet bloc. We were also promised both AMX and Sherman tanks from France. And Britain had agreed to sell us six Meteor night-fighter planes. The United States, however, remained adamant in her refusal to change her embargo policy, even though she was well aware that the sum total of weapons we could buy from the limited sources available to us was paltry, compared to the massive quantities now pouring into Egypt.

Still, bemoaning our fate while our enemy grew stronger was not the way to meet his threat, and I tried to suggest the appropriate course in an address to the troops later that month. We had no Czech arms deal, I told them, nor an American nor an English deal. What we could buy from France was minute compared to what Egypt was getting from the Soviet bloc. The countries that had weapons refused to make deals with us. However, there was one nation with which we *were* able to make a deal—the nation of Israel. An "Israeli deal" could uncover the hidden spiritual and material resources which would increase our strength. We could make a deal with our workers and teachers, with our pupils and youth movements to go out and help fortify our border settlements and establish new ones. We could make a deal with our veteran settlers to help and guide the new immigrant villages. We could make a deal with our serving soldiers and our reservists to fight to the bitter end for Israel's survival if war came upon us. The deal with ourselves was the most difficult of all, but it was the one with the most promise. Upon it hung the character of the state, the quality of the army, and, above all, the building of the nation.

However, this call for a supreme national effort in no way diminished our need to secure more quality weapons from an outside source. France had been the only manufacturing country to respond to our request. But shortly after our pilots had flown the first twelve Mystères to Israel, there was trouble in Paris. The French Foreign Ministry was at loggerheads with the French Defense Ministry and was urging that supplies be stopped. Only at the end of the month were we reassured that Prime Minister Guy Mollet had come out in support of Defense Minister Maurice Bourges-Maunoury and there was hope that supplies of both planes and tanks would continue. To make that hope tangible, I went to France on a secret mission, together with Shimon Peres, the director-general of the Defense Ministry, toward the end of June 1956, and after three days of talks we reached a firm agreement on the purchase of arms which would enable us to meet the quality, if not the scale, of Egypt's Soviet weaponry.

However, that weaponry, plus the Soviet political backing that went with it, had given Egypt formidable military might and her president, Gamal Abdel Nasser, a tremendous feeling of confidence. On July 26, 1956, he stunned the world with the announcement, made before a cheering crowd of tens of thousands in Cairo's Independence Square, that he had nationalized the Suez Canal. It was undoubtedly the most significant political event of the year, with far-reaching international consequences. One of them was an immediate decision by France and Britain to consult on the steps to be taken, and the French foreign minister arranged to leave for London the next day to meet Prime Minister Anthony Eden. I heard about this move from our representatives in Paris, who informed us that they had been approached by our friends in the French Defense Ministry. They said that Christian Pineau, their foreign minister, would be accompanied by military experts, suggesting that military action against Nasser was not ruled out. What the French wanted from us was up-to-the-minute information on the strength and locations of the Egyptian formations—land, sea and air—so that their delegation to London could be well briefed.

The day that followed was one of personal sadness for me. My mother died after a long illness and was buried in Nahalal. After the funeral I met with Ben-Gurion and proposed that in the situation created by Nasser's Suez action, and before Egypt attacked us, we should launch one of three operations: capture the Sinai Peninsula up to the Canal and establish international control of the waterway; capture Sharm el-Sheikh and lift the blockade of the Aqaba Gulf; take over the Gaza Strip.

Ben-Gurion said that we had not yet received the heavy weapons and equipment needed to fight a war. I assured him that from what

I knew of our army, we could gain our objectives even without the arms we had been promised by France. Ben-Gurion was afraid that it would cost us heavier casualties, whereas if we waited until we had acquired the French arms, we could deal Nasser a decisive blow in a short war and lose fewer men. True, he said, the current international situation was favorable for such action, but it was best to exercise patience, absorb our new weapons, strengthen our forces, and seek another suitable opportunity to nullify the Egyptian threat.

That opportunity was being busily developed in London and Paris in the weeks that followed. After the first meeting of the French delegation with Eden in London, the governments of Britain and France resolved to launch a joint military operation to seize and hold the Suez Canal Zone, cancel the nationalization order, and restore their rights in the Canal Authority. It was also their aim to topple Nasser. The General Staffs of both countries began planning a large-scale operation. Reserves were to be mobilized, forces were to be concentrated in Malta and Cyprus, and ships were to be assembled for a huge amphibious operation, almost on a World War Two scale, to follow up an initial paratroop drop in the Canal area. The operation was codenamed "Musketeer." It was to be under the Supreme Command of Britain's General Sir Charles Keightley, commander of British land forces in the Middle East. Admiral Pierre Barjot, commander of the French forces, was named deputy supreme commander.

France was the driving force behind the policy of action. Britain's Prime Minister Eden also favored military measures, but he faced serious opposition inside his own country. And the United States, even though she had been the object of gross vilification in Nasser's nationalization speech, was firmly opposed to the projected operation by her European allies against Egypt. There was to be doubt and wavering right up to the last moment—and vestiges of this mood were to linger even after the twelfth hour had struck.

13

THE FRENCH CONNECTION I

THE FIRST INTIMATION that France was interested in coordinated action with Israel against Egypt reached us on September 1, 1956. It came in a "Most Immediate" signal I received that morning from our military attaché in Paris informing me of Anglo-French plans and adding that Admiral Barjot held the view that Israel should be invited to take part in the operation. The message was brought to me while I was meeting with the General Staff. Ben-Gurion was present, and he instructed me to reply that in principle we were ready to cooperate. If what was required from us was only intelligence on Egypt's armed forces, this information would be furnished by the office of our military attaché. If the French had in mind the participation of the Israeli army in military action, the minister of defense was prepared to send me to Paris to discuss it.

After further exploratory feelers from the French General Staff, it was decided to send my chief of operations to Paris for talks with French military representatives. He happened to be in Europe at the time. The meeting was set for September 7. I sent him a summary of a written directive I had received from Ben-Gurion stating that we were ready to give the French all possible help. If they requested the use of our air and naval bases and the active participation of our military forces, the government in Jerusalem would consider and decide. I added that in answering French queries, he was to be frank about our ability—and our limitations—in the various fields. If asked for commitments, he was to weigh the advisability of my coming to France.

Admiral Barjot was the principal French representative at the Paris meeting, which took place in a private home. He was particularly interested in information on Egypt and wanted to know about the possibility of French aircraft landing in Israel in case they were forced to do so. He also asked about our capacity to tie down Egyptian forces by undertaking military action in Sinai, close to the Israeli border. Admiral Barjot made it clear that his questions at this stage were only for enlightenment, though he was asking them on the assumption that appropriate political conditions might arise in the immediate future for Israel to take part in the operations.

During the very days when the exploratory talks were under way with the French, we were being troubled by terrorist incursions from Jordan, and our small commando units stormed and blew up two strongly fortified Jordanian military posts on the border as a military reaction to the terrorist murder of Israeli civilians. The terror groups were directed by the Egyptian High Command, but we had no alternative but to react against objectives in Jordan when they operated from Jordanian territory. Such actions—terror and counter-terror—were to have a certain impact on the later course of the Suez negotiations.

With America and Europe divided over how to handle the Suez crisis, the day-by-day deterioration of the international political situation pointed to the near certainty of imminent war in our region. I therefore took the opportunity during September of preparing our military commanders when I visited their units. I wanted the Armored Corps to hasten the training of crews to man our tanks, and I asked that the Air Force gear its pilot-training program to the rapid absorption of our most recently acquired aircraft. All the warplanes in our possession, new as well as old, had to be employed if we should soon go into action.

I ordered the various branches of the General Staff to examine anew contingency plans for the Egyptian front, ranging from the capture of the whole of the Sinai Peninsula to such partial and limited actions as the capture of the Straits of Tiran or seizure of the Gaza Strip.

In the middle of the month, reviewing these plans with the Operations Branch, I presented the political and strategic background, in accordance with Ben-Gurion's directives. There were international problems, I said, and there were our own special problems, and we had to distinguish between the two. The nationalization of the Suez Canal was an international, not an Israeli problem, though of course it was of close concern to us. But it was no part of our purpose to reach the Canal and become involved in that dispute. The Straits of Tiran and the Gaza Strip, however, were different. They posed problems specific to Israel. The first was used by Egypt to blockade shipping to Eilat; the other was used by Egypt as a base of terrorist action against Israel. Another of our problems was the concentration of Egyptian forces in the Sinai Peninsula, readying for an attack on Israel. I stressed that military action to defeat Egypt's purposes was likely to be taken by us at our own initiative—either with or against the will of other forces operating against Egypt—if the government of Israel decided that the situation demanded it.

The director-general of the Ministry of Defense, Shimon Peres, left for Paris on September 19 to try to achieve an easing of the conditions of payment for the tanks and planes we had bought from France. Peres was a personal friend of France's minister of defense, Maurice Bourges-Maunoury, and he also knew Prime Minister Guy Mollet and Foreign Minister Christian Pineau. He was to use the opportunity to hold frank and informal talks with them on the subject of Franco-Israeli political cooperation in the Middle East.

Before he left, I suggested that he insist on three basic conditions for such cooperation. First, the initiative was to come from France, and she should officially invite Israel for talks on this subject. The importance of this point stemmed from the nature of our relations with France up to then. Our recent arms purchases from France had to be effected in a somewhat clandestine manner, since there was an agreement between the United States, France, and Britain to coordinate arms policy toward Israel. Now, if France sought our help over the Suez crisis, I thought we should try to extricate ourselves from the status of an infant, subject to a triple custodianship, and become an ally with equal rights, particularly when the subject of our common concern was on our very doorstep.

Second, it was essential to avoid a situation in which we might be drawn into a conflict with Britain that could lead to British military action against us. Such a possibility grew out of the complex character of British-Israeli relations. Britain had treaties with several Arab states that might go to Egypt's aid. If this happened, a situation could arise whereby we would be fighting together with the British on one front and suddenly find ourselves clashing on a second front with Jordan, to whom Britain would be rushing military aid under the Anglo-Jordan defense treaty.

Third, if war came, Israel should be able to rectify her border with Sinai to include Sharm el-Sheikh, Nakhl, Abu Ageila, and Rafah. These were desert areas, without water or inhabitants. The Sharm el-Sheikh locality was occupied at the time by Egyptian coastal batteries poised to open fire on any ships trying to reach Eilat. If an Israeli unit were there instead, the western shore of the Gulf of Aqaba would be a protective base for freedom of shipping. If not, the blockade would continue.

I confess that when I told Peres all this, I doubted his chances of success, but I thought it worth trying. Indeed, if there were anyone who might succeed, it was Shimon Peres. Time and again he had surprised me by managing to achieve in France what I had thought was impossible.

There was a cable from him three days after he had left telling me that in his talks with Bourges-Maunoury, the French defense minister had explored the possibility of joint Franco-Israeli action against Egypt—without the British. It transpired that in talks held in London on September 12 between Mollet and Pineau and their British counterparts, Prime Minister Anthony Eden and Foreign Secretary Selwyn Lloyd, the British informed the French that "Operation Musketeer" had to be deferred: they had to accept U.S. Secretary of State John Foster Dulles' proposal to set up the Suez Canal Users Association (SCUA). France regarded this decision as Britain's abandonment of her former readiness to take military action against Egypt, and so France was turning to us.

French Minister of Defense Bourges-Maunoury also sent a handwritten message of greeting to Ben-Gurion on his seventieth birthday, using the opportunity to hint at France's desire to "do something" with Israel in defense of the interests of both countries against Egyptian aggression.

Ben-Gurion replied, also in a personal letter, underlining Israel's readiness to cooperate on a joint policy in the Middle East. Timing was an important element, and timing seemed to be at the root of Anglo-French differences. Britain was suggesting postponement of military action until political conditions became more favorable, probably after a few months (if at all); France wanted immediate action. In Ben-Gurion's letter to Bourges-Maunoury, he supported the French on timing and was ready to act jointly with France, even without Britain.

Terror again stole our attention, and Ben-Gurion called a special meeting of the Cabinet to approve military reprisals against Jordan's Arab Legion. We had no wish to aggravate the Arab-Israeli conflict at a time when the West and the Arabs were in conflict over Suez, but we could not avoid taking vigorous action against Jordan. We had to convince Jordan that her attacks—or attacks by terrorists using her territory as a base—on Israeli civilians could end only in a loss of prestige to her government. The Arab public might regard terrorism against Israel as part of a noble national war, satisfying their yearning for vengeance, restoring something of their honor after the defeat of their armies in Israel's War of Independence. To overseas critics, the Arab governments, including Jordan's King Hussein, claimed that they were powerless to prevent acts of terror, which they said were the acts of Palestinian refugees. Among their own people, however, they made no secret of their encouragement of terrorism. I had no doubt that the only way to put an end to their attacks on Israeli civilians was to take sharp action against specifically military objectives in the countries from which the attacks were launched. This alone would have the desired impact on their governments, showing them that it was in their own interest to prevent *fedayeen* activity. If they did not, the Israeli army would strike back, demonstrate the weakness of the Arab armies, and expose them as incapable of meeting the Israeli army in the field. The consequence to the Arab leaders could only be a loss of standing in the eyes of their people.

That week in mid-September had seen a sharp increase in the scope and cruelty of terrorist acts from Jordan, beyond the point where we might normally exercise restraint. A group of Israeli archaeologists inspecting excavations at a site near the border just north of Bethlehem were machine-gunned from a few hundred yards away. Also, not far from Jerusalem, a girl gathering wood was shot and maimed by Arab Legionaries, who then crossed into Israel, stabbed her to death, and cut off one of her hands as a souvenir. In the Bet She'an Valley, where the Jordan River becomes the boundary between Israel and Jordan, Arab soldiers crossed the river, shot a young tractor driver who was out plowing, and dragged his body over to Jordan.

Ben-Gurion called a special Cabinet meeting for September 25 to consider appropriate military action against Jordan's Arab Legion. Shimon Peres and I met him before the meeting, I to suggest possible targets for our action, and Peres to brief him on his Paris visit, from which he had just returned. I gave Ben-Gurion my suggested targets, chosen because there were troops stationed in each, and the aim was to strike at them and not harm the civilians. Ben-Gurion was inclined to authorize limited reprisal action in the vicinity of Jerusalem so as to underline the link between that operation and Jordanian provocation. Otherwise he feared that a military engagement between Israel and Jordan might disturb the prospect of joint Franco-Israeli action against Egypt.

Peres then reported on his talks in France. Bourges-Maunoury had told him that Pineau had attended a second London conference on September 21 and had returned gravely disappointed. This was to have been the founding conference of the Suez Canal Users Association, as suggested by Dulles, but it became clear to Foreign Minister Pineau that the American design was really to nullify any attempt to oppose the Egyptian nationalization of the Canal and to prevent the British from taking military action against Nasser. Prime Minister Eden favored such action, but he was encountering strong opposition in Britain, including elements in his own party. According to Bourges-Maunoury, Pineau had told Eden before leaving that in such a situation France might act alone—and even be aided by Israel. Eden's reply, according to Pineau, was that he was not opposed to this plan as long as Israel did not attack Jordan.

As to how the other Powers would view such action, Defense Minister Bourges-Maunoury told Peres he thought Britain would, in the end, join the campaign against Egypt and that the United States would not interfere. As to the Soviet Union, he could not guess what her reaction would be. In the light of these facts, the French Cabinet had decided to empower Bourges-Maunoury to make contact with representatives of Israel's Ministry of Defense and invite them to Paris to discuss joint military action against Egypt.

Ben-Gurion said he would raise the matter for consideration at the political level. He personally did not think that anything would come of it, though he would like to join France in operations against Nasser. Israel's position would depend on the nature of the suggested cooperation. It would have to be an honorable partnership on a dignified basis. As to Israel's interests, Ben-Gurion was not enamored of the idea of annexing the Gaza Strip or the Sinai Peninsula. What he did want was control of the west coast of the Gulf of Aqaba and of the Straits of Tiran at its outlet, namely Sharm el-Sheikh. If the straits were open to Israeli shipping, Eilat could become a large port, and this would bring to life the whole of the Negev.

On the question of Israeli-Jordanian relations, Israel would not attack Jordan if Jordan did not go to the assistance of Egypt and if she did not allow the Iraqi army to enter her territory. Unlike Egypt,

Lebanon, Jordan and Syria, Iraq had refused to sign an Armistice Agreement with us after the War of Independence, and she was therefore formally in a state of war with Israel. If Iraq sent its army into Jordan, with which we had a common frontier, we would have to take action—moving in to the West Bank of the Jordan and establishing a defensible frontier. Ben-Gurion believed that Britain had enough influence to guarantee Jordan's neutrality and thereby prevent the unnecessary complications that would follow the entry of Iraqi forces into Jordan.

That evening, Ben-Gurion informed me that it had been decided to dispatch a delegation to Paris to clarify with representatives of the French government the possibilities of joint action against Egypt. The delegation would comprise Foreign Minister Golda Meir, Transport Minister Moshe Carmel, Director-General of the Defense Ministry Shimon Peres and myself.

A few nights before I left for Paris, one of our commando units was sent across the border on a retaliatory action against a tough Arab Legion police fort. As usual in such engagements, I spent the night at the forward headquarters of the unit, preferring to follow events as they were happening and close to the scene of the action. I left my car and driver at the rear headquarters in a border kibbutz and went forward on foot to a point on a hill a few hundred yards from the enemy post. When I got back to the rear headquarters just before dawn, I found that several of our men had been wounded when the Arab Legion had fired mortars at the kibbutz. Among them was my driver.

The operation was successful. The enemy fort was blown up and nearby Legion emplacements were overrun. But the price we paid was 10 killed and 16 wounded, mostly among the lead assault group when it stormed the Arab positions. The troops on such missions always had a difficult task. In the few hours of darkness available to them, they had to climb steep, boulder-strewn, unfamiliar hills, capture under fire the enemy's entrenched forward positions, move up their explosives across trackless ground to the main enemy fort, blow it up, and return, carrying their dead and wounded with them. And they had to do this without the element of surprise. The enemy would be waiting for them on emergency alerts, knowing by then that after terrorist actions against us, they could expect a reprisal operation. Some of our best men were usually among the casualties, for they were always at the head of our assault force. Only a fortnight before, the finest of our commando soldiers, Capt. Meir Har-Zion, had been gravely wounded in a similar action against a Legion fort. His life had been saved only by a daring tracheotomy operation performed under fire by the unit's doctor.

On the way back to General Headquarters at dawn, I pondered over the heavy losses we suffered in the repeated Arab terrorist actions and our reprisals. It seemed to me that we should try to reach a full-scale encounter with the enemy, which would bring in its wake peace along the borders.

I quickly became involved again in our mission to Paris. Before leaving for the French capital, our delegation met with Ben-Gurion and was given these directives:

• Israel would not launch war on its own. If our friends started, we would join. If we were asked to make a parallel start, we would consider it sympathetically.

• The United States should be apprised of the impending war and offer no objection (or at least express no specific opposition). We should be ensured that the United States would not impose sanctions or an embargo against Israel.

• Britain should be informed, should agree, and should undertake not to go to the assistance of the Arab states if they should join Egypt.

• It was our aim to gain control of the western shore of the Gulf of Aqaba so as to guarantee freedom of Israeli shipping through that waterway. Consideration might perhaps be given to the demilitarization of the Sinai Peninsula, even under the supervision of an international force.

To these I added three operational directives:

• The forces of each country would operate in separate sectors— ours in our sector, the French in theirs—even if there were a single overall headquarters. This affected primarily the land forces, less so the air forces.

• If we received aid in equipment, and if the French forces entered Egypt, Israel could take it upon herself to capture the eastern sector of the Suez Canal Zone (meaning the Sinai Peninsula).

• We should ask the French for equipment but not make their affirmative reply a condition of our participation in the operation.

Our direct communications link was with France, and we knew where she stood. But the attitudes of the United States and Britain gave us cause for concern. Ben-Gurion was apprehensive about the United States and suspicious of Britain. I personally was worried that Britain might wish to demonstrate her friendship toward the Arabs by dashing to the aid of Jordan and flinging her forces against us.

Furthermore, the nature of the relations between Jordan and Iraq were not at all clear at that time. Jordan was wavering between a pro-Egyptian and a pro-Iraqi orientation, with the odds on a strengthening of ties with Iraq, which then had a fellow Hashemite on the throne. In June of that year, the two countries had established a joint high-level defense committee to coordinate plans for Iraqi military aid to Jordan, and it was decided to station an expanded Iraqi division on the Iraqi-Jordanian border that would be ready to help Jordan in an emergency. Shortly afterward, the two Hashemite relatives, King Hussein of Jordan and King Feisal of Iraq, had met to consider the movement of the Iraqi formation into Jordan itself. Ben-Gurion had made no secret of his apprehension of such a move or of his determination to react militarily if it took place. The problem was what Britain might do if war broke out between Israel and Jordan.

We left for France on the evening of September 28, stopping off in Bizerta, on the Tunisian coast, for the night and arriving at a military airfield near Paris on the next day. It was a sunny autumn Saturday, and families relaxed peacefully in the gardens along the Seine, while fishermen stood calmly on the banks trying their luck. It was an incongruous curtain raiser to the dramatic talks we were about to hold.

We met on the next morning, Sunday, in an eve-of-war atmosphere, at the Montparnasse home of Louis Mangin, trusted aide and political adviser to Defense Minister Bourges-Maunoury. The French were represented by Foreign Minister Christian Pineau; Bourges-Maunoury; Abel Thomas, director-general of the Defense Ministry; and General Challe, deputy to the chief of staff for Air Force affairs.

Pineau, conscious as we all were of the solemnity of the occasion, opened with a frank and cogent background survey. After Nasser's nationalization of the Suez Canal, the foreign minister said, it had become clear to France that force would have to be used against Egypt. The United States was against it, having no desire to disturb the peace arrangements she hoped to advance with the Soviet Union. Dulles failed to recognize that the Russians were exploiting this American attitude and were penetrating deeper into Egypt. Even by that time "pilots" taking vessels through the Canal were Soviet naval officers.

For the French, he continued, the most suitable date for military action was some time before the middle of October: the Mediterranean would be relatively calm up to then but stormy later, and he thought it best for the action to take place before the U.S. presidential elections. Pineau believed that President Eisenhower would not wish to appear before the American electorate as one who was so anxious for an accommodation with the Soviet Union that he was prepared to sacrifice his allies—Britain and France.

The French foreign minister was leaving later that day for the United States to take part in the Security Council meetings. He expected the sessions to be long and tough. U.N. Secretary-General Dag Hammarskjöld wanted to propose a four-nation committee, composed of representatives of Britain, France, the Soviet Union, and one of the Asian states, to mediate between Egypt and the Western Powers. Pineau saw this as a device to force the West to surrender, and France would not hesitate to use her veto to defeat this proposal.

Likewise, France would try to convince the British that Anglo-French military measures were the only course, but he was doubtful that she would succeed. Though Anthony Eden favored action, British Foreign Office officials preferred a policy of passively waiting for some miracle. Pineau therefore requested that we explore the possibilities of joint action with Israel. He in no way wished us to feel that he wanted Israel to act only in order to help solve France's problems. If Israel took measures against Egypt, she would be doing so to defend her own basic interests, whereas France and Britain had to bear the responsibility for military action as their reply to Egypt's nationalization of the Canal. An indication of what was implied in this formulation emerged when Pineau reminded us that under the Anglo-Egyptian Treaty of 1955, in time of war Britain had the right to seize the Canal by force, so that war between Israel and Egypt could provide Britain with the juridical pretext to put her army back in the Canal Zone.

At all events, said the foreign minister, he would like to hear from us whether Israel was interested in taking military action against Egypt, together with France, in the event that Britain withdrew from an Anglo-French operation. If we were, then France would, of course, give us full military aid and full political backing in the Security Council—including unreserved use of the veto in favor of Israel. If Britain pulled out, Pineau believed that France and Israel could act together in one of two ways: either Israel could launch the action alone, receiving military aid from France, and after the campaign was under way France would send in her forces; or the action could be opened jointly by Israeli and French forces.

Pineau spoke for about forty-five minutes, and then our delegation presented Israel's position. First, we agreed with the French view that relations with Nasser could no longer be regularized by diplomatic means. There was now no alternative to military action. Second, we regarded France as our friend and ally and agreed wholeheartedly to act jointly with her. Third, we had to be certain of Britain's stand if she stayed out of the campaign. Would she invoke her treaty with Jordan and go to her aid if Jordan should attack Israel, or if Israel should move into the West Bank in reaction to the entry of Iraqi forces into Jordan? If she would, we could find ourselves in a situation whereby we were allied with France in a military operation against Egypt on one front, while Britain was fighting at the side of Jordan and Iraq against us on another. Fourth, what was the United States likely to do? During our War of Independence she had declared an embargo on arms to the Middle East. Now America might declare an economic embargo, which would be a grave hardship. And finally, what of the Soviet Union? Was she likely to send her forces to the aid of Egypt?

The French were very cautious in their replies and said they could only be in the nature of judgments, not information. The shorter the campaign, the better were the chances that the Soviet Union would not intervene directly. But to be on the safe side, we should keep in mind the likelihood that the Polish and Czech flying instructors presently in Egypt would take an active part in the fighting as pilots. As to the United States, the French believed that Dulles would persist in his "no action" policy, but they did not recommend that either France or Israel should approach him on the subject. They said that when it had been mentioned to Dulles that Israel might intervene in the Suez crisis, Dulles had said, "All right, but not before the end of the year," namely, not before the American presidential elections. Finally, the French did not think that Britain would make war on Israel as long as Israel did not initiate an attack on Jordan. During the latest border clashes between Israel and Jordan, Eden was reported to have remarked: "Pity they did not happen on the Egyptian border."

In the course of our meeting, it transpired that France had no suitable bomber aircraft, so that if Britain stayed out, the campaign might not be satisfactorily concluded—even if the Egyptian Air Force was knocked out of the skies—for the airfields near Cairo would remain intact and the Egyptians could receive new planes and continue the battle. For this and other reasons, the French returned to their suggestion that Israel open the campaign, and then they felt sure that Britain would join in—albeit at a later stage. On the other hand, they insisted that even if Britain agreed to a Franco-British action, it would be desirable for Israel to join the campaign later and capture the Sinai Peninsula east of Suez. Such Israeli action would tie down a sizable part of the Egyptian army and secure for Israel a better border arrangement at the end of hostilities. Moreover, if Israel held on to the Straits of Tiran, she would be able to lay an oil pipeline from Eilat to the Mediterranean.

France's foreign minister expected to get a final reply from the British about the middle of October, at the end of the Security Council discussions. It was clear that France could not finalize her plans for a Suez campaign until she had Britain's decision. On the other hand, Pineau wanted Israel's agreement to join in the campaign, fighting in an independent sector, under a separate command, and starting the war on her own before the British and French. If Israel were prepared to do this, he was confident that it would strengthen the chances of a British decision to participate.

With the conclusion of this political part of our clarification talks, I felt none too happy. The one point that emerged clearly was that the situation was unclear and it would remain so until the end of the Security Council meetings. This state of uncertainty was not only politically burdensome and psychologically frustrating, but it also added to our military headaches. In the absence of a clear-cut political decision, it was difficult to make the final military preparations, and if and when the decision was taken to go ahead, the time at our disposal would be very short indeed. How, then, would we be able to do what we would be asked to do?

The target of our complaints, France's as well as our own, was Britain. It was true that British participation in the campaign was of decisive importance. As we listened to Pineau, we recalled the justice of Ben-Gurion's observation that if Britain pulled out, France was likely to do the same. From the international political standpoint, it would be difficult indeed for France to face the opposition of the United States and the Soviet Union alone. And from the military standpoint, going it alone would mean France's loss of the important advantage which Britain could contribute—suitable bomber aircraft.

If the French suffered from Britain's reluctance to make a firm decision, we bore the additional indignity of British hypocrisy. Britain hated the very idea that her name might possibly be smeared as partners with Israel in military action against Arabs, but at the same time, she would welcome the chance of exploiting Israel's conflict with the Arabs to justify her action against Egypt. The most desirable development for Britain would be an Israeli attack on Egypt. She could then rush to Egypt's defense and drive out Israel's forces, and since British troops would then find themselves in the

Suez area, they would automatically stay to control the Canal. The Foreign Office was convinced that under such circumstances, no one could accuse Britain of being either anti-Arab or the aggressor.

Moreover, Britain wished us to fulfill this exalted function of villain, or scapegoat, without her having to meet us and discuss it face to face. She knew that the very act of our sitting together would carry the implication of "treaty making"—albeit limited to one-time action against Egypt—which would be highly unpopular in the Arab world. The British therefore wanted France to be their insulated link with Israel. Through France they would get us to do what was desirable for Britain while guaranteeing them freedom from contact with Israel.

We lunched at Louis Mangin's house, where we had been meeting, somewhat overawed by the gaze of our host's father, whose portrait dominated the dining room. He was the famed General Charles Emmanuel Mangin, hero in the battles of the Marne and Verdun in World War One. The house and its furnishing were still redolent of old-world French aristocracy. With us at the table were Bourges-Maunoury, Abel Thomas of the Defense Ministry, and military officials. The atmosphere was lively and gay despite the grimness of our morning's discussions. In France, not even politics were allowed to interfere with good food and good red wine.

Since Admiral Barjot was not present, and those of us who were serving officers were in the land or air forces, the fun at the table was mostly at the expense of the Navy. I liked what one of our irreverent French colleagues said about a certain admiral, known for his pursuit of publicity. Arriving at Orly Airport one day, he was greeted at customs with the usual "Have you anything to declare?" "Of course," said the admiral, "where's the microphone?"

The talks were resumed at 3:30 P.M. and were now directed at the military aspects of the program. The French indicated that they still hoped Britain would join. It was best, however, to plan the action as an Israeli-French venture on the assumption that Britain would stay out, or, of she came in, would do so at a later stage. The current plan, "Operation Musketeer," was an Anglo-French operation, and this now had to be changed or modified to bring in Israel in place of Britain. The French forces had several limitations. The most important was their lack of air bases close enough to the target. Under Musketeer, Britain's bases in Cyprus would also serve the French, and the first question was whether Israel could now be a substitute for Cyprus. From the technical point of view, could Israel's air bases be used by French aircraft?

I believed that the presentation of the problem whereby Israel would replace Britain in "Operation Musketeer" was oversimplified and unrealistic, and I suggested a different approach both for an examination of the problem and the search for the solutions. We would tell the French what forces we could muster and what military objective we felt we could tackle, and the French would tell us what they could do and what forces they would commit.

The French were very eager to hear our plans but seemed somewhat reserved in the presentation of their own. This might have been because they still felt themselves bound to the British or simply because they had not yet worked out their plans in detail.

The day's talks ended with the decision that we would meet the next day with the French chief of staff to clarify the operational data and intentions and to consider in practical terms the procurement of French military equipment for our army. It was also decided that a French delegation would return with us to Israel to examine on the spot the feasibility of our bases serving as a substitute for Cyprus.

We met French Chief of Staff General Paul Ely on the morning of October 1 at Louis Mangin's home. I was the only member of the Israeli delegation at this talk, but I was accompanied by several officers from our military attaché's staff. With General Ely were General Challe; General Martin, his deputy; Colonel Simon, chief of operations; a naval officer; and Mangin.

Though the stated purpose of our meeting was simply the exchange of information and clarification of certain technical points, it was my aim to strengthen the conviction of the French army chief that from the military point of view the operation could be undertaken with success even without British participation. General Ely spoke warmly of Israel. Gray-haired, tall, and thin, he looked very much the intellectual. He had lost the use of one arm. He was treated with great respect by his officers, and he was clearly more to them than just their chief.

The French opened by asking about the strength of Egypt's forces, and we told them what we knew. Our information seemed to tally with their own intelligence reports. They then went over to the question of the joint operational plan, and they asked how I envisaged the action of the Israeli army and in what way they could help us. I said we could mobilize for the Egyptian front 6 to 8 infantry and armored brigades and some 70 combat planes—Mystères, Ouragans and Meteors. Though this was a small army, I was confident that we could defeat the Egyptians on land and in the air even if we fought alone—not only without the British but even without the French. As for military aid, we needed equipment, and we had with us a list of requirements, but I said that the most important aid would be a simultaneous campaign with France.

The French asked whether we had thought of the division of the battle sectors. I told them that we saw our sector, for our land forces, as east of the Suez Canal, and the same for our Air Force, except for certain additional targets. The French, I thought, should capture the Canal Zone and put out of action the Egyptian airfields west of the Canal. The problem of Egyptian airfields was of special importance because of the presence in Egypt of foreign pilots, ground crews, and other experts. Additional pilots could be rushed over from Czechoslovakia or Poland if planes and airfields were left intact. Current Egyptian air strength stood at about 150 MiG fighters and about 40 Ilyushin bombers.

As to the naval sectors, I thought the functions should be divided so that the Israeli Navy would be responsible for the defense of Israel's coast and the French would tackle the Egyptian Navy. (We had no submarines at that time.) We saw our campaign against Egypt as primarily an encounter between land forces, and the task of our Navy would be to help our forces through the Red Sea and defend our Mediterranean coastline.

When I said that our operation would be limited to east of Suez, the French asked whether I had no intention of maintaining a bridgehead on the west bank of the Canal. I told them no. I did not know what was behind the question, but it was evidently linked to the next one they had in mind. This concerned Cairo. During the course of the talk, they had asked how I envisaged the end of the campaign and whether I did not think that Cairo should be taken. I said that the capture of Cairo would create severe political complications which would best be avoided. This, I said, was of course a political question of the highest order, and I was expressing only my personal view.

I was unable to get the French to disclose specific details of their plan. Asked about the strength of the French force that would be taking part, they said that the Anglo-French operation was based on four infantry divisions and on the heavy bombing of Egyptian airfields. The objective was the capture of the Canal Zone.

Summing up, the French said they were satisfied that the Israeli plan was feasible and that it would enable the French to gain their objectives even if the British withdrew their participation. They also assured me that we would find the French plan satisfactory. We were told later that the air strength allocated by France for the operation was 75 P-84s and 25 Mystère-4s.

The French confirmed that they were sending a delegation to Israel to see whether our air bases could serve the French craft, particularly transport planes, and could take emergency landings of other aircraft. I said we would offer them all facilities for inspection, but whether our bases could be used for French Air Force planes depended on the decision of my government.

They asked what equipment we would require, and I handed them the list. It included tanks, half-tracks, trucks with four-wheel drive to negotiate the sand, bazookas, and transport planes. They seemed somewhat surprised at the small and obsolete weapons and equipment, especially armor, of the Israel Defense Forces and particularly at the fact that the size of our units was roughly one-quarter that of their counterparts in the French army. Nevertheless, I told them I was convinced that with what we had—or rather, despite what we lacked—we could capture the Sinai Peninsula quickly. If we could not get additional tanks, we would use bazookas mounted on jeeps and command cars. Our big problem was vehicles fit for movement in the desert. I did not know how tough the opposition from Egyptian armor would be, but I did know how serious an obstacle the desert was. To get our troops, ammunition, and other supplies to Sharm el-Sheikh, we would need suitable transport.

On the subject of timing, I reminded the French that the Israeli army was based largely on its reservists. They could be mobilized very quickly, but for "comfortable" mobilization we would need five to seven days. If we took their estimate as the basis of our calculations, with the Security Council ending on the 12th of October and a final political decision taken on the 15th, the Israeli army could be ready for action on the 20th. The meeting ended with mutual expressions of friendship, and I returned to the hotel to reflect upon our review.

The French were still uncertain about two important factors in the campaign—the start and the finish. For us, these two problems were less uncertain. If the British or French needed a pretext for military measures against Egypt, we certainly did not. The Egyptians had given Israel sufficient legitimate excuse to take action: their military blockade of the Straits of Tiran; their terrorist activities against Israel; their military concentrations in Sinai and their preparations for an invasion of Israel; and their repeated declarations that a state of war existed between Egypt and Israel. As to the final objectives of the campaign, our aims were clear. It was our purpose to capture the Sinai Peninsula and drive out the Egyptian forces. This would guarantee freedom of shipping to Eilat, neutralize the direct threat to Israel by the Egyptian army, and put a stop to the terrorist operations launched from the Gaza Strip.

We, too, would have wished to see Nasser replaced by a new regime in Egypt which would establish peaceful relations with Israel. But this was not an integral ingredient of our military objective, as it was for the French and British. In capturing Sinai, we would gain our objectives even if Nasser remained in power.

I well understood Ben-Gurion's hesitation over the Anglo-French suggestions that we solve their launching problem by opening the campaign. There were sound political and military reasons why we should not do so. However, here was an opportunity, unlikely to recur, for action against Egypt in cooperation with France—and possibly Britain as well. We would not be alone. I thought this called for a supreme effort on our part, and in our interest, not to miss an historic chance.

We took off on the evening of October 1, together with the French representatives, from the military airfield of Villacoublay and arrived in Israel on the next day. This time, too, our route was via Bizerta, but now we flew in a comfortable passenger plane—the DC-4 which President Truman had presented to de Gaulle some years earlier and which he had turned over to the Defense Ministry. It was fitted out with comfortable sleeping, eating, and working arrangements, and indeed both we and the French used the time to good working advantage. Apart from studying the feasibility of using our air bases, the French had two further tasks: to rate the degree of urgency of the equipment we requested and the technical possibilities of its reaching and being absorbed by our army in time for the campaign; and to examine our operational plans and make a judgment on whether or not we could carry them out.

On our arrival home, my delegation colleagues and I went straight to the prime minister to report on our Paris talks, while the French delegates met with a small staff committee we had set up consisting of three colonels representing the three services. On my return to General Headquarters in the evening, I found there had been rapid practical progress on the subject of equipment. After detailed consultations, the French had decided that it was indeed essential to send us supplies quickly, even though they might not reach our units until after the start of the battle. Later that night, they showed us a copy of the cable they had sent to the French minister of defense and to their chief of staff. In it they made the urgent recommendation to supply us with Bren carriers, tanks, trucks with front-wheel drive, tank trailers, and fuel tankers for aircraft. They apparently accepted our view that our primary problem was movement through the desert. They had no worries about our ability to overcome the Egyptian army.

I called a meeting of the General Staff that same evening to give them the Early Warning Order. I told them of the imminent possibility of a joint campaign with France, and perhaps with Britain, against Egypt, although no final decisions had yet been taken either by our government or theirs. The estimated date of the opening of hostilities was October 20, eighteen days hence, and the campaign would probably last about three weeks. (In fact it would start later and take less time.) Our allies were expected to bomb the Egyptian airfields and seize the Canal Zone. Our task was to capture the Sinai Peninsula. We had to be prepared for the possibility that other Arab states might join in the fighting against us, and we had therefore to secure the Syrian and Jordanian fronts.

We would not mobilize our reserves at this stage, but the preparations for mobilization should be started. I also wanted the recall of all our officers who were on training courses abroad, so that they could take part in the campaign. This would give them more experience, learning, and confidence than anything they could acquire at an overseas staff college. It was also what they would most want. To preserve secrecy of intention, our preparations might be explained as a counter-move to the possible entry of Iraqi troops into Jordan.

The next morning, October 3, I received from the prime minister a memorandum he had written late the previous evening which, he said, summed up his considered reaction to "the Plan." It was more reserved and cautious than his reactions had been when we reported to him on our talks in Paris. I knew Ben-Gurion had met earlier with several members of the government and that some were apprehensive. Ben-Gurion pointed out that without British participation, Israel might face grave dangers, notably the bombing of her cities; for without the British, France's bombing power would be weakened. And since, under such circumstances, French aircraft might be operating from Israel and not Cyprus, Israel would be the sole target of Egyptian air attack. Ben-Gurion's memorandum did not conclude with a specific acceptance or rejection of the plan. But it ended with the recommendation that the French should be told directly and frankly of its implications for Israel.

It was not quite clear what this warning was expected to produce.

After all, the French, too, preferred joint action with Britain, and the suggestion of a Franco-Israeli operation was prompted by the absence of an alternative. Such an approach by Ben-Gurion augured ill for the chances of military action.

The French delegation was scheduled to meet the prime minister in Jerusalem later that morning. I arrived a little earlier, with Shimon Peres, for a prior talk with Ben-Gurion. I found him worried and less than enthusiastic. He said he was thinking of writing immediately to France's prime minister, Guy Mollet, expressing his doubts about the operation. I begged him not to do so but to wait until the conclusion of the French delegation's visit and until we heard their definitive suggestions. It would have been easy at that moment to quench the French government's ardor to wage war against Egypt. To fire it anew might have been well nigh impossible.

I told Ben-Gurion that I thought both his apprehensions and his estimate of the Egyptian capacity to bomb us were exaggerated. In my judgment, the French Air Force, even without the British, was capable of inflicting sufficient damage on the Egyptian Air Force. What limited Egyptian action might be directed against Israel thereafter could be met by our own Air Force, however small it was at that time. My tone was somewhat sharp, but I did not regret it. If France were willing to undertake joint action with us, it would be in the highest degree unfortunate if we rejected their offer and returned to our state of isolated struggle.

At their meeting with Ben-Gurion, and in reply to his questions, the French reiterated their hope that they would be permitted to operate from bases in Cyprus, with or without the British. If not, they would wish to use Israel's bases. Ben-Gurion asked how they envisaged the toppling of Nasser—their principal aim—if their plan called for the capture only of the Canal Zone? Egyptian forces could remain in the unconquered part of Egypt, carry out guerrilla warfare against the occupying French army, and Nasser could call for Soviet aid. The French agreed that this was possible, and they confessed that there was indeed no solution to this problem in their current plan.

The differences in approach between Ben-Gurion and the French were very evident throughout the talks. For Ben-Gurion, the launching of operations was dependent on satisfactory replies about the situation likely to develop in the later stages of the campaign and after. The French, on the other hand, were pressing for immediate action as the correct response to Nasser's nationalization of the Canal, even if they had no reasonable answers to the problems that would arise therefrom. Their approach was based on the recognition that no action was the worst course of all. Furthermore, the French still hoped that we would be joined by the British. Ben-Gurion, for his part, was not prepared to count on British participation. He was also disturbed by the possibility of military failure in an operation in which we were partners.

We returned to Tel Aviv in the afternoon and held a summing-up conference with the French delegation. We dealt first with two technical problems: the use of Israeli bases by the French as an alternative to Cyprus and French help with equipment for the Israeli army.

The Air Force representative in the delegation, who had visited our bases, had warm words to say about the standard of our Air Force, and he was now confident that effective coordination arrangements could be made. A list was drawn up of additional equipment our Air Force would require if it had to handle the French aircraft. We would also be getting equipment for our infantry and armored units, though not on the scale we had requested.

Our French visitors expressed their relief at finding our army so well organized and on a technical level so much higher than anything they had expected. Israel could certainly serve as a substitute for Cyprus without affecting the operational efficiency of the French forces.

When we came to consider the operational side of the campaign, the French delegation, while impressed with the concept of our plan, viewed it as rather ambitious, and they also thought that our Air Force, in particular, was assuming a very heavy load, stretching itself to the utmost. This might also be the case with our land forces—infantry, armor, and our first wave of paratroopers.

I asked them to try to see things as I saw them, although I knew this was not easy for foreign soldiers who devised their plans on data very different from ours. The fact was that speed was the key element, not only for the obvious political reasons but also for purely military reasons. A rapid advance was of supreme importance in enabling us to extract the essential ingredients from those elements in which we enjoyed an advantage over the Egyptian army. I was thinking not only of our advantage in the quality of the individual, but of the handling and behavior of our entire army and its fighting formations as against those of their Egyptian counterparts. The Egyptians tended to go by the book, and their command headquarters were far from the front. It took them time to make changes in the disposition of their units, such as forming a new defense line, switching targets of attack, or moving forces not in accordance with the original plan.

We, on the other hand, were accustomed to acting with greater speed, more flexibility, and less military routine, with our commanders right on the spot, in the midst of their fighting units, able to give split-second orders and adjust to the lightning changes on their front. This was a prized advantage we had to exploit. I was confident that we could run the campaign in such a way that the enemy would be given no time to reorganize and there would be no pause in the fighting. Each of our major formations would be told its special objective and receive orders to gain it in one continuous battle. This approach might not be appropriate for every campaign, but I considered it correct and feasible for this one, as well as suited to the character of the Israeli army and its commanders. Our plan called for opening with a paratroop drop in the vicinity of our final objective. The task of our paratroop units would be to block the paths of Egyptian reinforcements and capture dominant positions of tactical importance. They would have to hold their ground until our main forces linked up with them, which I estimated would be not more than forty-eight hours later.

After listening to our explanations, the French said they hoped we would really be able to carry out so ambitious a plan. Having seen some of our army units, they were prepared to give us credit which they would have been reluctant to concede before coming to Israel. They added that the approach in planning the Anglo-French "Operation Musketeer" had been completely different from ours. To this I said that we were a small army, and if we tried to adopt the military concepts of France or Britain, we would not thereby become a great power; we would merely lose the special qualities we did possess.

Though our meeting was concerned with military operations, it was inevitable that we should also touch on their political aspects. As at our other sessions in Paris and also with Ben-Gurion, the two traditional questions cropped up: how was the campaign to start, and with what was it to end? In my opening words on campaign plans, I had said we proceeded on the assumption that at the start of our action a simultaneous attack would be launched by French land forces. The delegation now asked whether I thought such simultaneous action was essential from the military point of view. I replied that it was of considerable military importance, for French landings on the coast of Egypt would compel Nasser to turn a good part of his strength to meet them, leaving his units in Sinai without reinforcements. But it was also of great political importance. The reaction of such Arab states as Syria and Lebanon, and even of Big Powers like the Soviet Union, the United States, and Britain, would be very different if Israel alone attacked Egypt.

The French said they agreed with this assessment, but they thought we should know that it would be difficult for the French forces to start their action on the same day as ours. Then they asked me the same question that Ben-Gurion had posed to them and which they would be asked by their own government when they returned: what would happen after we each captured our respective sectors without this resulting in a new Egyptian regime? What if Nasser started waging guerrilla warfare? Was there not a danger that instead of a brief and light campaign we would find ourselves up to our necks in a long, drawn-out struggle?

This was indeed a grave problem, and there was no simple or clear-cut answer. But it was more a problem for us than it was for France. Ben-Gurion had raised it in all its severity because he, after all, was the one who would have to make the final momentous decision, and because he knew, as I did, that a military-political defeat for little Israel, still taking its infant steps in statehood, could shake her to her very core. For France, the risk was nowhere as great. If at some stage she might have to remove her forces without gaining her objective, this would not undermine the foundations of her existence.

My reply was that with all the anxiety over grim post-campaign problems, there was no need to overestimate the power of the Egyptians to do us damage, particularly after a good part of their army and weapons would have been destroyed in the fighting. It was not we but the Egyptians who would be weak, and it was not for us but for them to be apprehensive. I added that neither Israel nor France had anything to lose. Nasser continued to conduct hostilities against us, and there was no prospect that his actions would stop without firm action by Israel. Would it be easier for France to solve her Moroccan and Algerian problem without action against an Egypt that aided and encouraged France's enemies?

Throughout our discussion of how the campaign was to end, I could not avoid the impression that the French had deliberately raised this issue almost in the same breath as the question of how the campaign was to open. They kept pressing us to launch our action ahead of them. They knew our security situation and were aware of my strong desire for joint action with them. They therefore stressed the doubts likely to worry the French government when it came to weigh how worthwhile the operation would be, and they wanted to spur us to respond to France's wish and be the first to start the action.

On the following day, October 4, I met with Ben-Gurion at 10 A.M. in Jerusalem to report on my summing-up talks with the French delegation and to receive his approval to continue our preparations. I found him relaxed, and he readily assented to my suggestion that we continue our operational planning jointly with the French without having to wait for Cabinet consideration and decision, while we accept from the French the equipment we requested on a tentative loan basis. If the campaign was called off, we would either return the equipment or pay for it. This, incidentally, was the original suggestion put forward by Shimon Peres, and the French were inclined to accept it.

A little later, Ben-Gurion met with a member of the delegation and told him, among other things, that he would not view with disfavor a situation wherein Israeli forces would be stationed for an extended period on the eastern bank of the Canal, while west of the Canal there was a French presence—even a small, token force. Both agreed that the operation should not be launched without the knowledge and agreement—even silent—of the British.

The talks ended and our French visitors returned to Paris. There had been clarification at the meetings, and contingency decisions had been taken on what each side would do if it were resolved to go ahead with the campaign. But the manner in which it was to be launched, if at all, had not been decided. It was agreed, however, that French supplies of equipment would be shipped immediately, and that the military staffs of both countries would start coordinating their plans without waiting for a final decision on the campaign from their respective governments. Ben-Gurion's impression after the talks was that the operation would not take place. He told me that he put the chances of French government ratification of the plan at 20 percent. I was more optimistic.

Whatever happened—or failed to happen—we had to proceed with our preparations with the utmost speed and urgency. I promptly scheduled meetings with heads of those branches of the army that would be closely involved in the pre-campaign arrangements (not least the Manpower and Quartermaster branches, the Ordnance Corps and my budgetary chief), and an immediate one with the Operations Branch to question some of the planning details. I felt that the plan leaned too heavily on the frontal attack and a gradual advance. I also saw that the paratroop drop had been designated for the El Arish area, on the Sinai Peninsula's Mediterranean coast. This had to be changed. I wanted a sizable landing at H-hour somewhere close to the Canal.

On October 8 I held an Orders Group—at which our Sinai Campaign was codenamed Operation Kadesh after the last site of sojourn in the Sinai wilderness by the Children of Israel before continuing to the Promised Land—and issued my directives. Among them was my insistence that our task was not to kill a maximum of the enemy's forces but to bring about their collapse and capture what we could of their weapons and equipment. We would do this by seizing at the outset the principal targets deep inside enemy territory through landings or paratroop drops, while our infantry and armored units embarked on a speedy advance. They would bypass enemy positions where possible, leave them cut off in isolated pockets in the rear, and resort to frontal attack only when this action was unavoidable. I also stressed the need to organize our forces so that the advance of one formation would not be dependent on the rate of progress of another.

In making our preparations, circumspection was essential. If we offered no clue to enemy intelligence, we might preserve the element of surprise. An example of this cautiousness was provided the very next day, while I was meeting with the General Staff. A request came in from Southern Command for authorization to carry out patrols in the Rafah region to test the sand dunes for tank movement. Fearing that this might draw unnecessary attention, I authorized only one small patrol and that only after being assured that it would make its way along the pebbled bed of the wadi, not more than two men would actually walk on the sand, and they would be fitted with Bedouin sandals made in Hebron, so that their footprints would not stand out against those of the habitual Arab smugglers.

Forty-eight hours later, on the night of October 10, while we were in the midst of feverish preparations for the Sinai Campaign, we put in a dramatic attack on the Jordanian Arab Legion police fort on the edge of the border town of Kalkilia. It was a large-scale action which had to be hastily planned, organized, and carried out, and the objective was gained. But our losses were heavy—18 killed (including 8 officers) and more than 50 wounded (including 14 officers). It also endangered our relations with Britain.

The immediate provocation was the murder on October 9 of two Israeli farm laborers working in an orange grove near the border, not far from Kalkilia, by a terrorist band from Jordan. But it climaxed several other flagrant terrorist acts—and a provocative order from King Hussein—only a little while earlier. On October 4 five workers on their way to the potash plant at Sodom, near the southern end of the Dead Sea, were ambushed and killed, their assailants returning to Jordan. When this happened, Ben-Gurion told me not to take reprisal action. It was important at this particular time to appear before the world as accusers and not aggressors. Our restraint was misunderstood by the Jordanians. They took it as a sign of weakness.

The terrorists at Sodom were the very ones who three weeks before had murdered three Israeli Druze in the north. Their identity was known to us, and we arranged for this information to be transmitted to King Hussein so that they could be brought to trial. They happened to be in a Jordanian jail—on a smuggling charge—where they had openly boasted about their actions in the north and at Sodom. Hussein's response to our message was an immediate order to release the terrorists.

Now had come the murder of the two farm laborers. After all that had gone before, it could not be overlooked. The prime minister, and the Cabinet, approved immediate retaliatory action. Within a few hours, the paratroops—quickly assembled from units in different parts of the country—were crossing the border on their way to Kalkilia.

Half an hour before midnight, after two-and-a-half hours of stubborn fighting against very stiff Arab Legion opposition, the police fort and its cluster of surrounding emplacements had been stormed, subdued, combed, and cleared and the fort blown up. The assault unit accomplished its mission. So did a second unit, which had penetrated deep inside Jordan and successfully blocked Arab Legion reinforcements driving to the aid of Kalkilia. But it ran into deep trouble on the way home. Trapped, outnumbered, and under constant all-round attack, the men held out until they were extricated by a daring rescue unit, which fought its vulnerable way to the beleaguered men and returned through heavy fire by first light. Only then, when all were back in Israel, did I cancel orders I had given during the night to prepare an armored and infantry force with air cover to break through to the trapped unit at dawn, if it had not been rescued by then.

Political complications emerged while the battle was still raging. The British consul in Jerusalem informed our Foreign Ministry that King Hussein had asked the commander of British forces in the Middle East to send the RAF to the aid of the Arab Legion in accordance with the Anglo-Jordanian defense treaty. On the next day, the British chargé d'affaires in Tel Aviv called on the prime minister to inform him that an Iraqi division was about to enter Jordan, and if Israel took military action, Britain would go to Jordan's aid. Ben-Gurion replied that Israel objected to the Iraqi move and reserved freedom of action if it took place. These political developments did nothing to improve Anglo-Israeli relations at the very time when there was talk of possible joint action against Egypt!

The military implications of Kalkilia led me to suggest that we stop costly night reprisal actions and carry out daylight operations instead, using armor and aircraft. This would be one way of compelling our Arab neighbors to choose between halting the terrorism themselves or meeting us in a full-scale war. A strong daylight action would reduce our casualties, and the affected Arab state would be unable to ignore the shock to its prestige. Another way would be to cross the border, capture commanding positions, and make our evacuation conditional upon the stopping of terror.

14

THE FRENCH CONNECTION II

IN A CABLE received on the night of October 18, Guy Mollet, the prime minister of France, invited Ben-Gurion to Paris. This cable had been sent before Paris had received our message containing the same suggestion from Ben-Gurion. Apparently the French had also realized that this was the most effective way to settle the matter. In earlier talks with our military attaché's office in Paris, the French had indicated that it would be better to begin the talks without the British. At the appropriate time, they would be brought in.

We arranged to depart for Paris on Sunday night, October 21. We now received details of the previous day's Anglo-French meeting in Paris. The British had handed the French a two-paragraph written declaration, signed by Prime Minister Anthony Eden, intending for the French to transmit it to us. The British felt that this would set our minds at rest and enable us to open the campaign alone and reach the Canal.

The first paragraph stated that Britain and France would demand of both Egypt and Israel that they retire from the Canal area, and if one side refused, Anglo-French forces would intervene to ensure the smooth operation of the Canal. The purpose of this paragraph was to provide the legal, political, and moral justification for the invasion of Egypt by Britain and France. The second paragraph declared that the British would not go to the aid of Egypt if war broke out between her and Israel. But this was not the case as regards Jordan, with whom Britain had a valid defense treaty. This paragraph was apparently designed to assure us that Britain would not turn her guns on us—even if Egypt asked her to.

Ben-Gurion, of course, did not regard this declaration as a basis for joint action. He insisted that we should not be the ones to launch the campaign and fill the role of aggressor, while the British and French appeared as angels of peace to bring tranquillity to the area. He was not prepared to accept a division of functions whereby, as he put it, Israel volunteered to mount the rostrum of shame so that Britain and France could lave their hands in the waters of purity.

I told Ben-Gurion that, to my mind, this issue could also be regarded from another aspect. For the actual military campaign, Britain and France did not need us. The five hundred warplanes they would be putting into action were enough to rout the Egyptian Air Force. The same held true of the land and naval forces. The sole quality we possessed, relevant to this context, and they lacked was the ability to supply the necessary pretext. This alone could provide us with a ticket of admission to the Suez campaign "club."

Moreover, our situation vis-à-vis Egypt was different from that of Britain and France. Nasser continued to proclaim that Israel and Egypt were in a state of war, and he followed his words with deeds by his blockade of the Straits of Tiran and the action of his terrorist gangs. This compelled us, without the slightest connection with the interests of Britain or France, to instruct our army from time to time to cross the border; and we often came into conflict with the Egyptian army. The British assumption was therefore correct: we had it in our hands to provide the pretext. We were in a position to "deliver the goods."

We also had to weigh very carefully what would happen if we refused the British proposal. To my mind, I told Ben-Gurion, we would lose an historic opportunity which would never recur. In our clash with Nasser, we would have to continue alone, without the forces of Britain and France and without the aid in equipment we would get from France within the framework of the joint campaign. In such circumstances and from the political point of view, could we on our own make war to capture Sharm el-Sheikh, so as to secure freedom of shipping to Eilat? Would we not be branded as aggressors and be subjected to even greater pressures by the United States and the Soviet Union? I thought Bourges-Maunoury was right when he told our people that it was more important for us to submit conditions about the results of the campaign than about its opening.

I was therefore convinced that if the French could take care of the naval side and their Air Force would help in the defense of Haifa and Tel Aviv, we should move toward the suggested plan and open the campaign, on the condition that the French and British would join within a couple of days and seize the Canal Zone.

On the morning of October 21, a plane arrived from France to take us to the Paris meeting. We would be leaving in the evening, and this would be a journey to decision. Both time and discussion had been exhausted. What was left was negotiation—on the extent to which each of the partners would be willing to concede and compromise—and a definitive ruling.

Two members of the earlier French delegation had come on the plane, and at 11 A.M. they walked into my office. Their arrival in Israel was unexpected, but their purpose was clear: they wished to start negotiating even before we reached Paris. The principal issue was the "pretext," or, as the French termed it, the "scenario." Britain had not moved from her position, and our French visitors had come specially to urge us to comply. They said they knew the British proposal was not a good one, but it was the only realistic plan, for Britain would agree to no other. She would join the campaign only if she could appear as an intermediary, as one who restored order.

The talk was tough. I asked them if the French Air Force would come to our aid if our cities were bombed within the first twenty-four hours—when our own planes would be needed over the battlefield. They answered in the negative, adding that the British were opposed to this idea as it would spoil the "scenario." At this point I just blew up, perhaps as much for the tiresome use of the word "scenario" as for the reasoning. Shakespeare, I said, was a genius of a scenario writer, but I doubted whether any in the British Cabinet had inherited his qualities. I, for one, would not support a partnership proposal based on the condition that one would do the job and the other two would come along and kick him out. If we had to fight the Egyptians alone, we ourselves would decide when and how to do so, being governed by what suited us best. In a partnership, however, if Egyptian planes bombed Tel Aviv because our own planes were away preparing the path for the Anglo-French conquest of the Canal Zone, it was inconceivable that our partners would not come to our aid so as not to spoil the "scenario"!

As to the air defense of Israel, they asked whether this problem might not be solved by stationing in Israel French squadrons that would go into action only in extreme emergency, namely, to defend Israeli cities attacked from the air? I replied that this was a new proposal and required consideration. Actually, my own solution was simpler. We would carry out land attacks on a comparatively small scale in the proximity of the Canal. This would not necessarily prompt the Egyptians to retaliate with the bombardment of Israeli cities, for fear that we would do the same to theirs, but it would be a sufficient pretext for the British and French. Still, the idea of having air aid in case of emergency was not to be dismissed.

We left before dusk for the airfield to take off for France—Ben-Gurion, his aide, Shimon Peres, head of my bureau Mordechai Bar-On, and myself. Only in the car on our way to the air base did I tell Ben-Gurion of the mission of the two Frenchmen. When he heard that they were again urging us to agree to the British plan, he wanted to cancel the flight. And when he saw them near the plane, Ben-Gurion, restraining his feeling with difficulty, said to them: "If you are thinking of pressing the British proposals upon us, the only useful thing about this trip will be the opportunity to meet your prime minister."

The aircraft took off after dark, and we all settled down for the night. Ben-Gurion had his nose in a volume of Procopius, the Byzantine historian who was born in Palestine's Caesarea in the late fifth century. During the course of the flight, Ben-Gurion suddenly called us over. His eyes lit up as he pointed to a passage he had just read, in which Procopius mentioned a Jewish realm that existed in the fifth century in the region of the Red Sea. The kingdom was located on the "isle of Yotvat," apparently the Hebrew name of what was later called the island of Tiran, at the eastern edge of the straits at the mouth of the Gulf of Aqaba.

Heavy clouds over central France prevented our landing in Paris and we had to turn back to Marseille to refuel. We returned and kept circling over Paris until, after seventeen hours of shaky and weary flight, the pilot saw a break in the clouds and we landed at last at the Villacoublay airfield on October 22.

Shimon Peres, Mordechai Bar-On, and I were quartered in a Paris hotel, while Ben-Gurion and his aide were staying at a villa in Sèvres, on the outskirts of Paris, where our talks were to be held. The villa was the home of the Bonnier de la Chapelles, a distinguished French family who were good friends of Bourges-Maunoury and had close associations with the leaders of the French Resistance. The only son of the house had been sent by the French underground to Algiers to assassinate Admiral Darlan. Eighteen years old at the time, he was caught and executed by General Giraud's men, who were then in control of Algiers. His room at the villa was kept just as it was when he left. Two candles framed his photograph.

After a few hours' rest, we started our first meeting at 4 P.M. The French participants were Prime Minister Guy Mollet, Foreign Minister Pineau, and Defense Minister Bourges-Maunoury. Our side consisted of Ben-Gurion, Shimon Peres and myself. The talks lasted until seven o'clock. At first they were fairly general. Both Guy Mollet and Ben-Gurion had theories and ideas about a host of weighty subjects and the major political happenings in the world, and they found it quite appropriate, in the midst of a discussion about Jordan's parliamentary elections, to dart off into an analysis of instability in communist Poland.

The discussion of our central theme was opened by Ben-Gurion, who warned the French in advance that he was about to present a proposal that might seem fantastic, or at least naive, at first sight. It covered a comprehensive arrangement of the problems of the Middle East. He said that Jordan was not viable as an independent state and should be divided. The areas east of the Jordan River should be given to Iraq against her undertaking to receive and settle the Arab refugees in her midst; and western Jordan should, as an autonomous region, become part of Israel. Lebanon, too, should give up some of her Moslem districts in order to guarantee for herself stability based on the Christian areas of the country. In such a Middle Eastern structure, Britain would exercise her influence over Iraq, which would include eastern Jordan, and over the southern parts of the Arabian Peninsula; and France's sphere would be Lebanon and possibly also Syria, with close relations with Israel. There should be a guaranteed international status for the Suez Canal, and the Straits of Tiran should come under Israeli control.

None of this could be achieved quickly, but attempts should be made to persuade the United States and particularly Britain to support these aims. Ben-Gurion saw the present situation—and that meeting—as a suitable opportunity for a comprehensive consideration of the future of the Middle East in order to reach a joint policy for the United States, Britain, France, and Israel. He suggested that we should not hurry with our military campaign but take the time to clarify the political possibilities. He considered the hour ripe for such reassessment, with Britain standing amidst the shattered fragments of her policy both in Egypt, where Nasser had nationalized the Canal, and in Jordan, where anti-British forces had just won the elections.

The French listened to Ben-Gurion's views with close interest, but they showed no disposition to be diverted from the down-to-earth subject of the military campaign. The prime minister of France did not believe the Americans could be persuaded that Nasser had to be thrown out. He said there was always a two-year time lag before the Americans understood any European problem. In World War One, understanding came only in 1917; in World War Two, it took from 1939 to 1941 until they joined. Even the gravity of Nasser's Suez action would sink in only in another two years. Moreover, the Americans were really interested only in problems connected with the Soviet Union.

Foreign Minister Pineau was even more outspoken than Guy Mollet. He warned Ben-Gurion that in trying to solve all problems at once, none would be solved. Neither the United States nor Britain was now prepared for a basic consideration of these issues. Eden, it was true, was genuinely in favor of action against Egypt, but he was having a difficult time. He faced opposition in Parliament from the Labor Party and also in his own party and Cabinet. The longer the delay, the weaker would be his position. Nasser, on the other hand, was getting stronger each day, and his ties with the Russians grew closer. Now, therefore, was the time to act, or the opportune hour would be missed.

Pineau cited three factors in support of immediate action. The first was technical: after October the Mediterranean starts getting stormy, making landings impossible. The other two were political. In his view, the United States would not take time off for the Middle East on the eve of her presidential elections in November, and advantage should be taken of the remaining weeks to launch our operations. The same held for the Soviet Union, which was currently engrossed in internal problems in Poland and other People's Republics.

Ben-Gurion tried again to draw the French into an all-embracing political review, not, he said, to solve all problems at once but to do so in stages. The first was to hold frank talks with Britain and to be assured of her goodwill. The second was to bring about a more reasonable regime in Egypt, which could also be the answer to other Middle Eastern problems. The third was to reorganize the Middle East. We had now to deal with the first two stages, but we should do this in the context of political aims for the future.

The difference in attitude between Ben-Gurion and the French arose partly from differences in personal character. Ben-Gurion always favored a comprehensive approach to a problem, even when this was unnecessary in tackling a concrete issue. The principal cause, however, was their differences in outlook and understanding of the object of the meeting. The French wanted to reach an arrangement which would make possible the military conquest of the Canal Zone by the British and themselves. Ben-Gurion wanted more than that. It was rare indeed in those years for the prime minister of Israel to consult with the leaders of France and Britain on a political development which had brought the three countries to a common point of departure. He wished to exploit this opportunity by trying to achieve an agreed policy covering all the problems of the Middle East.

The foreign minister again took the floor to return the discussion to the practical problems of the Suez campaign. Defense Minister Bourges-Maunoury followed, explaining that if the campaign were not launched within a few days, France would be compelled to back out. She could not continue to hold idle the merchant vessels and army units assembled for the operation. As to Israel's misgivings, Bourges-Maunoury, as defense minister of France, was prepared to guarantee that French warships would safeguard the coast of Israel and even help with anti-aircraft defense. He was also ready to agree that French Air Force units be stationed in Israel and, if necessary, take part in air defense.

At 7 P.M. British Foreign Minister Selwyn Lloyd and a senior official of the Foreign Office arrived, but they did not immediately come into the meeting room. Instead, they closeted themselves in another chamber, where they were briefed by the French delegation on Israel's position. The French returned without them, and we continued the talks. However, we had reached a stage where we were deadlocked, and there appeared to be no way out. Ben-Gurion was not prepared to accept the British proposals and said he had better leave for Israel in the morning. It seemed pointless to stay. Bourges-Maunoury, for his part, announced that he would have to consider disbanding his Suez units by the end of the week unless a positive decision were taken quickly.

Pineau again read out the principal moves and the timetable of the British suggestion:

• Israel to start military action against Egypt.

• Franco-British ultimatum to be issued to Egypt and Israel demanding their withdrawal from the Canal area.

• Egyptian airfields to be bombed after the expiry of the ultimatum.

It was decided to hold a further talk with the British, and this time we were asked to join. Ben-Gurion and I represented our side. This first tripartite meeting lasted an hour and a half, and it was resumed after a brief adjournment for dinner. Shimon Peres joined us for the second part of the session, which ended toward midnight when Selwyn Lloyd left for London to transmit our suggestions to his prime minister.

It was a strange meeting. In their opening remarks, both Selwyn Lloyd and Ben-Gurion presented extremist stands, yet at the end they showed a surprising measure of readiness to compromise. It is possible that their very inability to tune into each other's wavelengths made both feel it was useless to engage in further clarifications or mutual attempts at persuasion. So they went straight to the final points of concession.

Britain's foreign minister may well have been a friendly man, pleasant, charming, amiable. If so, he showed near-genius in concealing these virtues. His manner could not have been more antagonistic. His whole demeanor expressed distaste—for the place, the company, and the topic.

His opening remarks suggested the tactics of a customer bargaining with extortionate merchants. He said that in fact it was possible to reach agreement with Egypt over the Suez Canal within seven days. His talks in New York with Egypt's Foreign Minister Fawzi had been fruitful, and the Egyptians agreed to recognize the Suez Canal Users Association, to set the Canal fees in advance, to guarantee international supervision of the operation of the Canal, and to accept the imposition of sanctions, in accordance with the U.N. Charter, if they broke their commitments.

If all was so well and good, why, then, was he here? Because, he explained, such an agreement would not only fail to weaken Nasser, but would actually strengthen him, and since Her Majesty's Government considered that Nasser had to go, it was prepared to undertake military action in accordance with the latest version of the Anglo-French plan. This called for the invasion of Sinai by the Israeli army, whose units were to reach Suez within forty-eight hours. (Selwyn Lloyd added here that Britain's military experts had been persuaded by the French that the Israeli army was capable of doing this.) Some time during those forty-eight hours, the Anglo-French ultimatum would be issued to both sides, ordering them to withdraw from the Canal. If Egypt rejected it, the Anglo-French attack would be launched to capture the Canal Zone and overthrow Nasser.

Britain would not go to the aid of Egypt following the attack by Israel. Nor would she go to the help of Jordan, despite the Anglo-Jordanian defense treaty, if Jordan attacked Israel. But Britain would aid Jordan if she were attacked by Israel.

Ben-Gurion's reply was firm and brief. He said he had already rejected the plan as outlined by Lloyd. Israel was not anxious to be branded as an aggressor and to be the recipient of an ultimatum to evacuate the Canal area. If Israel were to attack Egypt under this plan, Egypt might react by bombing Israel's cities. With Israel fighting alone, one could not rule out the prospect that Soviet and Czech "volunteers" would be dispatched to stiffen the Egyptian Air Force. Ben-Gurion's answer, therefore, was that Israel would not start a war against Egypt, neither now nor at any other stage. If she were attacked, however, she would defend herself and eventually defeat Egypt, even at the cost of heavy casualties.

Ben-Gurion had explained what we were not prepared to do. With his permission, I now outlined what we *were* prepared to do, and I presented our plan. I said we were ready to take reprisal action against Egypt. For example, at 5 P.M. on D-day, an Israeli force would cross the border and carry out a limited action. This could be undertaken in the vicinity of the Canal by a paratroop unit that would be dropped behind the Egyptian lines. The British and French governments could meet that same evening and issue a demand that the Egyptians evacuate their forces from the Canal Zone, since their presence endangered the smooth functioning of the Canal. They could make the same demand of Israel, asking us not to advance beyond the Canal, and we would accept it. Since we had no intention of doing so anyway, such a demand had no practical significance. If Egypt turned down the evacuation call, British and French air units would start bombing Egyptian airfields the next morning.

Selwyn Lloyd was not shocked. He did not even seem surprised at my plan. He simply urged that our military action not be a small-scale encounter but a "real act of war," otherwise there would be no justification for the British ultimatum and Britain would appear in the eyes of the world as an aggressor. To this, Lloyd insisted, Britain could not agree, "for she has friends, like the Scandinavian countries, who would not view with favor Britain's starting a war." I did not dare glance at Ben-Gurion as Selwyn Lloyd uttered this highly original argument. I thought he would jump out of his skin. But he restrained his anger, though not his squirming, and all I heard was the scraping of his chair.

Bourges-Maunoury followed, and he promised French air aid to Israel. He even suggested putting French planes into action in an emergency, from the Cyprus base, to which Lloyd hastily responded that he could not agree.

This was too much for Ben-Gurion, and he asked Lloyd directly whether Her Majesty's Government had given thought to the damage that might be suffered by the cities of Israel during the two or three days when Israel would be standing alone on the battlefield? Lloyd seemed hurt by so unpalatable a question, and he said he had come to Paris only because he thought he would be discussing the plan as agreed upon between the British and the French, and here he was, being confronted by a new suggestion.

Nevertheless, despite his apparent reservations, it was evident that Lloyd did not rule out our proposal. He again asked what kind of force we would send across the frontier. Without going into figures, I assured him that it would be a "real act of war." In the course of the talks, Lloyd said that perhaps it might be possible to narrow the time between our action and the activation of their forces, so that they could issue their ultimatum on the morning after our D-day and go into action at night, twelve hours later—namely, thirty-six hours after our opening of the campaign.

When Lloyd left us, close to midnight, I had the feeling that it was possible to bridge the gap between the respective plans—if the parties were willing. Pineau, who was not happy about the kind of report Lloyd would present to Eden, got himself invited to London for a meeting with Britain's prime minister the next evening. He intended to return to Paris the following day, October 24, for the final summing up.

Ben-Gurion had allowed me to put forward my plan, but I was not unaware of the fact that he forbore from committing himself to it and was careful to refer to it as "Dayan's plan." I feared that his reservation was not just a tactical move vis-à-vis the British and the French, but was really sincere, and that he had many doubts about it.

Before going to bed, I went through the cables which had arrived from Israel. One of them informed me that the prospective new prime minister of Jordan was Suleiman Nabulsi, an anti-British Palestinian who had already announced that he would annul the British-Jordanian treaty and that Jordan would join the Syrian-Egyptian military command. A later cable contained the news that as a step toward the union of armies, a conference of the chiefs of staff of Egypt, Syria, and Jordan would be opening that day in Amman. The chairman of the conference would be Abd-el-Hakim Amr, chief of staff of the Egyptian army. The only consoling thought that popped into my mind as I read these cables was that on reaching London Selwyn Lloyd would also find on his desk the same heartening news!

On the morning of October 23, the military members of the French and Israeli delegations met in Mangin's home. It appeared that the French members who had taken part in the previous night's tripartite meeting did not share my impression that the gaps could be spanned. They thought we had come no closer to an agreement with the British, and they believed the negotiations were deadlocked. The obstacle to agreement between the British and ourselves, I said, was not a paucity of Israeli-Egyptian clashes but Britain's reluctance to consider us an equal partner. The suggested "partnership" was based on the condition that Britain and France would play the cops and we the robber, they the saints and we the sinner.

The French said they were sorry my reply was so dampening, but they would try their luck with Ben-Gurion over lunch, when the full delegations of France and Israel would be gathering again at the villa of Bonnier de la Chapelle. The house, half an hour's drive from Paris, was a large structure whose great virtue, for me, was the magnificent garden in which it was set, its lawns fringed with flower beds and surrounded by orchards. If our negotiations failed, hospitality would surely not be the cause. None could have any complaint on that score, and I especially had none against the heavily laden fruit trees.

Pineau and Bourges-Maunoury arrived for lunch after a busy morning in their offices. It seemed as though Providence in those few days had been working overtime orchestrating Middle Eastern affairs. After Jordan's harsh blow to Britain, with the installation of an anti-British premier and her army placed under a joint military command headed by Egypt, it was France's turn. An Egyptian vessel, the *Athos*, had been caught trying to smuggle weapons sent by Egyptian Intelligence to the Algerian insurgents. There had been an outcry in the French Parliament against Egyptian intervention in the internal affairs of France, and the French ambassador had been recalled from Cairo. (The day before had also seen the start of the Ben Bella episode, when a French fighter plane had forced down a Moroccan passenger aircraft carrying Mohammed Ben Bella and four Algerian rebel leaders.) The events in Jordan and North Africa heightened international tension and underscored Nasser's prime role in anti-Western activity. These were the natural topics of conversation at lunch.

Between dessert and coffee, Bourges-Maunoury and Pineau returned to our differences with the British. Selwyn Lloyd had told them after the tripartite meeting the previous night that Britain would not accept our suggestion as presented in "Dayan's plan." The two points at issue were the scope of our military action, the British demanding that we undertake "a full-scale act of war," and the duration of the period between the start of our operation and the Anglo-French attack on Egyptian airfields. The British insisted on forty-eight hours, but it might perhaps be possible to get them to cut it to thirty-six. They would not consider anything shorter, for then the whole business of the ultimatum would be exposed as a fiction. Pineau was to leave that night for London, and he was to take with him "our final word."

We promised him that he would receive our reply before he left, and our delegation adjourned for internal consultations. Such consultations were held from time to time by each of the delegations, ours and the French, whether by formal meeting in a separate room, informal gathering in a corner of the council room, or an exchange of notes during the joint session. But there was a difference in the nature of our respective consultations, arising from the difference in make-up of the two delegations.

The French comprised a group of friends with close ties forged way back in the days of the Resistance. The rank of their authority was largely a product of their functions. Guy Mollet had the last word primarily because he held the post of prime minister. Pineau determined foreign policy and Bourges-Maunoury commitments on defense. In the Israeli delegation, which consisted of the prime minister, the director-general of the Ministry of Defense and the chief of staff, not only was the difference in level between our positions so much wider, but the personal authority of Ben-Gurion for Shimon Peres and me was infinitely greater than that reflected by a formal definition of our respective functions. Our delegation, in fact, was a single representative, Ben-Gurion. He was like the traditional rabbi, and we, his aides or advisers, were his disciples. For this reason, even our internal consultations were basically not discussions leading to decisions but efforts by Peres and myself to persuade Ben-Gurion to accept our suggestions. We did this, as a rule, only when he showed interest and only as long as he himself had not yet reached a final decision.

When we adjourned that afternoon for such a private meeting, we were aware of its fateful importance. We would need to equip Pineau with a formula for his London journey which would determine whether the Suez campaign took place or was canceled. But Ben-Gurion had not yet made up his mind whether, in the present circumstances, Israel could join in the war. Though he did not say so, it was evident that he was disappointed with the meetings so far. He was particularly hurt by the refusal to view Israel as a partner of equal standing, which was the attitude of Britain and to which

France had become reconciled. He was also disheartened by the reluctance of the leaders of France, and undoubtedly also of Britain, to discuss a joint policy for the Middle East. In such a mood, Ben-Gurion was not disposed to show undue flexibility and a readiness to make concessions.

I thought he exaggerated the danger to Israel during the thirty-six or so hours when she would be facing Egypt alone. I was not sure whether he really believed in the dark picture he kept painting of Egyptian planes wreaking havoc and destruction on Israel's cities or whether he did so for tactical reasons. Or perhaps he was preparing the ground for a withdrawal from the whole affair.

He opened the consultations by asking whether we thought there was anything more we could suggest to Pineau for transmission to Eden. Peres came up with an idea to send an Israeli vessel from Haifa to Port Said. The Egyptians would undoubtedly stop it and prevent its passage through the Canal. Peres thought such action might offer a good pretext for war and for Anglo-French intervention. Ben-Gurion received this proposal in silence.

We returned to the subject of our differences with the British. I said we should not regard our day and a half of fighting alone as a critical problem that could not be overcome. From the military point of view, if this was the one stumbling block to a campaign in Suez, then I was in favor of accepting the British proposal.

Ben-Gurion observed that Britain was demanding not only that we fight alone for a time but that we should open the campaign with a large force and reach the Canal area. Paratroop units dropped behind enemy lines could be cut off, as had happened to the "blocking" unit at Kalkilia, and would suffer heavy casualties. Had we forgotten the mood of our people after that action?

Our public was depressed after Kalkilia, I told Ben-Gurion, because our considerable losses had been incurred in an operation that decided nothing. The public knew that despite the action and the casualties, terrorism was likely to continue. With the projected campaign, however, the situation was different. The public might not grasp its purpose on the first day of battle. But as it developed to its full scope, followed by Anglo-French action, they would recognize that this was a decisive war, and even if casualties were high, the public would endure it. I had no doubt that the majority of our people would see this campaign as an opportunity not to be missed. If it were, we would have to fight alone in the future and our casulties might be much higher.

I followed with an analysis of the operational plan. I thought it had intrinsic merit and could also satisfy the British requirements. I proposed that on D-day, after dusk, we drop a paratroop battalion close to the Canal at a place called Mitla, and the same night a mechanized brigade would capture the Egyptian border positions of Nakeb and Kusseima. The column would push on the next day, capture Thamad and Nakhl on the way to Mitla, and join up with the paratroop battalion at the pass.

Under this plan, we would not put our Air Force into action on the first day—apart from making the paratroop drops, which we would try to do without being spotted. We would not attack Egyptian airfields and would try to avoid air battles, unless our ground forces were attacked—and even then we would limit ourselves to protective air cover. In this way I hoped that on the first day the battles would be strictly localized. This should encourage the Egyptians to assess our actions as no more than a large-scale reprisal operation, which they would not wish to turn into a full-fledged war. They were unlikely to cross the border or to bomb Israel's cities and airfields.

This plan should satisfy the British, for it contained the elements they demanded: our forces would be operating close to the Canal (Mitla is about thirty miles from Suez); and they would be large enough to commit what Britain would call a "real act of war," comprising a paratroop battalion, a mechanized brigade, and air squadrons. We should tell the British the size of our force but not the location of the paratroop landings or the axis of movement of the mechanized brigade. This was not their affair. They would no doubt think we intended operating along the northern El Arish-Kantara axis and not in the south, in the desert area of Sinai.

The capture of the positions noted in the plan on the first night was also a good opening for our army, mainly because our primary political objective was Sharm el-Sheikh at the southern tip of Sinai, and we had therefore to continue advancing southward. As for the paratroop battalion, it would not be cut off for long. Reinforcements would reach it within forty-eight hours at the most. I did not expect it to be attacked on the first night, so that the longest it would have to fight alone was one day.

Ben-Gurion listened very carefully to my details of the plan, the main lines of which he had already heard at earlier discussions. He made no comment, just as he made none on Peres' proposal. It was clear that he had not digested all the information and that he had not yet made up his mind on the basic question of whether, under the present conditions, the campaign was acceptable to Israel. I asked

Ben-Gurion whether I should present my suggestion to Pineau. He agreed that I should on the condition that I indicated it was my personal proposal without committing him to it. He said the same about Peres' suggestion of sending an Israeli vessel to Port Said. To make his point even clearer, Ben-Gurion retired to his room, and only Peres and I continued the meeting with Pineau and Bourges-Maunoury. The absence of Ben-Gurion underlined the fact that our proposals had no official backing.

When we entered the conference room, we found the French awaiting us impatiently. Pineau kept glancing at his watch, for he had business to attend to at the Foreign Ministry before leaving for London. Peres opened with his suggestion and elaborated on the suitable consequences that would follow the attempt of an Israeli ship to pass through the Suez Canal. Pineau said that this might well be a good plan, but it was not wise to bring up a new scheme at this stage, for the British would use it as an excuse to delay and perhaps even shelve the whole project.

I now presented my plan together with Israel's requests that followed from it. I did not detail the operational part, but simply outlined it in general terms. When I had finished, Pineau asked me to repeat my proposals so that he could take them down in writing. When he had done this, he read me his notes and said that these would serve as his terms of reference in his talk that night with Eden. I stressed that these were my suggestions and had not yet been approved by Ben-Gurion. He brushed this aside and remarked with conviction: "I know, I know how you fellows work." I envied him his confidence!

Pineau left us to go to London. We were to meet the next day on his return. Ben-Gurion remained in his room, and Peres and I returned to our Paris hotel and decided to take the evening off.

For the "evening off," we went to a Montmartre nightclub called "Nouvelle Eve," where we sat in a small and crowded balcony and turned our eyes to the stage. But apparently when heart and head are absorbed in a totally different world, one becomes indifferent even to the displays of the most exotic Parisian stripteasers. We moved off to a small bistro for some coffee. As we were leaving, we heard a startled voice exclaim in good Galilean Hebrew: "Hey, boys, did you see who just passed? Moshe Dayan and Shimon Peres! I wonder what's up? It must be something secret, for Dayan is hiding behind dark glasses!"

We had promised ourselves an evening free from care, but when we returned to the hotel I could not help thinking about our problems. I tried to sum up for myself how things stood, in preparation for the final and decisive meeting on the next day.

From the French we would receive all the air aid they could give —two or three fighter squadrons. I thought we would manage with that. The divergences of view between the British and us had narrowed, and there was no point in continuing to plow that furrow. The distance between us was not great, and if they really intended to back out, it would not be on account of the few hours' difference between their request and our plan.

The problem was Ben-Gurion's stand. I had no doubt that his cool reaction to my plan that day had not been a tactical pose, as some thought, but a reflection of his doubts and anxieties. He was still grappling with the basic question: should we or should we not go ahead? He had given voice to his reservations both in our talks with the French and at our internal consultations. For one thing, he did not share the optimism of the French over the American stand. He even tried several times to persuade them to put off the campaign until after the American elections and to try to secure the U.S. president's agreement on the action. For another, he was disappointed over the French reluctance to enter into discussions on a comprehensive policy on the Middle East. He was disappointed not because he was turned down, but because he was convinced that the military campaign alone, if not part of a logical overall policy, would not secure its aims. Britain's behavior toward us, hardly "gentlemanly," also aroused suspicion and mistrust. Ben-Gurion was not at all convinced that if complications developed with other Arab states, Britain would not shake off Israel and rush to the aid of Jordan and Iraq.

On the other hand, I was equally certain that he was as aware as I was, even more so, of the significance to us of a campaign coordinated with France and Britain against Nasser. He knew that it bore fruitful prospects of settling some of our most burdensome problems, which would be difficult for us to solve without the campaign.

As to the military plan, I believed that Ben-Gurion was afraid of heavy casualties during the first few days, when we would be fighting alone. He seemed to assume that at the start of our offensive, the Egyptian Air Force would immediately send up its Soviet Ilyushin bombers to attack Tel Aviv and Haifa, causing massive loss of civilian life and widespread destruction. I did not share these fears. Of course we could not expect to wiggle between the raindrops and emerge completely dry, but I thought we could avoid getting drenched. I believed we would be able to give the initial stage of our operation the limited character of a reprisal action and at the same time do what was expected of us by the British and the French, namely, put a significant force close to the Canal. The Egyptians would not recognize it as the start of a comprehensive campaign.

It was in conformity with this aim that I had introduced two basic changes in our original operational plan. One concerned our opening ground action, which would now be the paratroop drop at Mitla and not the capture of El Arish. The earlier plan had called for us to control northern Sinai in the first stage, so it was to begin with an assault on El Arish, the capital city of Sinai commanding the main route between Egypt and Israel. This route extends across the northern edge of Sinai, running along the Mediterranean coast, and is served by a railroad, an asphalt highway, an airfield, and sources of sweet water. The region around it naturally held concentrations of the main Egyptian forces assigned to the Israeli front.

In contrast to El Arish, the Mitla Pass is close to the southern end of the Suez Canal, and its geographic link with Israel is an unpaved desert track which bisects the Sinai Peninsula. This track was defended by small Egyptian units, and the pass itself was uninhabited. I therefore thought that the Egyptian military staff would interpret a paratroop drop at Mitla as no more than a raid. I did not believe that Egypt's army commanders would conceive the possibility of a campaign to conquer Sinai that did not begin with an attempt to gain control of the two northern axes, El Arish and Bir Gafgafa. Moreover, I reckoned that on the next day, when our mechanized brigade captured the defense positions of Thamad and Nakhl on the Mitla axis, the Egyptians would view the development as a move to bring our isolated Mitla unit safely back to Israel.

The second change affected our air activity. We would not start by bombing Egyptian airfields but would limit ourselves in the first two days to giving air support to our ground forces and to protecting the skies of Israel. This change, too, was designed to strengthen the Egyptian impression that we were engaged in a limited action and not in a full-scale war.

There was naturally some risk in acting on these assumptions. If they should prove wrong, and Egypt launched an air attack on Israel's cities, we would pay dearly for having passed up the chance of surprise by failing to knock out the Egyptian Air Force while it was still on the ground. But I thought this would happen only if the Egyptians secured intelligence of our plans. In the normal course of developments, it was doubtful that the Egyptian General Staff would at first have any precise idea of what was happening. True, they would receive information from their units under attack. But such units often reported the presence of large Israeli formations even when they were faced by nothing larger than a platoon. Egyptian General Headquarters was thus already accustomed to false alarms. Only on the next morning, when the reality would confirm the warning, would the Egyptian chief of staff consider his reaction. He would certainly not hesitate to put all his forces into action against the Israeli units which had penetrated Egyptian territory. But I did not believe he would promptly send his planes to bomb Tel Aviv.

It seemed reasonable to predict that on the first day of fighting, the battles would be localized to the Nakhl-Mitla axis. A day later, at dawn, action was expected to be launched by the British and French forces. If this really took place, we would be able to develop our operations in two directions: continued advance to the south, to Sharm el-Sheikh, and an attack in the north on Rafah and El Arish. But if the plan were disrupted for whatever reason and we had to halt the campaign, we could evacuate our Mitla unit through the Nakhl-Thamad axis, which would then be under our control. It would be thought that we had been engaged in only a reprisal action, and with its completion our forces had returned to Israel. It was with these reflections that I fell asleep that night.

At 11:30 the next morning, October 24, Shimon Peres and I were summoned by Ben-Gurion for final consultations. We drove to the house where he was staying and found him enjoying the sunny autumn morning in the garden. Before we got down to the principal issues, he asked me to explain once again the main moves in the operational plan I had proposed. This was best done with the help of a sketch map showing the location and movement of our forces, as well as the main military objectives. I had no paper on me, so Shimon Peres pulled out a pack of cigarettes and handed it to me. That was good enough, and on it I traced the familiar triangular outline of the Sinai Peninsula bounded on the west by the Gulf of Suez, on the east by the Gulf of Aqaba, and on the north by the Mediterranean. I marked it with three arrows. The center one ran through the middle of Sinai, pointing west. This represented the flight of the paratroops to be dropped at Mitla and the line of advance of the mechanized brigade that would be linking up with them. The parallel arrow above it showed the westward movement of the armor through northern Sinai along the Mediterranean coastal strip. The third arrow showed the southward advance of the mobile force thrusting toward Sharm el-Sheikh. I was rather glad I did not have a proper map at the time. On the white and smooth cigarette box, with not a sign of mountain, sand dune, or wadi, the plan looked simple and very easy to carry out.

With this rough sketch before us, I described to Ben-Gurion the broad military moves I envisaged in the campaign—if he decided to go ahead. Whether he had or not I could not have told at that moment, though his very request for a repetition of this military information was encouraging.

He then drew forth a sheet on which he had written a number of questions that he had prepared for this meeting. As he read them to us, my mind grew steadily easier, for they were mostly "how," "what," and "when" questions, not "if," and it was evident that he had reached a positive decision on our joining the campaign.

The questions he asked can be gauged from the replies I gave:

• D-day for the Israeli army would be Monday, October 29, 1956, at 5 P.M.

• D-day for the British and French would be Wednesday.

• Upon Egypt's rejection of the ultimatum, British and French forces would start bombing Egyptian airfields at dawn on Wednesday, October 31, and on Friday, November 2, two French brigades would land.

• As far as I knew, British and French forces would total 4 infantry brigades, 400 fighter aircraft, and 120 bombers.

• I did not know if they intended to control both sides of the Canal or only the west bank.

• As to whether they would march on Cairo if this became necessary, I did not know, and I doubted whether they did.

• The French said their forces would remain together with the British in the Canal Zone, and they would not let Egyptian forces cross to the east of it or Israeli forces to the west.

• On their plans for the future of the Sinai Peninsula, all I knew was that Selwyn Lloyd's secretary had told me over dinner: "I hope you don't have dreams of seizing this opportunity to take Sinai."

• I had no idea whether the Egyptians would establish a new regime.

• As to whether Britain guaranteed the neutrality of Jordan and Iraq, Selwyn Lloyd had said that Britain would not countenance an Israeli attack. But if we were attacked by Jordan and we retaliated, she would not intervene.

• On what would happen with the British forces in Amman and Aqaba, I thought they would stay put.

• Would we be permitted to capture the Straits of Tiran? The French had said "By all means" and had told us that the British did not care if we captured areas of Sinai lying to the east of the Canal. Selwyn Lloyd's secretary had also told me that the British would not object to small border adjustments we might make in the course of the campaign.

• What kind of formation would we send to the Canal area on D-day? Not less than a battalion, though I thought the British might ask for at least a brigade. We were interested in using a small force.

• I thought we would delay the capture of Gaza and Rafah until the Egyptian units there had had a chance to digest the news of what was happening in the Canal Zone.

Egyptian forces in the Gaza Strip area consisted of two divisions, one a Palestinian. I thought that on the Monday and Tuesday, after the start of our action and before the Anglo-French attack, Egyptian reinforcements would stream from west to east, namely, from Egypt to Sinai and Gaza. After Wednesday, when our allies were to go into action, the Egyptian movement would be in the reverse direction, retreating to Egypt.

The consultations lasted until 2 P.M. with Ben-Gurion continuing to probe and question. When we had risen and were about to go, he said, almost as an afterthought: "Moshe's plan is good. It saves lives." In the next breath he switched to another subject which apparently had been puzzling him ever since he had read Procopius on the plane coming over. "I wonder," he said, "how a Jewish realm could have subsisted in Yotvat without water. Why, the Jews almost destroyed Moses over the problem of drinking water."

At 4 P.M. Pineau returned from London, and we were immediately called to the conference room. Pineau announced that within the hour, representatives of Britain would be arriving, and he believed it was possible to reach a final arrangement. He had met Eden and, as he hoped, had found his approach far warmer than that of Lloyd.

As for the pretext required by the British, they again stressed that it had to be a "full-scale act of war." The British agreed to advance the timetable and go into action on the night of the 30th, that is, at 4 A.M., dawn, on Wednesday. They also agreed that in the wording of the ultimatum, a paragraph would be included on a cease-fire, so that any subsequent Egyptian bombing of Israeli targets would be regarded as a breach of the conditions of the ultimatum.

In addition to the demand that both armies fall back from the

Canal, the ultimatum would contain the specific requirement that British and French armed forces enter the Canal Zone. The Egyptians would certainly not agree to this, so there was no chance of their accepting the ultimatum. The demands to Israel and Egypt would not include the word "ultimatum." The term used would be "appeal." Israel would be asked only to cease fire and to retire from the Canal.

At 4:30 P.M. the British representatives arrived. One was a Mr. Logan, who had been introduced to us on the previous occasion as Selwyn Lloyd's secretary. With him as head of the delegation was another "secretary," Patrick Dean. The level of this delegation had undoubtedly been lowered by the substitution of a Foreign Office official for the foreign minister, but from the practical point of view I thought the absence of Selwyn Lloyd would prove no loss.

Before we were joined by the British, we had sat on comfortable armchairs in a corner of the room. We now ranged ourselves around the circular table, and the meeting assumed an official air. Pineau opened and presented the main items as they had been agreed upon by all the parties. Ben-Gurion raised the question of British aid to Jordan if she should attack Israel. He also announced our intention to capture the Straits of Tiran, which were "Israel's Suez Canal." The British asked about our operational plan, but I declined to give details. I said only that we would stand by our commitments on time, place, and size of our forces. Neither did I give any details to the French, saying only that our paratroop unit would be dropped closer to the city of Suez than to Port Said.

At 5 P.M. a small group of us adjourned to a nearby room to sum up our consultations. Participating for Israel were myself and an aide from our military attaché's office. It was heavy going, and our discussions lasted two hours. When it was over we began to hear the professional tap-tap of a typewriter from an adjoining room.

The principles of the plan that emerged were as follows:

• On the afternoon of October 29, 1956, Israeli forces would launch a large-scale attack on the Egyptian forces with the aim of reaching the Canal Zone by the following day.

• After being apprised of these events, the governments of Britain and France, on October 30, 1956, would submit to the governments of Egypt and Israel, separately and simultaneously, appeals formulated in the spirit of the following basic lines.

To the government of Egypt:

Absolute cease-fire.

Withdrawal of all forces to ten miles from the Canal.

Acceptance of the temporary occupation of the key positions on the Canal by Anglo-French forces in order to guarantee freedom of passage through the Canal to the vessels of all nations until a final arrangement was secured.

To the government of Israel:

Absolute cease-fire.

Withdrawal of her forces to ten miles east of the Canal.

• It would be reported to the government of Israel that the governments of France and Britain had demanded of the government of Egypt that she agree to the temporary occupation of the key positions on the Canal by Anglo-French forces. If either of the two governments rejected the appeal, or failed to give its agreement within twelve hours, the Anglo-French forces were liable to take the necessary measures to ensure that their demands were met.

• The government of Israel would not be required to fulfill the conditions of the appeal sent to her in the event that the government of Egypt failed to accept the conditions of the appeal which she would receive.

• If the government of Egypt failed to agree to the conditions presented to her in the allotted time, the Anglo-French forces would launch an attack on the Egyptian forces in the early-morning hours of October 31, 1956.

• The government of Israel would dispatch forces to seize the western shore of the Gulf of Aqaba and the islands of Tiran and Sanapir in order to ensure freedom of navigation in that gulf.

• Israel would not attack Jordan during the period of the operation against Egypt. But if by chance Jordan attacked Israel during that time, the British government would not go to Jordan's aid.

Ben-Gurion was tense, and he made no effort to conceal it. He read and reread the articles in the plan with scrupulous care, knitting his brows in furious concentration and murmuring each word to himself. He then neatly folded the paper and placed it in the inside pocket of his jacket.

The primary importance of the plan lay in its very existence. It set out the actions of the parties to the campaign and the aims each wished to achieve. On this subject of aims, there was a marked parallel between the Anglo-French goal of holding the Suez Canal in order to ensure free passage for all nations and the Israeli purpose of holding the western shore of the Gulf of Aqaba and the islands of Tiran and Sanapir to secure freedom of shipping in that stretch of water. The only substantive difference was that whereas the Anglo-French occupation of the Canal Zone was spoken of as *temporary*, the west coast of the Gulf of Aqaba was spoken of as being held—not held temporarily.

There was another parallel. Israel would not be a partner in the capture of the Canal Zone, and so the British and French governments were notifying her of their intention to hold the Canal. And the British and French would not be partners in the capture of the western shore of the Gulf of Aqaba. Israel would do this alone and occupy it, and so she was bringing this to the attention of France and Britain.

Also noteworthy from the Israeli point of view was the fact that the plan solved the problem of the ultimatum. It removed every ingredient of threat and warning to Israel and set the Anglo-French appeal in its proper place as part of the overall plan of action. In this way, it was only to Egypt that the appeal bore the significance of an ultimatum, while to Israel it was part of the procedure.

Now that the decision had been taken, every moment was precious. I stole away from the conference room and sent a "Most Immediate" signal to my chief of operations: "Good prospects for Operation Kadesh soonest. Mobilize units immediately. Ensure secrecy in mobilization. Activate deception to produce impression that mobilization aimed against Jordan because of entry of Iraqi forces. Leaving midnight tonight, arriving tomorrow morning."

When I returned to the conference room, I found everyone standing around full of nervous tension and not quite knowing what to do with themselves. Planning to launch a campaign was not the kind of event over which one clinked glasses or indulged in comradely backslapping. However, there was a general sense of deep satisfaction that the effort had been fruitful. The first to leave were the British, mumbling as they went words of politeness tinged with humor and not quite comprehensible. We were the next to shake hands with our French hosts, and we did so with genuine warmth. Ben-Gurion went up to his room, and we drove to our Paris hotel.

We arrived back in Israel at midday on October 25 and drove straight to General Staff headquarters. In the plane I had drafted several orders and guidelines for the General Staff and field commands which were to be issued immediately. The most important was the one to Operations Branch, and I was now able for the first time to give clear directives on the framework of the campaign for its operational order.

This new order set the D-day and H-hour and also changed three of the instructions contained in the original operational order. The first concerned the paragraph on aims. Stress was now laid on the creation of a threat to the Suez Canal, in accordance with our commitment in the plan, and then came the two basic objectives of the campaign—the capture of the Straits of Tiran and the defeat of the Egyptian forces.

I had had several discussions with Ben-Gurion on this last point during our stay in Paris. It was clear that we had no interest in "destroying the forces of the enemy," as was customary with most armies in the framing of war aims. In the state of affairs that existed between Israel and her neighbors, it was best to shed as little blood as possible. I therefore established that our aim was "to confound the military array of the Egyptian forces and bring about their collapse." This meant that our army was to seize the crossroads, dominating emplacements, and key fortifications which would give us control of the area and thereby compel the enemy to surrender.

The second change in the operational order affected the phases of our action. Instead of starting with the capture of northern Sinai, we would begin with its central region, the Nakhl-Mitla axis, with the paratroop drop at Mitla.

The third change covered the use of our Air Force. In contrast to our earlier plans, the campaign would not open with an air attack by us. The Air Force would transport the paratroopers to the drop area and maintain a state of alert in its airfields. If the Egyptians sent their aircraft into action, we would try during the two days we would be fighting alone to limit the aerial war to the region under enemy attack. When I stepped out of the plane on my return from Paris, I hoped that these would be the final changes. Only four days remained to the opening of the campaign.

15

THE SINAI CAMPAIGN

WE WOULD BE fighting in the vast expanse of the Sinai—the northern half desert; the southern half mountainous, impassable; the total, thrice the size of Israel at the time. Our objectives were to neutralize the armed Egyptian threat, end the *fedayeen* terrorism from the Gaza Strip, and gain control of one pinpoint of land, Sharm el-Sheikh, near the southern tip of the peninsula. By capturing Sharm, we would automatically break the Egyptian blockade of the Gulf of Aqaba, a primary aim of the campaign. But we could reach it, and hold it, only by defeating the Egyptian army in the whole of Sinai, for the only road to Sharm lay at the extreme western edge of the peninsula, along the Egyptian-held Gulf of Suez.

Sharm el-Sheikh overlooks the vital Straits of Tiran, through which ships from the Orient and East Africa must pass to reach the Gulf of Aqaba and the Israeli town of Eilat. If ships could make that journey, then Eilat could become a large port and thereby bring life to the whole of the Negev. The straits themselves are formed by the Sinai coast, on one side, and the tiny island of Tiran, on the other. In between, the navigable narrows for ocean-going ships are only 650 feet wide. Thus the Egyptians were able to blockade the straits by simply placing a few guns on a bleak promontory three miles from Sharm el-Sheikh.

In describing the campaign, I have drawn on the diary I kept at the time.

The campaign opened in the late afternoon of October 29, when a 395-man battalion of the 202nd Paratroop Brigade dropped near the eastern entrance to the Mitla Pass, deep inside the Sinai and about thirty miles from the Suez Canal. They had taken off at 5:20 P.M. in sixteen Dakota transports flying low across the Sinai desert to evade Egyptian radar. Only when they approached the jump area, just two minutes' flying time away from the Egyptian air bases, did they rise to parachute-opening height. Two hours earlier, on a hair-raising operation to confound enemy communications, four of our piston-engined Mustangs flew over Sinai and cut the overhead telephone lines with their propellers and wings only 4 yards from the ground.

In the meantime, the other battalions of the paratroop brigade assembled on the Jordanian border as a feint to deceive the Egyptians and their allies. These soldiers then had to cover more than sixty-five desert miles across the Negev, from the eastern to the western border of Israel, before starting their battle drive through Sinai. They did it in nine hours and lost many vehicles to breakdowns and the sandy terrain. But the brigade commander, Arik Sharon, allowed none of his difficulties to stand in the way. With or without vehicles the column would maintain its advance, and he swept on to the first Egyptian position in central Sinai, Kuntilla. The Egyptians fled at their approach. The column pressed on westward and deeper into Sinai, crossing the stubborn desert track, which took a further toll of wheeled vehicles and another four tanks. Finally, with only 2 out of 13 tanks left, the brigade reached its next objective twenty-five miles away, the Thamad stronghold, where it fought its first major battle. The paratroopers aboard their half-tracks dashed across ditches and through minefields and broke right into the well-fortified and well-equipped Egyptian positions. After forty minutes of brisk fighting, Thamad fell. The sun had helped, shining on the backs of our men and into the eyes of the defenders.

While this battle was at its height, other units of Sharon's brigade advanced to the next major enemy stronghold, Nakhl, capturing it in twenty minutes. Soon thereafter, the first battalion of the brigade, 180 miles from its starting point, linked up with its sister battalion that had parachuted near the Mitla Pass twenty-four hours earlier. The southern axis was now secured, and with this opening move in the campaign, we had outflanked all the Egyptian positions in north-eastern Sinai—and the battalion that had been dropped near Mitla was no longer in danger of being cut off.

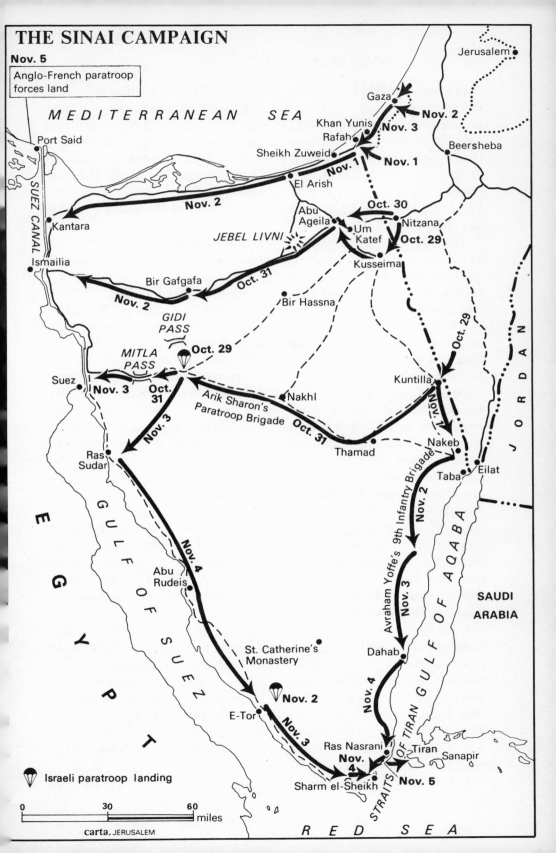

THE SINAI CAMPAIGN

Nov. 5

Anglo-French paratroop
forces land

MEDITERRANEAN SEA

Jerusalem

Gaza
Nov. 2

Khan Yunis
Rafah **Nov. 3**

Beersheba

Sheikh Zuweid
Nov. 1

Port Said

El Arish **Nov. 1**

Nov. 2

Kantara

Abu Ageila **Oct. 30**

Nitzana

Oct. 29

Um Katef

JEBEL LIVNI

Ismailia

Kusseima

Bir Gafgafa **Oct. 31**

Nov. 2

Bir Hassna

Oct. 29

GIDI PASS

Oct. 29

MITLA PASS

Nakhl

Kuntilla

Suez **Nov. 3**

Oct. 31

Arik Sharon's
Paratroop Brigade **Oct. 31**

Nov. 3

Thamad

Nakeb

J O R D A N

Ras Sudar

Taba Eilat

Avraham Yoffe's 9th Infantry Brigade **Nov. 2**

Nov. 4

Abu Rudeis

Nov. 3

SAUDI ARABIA

E G Y P T

G U L F   O F   S U E Z

St. Catherine's Monastery

Dahab

Nov. 4

Nov. 2

E-Tor

Nov. 3

Ras Nasrani
Nov. 4

Tiran
Sanapir

G U L F   O F   A Q A B A

STRAITS OF TIRAN

Sharm el-Sheikh **Nov. 5**

🪂 Israeli paratroop landing

0   30   60
miles

carta, JERUSALEM

RED SEA

In another action on the first night, the southern position of Nakeb, on the Negev-Sinai border, was also captured. And early the next morning our 4th Brigade took the vital crossroads of Kusseima, also near the Negev-Sinai border north of Kuntilla, thus opening an additional gateway into Sinai from the east and threatening the southern flank of the strong Egyptian forces to its immediate north. The capture of Kusseima completed the opening phase of our operations. The four objectives I had set for the first night of the campaign were in our hands.

The Egyptian military reacted to this first phase as I had expected. They simply did not exploit their advantage of massive superiority in Russian arms and equipment and their much larger Air Force, equipped with the latest Soviet jet fighters and bombers. In their strongholds, the Egyptian troops put up initial resistance. But when our forces attacked them and they saw other units bypassing their positions to cut them off, some chose to flee rather than to fight. And once our men broke through their defenses, the enemy soldiers who had remained to fight preferred to surrender rather than engage in hand-to-hand combat. In the air, too, our forecast of the Egyptian response proved correct: if we would not attack their airfields, they would not extend their air operations beyond the borders of Sinai. However, the Egyptian aircraft did take advantage of the fact that their air bases were far closer to the battlefield than ours, and thus could spend more time over the combat area. They did, indeed, harass our ground forces, but they came off second best in encounters with our planes, and they tried to avoid aerial battle. During the early hours of the morning, the Egyptian Air Force had a field day attacking the fully exposed 202nd Brigade advancing openly toward Mitla. But then our Air Force started patrols to protect the column and kept them up almost without a break. The Egyptian planes steered clear of them. After all, it was not the planes but the pilots who had to do the battling.

I was in the south when news came through that the 7th Brigade's reconnaissance unit had just seized control of the important Deika defile, a narrow pass about fifteen miles west of Kusseima, near the Negev-Sinai border. This meant that the brigade, the main armor of the central task force, could now come upon the key stronghold of Abu Ageila from the rear. The next two days could prove crucial, for we would then fight the major battles in the northern sector of Sinai, where the Egyptians had concentrated most of their forces. They would be battles of decision.

Returning to General Headquarters from the south, I learned that the Anglo-French forces had postponed their attack and would not start bombing Egypt's air bases at dawn the next morning, October 31, as planned. I went to see Ben-Gurion, who was in bed with influenza, and he was very worried about the effect this delay might have on the position of our men at Mitla. His immediate reaction was to ask that they be withdrawn that very night. He was evidently recalling the Kalkilia episode and was concerned that the Mitla paratroops might be similarly trapped deep in enemy territory. I tried to reassure him. Even if the British and French canceled their invasion, I was confident that we could proceed with our campaign and emerge victorious. I argued that rather than withdraw from Mitla, our forces there should be strengthened, and I hoped we would be able to do so. With great reluctance Ben-Gurion dropped the evacuation idea, but I could see that military logic did little to reduce his anxiety over the lives of our paratroops.

That evening Britain and France issued their ultimatum to Egypt and Israel, calling on both sides to stop the fighting and withdraw to a distance of ten miles from the Suez Canal. Egypt had to accept temporary Anglo-French occupation of Port Said, Ismailia, and Suez in order to guarantee freedom of transit through the Canal. Non-compliance with the ultimatum "within twelve hours" would bring about armed intervention. This would provide the British and French governments with their pretext to capture the Canal Zone by military force.

The U.S. government was equally active—in the opposite direction. That day Ben-Gurion received a cable prompted by President Eisenhower suggesting that Israel withdraw her forces from Sinai. Compliance would be deeply appreciated by the president. When the desired Israeli reply was not forthcoming, Henry Cabot Lodge, the U.S. representative to the United Nations, requested an emergency meeting of the Security Council, at which he tabled a resolution calling upon Israel to withdraw immediately, on pain of sanctions, and urging all other nations "to refrain from the use of force or threat of force in the area." The meeting was adjourned for five hours at the request of France, Britain, and Israel, and when it reconvened news had already come through of the Anglo-French ultimatum. President Eisenhower regarded this as an act of fraud and treachery by his allies. He ordered his representatives to throw the full weight of the United States against the consummation of the Anglo-French plan.

The eventual hostile U.N. resolution was vetoed by France and Britain.

In the meantime, Israel had replied to the ultimatum and accepted its terms on the assumption "that a positive response will also have been forthcoming from the Egyptian side." Egypt, however, replied as expected that she was not prepared to accept the Anglo-French demand, which meant that England and France could now move against Egypt.

Nevertheless, Anglo-French forces did not bomb Egyptian airfields in the Canal Zone after the expiration of the twelve-hour ultimatum, and Israeli forces in Sinai fought their heavy battles through the entire day of October 31 under the threat of massive attack by the Egyptian Air Force. Also on that day, Egypt moved additional heavy armored and infantry units into Sinai, sent its Navy into action against Israel's coasts, and rushed reinforcements by sea to Sharm el-Sheikh. Not until 5 P.M. that day did the Anglo-French force start bombing Egypt's air bases.

Failure of our allies to support us as promised did not prevent the 7th Brigade from conducting the most spectacular armored battles of the campaign, capturing Abu Ageila, the Ruafa dam, Bir Hassna, Jebel Livni, and Bir Hama in bitter fighting. By crushing the Egyptian forces in these formidable strongholds in northeastern and central Sinai, the way was opened for speedier advances and more varied outflanking movements of enemy formations in western Sinai. The armored brigade registered these successes despite grave misadventures, including—and arising out of—the malfunctioning of the air-support signal instruments, so that for two days the brigade was unable to summon Air Force aid.

Later in the day, the same battalion team that had captured the key stronghold of Abu Ageila in the morning was involved in the heaviest fighting of the armored brigade. This was at the Ruafa dam, a well-defended locality immediately southwest of Abu Ageila. Its capture would seal the Egyptians in the strongholds of Um Katef and Um Shihan to the east.

The men of this battalion had been fighting for three days without rest, and they were exhausted, but their battalion commander kept pressing them on, urging them to exploit to the full the momentum of their breakthrough.

The assault was put in from the southwest, and facing our men on this sector were well-entrenched defense posts consisting of more than twenty anti-tank nests, including anti-tank guns, 57 mm. guns, 30 mm. cannon, and six 25-pounders sited.

The attack started after sunset. In the dim, dust-laden twilight, the weary eyes of the tank crews could hardly see ahead. The Egyptians opened up their frontal fire with everything they had and right away scored a direct hit on one of the half-tracks. All the men aboard were wounded. This blow stopped the rest of the half-tracks, but they recovered in a few minutes and continued their advance. Soon darkness fell, and all that lit the black night were the illuminated flight paths of the criss-crossing shells and the bursts of flame from exploding Egyptian ammunition stores. Anti-tank fire struck the tanks of our assault unit, and we suffered casualties. But the men pressed on. In the final stage of the battle, our tanks ran out of ammunition and their crews fought on with hand grenades and sub-machine guns. After clearing the Egyptian posts and their communication trenches, the wounded were assembled and bandaged by the light of jeep headlights. If the Egyptians had counter-attacked at this moment, it is doubtful if our men could have stood up to them. Even the single tank that was comparatively unscathed was now without fuel and ammunition. But the Egyptian troops, too, needed a few hours to organize themselves for a counter-attack, and when it came, just after 9 P.M., our armored unit had already refueled its tanks and restocked them with ammunition and was properly arrayed for defense. Artillery from nearby strongholds and close covering fire from mobile anti-tank guns supported the Egyptian attack. But it failed, and then the enemy retired to nearby El Arish, on the Mediterranean coast, leaving behind their guns and their dead.

We were now in virtual control of the three southern routes across Sinai: Nakhl-Mitla; the one running through Jebel Livni; and the southwesterly route through Bir Hassna.

Apart from the armored battles in the Abu Ageila region, and the numerous aerial engagements in the skies over Sinai, the other major fighting that occurred that day, October 31, was in the Mitla Pass, and it involved the paratroop brigade. It began at 12:30 P.M. and it lasted seven desperate hours.

Long before the start, soon after the main body of the brigade had broken through the Nakhl axis and linked up with its battalion dropped at the Parker Memorial near Mitla, the brigade commander had sought permission to advance and seize the pass. However, he was only given specific permission to send out a patrol, on condition that it avoid serious combat. The unit that set forth was not "a patrol" but in fact a full combat team, quite capable of capturing the pass. It consisted of two infantry companies on half-tracks, a detachment of three tanks, the brigade reconnaissance unit on trucks, and a troop of heavy mortars in support. Commanding the unit was a battalion commander. The deputy commander of the brigade went along too.

As soon as the convoy entered the defile, it was fired on from the hillocks flanking it on both sides. The full combat unit continued through the defile on the assumption that it was held only by light Egyptian forces. As the spearhead of the convoy penetrated deeper into the narrow pass, the firing grew in intensity, and the half-tracks —and the troops they were carrying—were hit. The commander of the unit rushed forward to rescue them, but he, too, found himself trapped, unable to advance or to retire. Nevertheless, the forward portion of the convoy, totaling more than one company, succeeded in breaking through and reaching the western end of the pass, despite the murderous fire poured into the defile. The rest of the force remained pinned down, their casualties mounting under the continuous heavy fire from the heights above.

From one o'clock in the afternoon until eight in the evening, the paratroopers fought a tough and bitter battle until they finally overcame the Egyptian opposition and captured the pass. Not even a veteran combat-hardened unit like this one had ever experienced such a battle. Their casualties, too, were unprecedentedly heavy: 38 killed and 120 wounded.

The Egyptian troops had taken up position in natural and artificial cavities in the slopes of the hills on either side of the pass, covering the track beneath them with automatic weapons and anti-tank guns. Early the previous morning the enemy sent five infantry companies through the western entrance to occupy the pass. They were heavily armed with anti-tank guns, about 40 Czech recoilless guns, and machine guns, and 4 Meteors covered by 6 MiGs from a nearby base provided air support. The Egyptian planes operated without interference, for owing to faulty communications our men could not signal our Air Force for help.

At the very start of the battle the paratroopers' fuel truck went up in flames, to be followed by the ammunition truck and three other vehicles. The company commander who jumped from his half-track was killed on the spot. The supporting heavy mortars were knocked out of action. Enemy fire also hit and immobilized four half-tracks, a tank, a jeep, and an ambulance. The paratroopers were forced to scramble up to the hillside caves occupied by the Egyptians and in hand-to-hand fighting captured one position after another. They had no other course of action, for it was the only way they could end the battle as victors and extricate the scores of wounded and killed.

This, then, was precisely what they did. I doubt whether there is another unit in our army which could have managed to get the better of the enemy under such conditions. Those paratroopers who had succeeded in breaking through the trap, together with two additional companies of reinforcements, worked their way around the Egyptian posts, climbed to the ridges of the hills, and then scrambled down and broke into the line of enemy cave positions on the slopes. By the end of the battle, there were 150 Egyptians dead, and the rest of the enemy, the fit and the wounded, disappeared into the darkness and fled across the Suez Canal.

The valor, daring, and fighting spirit of the paratroop commanders were qualities to be applauded and encouraged. And certainly this bloody capture of the pass might have been justified if the task of the brigade was to reach Suez. But in the circumstances, when our aim was to proceed southward to capture Sharm el-Sheikh and not get any closer to Suez, there was no vital need to attack the Egyptian unit defending the approaches to the Canal. Moreover, after capturing the pass, the paratroopers continued to base themselves near the Parker Memorial. The pass was therefore attacked, captured, and abandoned.

Several officers of the General Staff told me, with disapproval, that I was too forgiving of the paratroopers, when I knew that they assaulted the Mitla defile against my orders and that their action had such murderous consequences. There was no need to say how much we all deplored their heavy casualties. But my complaint against the paratroop command was not so much over the battle itself as over their subterfuge in terming the operation a "patrol" in order to "satisfy" the General Staff. This made me sad, and I regretted that I had not succeeded in molding such relations of mutual trust that if they had wished to defy my orders, they would have done so directly and openly.

In analyzing the actions at Mitla, I made a distinction between the errors and the breach of orders. I was angered by the decision to attack in defiance of orders, but I could understand it. It was only eight years since the War of Independence, when I had been in charge of a commando battalion, and I could imagine a situation where I would decide to seize a tactical position to give a secure base to my unit even if my action went contrary to orders from General Headquarters. I could well believe that a commander could behave quite innocently, in the conviction that staff officers could not know the conditions or the enemy positions, and that only the man on the spot was capable of appreciating the situation and taking a correct decision.

The paratroopers' principal mistake was tactical. The unit command estimated that the Egyptians had not placed a strong force at Mitla, and they therefore allowed themselves to proceed along an easy topographical route, through the wadi, with their men bunched together aboard vehicles in column formation. They thought that even if they encountered enemy forces, they would be able to deploy and ready themselves in time for attack.

These paratroopers had plenty of self-reliance, and they had developed battle procedures based on speedy organization and the dash into action. But the special topographical features of the Mitla Pass did not suit such procedures.

In other circumstances, the paratroop command would doubtless have reconnoitered the area, either on the ground or from the air, before going into action. But with the brigade hundreds of miles inside enemy territory, cut off from the rest of our forces, and only a comparatively few miles away from the Egyptian tank and air bases, small wonder that they had been anxious to consolidate their position quickly.

For their mistaken judgment and tactical errors, the paratroop unit paid heavily in blood. As for the breach of my orders and my forgiving attitude, the truth is that I regard the problem as serious when a unit fails to fulfill its battle task, not when it goes beyond the bounds of duty and does more than is demanded of it.

The world strongly condemned our operations in Sinai, and the criticism grew even more intense with the Anglo-French intervention —first with the ultimatum and then with their bombing of Egyptian airfields on the evening of October 31. The United States led the campaign for the West, and Russia, of course, took a similar position, vigorously protesting against the military attack on her friend Egypt. Both these Powers were joined by an assorted choir of "peace at any price" enthusiasts, particularly vocal when the price did not have to be paid by them.

The gravest reaction to the Anglo-French venture occurred in Britain, where criticism was directed primarily against Prime Minister Eden. There was no doubt that the general public and even the majority of his Cabinet did not support his Suez action. Britain's army commanders made Eden's task no easier. They said they had been persuaded that Egypt had strong forces, and they had accordingly planned a complicated military operation and set a later date for the landing of their ground forces.

At the United Nations there was feverish activity to bring the fighting to a halt, particularly after the Anglo-French air attacks, and since Britain and France had vetoed action in the Security Council, an emergency meeting of the U.N. General Assembly was convened for the night of November 1.

It was clear to me even before this that the political clock was working against us and that international pressure to halt the military action would mount. The successes we had gained in only two days of fighting now made it possible for our task to be completed in another few days, but there was no certainty that those days would be given to us. We had to press on quickly. Our troops could have little rest.

It was with these thoughts that, together with the GOC Southern Command, I visited the 10th Brigade that day, Wednesday, October 31, and urged them to capture Um Katef with all due speed. This fort and nearby Um Shihan were the two places in the Abu Ageila stronghold area that remained in enemy hands and barred our breakthrough into Sinai on the central sector. Though we had nevertheless emerged into central Sinai by capturing Kusseima, Abu Ageila itself, and the Ruafa dam and were advancing westward, we were forced to go across dirt tracks in poor condition. This meant that they could create bottlenecks among our supply convoys and thus hold up our advance. Um Katef controlled a key stretch of the asphalt road which would solve our problem, and its capture would open a new axis of movement.

I did not find my meeting with the brigade officers at all agreeable. True, they were not a crack formation, like the paratroops or the armored corps. They were a reservist brigade of insufficiently trained infantrymen above average age. Furthermore it was apparent that their own officers doubted their capabilities as soldiers. Nevertheless, I became impatient with the officers and had no ear for their complaints about difficulties. I knew that their men were tired, supplies did not reach them in time, the nights were cold, the days hot, their dust-clogged rifles got jammed, their vehicles became stuck in the mud. But I had no solutions to such problems, except to stick it out. I could not change the Negev, and I had to have that new route opened.

They attacked Um Katef that night, but their heart was not in it. Nothing came of it. On the other hand, a unit of the 37th Armored Brigade, which advanced later that evening with determined spirit, also failed. Indeed, the officers were over-eager to rush the enemy defenses, dashing in on half-tracks without waiting for support tanks, which had been delayed. Faulty intelligence at Southern Command, lack of a sound operational plan, and the insufficient concentration of available strength also contributed to our failure. So did I in some measure. I had put pressure on the GOC Southern Command to hasten the opening of the new route through Um Katef. He in turn had put pressure on the brigade commander, saying that he had promised me it would be opened by first light. My orders had indeed been to speed its opening—though he could have had up to noon next day—and I had indeed demanded that this be done even if it meant a difficult frontal attack involving heavy casualties.

After the poor use of the 10th Brigade, the GOC Southern Command replaced the brigade commander, and I confirmed this change. I said at the time that the supreme function of a unit commander was to lead it in battle. If he did not stand the test, he should not be punished but he should give way to someone who could. Without going into all the misadventures on the night of the brigade attack, it was not poor direction, lack of skill, loss of control, or tactical error that led to failure. To my mind the fault was more grave from the military point of view: the unit did not make the effort required to enter into effective combat.

It was already possible to assess the fighting qualities of the Egyptians and their concept of warfare. In general, they fought well during the static phase of their combat. Dug in and using their anti-tank, field, and anti-aircraft guns from fixed positions prepared in advance, they fought effectively. But they became poor soldiers when we forced them to leave their entrenched posts or change their plans. They carried out few counter-attacks, and when they did their action appeared feeble. They clearly exaggerated the power of the defensive bastion, like their Abu Ageila cluster of strongholds, to block a penetration force in the terrain of Sinai without calling upon its counterpart mobile units, armor, paratroops, mechanized infantry, with air support. The Abu Ageila defense complex could play a decisive role only if it served as a base for mobile forces who could go out to engage an enemy seeking to break into Sinai.

Forty-eight hours after the start of the campaign, on the night of October 31 and right through to nightfall on the next day, the center of fighting shifted to the northern sector of Sinai, with attacks on the powerful defense positions of Rafah, at the southern end of the Gaza Strip, and a breakthrough to the approaches of El Arish on the Mediterranean coast. The defense area of Rafah was a veritable labyrinth of numerous entrenched positions, and our attack plan was adapted to these conditions. We split our forces into many small units, and each beat a path for itself through the minefields and barbed wire, broke through on its own to its target, and fought an independent battle. Reaching the heart of each stronghold required skill, daring, and ingenuity, and our men displayed these qualities. When lead vehicles hit a mine and started burning, their flames lit up the targets for the Egyptian gunners, and Israeli sappers had to crawl between exploding shells to clear new paths through the mine-fields. But they pressed on, reached their objective, deployed for the assault, and stormed the enemy.

When the lead tanks of the 27th Brigade approached the vital crossroads that would enable them to advance toward El Arish, they received the most joyous greeting from the infantrymen of the 1st Brigade, who had just captured it. Scattered shooting still continued, and from time to time the heads of Egyptian soldiers would pop up behind the cactus hedges. But the infantrymen could barely restrain their feelings. They came out of their positions and rushed forward to meet the oncoming tanks. Within minutes, tanks and half-tracks jammed the crossroads and huge grins lit up the dust-covered faces of the enthusiastic troops. Even hardened veterans fell upon their comrades in spontaneous embrace. I had followed the 27th Brigade throughout this attack, and my particular victim was the second in command of the 1st Brigade. We fell into each other's arms in the classic tradition of a Russian movie.

At 10:30 A.M., the 27th Brigade started its advance to El Arish, and we drove westward along the tarred road through the sand dunes in a light breeze that blew in from the Mediterranean. We encountered little opposition until we reached the El Jeradi salient, about halfway to our objective, where we fought a battle lasting more than an hour. There were further enemy posts that held us up, and it was not before nightfall that we reached the outskirts of El Arish. By now our brigade convoy had scattered and could not deploy for attack. The men were tired and the tanks needed refueling and maintenance. We postponed our entry into El Arish till the next morning. Before getting myself ready for the night, I looked through and replied to the signals which had come in from General Headquarters. I also confirmed my orders for the 9th Infantry Brigade to begin its march at dawn next morning, November 2, on Sharm el-Sheikh, and for the 11th Infantry Brigade to start its operation in the Gaza Strip. We were about to open the final phase of the campaign.

We entered El Arish without opposition at 6 A.M. The last Egyptian units had withdrawn during the night, having begun their flight at our approach. The fleeing soldiers had set a few military stores on fire, but these formed only a trifling part of the huge quantity of military equipment that was left. It was apparent that when the with-

drawal order was given, everyone had simply left his post and rushed
to join the convoys leaving the city. The hospital offered a gruesome
sight. On the operating table lay the body of a dead Egyptian soldier
with a leg just amputated. He had been abandoned in the middle of
the operation without a doctor or a nurse stopping to bandage him,
and he died from loss of blood. The hospital wounded, some of them
in the wards but most of them trying to hide in the courtyard and
garden, told us that when the medical personnel were informed that
ambulances awaited them, they ran from whatever they were doing,
pushed their way into the vehicles, and vanished. Not even a single
male nurse remained behind to treat the wounded, and casualties who
were in need of immediate attention—eighteen men—expired during
the night. They lay in the same position in which they had been left
when the flight started.

Those enemy troops not able to get away surrendered. But not all.
Some took to sniping, as I soon discovered. I was standing near the
open window of a building looking out onto the street when a sniper
crouching behind a fence fired a burst from his machine gun and hit
my signalman, who fell dead at my side.

The brigade did not linger long in the city. Combat teams went
off to secure the El Arish airfield and the road to Abu Ageila, and
others hurried westward to pursue the fleeing enemy toward Kantara
on the northern part of the Suez Canal. Inert enemy vehicles knocked
out by our Air Force cluttered the roads.

At 11 A.M. I took off in a Piper Cub from the El Arish airfield to
return to General Headquarters. I asked the pilot to circle low over
the city. But we quickly had to climb out of range of rifle and
machine-gun fire from Egyptian troops. They had taken cover among
bushes and folds in the surrounding dunes. From that height I could
see our armored brigade moving westward. Five hours after our entry
into El Arish, our lead vehicles were already tens of miles on their
way to the Canal. The battle for the northern axis acros Sinai, Rafah-
El Arish-Kantara, was virtually over.

As soon as I had returned from El Arish, I went to see Ben-Gurion
and found him fully recovered from the flu and in high spirits. He
questioned me about the battles of Rafah and El Arish and also on
what was happening on the other fronts. I told Ben-Gurion that British
naval vessels were patrolling the waters near Sharm el-Sheikh and I
asked whether he thought the British were likely to shell our forces.
"About the British," he replied, "I do not know, but about the British
Foreign Office I am prepared to believe anything."

Before leaving his room, I heard Ben-Gurion amiably chiding

officials who had come to him with Job-like tales of what was happening at the U.N. General Assembly. "Why are you so worried?" he asked. "So long as they are sitting in New York, and we in Sinai, the situation is not bad!"

Our overall casualties so far were a little more than 100 killed and almost 700 wounded—including the sick and those injured in traffic accidents. As to Egyptian casualties, we had not counted the enemy who had fallen. We had several thousand prisoners, despite all our efforts not to accept them. The adjutant general assured me that the behavior of our troops toward them was good and that possible revenge takes only one form—the prisoners are being fed Israeli army "rations"!

Also on that day, November 2, and the day before, the 27th Armored Brigade had completed its capture of the central axis, Kusseima-Jebel Livni-Ismailia. That day, too, our forces captured the Gaza Strip. The enemy was in a hopeless position there once Rafah and El Arish had fallen, and their resistance reflected the state of their morale.

The final task to be accomplished was the capture of Sharm el-Sheikh, and the 9th Brigade, which had been given that assignment, had begun its trek at five o'clock that morning, moving south along the western shore of the Gulf of Aqaba. Later in the day, we decided to strengthen the attack force. In the evening, two paratroop companies were dropped at the airfield at E-Tor, on the Gulf of Suez, and when this airfield was secured we began an air shuttle and flew in an infantry battalion. At midnight, another unit from the 202nd Paratroop Brigade, a battalion, left the Parker Memorial and moved southwestward over rough terrain to Ras Sudar, on the gulf, and continued south from there over the tarred road to E-Tor, 105 miles away. Later in the day, they carried out a reconnaissance of the road to Sharm el-Sheikh. The plan was for the 9th Brigade to come upon Sharm from the north, while the paratroops would approach from E-Tor and attack it from the south.

The next morning, November 3, I took off in a Dakota; flew over the 9th Brigade column, which was now forty-five difficult miles from Sharm el-Sheikh; spoke to the brigade commander by radio, since there was nowhere to land; continued over the central Sinai mountains to E-Tor; ordered the paratroops there to press on to the outposts of Sharm; discussed civilian administration problems with the infantry battalion that would be holding that area; returned via Mitla, where I briefed the 202nd Brigade commander; flew on to Bir Hama to see the 27th Armored Brigade commander, whose men had fought and captured more enemy positions than any other unit in this campaign; and made a last stop at El Arish, where I discussed steps to restore civilian life to the city with the formation commander. I returned to the General Headquarters command post at 7 P.M.

While the Sinai became a raging battleground, the international political front also seethed. The United Nations had held its emergency General Assembly meeting on November 1 and had adopted the resolution presented by John Foster Dulles, the American secretary of state, calling for an immediate cease-fire—which was directed against Britain, France, and Israel—and a withdrawal to the Armistice Line—which was directed specifically against us. The next day, Egypt had towed two vessels into the Canal and sunk them, thus blocking the waterway. This marked a serious blow to Britain, where the government had told the public that the purpose behind the Anglo-French air action was to keep the international waterway free and open. Curiously enough, the British had known of Egypt's intentions and had planned to bomb the blocking ships at their anchorage in Port Said before they could reach the Canal. Yet they had failed to do so.

A representative of the French Military Attaché's Office called to tell me that the French were feeling frustrated at the British insistence on November 6 as the date of the Anglo-French landings in the Canal Zone. France wanted the invasion date advanced by two days, as they feared a hostile U.N. Assembly decision and wished already to be in the Zone. The British, however, were unable or unwilling to modify their complicated large-scale plan to make an earlier landing possible. November 6 would remain their D-day. For us, whenever they landed was already of no military significance. Fighting alone, we had already secured all our aims except Sharm el-Sheikh, and I hoped we would gain that soon. But for political reasons I was sorry the invasion would not be advanced. At the United Nations pressure against the use of military force in Suez was becoming increasingly vigorous. And an awkward situation was created at the resumed U.N. Assembly session on November 3.

Dag Hammarskjöld, the secretary-general, had announced that Britain, France, and Israel had given negative replies to the Assembly's demand the previous day for a cease-fire and withdrawal. On the other hand, he said, Egypt had accepted. Russia and her satellites demanded full compliance by the "three aggressors." America's Henry Cabot Lodge suggested the establishment of two international committees to deal with the Israeli-Arab conflict and the Suez problem. The Assembly finally accepted the proposal of

Canada's Lester Pearson to set up an international military force to secure the fulfillment of the Assembly resolution. Toward the end of the session, which went on till the early hours of November 4, there was a renewed demand that Britain, France, and Israel immediately declare their acceptance of a cease-fire. Israel's representative thereupon announced Israel's agreement "provided that a similar answer is forthcoming from Egypt." Our representative no doubt thought that by the time Egypt replied, we would have secured Sharm el-Sheikh. For Israel, now under the heaviest pressure, the important political point was that we were complying with U.N. resolutions.

The British and French representatives almost jumped out of their skins, for if both combatants ceased fire, there was no justification for Anglo-French intervention. For Britain, it removed the basis of her "pretext" and added greatly to the difficulties of Prime Minister Eden. She therefore sought French help in persuading us to retract our announcement. After weighing all the factors—notably the difficulty of refusing French entreaties—Ben-Gurion instructed our representative to notify Hammarskjöld that our announcement had not been properly understood. We accepted the cease-fire on condition that Egypt unequivocally did the same, renounced her declared and long-maintained position that she was in a state of war with Israel, was prepared to negotiate peace with us, cease the economic boycott, lift the blockade of Israeli shipping, and recalled the terrorist groups under her control in other Arab countries.

This step did not enhance our political position in the international arena. Ben-Gurion had met the French request, but he was very angry. If Britain and France had wished to exploit the fact that hostilities had broken out between Israel and Egypt, they had had six days at their disposal, from October 29 to November 4, during which there was fighting between Israeli and Egyptian forces near the east bank of the Suez Canal. But throughout that period the British army occupied itself with meticulous preparations for "Operation Musketeer" as if it had all the time in the world. Now, when the U.N. Assembly called for a cease-fire, Britain was asking Israel to reject it for the sake of her political convenience. Israel had done her utmost, made a supreme effort to end the campaign before finding herself in grave conflict with U.N. resolutions, and had in fact succeeded. Now Israel had to add to her burdens by rejecting the cease-fire, which, on her own, she would not have needed to do.

One effect of the frantic activity at the United Nations was evidently to persuade Britain to hurry with her military action. She kept November 6 as D-day for the seaborne landings but sent a paratroop battalion at dawn on November 5 to seize the Gameel airfield at Port Said, while a French paratroop battalion captured the bridges linking Port Said to the mainland.

That night, November 5, Soviet Premier Nikolai Bulganin sent rocket-rattling threats to the prime ministers of France, Britain, and Israel. The one to Ben-Gurion expressed Russia's "unqualified condemnation" of the "criminal acts of the aggressors" against Egypt, and called on Israel to stop the military operations at once and withdraw from Egyptian territory.

The letter added that the "whole of peace-loving humanity indignantly condemned" us, yet despite this "the government of Israel, acting as an instrument of external imperialistic forces, perseveres in the senseless adventure, thus defying all the peoples of the East who are conducting a struggle against colonialism and for freedom and independence of all peace-loving peoples in the world."

Bulganin's letter continued: "The government of Israel is criminally and irresponsibly playing with the fate of peace and with the fate of its own peoples, which cannot but leave its impression on the future of Israel and which puts a question mark against the very existence of Israel as state. Vitally interested in the maintenance of peace and the preservation of tranquillity in the Middle East, the Soviet government is at this moment taking steps to put an end to the war and to restrain the aggressors."

The message ended with the information that Russia was recalling her ambassador—she later broke off diplomatic relations with Israel—and the advice that Israel should "properly understand and appreciate this notification of ours."

When I saw Ben-Gurion, I noted that while he did not hide his deep concern over the Soviet stand, or seek to ignore the full gravity of its significance, his reaction was not a trembling at the knees. He was not seized by panic. On the contrary, the emotional effect of the Soviet ultimatum was to spur him to struggle. What particularly infuriated him was the difference between the letters sent to Britain and France and the letter sent to Israel. The one to us was couched in terms of contempt and scorn, and it threatened the very existence of Israel as a state. The messages to France and Britain also contained the clear and explicit threat to use military force and to bombard them with ballistic missiles, but there was no calumny, no threat to their political independence, and there was none of the coarse mockery that marked the text of the ultimatum to Israel.

I was very pleased about the cool composure with which Ben-Gurion analyzed this new development. I could think of several political leaders who might have filled the premiership if Ben-Gurion were out and whose reactions in such a situation would have reflected more than a dash of panic.

It was perhaps just as well that Russia's intervention to suppress the Hungarian revolt had delayed Bulganin's threatening messages until this date, the night of November 5—exactly twelve hours after the last shot had been fired in our Sinai Campaign. That morning, we had captured Sharm el-Sheikh, after a race between the 9th Infantry Brigade, the 202nd Paratroop Brigade, and the Israeli Navy to hoist the Israeli flag on its towers.

The day before, I had flown to E-Tor on the Gulf of Suez with the object of picking up a Piper Cub there and flying to the 9th Brigade to ensure that it would attack Sharm el-Sheikh that day. I was pretty certain it would have done so without me, but I wanted to leave the matter in no doubt. Perhaps I might find that the paratroops at E-Tor could reach Sharm more quickly. When I landed at E-Tor, I found that the Piper had not yet arrived and that the paratroop battalion had already left. It had set off before dawn on the tarred road from E-Tor with the aim of seizing the southern opening to Sharm el-Sheikh.

I decided not to wait for the Piper, to abandon my plan of reaching the 9th Brigade, and to leave instead by vehicle and try to overtake the paratroopers. These were our finest troops and they were in excellent fighting condition. I therefore resolved that if Sharm el-Sheikh had not yet been taken by the 9th Brigade, I would order these paratroopers to attack it and try and capture Sharm, alone.

We set off in three vehicles—a command car and two rather doubtful civilian vans—and with a few soldiers from the reserve unit holding E-Tor. The road was good, but the vehicles were dreadful, and we were afraid to overtax them with fast driving. At the beginning of the journey, we did not meet a living soul. The black strip of road unwound before us, on our right the waters of the Gulf of Suez and on our left, beyond the sand, the rising mountain range. But after thirty miles, about halfway, we began to pass Egyptian soldiers coming singly and in groups from the direction of Sharm el-Sheikh. They had started escaping the night before. Here and there we also came across dead and wounded lying near the road, casualties from clashes with the paratroop battalion which had passed by a few hours earlier. As we drew closer to Sharm el-Sheikh, we encountered even more Egyptian troops. I ordered our escort not to reply if we should be fired on with isolated shots. The last thing I wanted was to get stuck that day between E-Tor and Sharm el-Sheikh and become involved in skirmishes with fleeing Egyptian soldiers.

I got out of the driver's cabin—from inside I could not tell what was happening on the sides of the road—and mounted the open rear of the vehicle, where I could stand and get an all-round view. There was, of course, nothing to stop any of the groups of Egyptian soldiers from taking cover behind the bushes or a fold in the ground and riddling us with machine-gun fire. But none did.

The whole picture—though it was the middle of the day—had a nightmarish quality. The scorching desert sun blazed without pity. One could see the heat haze rising from the melting surface of the tarred road. The Egyptian troops in khaki fatigues merged with the sandy landscape and only at the last moment did they spring into sight amidst the dunes. There is no doubt that they knew we were Israeli soldiers, but they neither fired at us nor tried to hide from us. They simply let us pass by. Their faces reflected their exhaustion. The wounded among them dragged one foot after the other with difficulty, and some who were on the road did not even bother to move aside to let our vehicles pass. We had to move around them.

Nevertheless, not for one moment did the thought leave me that if anything happened to make us stop, it would be the end. We were so few, exposed, and vulnerable that even if all they had were their bare hands, they could tear us apart. I knew that our chances of reaching Sharm el-Sheikh depended on not a shot being fired and on not pausing for a moment. Each meeting with an escaping enemy group would pass in a flash, so that by the time they had absorbed what they had seen, we would be out of range of their fire. At last the road curved and turned toward the hills, and we could breathe freely again. In the distance we saw the trucks and half-tracks of the paratroop battalion.

The commander of the company assigned to protect the newly seized road told us that the battalion had captured this southern defile leading to Sharm el-Sheikh at five in the morning. At 6:30 A.M. a Piper had flown in from the 9th Brigade requesting the battalion to advance to about a mile from the emplacements on the outskirts of Sharm el-Sheikh. The commander decided to break through. The battalion advanced, the half-tracks leading and after them the motorized companies. Resistance was not stiff—the Air Force had given close, powerful, and effective support—and by 9:30 A.M. the battalion commander with the first half-tracks reached the entrance to the Sharm stronghold, while the dominant defense positions opposite him were already in the hands of units of the 9th Brigade.

After hearing this roadside report, we pushed on to the Egyptian base. The sight that greeted us was a combination of battleground and enchanting scenery. The Sharm el-Sheikh harbor, at the southern tip of the Sinai Peninsula where the Gulf of Suez and the Gulf of Aqaba meet and join the Red Sea, offers one of the most spectacular views I have ever seen. Its waters are deep blue—Egyptian prisoners warned us against swimming there for they are teeming with sharks— and they are framed by hills of crimson rock. Even the building on the shore, the white mosque with its tall minaret, matches the picture of a wonderland hidden among lofty mountains.

On the ground, however, there were still fresh signs of battle. Smoke was rising from the defense posts and stores which had been bombed a few hours before by the Air Force. Many Egyptian Bren carriers—some damaged, others serviceable—lay scattered in confusion in the port area. And troops of the 9th Brigade could be seen moving over the surrounding ridges, their weapons at the ready, combing the region and assembling the prisoners.

The most ambitious mission in the Sinai Campaign was undoubt- edly the one entrusted to the 9th Brigade, a reservist formation com- manded by Avraham Yoffe. It had had to move south along the western shore of the Gulf of Aqaba, a distance of some two hundred miles through enemy territory over trackless sandy and boulder- strewn ground, to reach and capture the Egyptian stronghold of Sharm el-Sheikh, which was manned by two battalions, fortified, and organized for lengthy siege. Both the march and the end battle could have met with misadventure and even failure.

The brigade column consisted of some 200 vehicles and almost 1,800 men. It was self-sufficient, carrying its own supplies: food for five days, fuel for 375 miles, and enough water carried in eighteen tankers to provide five liters a day per man and four per vehicle for five days. Neither in the course of its march nor in battle would it be possible to send it reinforcements. The 9th Brigade was thus an expeditionary force which had to rely on itself alone and had to suc- ceed in its mission. If it captured its objective, Sharm el-Sheikh, it would have at its disposal a port, an airfield, and a landward route to Israel. If it was blocked on its way south, or defeated in combat, it could expect to be cut off. It would be unable to return to Israel by retracing its steps. It would lack the necessary water, fuel, and spare parts, and there were lengthy stretches of sandy incline which could be negotiated only from north to south.

Politically, the mission was of supreme importance, for control of Sharm el-Sheikh meant control of the Straits of Tiran, which in turn controlled shipping through the Gulf of Aqaba. Egypt had used that control to blockade Israeli shipping. The principal aim of the cam- paign was to break that blockade.

The time element was crucial. It is doubtful whether Israel could have continued fighting, in violation of U.N. Assembly resolutions, when even powers like Britain and France eventually found themselves compelled to accept the verdict and halt their military operations. It was not inconceivable, therefore, that if Egyptian forces at the Straits of Tiran could have held up the 9th Brigade while it was on the march, or could have staved off its attack for a few days, Israel might have been forced to stop fighting before gaining possession of Sharm el-Sheikh.

It was for this reason that we at the General Staff had decided to add another string to our bow and advance the paratroop units from Mitla to Sharm el-Sheikh through E-Tor. However, if pressing this additional formation into service for this engagement—acting independently of the 9th Brigade—was a correct step, it did not ease the brigade's major problems. In the event, the brigade was helped by the paratroops only on the last day, when the battle for Sharm el-Sheikh was already at its height.

The brigade trek was easiest along the first section, from Nakeb to the oasis of Ain Furtaga. Here the convoy proceeded at an average speed of seven-and-a-half miles an hour and covered sixty miles by one in the afternoon of November 2. But then came the toughest part of the journey. The next nine miles were uphill, and the route lay through deep sand which no vehicle except the half-track could traverse under its own power. The most difficult items to move were the 25-pounder field guns which sank up to their axles. Even with the other vehicles, the tires had to be deflated so that the wheels could get a better grip. The average speed of the convoy along this stretch was two-and-a-half miles an hour, and even this was attained only by supreme efforts of pushing and towing both by hand and with the aid of half-tracks. The brigade reached the "watershed"—the peak of the ascent, after which it was almost all downhill—two hours after midnight. Eight vehicles which had got stuck in the sand and could not be pulled out quickly were left behind, after removing whatever could be dismantled. The men were utterly exhausted.

Even the next section had a five-mile stretch which was sandy, but now, with the "watershed" behind them, they were on a slight descent and their vehicles could proceed with less difficulty. They covered the next thirty miles in five hours, and shortly before noon, on November 3, reached Dahab, the largest oasis on the Gulf of Aqaba.

The Egyptian guard unit at Dahab was the first enemy detachment encountered by the brigade. It consisted of ten camel-mounted sol-

diers and a radio transmitter. They put up a fight when the reconnaissance scouts appeared, but were quickly overcome. However,
through lack of caution we lost three killed.

At Dahab the brigade enjoyed its first long rest. The men were able
to wash in the waters of the abundant springs and to relax in the
shade of date palm and tamarisk. The vehicles, too, were in need of
maintenance and refueling. During the evening, two naval landing
craft arrived, according to plan, laden with fuel. They came just in
time. Owing to the unexpectedly stubborn track, far more fuel had
been expended than the prescribed allowance.

The brigade set out on the third stage of its journey at 6 P.M. on
November 3, reaching its next stop, Wadi Kid, at two in the morning.
The grimmest problem here was getting through the rocky section.
The route is a goats' pass on the mountain slope, less than 2 yards
wide and in some parts narrower, and covered by boulders. The only
course open was to widen the narrow sections and blast the obstructing rock. The dynamiting was done by the engineers, and the rest of
the men were mobilized to remove the blasted rocks and level the
track.

Apparently the Egyptians also knew that this narrow defile in the
Wadi Kid was a most difficult stretch to cross, and when the reconnaissance unit, several hours ahead of the column, reached a point
one-and-a-quarter miles from the exit, they ran into an ambush.
Their first jeep went up on a mine, and this blow was immediately
followed by a hail of fire from enemy machine guns and bazookas
and the tossing of hand grenades. Our unit returned the fire, left the
damaged jeep behind, and retired. It was now 6 P.M., and in the thick
darkness of the wadi they could see nothing. They could certainly
not spot mines or locate the Egyptian positions.

At first light on November 4, the reconnaissance scouts returned
to the roadblock, to find that the enemy unit had abandoned its posts.
However, before leaving, it had laid a large number of vehicle mines
just beneath the surface of the ground further along the wadi. The
mines were located, a path marked through them, and at 9 A.M. the
brigade went forth on the final stage of its advance, with only twenty-
five miles more to go. At 11:45 A.M., it reached the end of its journey,
coming within sight of the Egyptian defense positions of Ras Nasrani
and Sharm el-Sheikh. The men had been en route to their objective
three days and two nights. They now faced the decisive phase of the
expedition—the battle for the Straits of Tiran.

The arrival of the brigade from the direction of Eilat was a complete surprise to the Egyptian command. In planning the defenses of

the straits, the Egyptian General Staff had proceeded on the assumption that no sizable Israeli force could possibly reach them by this route. When the Egyptian guard unit at Boasit, forty miles south of Eilat, reported to Sharm el-Sheikh that an Israeli brigade was advancing southward along the shore of the gulf, the commander there assumed that the information was exaggerated, since he was convinced that only a tiny force could possibly cross this trail. Later, when he received similar reports from his unit at Dahab, he began to suspect that he may have been mistaken. The full measure of his mistake, however, became apparent to him only at noon on November 4, when his eyes took in the sight of two hundred Israeli vehicles approaching Ras Nasrani.

Nevertheless, this surprise brought almost no tactical advantage to the 9th Brigade, for both Sharm el-Sheikh and Ras Nasrani had been organized for all-round defense. The Egyptians had not expected an overland force, but they had certainly considered the possibility of a paratroop attack from the north. The 9th Brigade did not therefore find the northern flank of Sharm el-Sheikh exposed and unprepared. However, being a land force and not an airborne unit, they possessed heavy equipment, and indeed the brigade's light-armored half-tracks played a decisive part in storming the Egyptian defenses.

The column reached Ras Nasrani, about three miles north of Sharm el-Sheikh, and found it empty. The Egyptian regional commander had decided to concentrate all his forces inside Sharm el-Sheikh. Ras Nasrani is located on a promontory at the edge of the gulf exactly opposite the isle of Tiran, where the straits are at their narrowest. It was here that the Egyptians had sited six coastal guns, two 6-inch and four 3-inch guns, to control the straits and maintain their blockade against Israel. They could blast any ship out of the water with the utmost ease. The brigade found that the Egyptians had spiked these guns before evacuating their posts.

Pressing on to Sharm, the reconnaissance unit encountered heavy and accurate fire from the enemy posts on the intervening ridges. It was now dusk, and there could be no air support until morning. The brigade commander had to decide whether to wait or put in an immediate night attack. He resolved not to wait. An assault was launched against strongly held emplacements, over difficult terrain and minefields, and under fire also from neighboring enemy posts. At 4:20 A.M. our men withdrew, but they renewed the attack at first light, this time with accurate support from their 120 mm. heavy mortars and with the participation of the Air Force. Leading the attack were the half-track company and the reconnaissance unit, with the infantry units right behind. The fighting was hard and lasted fifty minutes, after which the reconnaissance unit's jeep detachment, with covering fire from the half-tracks, stormed and broke right into the Egyptian emplacements, and the enemy started to run.

The steamroller operation of diving attack planes followed by assaulting half-tracks and jeeps rolled forward along the entire stretch of road that runs through the defended locality of Sharm el-Sheikh. And one after another, the emplacements in the western flank, which dominate the whole locality, were captured, while at the same time, a second battalion, moving parallel to the half-track and jeep units, advanced along the eastern flank and cleaned up the enemy posts there. One emplacement showed particularly sharp opposition and let fly with bazookas and machine guns at anyone trying to approach it. But this position, too, was eventually silenced by a direct hit from a bazooka through its embrasure. By 9:30 A.M., November 5, surrender came from the last Egyptian outpost in Sinai—Sharm el-Sheikh.

In the campaign, Israel achieved its three major aims: freedom of shipping for Israeli vessels in the Gulf of Aqaba; an end to the *fedayeen* terrorism; and a neutralization of the threat of attack on Israel by the joint Egyptian-Syrian-Jordanian military command.

Israel, however, did not gain its "war aims" by direct negotiation with Egypt. Rather, this agreement was worked out with the secretary-general of the United Nations, who served as an intermediary separating the two sides. The secretary-general had demanded the unconditional withdrawal of the Israeli army from Sinai. As a condition of evacuation, the Israeli government had insisted on guarantees for the freedom of her shipping through the gulf and a cessation of Egyptian acts of hostility.

On March 16, 1957, four-and-a-half months after the Sinai Campaign began, the conflict was brought to an end when Israeli units returned to their borders. The last British and French troops had departed the Suez area two-and-a-half months earlier. Sharm el-Sheikh and the Gaza Strip were not handed back to Egypt but were put under the control of the United Nations Emergency Force. Significantly, Nasser had accepted the decision to give freedom of shipping to Israel and to end terrorism against her, at least for the time being.

PART IV

From Minister
to
Private Citizen

[1958~1967]

16

FREEDOM AND POLITICS

AT THE END of my term as chief of staff, I shed my uniform and, at the age of forty-one, enrolled at the Hebrew University of Jerusalem as a regular student in the Political Science Faculty, with the accent on Middle Eastern affairs. I did not find the transition difficult. For one thing, I had already studied law several years earlier when I served as a soldier, attending evening lectures at the Tel Aviv School of Law and Economics. For another, my assignments as an army commander had called for a good deal of thinking, writing, lecturing, and reading reports on a variety of political, diplomatic, technical, and military subjects. Army service in the top commands did not consist of squad drill and standing in trenches. It often meant sitting chained to a desk, grappling with paper work, conducting meetings, deliberating with colleagues.

The main difference as a student was the absence of responsibility, and my two years of university life passed like a vacation. And like a vacation, it left no deep imprint.

Then the political field opened up. Parliamentary elections were scheduled for November 3, 1959, and I was asked to stand as a candidate for Mapai, Israel's Labor Party, headed by Ben-Gurion. Our parliament, called the Knesset, a biblical name for an assembly or gathering, is a single house with 120 members. The electoral system is a pure form of proportional representation. Each party presents a list of 120 candidates for the entire country, and the number of Knesset seats it receives is proportionate to its percentage of the total national vote. The candidates are listed in the order in which they will secure a parliamentary seat if their party gains the requisite number of votes, and heading the list are the party's leading personalities. They are the candidates from whom the ministers are usually drawn if the party forms or joins the government.

The election results gave Mapai fifty-two seats, more than it had ever obtained. Once more it was the largest party, but, again, it did not obtain a decisive majority, and had to form a coalition. Ben-Gurion became the prime minister, and on December 16 he presented his Cabinet to the Knesset. I was included in the new government as minister of agriculture.

The world of politics and government was not strange to me, but until now I had been spared the personal involvement in interparty strife. I was also protected like a hot-house plant from attack by opponents, for it was the minister of defense who carried parliamentary responsibility for the chief of staff's conduct of military affairs.

All this changed when I became a Mapai Knesset representative and a member of the government. But, of course, my primary concern involved the work of my Agricultural Ministry, and this suited me perfectly. Born and brought up in a farming atmosphere, even during my army years I had never cut myself off from the people who worked the land and the problems of agricultural settlement. Nahalal continued to be both my place of residence and my real home. The fields, the orchards, the cowsheds, the seasons of planting and harvesting were deeply infused in my blood, more so than tanks and guns and fighting. The tanned farmers and their wives, Jews and Arabs, with their leathery faces and coarse hands, touched a stronger chord in my heart than did uniforms and festive parades. The sight of a woman bending over a vegetable plot always evoked the vision of my mother weeding the beetroot and cauliflower plots.

As in any country of pioneers, but particularly in Israel, defense and security were synonymous with settlement on the land, and this had been so ever since the First and Second Aliyot, or waves of immigration, when the Jews began returning to the Land of Israel. After the state was born, the government gave special emphasis to the establishment of frontier settlements, particularly in the hill regions of the north and center, and in the Negev, the southern portion of the country. As chief of staff, I had done everything I could to encourage the veteran members of older, established settlements to assist the young settlements, especially in the Negev. Without the assistance of the veterans, it was doubtful whether the new immigrants could hold their own under the arid conditions of the southern desert or on the stony slopes of northern Galilee, where they also had to contend with the unremitting attacks of Arab saboteurs.

Furthermore, when I became minister of agriculture, I found that all the settlements were in the throes of an economic crisis. A farmer's income was 20 to 30 percent below the general average—and that was low enough. Hurt most were the young kibbutzim and moshavim that were least financially capable of overcoming the drop in prices paid for agricultural produce, the increased cost of production, and the lack of revolving capital and credits, which they needed to acquire new tools and farm machinery. To add to their burdens, the Negev had suffered a drought for three years in a row.

What was needed was central planning to bring order out of increasing chaos, control of production to avoid gluts and low prices, the channeling of profitable branches to the new immigrant farmers—who also had to have more land and water allocations, as well as professional guidance. I established a Planning Authority, production and marketing councils for each branch of agriculture, and regional offices throughout the country where local farmers could receive agricultural guidance and services without strangling in a maze of red tape.

My first battle to direct production involved milch cows, and it typified the kind of problem I had to contend with in the five years I served as minister of agriculture. Though farm incomes were low, the veteran farmers were far better off than the new settlers, particularly the new immigrants. I had to help them. The young settlements went in for dairy farming and needed an additional ten thousand milch cows to subsist. But in a non-expanding market, increasing production would only send prices tumbling. I decided to cut production quotas in the veteran settlements, shut down urban dairies—small herds kept close to towns—and transfer their quotas to the young settlements. A town was not the ideal place for a dairy farm. Laborers close to town had access to other means of livelihood, while the border settler did not. As for the owners, we promised compensation. "Farming for the farmers" was our slogan. But the urban dairies were up in arms. They staged stormy demonstrations in front of my office shouting slogans of protest. There were days when it was so noisy that it became impossible to work, so I picked up my papers and moved to another office. However, my decision remained in force, and the urban dairy farms were abolished, while the new settlements received additional cows.

There were many other problems, among them the grant of more land and increased supplies of water to the new settlements. Of paramount interest to me was how to use state land to secure a healthy distribution of the population, improve public amenities, and protect our natural environment.

About 90 percent of the land in Israel belongs to the nation. Prior to the establishment of the state, most of the land owned by the Jewish community had been purchased by the Jewish National Fund, the organization created by the Zionist movement in 1901 to acquire and reclaim land in Palestine for settlement. This land remains the national possession of all the Jewish people and no single individual can buy or own it. With the establishment of Israel, all public lands owned by the preceding British Mandatory power came under state control, and this amounted to 71 percent. The state also became custodian of the lands abandoned by the Arabs who had fled Israel during the War of Independence in 1948.

My main land policy recommendations were approved by the government. One of them was designed to make state lands available for public housing projects in the center, the south, and the north of the country but not in the crowded coastal strip. Another, to protect the environment, involved the Mediterranean beaches that stretch half the length of Israel from its northern tip near the Lebanese border to the Gaza Strip in the south. The hotels on the seashore cater to tourists and a small number of well-to-do Israelis. But the lands along the sea must serve all the people as one of their principal places of recreation. During the year we are blessed with seven warm summer months, and one of the most enjoyable ways those with limited means can spend the weekend is to take a trip to the seashore. I would often watch entire families, both Arab and Jewish, flock to the beach, stretch out on the sand, and frolic in the water. I realized there was the danger that private investors might take over some of these beaches for their exclusive use. I told the Israeli Lands Authority, which administers public lands, not to sell any of its plots on the shore or hand over its rights to these lands to private parties. I also asked the authority and the Ministry of Tourism to provide three public beaches and to make sure that those beaches set aside for hotels would in no way infringe on the areas created for public bathing.

While we were seeking solutions to our own problems, we were inundated with requests from the developing African nations to send them agricultural experts. Latin American countries also sought our aid, and eventually our agricultural experts worked as close to home as Cyprus, Turkey, and Crete and traveled as far away as Nepal, Thailand, the Philippines, Ceylon, and Cambodia.

Our foreign aid began when many African countries gained their independence. Israel welcomed the visiting African leaders who would take tours of kibbutzim and moshavim during their stay. They were shown the Negev settlements, and our people would explain how it was possible to transform a desert into a lush, smiling countryside and how new immigrants without any previous farming experience could be turned into successful modern farmers. Our problem began when our guests asked us to organize a settlement movement such as we have to instruct their youth to settle on the land. We found it difficult to explain why it was possible to set up a kibbutz and a moshav in Israel, but impossible to transplant in other countries what had been created as the result of the special character, history, and circumstances of the Jewish people and the Land of Israel.

Undoubtedly we could help the people of Africa to develop and modernize their agriculture, but this had to be done by adapting methods suited to their conditions and not through mechanical translation of what we had achieved in Israel. We did it by selecting not just any expert but experts who cared, men and women who would be as dedicated to helping and guiding the peoples of other countries as they were with our own immigrants. We studied the agricultural problems in Africa as though they were problems facing our own settlements in the Negev desert and the Valley of Jezreel.

By 1963 our people in Africa had worked long enough for me to judge what they had achieved and to learn how our activities were regarded by the Africans themselves. I had, of course, frequently met with and heard reports from our people when they returned from the field, but reports were never as useful as an on-the-spot visit. I discussed the matter with Golda Meir, who was then minister of foreign affairs, and at her suggestion I left for a tour of West Africa in the autumn of 1963. I paid visits to Togo, Cameroun, Ivory Coast, the Republic of Central Africa, and Ghana. In July of the following year I represented Israel at the Independence celebrations of Malawi (formerly Nyasaland) and then completed my tour of East Africa, visiting Kenya and Tanzania—Tanganyika and Zanzibar, as Tanzania was then known. I met with the presidents of those countries, with ministers of state and with the local people working with our experts. But I devoted most of my time to visits in the field. Our services were much appreciated by the African leaders, and many asked me to extend our activities.

Other nations were assisting the Africans. The Russians established a farm in Ghana; instructors from China were also at work in Africa, as were the French, British and the American Peace Corps. Indeed, people from all parts of the world were knocking at Africa's door offering them aid. However, all these foreign groups, with the exception of the Israelis and the Chinese, did not work with the African farmers themselves or with their hands. The French, English, and Russians set up experimental stations from which they distributed seeds and saplings. The Peace Corps consisted of idealists and true pioneers, but for the most part the Americans taught English, built experimental stations, and provided high-level instruction in agricultural planning.

On the other hand, our representatives, most of whom were raised on kibbutzim and moshavim, came into contact with the individual farmer in his own village. The Israelis and the Chinese were the only people who had gone out into the fields to give guidance and instruction on the practical level, who sat together with the African farmers on their tractors, and who worked with them in the cotton fields and in the chicken runs. In large measure, it was this total involvement that proved the key to our success.

On my return from Africa, I suggested to the government that we extend our technical aid in agriculture, and we increased the number of Israeli experts sent into the field. A study center was set up with training courses for instructors before they went out in the field, and a committee which I headed directed their activities and dealt with their problems.

Despite the sincere efforts made by Israel as a state, as well as by the individual Israeli emissaries who worked with all their hearts and souls, I cannot claim that our foreign assistance program was wholly successful. Sooner or later we reaped disappointment in almost every place we had worked. Our people were forced to return to Israel. And most of the projects we had set up—kibbutz-type villages, model farms, modern chicken runs—were abandoned. One reason for this failure had to do with international politics, the rapprochement between the developing African countries and the anti-Israeli Arab bloc. But there were other, more profound reasons that explain our lack of ultimate success.

It is impossible to span generations and bring progress to any developing society—whether to individuals or communities—within the short period of a few years. Even when the people of these countries spoke our own ideological language and tried to adopt the life-style and social structure of the kibbutz and moshav, they were only repeating what they had learned by rote, and these words did not really represent their own feelings and points of view. True, we could give them the technical instruction, teach them how to use tractors and water sprinklers, show them the ways to spray against pests, to fertilize their soil, and plant new crops. But we could not change their way of life, their tribal system, their outlook. It could be done, but not overnight. Nor could one change at a stroke the fatalism and lack of personal initiative induced in them by centuries-old circumstances.

There was also the problem of the governments themselves. Revolutions by military junta followed one another in rapid succession, and it was sad to see that some of the African leaders were interested in status rather than the development and progress of their people. Indeed, our emissaries were often more concerned than some African officials in improving their farming and raising the living standards of their peasants. Our people worked day and night to make the development projects succeed, chafed at every delay, agonized over failure. By contrast, many local African leaders and governments looked upon our assistance as an instrument for their own ends, proudly displaying a new model village, a modern farm, to impress foreign visitors and gain political prestige. The projects were a showcase. Our representatives would implore them to allocate funds for an access road or provide a tract of land for a new farm settlement. They would keep putting off our requests—made on behalf of their own people—and in the end offered insufficient funds, so that the overall projects were doomed to fail.

I am convinced that a tangible change in the mode of agriculture and in the life of the farmer in the emerging nations can be achieved, but only gradually. This can be done as part of the country's general development and on condition that the people and their leadership truly desire such change. To accomplish it, they must be willing to do everything possible to bring it about, knowing that the road will be long and hard and demand great sacrifice.

Not that any of us regretted the efforts we put in to help the developing nations at the grass-roots level. Ben-Gurion himself followed the progress of our technical aid program with the keenest interest throughout his premiership. He relinquished that office before his term was up, resigning both as prime minister and minister of defense on July 16, 1963. Eight days later, Levi Eshkol succeeded him in both offices.

The events that had brought about this change had begun three years earlier and harked back to the 1954 security mishap known as the Lavon Affair. Pinhas Lavon, who in 1954 was minister of defense during Ben-Gurion's temporary retirement to Sdeh Boker, had denied that he had given the order for the security action which had misfired. He claimed that a senior officer involved had acted on his own. The officer insisted that Lavon had issued the order. A private investigation called for by the then prime minister, Moshe Sharett, failed to establish the correct version. In the political crisis which followed, Lavon resigned.

In September 1960, as a result of what had transpired at a secret defense inquiry into a totally different matter, but which contained a reference to the 1954 mishap, Lavon turned to Ben-Gurion, once more prime minister, and asked that he be rehabilitated. Ben-Gurion replied that only a judge could do that.

Lavon was not satisfied, and was instrumental in having the matter brought before a Knesset committee. Its proceedings were leaked to the press. They included Lavon's charges against the Defense establishment.

The senior officer thereupon wrote to the chief of staff requesting a judicial inquiry to establish definitively who had given the order, he or his minister, Lavon. The chief of staff passed on the request to Ben-Gurion, who brought the proposal to the Cabinet. They were to decide only whether to establish a judicial commission. But the majority of ministers decided instead to set up a ministerial committee of seven to examine the material and to report back to the Cabinet their recommendations on the steps that should be taken. Their report to the government in December 1960 exonerated Lavon and held the senior officer responsible. The Cabinet endorsed their report in a vote in which there were four abstentions. I was one of the abstainers.

Ben-Gurion himself did not take part in the vote. He held that there had been a miscarriage of justice. The Cabinet had been asked to consider a procedural question—whether to establish a judicial commission. Instead it had appointed a ministerial committee which had carried out a substantive inquiry. This committee was not an authorized court of law, had not conducted its inquiry as a court, and had no right to issue a verdict in a conflict between two contestants. Only a full-scale judicial inquiry could do that.

Ben-Gurion then told the Cabinet that he dissociated himself from the committee, its findings, the government endorsement, and washed his hands of the whole matter. He left his office the same day and came back several weeks later only to hand in his resignation.

Thirteen years later, on the day that Ben-Gurion died, Chaim Yisraeli, who was head of my bureau and who had worked in the Defense Minister's Office when Ben-Gurion held that portfolio, recalled to me the following episode about that stormy period. In December 1960 the Central Committee of the Mapai Party was called into urgent session. A letter from Ben-Gurion was read out to the assembled members stating that following the decision of the Committee of Seven on the subject of the Lavon Affair, he had resolved to submit his resignation to the president. The assembled members were shocked, and in the discussion which followed, a resolution was proposed that if Ben-Gurion insisted on resigning, then Mapai would not form a government. I, too, was present and took part in the discussion. I strongly opposed this draft resolution. "Ninety-nine percent of my pro-Ben-Gurionism," I said, "is not pro-the person of Ben-Gurion, but for the identification of Ben-Gurion with the state. The state takes precedence over all, even over Ben-Gurion. If a situation arises in which Ben-Gurion decides to resign, and I consider that the good of the state demands that Mapai form a government even without Ben-Gurion, and it is given me to join such a government, I shall do so."

Some four years later—so Chaim Yisraeli told me—Ben-Gurion was writing an account of the period and wished to see the minutes of the 1960 Central Committee meeting. Yosef Almogi, a veteran Mapai leader who was then secretary-general of the party, brought around a copy and left it with one of Ben-Gurion's aides. A few hours later, Almogi telephoned Yisraeli in a panic and told him to hold on to the record and not let Ben-Gurion see it. Almogi had just glanced at it and had spotted the reference to the possibility of a government without Ben-Gurion. "Such a suggestion by Moshe Dayan," he said, "will only distress Ben-Gurion. Just as well not to show it to him." Yisraeli told him that it was too late. The record was already with Ben-Gurion.

Shortly afterward, Ben-Gurion walked into Yisraeli's room, a smile on his face, the record in his hand. "I enjoyed the words of only one person," he observed to Yisraeli, "those of Moshe. Words of understanding. He is the only one who made sense. He is a wise fellow. How could the others say that without Ben-Gurion we shall not form a government? Ben-Gurion is only flesh and blood. It's not the man who is important—he passes from the scene. It is his path that is important—and that goes on."

I was touched. A word of praise from Ben-Gurion had always meant much to me.

General elections were held in August 1961, and Ben-Gurion again headed the government. But strained relations continued between him and his Mapai colleagues who had opposed him on the Committee of Seven's report. They became even more strained as Ben-Gurion himself persisted in his efforts to reverse what he deeply felt to have been a miscarriage of justice. Two years later he left office and never returned.

I continued to serve in the Cabinet for sixteen months, and then I left, sending the prime minister my letter of resignation on November 3, 1964. My problem was not Ben-Gurion's absence from affairs of state but the stifling atmosphere in which I found myself in Eshkol's government. I felt like the prisoner in a story I had once read, an unpopular member of a work party who were taken one day under guard to their labors along a narrow goat's path on a steep hill. One after another his comrades elbowed past our prisoner until he was close to the man at the end of the line, who promptly pushed him over the slope.

I knew that I would not be allowed to remain for long in the same line with the other Mapai members of the government. I would be jostled and shoved and eventually pushed until I stumbled. It was better to get out while I still stood on my feet.

Ben-Gurion, out of office and back in Sdeh Boker, continued to absorb himself in the moral issue over the Lavon Affair, and did not spare his sniping at the Eshkol government. Matters came to a head in June 1965, when Ben-Gurion formally broke with Mapai and formed a break-away party called Rafi. Seven Mapai Knesset members joined Rafi immediately and were registered as a new party in the Knesset in July. I myself joined Rafi only several months later.

When I left my office at the Agricultural Ministry, I gathered up the books and pictures I like to have near me when I work. Among the books, apart from the Hebrew Bible and the collected works of Bialik, our national poet, are the writings of Natan Alterman, the poet who spoke to my own generation. Alterman also appears among the three portraits that stand in the center of my office bookshelf to this day. The other two are Ben-Gurion and Chaim Sheba, a physician. These three men were head and shoulders above anyone I had ever met. I am not by nature a hero worshiper, but if I try to put into words what I felt about them, I would say it was a combination of appreciation, respect and love.

I got to know Alterman well only after I became chief of staff in 1953 and began working closely with Ben-Gurion. I had met him several times before, but I knew him only through his Hebrew translations of the classics and through his poetry, with which I was familiar. Indeed, I knew most of his poems by heart, and somehow looked upon them as personal and esoteric, their hidden secrets known only to Alterman and myself. It was Ben-Gurion who brought us together. The two were very close.

When I came to know him, I found him to be a man whose character was without blemish. He had his failings, but no flaw. He had his weaknesses, but they left him untarnished. The more I saw him, whether during a working day or at a party at night, whether he was depressed or animated, in somber or buoyant mood, I was inspired by his richness of spirit, his wit, his sincerity, and his integrity.

It was not by chance that Alterman wrote both love poems and political commentary, light ballads, lyrics and theatrical satire. This was not the versatility of a bard but the full expression of the varied hours and moods of an individual. It was therefore not possible to separate his works into different categories. All were parts of the whole. His weekly column for a large Hebrew newspaper in Israel would often be an entire poem whose lyrical power was so strong and deep as to be positively painful. I once told him, rather late at night, that on occasion his words set me shivering and grinding my teeth like the scratching of a rusty nail on a tin can. Nor was there any triviality about his ballads or his popular songs.

He encompassed in his being all the triumphs and tragedies of his people. Brought up on the chronicles of our biblical past, tortured by the hardships of our centuries' old exile, agonizing over the ineffable cruelties of Hitler, he was a staunch believer in our future and an equally staunch fighter. All this came through in his work, whether in song lyric or sketch or political comment on the events of the day. And all were marked by subtle sensitivity and clarity of thought.

Alterman's roots reached out to all the strata of our turbulent history, and were nourished by them, in their glory and their squalor, their splendor and their suffering. His overpowering poetry was a reflection of the man. His father was a teacher. Alterman himself was the greatest educator of my generation. He bequeathed to us a sense of sublime mission, to bring about the revival of Jewish independence. He spoke to every youngster, electrified him with the demand that he meet the challenge of the nation and regard its fulfillment as his personal ideal. He wanted us to be idealists, but also to savor the wonders of life, sense the beauty of nature's greenery, in the flight of an eagle, taste the salt of the sea, experience the headiness of wine, be enraptured by the stars. Not only in its content but also in its style, in the delicate use of the Hebrew language, his writing bespoke simplicity, noble, pure, aesthetic. I noticed myself, and heard it also from other friends who had spent more time with him at night when he had drunk more than a little, that they had never heard a coarse word pass his lips, never an obscenity. It was not that ugliness was repressed. Within him it just did not exist.

He once gave me a variation of a joke that was going the rounds at the time. It concerned a *"Yekke,"* the endearing term for a German Jewish immigrant from the 1930s who had not yet managed to learn Hebrew. He wanted to know the time, but the very people he asked happened to be without a watch, and they replied, "No idea." The *Yekke* therefore thought that "idea" was a watch, and when he went to buy one he asked the shopkeeper for "an idea." Alterman's variation was that the *Yekke* was more of a philosopher than he knew, for after all to know the time in which we lived, we needed an idea rather than a watch. Alterman was certainly a man who turned the private time of an individual into the eternal ideas of a nation.

Out of government, no longer in the army, but still a member of the Knesset, I divided my time between sitting on the parliamentary benches as a member of a small opposition party, attending to the affairs of a small fishing company of which I had become a director, and writing a book on the 1956 Sinai Campaign. But I was still deeply concerned with the grim dangers to my country, and profoundly interested in matters of defense and security, with which I had been involved all my life. Whatever the future held for me, whether in or out of office, I still hoped to contribute in some measure to the shaping of the country's defense policy.

I had kept abreast of military developments, read public and private reports and received information from a variety of sources on advances in weapons technology and tactics. But first-hand experience added a dimension to understanding which second-hand description could never provide. It was now, in 1966, ten years since I had been in battle, ten years since I had been at the wrong end of an enemy tank, field gun, and attack plane—and the right end of our own. I wanted to see for myself, on the spot, what modern war was like, how the new weaponry was handled, how it shaped up in action, whether it could be adapted for our own use.

The best, and only, military "laboratory" at the time was Vietnam. So I agreed to write some newspaper articles for *The Washington Post* and was accredited as a war correspondent. When he heard about it, and as I discovered later, United States Defense Secretary Robert McNamara had been kind enough to send a signal to the American commander in Vietnam, General Westmoreland, to open all doors, but advising him not to expose me to too much danger. However, out in the field, the very friendly local commanders let me see all the action I wanted. So in early August 1966 I found myself in an American helicopter flying from Danang to the rear headquarters of the 1st Air Cavalry Division. From there I would be flown forward to join a jungle patrol.

We circled the camp before landing. The precious helicopters were grouped in the center. Round them were the tents, and just beyond them the 105 mm. and 155 mm. gun positions. Encircling them were barbed-wire entanglements, watchtowers, searchlights, communications trenches, bunkers. Beyond the barbed wire was a "firing area" stripped of trees and bush. And beyond that, closing in from all directions, the jungle, a thick, dark-green mass of vegetation, unlike any terrain I had ever fought over.

From the air I had seen the streams flowing in the valleys, the flat strips along their banks still holding traces of peacetime rice paddies, now abandoned. Each month produced a new crop—not of rice but of more than 20,000 refugees, farmers fleeing the battle zones for the coastal towns.

It rained heavily the whole morning, and visibility was zero. But by late afternoon the skies cleared a little and I could be moved on to advance headquarters at Pleiku. We flew over Route 19, made famous by the French battle there twelve years before. Just where the highway entered the mountains, more than 1,000 French troops had been wiped out in a Vietcong ambush. Even now, the Vietcong were obstructing the normal use of this route, mining it, blowing up bridges, firing from the jungle at passing traffic. Civilian vehicles did not use it at all, and even military convoys found it heavy going. They were always led by tanks to detonate the mines, and they had to resort to improvised tracks to skirt the blown bridges. Vietcong saboteurs often laid a 105 shell—usually American—underneath a mine. When that went off, it often took the tank with it.

At advance headquarters I received a warm welcome from the commander of the 1st Cavalry (Airmobile) Division, as it was officially called, Maj. Gen. John Norton. "I've had word from General Westmoreland," he said. "For you, *mon général*, all doors are open. Just take care of yourself, and for heaven's sake don't pick one of my units to get killed in."

Norton took me into dinner. With us was Col. Brendswieg, commanding the 2nd Brigade, which was soon to go into action. I would be with them.

The division was currently engaged in Operation "Paul Revere."

A continuation of Operation "Hastings," it was being carried out in the highland area near the Cambodian and Laotian frontiers to search for Vietcong units and engage them in combat. This was the operation I had asked to join.

American warfare in Vietnam was primarily helicopter warfare. There were altogether 1,700 helicopters in the country when I was there—more than all the helicraft in Europe. The 1st Air Cavalry Division was the "Cavalry and I don't mean horses" foreshadowed in General Gavin's brilliant article, an organizational and tactical expression of the imaginative use of the helicopter in battle. It was the American answer to the problem of movement in the jungle, and was certainly applicable to territory with which I was more familiar, providing mobility that was not dependent on roads, ground vehicles, or airfields.

Within four hours of the warning order, an entire battalion with all its equipment could be lifted to the combat area, landed in the heart of the jungle or on a mountain summit.

We were scheduled to take off in the morning, but it was impossible to do so. There was no letup in the hard driving rain, and the clouds were so low they were almost resting on the treetops. Just before noon it cleared slightly and H-hour was set for 1 P.M.

According to Norton's information, there was a Vietcong division in this highland area. It was not concentrated in a single base but split into several battalions, each of about 350 men. It was Norton's plan to land a battalion from Brendswieg's brigade in the Vietcong divisional area and then, in accordance with the developments of the battle, to rush in additional "reaction troops" to reinforce, seal off, and carry out flank attacks.

All this was fine, except for one small item missing in the plan: the exact location of the Vietcong battalions was not known. Air photos and air reconnaissance had failed to pick out their encampments, entrenched, bunkered, and camouflaged to merge with the jungle vegetation.

The American intelligence sources were largely technical—air photos and decoded radio intercepts, for Vietcong units from battalion strength and up used transmitters. Only scanty information could be gleaned from prisoners of war.

At 1:05 P.M. D Company, to which I was attached, got the take-off signal for the enemy's divisional area. The helicopter doors were removed and the machine-gunners took up their ready-to-fire positions. The helicopters rose like a swarm of hornets and slid above the tree tops. Each company flew in a tight group of sixteen craft and was assigned its own landing zone. When we climbed higher, we heard the salvos of the artillery engaged in "clearance" shelling of the landing areas. In Operation "Hastings," an American company had been wiped out when it landed in an area which appeared to be empty but which was held by a camouflaged Vietcong battalion.

The battle procedures of the 1st Cavalry operated like an assembly belt. First came the shelling of the landing zones by ground artillery. Then came aerial bombardment. And the landings themselves were covered by "gun-ships," the accompanying, close-support, heli-borne units firing their rockets and machine guns almost at our feet.

The landing zone of our company was a long thin strip. This was a field in the jungle which at some time had been cleared of trees and undergrowth by Vietnamese farmers and prepared for rice cultivation. Since then most of it had become overgrown with tall elephant grass, but helicopters could land.

As we approached the strip, smoke still rose from the shelling. The ground was scarred by large black patches of scorched grass. The smell of burning penetrated the open doorway of our aircraft.

We had released our belts while in the air, and even before the helicraft touched down we jumped and quickly took cover in the grass. Landing our company took less than two minutes. The helicopters whirred off. All around came sounds of exploding shells and machine-gun fire. I tried to poke my head out to discover their source, but the grass was too high. So I climbed a slight rise from which I could see the terrain. The forest was silent. The firing came from the neighboring landing zones which were still being "cleared." Our company commander signaled the platoon commanders to take up battle positions.

The assembly line of the 1st Cavalry's fighting machine continued in full production and at full speed, landing units, equipment, weapons, and ammunition. Heavy Chinook helicopters flew over the area of battalion headquarters, and one after another deposited 105 guns and shells. Guns and ammunition bales were carried hanging below the bellies of the aircraft, which came down low, released their load and flew off, almost without stopping.

These were followed by the giant Crane helicopters dangling heavy 155 guns, bulldozers, and command-communications caravans. As I watched them, I could not help recalling my tussles with the Ministry of Finance when I was chief of staff. Each of these huge helicopters cost $3 million at the time, and I remembered an occasion when I had postponed an overseas study trip for some of our officers to save the $70,000 I needed for urgent spare parts. O America. O Israel.

But where was the war?

It was like watching military maneuvers—with only one side. Could they have operated in this way, I wondered, if the Vietcong had also possessed warplanes, artillery, and armor? The heaviest weapon in a Vietcong unit, a medium mortar, could be carried on a man's back. But anyway where were the Vietcong? And where was the battle?

The Vietcong were there, a few hundred yards away. And the battle came half an hour later, when the company which had landed 300 yards to our south ran into an ambush after it had started moving off. I transferred from D Company to battalion headquarters, where I found Gen. Norton, Col. Brendswieg and Gen. Walker, commander of the neighboring 25th Division, part of whose formation was attached to the 1st Cavalry. They were bent over maps spread out on the grass near the command post.

The southern company had landed, as we had, without interference. The company commander had then decided to advance to a hill on the other side of a stream. The unit had moved off in single file across the narrow path leading to the stream, one platoon after the other. Even though the scouts had proceeded with great caution, stopping every so often to listen, they had failed to detect the presence of the Vietcong until they found themselves under fire. The Vietcong battalion positions were dug in a little way from the path and were covered by branches supporting the dug-up earth with its grass. Only narrow firing slits were left open, and these, too, were skillfully camouflaged.

The Vietcong commander let the first American section go through and then opened up with all the unit's machine guns and rifles on the platoons along the path. Within minutes, the company was put out of action, sustaining more than 70 casualties—25 killed and about 50 wounded. The company commander was among the wounded, and his second in command was killed when a chance bullet hit and detonated the grenade hanging from his belt.

The company lost its fighting capacity, but not radio contact with battalion headquarters and support units. The firing officer requested reinforcements, and the shelling and bombing of the Vietcong positions. Battalion command informed him that a company would be landed near them within a few minutes. They would help remove the wounded and dead, but they would not assault the Vietcong emplacement.

The Americans carried out their counter-attacks and "pursuit" in the jungle not with infantry but by firepower. The artillery and Air Force were summoned to bombard an area as soon as it was shown to be holding enemy troops, even when these were few and even if "they" turned out to be a lone sniper.

The problem faced by an American infantry unit in engaging the Vietcong was not how to storm the enemy positions but how to discover where they were. The "storming" and "assault" would be done by artillery and air bombing. These were not restricted to jungle paths and were not vulnerable to ambush.

The most effective weapons the Americans had for this function were their heavy bombers. They flew high; their bombing, directed electronically, was accurate and destructive; and they could operate no matter what the weather or visibility.

The clash between American forces and Vietcong units, like that which occurred that afternoon, would have seemed, on the face of it, to have been accidental—the chance ambush of an American company. It was not. The fact was that most of the U.S.-Vietcong engagements at the time of my visit started out in this way, and this was the joint product of Vietcong tactics and American strategy.

The Vietcong tactic was to attack American units with the aim of destroying them when the prospect of success seemed bright. Even that afternoon, if the Vietcong unit had wished to evade battle, it could have withdrawn from the area without detection. But when the American battalion landed nearby, the Vietcong troops remained, hoping they would be afforded a favorable tactical situation in which to assault it. And this was what happened when the American platoons had passed close to their positions, in single file, and exposed to their fire. Ninety out of every one hundred battles in the Vietnam war began, as this one did, on Vietcong initiative, when they deemed the circumstances favorable.

The American forces, too, had as their aim destruction of the enemy. But they did not make its execution conditional on a favorable tactical situation. The American commanders were eager to make contact with the Vietcong at all times, in any situation, and at any price. They were not put off by the possibility that at the first contact the Vietcong might have the upper hand. They were convinced that as the clash developed they would come out on top. Their main problem was to shake the Vietcong from their hiding places, and if

American patrols served as bait, that could not be helped. It was the price they had to pay. For the Americans, coming under fire was not the climax of the battle. It was just the opening, to be quickly followed by the full might of their artillery and aircraft, thereby smothering the initial advantage of the Vietcong troops, equipped only with personal weapons.

The aggressiveness of American fighting in Vietnam stemmed not only from the character of the American army. Its source lay in policy, in strategy, in the way in which those who determined the military steps of the United States hoped to achieve victory.

To hear about American strategy in Vietnam, I had flown to Saigon via Washington. I had posed the question to Gen. Maxwell Taylor. I had also raised it with Robert McNamara, whom I had met at a dinner party. But at its simplest and baldest, Washington saw the key to victory in the breaking of Hanoi's fighting spirit. This could be secured by keeping up the heavy bombing of North Vietnam and wiping out the Vietcong units in the south. McNamara and Taylor believed that if this American military activity was maintained and strengthened, Ho Chi Minh would not be able to withstand it for long. He would be forced to end hostilities and accept the American demand to sit down with them at the negotiating table.

The American army in Vietnam had therefore to penetrate every likely area in every way in an effort to expose Vietcong units and wipe them out. Search and destroy was the policy, and therein lay the path to victory.

This military policy of Washington well matched the aggressive character of the American commanders. Anyone witnessing Gen. Norton spurring his men "to be quick on the trigger" as he jumped aboard his helicopter, took the controls in his hands, and soared off, skimming the trees, could not fail to see in him a kind of latter-day sheriff of the old Wild West, fighting it out to the bitter end. In place of a couple of revolvers, he twirled 155 mm. guns; and his faithful steed was his helicopter, UH-ID.

At 5:30 P.M. we left battalion headquarters. Monsoon clouds again began to blanket the skies. Norton invited me to join him in the flight to Gen. Walker's headquarters for dinner and the continued review of the operation.

As we flew I noticed large clearings in the jungle, which turned out to be extensive tea plantations. They looked for all the world like beds of ornamental trees. Such careful cultivation was in stark contrast to the wild and primitive vegetation all around. The tops of the bushes glistened with the fresh green of the new leaves, which were cut young and dried to make the best tea.

The plantations were old. Their owners, French and Chinese, continued to tend them in the midst of what had been a battle zone for twenty years and to sell their produce in orderly fashion to the world markets. Coexistence was apparently possible even in war. Neither the government troops nor the Vietcong interfered with the plantations, their workers, or their installations. The surrounding jungle was heavily marked by craters from aerial bombing. The bridges on the adjoining Route 19 had been dynamited by the Vietcong. But the plantations were untouched. Not a building had been wrecked, not a worker scratched, not a branch lopped off. Tea prices were high, labor was cheap, and profits were ample enough to cover taxes and bribes to the government and ransom to the Vietcong. Tea for two.

Gen. Walker's advance divisional headquarters looked like a field unit. Two tents served as the officers' mess, plates were standard field issue, and the food, apart from cans of beer, was the same as that which I had eaten with the troops.

Gen. Norton took charge of the operational review. The question was whether the Vietcong would exploit the hours of darkness and the early morning monsoon rains to withdraw from the area; and if so, how they could be stopped. They were expert at moving through the jungle, and when they wished to avoid combat, they split their units into small groups of not more than fifteen men and each took a different path to reach the new rendezvous.

Walker thought they would try to retire to Cambodia during the night. The frontier was less than ten miles away. Norton was not so sure. He thought they had stocks of ammunition and rice in the area, and perhaps also an underground hospital, and they needed time to shift them. Moreover, they had put enormous effort into concentrating their forces in this zone; their men had marched for more than three months from North Vietnam to get there, and they were unlikely to make a hurried retreat. They had come to attack the American army, and they would try to do so.

After listening to the discussion, and after what I had seen, I did not have the feeling that Operation "Paul Revere" was achieving its objective. The U.S. units had concentrated their might to destroy the Vietcong force. What the Americans had at their disposal was a commander's dream: helicopters to rush his men to any location; well-trained troops with aggressive spirit and ready for action; air and artillery support; equipment, ammunition, and fuel in virtually unlimited supply. Yet with all this, they had not routed the Vietcong. Indeed, they had not succeeded in bringing them to decisive battle. They did not always know where the Vietcong units were. And when they did run across them, usually when this suited the Vietcong, after the initial encounter the enemy slipped from their grasp, defeating attempts to seal him off.

I said to Norton that the Air Cavalry was the perfect, though expensive, answer to the problem of mobility in the jungle. There was no place they could not reach. But there was one thing they seemed unable to do—land their units quietly, secretly, without detection. The helicopters announced themselves every inch of the way and advertised every landing in the jungle. The Vietcong, on the other hand, might take three months to walk from the north, but neither en route nor before their engagements did they give themselves away.

Norton listened attentively. When I finished, he fixed me with his eyes and said in jesting tone—but he meant it: "Don't worry, *mon général*, we'll get 'em!"

After the meal, I was flown to Plei Me, three miles from the Cambodian border, to join a two-day patrol of a Special Forces group, the "Green Berets." They were going out the next day.

But early in the morning, a signal came in from 1st Cavalry headquarters reporting that there had been a heavy Vietcong attack on a Korean defensive position close to where I was now, and Gen. Norton thought I might like to get there fast while the signs of battle were still fresh. I postponed the patrol and a Special Forces jeep drove me to the scene of the action.

During the night, this defensive position, manned by a company of about 130 Koreans, was attacked by a Vietcong regiment comprising three battalions—more than a thousand men. The attack failed, and the regiment left 237 killed on the battlefield.

When I got there, the Koreans were still glued to the firing slits of their defense posts, still in their steel helmets, tense and alert as though not yet sure that the danger was over. On the flanks of the camp, the American support tanks which had been rushed to the battle after the start of the attack were still in position ready for further action.

The Korean company had arrived six days earlier and had had enough time to dig themselves in. They had done it with care and skill. Every defense post was overhung with slate bearing a thick layer of grass-topped earth, and all were linked by deep narrow trenches. The entire position was ringed with concertina wire sown with mines and illumination shells.

The main attack was launched on the western defenses. The distance from the barbed wire here to the edge of the jungle was just under 200 yards, covered with tall grass.

The Vietcong commander had apparently assumed that he could reach the fence on this sector without being exposed, and it was here that he concentrated his assault force, and against these western emplacements that he directed his deterrent fire—machine gun and mortar. It turned out later that Vietcong patrols had reconnoitered the defense position and noted the Korean firing posts despite their camouflage.

The Vietcong commander had made the fatal mistake of thinking only of the Korean company which he could see, and not of the artillery, aircraft, and tanks which would be summoned to its support. There is a primitive and leaden logic to warfare: in an open engagement between two unequal forces, the strong defeats the weak. The victories of the Davids over the Goliaths were rare enough in my country in biblical times. They are rarer still in the kingdom of tanks and guns.

What happened to the Vietcong soon after their attack was that along the 200-yard-wide strip between jungle and fence, the American support units laid down no less than 21,000 shells! (This was more than the total volume of artillery fire expended by the Israeli army during the Sinai Campaign and War of Independence together.) Every barrel within range opened up—155s, 105s, tank guns, heavy mortars—covering the area with fire and explosives.

The wonder is not that the Vietcong failed to capture the position, but that a few managed to reach the fence and even lob hand grenades.

As I walked through the devastated battlefield, I was struck by the extreme youth of the Vietcong dead. Vietnamese males in general have young faces, but these looked particularly youthful. Perhaps it was the pallor of death. Most of them were without helmets. Many wore sandals, but some were barefoot—they may have lost their sandals while rushing to the assault. Despite their poor clothing and the murky puddles in which they lay—the rain was unceasing— they looked quite smart and clean. I got the impression that in preparation for the attack, they had paid careful attention to their appearance—haircut, shave, change of uniform.

The weapons they bore were of varied type—Mausers from World

War Two, semi-automatic rifles of Soviet design and Chinese make, light machine guns with 30-round arc magazines, and even a few medium machine guns.

Deeper in the jungle we found their support weapons—mortars —and their knapsacks, which they had removed before going off to the attack. I inspected one. In it was a spare uniform and a nylon bag containing 1½ pounds of rice, a packet of salt, a cooking pot, a spoon, a lighter (flint and wick), and ink powder.

I had witnessed a lot more in Vietnam, and heard a good deal, and I was glad I had been there. I had seen what war was like in the mid-1960s. I could not know then, as I was leaving for home, that barely ten months later I would be back in government, at the center of military affairs and actively involved in the direction of one of my country's most dramatic campaigns.

PART V

The Six Day War

17

THE LONG WAIT I

ON SUNDAY EVENING, the 14th of May 1967, during a torchlight tattoo
in the Jerusalem stadium to mark the opening of Israel's nineteenth
Independence Day celebrations, intelligence reports were received
that the Egyptians were moving huge forces across the Suez Canal
into Sinai. Three days later, Nasser demanded the ousting of the
U.N. Emergency Force (UNEF), which had been stationed along
the Sinai and Gaza Strip border following the 1956 Sinai Campaign.
The U.N. secretary-general agreed to its removal. Within another
few days, some 80,000 Egyptian troops and 800 tanks were in Sinai,
with advanced formations approaching Israel's border, swelling the
forces already stationed there.

On May 22, Nasser declared the blockade of the Straits of Tiran
to all ships bound to or from Israel. When Israel had withdrawn her
troops from Sharm el-Sheikh after the Sinai Campaign, she had
clearly stated that reimposition of the blockade by Egypt would be
an act of war. Not only the United States and other Maritime Powers,
but Egypt, too, fully understood that this was our position. On May
26, Nasser announced that Egypt intended to destroy Israel. Four
days later, King Hussein placed Jordan's armed forces under Egyptian command. So did Iraq. Expeditionary units arrived from Kuwait

and Algeria to add to the Egyptian strength in Sinai. By the opening days of June, Israel was threatened on all fronts by Arab armies vastly outnumbering us in troops, tanks, artillery, and warplanes. To the world Israel seemed doomed.

Inside Israel, there was a partial (later a full) mobilization of reserves who were deployed to forward positions. There they waited, not knowing whether they would remain inactive until attacked by the enemy or whether they themselves would be launching the first strike. At army headquarters, contingency plans were being brought out, dusted off, and adapted to the new circumstances. The Israeli government, headed by Prime Minister Levi Eshkol, was faced with two choices: ordering its troops into immediate action, or engaging in urgent diplomatic efforts to bring international restraints to bear upon Nasser. Despite the danger that the Egyptians would attack while the diplomatic process was continuing, the government decided to try diplomacy first. For twenty-two days the mobilized troops remained in their positions while their families anxiously waited at home, listening intently for the next news bulletin. The tension mounted hourly until finally, on the morning of June 5, the air-raid sirens once again screamed out their warning that Israel was at war.

The Six Day War, as it was later called, was the third major armed conflict Israel had had to fight since the nation's birth nineteen years earlier. This war stemmed from the flawed judgments of President Gamal Abdel Nasser of Egypt. The immediate roots of the conflict were grounded in a series of incidents between Israel and Syria (and Jordan, too) and in Egypt's reaction—or rather the reaction of its president. Nasser well knew that his aggressive moves—particularly closing the Straits of Tiran—would be viewed as an act of war by Israel, but he presumed that the Big Powers would prevent Israel from taking action, or, if the Israeli army did attack, it would be unable to penetrate the Egyptian military lines in Sinai. In any event, the Security Council would quickly impose a cease-fire and the episode would end with Nasser achieving two goals: removal of the U.N. Emergency Force while imposing a permanent blockade of the straits. He recalled what had happened after the Sinai Campaign in 1956, when the United States and the Soviet Union forced France, Britain, and Israel to withdraw their forces and reconcile themselves to the nationalization of the Suez Canal. This time not only America and Russia, but France and Britain as well, were against war. All that Nasser had to do was overwhelm Israel.

One of the first seeds of the Six Day War was planted eight months earlier in the shape of a mine. Its explosion was to result in a taunting challenge flung at Nasser by one of his allies, Jordan. On November 12, 1966, an Israeli detachment patrolling the Israeli-Jordanian border south of Mount Hebron ran over the mine, which killed three and wounded six. In a reprisal action on the next day, an Israeli unit crossed the frontier; fought an engagement with Jordanian troops; entered the village of Samua near Mount Hebron, which the saboteurs had used as their base; and blew up ten houses, after evacuating their occupants. In the course of the action, an Israeli Mirage shot down a Jordanian Hunter aircraft. Other Jordanian casualties included 20 killed—14 soldiers and 6 civilians—and 35 wounded. The Jordanian press and radio were filled with sarcastic references to Nasser, who had promised to rush to the aid of Arab states that came under Israeli attack. His promises were now seen to be empty. The Egyptian army, they said, was hiding behind the skirts of U.N. troops who were stationed on the Israeli-Egyptian border and who ensured freedom of shipping for Israeli vessels to and from Eilat.

The next challenge to Egypt came from Syria. The heightened tension that developed between Israel and Syria in the period preceding the Six Day War sprang from the extremist character of Syria's regime; a fanatical hatred of Israel; attempts to divert from Israel the water sources of the Jordan River; and the Syrian army's sponsorship of terrorist action.

Syria followed a more hostile policy toward us than the other Arab states. Apart from trying to prevent Israel from using the waters of the Jordan or working the lands in the demilitarized zones on the Israeli side of the international frontier, she also repeatedly shelled Israeli border settlements. In pursuing this aggressive policy, Syria enjoyed a topographical advantage, since she was able to dominate the Jordan and Huleh valleys from the Golan Heights. Syria also received unlimited support from the Soviet Union. To Russia, Syria's rulers, the leaders of the left-wing Ba'ath Party, were "Moscow's darlings," to be petted and pampered, for their country was part of the land route from the Soviet Union to the Persian Gulf.

Israel suffered considerably from Syria's hostile actions but found it difficult to reply by comparable military means. Her artillery could not reach Syrian army bases on the high ground, and Israel had no wish to fire on civilian villages in reply to the shelling of her own. Border incidents between Syria and Israel increased in number and gravity. On March 5, 1967, an Israeli tractor plowing near Kibbutz Shamir, close to the Syrian border, went up on a mine, and the farmer was seriously wounded. A month later there was an exchange of fire when Israelis were plowing their fields in the demilitarized zones near the Sea of Galilee. The most serious incident occurred on April 7. After the Syrians had shelled three kibbutzim at the foot of the Golan Heights, Israeli Air Force planes were brought into action. Syrian aircraft flew to meet them, and in the ensuing air battle we shot down six Syrian MiGs, two of them over the approaches to Damascus. The Israeli Air Force suffered no losses. Thousands of Arabs saw the Syrian planes go down in flames.

Israel also found terrorist activity very painful. It always seemed to me that the Arab authorities never quite understood our feelings or their implications, never grasped why we were so deeply concerned and reacted so sharply when our people were murdered, houses attacked, or roads mined by infiltrating terrorists. On the eve of the Sinai Campaign eleven years earlier, the terrorist murder of Jewish workers at the Dead Sea potash works and raids on Jewish villages near Kalkilia brought Israel and Jordan almost to the brink of war.

Israel's reprisal actions against Samua in Jordan on November 13, 1966, and against Syria on April 7, 1967, were particularly firm. But while Jordan began thinking seriously of checking terrorist operations from her soil, Syria became more militant. She turned to Russia for more military equipment, mostly surface-to-air missiles, and to Nasser with the categorical demand that Egypt join in the active defense of Syria, either by sending Air Force units to be permanently stationed on Syrian territory, or by taking military action against Israel near the Egyptian border. Israel need not have been surprised by these moves. It was to be expected that Syria would be deeply shaken when her planes were shot down by Israeli pilots over Damascus. To Syria, the most calamitous aspect of this episode was not the rout of one of her units in a border incident but her evident inability to protect her capital from the Israeli Air Force. The damage to her national prestige was enormous.

In the wake of these armed engagements came the war of words. Syrian spokesmen compared their fight against Israel to that of the Vietcong and declared that they would not stop until they had conquered Israel. And they seized upon expressions used by our own spokesmen, including the prime minister and the chief of staff, flaunting them as threats to attack Syria if she did not desist from her hostile acts against Israel.

Then came Syria's complaint that Israel had concentrated forces all along the border. This charge was completely untrue. Israel certainly had no intention of attacking Syria. It seems, however, that at first the Syrians may well have believed that there was increased military activity on the Israeli side of the border, and against the background of the disastrous air battles, they took the shadow of the mountain for the mountain itself. Israel—above all Prime Minister Eshkol—grasped the danger in this false complaint and sought to refute it. But the Soviet Union was loath to give up so welcome and provocative an "argument." The prime minister invited the Soviet ambassador to Israel to travel with him along the Israeli-Syrian border and see for himself that there were no military concentrations. The ambassador declined to go.

The downing of Syrian MiGs over Damascus and Syria's militant response posed the problem to Nasser in its sharpest form: how, if at all, could Egypt go to the help of other Arab states—particularly Syria, with whom Egypt had signed a joint defense pact in November 1966. Furthermore, following this incident Egypt began receiving "information" from Syrian and Soviet sources that Israel was concentrating forces near the Syrian border and was aiming to invade Syria, capture Damascus, and topple its leftist regime.

Nasser could either turn his back on Syria's difficulties, even if this damaged his standing as leader of the Arab world, or consider himself obliged to respond to her appeal and take appropriate action. He chose the second course, and on May 1, 1967, announced in a May Day speech that he would place at Syria's disposal all the planes and pilots needed for her defense.

The Russians fed the flames. On May 12, 1967, an intelligence officer in the Soviet embassy in Cairo transmitted to Egyptian intelligence "confirmation" of the Syrian report that Israel was massing troops on the Syrian border. The next day Soviet President Nikolai Podgorny repeated this claim in his talk with Egypt's Anwar Sadat (Nasser's close colleague), who was visiting Moscow at the time. Podgorny added that Israel's aim was to invade Syria, that the Soviet Union would help Syria and Egypt in their war with Israel, and that Egypt should be ready for such action. "You must not be taken by surprise," he said. "The coming days will be fateful." The Soviet foreign minister spoke to the Egyptian visitor in a similar vein and added the "intelligence" detail that Israel might attack Syria between May 16 and 22. Ironically, Israel's announcement that for reasons of economy there would be only a modest march on Independence Day, May 15, was adduced as further "evidence" by the Syrians and Russians that most of Israel's troops and weapons were "otherwise engaged"—preparing for the invasion of Syria.

Sadat hastened to inform Nasser of what he had been told in Moscow, and on Sunday, May 14, the Egyptian president decided on a demonstration of strength by moving two divisions into Sinai to join the one already there. This act, which our chief of staff learned about that evening in the Jerusalem stadium, was the first military step taken by Egypt, and it marked the start of the procession of armies marching toward the Six Day War. According to Muhammed Hassanein Heikal, the leading editor in Egypt and close confidant of Nasser, the Egyptian president's action was prompted by a twofold motive: showing Syria that Egypt was ready to fight at her side, and obliging Israel to transfer forces from the Syrian border to the south to meet the Egyptian threat.

Nasser's next step was the demand that the UNEF remove its troop units along the Egyptian-Israeli border, namely, from Gaza to Eilat. Egypt's General Sharkawi explained to Indian General Rikhye, the UNEF commander, that Egypt was making this request since hostilities were likely to break out with Israel, and Egypt therefore wished the border to be free for her military actions. However, he said, Egypt did not wish the UNEF to leave Sharm el-Sheikh, which controlled the Straits of Tiran, or the Gaza Strip.

U.N. secretary-general U Thant, on the advice of Dr. Ralph Bunche, refused to leave UNEF units at Sharm and Gaza, arguing that for the UNEF to carry out its assignment, it could not abandon some of its positions and remain in others. All were part of an integral system. Nasser's reaction came on May 17 with the order for all UNEF troops to get out, including those at Sharm el-Sheikh. U Thant acceded to Nasser's demand, and two days later all U.N. forces were withdrawn. The Palestine Liberation Army promptly took over the U.N. emplacements in the Gaza Strip.

Then came Nasser's decisive step to war. The Supreme Committee of the Arab Socialist Union—Egypt's only political party—met at Nasser's home on May 21. It was decided then to blockade the Israeli port of Eilat by stopping all Israeli vessels and all foreign vessels carrying "strategic materials" to Israel that sought passage through the Straits of Tiran. The next day, visiting the Air Force base of Abu Suweir, the Egyptian president publicly announced that "the Gulf of Aqaba is closed to the Israelis." The blockade was imposed that very day, May 22. Two German ships were stopped at the Straits of Tiran, checked, and only after it was found that their destination was the Jordanian port of Aqaba, not Israel, were they allowed to proceed.

On the same day, after making his blockade announcement, Nasser met with the Soviet ambassador to Cairo. The ambassador asked him whether he wished Russia to repeat its warning to Israel that if she

Moshe at the age of five with his father and mother.

Dayan's father's family in Russia in 1910.

Dayan's namesake, Moshe Barsky, who was killed by marauding Arabs near Deganiah.

Most of Moshe's youth was spent working the family farm in Nahalal.
(I.P.P.A.)

On his horse, Tauka, Moshe and four other teenage riders guarded the fields of Nahalal against marauding Arab bands.

In 1937, Moshe Dayan joined the Jewish Settlement Police, under the British army, and commanded the mobile guard shown here.

In October 1939, the British arrested forty-three Haganah members for illegal possession of arms and imprisoned them in the Acre fortress, where this group picture was taken. Dayan is shown at the extreme right.

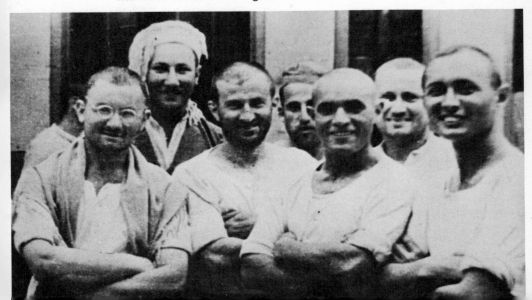

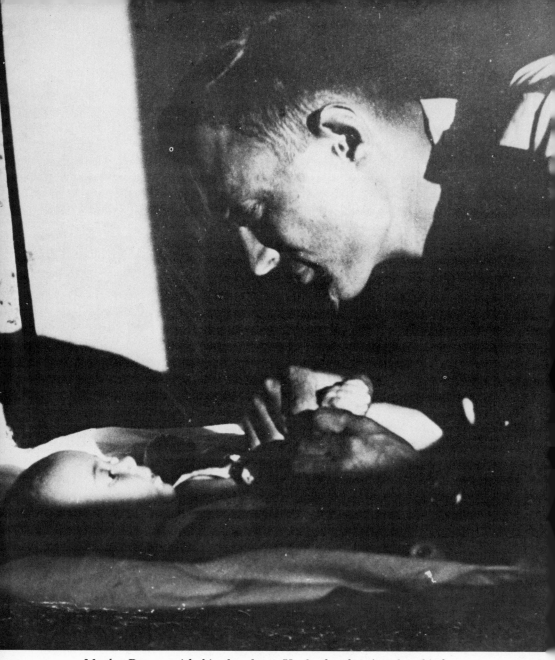

Moshe Dayan with his daughter, Yael, shortly after her birth.
(I.P.P.A.)

►

Dayan's brother, Zorik, who fell during the War of Independence, with his wife, Mimi.

(I.P.P.A.)

Before assuming his first field command in the War of Independence, Dayan accompanied the body of Col. David Marcus to the United States, where Dayan joined the funeral cortege at West Point. An American army officer, Col. Marcus had served as the commander of the Jerusalem front.

On the night that the United Nations voted in favor of the partition of Palestine, thereby heralding the establishment of the State of Israel, Dayan took his three children to the village hall in Nahalal to participate in the evening of celebration. Here they are pictured at the time: Assaf (left), Yael, and Ehud.

Ruth and Moshe Dayan during the period he served as the commander of Jerusalem.

It can snow in Jerusalem, and a commander's life is not all work.
(HERBERT MEYEROWITZ)

During his term as commander of Jerusalem, Dayan became friends with his Jordanian counterpart, Abdulla el-Tel, with whom he negotiated the postwar arrangements for Jerusalem.

(DAVID RUBINGER

Before the war in Sinai in 1956, the army aided the civilian border settlements along the Gaza Strip in digging protective trenches against terrorists who crossed the frontier, and Chief of Staff Moshe Dayan is shown taking his turn.

In the autumn of 1966, Dayan, now a private citizen, covered an American jungle patrol in Vietnam as a newspaper correspondent.

(I.P.P.A.)

After the liberation of Jerusalem in the Six Day War, Dayan paused to pick some wild cyclamen for Rahel that were sprouting near the Western Wall. She preserved them between the leaves of a book.

With Chief of Staff Yitzhak Rabin (right) and GOC Central Command Uzi Narkiss (left), Defense Minister Dayan enters the Old City shortly after its liberation in the Six Day War.

(ISRAEL GOVERNMENT PRESS OFFICE)

With Prime Minister Levi Eshkol, under whom Dayan served as minister of agriculture and later as minister of defense.

With Chief of Staff Yitzhak Rabin on a helicopter flight to Sinai during the Six Day War.

(DAVID RUBINGER)

With his daughter, Yael, near the Suez Canal, at the close of the Six Day War. Yael had been in Greece and returned to Israel shortly before the outbreak of the war to join a reserve unit.

(ASSAF KUTIN)

As minister of defense, Dayan surveys the Egyptian side of the Suez Canal.

The minister as a guest of the Bedouin in the desert.

Relaxing with Mahmed Ali Jaberi, then the mayor of Hebron and a leading Arab statesman on the West Bank.

After terrorists attacked and killed nine children in a schoolbus along the northern border in May 1970, Defense Minister Dayan attended the youngsters' funeral, where he comforted one of the mourners.

(NEWS PHOT)

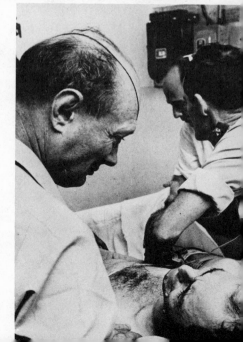

Pursuing the terrorists along Israel's eastern border was a protracted campaign and took a high toll among her officers. Here Dayan visits one of the wounded men.

(ISRAEL SUN)

With David Ben-Gurion.

With Golda.

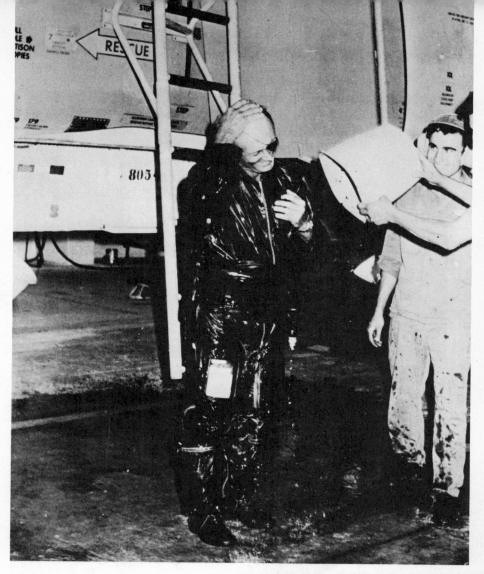

It's an old Air Force custom to douse the man who has just returned from a maiden flight, so this was Dayan's reception after his first trip in one of Israel's newly acquired Phantoms.

As a member of the Knesset, Israel's parliament, Dayan is seen here at the Cabinet table during a vote.

(NEWS PHOT)

Dayan's interest in archaeology began when he was still a front commander. Here he inspects a discovery at an archaeological excavation.

(ANDRÉ LEFEBVRE)

While minister of defense, Dayan was engaged in an archaeological dig when he had a serious accident that almost cost him his life. During his hospitalization, he was visited by a worried Ben-Gurion (right) and attended by Dr. Chaim Sheba (left).

(A. VERED)

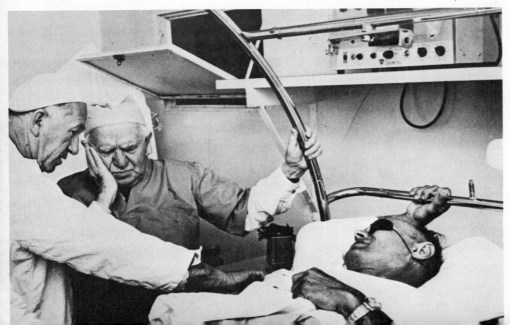

Israeli soldiers preparing to cross the Suez Canal during the Yom Kippur War.

With Lt. Gen. Chaim Bar-Lev (left) and Maj. Gen. Arik Sharon (right) on the Egyptian side of the Suez Canal during the Yom Kippur War.

With Prime Minister Golda Meir at a ceremony for the war dead.

(NEWS PHOT)

Secretary of State Henry Kissinger and his wife, Nancy, join Mr. and Mrs. Moshe Dayan near the patio of their home in Zahala.

(BAMAHANEH)

Moshe and Rahel Dayan at Ben-Gurion Airport shortly before leaving on a mission overseas.

(DAVID RUBINGER)

Moshe Dayan in his garden surrounded by his antiquities.
(GENEVIEVE CHAVEL–GAMMA)

attacked any Arab state, Soviet troops would be sent to help the embattled Arabs. Nasser replied that such a warning had better be sent to the United States.

Nasser's aggressive military moves came upon Israel like thunder out of the blue. It may be that the immediate prompting was Syria's call for help against an Israel that was stronger than she, but after May 15 the picture was reversed. The concentration of forces and threat of war were not made by Israel against Syria but by Egypt against Israel. Egypt had moved more than half her armed strength into Sinai, removed the UNEF, and blockaded the straits. Israel was shaken and bewildered. Neither the government nor the people expected such action. Israel did not want war, but she could hardly reconcile herself to the closing of the Gulf of Aqaba, which would mean the end of Eilat as an Israeli port, or calmly ignore the tangible threat of the Egyptian army advancing in full strength toward her borders.

There then began a round of nonstop consultations inside the country and diplomatic meetings in the capitals of the world to secure the lifting of the blockade and the Egyptian military threat. Israeli ambassadors kept urging all freedom-loving countries to work toward the same end. But as each day passed it became increasingly evident that we could not expect effective measures from the outside world.

As it turned out, Nasser was mistaken over the outcome of his military confrontation and over the political developments, but he was fairly accurate in his judgment of the stand that would be taken by the Big Powers. The Soviet Union championed all his activities and even spurred him on. Russia's representative fed Egypt with false reports about Israel's alleged concentration of forces on the Syrian frontier and even promised to help the Arabs with an expeditionary force in the event of war.

France did not want war, but President de Gaulle helped Nasser to try to gain what he wanted without war. The arms which Israel had ordered from France—and paid for—were held up. De Gaulle justified this "delay" to Israel's representatives as an action to "prevent Israel from being able to start a war"—this French decision coming at a time when Egypt was receiving unlimited quantities of arms from the Soviet Union. De Gaulle took the position that Israel had to submit and reconcile herself to the blockade of the straits. He went further, insisting that the rest of the Arab demands, such as the return of the refugees and the "rights of the Palestinians," should be studied anew by the Big Four. In advising Israel to entrust her affairs to him (France being one of the Big Four), the imperious de Gaulle did not forbear from stressing that the period of Franco-Israeli cooperation that had flourished in 1956 was over, and that France was now interested in fostering good relations with the Arab states.

Britain's activities were well intentioned, but nothing came of them. Prime Minister Harold Wilson, in Washington at the time, energetically supported President Johnson's suggestion to set up a naval task force, but the initiative fizzled out. His foreign minister, George Brown, also tried to help, often acting on his own when his Cabinet colleagues disagreed with his proposals, but he too failed. Italy and Spain refused to cooperate for fear of upsetting Egypt. France refused to sign the Freedom of Shipping Declaration proposed by the United States. Finally, Brown flew to Moscow on May 24 and put his suggestions to the Soviet leaders. Kosygin brushed him off with a coarse reminder of the Anglo-French failure in their 1956 Suez war. "Do you want a second Suez?" Kosygin asked him. The Russians also rejected two further proposals by Brown: that the Soviet Union cooperate with Britain, France, and the United States in securing the return of the UNEF to its buffer positions, and that Russia should press Egypt to evacuate her troops from Sharm el-Sheikh. It was a disappointed British foreign minister who returned to London after two days of fruitless talks in Moscow.

The United States, for her part, did not respond with an "Amen" to Nasser's provocative actions. Nor did she sit back and do nothing. But none of her proposed measures proved practical, and none reached the implementation stage. On May 23 the American ambassador to Cairo met with Egyptian Foreign Minister Mahmud Riad and informed him of the United States' position: America was opposed to the evacuation of the UNEF; Egyptian troops were not to occupy Sharm el-Sheikh unless Egypt declared that she recognized the principle of freedom of shipping through the straits; the Egyptian army was not to enter the Gaza Strip; the United Nations was to continue to be responsible for administration in the Gaza Strip.

About a week later, on June 1, President Johnson sent a special emissary to Cairo. He was Robert Anderson, who knew Nasser well and who handed him a personal message from the president. In it, according to Muhammed Hassanein Heikal, Johnson told Nasser that the United States would not participate in sending an international maritime force through the straits but that he, Johnson, was committed to the security and development of Israel, which also covered Israel's right to freedom of navigation. The president therefore thought that a compromise solution should be found and war avoided.

Nasser's official reply was that he agreed to the proposal made by U Thant, whereby Egypt would postpone her blockade for two weeks and during this time Israel would refrain from sending vessels through the straits. The fortnight would be spent in trying to reach a solution agreed to by both parties. In other words, Nasser was willing not to stop Israeli shipping provided none tried to get through! The main consequence of the Anderson visit was to strengthen Nasser's conviction that the Big Powers were opposed to war and that if it erupted, the United States and the Soviet Union would join together —as they had done in 1956—to bring it to an immediate halt.

In the meantime, the Egyptians continued to strengthen their force in Sinai, received reinforcements from the armies of other Arab states, and put the finishing touches to their war plans. In the south, Egyptian units were to cut off Eilat by linking up with Jordanian forces. In the north, the Syrian army, with the help of Iraqi units, was to isolate the northern part of Upper Galilee.

On May 26, speaking at a public meeting of Arab trade-union delegations, Nasser distributed warm praise to the Soviet Union and threats of destruction to Israel. He told his audience that Egypt had allowed the UNEF to remain on her soil until she had completed the build-up of her armed forces. As soon as that was done, "we went to Sharm el-Sheikh, knowing that this would lead to war. We chose the appropriate time for this, when Israel threatened Syria." The Egyptian president declared that the armies of Egypt and Syria were now one and expressed the hope that all the Arab states surrounding Israel would form a single military front.

On May 30 Jordan responded, joining her forces to those of Egypt and Syria and adding sharp reality to the projected Arab attack on Israel. King Hussein had been on bad terms with Nasser, and with good reason. For years Nasser had openly tried to get him deposed. Indeed, when Hussein decided to fly to Cairo, without receiving the prior agreement of Nasser to receive him, he was taking a chance. He might have been arrested on arrival. But he was not. A few hours later he was signing a defense pact linking him with Egypt and Syria. With King Hussein joining this triple treaty organization, there could only be one meaning—war. If Hussein had not feared that the other Arab armies would attack Israel and win, leaving him in a vulnerable position if he stayed out, he would never have linked his fate with theirs. On his return to Amman from Egypt, Hussein gave an interview to the correspondent of the Beirut journal *Al Hayatt* in which he said that the joint defense pact which he had signed in Cairo was an historic event. It was a document embodying a forceful decision for action.

Hussein's visit and the pact dispersed the last remnants of cloud which darkened the skies of the Arab peoples. The king said that he looked forward to further cooperation with Egypt and other Arab states both in the Orient and in the West "so that we can tread the proper road leading to the erasure of our shame and the liberation of Palestine." Egyptian General Abdel Munim Riad was appointed the responsible commander of the eastern front and of the Jordanian forces.

The ring round Israel was completed on June 4 with the signing of the joint defense treaty between Egypt and Iraq and Nasser's notification to Hussein that the pact now included Egypt, Iraq, and Jordan. The following day Egyptian warplanes reached Jordan, together with two Egyptian battalions. An Iraqi Expeditionary Force also began moving into Jordan, headed by a mechanized brigade and an armored battalion.

In the light of Hussein's Cairo visit, the pact, and the placing of Jordan's forces under Egyptian command, Israel could no longer remain passive while enemy armies were poised to invade her from the north, the east, and the south. Even those who tended to discount the florid phraseology of Arab leaders could not seal their ears against the whooping war cries that burst forth in the speeches of Nasser, the utterances of Hussein, the Order of the Day of Egypt's top field commander, General Murtagi. The question then for Israel was not whether to reconcile herself to the blockade and not even whether there would be a war, but whether to wait until she was attacked by the Arab armies or to get in the first blow.

When Egyptian forces began moving into Sinai in mid-May, and four days later mobilization was begun of Israeli army reservists, the immediate effect was a partial paralysis of the Israeli economy and the generation of an atmosphere of anxiety among our people. Once Nasser followed up his military move by declaring the blockade of the Straits of Tiran on May 22, it was obvious that Israel could not reconcile herself to this act of aggression. The Israeli public expected its leaders to take a firm stand and to express themselves clearly on this crucial action. But neither was forthcoming. The feeling spread that Prime Minister Eshkol was torn by uncertainty and incapable of decision. Public doubt in the leadership turned into public contempt, with wry "gallows-humor" making the rounds of the market place. What was at stake was the very survival of Israel, and general confidence in the government's capacity to direct the affairs of state was undermined. Since the departure of Rafi from the ranks of Mapai in 1965, the governing party had lost not only Ben-Gurion but also its most prominent defense experts, including Ya'akov Dori, who had been Israel's first chief of staff; Shimon Peres, who had been director-general of the Defense Ministry and later deputy minister of defense; and myself, a chief of staff for close to five years. We were joined by Zvi Zur, who had also served a term as chief of staff.

I have been called a "loner," and if ever the term were apt, it was particularly so in the fortnight before the outbreak of the Six Day War. During this waiting period, I scrupulously refrained from intimate talk or discussion of the situation with personal friends and most political colleagues. Yet at no time did I feel a sense of loneliness or isolation. Indeed, I had never felt so close to the people, so integral a part of the community of Israel, from the troops in the line to the farmers in the border settlements and the lively eager crowds in the bustling streets of Beersheba, the town closest to Sinai. I sensed with my entire being the tension that gripped the country, and I was completely absorbed by the problems with which we were suddenly faced. On the surface, these seemed to be political-military problems. But I knew in my bones that they were basically historical Jewish problems which were rooted in our past. How we tackled them would determine our future.

I also knew that war was inevitable. Diplomatic efforts within the international community would come to nought. And when war broke out, I had to be personally involved—even if only as a private soldier, though hopefully in a command function.

From the public point of view, I had two possible courses of action: the first was to carry out my responsibility as a member of the Knesset—to take part in parliamentary debates on the budget of ministries in whose functions I could not claim a passionate interest; to attend meetings of the Foreign Affairs and Security Committee, where ignorance, in some members, proved no bar to their delivery of advice and long speeches; to drink tea in the Knesset restaurant and then drive home without having had any impact on decisions affecting the major issues of the day. True, I could also join with Ben-Gurion, Shimon Peres, and others in discussions within the Rafi Party. But I felt such discussions to be sterile, since we were cut off from any influence on government policy or action.

The alternative course was to spend my time with the army and frontier settlements in the south. There might be no public value to my presence there. But similarly the public would in no way benefit by my presence in Jerusalem. On the other hand, the personal reasons were very compelling. Whether in or out of office, I was and would continue to be closely concerned with and about military affairs. This interest had prompted me only a few months earlier to go to Vietnam to see the war there at close quarters, so how could I stay away from the area of conflict in which my own country was about to become involved? Rather than hang around the parliamentary or other cafés in Jerusalem, I preferred, as long as I was physically able, to take part in the fighting, even just as a private.

It was against this backdrop and developing drama, while the tension among the Israeli people became almost overwhelming, that I began a journey to our outposts which would have to face the Egyptian onslaught. On May 20 I telephoned Col. Yisrael Lior, aide de camp to the prime minister and minister of defense, and asked him to tell Eshkol that I sought permission to visit army units in the south to apprise myself of their combat capability and of the operational plans. Permission was granted. A few hours later, however, I was telephoned by Maj. Gen. Aharon Yariv, chief of Intelligence, who asked me whether I would not care to wait a couple of weeks until the dust settled and the men would be less busy. Seeing *how* the "dust settled" and how busy the men were was precisely my purpose, I told him. I was not proposing a Cook's tour. I wanted to get my teeth into what was happening in the line. My departure for the south was then set for May 23. It was decided that I would wear a uniform. A car and driver were placed at my disposal, and a conducting officer, Lt. Col. Bar-Niv, was assigned to me from the Adjutant General's Office.

Two days later, on the eve of my departure, the chief of staff, Lt. Gen. Yitzhak Rabin (later to become prime minister), came to my home for a talk. He asked me for my appreciation of the situation. I told him that I thought Nasser would close the Straits of Tiran, which he did forty-eight hours later; that Israel would be obliged to counter with military action; and that the immediate move in such action should not be seizure of the straits by capturing Sharm el-Sheikh, but bringing the enemy to battle and routing it at a location favorable to us, and only thereafter extending the campaign southward to the straits.

Yitzhak said these were also his views and he thought the most suitable place for the first clash was Gaza, on the assumption that the Egyptians would rush troops there. I said this did not seem feasible to me because of the presence in the Gaza Strip of Palestinian refugee camps and because of the area's largely civilian character. A military clash was more appropriate against a purely military objective. Rabin also said that a condition for our success was a pre-emptive air strike. I said that I doubted whether he would get authorization for this plan under the present political conditions and with the existing Cabinet leadership.

Yitzhak seemed not only tired, which was natural, but also unsure of himself, perplexed, nervously chain smoking, with hardly the air of a man "impatient for battle." He complained that instead of being allowed to do his work in the army, he was being rushed to Jerusalem each day to take part in government consultations, and that he was not getting from Eshkol a clear political-military line or definitive instructions. He had met Ben-Gurion the previous evening, and I was interested in his impressions. He said that Ben-Gurion had given him the same political and defense judgment that I had just given him. On the operational side Ben-Gurion had shown little understanding, but it was a novel pleasure for him to talk to a man who spoke clearly and decisively, in Yes and No terms, on what to do and what to avoid. My principal impression of the evening was that Rabin was in a state of dejection, and if this were also apparent to his officers and men, it would be most unfortunate.

On the morning of May 23, I set out for Southern Command accompanied by Lt. Col. Bar-Niv, my conducting officer. On the road, however, we were stopped by a military policeman who informed me that I was to return to Tel Aviv for an urgent meeting in the Prime Minister's Office.

It turned out to be a joint meeting of the Ministerial Defense Committee together with leaders of the parliamentary opposition. On the government side there were Prime Minister Eshkol, Foreign Minister Eban, Minister Without Portfolio Galili, Minister of Education Aranne, and Minister of Interior Shapiro. The opposition was represented by Menahem Begin, Shimon Peres, myself, and others. Also present were Chief of Staff Rabin and Chief of Operations Ezer Weizman. A special invitee was Golda Meir, who was secretary-general of the Mapai Party at the time.

We were given a general briefing, and the prime minister then turned to the problem on which he sought our views. We had been urgently summoned for it was a problem which required an immediate decision: the United States had requested that we wait forty-eight hours—following Nasser's announcement the previous night that he was closing the Straits of Tiran—before sending an Israeli ship on a demonstrative journey through the Gulf of Aqaba.

Abba Eban suggested that we ask the United States for an American destroyer to accompany the Israeli ship, for this would test the United States' attitude. We were told that the United States had informed Israel that if we wished her to share responsibility for what happened, we had to consult with her before we took any step.

My own view, which I put to the meeting, was that we should give the U.S. the forty-eight hours she wanted. If she were prepared to use her forces to guarantee freedom of Israeli shipping, I would be very pleased. But I did not think anything would come of it. Therefore, at the end of forty-eight hours, we should launch military action against Egypt with the aim of inflicting heavy losses on her armed forces. If possible, it would be well to select a battleground close to the Israeli border. We should take into account the likelihood that all the Arab states would join in the war against us soon after the initial action. This would include Jordan, and we should therefore prepare ourselves against a Jordanian attempt to capture our enclave on Jerusalem's Mount Scopus. Israeli Arabs, too, might take action against us in areas where they might feel they were in an advantageous position.

I also pointed out that we had not heard any overall political-military plan for the campaign. Nor had we heard of the link between the military campaign and the opening of the straits to our shipping. How would such a link be apparent? I added that we had to take extreme care that there would be no setback in our initial action, for this would have grim results. We should aim to destroy hundreds of tanks in a two- to three-day battle.

Eban appeared more tense than the others. It seemed to me that he was the only one who recognized the full gravity of the situation. Eshkol maneuvered so as to secure an agreed formula which would permit him not to take military action in response to Egypt's blockade of the straits. He spoke of a "device"—an American destroyer escort for an Israeli ship. It appeared, however, that Nasser would give orders not to open fire on Israeli shipping which was escorted by American vessels. Thus, the suggestion to request an American escort would be valueless, for freedom of Israeli, rather than American, shipping would neither be put to the test nor guaranteed.

In his reply, Eshkol addressed himself to my point about there being no overall political-military plan. "The Israeli army," he said, "has operational plans for all the fronts." It was a strange observation. Either he failed to understand my meaning, or he really thought there was no need for a detailed operational plan for a particular campaign and that it was enough to have a general contingency war plan, as the Israeli army, like every army in the world, had in its files for every front.

At the conclusion of the discussion, it was agreed by the majority of those present to respond to the American request to wait forty-eight hours, but not to ask for a U.S. naval escort. It was also agreed that the Israel Defense Forces would order full mobilization of reservists.

When we adjourned, Shimon Peres, my colleague in the Rafi Party, suggested we call on Ben-Gurion, the party leader. I refused. I imagined that Ben-Gurion's political stand would be that we demand Eshkol's resignation. He might even insist that we refuse to cooperate with the prime minister, and that was a position I was not prepared to accept. I told Shimon that in my view we should certainly participate in meetings like the one we had just had, but only with the status of representatives of the opposition. We should not join the Eshkol government if this were proposed. As to the suggestion that Eshkol be replaced, that, I said, should be raised before his party, Mapai, for it to recommend. Some had thought that we should propose it to the Knesset's Foreign Affairs and Security Committee. I was against it. In the sessions of this committee, we should simply say that we had no confidence in the government and did not consider it capable of directing the affairs of state either in war or peace.

18

THE LONG WAIT II

IT WAS NOT until that afternoon of May 23, nine days after it was learned that Egypt was moving her armies into Sinai, that I finally reached Southern Command. I found that the GOC, Maj. Gen. Shayke (Yeshayahu) Gavish, was away at General Headquarters in Tel Aviv. From his chief of staff I learned about the deployment of both the enemy and Israeli forces, as well as about our operational plans. We had three armored divisions in the south, commanded by Maj. Gens. Yisrael Tal (Talik), Avraham Yoffe, and Arik Sharon. The operational plans were not final, and they contained various options, ranging from the capture of the Gaza Strip to deep outflanking actions further south. At first glance they seemed to me to be too complicated. They also lacked what I considered an essential Israeli element—compelling the Egyptian army to change its plans and deployment. One of our basic advantages over the enemy was our ability to improvise during the course of a battle and to do so quickly. Thus, our plans should have been designed to create situations in which the Egyptians would have to make operational changes, which they would do slowly and ineffectually. But I found this factor missing in the plans I saw. I kept these reflections to myself at the time. I had been cut off from army affairs for ten years, and I had to learn things thoroughly before I could reach the right conclusions.

From Southern Command I drove to the armored division commanded by Talik and was then helicoptered to the division's 7th Brigade. This inspection was a real pleasure. The brigade commander, Col. Shmuel Gorodish (Gonen), exuded confidence in his brigade, his men, and his plans, and indeed I felt after my inspection that his confidence was fully justified. He was ready to go into action at once on any assignment, convinced that with the accuracy of his tank gunners at long-range targets, he would get the better of both the Egyptian anti-tank guns and their tanks, and he was prepared to fight even without artillery or air support.

I returned to the Desert Inn in Beersheba, where I would be spending the night. Summing up my feelings after a day in the field, I was vastly impressed by the fighting ranks. True, this feeling was induced by the spirit and character of one man—Col. Shmuel Gorodish, commander of the 7th Brigade—but I considered that he reflected the true mood of the entire brigade.

At 10:30 I met Shayke Gavish at his Southern Command headquarters. He reported on his General Staff meeting in Tel Aviv. Full mobilization had been ordered, and D-day had been provisionally set for seventy-two hours from Nasser's closing the straits. Authorization had been given for the aerial bombing of Egyptian airfields and for the capture of the Gaza Strip.

I made no effort to hide my disappointment, though I was still hesitant to express my views at this early stage and at this forum. With Shayke were his staff officers. I had come to see and listen and not to air opinions, I said, after Shayke had suggested that we analyze the various operational possibilities. But he repeated his request, adding that he had spoken to the chief of staff and received permission to discuss these matters with me, so I agreed.

Shayke explained the difficulty of breaking into the heavily fortified Egyptian strongpoints, whereas by capturing the Gaza Strip, we would gain a valuable bargaining card, being able to trade off the return of the strip for freedom of shipping through the straits. Nasser's prestige would be tarnished, and would be vulnerable to our attack under conditions favorable to us.

I said that this plan did not seem feasible to me for both political and military reasons. The Gaza Strip bristled with a variety of problems. Israel was liable to find herself stuck with a quarter of a million Palestinian refugees. At the same time Egypt was unlikely to consider the strip an important enough card to make a trade. But the more decisive reason was a military one. The aim of this war was armed confrontation with Nasser. The real gravity of his closing the Straits of Tiran lay not simply in the blockade itself, but in his attempt to demonstrate that Israel was incapable of standing up to the Arabs. If we failed to disprove this thesis, our situation would steadily deteriorate. We therefore had to embark on a test of strength, and we could do this in one of two ways. We could capture Sharm el-Sheikh. But if this was too difficult for the moment, the alternative was to meet the Egyptian forces at a more convenient location. Such a confrontation should be on a large scale, however, so that much of Egypt's military strength could be destroyed or impaired.

The capture of Gaza would not provide these results. Gaza was not an outright military target, and Nasser would not rush military reinforcements to save it when he saw that its situation was hopeless. Therefore, I said, we had no choice but to go out to the very center of his armed might.

Our review of possible military operations lasted until midnight, and I left Southern Command in a somber mood. There had been no differences of view as to our war aims. But I detected a certain doubt on the part of some of the officers as to whether we had the strength to rout the Egyptian forces. And one asked if we were justified in risking heavy losses for such a campaign, or whether we should not try to avoid such casualties—even if this meant failure to gain our full purpose.

Well, it had apparently been decided at the army level that the target would be Gaza. The government—or, more accurately, Eshkol—would certainly not have challenged this view, even though it was a political problem, and even though, from the military side, such a decision required governmental consideration and approval. But with the current composition of the Cabinet, the chief of staff would announce the nature of the operation and no one in the government would dare to demand that a greater effort be made by the army. I was told that the chief of staff would be inspecting units in the south, so I decided to visit formations which were not on his itinerary, so as not to get in his way. But this turned out to be unnecessary, for my escort officer was told during the night that Rabin would not be coming south after all. The next morning, May 24, Avraham Yoffe told me that Rabin was in bed sick, suffering from nicotine poisoning.

I accordingly went off to visit Arik Sharon, commander of an armored division, whose eyes sparkled as he explained his plan of breaking into the heavily fortified enemy defense system around Kusseima-Um Shihan-Um Katef if he got the green light. But for the moment he had received no permission and none of the forces required for such an operation. The only plan which had been confirmed by General Headquarters was the capture of the Gaza Strip.

From Arik I drove to inspect some of his subsidiary formations. I called on Kuti (Col. Yekutiel Adam), commander of an infantry brigade, and found him in excellent spirits. His forces were scanty, but he was ready—and, I was sure, also able—to storm the forward enemy strongpoints facing him without waiting for reinforcements. Kuti shared my interest in archaeology, and on this visit he gave me some ancient arrowheads and a flint ax which he had just discovered near Nitzana, right on the Negev-Sinai border. Some of the arrows had been fashioned not by cutting but by the improved, though more complicated, pressure method, which was fairly common in Egypt during the second millennium B.C. but rare in ancient Israel. Kuti poured his heart out to me at his being unable to use the bulldozers at his disposal for archaeological digs. If only, he said, he could find a tomb in this region like the one he had discovered in Yissor! Some time before, he had found several beautiful jugs in that tomb and had offered me one. To this day he cannot forget his chagrin over my having chosen the one jug which turned out to be adorned with the most exquisite decorations. He again asked me, for the thousandth time, how I picked on that jug and how I could know that beneath its thick white patina there would be decorations. I consoled him with the thought that we would discover other jugs, and he promised he would one day find and show me an untouched tomb which we would open together. That, I vowed, was a promise I would not forget.

At noon I returned to Southern Command headquarters just as the senior commanders had assembled for an Orders Group. I sensed an eve-of-battle tension, and, indeed, they were told that the long, depressing, nerve-fraying period of waiting was about to end. They were going to war. D-day was next day, May 25. It would start with an air attack in the morning. Ten days had passed since we had first learned of the movement of massive Egyptian forces into the Sinai.

With our attack about to start I arranged to be attached to the 7th Brigade in Talik's armored division. Its commander, Shmuel Gorodish, who had so impressed me with his confidence two days earlier, would be spearheading the offensive. It would be interesting to return and break through the same ground that I had traversed eleven years before in the Sinai Campaign. So—unless there was a change—we would be at war in the morning.

During lunch, it became clear that there was still no confirmation of a green light from the government for military action. Rabin, the chief of staff, was still sick, and Ezer Weizman, the chief of operations, was running the show in his place. The present operational order was better than the one that had been reported to me on the previous day. Action in the Gaza Strip was still part of it, but at least the 7th Brigade would now advance deep into Sinai, capture El Arish, and continue west toward the Canal. Perhaps my comments had had some effect after all, though I could have wished for two additional routes opened into Sinai at the same time. After lunch I found the local quartermaster and got from him combat fatigues (without badges of rank), boots, and a revolver. When I joined the 7th Brigade, I would abandon the civilian car and my escort officer and become a simple combat private. At 5 P.M. I was told that H-hour had been postponed for twenty-four hours, so I returned to Beersheba. It was teeming with troops. Vehicles rumbled by in a ceaseless stream, watched by the curious citizenry crowding the sidewalks. In the eyes of all hovered the question—when will the war be launched?

I drove on to the Desert Inn, the hotel on the outskirts of Beersheba where I was staying, and after dinner I went into the garden to breathe the air of this northern Negev region, dry, fresh, limpid. The lights in the distance beckoned, and I suddenly decided to stroll into town. I started walking along the main road, which boasted no pavement, keeping carefully to the side and out of the way of the convoys rumbling by. There was no point in trying to thumb a lift, as I knew no vehicle would—or should—stop. The traffic was all military transport, and everything was streaming one way—south, toward the Sinai border. All at once I noticed that a car which had passed me was slowing down, and the driver was motioning me toward him, managing at the same time to indicate by the twisting motion of his hand that he was unable to reverse toward me and against the press of vehicles behind him. I thought he must be a kind-hearted driver trying to help a stray pedestrian. It could not be anyone I knew, or some anonymous person who had recognized me from a press picture, for it was pretty dark, and the car had been traveling at top speed. No one could have spotted me. All became clear, however, when I reached the car, which had stopped long enough for me to get in. I saw the driver was Amos Yarkoni—formerly Abed el-Salim—the finest tracker I have ever met. True, over the years, wounded time and again in battle and getting blown up on mines, he had lost a hand and damaged a leg. But his acute tracking sense and uncanny powers of observation had remained unimpaired. He had recognized my walk in an instant.

I had known him when he was a child and I was in my teens. His family belonged to the Bedouin tribe of Arab el-Mazarib, who were encamped near Nahalal. I first met him some forty years earlier, when I was working in the Jewish National Fund forest in the hills of Nazareth and he was tending his father's sheep. He was a sweet little fellow of about ten, rather small for his age, who played his flute and eagerly devoured the bits of bread and jam we gave him from our lunch satchels. When he grew up, he naturally gravitated to the bands of Arab marauders who attacked Jewish settlements. I met him again in 1939, when we were both prisoners in Acre jail, he for being caught in an action against the Jews, and I for my membership in the Haganah. I felt no hatred toward him whatsoever. Indeed, I used to give him a little money in prison so that he could buy himself cigarettes.

After our War of Independence he became friendly with our people, joined our army as a volunteer, and was eventually picked for an officers' course. I was chief of staff by then, and I attended the parade at the end of the training. It is the custom for the outstanding cadets to receive their badge of rank from the general reviewing the parade. Abed el-Salim was one of the cadets to be honored. He had distinguished himself during the course, and as he stood before me while I pinned on his badge, I could not hide my emotions. It was amazing. Here was a young lad who had never been to school but who by native intelligence and unswerving persistence had learned not only to read and write Hebrew (I was not at all sure he could do the same in his native Arabic) and follow a map, but also to meet so successfully the difficult challenges of the Israeli army's deliberately tough officers' course.

I had hoped—and I was not to be disappointed—that a Western education had not smothered his natural abilities and the tracking talents he had acquired as a child, when he was able to discern, even on rocks, the tracks of a stolen cow. (I had once seen him do this!) During his years of army service, he was decorated no less than three times for conspicuous bravery, and though maimed and seriously wounded, he remained as lively and exuberant as ever, a man of iron character and independent spirit.

He was now living in Beersheba, and he drove me to his home. We drank the ritual coffee and I met his children, three charming girls and a boy. I also met his wife, a Christian woman who had converted to Islam. Like him, she spoke fluent Hebrew. At the end of my visit he drove me back to town and dropped me in the center, as I felt like walking through the streets.

That was a mistake. People sitting at roadside cafés recognized me and began calling my name. I soon had a procession behind me. One old fellow, obviously drunk, fell upon me, tears in his eyes, and tried to kiss me. Another buttonholed me with a story that he had tried to volunteer for the army but had been rejected and begged me to intercede. The crowds around me were becoming thicker and a policeman tried vainly to keep them away. Help came eventually from an unexpected quarter. Reuven, who was my driver when I was minister of agriculture, happened to be sitting in a café when he heard people shouting "Moshe Dayan, Moshe Dayan," and he had come looking for me. He got his car and drove me to the hotel.

Public opinion in Israel was reflected not only in the streets but in the general press. An editorial published in one of the more respected newspapers on the next day, May 25, called for "the inclusion in the government of men whose ability, experience, and prestige would ensure the maximum response on the part of Israeli citizens and maximum consideration for our position on the part of the nations of the world." Another editorial three days later spoke of the "widespread feeling of lack of confidence in the government in its present composition. It is the personality of Ben-Gurion that symbolizes to all the firm resolve of Israel to stand up to the most difficult challenges." But the government still stood firm in its posture that Eshkol would remain prime minister and minister of defense—and I continued my survey of our forces on the southern front.

The next morning, I joined a patrol of Yehuda Reshef's brigade along the entire border of the Gaza Strip and visited some of the border kibbutzim. The UNEF observation posts, which were right on the border, were abandoned, and the nearby UNEF camp had been completely stripped of anything movable—roofs of buildings, doors, window frames, right down to the last screw, in the best Arab tradition. The Egyptian troops were entrenched in their old line along the first ridge, a few yards from the border. Throughout the drive, not a single shot was heard. The fields in the strip were being worked as usual. This was the harvest season, and the area was dotted with bent-backed figures—peasants in white and Bedouin swathed in black—gathering vegetables or cutting and sheaving barley and wheat. On the Israeli side, too, work continued normally, except that with us the harvesting was done with combines and the farmers were accompanied by soldiers. But all on our side, farm settlers as well as troops, were aware of the gravity of the situation with the dismissal of the UNEF.

I drove to Tel Aviv and saw Ezer Weizman, who told me that the operation would begin the next morning, May 26. I again asked him to try and get me mobilized. From him I went to Meir Amit, head of Special Services, who gave me his appreciation of the situation, told me of our exchanges with Washington, and briefed me a little on the domestic political picture. On the general military situation, he said that all the neighboring Arab states were geared for an overall attack on Israel, that Egypt already had some eight hundred tanks in Sinai, and was continuing to secure reinforcements. The attack would be launched very soon. We had transmitted this information to Washington, stressing its gravity and asking whether the United States would now declare her readiness to "come to the defense of Israel as if it were the United States."

I explained to Meir, before he had to ask me, my reasons for being in the south at this time. To my considerable pleasure, though little surprise, he agreed wholeheartedly. However, he asked one question: if I were offered a responsible appointment, would I accept it? I told him I would, and indeed I had written a note to the prime minister, which I now handed to Meir and asked him to deliver in the morning. The note said:

"Dear Eshkol, I have asked Ezer Weizman to arrange my formal mobilization for active service so that my presence in an army unit will be legal and proper. If you or the chief of staff consider that I may be of help in this war by being given a specific task, I shall, of course, accept. If not, I shall continue in the meantime to be attached to combat units so that I may see developments at close quarters and be able to express practical views on the strength of the army and on what may be done. Moshe Dayan. 25.5.67."

Then I went to meet my daughter, Yael, who arrived from Athens that day. I had cabled her earlier to return home, as I had done on the eve of the Sinai Campaign in 1956. I believe that for an Israeli no feeling could be more dreadful than that of finding oneself abroad when war breaks out at home. I am very much attached to Yael, with bonds of love and high regard, and the one way to behave toward her is to try to guess what she would wish to do. I had no doubt she would wish me to call her in good time so that she could take part in the war. It transpired that she was more efficient than her father. En route home from the airport, she managed to get herself mobilized and was due to receive her posting the next day.

I took Yael to dinner at a festive restaurant, and at 11 P.M. I left Tel Aviv for the south, expecting to be taken to the 7th Brigade, which was scheduled to go into action a few hours later. But at divisional headquarters they were all asleep. The duty officers said they had been notified that H-hour would not be before 9 A.M., and like good soldiers they were using the respite to catch up on sleep. I realized that once more action had been delayed, for ground operations would start only after the pre-emptive air strike, and I did not see how that could be undertaken before Eban's meeting with President Johnson in Washington the next day. We could not have it both ways. We could either refrain from appealing to Johnson, or we could postpone our action until we had received Johnson's response. In the end, H-hour was again put off.

However, I was more disturbed by two developments. The approach to Johnson was apparently not over freedom of Israeli shipping through the Straits of Tiran but over an American guarantee to Israel against attack by the Arab armies. If this indeed was to be the focal point of our address to the United States, with its emphasis on the defensive aspect—namely, America's support for Israel as a victim if, when, or after she was attacked, and not America's support for an Israel that launched an attack in order to break the Egyptian blockade—then this was tantamount to our reconciling ourselves to a closure of the straits.

The second disturbing development was Eshkol's suggestion to the Gahal and Rafi parties that they join the Ministerial Defense Committee. Praise the Lord, that committee already had seven members. The prime minister's proposal would mean enlarging it with additional political leaders, when what was urgently required was a small war Cabinet of three or four people.

I was convinced that the most important step for us now was to meet the challenge of Egyptian might and defeat it. It would be catastrophic if Israel were to be seized by hysterical fear and start banging on the doors of the Big Powers, begging them to come to her rescue. Such an entreaty would immediately invite "conditions"— and all this when in fact, as I firmly believed, we were capable of putting the Egyptians to rout. To approach other countries and the United Nations, to present the facts of the situation, to show that right was on our side, to underline the seriousness of Egypt's blockade of the straits, and then, after convincing them of the justice of our case, to end up by proposing that *they* should settle the matter for us was both naive and foolish. Rather it should be our purpose to convince them that because of Nasser's dangerous acts, we were compelled to strike immediately at Egypt.

I was right about the operation being postponed again. I spent the morning of May 26 visiting two of Avraham Yoffe's brigades (commanded by Col. Iska Shadmi and Col. Elhanan Sela), reviewing battle plans with Yoffe, and finding that there was a growing sense of dissatisfaction on the part of the field commanders with the top army command and its operational approach. During that morning Eshkol got a message through to me saying that he wanted to see me. Flying back to Beersheba, I thought without relish of the meeting I was about to have. I also wondered about the next day. Would we attack? I thought it was time we did!

At 7:30 P.M. I met the prime minister at the Dan Hotel in Tel Aviv. He said he wished to establish a Ministerial Defense and Foreign Affairs Committee consisting of seven members: five (including himself, Eban, and Minister of Labor Yigal Allon) representing the several parties in his coalition government, and two members of the opposition, Menahem Begin, leader of Gahal, and myself from Rafi. I told him that I would not join this committee. On the other hand, if he, or the chief of staff, or any other responsible authority should invite my views (once I was mobilized, as requested), I would, of course, express them. I stressed, however, that I was *not* suggesting that I be appointed "adviser to the minister of defense" or be given any similar appointment. I wanted a combat task.

He then asked me about my impressions of the army and the nature of my visits to our formations in the field. At the end of the talk, he promised a reply within twenty-four hours to my request to be called up for active service. If this request was granted and I was offered a command, I would, of course, accept. If not, I wished to continue my current activities of visiting the men in the field and be attached to a fighting unit.

After leaving the prime minister, I again met with Meir Amit, and to him I set forth my objections to the present operational plans and my proposed changes, as follows:

• Since our *casus belli* was Egypt's blockade of the straits—a clear act of war against Israel—our campaign should be presented for what it was: a measure aimed at reopening the straits. In the nature of war, the campaign would take in all Egyptian forces in Sinai, including airfields, armor, and other formations lying between Israel and Egypt.

• The aim of the campaign should be to meet and destroy Egypt's military strength. This should be confined to the eastern half of Sinai. I rejected the assumption that seizure of territory and holding onto it could be used as a bargaining card in exchange for freedom of shipping. By "territory" I included the territory of Egypt proper. I was also against the capture of the Gaza Strip, which bristled with problems, and even more against reaching the Suez Canal, which could provoke an international crisis.

The Gaza Strip was a nest of wasps, the Canal a nest of hornets, and we should avoid involving them in the campaign. The idea that we would blockade the Canal and make its opening conditional upon the opening of the Straits of Tiran was gravely misguided. We would arouse all the Canal users against us, and they would do Egypt's work for her and help to destroy us. In the second phase, once we had routed Egyptian air and armored forces, and if political conditions permitted, we could proceed to capture the straits.

Though Meir disagreed with some of my proposals—he was in favor of advancing right up to the Canal—he was impressed with most of what I said and sought my permission to report it to the prime minister and ask him to hear it directly from me.

I repeated my remarks to Ezer Weizman, chief of operations, when he came to see me early the next morning, May 27, and he said that from the Air Force point of view, my plan was feasible. But he had two immediate problems. The first was the chief of staff. He said that Yitzhak Rabin had come to him a few days before with the announcement that he felt he should resign. Ezer had talked him out of it. The second was the timing of our attack. He thought that unless we acted at once, we would be too late, and Egypt would get in the first blow. I said I was not certain of Egyptian intentions and would like to see the intelligence material so that I could form my own conclusions.

At 3 P.M. the deputy chief of Intelligence brought me the intelligence data I had asked for. Within Sinai, the Egyptians already had some 900 tanks, more than 200 warplanes, and about 80,000 troops. From the data and a good deal of additional information he showed me, together with his own conclusions, it seemed that apart from the operational plans for her ground forces, Egypt also had plans for an air attack, which might be launched simultaneously with her ground attack or in response to action by us. He also gave me a nutshell report of President Johnson's reply to our approach to him: "First, give us [the United States] time and we will open the straits and guarantee freedom of shipping. Second, if you act alone, you will remain alone. If you refrain from attacking and the Egyptians attack you, we will help you."

On the other hand, we had information that the Americans were trying to appease the Egyptians. Johnson was ready to invite Nasser to Washington and to give him grants and loans, and the American ambassador in Cairo had told Nasser that the United States was not with Israel. However, there was no information repudiating the report that the same ambassador had officially requested that Egypt open the straits, restore the UNEF, and withdraw her troops from the border.

The instructions given to Eban by the government were to present the Egyptian actions as preparations for an all-out attack on Israel, and *not* to set the blockade of the straits as the central and principal issue. Eban, however, had concentrated on the straits. The Americans, for their part, had not accepted our assessment of an imminent Arab attack and presented us with an interminable list of questions for clarification. And so it continued, the tension increasing with no indication that Israel was prepared to take the ultimate step that would cut the noose now hanging around her neck.

On the evening of May 28, Eshkol broadcast to the nation. Two weeks had passed since Egypt began moving huge forces across the Suez Canal. The speech was awaited with expectancy. In every house throughout the country, in every tent and tank in the field, ears were glued to the radio set. At last there would be a clear analysis of the crisis, a lucid presentation of government thinking. But the prime minister faltered and bumbled through his address, stumbling over the words. (I learned later that the speech had been hurriedly prepared and hastily typed—with many errors—and Eshkol had not had time to go over it before being rushed to the microphone.) What the public heard were the halting phrases of a man unsure of himself.

The effect was catastrophic. Public doubt and derision gave way to an overwhelming sense of deep concern. An editorial the next morning said: "If we could believe that Eshkol was really capable of navigating the ship of state in these critical days, we would willingly follow him. But we have no such belief, and apparently this skepticism is felt by more and more people. Eshkol's radio address last night has increased their number. He is not constituted to be prime minister and minister of defense in the present situation. The proposal that Ben-Gurion be entrusted with the premiership and Moshe Dayan with the Ministry of Defense, while Eshkol is given charge of domestic affairs, seems to us to be a wise one."

At ten that evening I left for the south. Eban was expected back in Israel from his diplomatic missions that night, and there would be a Cabinet meeting immediately. If there was a decision to go to war, we would be moving off before dawn. But the next day, May 29, passed without any action. I thought it absurd to hang around doing nothing, just waiting for the government's order to the army to go ahead. What was worse was the on-again, off-again process, with the signal given and then canceled almost at the last moment. So I spent the day inspecting the regional defense system and again visiting frontier kibbutzim.

I stopped off at Kibbutz Nahal Oz on the Gaza Strip border. I had called in there on my patrol four days earlier and had been pleased to discover that Re'udar was now in charge of defense. He is a relative of mine, and I remembered him as an apple-cheeked little urchin in his Petach Tikvah home. He was now a serious young man, one of the pillars of the kibbutz, in charge of the poultry division—one of the most up-to-date in the country and the last word in automation—and now apparently responsible also for security.

I had found him in the poultry run on my previous visit, but the calm had been broken in the four-day interval, and my young friend was in his forward command post. The kibbutz field workers had been harvesting with their combines when armed Palestinian bands in the strip opened fire with mortars and machine guns, hitting a jeep and setting the standing corn on fire. The crop was ripe and dry and easy to set alight. The harvesters had evacuated the field, leaving behind two tractors and the damaged jeep.

We inspected the shelters. The children were having their lunchtime sleep. The walls were adorned with their drawings—surrealist or just paint daubing, I would not know. Outside the fields went on burning, darkening the sky with black smoke. It seemed to me that area defense had made little advance in the eleven years since the Sinai Campaign.

I went on to another border kibbutz, Mefalsim. When the members heard that I was there, they came crowding into the secretariat office, and the usual kibbutz debate inevitably followed. They plied me with questions, complaints, and demands. I found myself having to defend the government's position of postponing military action until all political clarifications with other countries had been completed. At the same time I stressed that I was only an ordinary citizen, with no authority whatsoever, and powerless to promise them more arms, more men, or more anything. But I was glad I had met them. I must say that in every place I visited, the attitude of the people was very friendly. It was particularly warm in Mefalsim, whose members are mostly from Latin America. They all seem to be very outgoing, more open and more cordial than *sabras* or even than Europeans and what the Israelis call Anglo-Saxons—people from English-speaking countries. When I left to return to Beersheba, dark clouds still hung over the smoldering fields of Nahal Oz.

Early the next morning, May 30, I flew to Eilat to talk to the regional commander and then lunched with the commander of the Navy. On our flight back, my escort officer spoke of what he called the "overwhelming" enthusiasm of the general public toward me. In Eilat, as in other places, owners of restaurants refused to present a bill for the meal. "Just keep well and bring us victory," they said. The same thing happened when we would stop off at a filling station for coffee. All kept saying they wished I was back in government and in charge of defense. Of course, they all read the newspapers, and for days the press had been full of lively political discussion on the subject of my possible return to office.

A front-page advertisement in one newspaper on that same day called for "changing the present bankrupt government by a government of national unity before it is too late." The irony was that this advertisement was signed by a member of Citizens for the Support of Eshkol, a group of distinguished men and women who had organized themselves during the 1965 elections to defeat Ben-Gurion and ensure Eshkol's return as prime minister.

The initiative—which developed into an ultimatum—to widen the framework of the government and establish a national unity administration was taken by the National Religious Party, headed by Moshe Chaim Shapiro, minister of interior. Shapiro himself was opposed to Israel's taking military action, but he was alert to the mood of the general public. (Actually, it was his view that only Ben-Gurion was capable of making a decision not to go to war and carrying the nation with him.) Even Menahem Begin, Ben-Gurion's political opponent, asked Eshkol to hand over the premiership to Ben-Gurion and serve under him. But the scars of the past could not yet be healed—or, as Eshkol had observed on an earlier occasion, "these two horses can no longer pull together."

During this period of ceaseless inter-party contact, the secretary-general of Rafi, Shimon Peres, was extremely active and effective, setting for himself one aim: the establishment of an incisive Cabinet capable of making decisions and restoring the faith of the nation in its government. He even proposed that Rafi should rejoin Mapai if that was the main condition for my appointment as minister of defense.

On May 30, when King Hussein of Jordan flew to Cairo and signed an Egyptian-Jordanian defense pact, the feeling that we had waited too long and were now faced with a threat on three fronts was too much: the prime minister had to give up the Defense portfolio. On the afternoon of the next day, I received a message from the prime minister asking me to see him at 4 P.M. Eshkol suggested that I join the government as deputy prime minister, while Yigal Allon would be given the Defense portfolio, an appointment supported by Golda Meir, then secretary-general of Mapai. I rejected the proposal out of hand, insisting that I would not take any job which was purely advisory. Indeed, I made a counter-proposal: that I be appointed commander of the front against the Egyptians, namely, GOC Southern Command—under Chief of Staff Rabin, of course, and accepting the usual channels and chain of command.

Shortly after I reached home, following this meeting, I was asked to return. Eshkol now had the chief of staff with him, and Rabin asked me exactly what I was proposing. I told him that I wished to command our forces confronting the Egyptian army, but he kept questioning me as to what I *really* wanted, underlining all the time that he was asking with the utmost sincerity: did I wish to replace him and return as chief of staff? My answer was a definite no. I explained that I had not approached the prime minister. He had approached me and had asked me to be involved in the war effort, but I did not want an advisory post. I wished to fight the Egyptians, and command of the southern front was the job I wanted above all others.

Yitzhak said he would like to think it over and give his reply the following day. Eshkol pressed him to give an immediate response, since he had called a Cabinet meeting for that evening and they had to reach a decision on military action. Apparently there was pressure from Mapai's coalition partners in the government. I left Eshkol and Yitzhak to work it out between them and went home.

Early the next morning, Thursday, June 1, I left for a visit to Central Command, where I was to inspect the Jerusalem area. At 8:30 A.M. I telephoned Yitzhak and asked whether my Southern Command appointment had been decided and if so whether I could proceed to take up my post. Yitzhak said he would speak to the prime minister and, if necessary, would get word to me while I was on my inspection trip. If not, I might telephone him on my return. He added that he had not yet spoken to Shayke Gavish, the current GOC Southern Command. I asked him, if he did speak to Shayke, to tell him that I would like him to stay on with me as my deputy or as the command chief of staff. But later, at a meeting of the Mapai secretariat held at noon that day, it became evident that Eshkol and Golda Meir were in the minority on the proposal to turn the Defense portfolio over to Yigal Allon and that the decisive majority favored my appointment as defense minister. Following the Mapai meeting, Yigal Allon informed the prime minister that he was withdrawing his candidature for the post. While this session was in progress, there was a demonstration of women outside Mapai headquarters demanding "the establishment of a national unity government and the appointment of Dayan to the Defense Ministry." Eshkol, whose sense of humor never abandoned him, promptly dubbed these earnest, zealous, sober-faced ladies "The Merry Wives of Windsor"!

At 4 P.M. the Prime Minister's Office telephoned and asked me to come. Eshkol told me that he proposed to recommend to the government that I be appointed minister of defense. In the evening, the Mapai secretariat met again, and the prime minister reported on the conclusions reached by the small special committee he had set up to negotiate with Gahal and Rafi on the broadening of the coalition. The Mapai ministers then left to attend a Cabinet session which was to make a formal decision on the inclusion of the new ministers in the government.

At 7 P.M. Eshkol telephoned to report that the Cabinet had just met and approved the decision to give me the Defense portfolio. As it was put in a newspaper interview I gave to young Winston Churchill the next day, it took the entry of eighty thousand Egyptian troops into Sinai to get me back into the government.

19

DECISION

Soon after the evening session on June 1, at which the Cabinet had endorsed the widening of the coalition, the enlarged Cabinet held its first meeting. Eshkol opened by announcing that the new government would be called the Government of National Unity, and he welcomed the new ministers. Menahem Begin, now a member of the Cabinet, replied in a brief speech, passionately sincere and studded with biblical epigrams, which a good-humored Eshkol punctuated with "Amen, Amen." The chief of staff then gave us a review of the enemy's strength and deployment, observing that if we had launched an attack five days earlier, we would have done so with a marked advantage in our favor. Eban reported on the diplomatic front, and this was followed by a discussion which was general but inconsequential. It lasted till after midnight. The new ministers had to familiarize themselves with the facts before they could present concrete proposals. That was certainly the case with me. I had to sit with the General Staff for a thorough review of the military scene. It was resolved that the next morning, at 9 A.M., the Ministerial Defense Committee would meet in the Emergency General Headquarters, together with senior officers of the General Staff.

I started the day of June 2 by a breakfast meeting with Zvi Zur, a former chief of staff. I had asked him, and he agreed, to be my number two. He could call himself adviser or assistant or any title he wished. (His title was later formalized as "assistant.") I told him to make arrangements whereby Ben-Gurion would be kept in the picture. I was also anxious for the ministry to make use of the considerable knowledge and experience of Shimon Peres, and I asked Zur to arrange for him to be given high-level assignments. As to the hierarchy inside the ministry, I told Zur that he would be responsible for the entire civil side of the defense establishment, but he would have no say on the military side. That would be for me and Chief of Staff Yitzhak Rabin to deal with, and I met Rabin immediately afterward. Later I met with the Ministerial Defense Committee and the General Staff. The generals were asked to speak their minds and they did so without inhibition, but it seemed to me that the issues—time and our operational plans—were not presented in the most appropriate way. I thought that stress should be laid on three critical points. One, that if we were going to war, the longer we waited the worse it would be for us, since in the meantime the Egyptians were fortifying their positions. Two, the duration of the campaign—if we were winning— would assuredly be limited because of the inevitable Security Council resolution and Big Power pressures to stop the war. If we had to stop in the middle, before the rout of the Egyptian army in Sinai, our subsequent withdrawal, under political pressure, would be hailed as a failure. Three, the campaign should be conducted in two stages: first, capture of northern Sinai; second, capture of the Straits of Tiran and Sharm el-Sheikh. If the first stage ended in victory, we could proceed to the second. If not, we would be unable to embark on action in southern Sinai.

At 11.30 A.M. I attended a meeting limited to Eshkol, Eban, Yigal Allon, and Rabin, and this was the most important meeting in which I had participated up to then. The prime minister asked for a clarification of our views, preparatory to a session of the Ministerial Defense Committee which he had convened for the following evening, Saturday night, in Jerusalem. He called on me to open. I said that we should launch a military attack without delay. If the Cabinet should make such a decision at its next scheduled session on Sunday, June 4, we should strike the next morning. The aim of our action should be to destroy the Egyptian forces concentrated in central Sinai. We should have no geographical aim whatsoever and we should not include the Gaza Strip in our fighting plans—unless, as was threatened, Iraqi troops entered and occupied it. The campaign would last from three to five days.

Yigal Allon spoke after me, and I must say I was disappointed. It had been many years since we had taken part together in a political-military discussion. Yigal agreed generally with what I had said, but he added that we should try to get close to the Suez Canal, so as to constitute a threat to it. It would then be clear that we could block its navigation if ever the Egyptians again blocked the Straits of Tiran. He also said that we should take the Gaza Strip and plan the transfer of its Palestinian refugees to Egypt.

I promptly raised objections to both proposals. I said that our proximity and threat to the Suez Canal would be a serious error. It would affect the interests of powerful forces in the world and turn some of our friends against us. We should therefore avoid getting too close to the Canal and certainly not adopt as a political tool the threat of its closure. As to the suggested movement of the refugees to Egypt, this was simply not possible. Such an operation would require the assent of the second party, Egypt, otherwise it would be a barbaric and inhuman act. On the contrary, we should strive to ensure that the United Nations Relief and Works Agency (UNRWA) continued to assume responsibility for the refugees. This might not be easy, for our operations in Sinai were likely to cut off the Gaza Strip from Egypt, UNRWA would have to receive its supplies via Israel, and UNRWA might not agree to this arrangement. At all events, Yigal's proposals did not seem at all feasible to me.

It was clear from Eban's general remarks that he was not enthusiastic about military action. Eshkol, on the other hand, without saying so explicitly, indicated that he was in favor of military measures. It was agreed that the consultations would be continued in Jerusalem the following night.

I lunched with Lt. Gen. (Res.) Yigael Yadin, a former chief of staff and now professor of archaeology at the Hebrew University, who had been asked by Eshkol to suggest procedures of work and cooperation between the prime minister and the minister of defense and to delineate their respective powers and responsibility. This was the third time in the brief period of Israel's statehood that the Defense portfolio was separated from the premiership. The first was in 1953–1955, during Ben-Gurion's temporary retirement, when Sharett was prime minister and Pinhas Lavon was defense minister. The second was from February to November 1955, when Ben-Gurion returned as defense minister under the premiership of Sharett. Yet no clear division of authority between the premier and the minister of defense had ever been defined, established, or even discussed. This time such definition was especially required for two reasons: the separation of the two posts occurred on the eve of war, and I had been appointed defense minister against the will of the prime minister. Furthermore, Eshkol and I did not have the close and informal relationship that existed—or was thought to have existed—between Sharett and Ben-Gurion or Sharett and Lavon. Yadin had prepared a draft, and I accepted it with only minor amendments.

The main points of the agreement reached by Yadin and myself were that "the minister of defense will not act without the approval of the prime minister" in launching a war against any country or attack any country which up to that moment had not taken part in hostilities. Nor would the defense minister on his own order the bombing of an enemy country unless that nation had first bombed Israeli cities. Eshkol later confirmed this agreement.

In the evening there was a review of the operational plan for the Sinai action. The original plan had undergone various revisions, and the one now before us received my approval. It called for penetrations along four axes, two parallel to each other, in the Rafah area at the southern end of the Gaza Strip, and two in central Sinai. There would be no conquest of the Gaza Strip, no reaching the Suez Canal, and no advance, for the time being, to the Straits of Tiran, since the issue of freedom of shipping was being handled, for the moment, by the United States. Our meeting lasted until 11 P.M., and I then went to the home of Shimon Peres, where Ben-Gurion and others were gathered to drink a toast to the occasion of my appointment.

I spent the next day, Saturday, June 3, our Sabbath, organizing the work procedures of my ministry, meeting with senior officers on the General Staff, holding a press conference with foreign and local correspondents, and consulting with the prime minister in Jerusalem about the Cabinet session to be held the next morning. At the press conference, I made a brief opening statement and then answered the many questions; most of them, of course, on whether I thought the crisis would be settled at the council table or on the battlefield. Without being explicit, I was hoping that despite the popularly drawn implications of the establishment of the National Unity Government and my own appointment to the Defense post, the impression might be gained that we were not about to go to war but were intent on exhausting all the diplomatic possibilities. Moshe Pearlman, my special assistant, told me later that he thought this was indeed the impression of the correspondents, judging from what they were saying and their reports of what they had filed.

At 5:30 P.M. I left Tel Aviv for Jerusalem and my meeting with the prime minister. Yigal Allon, Yigael Yadin, Meir Amit, and our ambassador to Washington were also present. Amit had returned that day from his lightning visit to Washington and reported on his meeting with Defense Secretary McNamara and others. His private conclusion was that the United States would do nothing to open the straits—Amit's friends scoffed at the idea of the proposed "naval task force"—but would also do nothing if we went to war. There was even a possibility that the United States might help us in the political sphere—at the U.N. Security Council and General Assembly.

The tenor of the meeting was that the die was cast. I was not the only one who urged that military action be launched at once. Eshkol, too, said there was no escaping war now, and it should be started as soon as possible. I asked him to convene the Ministerial Defense Committee so as to secure an authorized decision on the matter.

The Ministerial Defense Committee met in Jerusalem at 8:30 the next morning, Sunday, June 4. Eban opened with a report on the diplomatic developments. The latest was an official notification to the prime minister by President Johnson that America hoped to secure the signature to a declaration on navigation in the straits from all the states it had approached, except France. De Gaulle had refused to sign, although in 1957 France had signed the original pronouncement guaranteeing freedom of shipping through this waterway. The United States was still working toward the establishment of a naval task force which would demonstrate this freedom, and she hoped that at least six other countries, including Britain and Holland, would join such a force. For the present, only Australia and one Latin American state had agreed to take part. The intended arrangement was for this naval demonstration to take place one week from that day, namely, June 11. Under this plan, an Israeli vessel would be escorted through the straits by the task force, and if the Egyptians opened fire on it, the escorting warships would return the fire.

Furthermore, the Americans stressed the importance of "who fires the first shot." That was the criterion by which the United States would determine her stand, and we, therefore, should refrain from being the first to fire. It was the American view that hostile action had not yet been perpetrated—despite Nasser's action in ordering out the UNEF and blockading the straits. Nasser's deeds could not be considered the opening act in a war against Israel.

Two days earlier, Israel's ambassador to Moscow had been summoned by Soviet Foreign Minister Gromyko and given an official notification to be transmitted to the Israeli government. Its concluding paragraph stated: "The Soviet government wishes to repeat and make clear that it will do everything to prevent the possibility of military conflict. Its efforts are now concentrated on this aim, but should the government of Israel take upon itself the responsibility of an outbreak of war, it will have to pay the full price for the results."

In France, there were mass demonstrations of support for Israel, but they had no impact on de Gaulle. On June 2, the French Cabinet decided that France did not consider herself bound by any commitments to any of the parties in the Middle East. France recognized the right of existence of all states in the region; all should refrain from any form of violence; and the first to use armed force would lose her support. The problems connected with navigation in the Gulf of Aqaba, together with those of the Arab refugees and of the relations of the neighboring states in the region, should be solved jointly by the Four Powers, the United States, Russia, France, and Britain.

On the next day, June 3, there was an announcement that France had decided temporarily to delay the supply of arms to Israel. In a talk with our ambassador in Paris, de Gaulle emphasized that France was in favor of Israel's existence, but "1967 is not 1957. I was not then in power," he said. In the meantime, France had renewed its association with the Arabs and was anxious to foster this relationship. France was stopping supplies to Israel, he insisted, because she wished to prevent us from going to war. The problems of the Middle East had always been solved by the Great Powers—in the past by Russia, France, and Britain and now also the United States.

England, for her part, was coordinating policy with the United States. British Premier Harold Wilson was in Washington at the time and would apparently be ready to take part in the procedures suggested by President Johnson, namely, signing an appropriate declaration and joining a demonstrative naval task force.

After this report from Eban, Intelligence chief Yariv outlined the moves and intentions of the Arab states. Egypt considered a military confrontation with us as unavoidable and was pouring armed forces into Sinai. A Kuwaiti armored brigade was about to land in Sinai, and an Iraqi battalion was en route to the Gaza Strip. Libya and Sudan had also promised expeditionary forces to Egypt, but these had not yet reached Sinai.

There were very evident signs that the Egyptians were about to launch their attack. The previous day, General Murtagi, commander of Egyptian forces in Sinai, had published in Cairo the following Order of the Day:

"The eyes of the world are upon you in your most glorious war against Israeli imperialist aggression on the soil of your fatherland . . . your holy war for the recapture of the rights of the Arab nation. . . . Reconquer anew the robbed land of Palestine by the grace of God and of justice, by the power of your weapons and the unity of your faith."

Nasser was also working on Syria and Jordan to secure their participation in the war. In Jordan, a front command subordinate to the United Arab Command had been established under Egyptian General Abdel Munim Riad. Riad was in control of all Jordanian forces, and he had ordered them deployed along the entire Israeli border. Iraq had promised the immediate dispatch to Jordan of four infantry brigades, as well as an armored force. In a demonstrative act, Jordan had canceled her order of aircraft from the United States and waived delivery.

When the head of Intelligence completed his report, Eban added the postscript that, according to the U.S. secretaries of state and defense, Dean Rusk and Robert McNamara, it was the American judgment that while Egypt would probably take military action against Israel, an *immediate* attack was not expected. As to our arms requests to the United States, the Defense Department had pointed out that even if they were granted, much time would elapse before the weapons reached Israel, so they would have no impact on the current crisis.

After the reviews by Eban and Yariv, Eshkol asked for my assessment. I had handed him in writing the proposed decision I thought we should take, and I now said that two major changes in the situation had occurred in the last few days. One was the Egyptian aim and efforts to get Jordan to open the eastern front. The second was Egypt's preparations for an immediate military attack. Two Egyptian commando units that had been sent to Jordan within the past two days were out-and-out assault forces. The Egyptians might not strike the next morning, but I believed they were anxious to get in the first blow. If they thought that was our intention too, they would not hesitate to beat us to it and launch their attack the day before we did. If they succeeded, the implications for us would be the loss of our advantage of surprise and the opening of a second Arab front.

There were two aspects to our loss of surprise. What we failed to gain in a pre-emptive strike we would be unable to achieve later. Though we all confidently proclaimed we would win, we had to remember that the size of our forces was limited, and if we lost many troops and pilots, victory would not easily be gained. We were not like the United States, which could throw in wave after wave of reserves. For us, each soldier counted. When the chief of Intelligence reported that Egypt had received another Iraqi air squadron and additional MiGs, we tended to nod and say "So what?" But all these additions posed greater difficulties, which were not lightly overcome. Members present at this meeting, I said, were preening themselves over their great accomplishments in the past week: they had staved off war for that period. I wished them well in their self-satisfaction, but I had to point out that each passing hour had made our task more complicated and bloody. Now, a march on Rafah or Gaza, which had been sparsely armed a week before but which were now filled with enemy tanks and infantry—brought in during the week our ministers had "saved"—would cost us many more in killed and wounded. It was not possible to assault one fortified emplacement after another without casualties.

Whoever argued that we should wait another week in order to ensure our political rear presumably knew what he was talking about. But anyone who felt that in the end we were likely to be involved in war should know the value—and the cost—of each day. How then could we speak so lightly of waiting another week?

We now had to make our decision on whether or not to carry out a pre-emptive strike. If we took the enemy by surprise, we would knock at least one hundred of their warplanes out of action. This, for us, would be the equivalent of all additional arms supplies we might receive for the next six months—if indeed there was a country that would agree to supply us with weapons, for in my opinion we would not receive a single plane over that period, whether or not there was an official arms embargo. De Gaulle would not let us have aircraft even if Egypt started the war. The first shot would determine which side would suffer the heaviest casualties, and would assuredly change the balance of forces.

But of far greater importance was the basic prospect of victory. Put bluntly, I said, our best chance of victory was to strike the first blow. The course of the campaign would then follow our dictates. If we opened the attack and effected an armored breakthrough into Sinai, the enemy would be forced to fight according to the moves we made. We would probably also be able to hold the other fronts with small forces.

Considering the situation in which we found ourselves, I said, with hundreds of enemy tanks poised on each of the axes leading into Israel from the Egyptian bases in Sinai, together with the last-minute preparations they were making, it would be fatal for us to allow them to launch their attack. We should decide to strike the first blow.

The prime minister followed me. While he spoke, a signal arrived from the president of the United States. It was long, convoluted, and negative in tenor. Apart from the traditional sentence which had been uttered by all four American presidents since the establishment of the state respecting the "territorial integrity of Israel and the other states in the region," the message was discouraging. The president cabled that he hoped by strong action to reach a satisfactory solution to the problem of freedom of shipping through the straits, but that such action had to be taken by the United Nations or the Maritime Powers, and at all events not by the United States alone. The United States was studying the British suggestion calling for an international presence in the waters of the straits.

Eshkol called Johnson's message disappointing. Its one virtue, he said, was that it was an improvement over de Gaulle's. Our situation was grave indeed, and in our return cable to the president we should explain why, but we should neither invite nor wait for a reply. We should now do what had to be done—Eshkol was reluctant to utter the word "war"—and perhaps, he added, we would have been better served had we acted three or four days sooner.

Eshkol ended the meeting with the proposal that orders be given to the army to choose the time, place, and appropriate method. In the special style of the prime minister, this meant launching our attack at what the army considered the right moment.

Our meeting of the Ministerial Defense Committee had been conducted in two sessions. There was a break in the middle for a regular session of the full Cabinet—and for the new government to be officially photographed. All ministers were present when the prime minister put two resolutions to the vote, one by me and one by the representative of Mapam, the left-wing labor party within the coalition.

I proposed that the government take armed action to liberate Israel from the military stranglehold that was being increasingly tightened and to prevent the attack that was about to be launched against her by the forces of the United Arab Command. The government should authorize the prime minister and the minister of defense to approve the timing of the action to the General Staff of the Israel Defense Forces.

The Mapam ministers proposed that the government, in order to break out of the aggressive and strangling ring of the enemy, should press on with the move it decided upon on May 27—namely, that we postpone any decision for the time being and follow the efforts of President Johnson to set up a multi-national fleet to break through the straits, while making clear to the Powers that our security and our existence were in grave danger and demanding immediate supplies of arms as required by the increasing seriousness of our security situation.

The Mapam resolution received only the two votes of the party's ministers. All the other ministers voted for my resolution, which thus became the government decision. I telephoned Rabin and informed him that the operational plan, including H-hour set for 7:45 the next morning, was approved for action.

Following the Cabinet meeting, I returned to Tel Aviv and met with the chief of staff and with the deputy chief of operations to review our projected action in the south. I then flew north for a meeting with Dado (Maj. Gen. David Elazar), the GOC Northern Command, and heard his situation report and proposals. I emphasized—against his urging—that the Syrian front was not to be activated, and no action was to be taken to capture, as he wished, three Syrian border emplacements. Instead, I thought he should strengthen our defensive arrangements, extend our minefields and add to our fortifications. The one area where I thought we might advance was the demilitarized zones, but we should move only up to the former international line and not beyond. This was also to be done in the El Hamma area, where we might advance eastward along the Yarmuk River, so as to be able to divert our share of the waters of this river into the Sea of Galilee—as envisaged in the Johnston Jordan River Plan. Under this plan, worked out in 1953–1955 by President Eisenhower's special emissary, Eric Johnston, we were entitled to share the waters of the Yarmuk with Syria and Jordan. But at the last moment, Syria, prodded by Egypt, decided not to sign the agreement for political reasons, and Israel was denied her share of the water.

A Cabinet session had been scheduled for ten o'clock the next morning. A room had been placed at my disposal in the Emergency General Headquarters, and I would sleep there. If there were no unexpected developments, the war would begin as scheduled at 7:45 A.M.

Nothing special happened during the night. Toward dawn all our forces were ready for action. I telephoned Rahel and asked her to breakfast with me. The war was an hour away, and I wanted to see her, if only for a few minutes, if only in a café. We went to a small one a few hundred yards from General Headquarters, sipped our coffee and ate hot rolls. I, of course, told her nothing of what would be happening soon, simply saying that I had to be back at my office at 7:30. Later, she was to complain—or rather make a slight show of complaining—that I had not even offered her the slightest hint.

This was the third time in my life that I had been appointed to a central position in state affairs. The first was on December 6, 1953, when I became chief of staff. The second was in 1959, when I joined the government under the premiership of Ben-Gurion as minister of agriculture. This time, however, the "feel" was different. In the present post, my all-absorbing concern and interest were the war and my responsibility for it, and not the ministerial member-of-the-government part of the job. Indeed, my membership in the Cabinet was very tenuous. I took no interest in subjects not associated with defense, and the veteran ministers, mostly members of Mapai, the major party in power, regarded me as an outsider whom they were compelled to accept as an expert on military matters. But my pattern of life underwent a radical change. From being a member of the Knesset who remained uninvolved in the work of parliament, who was in the political wilderness as a member of the small Rafi opposition party, as one who did not quite know what to do with himself and who filled in time by directing a fishing company or visiting Vietnam, I had suddenly become one of the key office holders in the state, with a determining voice in the direction of Israel. This sense of personal revolution, however, quickly evaporated in the vastly changed atmosphere that enveloped the country as it plunged into war.

Not that I was unmindful of the prestige of the office or the publicity attendant on my being in the news. This assuredly added something of a new style to the life I was living. But it was all part of the overall mood of war, and war changed everything anyway. Of course, I was on the crest of a wave, but it was the strong wave of the entire people of Israel, army and civilians, surging forth to break the shackles by which they were being bound. I confess that I felt a deep sense of satisfaction, proud that I had been chosen to bear responsibility in the nation's grimmest hour and gratified by the demonstrations of support shown both in the army and in the country. I was confident that I would know what to do—and what not to do—about the military and political developments associated with the war.

Nevertheless, I was conscious at all times of the heavy burden that had become mine. I could not dismiss lightly the words of Ben-Gurion, who had warned against embarking on this war. Nor could I ignore the stand taken by de Gaulle, the cautionary advice of Dean Rusk, and particularly the threats of the Russians. And I could hardly forget that if the previous war, the Sinai Campaign, had lifted my spirits in victory, it had also left me with the scars of our withdrawal.

Moreover, this was the first time I would be acting without being subject to higher authority. True, I was subordinate to the prime minister, Levi Eshkol. But in fact, and psychologically, there was a great difference between my current position and my post during the 1956 war, when I was chief of staff working under Ben-Gurion. I thought well of Ben-Gurion, and even when we differed and I considered him mistaken, I would carry out his orders with an easy heart, knowing that in the end he might well turn out to have been right. This was not the case now. As a minister in Eshkol's government, I did not feel myself absolved of the need to weigh the issues as though there was no one above me. Ben-Gurion, whose political wisdom I had always admired, was now staying not far from my office, but I forbore from taking counsel with him. I thought that he had an imperfect vision of our situation, that he was living in a world that had passed. He still admired de Gaulle, had an exaggerated opinion of Nasser's power, and underrated the controlled strength of the Israel Defense Forces. For good or ill, this was how the wheel had turned. In this war I would be on my own.

20

EXPLOSION

D-DAY, JUNE 5, 1967. H-hour, 07:45.

At 7:30 A.M. I was in the Air Force command post. The tension was almost tangible. Not an eye moved from the war table, not an ear from the radio network. When our aircraft reached their targets and it became clear that they had not been detected, a stone—just one, but of agonizing weight—rolled off the heart. The opening move had succeeded. The planes began their bombing runs, and Southern Command received the coded order: "Nahshonim, action. Good luck." Nahshon, leader of the tribe of Judah during the Exodus, is traditionally believed to have been the first to enter the waters of the Red Sea as they parted, setting an example to the rest of the Children of Israel, who promptly followed. Our armor, too, began moving.

Within an hour the pilots' reports began coming in: hundreds of enemy planes destroyed, most of them on the ground! Surface-to-air missile sites had also been destroyed or put out of action. Only rarely was a plane of ours hit. So we had crushed the enemy's air strength. But this was only part of the enemy's armed might, and our tanks had not yet encountered the Egyptian armor. However, already, within a few moments, the nightmare of the previous weeks had vanished. True, the war had only just begun, but it was the kind of start which augured well for the remaining phases. Egypt was left without an Air Force. This not only removed the danger of her bombing our civilian population, but it also gave our land forces a decisive advantage. They would enjoy air support; the Egyptian army would not.

Our attack on Egypt's air bases was carried out in two waves. In the first, 183 aircraft took part. Between 7:14 A.M. and 8:55 A.M., 11 Egyptian airfields were attacked; 197 enemy aircraft were destroyed, 189 on the ground and 8 in aerial battle; 6 airfields were rendered inoperable, 4 in Sinai and 2 (Fayid and Kabrit) west of the Suez Canal; and 16 radar stations were put out of action. In the second wave, 164 planes participated. They attacked 14 air bases and destroyed 107 enemy aircraft. Our casualties were 11 pilots—6 killed (5 in the first wave, 1 in the second), 2 taken prisoner, and 3 wounded—and we lost 9 planes. Six were hit but returned safely and could be repaired. Altogether, the Egyptians that morning lost three-quarters of their air strength—304 of the 419 warplanes in their possession.

The operation of the first wave went off exactly as planned, and the considerations underlying the planning turned out to be correct. H-hour had been set for 7:45 A.M. on the assumption that at that hour the senior Egyptian officers would be on their way from home to headquarters. This proved right. Flying at low altitudes and maintaining radio silence brought our aircraft to their targets without detection. The order for radio silence was so strict that it was not to be broken even in the event of a crash or the abandonment of an aircraft, and the maximum altitude allowed any plane was extremely low.

The briefing to wing commanders was given by the commander of the Air Force, Maj. Gen. Mottie (Mordechai) Hod, on the afternoon of the previous day, Sunday, June 4. The wing commanders briefed their squadron leaders that same evening, at 8 P.M. And next morning, the pilots were awakened at 3:45 so that they could bone up on the briefing. The first formation to take off made for the Bir Gafgafa air base in Sinai. One minute later the second formation took off for Abu Suweir, west of the Canal. The planes that followed attacked Beni Suyeif and Cairo West. The attack on the airfield of El Arish was carried out without bombs, so as not to damage the runways. It was presumed that El Arish would be captured in a day or two, and our Air Force would wish to use it.

The enemy air bases which received the heaviest attention were Abu Suweir (where we carried out 27 sorties); Fayid, close to the

Great Bitter Lake (24 sorties); and Cairo West (22 sorties). These three held the largest concentration of warplanes. Through a navigational error one of our formations of four planes reached Cairo International Airport. There were no military aircraft, so it was left untouched.

At 9:34 A.M. the second wave took off. In this one, unlike the first, there was some improvisation and change from the original plan, for now account had to be taken of the results of the first attack wave and possible unexpected developments. There were some airfields where all the aircraft had been destroyed and there was no need for a repeat assault. As against these, some enemy aircraft had succeeded in escaping and landing at other, more distant, airfields which had not been included in the original plan. Of the 164 sorties carried out by the second wave, 115 were attacks on air bases, 13 were against radar stations, and the rest were engaged in patrol and close support to the attacking planes. This wave bombed 14 air bases, of which 6 had not been attacked by the first wave and where escaping enemy craft had landed. These were the most distant targets—Mantzura, Bilbis, Helwan, Minis, Gardake and Luxor. The air base most heavily pounded in both operations was Abu Suweir, where 61 warplanes were destroyed in 52 attack sorties.

By the time the second wave went into action the Egyptians were on full alert, and at some of the targets our planes met heavy anti-aircraft fire. Yet on the whole the conditions were easier this time. The dense pillars of smoke that rose from the bombed airfields helped navigation, and there was now no need to keep radio silence or to fly at dangerously low altitudes.

While our Air Force was engaged on the Egyptian front, the Syrian, Jordanian, and Iraqi Air Forces began attacking Israel. The Syrians were the first. Twelve MiG-17s took off from Damascus at 11:50 A.M. Two of them attacked Kibbutz Deganiah, setting fire to a silo and a poultry run, and then went on to bomb—and miss—a company strongpoint at Bet Yerach, also on the Sea of Galilee, and a dam on the Jordan River. Three others attacked an airfield in the Jezreel Valley, and one was brought down by the field's anti-aircraft guns. Another flight of three set a haystack and a granary on fire near Kibbutz Ein Hamifratz in the mistaken belief that they were bombing the Haifa oil refineries. The rest strafed and rocketed the convalescent home of Kfar Hahoresh, near Nazareth, damaged buildings, and wounded one Jew and one Arab.

The Jordanian Air Force was the second to go into action, its Hunters taking off at noon and attacking the coastal resort of Netanya and the Kfar Syrkin airfield near Petach Tikvah. At Kfar Syrkin they destroyed a Nord transport plane that was on the ground. Two hours later three Iraqi Hunter planes flew over, sending rockets in the direction of my own settlement of Nahalal, no doubt believing it was the Ramat David airfield. They caused no damage and returned to Iraq.

As soon as the reports came in of Syrian and Jordanian air attacks, Mottie Hod ordered his staff to "Plan Syria and Jordan—fast!" Within minutes, eight flight formations that were on their way to hit other targets were diverted in the air to Syrian and Jordanian air bases.

Thus, at 12:15 P.M., a third wave of Israeli warplanes went into action on basic missions to wipe out or reduce the enemy's air strength. Fifty-one sorties were carried out in Jordan in attacks on the two air bases of Mafrak and Amman and the entire Jordanian Air Force of twenty-eight warplanes was destroyed. In the process the runways were damaged, but in any case there was no plane left to use them.

Syria lost almost 50 percent of her Air Force—53 planes destroyed out of a total of 112—in 82 attack sorties on the air bases of Damir, Damascus, Seikal, Marjarial and T-4. Iraq lost 10 planes in a 3-sortie attack on a single field, 3-H. Our own losses in this third wave were 10 planes, 5 pilots killed, 2 wounded, and 2 taken prisoner.

For the men of our Air Force, it had been a long, arduous, and hazardous day. It was their day. By brilliant planning and by daring combat between dawn and sunset, they had assured the successful outcome of the campaign against three countries.

We had taken the first step in the war with Egypt. We were now faced with two additional problems that required an immediate answer: the nature of our military response to the two other Arab belligerents, Syria and Jordan, and how to cope with the inevitable charge in the world that we had "fired the first shot."

Throughout the intensive air activity in the morning, I tried to spend as much time as possible in the Air Force command post. Mottie and his senior staff officers sat in the front row facing a glass partition, and I sat just behind them. There was continuous chatter from the signals equipment, with the receiving of information and transmission of orders. And there was the constant movement of duty officers coming and going. Yet all seemed to freeze, all sound was cut off, at critical moments, allowing Mottie to concentrate in silence, to listen, reflect, decide, and issue his fateful orders.

As we followed the pilots' reports, there were lightning changes of mood, silently registered by the expression in everyone's eyes. They shone when we heard: "Shot down MiG," "I'm hit, but okay," "Returning to base." And there was sadness at "I'm bailing out" or "Can't see the parachute." The officers in the command post knew every man in the air and could identify each one of them. The professional jargon was economical, terse, dry. It was their language, the language of their lives, and it gave them a tangible feeling of what was happening in the air battles, as if they themselves were sitting in the cockpit. When things were going well, there was a quick smile. But when a pilot was hit, wounded, bailing out, or landing by parachute and seeking a hiding place in the dunes, behind a shrub, or between rocks, their thoughts were with him at every moment. Helicopters, a doctor, and protective fighter planes were sent racing to his aid. But it was as though the men in the command post were with him all the time, bound to him by an unbreakable physical link.

I had known Mottie for many years, as I had known his predecessors, Ezer Weizman and Dan Tolkowski. But Mottie and I shared a common background. Mottie was also a son of Kibbutz Deganiah. True, when he was born, I was already with my parents in Nahalal, but the special bond with his family had never been cut. His uncle, Zvi Fein, was a member of Nahalal, and his late father, Yosef, had guided me on the eve of the action in Syria in 1941. Yosef was among the first settlers of Metulla, the northernmost Jewish village in the country, right on the Lebanese border, and he knew the Arabs, their language, customs, and pattern of living extremely well. He was also a close friend of many Arab families in the Galilee, in Syria and Lebanon. During the long nights we had spent together, when I was preparing myself for my mission, he had instructed me in the "do's and don'ts"—and above all "when to believe and when not to believe"—when going on a joint operation with Arabs. Before the Allied incursion into Syria, which was then under Vichy rule, I went on night reconnaissance patrols across the border together with an Arab guide, and Mottie's father was fearful of what might happen if I were caught. If all went smoothly, he said, and I remained undetected, the Arab would not give me away. But if I got into trouble, who knew what he might do? Now, in the command post, watching Mottie drink jugful after jugful of water, as he followed his pilots with deep anxiety on their bombing runs over the enemy air bases, I could not help recalling the figure of his father, standing on a hillock on the northern border, anxiously waiting till dawn for my return from a Syrian night patrol.

The question of "who fired the first shot" was asked me at 8:30 that morning by a member of the Knesset Foreign Affairs and Security Committee. I had reluctantly left the air command for a short while and met the committee at Sdeh Dov, the Tel Aviv airfield. They were there waiting to emplane for a tour of the northern front, which had been arranged the previous week. I had not canceled it, so as not to arouse speculation and jeopardize secrecy. Now, when I saw them, I read them the announcement put out by the army spokesman shortly before: "As of this morning, stiff fighting is in progress between Egyptian air and armored forces advancing toward Israel, and our forces who have gone out to stop them." I then briefed them on the morning's events. I did not reply directly to the "first shot" question, but since they had already heard my views on the importance of initiative and surprise in battle, they did not need to do much guessing.

In the meantime, Cairo Radio announced that the Egyptian Air Force had shot down forty Israeli planes. There was, of course, no substance to this claim, but Arab vanity and extravagance now served us well. I told those concerned with public information to make no mention of our victories for at least the first day, to keep the enemy camps confused.

But it was not only the outside world that mattered. We had to say something to our own people and to our troops. The prime minister accordingly gave a radio address to the nation, and I spoke to the troops over the army broadcasting service, saying that the Egyptian General Murtagi, commander of the Arab forces in Sinai, had told his men that the world expectantly awaited the results of their "holy war" and called upon them to capture by force of arms and fraternal unity "the stolen land of Palestine."

"Soldiers of Israel," I said, "we have no aims of conquest. Our purpose is to bring to nought the attempts of the Arab armies to conquer our land, and to break the ring of blockade and aggression which threatens us. Egypt has mobilized help from Syria, Jordan, and Iraq and has received their forces under her command. She has also been reinforced by army units from Kuwait to Algeria. They are more numerous than we; but we shall overcome them. We are a small nation, but strong; peace-loving, yet ready to fight for our lives and our country. Our civilians in the rear will no doubt suffer. But the supreme effort will be demanded of you, the troops, fighting in the air, on land, and on sea. Soldiers of the Israel Defense Forces, on this day our hopes and our security rest with you."

Syria and Jordan joined the war. At 11:45 A.M. the Jordanians opened up with artillery and mortars on the Jewish quarters of Jerusalem and followed shortly afterward with artillery and light-weapons fire all along the cease-fire line. Half an hour later, Syria went into action with her Air Force, bombing the cities of Tiberias and Megiddo.

The hostile move by Jordan raised three questions. The first concerned Jerusalem, which was held only by a reserve brigade of elderly men: what action to take, and when. The second involved the order of priority in the allocation of our forces. We had to assign all the required formations to the Egyptian front in order to achieve a decisive and speedy victory. From where, then, could units be taken and diverted to the eastern front? The third problem was how to protect our civilian population from Jordanian fire. The Jordanian front, unlike the Egyptian, adjoined our most densely populated centers—the Jerusalem area, the crowded coastal plain, and the valleys of Jezreel and Bet She'an.

The basic problem posed by Syria's entry was whether to respond with all-out war or to limit ourselves to local raids, shelling, and air strikes. My own view was that two fronts were enough, and we should avoid, insofar as the matter rested with us, a third front. Moreover, there was no objective in Syria as vital to our interests as, for example, Sharm el-Sheikh, the key to freedom of shipping to Eilat, or as Jerusalem and the West Bank, which were part of the flesh and bones—indeed, the very spirit—of the Land of Israel.

After consultations in the war room with the chief of staff and his senior officers, I finalized the following orders:

• Our Air Force was to go into action against any state whose aircraft attacked us.

• In the Jerusalem area, our forces were to return fire against the sources of Jordanian fire but were not to bomb or shell the Old City.

• Forces were to be readied for offensive action in Jordan, both in Jerusalem (by the 10th Brigade) and in the north (by units of Northern Command).

At 12:30 P.M. there were consultations with the prime minister. He approved my directives that the 10th Brigade should capture Mount Scopus; the Air Force was to deal with military objectives in Jordan and Syria; and that Northern Command was to capture the Jenin area, so as to remove our Ramat David airfield from the range of Jordanian artillery.

After the meeting the chief of staff asked me whether in the operations against Jenin we should not also capture Ya'abad, a few miles to the west. I approved. Ya'abad is a large Arab village located on top of a mound which dominates the Valley of Dothan, and it had a history both ancient and recent. It was here, some 3,500 years ago, that

Joseph was sold by his brothers to the Midianite merchantmen. And it was here, during the Mandatory administration, that an Arab woman who was out gathering wood came upon the terrorist-zealot Az-el-Din el-Kassam and his friends. They were hiding in a cave, and she gave them away to the British. The biblical episode of Joseph the dreamer had a "happy ending." The Kassam band were shot. Modern times.

21

WAR

In the ten years since the 1956 Sinai Campaign, the Egyptians had moved considerable forces into the Sinai Peninsula and built a series of powerful strongholds to serve the twin purposes of offense and defense. Those closest to Israel's Negev border were both springboards for an Egyptian invasion of Israel and barriers against an Israeli penetration of Sinai. The fortifications established deeper in the interior were rear bases to serve the forward positions, holding concentrations of reserve forces and supplies to nourish the fronts, and provide defensive fallback lines if the advance positions fell.

The most formidable of the eastern strongholds were those which commanded routes of entry into Israel for an Egyptian invasion force and at the same time barred access to routes across Sinai if Israel invaded. The only routes across Sinai capable of carrying heavy-combat vehicles were in the northern half of the peninsula, a largely flat, sandy expanse of desert covered by treacherous dunes, but also marked by hills and wadis. This was the main battle area of Sinai, as distinct from the mountainous, impassable, trianglar southern half. This southern part is bounded by the Gulf of Suez in the west and the Gulf of Aqaba in the east. Sharm el-Sheikh, near the tip of the triangle, was normally accessible only by a coastal road along the eastern shore of the Suez Gulf. Effort, stamina, and resourcefulness alone enabled our 9th Brigade to make their battle trek along the trackless shore of the Aqaba Gulf which so surprised the Egyptians at Sharm el-Sheikh in 1956.

But even in the northern half of Sinai, the routes are limited to two main ones, the northern and the central, and a rough subsidiary southern route. These routes are themselves linked by occasional roads and rough tracks. To guard against the entry of an Israeli force to the northern route, which runs along the Mediterranean coastal belt to Kantara on the Suez Canal, the Egyptians established a fortified base at Rafah, in the northeastern corner of Sinai and at the southern edge of the Gaza Strip. But this base could also be a jump-off point for an Egyptian penetration of Israel's southern coastal plain. It was indeed through Rafah and up the Gaza Strip that Egypt invaded the new State of Israel in 1948.

To bar Israel from the central route, running from the Israeli border in the east to Ismailia on the Canal in the west, Egypt built a cluster of fortified bases in the defended locality of Abu Ageila and nearby Um Katef. And again, an Egyptian invasion force could use Abu Ageila to invade Israel and threaten Beersheba.

Bases were also established at Kusseima, to the south of Abu Ageila, and further south at Kuntilla. Both offered access to the southern route, which reached the Canal at Port Tewfik and the city of Suez, at the head of the Suez Canal. And both Kusseima and particularly Kuntilla could serve an Egyptian force seeking to cross the Israeli border to cut off Eilat.

These Egyptian frontier strongholds were large defensive localities often as deep as twenty miles. At the core were powerful fortifications, stiffened by artillery and anti-tank gun positions and machine-gun nests, with tank detachments and long rows of trenches and surrounded by extensive minefields. Guarding all approaches were outposts which were themselves miniature editions of the central bastion. Further back toward the Canal at intervals along the routes, usually where they were crossed by a lateral road or track, were further strongholds and military bases.

Now, on the eve of what was to become known as the Six Day War, not only were all these strongholds manned in great strength, but they were the centers of huge concentrations of armored and infantry divisions which had poured into Sinai in the previous three weeks.

The basic Israeli attack plan was to break through the Rafah

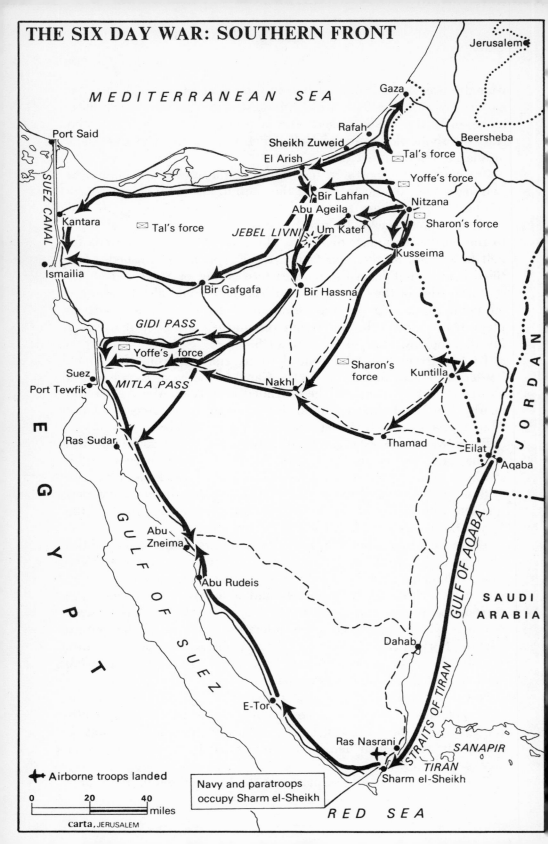

THE SIX DAY WAR: SOUTHERN FRONT

MEDITERRANEAN SEA

Jerusalem

Gaza

Port Said

Rafah

Beersheba

Sheikh Zuweid

El Arish

Tal's force

Yoffe's force

Bir Lahfan

Abu Ageila

Nitzana

Kantara

Tal's force

JEBEL LIVNI

Um Katef

Sharon's force

Ismailia

Kusseima

SUEZ CANAL

Bir Gafgafa

Bir Hassna

GIDI PASS

Yoffe's force

Sharon's force

Kuntilla

Suez

Port Tewfik

MITLA PASS

Nakhl

Ras Sudar

Thamad

Eilat

Aqaba

E G Y P T

GULF OF SUEZ

Abu Zneima

SAUDI ARABIA

Abu Rudeis

GULF OF AQABA

JORDAN

Dahab

STRAITS OF TIRAN

E-Tor

SANAPIR

Ras Nasrani

TIRAN

Sharm el-Sheikh

✈ Airborne troops landed

Navy and paratroops
occupy Sharm el-Sheikh

0   20   40
miles

carta, JERUSALEM

RED SEA

stronghold in the northern sector and the Abu Ageila bastion in the central sector by coming at them from unexpected directions and in unexpected ways; advance through the gaps and engage enemy concentrations in the rear; race toward the Suez Canal, capturing or outflanking enemy bases on the way, engaging enemy armor, and trapping forces left in Sinai by sealing the escape routes; and securing the land route to Sharm el-Sheikh and lifting the blockade on the Gulf of Aqaba.

The offensive against the Egyptians in Sinai was carried out by three divisional task forces commanded by Maj. Gens. Yisrael Tal, Arik Sharon, and Avraham Yoffe, under the GOC Southern Command, Maj. Gen. Yeshayahu (Shayke) Gavish.

While the Israeli Air Force was delivering its strike on Monday morning, June 5, Tal's force, operating in the northern sector and spearheaded by Shmuel Gonen's (Gorodish's) armored brigade, routed an Egyptian division, broke through the fortifications of Rafah, opened the coastal route, went on to capture a divisional headquarters, and reached the approaches to El Arish, on the Mediterranean, by dusk. Overcoming the strong Rafah bastion took a whole day of tough fighting. In a two-brigade pincer movement, Gonen's armored force assaulted from the north and Raful Eitan's paratroops, as well as an infantry and an armored unit, made a deep flanking movement through the sand dunes to attack from the south. There was also stiff fighting that day at one of the bases along the westward route before El Arish. El Arish fell the next day, as did its airfield, which was put to immediate use by our Air Force. From El Arish, a reconnaissance unit and paratroops on half-tracks sped westward toward the Suez Canal, while armored units advanced to tackle the enemy in the heart of Sinai and link up with other of our forces that had broken through in the central sector.

The breakthrough in this sector was carried out by Sharon's task force. In a complex night operation requiring meticulous timing and coordination between armored, infantry, and paratroop forces, Sharon launched his attack on the fortified positions at Um Katef, covering the crossroads at Abu Ageila, at one hour before midnight. Heliborne paratroops landed behind the enemy lines and wiped out several artillery batteries that were shelling the approaches to Um Katef and Abu Ageila. An infantry brigade marched across the dunes and under heavy fire burst into the long trenches of the stronghold and cleared them in bitter hand-to-hand fighting. An armored unit engaged the tanks within the Um Katef stronghold, while another tank battalion advanced westward and then swung round to break into Abu Ageila from the rear. Before the battle was over, an armored brigade from Yoffe's task force performed the complicated operation, in perfect coordination with Sharon, of moving through Sharon's lines and pressing on westward. It soon caught up with a sister brigade of Yoffe's force whose tanks had laboriously driven over stubborn terrain between the northern and central sectors and emerged beyond the enemy's forward strongholds.

The breakthrough phase was completed in just under two days, and our troops now had space to maneuver as they tackled the enemy forces and bases in their advance toward the Canal. But the breakthrough battles had been very tough indeed. The Egyptians in the strongholds had not been taken by surprise. They were ready for our assault and had all the armaments and defensive installations to meet it. They were defeated because our three divisional task forces showed a superior fighting capacity in two main areas. First was their persistence and stubborn determination to advance and capture their objective in spite of all the difficulties—heavy casualties, numerical inferiority, and at times even the knowledge that they were running out of ammunition and fuel. The second was their professional expertise: close cooperation between armored, artillery, infantry, and engineering forces; accuracy of fire and sophisticated use of terrain; and flexibility in combat deployment to meet the rapid changes in the battle situation. Included in this factor of high professional ability was also the skill shown by all three task forces in advancing through sand dunes in areas which the Egyptians had considered impassable. This factor carried great weight in the overall planning of the battles.

By the end of the second day, the Egyptians in the forward positions who had not been trapped began to retreat, following a withdrawal order they had received from Cairo. When we learned that the enemy troops in Sharm el-Sheikh had begun to leave, we quickly advanced the date we had set for its capture and decided to dispatch a paratroop unit without waiting for our land forces to secure the land route. At 1 P.M. on June 7, helicopters carrying the paratroops reached Sharm. Flying round it, they saw two Israeli torpedo boats tied up at the quay. A naval force under Col. Botzer ("Cheetah") had reached it at 11:30 A.M., found it empty, and put two detachments ashore. Three-quarters of an hour later, it ran up the Israeli flag on the roof of the hospital which the UNEF had established before being ordered out by Nasser. The first enemy prisoners in the area also fell to the Israeli Navy. Thirty-three Egyptian commandos who had been holding the island of Tiran were caught together with their weapons when trying to escape to Egypt in two fishing boats.

It was in this fortunate but undramatic manner that the flag of Israel was restored to Sharm el-Sheikh, the blockade of the gulf lifted, and one of the main objectives of the campaign gained.

In the evening of June 7, we heard that the Security Council was about to meet in emergency session and was likely, under Soviet pressure, to impose a cease-fire for the following morning. We held hurried consultations, and the General Staff issued orders at 10 P.M. to two divisional task forces to advance immediately to the Canal, and also to Ras Sudar on the Gulf of Suez. Tal's force was to prevent the retreating Egyptian forces from crossing the Canal to the west bank. Yoffe's force was to secure a continuous land link with our units in Sharm el-Sheikh.

One of Tal's units set off one hour after midnight and before dawn had gotten to within ten miles of the Suez Canal. It was followed by a paratroop brigade. After battling a strong Egyptian combat team of commandos, paratroops, heavy tanks, and artillery, our men reached the Canal by capturing Kantara East. They advanced south at first light and at 7:30 A.M. on June 9 reached the Ismailia crossroads and the Firdan Bridge. Seven hours later, they were joined there by an advance armored unit from Tal's force which had fought its way through the central sector, capturing the large enemy base of Bir Gafgafa and smashing the Egyptian armored concentration in the area. With our troops at the Firdan Bridge, this retreat exit for Egyptian troops across the Canal was now sealed.

In the meantime one of Yoffe's brigades had swung southwest in pursuit of the retreating enemy trying to get through the Mitla Pass to reach the Canal. The route was strewn with burned-out enemy vehicles that had been attacked from the air, as well as with unprimed mines that had been hastily laid by the fleeing Egyptians. As the lead unit caught up with them, hundreds of enemy tanks, armored personnel carriers, and transport vehicles were moving in long convoys toward Mitla. One battalion took a short cut across a difficult track to block the entrance to the Mitla Pass and reached it with nine tanks. Many Egyptian formations had managed to enter Mitla before it was blocked. Some had got through, but a large number had been attacked by our Air Force, and the pass had become a huge graveyard of enemy combat vehicles. But there were still many vehicles belonging to rear units that now tried to force their way through the barrier by frontal attack. The small blocking unit of nine tanks, which was reinforced only the next morning by another ten, fought with the utmost stubbornness and kept the pass barred from 5 P.M. on June 7 until noon next day, when it was relieved by another unit.

Yoffe's force captured the Mitla and Gidi passes and went on to the Canal after fighting stiff tank battles with well-deployed Egyptian units that battled hard to hold us up and give their fleeing comrades a chance to get away. One of the brigades then moved south along the eastern shore of the Gulf of Suez.

Sharon's task force, after the breakthrough battles, had raced south and southwest to pursue and destroy the retreating Egyptian armor. After a large-scale ambush of enemy tanks at Nakhl on the southern route, his units advanced to Mitla.

The Gaza Strip had been attacked on the first day of the war—though I had opposed such action in the opening phase, since I believed that the strip would be cut off and surrender without a battle once Rafah and El Arish had been captured. But after enemy units had shelled Israeli border settlements, the GOC Southern Command and the chief of staff had urged that the strip be captured immediately. In the event it took more than two days of fighting to secure it. The battle for Gaza could have been avoided.

The completion of the conquest of all Sinai was marked by a link-up on the evening of Saturday, June 10, at Abu Zneima, a small fishing village midway along the eastern shore of the Gulf of Suez, by a force from Ras Sudar moving south and the paratroops who had landed at Sharm el-Sheikh moving north. On their way, the paratroops had captured E-Tor and gone on to gain control of the Abu Rudeis oil wells. The link-up should have taken place forty-four hours earlier, and when I got to Abu Zneima, I was furious over the delay. But Abu Zneima was serene and relaxed. After all, it was from here, more than 3,500 years ago, that ships laden with turquoise quarried at the mines of nearby Serabit el-Khadem had carried their opulent cargo across the gulf to decorate the palaces of the Egyptian Pharaohs.

After four days of bloody battle, failure, and traumatic shock, experienced by both his soldiers in the field and by their superiors—political as well as military—Nasser accepted the cease-fire. It came at the close of Thursday, June 8. Nasser and his military chiefs had failed to read Israel's intentions to react to his naval blockade, though the signs were evident. It should have been clear to them, particularly after the establishment of the National Unity Government, that Israel was bound to break the blockade by capturing the Straits of

Tiran—which could be achieved only by first battling in the heart of Sinai. Yet the Egyptians convinced themselves that Israel would not dare to take action. Nasser learned through his ears that the war had started—he heard the explosive sounds of the attack on Cairo West airfield. His army commander, Gen. Amer, learned through his eyes—the sight of pillars of smoke rising from the air base at Abu Suweir.

Nasser and his military commanders also failed to grasp Israel's operational plan after battle had been joined. And they failed to judge correctly the events on the battlefield—they were often unaware of them until it was too late to take counter-measures. And finally they failed to display the required resilience after the shock of our pre-emptive air strike. The effect of the shock was more psychological than operational in the opening phases of the war, for though Israel gained command of the skies, Egypt's cities were not bombed, and the Egyptian armored units at the front could have fought even without air support.

At 9:35 Thursday night, June 8, U.N. Secretary-General U Thant told the Security Council that the Egyptian representative had just notified him of Egypt's unconditional acceptance of the cease-fire. This was a complete reversal of Egypt's position up to that moment. Only seven minutes before, the Soviet representative had submitted a draft resolution calling not for an *unconditional* cease-fire, but for an Israeli withdrawal to the 1949 lines. And twenty-four hours earlier, Nasser had informed the presidents of Algeria, Iraq, and Syria and the King of Jordan that Egypt would not stop fighting as long as a single Israeli soldier remained on Egyptian soil. He made this statement an hour and a half after the Security Council had adopted a resolution demanding acceptance of a cease-fire by all parties, to take effect at 10 P.M., June 7. Nasser had not been mouthing empty slogans. He really wanted to go on fighting and believed he could do so. That same night, the Cairo High Command ordered the Egyptian forces to launch a counter-attack against the Israeli army, and one unit had indeed tried to do so.

Nasser became painfully aware of the true state of affairs only on the night of June 8, when he heard that Kantara East had fallen and that his Sinai forces were in panic flight and had no hope of establishing a defense line. It was then that he had instructed his U.N. representative to accept the cease-fire.

Our troops were already at the Canal when Egypt accepted the cease-fire. Nevertheless, I thought we might be able to establish a line some distance from the Canal after the war. I wanted a line that would prevent Egypt from re-introducing her armed forces into Sinai yet enable her to maintain normal life in the Canal area. After we had captured Kantara East, I had requested a consultation with the prime minister and the chief of staff, and we decided that our forces would halt twelve-and-a-half miles from the Canal. But there were two new developments. First, despite Egypt's acceptance of the cease-fire, remnants of her forces continued to harass our units east of the Canal. Second, America was about to submit a resolution to the Security Council calling on each side to remove its armed forces to six miles from the Canal, and we thought it well to have an area from which to withdraw. Our General Staff had accordingly issued a correction to its previous order and said that only after the fighting ended would the new deployment go into effect.

Shortly after our opening air strike against Egyptian air bases on Monday morning, June 5, we sent a message to King Hussein of Jordan recommending that he refrain from hostile acts against us and no harm would befall him. The message had been sent through Norwegian General Odd Bull, commander of UNTSO, the U.N. Truce Supervision Organization. Hussein's answer was given to us only after 11 A.M. It said that since we had attacked Egypt, we would get the Jordanian reply from the air. Shortly thereafter, Jordanian Hunter warplanes took off for targets in Israel.

Jordan followed up this aerial bombardment by shelling the Jewish part of Jerusalem and other Israeli centers, as well as our international airport at Lod. At 1:55 P.M. we received a call from General Bull to say that his headquarters building on the southern outskirts of Jerusalem between the Israeli and Jordanian lines had been seized by the Jordanian army. A unit of the Arab Legion had entered the demilitarized zone and taken control of the entire U.N. compound.

We now had no option but to engage in full-scale action against Jordan, reluctant as we were to divert resources from the fighting in Sinai. Our Air Force quickly reacted to the air attacks, and within a few hours the Jordanian Air Force was completely wiped out. Maj. Gen. Uzi Narkiss, the GOC Central Command, received permission to retake the UNTSO building and to go on to capture an Arab village, which cut off the Arab part of Jerusalem from Bethlehem and Hebron. Later, units from our Northern Command broke through the Jordanian lines in the north to enter Samaria and capture several Arab Legion forward positions.

The campaign on this front now had to continue at full strength, and the focal point, geographic and political, was of course Jerusalem, divided into Arab and Jewish halves since 1948, with the Old City in Arab hands. A reservist armored brigade under Col. Uri Ben-Ari was accordingly summoned to a point ten miles west of Jerusalem. And a reservist paratroop brigade under Col. Motta Gur, waiting near an airfield to emplane for an operational drop in Sinai, was ordered to Jerusalem instead.

While these units were on the move, I myself was on my way to Jerusalem to perform a constitutional duty. My appointment four days earlier as minister of defense required formal approval by the Knesset, and I had to go to Jerusalem to take the oath of office from the rostrum at a parliamentary session. One had been convened for that afternoon. But when I reached the Knesset, Jewish Jerusalem was being shelled and everyone was in the shelter. I hung around for a while, grew impatient, and returned to General Headquarters. That night I was informed that the Knesset had convened later and approved the new ministerial appointments. I could take the oath at a convenient time after the war. The only Knesset members to register a negative vote were the four representatives of the Communist Party. One of them, Taufiq Toubi, an Arab, had heckled when the voting results were announced, and called out: "This means that four members favor peace and condemn war!" He had to shout these words of wisdom to make himself heard above the noise of exploding Jordanian artillery shells!

While the Knesset was meeting, Ben-Ari's brigade was breaking through the Jordanian hill positions west of Jerusalem. It continued advancing during the night and battled its way around to come upon Jerusalem from the north, arriving near the Israeli enclave of Mount Scopus overlooking the Old City at noon next day, June 6. There it met with the surviving remnants of a paratroop battalion that had fought its way at great cost to open the road to Mount Scopus, which ran through Arab-held suburbs, and restore its link with the Jewish part of Jerusalem.

Motta Gur's paratroops had gone into action at 2:30 A.M. on June 6 with no time for a thorough reconnaissance because of the hasty switch of assignments. Their first task was to break through to the dominating ridges of Mount Scopus and the Mount of Olives. To do this they had to make frontal assaults on the Jordanian Police School compound, which had been turned into a fort, just inside the line separating an Arab from a Jewish suburb, and a formidable fortification known as Ammunition Hill beyond. Led by the officers, the leading assault company stormed the Police School under withering fire. Suffering casualties every minute, the assault troops cut their way through four fences, reached the peripheral trenches, cleared them in hand-to-hand fighting, and captured their target.

Without pausing they raced toward Ammunition Hill, followed by other units of the battalion, and advanced against this bastion. Complete with bunkers and all-round embrasures for machine guns, it contained forty firing emplacements, also protected by stout walls of stone. They were trained on all possible approaches. Blood was shed with every forward move, but our men went on, fighting in bunkers, emplacements, and trenches. The last enemy post was captured at 6:15 on the morning of June 6.

The battle for Ammunition Hill was the toughest in the war against the Jordanians. The best fighting men in the Israel Defense Forces took part, and twenty-one were killed. More than half of the troops and the majority of the officers who fought at Ammunition Hill and the Police School were wounded. It was not only the difficulty in capturing the objectives, nor the heavy price that was paid, but the heroism displayed by each fighting man that made this battle unforgettable and gave it a permanent place in the military annals of Israel.

When I reached Mount Scopus shortly thereafter, Uzi Narkiss told me that in the afternoon the paratroops would attack the Augusta Victoria building, between Mount Scopus and the Mount of Olives, in order to reach the Jericho road and cut off Jerusalem from the east. But due to various mishaps, in which we suffered heavy casualties, the attack had to be put off till the next morning, by which time the Jordanian unit had withdrawn and fled across the Jordan. With our occupation of Augusta Victoria on Wednesday morning, June 7, and with it control of the Jericho road, the encirclement of Jerusalem was complete. From the observation plaza in front of the Intercontinental Hotel on the Mount of Olives, brigade commander Motta Gur issued the order to his battalion commanders to advance to the Lions' Gate and enter the Old City. They burst through the gate, turned left onto the Temple Mount, and from there went to the Western Wall.

As they were entering the Old City from the east, Eliezer Amitai's Jerusalem Brigade was about to enter it from the south, through the Dung Gate. His troops did so half an hour later, having captured several Arab positions and cleared the minefields between Mount Zion and the Church of Peter in Gallicantu. It was soon after this that I entered liberated Jerusalem and visited the Western Wall.

THE SIX DAY WAR: CENTRAL FRONT

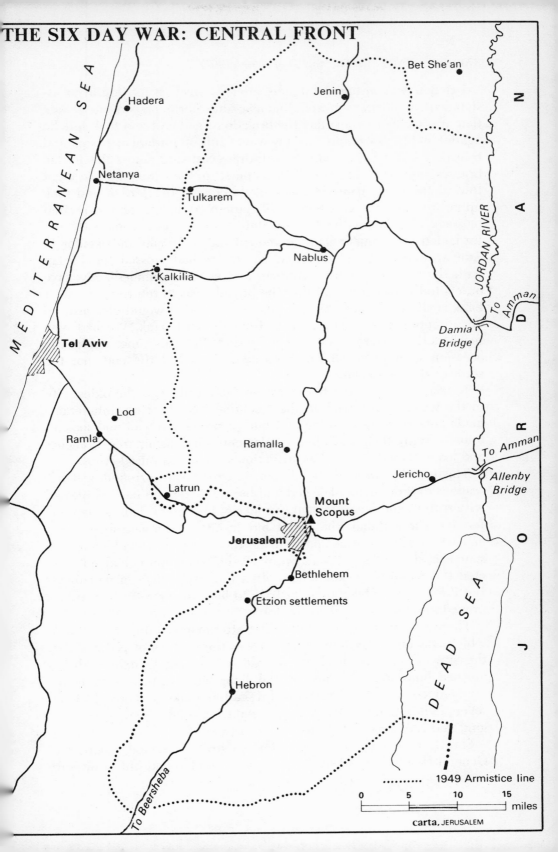

MEDITERRANEAN SEA

Hadera

Jenin

Bet She'an

Netanya

Tulkarem

Nablus

Kalkilia

JORDAN RIVER

To Amman

Damia Bridge

Tel Aviv

Lod

Ramalla

Ramla

To Amman

Jericho

Allenby Bridge

Latrun

Mount Scopus

Jerusalem

Bethlehem

Etzion settlements

DEAD SEA

Hebron

To Beersheba

N A D R O J

······· 1949 Armistice line

0   5   10   15
miles

carta, JERUSALEM

Uri Ben-Ari's armored brigade, after completing its Jerusalem assignment at noon, captured Ramalla, due north of Jerusalem, late that afternoon. The next day the brigade turned east and took Jericho against light opposition. The town was full of Jordanian troops and transport waiting their turn to withdraw eastward across the Jordan bridges, and when the Israeli tanks burst in, there was a panic flight toward the river. Units of the brigade crossed the Jordan and took up positions on the east bank. This prompted an urgent and excited message to us from the United States ambassador. Apparently the Jordanian government had summoned the American ambassador in Amman and informed him that our forces had crossed the Jordan with the aim of capturing Amman and es-Salt. I immediately gave orders to the General Staff that the brigade was to return to the west bank of the Jordan and blow up the bridges. This would demonstrate our intention to cut ourselves off from the east bank. We had now reached the eastern limit of our fighting. But this time, unlike the occasion with Joshua 3,300 years ago, it marked the end, not the start, of the campaign.

Jericho, "city of palm trees," as the Bible calls it, is the oldest city in the world, going back to the Neolithic Age. Its early inhabitants made constructions of stone and built a protective wall and lookout towers. With their primitive implements, and using tree branches and loam, they developed an irrigation system and raised crops.

This is the lowest inhabited spot on earth. The surrounding landscape is dry, desolate, bleached and bare. But Jericho itself is blessed with springs and seems to float in a lake of lush grass. This is the same Jericho where Rahab the harlot hid Joshua's reconnaissance scouts and where Elisha miraculously made the foul water wholesome—the source is still called Elisha's Spring. Which conqueror had not coveted this oasis? Who knew how often the city had been destroyed? But it had always been brought back to life. The sweet-water springs proved more enduring than the forces of destruction.

There was another tank battle that afternoon, Wednesday, June 7, which was far more dramatic. This was the capture of Nablus, near the site of biblical Shechem, in which a young lieutenant distinguished himself by pitting his four light tanks against a Jordanian armored column of more powerful Patton tanks and knocked out seven, in addition to an armored personnel carrier, a jeep, a recoilless gun, and a truck laden with Jordanian troops.

Shortly before noon on Thursday, Central Command reported to General Headquarters that its Jerusalem Brigade had linked up with

Southern Command, having advanced south from Jerusalem and seized Bethlehem, Hebron, and Dahariah. I promptly set off for Hebron, meeting Uzi Narkiss in Jerusalem and driving south with him. Crossing the old border between Jerusalem and Bethlehem, we still had to be careful not to go off the track which had been cleared through the minefield. But after that there was almost no sign of war. The Hebron hills were in full bloom. While the valleys at that time of the year were fiery in the summer sun, the fields parched, here it was still spring. All was green and fresh. There was no traffic along the roads, apart from military vehicles, and in the groves and vineyards the farmers were at their usual tasks. Every inch of soil between the rocks was carefully nurtured and planted with vines and olive and fig trees.

We looked in at the Pools of Solomon and then turned off to the Etzion bloc, the group of religious kibbutzim which had been destroyed by the Arabs in 1948. Virtually nothing remained of these four Jewish settlements. In their place the Arab Legion had erected army camps and a mosque. As I looked around, reflecting on what had happened to the original pioneers, I felt quite certain that new kibbutzim would soon spring up on this site. And, indeed, a few months later the restoration was started by the children of the founding members who had been killed in 1948. They were determined to build houses and schools and renew the fields and raise children for whom the Etzion bloc would be a permanent home.

We moved on to Hebron. It was under curfew. The streets were deserted. The mosque over the Cave of Machpelah, burial place of the Hebrew Patriarchs, was guarded by a single soldier against the entry of any of the troops. As our jeep swung into the entrance and screeched to a stop, the guard sprang to alert and turned his rifle at us, shouting "no entry." He then pointed to a sign on the door which our men had put up noting that this was a holy site and out of bounds to the troops. We sat back in the jeep, unmoving. He was about to harangue us when he suddenly gulped, apparently having registered who we were. His rifle still in his hands, he waved it toward me and said, "I suppose it's all right for you. You can go in." I thanked him and we went up the steps and into the building.

It was the first time I had been inside. Entry to the Cave of the Patriarchs had been prohibited to Jews. Under Moslem rule, they were allowed only up to the seventh step outside the building, and there they could look through a hole and catch a glimpse of caves down below. We went beyond the seventh step and up into the hall. On the left was a Moslem prayer chamber. On the right were the traditional tombs of the Patriarchs Abraham, Isaac, and Jacob and their wives.

I was, of course, moved by the idea that Jews would again be able to visit one of the ancient holy places to which they had been denied access for so long. But I cannot say that I was impressed by the actual structure built on the site. The biblical Cave of Machpelah, which Abraham bought for "four hundred shekels of silver" from "Ephron the son of Zohar" for "a possession of a burying place," had no doubt been a typical cave scooped out of the gray rock of the slopes above a field of barley. But there was nothing in the building to suggest this. Two thousand years after Abraham's death, during the Christian period, the original Jewish burial place had become the site of a church, and later still, with the birth of Islam, it was turned into a mosque. But it was not only the Byzantine, crusader, and Mameluke additions which were out of character. Even the huge, basic, rectangular building erected during the Herodian period in the first century B.C. failed to evoke the image of wandering shepherds, one of whom tended his father-in-law's flock for seven years as the price of each wife!

I decided that arrangements would have to be made for both Jews and Moslems to come, pray, and pay homage at this shrine. On my arrival, I had noticed that an Israeli flag flew from the building. I ordered it to be taken down. The flag should be flown from the office of the governor, not from the roof of a sacred tomb. The flag was removed.

During this tour, I gave the policy directive to the GOC Central Command that he was to act in accordance with our intention to establish permanent Jewish settlements in the Mount Hebron and Jerusalem areas. Further north, on the central range above Jenin, Nablus, and Ramalla, we would have to establish army camps so that we could hold the Jordan River with a small force.

For the moment, only Jordan and Israel had announced their readiness to accept the cease-fire. Egypt and Syria had refused for the time being to obey the Security Council resolution. We requested a meeting with representatives of Lebanon, considering that perhaps the time was now ripe for talks with them. If they were unwilling to sign a peace treaty with us, perhaps we could conduct negotiations for some other arrangement that would be helpful. They rejected our approach, stating that Lebanon was officially in a state of war with

Israel. This meant that even the Armistice Agreement that had existed between us since 1949 was no longer valid.

Jordan's rapid exit from the campaign had two important effects. The immediate one was military—we were able to transfer our forces from the Jordanian to the Syrian front. The second was political—the Palestinians on the West Bank had not taken part in the war. Most of the battles took place outside the populated areas, so that the clashes were between professional Jordanian armed forces and the Israeli army. Almost no harm or damage was suffered by the civilian inhabitants of Judea and Samaria. From my point of view, and my understanding of the system of relations we should strive to fashion with the Palestinian Arabs, this fact was to have decisive implications.

On the first day of the war, Egypt appealed to Syria to launch an all-out attack on us. Syria's response was trifling—a few bombing sorties by her Air Force and the shelling of a village. Israel's Air Force struck back at Syrian air bases and destroyed fifty-three of her planes. That night, the government of Syria made its most important decision of the war. It decided to cancel "Operation Nasser," whereby Syria was to join Egypt in an overall attack, and substitute the less grandiose "Operation Jihad" (holy war). This involved a defensive deployment, coupled with minor offensives with small forces across the border. In line with this plan the Syrians carried out two unsuccessful attacks on a northern kibbutz and a military post on June 6. Thereafter, they confined themselves to shelling our kibbutzim and a few of our army camps.

At 11:30 A.M. on Friday, June 9, after Jordan was completely and Egypt almost out of the campaign, our forces attacked the Syrian fortified positions on the border. The cease-fire went into effect a day and a half later. In fact, the breakthrough operations lasted seven hours, until evening, and they were indeed violent hours. But during the night, the Syrians continued strong opposition only in one position. In all other sectors, after we had broken into their fortifications, the Syrian military system collapsed. At the highest level, the Army Command in Damascus even preceded its forces in the field by deciding to abandon the campaign. At noon on Friday, when Syria's leaders realized the threat to the Golan Heights, they took action in two spheres. Politically, they increased their efforts to bring about a cease-fire. Militarily, they ordered a withdrawal from the line of the Golan Heights and the concentration of all forces in a deployment

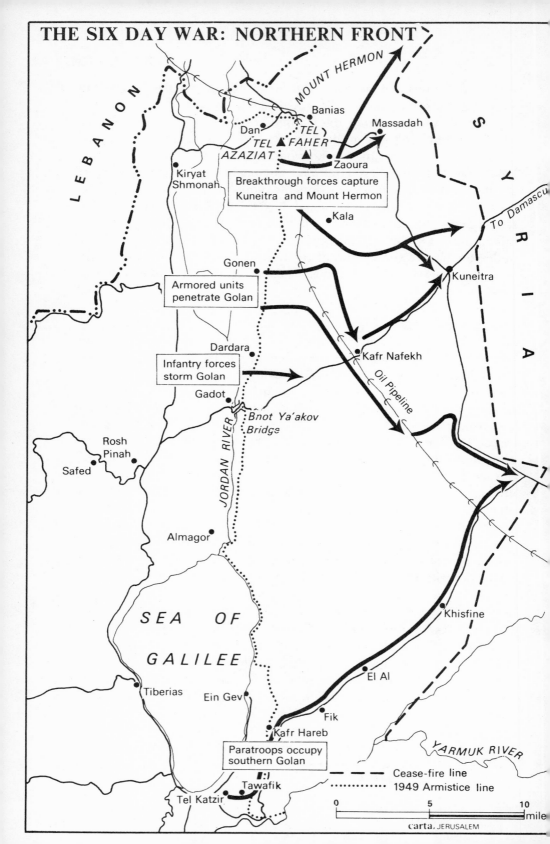

THE SIX DAY WAR: NORTHERN FRONT

LEBANON

SYRIA

MOUNT HERMON

Banias

Dan

TEL FAHER

TEL AZAZIAT

Massadah

Zaoura

Kiryat Shmonah

Breakthrough forces capture Kuneitra and Mount Hermon

Kala

To Damascus

Gonen

Kuneitra

Armored units penetrate Golan

Kafr Nafekh

Dardara

Oil Pipeline

Infantry forces storm Golan

Gadot

Bnot Ya'akov Bridge

JORDAN RIVER

Rosh Pinah

Safed

Almagor

SEA OF GALILEE

Khisfine

El Al

Tiberias

Ein Gev

Fik

Kafr Hareb

Paratroops occupy southern Golan

Tawafik

Tel Katzir

YARMUK RIVER

— — Cease-fire line

.... 1949 Armistice line

0   5   10
                              mile

carta, JERUSALEM

for the defense of Damascus. The battle for the Golan turned out therefore to be a one-phase operation, the breakthrough phase. Thereafter, the Syrian troops retreated—and in many places fled—in confusion and disorder toward Damascus.

At the start of the operation, the Syrian front line appeared impregnable. From their commanding and well-fortified positions on the heights, the Syrians completely dominated the narrow routes up the steep escarpment our forces had to use, so that they were pounded by artillery before they could get anywhere near the enemy.

We decided to make the main breakthrough effort in the northern sector of the Golan Heights, and the brunt of the fighting was borne by Albert's armored brigade and the Golani Brigade commanded by Yona. While other border positions were being attacked by other units, the armored brigade and the infantry brigade crossed the border to attack strongly defended Syrian positions and were engaged in the very toughest combat. They fought with heroism, persistence, and stubbornness, and although they suffered heavy casualties, they gained command of the Syrian positions by nightfall.

The armored brigade set off on its operation at 10 A.M., and suffered casualties from artillery before it was across the border. Upon entering the Golan Heights, the lead assault battalion made a navigational error and instead of turning north to attack Zaoura, their first target, which would later have taken them to the second target, Kala, at the same altitude, they took a route which led to Kala up a steep incline, mined, covered by anti-tank fire, and barred by natural obstacles and concrete dragon's teeth. Nevertheless, even when the assault commander realized his mistake, he decided to launch his attack from this mistaken direction, and Northern Command approved it. Attacking Kala from the south, instead of the north, exposed the Israeli tanks to murderous fire from the enemy's tanks and anti-tank guns, and from the beginning to the end of the battle the assault force went on being hit and taking casualties. Time after time, tanks and half-tracks were knocked out, either by shell fire or by mines as they tried to clear a track through the obstacles. The tank crews and the troops in the half-tracks fell prey to the enemy's bullets or to the flames which enveloped their shelled vehicles. The battalion commander was wounded at the outset of the assault. His replacement was killed ten minutes later. The command then passed to a junior officer. Only two tanks were still in operation out of its entire armored complement, and its troop losses were 13 killed and 33 wounded. Brisk air support turned the tide and brought about the retreat of the Syrian armor—Soviet TU-100 tanks. The capture of Kala ended at 6:30 P.M.

The Syrian force at Zaoura put up a stubborn defense and fought well. But it was soon overcome.

The capture of the third Syrian position in northern Golan, Tel Faher, was assigned to a mechanized infantry battalion on half-tracks from Yona's brigade, with a tank company in support. En route to their target, they came under heavy fire from the fortified Syrian positions above them, and six half-tracks were hit one after the other. Of the armored company four tanks were hit and two others were unable to continue and blocked the track. A few minutes later the mortar half-track received a direct hit and exploded, and the command half-track was stopped by a shell, leaving the battalion commander and four of his officers cut off in the field. The lead unit of the assault force abandoned its vehicles and proceeded to the target on foot. One officer and twelve soldiers made their way toward the northern part of the mound of Tel Faher, and another officer with a similar squad attacked from the south. Under artillery cover, they crossed the mine belt and protective fences without mishap, broke into the fortified position, sprang into the communications trenches, and started to clear them. But they encountered fierce opposition, and in a short time both Israeli squads were decimated. Out of the 13-man southern unit, 10 became casualties. And out of the squad attacking the northern section of Tel Faher, all except one were hit, including the commander, who was killed. A few minutes later the battalion commander and a company commander were killed, and the second in command of the battalion was seriously wounded.

Tel Faher was captured only after the units were reinforced and reorganized. Under the command of the deputy commander of the Golani Brigade, the remnants of the assault force, together with a reconnaissance company, a tank platoon, and a few half-tracks, were assembled. They stormed the northern section of the enemy fortifications and overcame the Syrian troops.

On the second morning, Saturday, June 10, our forces found the Syrian positions empty. The enemy had abandoned them in panic during the night, leaving their anti-tank guns and heavy and light machine guns behind. The defeat of the previous day and the ceaseless bombing by the Israeli Air Force had broken their spirit. Specially destructive to their morale was the announcement by their own Damascus Radio that we had captured Kuneitra. The Syrian government, realizing its desperate plight, had issued this announcement at 8:30 that morning in order to spur the Security Council to adopt a cease-fire resolution. In fact, at that hour, no Israeli soldier was in sight of the city. As soon as the Syrian troops in the field heard the news of Kuneitra, they began to flee, and there was therefore no point in continuing to hold it.

Toward noon, when our troops reached Kuneitra, Massadah, and Butmia, the final targets in the conquest of the Golan Heights, they found them empty.

The cease-fire line that we held ran to the east of Massadah, Kuneitra, and Rafid. This was the line which appeared in a directive I sent to Northern Command at noon on June 9—the line I said our forces should reach. On the Syrian front there was no Suez Canal and no Jordan River, and we therefore had to establish a frontier between the Syrians and ourselves, which reflected military logic and political significance. This line offered topographic advantages of defense and was fifteen miles from the Jordan River, which meant that our farm settlements in northern Galilee would be outside the range of Syrian artillery. The Syrians, of course, would view our presence there with great concern, not only because of our occupation of a portion of their territory, but also because we were now on the high ground and at a distance of less than forty miles from Damascus, without any natural obstacles to stop our advance. In their mind's eye, they would see us getting into our tanks and galloping on to Damascus whenever the fancy should take us. This may have been thought a flight of Oriental fantasy, but anyone going up to the Golan Heights and seeing the vast plain stretching away toward Damascus could hardly rule out such a possibility.

It was indeed in this context that there was great political tension even during the two days of battle. The Syrians feared that it was our intention to capture Damascus, and Russia, turning to the president of the United States, warned that if America did not stop our advance, the Soviet Union would intervene to help the Syrians. The Americans reacted "firmly and effectively," according to one informant. But at the same time, Secretary of State Dean Rusk got in touch with our foreign minister, Abba Eban, and our ambassador in Washington and asked them in near panic where we thought we were heading. He warned that our situation in the Security Council was getting worse, and he demanded that we obey the Council's cease-fire decision forthwith. We replied to the Americans that we had no intention of reaching Damascus but only of putting our settlements beyond the range of Syrian artillery, and that we were ready for a mutual cease-fire.

I did not know what the Americans told the Russians in our name, but I did know that the Russians did not limit themselves to an approach to the United States. In Moscow our ambassador was handed an extremely sharp note containing threats as well as the notification that the Soviet Union was breaking off diplomatic relations with us.

In the meantime, things were happening in Egypt, too. At 4 P.M. on June 9, Cairo Radio announced that President Nasser had accepted the resignation of the commanders of his army, Air Force, and Navy. Two and a half hours later, at 6:30 P.M., it was announced that he himself had resigned, but at 11:10 the next morning, the radio said that he had withdrawn his resignation.

Four days later, on June 13, I gave my colleagues a summing-up report on the war. With me was the chief of staff.

I told them I would speak frankly, and I did. I said that in the period preceding the war, the army and the government had made incorrect assessments in three basic areas. The first concerned the possible reaction to our military reprisals against Syria. We did not properly judge how far Egypt would consider herself bound to go to Syria's aid. It was thought that Egypt was too involved with her war in Yemen to be available for other action. We seized upon Nasser's warning to the Syrians not to go to war with Israel simply because of a bombing here or a shelling there. This was also the case with our reprisal action in Jordan's Samua. We failed to estimate correctly the weight of Jordan's complaint to Egypt that the Egyptian Air Force had not come to her aid and that Egypt was permitting Israeli vessels to pass through the Straits of Tiran without hindrance. At the time we did not believe that our actions would prompt so sharp an Egyptian response.

The second incorrect assessment was to regard the entry of Egyptian forces into Sinai as window dressing. The army and the government did not believe that the Egyptians were ready to make war. This judgment was incorrect. The movement of the Egyptian army into Sinai was not simply a demonstrative move.

The third area in which we were mistaken was the facility with which Nasser was able to order, and secure, the removal of U.N. forces from Sharm el-Sheikh. It was not thought that he could do so with such ease, and therein lay a profound lesson for us. It was evident there was no difficulty in getting rid of this international instrument known as the United Nations Emergency Force.

I went on to explain to my colleagues in what way I thought our policy immediately prior to the opening of the campaign had been wrong. The principal mistake had been Israel's failure to react at once to Egypt's blockade of the straits. Thereafter, the term "who fired the first shot" acquired a special value. Of course, there was important political significance to the question of who started the war, but to my mind it was the Egyptian blockade that was the opening shot. This was a clear act of war, which surely justified military counter-action on our part. Yet the government of Israel allowed Nasser to push this belligerent action down our throats without any reaction from us. True, the U.S. government asked us to let it have forty-eight hours to deal with the matter. But after that, Israel was faced with the critical decision of whether to regard the blockade as an act of war and go out to meet it with war, or whether to take no immediate action, in which case the fact that Egypt had indeed fired the first shot would lose its significance and value. In the event, we waited, and this plunged us into a complex situation. The government had maneuvered itself into a position whereby we had to be the first to open fire, for we had reacted to the Egyptian blockade as though it were a problem that might be settled without war.

Nor was the assumption correct that the United States was capable of lifting the blockade for us. America soon demanded two or three weeks to try to arrange a solution to the problem. We agreed, and then nothing came of it. The United States was not prepared to complicate her relations with Egypt in order to guarantee freedom of shipping for us. But even if America had managed to achieve some remedy in this field, this would in no way have corrected the disturbed balance of forces. The Egyptians had thrust eighty thousand troops and a vast number of tanks into Sinai. Even if the Straits of Tiran had been opened, the problem of Egyptian armor on our borders would have remained.

Though the Egyptian blockade was the opening move of the war, the first shot in the literal sense was, of course, fired by us, and fired well, destroying 70 percent of the warplanes of the Arab states on the first day. Yet the issue became blurred. The Arabs, as usual, announced that they were winning and that they had shot down forty-seven Israeli planes. The next thing that happened was that Jordan and Syria immediately entered the war, with Jordan shelling Jerusalem and Syria shelling and bombing in the north. Thus, the question of who started the war was relevant not only to Egypt but to Jordan and Syria, too, when it was perfectly clear that on those two fronts it was Jordan and Syria who had fired the first shot against us.

The problematic factor in the war was Syria. It was true that the Syrians had made several attempts to break into a kibbutz and a few other places in the opening days of the Six Day War, but these were not serious enough for us to wage all-out war. The fighting might have ended with the Syrian front coincident with the pre-war borders. We were not forced to go to war with Syria because of the Syrian-initiated attacks during that week. The reasons we campaigned in Syria were primarily to save our settlements in northern Galilee from incessant Syrian shelling, and also to show the Syrians that they could not continue to harass us with impunity. The Israeli Cabinet agreed unanimously that the Syrian front would be the one we would deal with last. We set off to capture the Golan Heights on the morning of June 9. The night before, when the question arose of whether we should undertake action against Syria, I opposed such action in the most extreme terms. But conditions changed.

At midnight that night, after I had had my say, I went to General Headquarters. There I learned that Nasser had agreed to a cease-fire. At three in the morning, Syria announced that she, too, accepted a cease-fire. There was also an intelligence report that Kuneitra was empty, and that the Syrian front was beginning to collapse. These announcements and reports prompted me to change my mind. At 7 A.M. I gave the order to go into action against Syria.

The General Staff had been in favor of the attack and had a contingency plan for the operation, but it was limited. The plan did not include the capture of the Golan Heights. It served, however, as the core of the opening phase. The final plan was given a wider aim, with the purpose of pushing the Syrians back twelve-and-a-half miles so as to take the Galilean settlements out of their artillery range, and for this our forces had to reach Kuneitra and Rafid.

We ended the Six Day War with maximum lines on all fronts.

I then told my colleagues that I had asked the General Staff to prepare an appreciation of the future situation as to how long it would take the Arabs to rebuild their military strength. The destruction to the Arab armies, particularly the Egyptian one, was extensive. In the meantime, we had to be ready for two onslaughts. One was an Arab political campaign against us. The Arabs would not be able to renew their armed forces in the short run, so they would concentrate their hostile activity in the immediate future in the international political arena. The other concerned the Soviet Union and the possibility of her active participation in the war against us.

I thought this had been a good meeting, yet I left it with a less than pleasant feeling. I could not help sensing a chilliness in the atmosphere, its source the prime minister and the Mapai leadership. I realized that they would always have it in for me. They had not reconciled themselves to my having been appointed minister of defense against their will and would look for faults in whatever I did.

PART VI

Open Bridges

[1967~1973]

22

NEW TIMES

WITH THE FIGHTING OVER, I gave orders for all barriers which had marked the division of Jerusalem to be removed. East and West Jerusalem were to become one again. The Jewish and Arab communities were once more to have access to each other. The orders called for the demolition of the anti-sniping walls, clearance of minefields and disposal of the barbed-wire fences which had been a constant reminder of the partition of the city. I wanted the unity of Jerusalem to be given full practical expression, and I wanted it done quickly.

No sooner had the orders been issued than I was regaled with howls of protest from various officials who tried to persuade me that I was being hasty. There were urgent pleas from the Ministry of the Interior and from Teddy Kollek, the mayor of Jewish Jerusalem, whose Municipal Council would now be responsible for handling the city affairs of Arab Jerusalem as well. They begged me to postpone these measures. My decision stood. The barriers would come down, now. However, two days before the orders were to go into effect, I agreed to meet with them and others, including the representatives of the police and the local army command. While other people expressed their apprehensions in muted terms, Mayor Kollek and the representative of the Interior Ministry entreated me to put off my decision, prophesying wholesale bloodshed. Jews entering the narrow alleyways of the Old City would be massacred by Arab fanatics, and Jewish hotheads would retaliate against Arabs found in the New City.

I heard them out, brushed aside their highly colored predictions and told them I saw no reason to change the orders. My reading of the situation and of the mood of the people, Arab and Jew, suggested that nothing untoward would occur, and if it did it could be handled. Free movement in both directions would be permitted forthwith, without hindrance, without checkposts, without special permits. We had to act immediately in accordance with the new reality, I said, and we could deal later with whatever problems would arise.

The measures were carried out. The bars and barricades were pulled down and the two halves of Jerusalem were reunited. The Old City and its environs and Israeli Jerusalem became one. There was no murder, no bloodshed, no clash, no incident, no trouble. The united capital of Israel wore a festive air. Arabs crowded Zion Square in the heart of the New City and Jews swarmed into the Old City bazaars. The only thing the police had to do was try to unsnarl the traffic jams.

The government next had to deal with the status of the Jewish, Moslem, and Christian holy places in Jerusalem and its environs. I proposed that all the barriers and limitations on access to these shrines, which had been imposed by the Jordanian regime, be removed. We should now allow all Moslems and Christians, whether citizens of Israel or residents of the West Bank and the Gaza Strip, to visit and pray at their holy sites—the Dome of the Rock, the Mosque of El Aksa, and the Church of the Holy Sepulcher.

For many years, the Arabs had barred the Jews from their most sacred site, the Western Wall of the Temple compound in Jerusalem, and from the Cave of the Patriarchs in Hebron. Now that we were in control, it was up to us to grant what we had demanded of others and to allow members of all faiths absolute freedom to visit and worship at their holy places. I took upon myself responsibility for the security risks involved. I believed that from the points of view of our relations with the Arabs, our international standing, and even our security, the less our government interfered with the private, religious, and communal lives of the Arabs, the better. At all events, we had to try this method. It was wiser to deal with its possible harmful exploitation by hostile elements than to stifle in advance the chance of developing correct relations between the Arabs and the Israeli regime.

The two Jewish holy places which raised special problems were the Temple Mount in the Old City of Jerusalem, site of the Jewish Temple built by King Solomon in the tenth century B.C., rebuilt in the sixth century, and destroyed by the Romans in A.D. 70; and the Cave of the Patriarchs in Hebron.

Some seven centuries after the Romans destroyed the Temple, the Moslems constructed two holy mosques—the Mosque of the Dome (or the Dome of the Rock) and the Mosque of El Aksa—on the Temple Mount. The site itself, a huge platform which enclosed the Jewish people's Temple and its courts, became the Moslem's holy Haram esh-Sharif, and in recent years the local Supreme Moslem Council has maintained its offices there. As with the Cave of the Patriarchs, the problems posed by this site stemmed from the fact that two religions, Judaism and Islam, viewed it as holy, and thus there was the danger that religious fanatics of either faith would claim the site as their own.

It seemed to me that we had to find a way of removing the artificial barriers which the Moslem authorities and the British Mandatory administration had imposed on Jewish visitors who wanted to worship at their holy places without disturbing Moslem sensibilities. At the same time we had to ensure that so sensitive a matter would not create a conflict that would inflame passions, ignite clashes and demonstrations, and cause an international uproar, particularly in Moslem countries.

I thought that the first unequivocal decision that had to be made concerned the direction and supervision of the compound of the mosques and the Moslem offices. On the morning of the first Saturday after the war, I visited the El Aksa Mosque and met the Moslem religious personnel responsible for it. I reached the court of the mosque by way of the Western (Wailing) Wall. Access to the Wall had been denied to Jews for the previous nineteen years, and now, as we passed it, thousands of Jewish worshipers crowded against its ancient stones in ecstatic celebration. As we continued through the Mograbi Gate above to reach the mosque compound, it was as though we were suddenly cut off from a world filled with joy and had entered a place of sullen silence. The Arab officials who received us outside the mosque solemnly greeted us, their expression reflecting deep mourning over our victory and fear of what I might do. The group was headed by Sheikh Abdel Hamid Sa'iah, the chief Moslem judge, and with him were the mufti of Jerusalem and the guardian of the mosque compound, who was responsible for the religious services.

Before entering the mosque, I asked the Israeli officers who were with me to take off their shoes and leave their weapons behind them. After hearing explanations about the mosque and the customary arrangements for worshipers and visitors, I asked my hosts to talk of the future. At first they refused, but when I sat down on the carpet and folded my legs Arab fashion, they felt it necessary to do the same, and inevitably we engaged in talk. As a consequence of the battle for Jerusalem, their water and electricity had been cut off. I promised that both would be restored within forty-eight hours. I then plunged directly into the main issue. I said that the war was now over and we had to return to normal life. I asked them to resume religious services in the mosque on the following Friday. I said I had no wish and no intention of continuing the practice which the Jordanians had instituted of censoring Friday's sermon before it was broadcast. Under Jordanian rule, Friday's sermons, which were broadcast over the radio, were subjected to strict censorship. I questioned in my own mind whether such a practice was proper for a Moslem ruler, but a Jewish ruler should certainly refrain from acting in the same fashion. I added my hope that the Moslem religious leaders would not take advantage of such freedom by indulging in rabble-rousing sermons that would incite some of their followers. If they did, we would of course take appropriate action.

I said that Israeli troops would be removed from the site and stationed outside the compound. The Israeli authorities were responsible for overall security, but we would not interfere in the private affairs of the Moslems responsible for their own sanctuaries. These were two Moslem places of worship, and they had the right to operate them themselves. My hosts no doubt knew that on the day we had captured this site, I had given orders that the Israeli flag be removed from the Mosque of the Dome, where it had been hoisted. We had no intention of controlling Moslem holy places or of interfering in their religious life. The one thing we would introduce was freedom of Jewish access to the compound of Haram esh-Sharif without limitation or payment. This compound, as my hosts well knew, was our Temple Mount. Here stood our Temple during ancient times, and it would be inconceivable for Jews not to be able freely to visit this holy place now that Jerusalem was under our rule.

My hosts were not overjoyed at my final remarks, but they recognized that they would be unable to change my decision. They would have wished the entire area, not just the mosques, to remain under their exclusive control, with the continued ban on Jews. But they also realized that Israeli troops had been removed from the compound and that we had recognized their rights to control their own holy places.

A sticky problem cropped up on August 16. This date coincided with the ninth day of the Hebrew month of Av, a millennia-old Jewish fast day in commemorative mourning for the destruction of the Temple. Rabbi Shlomo Goren, the chief army chaplain, and several *minyanim* (religious quorums) decided to pray on that day on the Temple Mount, namely, the Haram esh-Sharif. They brought with them a Torah (Scroll of the Law), an Ark of the Law, and a pulpit. I learned about the incident only later, when Maj. David Farhi, the military government's liaison officer with the Arab leaders, failed to prevent the rabbi and those with him from praying there. The matter came up for consideration by the government. Although, understandably, no minister wished to take a formal position stating baldly that Jews were forbidden to pray on the Temple Mount, it was decided to "maintain the current policy," which in fact banned them from doing so. It was evident that if we did not prevent Jews from praying in what was now a mosque compound, matters would get out of hand and lead to a religious clash. Rabbi Goren fought determinedly against the *de facto* ban, but he eventually accepted the verdict and tempers were calmed. As an added precaution, I told the chief of staff to order the chief army chaplain to remove the branch office he had established in the building which adjoins the mosque compound. I was convinced that precisely because control was now in our hands, it was up to us to show broad tolerance, so rare an attitude among the regimes of the preceding decades and centuries. We should certainly respect the Temple Mount as an historic site of our ancient past, but we should not disturb the Arabs who were using it for what it was now—a place of Moslem worship.

The arrangement we made for the Cave of the Patriarchs in Hebron had a different purpose from the one in Jerusalem. The aim here was not a division of authority and rights but harmonious coexistence. According to Jewish tradition, the Cave of the Patriarchs is the most ancient Hebrew burial place. The first Hebrew was Abraham, and he, his son Isaac, and his grandson Jacob were buried there. So were the Matriarchs Sarah, Rebecca, and Leah. (The tomb of Jacob's favorite wife, Rachel, is a few miles to the north, "in the way to Ephrath, which is Bethlehem," as the Bible puts it.) The Moslems also respected this tradition, for Abraham was their "Friend," father of their forebear Ishmael, so that for them, too, the Cave of the Patriarchs holds a special reverence.

During the four hundred years of Ottoman rule and thirty years of British Mandatory control, the Moslems forbade any Jew from entering the cave or even the building erected over it, which had been converted into a church and later still into a mosque. The closest the Jews had been allowed to approach their ancient shrine was the seventh step of the outside staircase leading to the building. We were now in a position to lift this shameful ban, but I wished to do so without causing the Moslems to suffer, as they had caused our people to suffer for centuries. What I sought was an arrangement whereby Jews would be able to visit, make the pilgrimage, and worship at the shrine of the Patriarchs without disturbing the Moslems at their prayer services.

The key to this conundrum lay in a geographic division of this holy place and coordination of timetables for the respective rituals. The geographic division was relatively simple, for the tombs of the Patriarchs—or rather the monuments symbolizing the tombs—were located in the western half of the building, while the praying hall of the mosque was situated in the eastern half. The timetable arrangement, namely the timing of Jewish visits so as not to clash with Moslem prayers, proved more complex. Moslem prayer services are held five times a day, but they go on all day long during the month of the Ramadan fast. The Jews have three services a day, but on the Sabbath and during festival and fast days, which draw large numbers of pilgrims, it is difficult to curtail the length of the services. I personally had not been in favor of holding formal Jewish prayer services in this holy place, which virtually turned it into a synagogue. I believed it should remain solely a shrine for pilgrimages and informal prayers. But once Jewish visitors and pilgrims had begun holding formal services, I was unwilling to stop them. I had to make provision not only for visiting hours but also for the customary times of Jewish prayers. It was evident that no suitable arrangement could be reached without compromise and mutual respect.

In the search for such an arrangement, someone came up with the idea of adding a small synagogue to the building at a level below the mosque with access, through a special opening, to the very cave traditionally held to contain the sepulchers themselves (as distinct from the symbolic tombs of the Patriarchs in the hall above). It was believed such an entrance had existed at one time and had subsequently been sealed, so that it might now be reopened. But upon investigation no opening was found, and the idea had to be shelved. The cave, I might add, can be glimpsed from inside the building through a grating in the floor of the mosque.

We thus had to revert to a compromise arrangement, and the first coexistence procedures acceptable to both communities were set out by me at a meeting with Moslem representatives held on August 1, 1967, in the office of the military governor in Hebron. In the six weeks that had passed since Hebron had come within our control and been opened to Jews again, the city was thronged each day with multitudes of pilgrims who converged on the Cave of the Patriarchs, taking in the grandeur of the huge Herodian stones in the surrounding walls, exploring with reverence the hushed interior, and standing in prayer near the tombs.

A day before my meeting with the Moslem notables in Hebron, I had reviewed the subject with the Ministerial Committee on the Holy Places and presented my proposals, which were approved. The one problem left open was whether to tell Jews to remove their shoes before entering the building. This is a practice which all visitors should follow when entering a mosque. But in this case, it would have signified for a Jew the cession to another faith of what was in fact a Jewish holy place. The site had undergone several conversions. Apart from the burial of the Jewish Patriarchs in the middle of the second millennium B.C., it had been a synagogue in the latter half of the first millennium B.C., a Christian basilica nearly a thousand years later, then a mosque, then again a church in the crusader period, and after that a mosque once more. The Ministerial Committee left it to me to decide, and I privately resolved not to compel Jewish pilgrims to remove their shoes but to ensure that they avoided the Moslem praying area.

With me at the Hebron meeting were members of the Military Government, as well as Raphael Levi, who was then serving as an adviser on Arab affairs. He was himself a Hebron man, knew the people of the city, and was familiar with their language and customs. The Moslem representatives were headed by the mayor of Hebron and included the mufti of Hebron and the sheikh of the mosque. After a thorough discussion, we reached the following agreement, which the Arabs viewed as the lesser of the evils and the Jews the lesser of the good. The agreement laid down that:

• The curfew would be lifted so that the Moslem community would be able to pray at 3 A.M.

• Non-Moslem visitors would be allowed to enter the building between the hours of 7 A.M. and 11 A.M. and 1:30 P.M. and 5 P.M.

• The muezzin would be allowed to call the faithful to prayer five times a day.

• Between the hours of 1:30 P.M. and 5 P.M., the Moslem community would be allowed to pray in the mosque but would use a separate entrance.

• Non-Moslem visitors would be requested to wear appropriate and respectable attire. There would be no smoking and no sale of candles or strong drink.

Signing for the Moslems was the head of the Supreme Moslem Council and for the Jews myself and Raphael Levi.

This agreement was not the comprehensive answer to all problems, but it offered a base for further arrangements that could be made from time to time. The principal subsequent additions were occasioned by the need to enable the growing number of worshipers to hold religious services on the "Days of Awe" between the Jewish New Year and the fast of Yom Kippur without disturbing Moslem prayer in the mosque. Here, too, a solution was soon found. Just west of the tombs was an open court which could be covered with a canopy. Indeed, there were iron hooks in the walls, which showed that this sort of covering had been used in the past, so there was a precedent. But, of course, the basic difficulty in such issues lies not in finding answers to technical problems but in generating the necessary goodwill on both sides to reach an understanding.

I spent a good deal of time on securing harmonious arrangements over the holy places in Hebron and, above all, in Jerusalem because they held the seed of an approach which might solve the much wider and deeper problems of Arab-Jewish coexistence in a united Jerusalem. We had to determine those areas which should be left separate and handled autonomously by each community—Moslem, Christian, and Jewish—as well as those areas in which communal cooperation was possible, and we had to work out how Arabs and Jews were to behave toward one another.

During the month of Ramadan, a Moslem religious festival, I ordered a shortening of the Jewish visiting hours in the Cave of the Patriarchs. I considered that Abraham, Isaac, and Jacob, and we, their modern descendants, were strong enough to bear this limitation. Whenever I visited the mosque during Ramadan and saw fasting Arabs on their knees praying with deep devotion to the one and only merciful Allah, I would try to walk on tiptoe so as not to disturb them. I never felt I was thereby abandoning my own faith. In the same way, I was certain, it would signify no diminution of their Islamic faith if the Arabs did not disturb the Jews praying at the Western Wall, their eyes shut tight in religious concentration as they sent up their prayers to heaven.

In Jerusalem, the question of coexistence had to encompass both the secular life of the city's inhabitants and the holy places and times of prayer. It was possible to congregate—and jostle each other—in the same crowded bazaars, to do business together, to maintain electricity, sewage, and water networks together. Arabs and Jews could live in the same city, impose uniform taxation, travel in the same buses, and receive equal pay for equal work. At the same time, one had to enable the Arabs to maintain separate schools, so that every Arab child could learn in his own language the history of his people, admire their heroes, believe in their faith, celebrate their festivals. I believed that the Moslems should be granted sovereignty over their holy places, and any Moslem from any land, whether or not it maintained diplomatic relations with Israel, should be allowed free access to these places. I was convinced that the cornerstone of Arab-Jewish coexistence was that each community should ensure the satisfaction of its basic yearnings, while showing toleration for the basic yearnings of the other.

I also made it my business to meet the Arab mayors of all the cities on the West Bank and the Gaza Strip during the week immediately following the war. On the West Bank, war casualties among the civilian population had been low and damage to property light. Indeed, outside the cities, although one would come across burned tanks and half-tracks, there was almost no other sign that there had been a war. The curfew imposed during the battles was lifted. Movement along the roads and work in the fields returned to normal. Through the clear air came the monotonous chant of camel drivers, their animals laden high with sheaves of wheat carried from the fields to the village threshing floor.

What is properly called the West Bank, but was always known to us by its biblical name, Judea and Samaria, held special boyhood memories for me. Nahalal in the early 1930s was a poor cooperative farm village. Apart from the community fields, each farmer had, as we did, a small vegetable garden next to the house, a few cows of mixed breed (products of a Dutch bull and an Arab cow), and chickens who flapped about and pecked away in the dirt and muck and laid their eggs in the darkest places, the haystack or under a heap of twigs. Most of our work was out in the cornfields, and the end of summer, between harvest and sowing, was a dead season, of which we took prompt and full advantage. My friends and I would set out on what we called "the long excursion," a walking tour through the country. Sometimes we would go with a guide—David Barash from the nearby village of Kfar Yehoshua, the finest of teachers. Mostly we would go on our own. With a knapsack of food and an army blanket on our backs and a few pennies in our pockets, we would wander round the land, along the Jordan Valley, across Samaria, up to Jerusalem and through Judea. We would vary the route each year.

My re-encounter with this part of the country, now open to us once again, was different. This was no youthful excursion, and I was no longer the boy hurriedly trying to take in as much as possible before dashing back to the farm in Nahalal. This was a renewed experience of getting to know the familiar land of my childhood which—though I had been cut off from it—had become much dearer to me with time.

There was another special feature about Samaria and Judea. I moved through these ancient territories thrilled by the view and thought of their biblical sites and the sound of their names: Shiloh, where the Israelite tribes assembled before the Ark of the Law; Tekoa, birthplace of the prophet Amos; Beth-El, associated with the Patriarch Abraham, with Jacob's dream, with Samuel's judgment, and with the concentration of Saul's forces when he fought the Philistines; Anathoth, of Jeremiah and two of David's "mighty men"; and so many others. Even when nothing was left of these places beyond piles of archaeological ruins, their names continued unchanged down the centuries.

The biblical characters were usually remembered in association with the places which gave them birth, and were so recorded— Elijah the Tishbite, Nabal the Carmelite, Micah of Moresheth. In the course of time, some of these Hebrew names underwent a certain corruption, accommodated to newer tongues. But this fact never bothered me, for the authentic ring of the original Hebrew or Canaanite was preserved: Yericho (Jericho), Yafo (Jaffa), Acco (Acre). The years, the battles, the nations that had passed over the sites had failed to destroy the source of their names.

Now there were Arab dwellings in Judea and Samaria. The young boys threshing the mounds of wheat, the field hands behind a wooden plow and pair of oxen, the women moving sedately from well to village with a pitcher on their heads were all part of the scenery. I did not think of them as being interposed between me and the land. Never have I harbored feelings of hostility toward the Arabs. The background of our wars and our conflicts was political and national ambition, not personal enmity. The encounters over *pitta* (flat Arab bread), olives, and dark coffee and the *"Ahalan wasahalan"* with which I was greeted whenever I reached the threshold of their homes were broken off from time to time by war, but they were always renewed after the dust of battle had settled.

There were three small districts in Judea and Samaria which had suffered badly in the war. One was the Latrun salient, where there had been brisk fighting. When the Jordanians initiated military action without cause, Arab Legion artillery in Latrun shelled Israel's international airport at Lod, and Arab strongpoints on the dominating hills threatened the stretch of the coastal plain which included Tel Aviv.

Quite different were the circumstances in which the other two affected areas had sustained considerable ruin. One was the town of Kalkilia in Samaria, the other were two villages in Judea. Here, the Israeli government gave the inhabitants building materials and financial grants to enable them to rebuild their ruined houses. Indeed, their plight was the subject of serious consideration at several Cabinet meetings, for it transpired that many houses had been damaged not as a result of battle but of punitive action by Israeli soldiers. Not only was this not dictated by Israeli government policy, but it was done in defiance of that policy, which laid down that in war the army was to do everything possible to avoid harming civilians and their property. I saw no point in embarking on a series of special investigations in the army. Instead I promptly visited the places to discover exactly what had happened and how we could help. I went first to Kalkilia.

When I got there, I found that more than one-third of the buildings in this town and its suburbs had been ruined, most of them not by shelling but by dynamiting. When I inquired of the army, I was told that this was done in reprisal for Arab sniping at our troops. The practical question for me was how to repair both the physical damage and the damage to Israeli-Arab relations. The mayor of Kalkilia, Haj Hussein Ali Tzabari, explained that some 800 houses had become uninhabitable, and that the number of people who had left the city totaled 12,000. Some were now living with relatives in Nablus and in nearby villages, but most were taking shelter in the olive groves just outside Kalkilia. I went to visit them.

If their ruined houses had not been visible across the way, one might have thought that these people were out enjoying a mass picnic. Under each tree sat a family. The children cavorted on blankets spread on the ground and were having a great time unraveling bundles of clothing; the women were bent over the fire with their pots, while the men in their *abayas* (long Arab cloaks), with their *kefiehs* (head cloths) wrapped round their faces, dozed peacefully.

When they recognized us, they gathered round, bombarding us

with questions. They did not grumble and they did not complain. They asked only for permission to return to Kalkilia and to receive mechanical equipment to clear the ruins. Permission to return was granted immediately. I also promised them the help they wanted. But I could say nothing in reply to what they had not asked but which hung in the air like a giant query: what did we want from them? I knew well that had their hopes been realized and the Arabs had been the victors in the war, they would not only have destroyed our homes, villages, and cities but would also have slaughtered us. They knew this too, and they had therefore accepted the ruin of their houses as the natural consequence of their defeat. Yet I could not hide behind this explanation. What the Arabs would have done to us could not serve as a guide for our action or behavior. But neither did I wish to say to them that I, the minister of defense, was sorry and ashamed at what some of our soldiers had done. Relations between us and the Arabs are, after all, relations between nations, and it would have been improper for me, in my official position, to speak to them as a private individual. So I simply assured them of government help and thereafter remained silent.

The same circumstances were also true of the two villages to the west of the Hebron hills. There, too, a local Israeli commander had decided to blow up a number of houses, and there, too, I promised the inhabitants in the name of the government that they would be supplied with cement and steel so that they could repair their concrete roofs. They did not require stones. Judea had an abundance of stones. Indeed, each generation had had its wars, and each its destruction. But even when roofs and walls were shattered, stones remained. These would be gathered from their own and from older ruins, as had been the practice for centuries, and for perhaps the hundredth time, maybe more, would form the foundations of their new homes.

23

LIVING TOGETHER

ONE OF MY FIRST ACTS after the war, when I came to deal with the administration of the occupied territories, was to abolish travel restrictions. I issued orders that any Arab, whether a resident of the West Bank or a refugee in the Gaza Strip, was free to travel anywhere in Israel and anywhere in the territories without requiring a permit. This act came as a welcome surprise to the Arabs directly affected. It was the last thing they expected from an occupying administration. There were many in Israel, however, who thought it would endanger our security by offering greater freedom of movement to terrorists.

I was prompted to take this measure largely by my recollection of the system of travel permits devised by the Military Government for Israel's Arabs in the early years of the state, and I was determined not to follow that path. The very requirement of a travel permit underscored the limitation of freedom, and the ponderous procedures added to the psychological bitterness, souring the relations between the inhabitants and the administration. The long wait to secure a permit, the lines at the checkpost, the inspection of documents, the searching of luggage, the overall dependence on the goodwill of the authorities were frustrating and degrading.

What hastened my resolve to prevent all this was an incident that occurred shortly after the war. Some enemy troops were still at large, weapons were still in hostile hands, the danger of sabotage was very real, and movement along the roads was accordingly subjected to checks by our troops. I happened to witness a spot check being carried out on a truck that had come from El Arish. The driver and his companion had said they were on their way to Hebron with a cargo of fish.

When I arrived, the soldiers had already pulled out the crates and tipped them over to see if there were weapons hidden beneath. The fishermen of El Arish, the Sinai city on the Mediterranean, must have spent hours carefully packing the fish for the Hebron and Jerusalem markets. They had laid the fish neatly head to head and layer upon layer on a bed of crushed ice, and over the crates they had spread branches and green leaves to shield their freight from the rays of the sun. In a quarter of an hour, nothing remained of their careful labors. The fish were on the floor of the truck, the leaves had dried up, the ice had melted. Of course we had to stop the smuggling of arms, and certainly we had to be alert to the danger of raids and sabotage, but I was determined that such incidents should be avoided as far as possible, even if it put our security at risk.

Undoubtedly the most significant and revolutionary change we introduced in our relations with the Arabs was the policy of "open bridges." This was the free movement of people and goods between Israel and the Arab countries across the Jordan River. The crossing near the destroyed Allenby Bridge, just east of Jericho, served the inhabitants of Jerusalem, Bethlehem, and Hebron, as well as Gaza. The one at the ruined Damia Bridge served Nablus and Jenin. Damia was the site of the biblical city of Adam mentioned in the Book of Joshua 3:16.

This policy was devised so that the Arabs of the administered territories would not be cut off from their brothers in the Arab world. The open bridges allowed their children to study at universities in Egypt, Syria, and Lebanon, their elected officials to be members of parliament in Amman, their representatives to meet openly with the leaders of Arab states—and even with leaders of the Palestinian terrorist organizations. Families could also exchange visits with their relatives anywhere, from North Africa to Saudi Arabia, for the open bridges, carried two-way traffic for Arabs. Indeed, something like a million visitors from various Arab states have crossed the bridges into the West Bank, Israel, and the Gaza Strip. All these states were of course hostile to Israel—and still are.

I was also alive to the opportunity open bridges would provide to bring Israelis and Arabs in touch with each other. The Arab countries allowed no Israeli to visit them, but it was within our power to allow their citizens to visit us. I did not believe for a moment that when they got to know Israelis at first hand, our neighbors would suddenly begin to love and admire us. But they would at least discover that it was possible to live with us. We are an open and classless society, a nation that considers all men to be equal in status and entitled to equality of opportunity. We are also a progressive state, and quite advanced. Obviously we have not reached the technological level of the United States. But there are areas in farming, industry, water conservation, medicine and public health, and probably others, in which I think inhabitants of the Arab states could find something of helpful interest.

I first learned of the border crossing immediately after the end of the war. Trucks were fording the Jordan River bringing farm produce from the West Bank to the east bank. The Arab farmers in the Jordan Valley were continuing to market their produce in Amman and even further afield in Iraq and Kuwait. I welcomed the news and was pleased that these Arab marketing activities, though unusual in the new circumstances, were proceeding without obstacle on our part. In my directives to the officers of the Military Government and in my talks with them, I had stressed the need to allow the Arabs to go about their normal business without unnecessary interference. I even ordered our army units out of the Arab towns. They were to set up their posts at strategic positions on the hills outside. I explained to their commanders that their task was to ensure the security of the Israeli community and not to dominate and direct the lives of the Arabs.

On August 2, 1967, together with the GOC Central Command, Uzi Narkiss, I paid a visit to the Damia crossing. During the summer, the Jordan River is shallow at this point, and trucks, tractors, and even private cars can cross without difficulty. This was the place which our troops on the spot had begun to call "the vegetable market."

It was an extraordinary sight, a Hollywood Wild West scene, except that instead of cowboys, cattle, and horse-drawn wagons converging on a river ford, there was a huge assembly of heavily laden trucks, vans, and carts being towed across by tractor. Up to one hundred trucks a day were crossing the Jordan, carrying vegetables, fruit, and olive oil, for the most part, but also other goods—plastic containers made in Bethlehem, building stones from the Ramalla quarries, as well as furniture and household goods belonging to families that had hastily left during the fighting and crossed into Jordan.

The visit was not without its distressing side. Having been recognized, I was approached by several of the Arabs with a plea for a *warkah*, Arabic for "paper." They wanted a document from me to permit their relatives who had fled to Jordan to return. My heart was with them, but I tried to explain to them—without success—why they had to follow the stipulated application procedure. During the war, some 200,000 persons from the West Bank had fled to Jordan. Half were from Palestinian refugee camps; the other half were residents who had left their homes and gone to their relatives in Jordan, Lebanon, and Kuwait in order to escape the fighting. The Israeli government was prepared to have them back, and, following a Cabinet decision, announced that all who wished to return would be allowed to do so up to August 10, 1967. But very few did. They had to submit their applications through the Jordanian government. Jordan held them up and placed obstacles in the way of potential returnees.

I watched the "vegetable market" and told the officer in charge to ease the formalities. There was no need for a long and detailed check of goods going from the West to the east bank. Why interfere? Why make it difficult? What were we looking for? Arms? That would concern us if they were being smuggled into our territory. But in the somewhat unlikely case that arms were being taken to the other side, why should we worry? Why hold up all farmers?

I spent quite a time at the edge of the river watching the departing vehicles. They were of all ages, types, and colors, and they moved in a convoy. As they passed me, I waved to the drivers and wished them good luck, and their response, after a moment of surprise, was a warm smile. It took so little, I reflected, to evoke a little warmth, even in men who only a few days earlier had fought us on the battlefield.

As winter approached, to make things easier for the West Bank farmers I asked Hamdi Cnaan, the mayor of Nablus, to go to Amman and propose to the government of Jordan that we construct permanent bridges across the river, in place of those which had been destroyed in the war. He did so, and the Jordanian authorities agreed —on condition that the bridging be done by them and not by Israelis. I raised no objection and the Jordanian Arab Legion put up two Bailey bridges, one on the Jericho road next to the destroyed Allenby Bridge and the second at Damia.

The open-bridges policy could not have been carried out unless both sides had desired it. Israel had not only wanted but had deliberately initiated such a policy. On the part of Jordan, it was the acceptance of a reality. Throughout the nineteen years of Jordanian rule over the West Bank, the border between the Kingdom of Jordan and the residents of the West Bank had become blurred, and by now the Arabs of both banks had become a single population. Each time the Jordanian government had tried to limit contact between the two banks—and there had been many such occasions—there had been outcries on the part of the West Bankers. Delegations of notables as well as city mayors had waited upon the king and government of Jordan and begged them not to do so. Many residents of one territory had relatives in the other. Well-known families like the Toukans, Masris, and Jaberis had branches in Jerusalem, Nablus, Hebron, and Ramalla on the West Bank, as well as in Amman and other towns on the east bank. Property, business, and commercial and family ties bound the residents of both sides of the Jordan, and any attempt to separate them was artificial and doomed to fail.

On the whole, relations between the Arabs in the territories and the military administration were normal, as they were with the Jews of Israel. In the matters which affected their daily lives, the Arab community had no complaints. On the material side, their standard of living rose by leaps and bounds. There were plenty of labor opportunities, and Arab workers—women as well as men—received the same pay as Jewish workers. The Jewish labor market was open to them, and in a short time they acquired skills in a variety of crafts and services. Their jobs ranged from mechanics and construction workers to staff duties in hotels. The self-employed Arab began to get higher prices for his products. Fish, vegetables, and fruit from the Gaza Strip, El Arish, and the West Bank were much in demand in Israeli stores.

In the refugee camps in the Gaza Strip, there was a veritable economic revolution. Refugees who for nineteen years had spent their time sitting outside their huts playing backgammon and talking politics, and seldom shedding their pajamas, began going to work. They continued to draw their rations and receive free health and educational services from the United Nations Relief and Works Agency (UNRWA). But now they could add to it by bringing home hundreds of Israeli pounds a week in wages. Indeed, thanks to the high wages in Israel, they were able to improve not only their standard of living but also their way of life. For the first time, they could acquire new clothes, furniture, and kitchen appliances. Many refugees even left the camps and went to live in one of the new housing estates which began to spring up on the outskirts of the towns. Television antennae sprouted from every rooftop, and refrigerators, hitherto the pride only of a few Arab notables, were now part of every home.

Nevertheless, there was friction and difficulty. The background was Arab terrorism. It was officially accepted by the Arab leaders, the town mayors and village *mukhtars,* that they were to give no help to the terrorists or support acts of violence against us. The agreed formula was that while they were opposed to our rule and wished us to evacuate the territories we had captured, as long as the existing situation continued, normal life was to be maintained. For this the government of Israel would bear state responsibility, ensuring work, food, health, education, public transport, and other public services for the Arab community. The Arabs would be free to work against us by political means and to express their criticism in speech and writing, but they were not to take lawless action.

On the whole, these general lines were followed. But there were exceptions. Terrorists who infiltrated from Jordan, Syria, and Lebanon found hiding places in the homes of their relatives and in their former villages. From time to time local residents of the administered territories joined the terror organizations and took part in their operations. We had to take stern measures. We would blow up houses—after evacuating the occupants—that had served to shelter saboteurs or where stores of weapons and explosives had been found. Naturally, this caused a furor, particularly when the householder was well known. But it proved effective and deterred many. Another measure was exile. We used this punishment against leaders who had taken an active part in incitement to terror or in helping saboteurs. In most cases we gave them a warning, and many indeed took heed and desisted. But there were some who ignored it, continuing their hostile activity in the belief that it would not be discovered.

The first to be exiled was Ruhi el-Khatib, the former Arab mayor of Jerusalem, followed by a former judge and the mayor of the town of Bira. Exile, like the blowing up of houses, was an effective method and helped to keep down terrorism, but it also roused popular anger.

The most difficult period on the West Bank was September and October of 1967, the end of the first summer of our rule. Religious and political leaders got together and raised the banner of rebellion. Its center was Nablus, where a general strike was declared and lasted several weeks. The start of the revolt was marked by the closing of schools. The next stage was timed to coincide with the opening of the U.N. General Assembly on September 19. Shops were shuttered and public transport ceased. After a short time, however, the people of Nablus realized that the rest of the West Bank had failed to join them and was even taking advantage of their strike. Merchants and truck drivers of nearby Jenin replaced them as exporters to Jordan and suppliers to the villages. Furthermore, the leaders discovered that their revolt was achieving no results: their strike would not bring about our withdrawal from the West Bank. At the beginning of November, life returned to normal. There were occasional clashes, but these were local and isolated episodes. The strike in Nablus, demonstrations in Ramalla, terrorism in Gaza all produced tension between the local Arab leaders and the Military Government, but they did not draw in the wider Arab community. The dominant factor which determined the pattern of life and thinking in the territories was the freedom of the individual and his material prosperity. Even when Arab terrorists opened fire on Arab workers traveling from their villages to jobs in Israel, they succeeded in killing a few, but not in halting the practice. The ties between Israel and the residents of the territories continued to develop. The Arab had equal status with the Jewish worker on the building site, in the factory, in trade, on the farm. The beaches, cafés, shops, buses, and all public places were open to the Arabs without discrimination. This engendered an atmosphere of calm and stifled all attempts to bring about national clashes. When Arab terrorists set off explosives in a Tel Aviv movie theater and booby-trapped a car in the main Jerusalem open market, the Jewish public was roused to fury at the sight of the dead and wounded, but they did not turn on the Arab workers and visitors in their midst. The differences of view did not develop into vendettas. The open bridges, the freedom of movement, the equality of pay and status, and the economic prosperity formed a sound basis on which the two nations could live together.

The acting leaders of the Arab population in the occupied territories were the city mayors. They were the link between the Arab community and the Israeli authorities. It was through them that the administrative procedures were conducted governing commerce —the grant of export and import licenses; entry permits for relatives in the Arab states to visit their families; education and health services; grants and loans for municipal projects; and other affairs of local government requiring the help of the central administration.

The "Big Three" were the mayors of Nablus, Hebron, and Gaza, but only one, Mahmed Ali Jaberi, the mayor of Hebron, was a natural leader, and was so regarded by his constituents. He alone had the strength to ignore the voice of Amman and conduct policy according to his own understanding. None of the others was of his stature. In Nablus the mayor was Hamdi Cnaan, but the real leaders of that city and the ones with the most influence and authority were the Masri and Toukan families. The mayor of Gaza, Rashid Shawa, could well have been the principal leader in his region. But his fear of the terrorist organizations and his frequent visits to Beirut to meet with their leaders and receive their blessing undermined his authority. He seemed wholly preoccupied with treading a tightrope between the Israeli authorities, on the one side, and the terrorist heads, on the other. I know little of the pleasure that Rashid Shawa may have enjoyed in his life, but I was a witness to what was assuredly the worst hour he ever suffered.

On the last day of the Moslem fast of Ramadan in 1971, Brig. Gen. Pundek, our military governor in Gaza, telephoned me. Rashid Shawa, he said, had just called on him with the information that the leader of the saboteurs in the Gaza Strip, Ziad el-Husseini, had committed suicide in the cellar of the mayor's house. Shawa asked to see me urgently. I told Pundek to send him along, and an hour later Shawa entered my office. He was pale as a sheet, and with good reason.

He said that a few weeks earlier, Ziad el-Husseini had come to his home asking for help to get him out of the country. In actual fact, our people were in hot pursuit, and he was trying to evade them. He had attempted to leave the Gaza Strip and flee to Lebanon, but had been unsuccessful. On November 3 Shawa had come to me to propose that we allow Husseini and his terrorist group to depart quietly, without fuss or hindrance. I had refused. These men had committed murder and sabotage, I said, and they should give themselves up and stand trial. Apparently Husseini had realized that this was the end of the road and had decided on suicide. He shot himself.

He left behind two letters. One was to his "host," Rashid Shawa, in which he thanked him for helping him hide from the Jews and for attending to all his needs—including contact with his terrorist group. In the second, headed "Will," he settled accounts with the Arab collaborators who, he said, had tried to deliver him into our hands. In this document, the same Rashid Shawa was transformed into the accursed villain. Husseini wrote: "I was deceived by the man called Haj Rashid Sa'id el-Shawa from Gaza, who is the greatest traitor, a Zionist agent . . . and Manzur, son of the filthy Rashid el-Shawa, who was once a noble man, but the son of the duck swam like the duck himself, and was a traitor. . . ."

I spoke to Golda and Minister of Justice Shapiro and explained the various aspects of the affair. The opinion I got from Shapiro was that under the Military Government, the governor had the final authority to act as he saw fit. He could send Shawa for trial for co-operating with the saboteurs. But he could also let him off with a warning and keep him as mayor. Golda left the decision to me.

I decided to leave him in office and not prosecute. I had not con-doned his act; I had not overlooked it; nor had I shown weakness. My decision was a deliberate move to improve Arab-Israeli relations. From their point of view, it was good for the Arab leaders to see that we fully understood their problems. As for the Arab public, despite the drama of the incident—or perhaps because of it—a diplomatic solution was likely to produce good results. The villain—or hero—of the piece had taken his own life. Our military authorities did not need the assistance of Arab leaders in their war against terror, and we now showed that we were strong enough to ignore the derelic-tion of Rashid Shawa. His family would make sure that Ziad el-Husseini would be buried without pomp, no shops would be closed, there would be no demonstrations and no graveside speeches of in-citement. They would do all they could to minimize the importance of the episode and help Rashid to make good his narrow escape from the mess of his own making. My main consideration in acting as I did was thought of the future. We had to clear the minefields that lay in our path and seek by all means to restore calm and normal life to the territories.

In my personal relations with the Arabs, I was closest to the Bedouin in the southern part of the Gaza Strip. Though now per-manently settled and working their own land, they have lost neither their tribal traditions nor the acute desert senses that had preserved them when they were a wandering people. They have vegetable plots and orchards, and some of them fish. They find the soil they need for their crops by digging for it, clearing huge mounds of desert sand beneath which it is buried. At first they used their hands to pour the sand into buckets and their heads to carry the buckets to the dump. They now use bulldozers to remove the dunes. Close to the coast the height of the sand is almost 20 feet, and further inland even higher. Enormous quantities of sand have therefore to be cleared before they reach the first level of soil. Today one can see patches of cultivated land, called *muassi*, tiny plots of a quarter or half an acre surrounded by the steep sand cliffs from which they have been scooped out.

Even after the plots are exposed, the Bedouin's work is not done. Before planting, they mix the soil of the *muassi* with sheep manure to nourish the roots of their crops. And they dig a drainage pit in the lowest part of the plot to ensure a reserve of irrigation water.

Preparing a *muassi* is a prodigious effort, but worthwhile. This region is the southern part of the biblical "rose of Sharon," the coastal belt stretching from here to Acre in the north, which even in antiquity was considered blessed by nature, with an equable climate for men and ample sun and rain for the crops. The Shamuti orange that grows here has a special flavor, and so have the strawberries and melons. Vegetables produce a crop in 90 to 100 days, cucumbers, tomatoes, eggplant and peppers in the summer and cabbages and cauliflower in winter.

Farming instructors from Israel's Ministry of Agriculture have taken the Bedouin under their wing and have taught them how to enrich the soil with chemical fertilizers and protect the tender plants with plastic covering. They have also replaced local seed with improved species. Export markets have welcomed their produce, and the honeydew melons and red and juicy Tayoga strawberries are welcomed by diners in Zurich and London. These Bedouin fruits are unmatched. The Sharon flavor is unique.

There were two Bedouin in particular whom I loved to visit, Haj Mahmoud abu-Selim and Hamed. The Haj was the head of the wealthiest Bedouin family in the Dir el-Ballah area of the Gaza Strip, and his word was law to the local residents. He had built a separate house for each of his sons, and he himself lived in a spacious villa in the middle of a veritable forest of palm trees. They were so numerous that from his roof the tops of the palms looked like a vast green sea stretching westward until it merged with the blue waters of the Mediterranean.

Haj abu-Selim was a tall, impressive figure of a man. In bearing and movement he was a Bedouin to his marrow, but there was vision in his eyes and he saw which way the world was heading. He sent his soon Farhan to study medicine in Germany, and, most unusual for a Bedouin, he allowed his daughters to be educated abroad. By the time I met him, he was very ill. He had long been an asthmatic. After the 1956 Sinai Campaign, when we withdrew from the Gaza Strip and the Egyptians returned, they jailed all whom they suspected of having collaborated with the Israelis. Among them was Haj abu-Selim, even though we had had no contact with him then. He remained behind bars for several years. He had returned to the Gaza Strip when we captured it in 1967, and our doctors did all they could for him. But the damage done in an Egyptian jail could not be repaired. In 1969 he was very ill. He would walk a few steps and then stop to catch his breath. He died a year later in the Tel Hashomer Hospital in Israel, with the most beloved of his wives, Um-Muhmad, at his bedside.

At the other extreme in the hierarchy of Bedouin society stood the second of my two favorites. With Hamed, there was no villa, no wealth, no social standing. He lived in a goatskin tent and made his living as a watchman, with a little pilfering on the side. But what was common to the homes of both men was the mood of leisurely grace. They were not places for people in a hurry, who find heaven in the Knesset cafeteria or a quick-lunch counter. In the house of the Haj I would be given coffee in an exquisite cup and a plate of dates filled with almonds. In Hamed's tent he would boil up tea in a sooty kettle over a wood fire and stir the sugar with a dry twig. But in both homes the proprieties of hospitality and politeness were meticulously kept. The meetings would open with noisy kisses on both cheeks, blessings and greetings of *salaam*. They would end with pleas for the release of a relative who was always "innocent of all guilt" but who was "unfortunately in prison," pleas which would assuredly not go unanswered, for as the "honored vizier" well knew, nothing in life was more noble than forgiveness. As for justice, the trial, and the offense for which the relative had been sentenced, the "honored vizier" would need have no worry. The sinner had already learned his lesson and would never again repeat his offense.

I too had my requests. From Haj abu-Selim I would seek direction on who in a particular Arab community decided what, how I might go about preventing assistance to the terrorists, when to show the mailed fist and when the gloved hand. From Hamed I hoped to learn something of his art in discovering antiquities. He was a veritable magician. His eye could detect bits of bone which the wind had swept along with the shifting dunes, and potsherds which had been carried into the wadis by the rain. He would hunt around and follow the course of wind and rain until he had reached the source of the relics—a millennia-old ruin of a settlement or a burial cave.

His most remarkable archaeological finds had been made beneath a stretch of sand belonging to Judge Abu Me'ilak, a wealthy property owner in Dir el-Ballah who had decided to turn this large tract into a *muassi* and plant a citrus grove. After the bulldozers had cleared the sand and holes were being dug for the planting, Hamed the watchman did some watching on his own account. At first his surveillance proved unrewarding. It was discovered that this area had been the site of a Canaanite cemetery some 3,500 years ago.

But the few Canaanite artifacts that were left were of little interest to Hamed.

He continued to watch. One day he spotted the tip of something while the men were at work and went to investigate. What he eventually brought out was an Egyptian sarcophagus of clay, the lid beautifully decorated with reliefs of the human form. Apparently, interspersed among the Canaanite remains were coffins of Egyptian officials who had served in the Gaza Strip as representatives of Pharaoh Rameses ii in the thirteenth century B.C. In the traditions of their homeland, their bodies had been placed in sarcophagi, together with precious personal effects—seals, nose rings, earrings, beads, and bracelets.

There had not been many of these Egyptian burials, and to this day I cannot fathom how Hamed was able to discover exactly where the coffins were likely to be. After finding the first, and when the owner of the property perceived that the Jews were ready to pay a fabulous price for it, Hamed was set to searching for others. He was successful, but the owner refused to share the proceeds with him. Hamed thereupon refused to take any further part in the search. The owner put his laborers on the job, but now the devil took a hand. Not another coffin was found. All the digging and the sifting proved fruitless. Only when Hamed was asked to return— and was paid his share—did the Egyptian sarcophagi reappear.

The owner's earlier parsimony still rankled, and Hamed now saw to it that he got more than his share. Upon the discovery of a sarcophagus he would extract it with artistry, raising it with thin and sensitive fingers inch by inch without breaking it. At the same time, keeping watch out of the corner of his eye that no one discerned his actions, he would cover with his bare feet the precious contents that had fallen from the coffin and thrust them behind him into a corner of the pit. With the coffin raised, he would seat himself on the rings and bracelets he had deposited in the corner, scratch, mop his face, and send the laborers to fetch him water, wrapping paper, anything to get them away. He would secrete his treasure beneath the sand, retrieve it at night, and bring it to his tent. Eventually, collectors would be able to acquire these objects for a handsome price from Hamed himself.

In the work of the Military Government, my own contacts were mainly with the municipal Arab leaders. With a few of them, especially Sheikh Mahmed Ali Jaberi of Hebron, I held serious and frank talks, and we found a common approach. But I knew this was not enough. Close ties at this level could perhaps smooth out technical problems, but they could not open out to create the human understanding that I wanted to achieve in our relations with the Arabs. Although they looked upon me, the Israeli defense minister, as a foreign conqueror and ruler, and upon all Israelis as invaders who had turned their country into a Jewish state, I believed and still believe that serious face-to-face talks with influential non-office-holding Arabs—thinkers and writers—would bring us closer together. We might still remain divided in our views, but at least we would understand one another.

I had heard of the Arab poetess from Nablus, Fadua Toukan. I had read her poems and been impressed by her sincerity and her nationalist spirit, and I wished to meet her. She accepted my invitation and came to my home in Zahala on October 12, 1968. She arrived in the company of her uncle, Dr. Kadri Toukan, and the mayor of her city, Hamdi Cnaan. I had with me David Farhi and David Zechariah, Arabists not only familiar with day-to-day affairs in the territories but also well versed in Arabic literature, traditional and modern.

Though Fadua was the reason for the visit, she herself did less of the talking than her companions. She was a woman in her late thirties, I thought, with a pleasant and open expression and thick black hair falling to her shoulders. When she spoke, or when she listened with concentration, her face became grave and there was a touch of sadness about her. When political topics were discussed, Hamdi Cnaan was the principal protagonist, and on relations between Israelis and the Arabs, it was her uncle, Kadri, who spoke in her name. Though he must have been well over seventy, Kadri was alert and full of vigor. He confessed that since our occupation, he had closed himself in his house and seldom left Nablus. His heart would not permit his eyes to see his land under foreign control. He was a teacher by profession, with a high reputation in educational circles in the Arab countries. He was also an author. He kept insisting throughout our talk that the Arab attitude toward Israel had undergone a change and that now, if we withdrew from all the territories we had conquered and allowed those of the 1948 refugees who wished to return to do so, the Arabs would recognize Israel, and we could live in peace with each other.

I did not think that Fadua was quiet because she was indifferent. She seemed to be very interested in the house and the antiquities in the garden, and she also asked my daughter, Yael, many questions about her childhood and about Nahalal, the village in which she had been born. She was probably better able to express her thoughts and feelings through the written rather than the spoken word, particularly with strangers. But perhaps the unbridled language of her poems, their power, and their bloodthirsty imagery came from the privacy of her soul, a soul that cried out but could not be heard.

Toward the end of their visit, Dr. Kadri Toukan again said he thought there were prospects for peace, whereupon I suggested that he go to Egypt, see Nasser, and find out if he was ready to come to terms with us. I told him that only a few days earlier Ben-Gurion had said that if we were faced with the option of peace or territories, he would choose peace and give up the territories we had conquered—except Jerusalem. Kadri said nothing, but Fadua suddenly sat up, turned to her uncle, and said, "Kadri, go to Gamal [Nasser]." Kadri tried to evade the issue, laughing it off with "Who is Gamal?" But Fadua persisted: "Tell Gamal to sit down with the Israelis and conduct peace negotiations. Kadri, go to Gamal!" Her tone was a mixture of pleading and ordering. For a moment I thought she would burst into tears.

Some two months later, I again met with Fadua, this time in the King David Hotel in Jerusalem. The only other person with us was David Farhi. Fadua had been to Egypt and had seen Nasser. Nasser told her that U.S. Secretary of State Dean Rusk had urged him to reach an arrangement with Israel on the basis of the Israeli army's withdrawal from the whole of Sinai, but Nasser had refused because the arrangement had not included Israel's withdrawal from the West Bank. Fadua said she had told Nasser of her talk with me and he had rebuked her for it. The one person she had met in Cairo who had encouraged her to continue to meet me was Muhammed Hassenein Heikal, the newspaper editor and Nasser's close friend. She had returned without any positive news. Not only in Egypt but in Jordan, too, the road to peace seemed to be blocked. According to her, even if we withdrew from the West Bank and came to an understanding with King Hussein, the Fatah organization would object and prevent an agreement. She was convinced that the majority of the people in the West Bank wanted peace and a solution to the Palestinian problem, but their leaders were cowards. Even her uncle, Kadri, was afraid and would not risk personal danger and political unpopularity.

I told her that I had recently spoken to a member of the Fatah terrorist organization who had given himself up to our troops. I had suggested to him that he be released and go to Abu-Amar, better known as Yasser Arafat, and tell him that I would like to meet him.

The prisoner refused to undertake this mission, preferring to remain in our custody. Fadua said: "I am a woman, but I am not a coward. I want peace. Nasser won't make peace with you. When I am in Beirut I will meet Abu-Amar and suggest that he meet you. We must make peace."

Fadua is no doubt a woman of courage. Whether or not she met Abu-Amar, I do not know. I did not hear from her again.

24

AN ARCHAEOLOGICAL MISHAP

WHILE WE FOUND we could live in harmony with the Arabs within our borders, terrorists from neighboring countries would cross the frontier to attack civilians in our border settlements. For the three years following the Six Day War, most of these Arab terrorists came from Jordan, even though King Hussein, unlike the Egyptian and Syrian rulers, did not adopt the slogan after the war that "what has been taken by force will be retrieved by force." King Hussein had learned something from the decisive and lightning defeat suffered by his armed forces, and he chose the political course rather than the battlefield as the means of gaining his ends. Moreover, Jordan had close links with the inhabitants of the West Bank, and the interests of both would be gravely jeopardized by another war.

Despite this, the Jordanian sector was the most violent for a considerable time. The terrorist organizations were the cause. True, they had announced only ten days after the Six Day War that they were posting their "High Command" from Jordan to the territory conquered by Israel, and Yasser Arafat did indeed spend a short time on the West Bank trying to organize a rebel movement there. But he was unsuccessful, and he returned to Jordan in September. Local terrorist leaders from the West Bank and the Gaza Strip followed him, leaving for Jordan or Lebanon when they found their cells exposed and their scope of operation restricted. Jordan became the main base of terrorist activities. It was through the Jordanian frontier that sabotage squads infiltrated into Israel to lay mines along the dirt roads of our farm settlements, and it was from Jordanian territory that they shelled Israel's border villages in the Jordan and Bet She'an valleys. Although the Jordanian army did not initiate action against Israel, its border units helped the saboteurs to cross the Jordan River, gave them covering fire on their return, and joined them on occasion in shelling and mortaring the Jewish settlements.

Action by the terrorists and counter-action by Israel ended only three years later in the autumn of 1970—Black September. A few statistics are enlightening. In that three-year period, 5,840 hostile acts were committed against Israel by Arabs operating from Jordan. Our casualties were 141 killed and some 800 wounded. Kibbutz Kfar Ruppin near the Jordan River was shelled 58 times, and nearby Bet She'an 40.

The first terrorist action was carried out nine days after the cease-fire, on June 19, 1967, when an explosive device was planted near Kibbutz Gesher in the Jordan Valley. Six weeks later shots were fired by a terrorist ambush party at a truck driving between Kibbutz Maoz Chaim and Kfar Ruppin. On October 1 terrorists ambushed and killed a member of Kibbutz Hamadiah and blew up one of the settlement's buildings.

I went to Zemach on November 2, 1967, to meet representatives of all the farm settlements and townlets in the Jordan Valley and then made an inspection tour of the border. The local representatives complained about the heavy guard duties the settlements now had to perform and the lack of weapons, shelters, trenches, illumination, and fencing. If here and there they exaggerated somewhat, they were basically justified in their complaints. Sabotage action launched from operational bases in the Kingdom of Jordan had turned our villages along the Jordan River into a front line. Though the big war was officially over, we clearly had to prepare ourselves in this sector for a new phase and style of hostilities.

I was back two weeks later, this time with an army brigade. We decided to station tanks and artillery in the area so as to react immediately with effective fire. However, I firmly rejected a suggestion that our response to the shelling of our villages should be to open fire on Arab farmers working their land on the eastern side of the border. If we did that, they would soon take flight, and we had no interest whatsoever in causing them to flee. Rather we should follow a policy which encouraged the Arabs to go on working their lands right up to the border, just as we did.

I had a similar discussion a few weeks later when I visited the kibbutzim Maoz Chaim and Kfar Ruppin, which had just come under artillery fire. Their members argued that if we retaliated by denying the Arab farmers access to their lands, the terrorists would think twice before shelling us. I told them that resultant misfortunes to local Arabs had not stopped terrorist operations in the past, and sharp measures by us against Arab peasants on the other side of the line would not produce the desired calm. The terrorists were active because King Hussein failed to stop them. What we had to do to force him to take control was not to harm local civilians but strike hard against the Jordanian army units that were cooperating with the terror squads.

I was again in Maoz Chaim, Kfar Ruppin, and Gesher on the night of February 15, 1968, when they were being shelled from Jordan. In Maoz Chaim and Gesher, farm buildings, silos, and stables were damaged, but in Kfar Ruppin there had been a direct hit on the children's dormitories. Fortunately, the children had been taken to the shelter and none was harmed. While I was in Gesher, the kibbutz came under renewed and rather heavy artillery bombardment. In accordance with government policy, I promptly ordered the chief of staff to use the Air Force and artillery against military targets, and they put in a strike against Jordanian artillery batteries and fortified military positions along the border. It was the first time since the war that our aircraft had gone into action.

A month later, on March 18, 1968, a bus carrying children from the Herzliya secondary school in Tel Aviv on a trip through the Negev went up on a mine. The incident occurred at Be'er Ora, some twenty-five miles north of Eilat. Two of the children were killed and twenty-seven were wounded. In response to this action and to the mounting raids and sabotage along the Jordan Valley, three days later the Israeli army carried out attacks on two important terrorist bases inside Jordan, one at Karameh, east of the river, and the other at Zafi, south of the Dead Sea.

The operation against Karameh turned out to be tougher than had been expected. Our forces, mainly armor, did not remain close to their target after its capture, as had been planned, but advanced eastward, climbed the ridges, and came up against Jordanian tank units. Even in the assault on Karameh itself, our men encountered tough terrorist opposition. The operation lasted until dusk, and our casualties were considerable—twenty-nine killed and some ninety wounded. We also left four damaged tanks and four armored vehicles on the battlefield. Casualties among the Jordanian troops and Palestinian terrorists were 232 killed and 30 tanks knocked out; 132 terrorists surrendered and were taken into captivity.

Because of persistent ground mist, our heliborne troops could not be flown and landed in time on the hills round Karameh, and a number of terrorists managed to escape. Among them was Yasser Arafat, who fled with some of his henchmen by car to Amman.

I was unable to follow the Karameh action at close quarters, as I had hoped, for I was in a hospital bed trying to recover from an accident that had occurred the previous day. While doing a little archaeological digging in a small cave in a mound at Azur, near Tel Aviv, I suddenly found myself under an avalanche of sand and soft limestone, and for the second time in my life I thought the end had come. The other had been in the 1941 Syrian action.

I had been up much of the night of March 19 at General Staff headquarters going over the operational plans for Karameh, which had been set for thirty-six hours later, and I thought I would take a few hours off from the office before the action. I would spend them at Azur, having been tipped off by my young friend Aryeh Rosenbaum that I might find it of special interest that morning.

I had come across Aryeh when he was a boy of ten, the son of immigrant parents, who had watched me at work when I had first begun digging in Azur and had caught the archaeological malady. He soon became familiar with the remains of antiquity in Azur and would get in touch with me whenever there was something he thought would interest me. Azur was an ancient site mentioned in the late eighth-century B.C. Assyrian texts and where the crusaders, some two thousand years later, built their Château des Plaines. But it had been settled very much earlier, and on previous digs I myself had found in its age-old caves superb sarcophagi dating to the Chalcolithic Period, more than five thousand years ago.

The Azur region was now undergoing rapid development. Some of its limestone mounds were being quarried, and the thick layers of sand covering them were removed for use on construction projects. The tip I received from Aryeh was that the bulldozers and power shovels would be working at a particular mound that morning, so shortly after dawn I drove out to meet him. We wandered round the site on the chance that in the course of excavation some relic of antiquity would be brought to light.

Half of the mound had already been sliced away, leaving a steep wall in the center. Against the wall was a huge pile of sand ready to be carried off to the construction sites. As I glanced over it, I spotted a few potsherds protruding from the sand. Upon examination, I identified them as parts of vessels from the Early Bronze Age (3150 to 2200 B.C.). This period predated the use of the potter's wheel, and the pots were therefore not symmetrical, for they had to be shaped by hand, like the kneading of clay in a kindergarten. The shards I picked out were hand-molded. They also conformed to the typical style of this period and were parts of what had been huge jars and jugs with handles specially set above the lip of the vessel.

I decided they must have come from a cave dwelling in the original mound, now cut through by the excavators. I climbed onto the sand heap to find it. Scanning the face of the wall, I noticed one patch where the lines of the strata were irregular. Instead of continuing horizontally, they turned downward, suggestive of the cross-section of a cave whose roof had collapsed inward. I scratched at the surface with my hands and found it crumbled and could be probed with ease. So I sank my spade into it and was soon able to squeeze half my body through the hole I had dug.

It had indeed been a cave in which people had lived some five thousand years ago. But nothing was left of their dwelling or of their possessions, though bits of pottery and flint implements might still be found embedded in the crushed floor of this stratum. The pressure of layer upon layer of sand and the ravage of earthquake, rain, destructive roots, and the organic processes of nature had had their effect. The modern dipper shovels had also contributed their destructive bite. They had cut away the lower strata of the mound, leaving the top precarious. I had not noticed it at first, but now I suddenly heard the light whoosh of showering sand. The entire wall of the mound was falling toward me.

There were two split-second stages to the mishap. In the first, part of the roof collapsed and knocked me out. But I must have come to almost immediately, only to discover that I was buried up to my armpits. The second stage came a moment later—and that was when I had heard the sound of falling sand: the upper part of what had been a compact segment of the mound above the cave split, disintegrated, and enveloped me. In the flash of time between seeing the collapse and realizing that I was buried, I thought: "I can't breathe, can't move, can't get out. This must be the end." There was nothing I could do, so I just passed out.

Aryeh, who had been behind me, was untouched, and he quickly summoned help from the people living nearby—two brothers who ran a local metal workshop and a wagon driver and his young son. Under Aryeh's precise direction, they dug with hoes and spades, found me, and pulled me clear.

With my head exposed, I soon regained consciousness, and my first recollection was of the thought that had raced through my mind when the mishap occurred. My next reflection was that although I felt pretty awful, this, after all, was not the end. I was told later that had I been able to see what I looked like, I might have stuck to my original thought. But now, above ground, bathed in the brilliance of a bright spring day and once more inhaling the freshest of fresh air, I felt alive again.

I was rushed to Tel Hashomer Hospital just outside Tel Aviv still conscious but unable to speak. With great difficulty I managed to produce some sort of grunt. The doctors examined my blue and swollen body and quickly established that I had sustained injuries to two spinal vertebrae and my ribs and that one of my vocal cords was severed. They feared there might be internal hemorrhaging and damage to the liver and spleen, but as there were no obvious signs of these injuries, they decided against opening me up. The body would be allowed to heal itself. Only the back and throat needed immediate attention. For the first, the upper part of my body was encased in a cast. For the throat, or rather for the restoration of speech, they brought in Dr. Ezrati, a superb specialist.

My immediate question, as soon as I could make myself understood, was whether, when, and in what kind of condition I would be able to leave the hospital and get back to work. The director of Tel Hashomer, the late Dr. Chaim Sheba, a wonderful man and a top physician, said that if all went well I could leave the hospital in about three weeks, when the cast was removed. I made a quick calculation, added a day for good measure, and decided that I would get out on April 14, twenty-five days hence. And that is what I did. On the morning of the 14th, I was back in my office.

While lying in the hospital, I recalled my feelings when I had last been in a similar state. It was when I lost the eye and had sunk into a deep depression, believing that my fighting days were over and I would never play an active role in positions of responsibility. I had also thought that for the rest of my life I would worry lest anything happen to the other eye. This time, however, soon after the ambulance deposited me at Tel Hashomer, I was determined to follow the reverse course—not to dwell on the accident, its effects, and the problems they might create, but to return to work as soon as I was able and behave as though nothing had happened.

For several months my body was locked in a stiff vest of plaster to keep the backbone in its correct position; but with the aid of a special chair I was able to move, sit, and work until my back was healed. Speech restoration was more complex. The remaining vocal cord had to be trained to take over the work of the severed one and to cover twice the distance in its vibrations. I also had to learn to enunciate the various letters and tones to fit the changed vocal structure in my throat. At first, the sounds I managed to extract from my lone cord induced not coherence but a sense of despair. The only hopeful element was the word of Dr. Ezrati: he assured me with a twinkle that a combination of my diligent effort and his extraordinary brilliance would give me normal speech once again! He proved right. True, the double strain on my single vocal cord is still very tiring on my voice, but this happens only when I talk a lot, and usually my listeners get worn out first.

In the hospital, and even afterward, I was inundated with visitors, flowers, letters, and cables. I told the chief of staff to act in my absence as if I were on leave and get his instructions from the prime minister. I did not think that defense affairs should be entrusted to the bedridden. I said this also to the prime minister when he came to visit me. Among other callers were Arab notables from the occupied territories, including the mayors of Nablus, Hebron, Gaza, and others.

I was particularly touched by the visit of the mayor of Kalkilia, who brought me oranges still on their fresh leafy branches. Ever since the partial destruction of his town by our forces and my personal efforts to get it rebuilt and rehabilitated, a special relationship had sprung up between us. It was the relationship of two men who shared a joint responsibility and concern for the fortunes of a community, its livelihood, housing, work, and health, a relationship vastly different from the normal administrative contact that might have been expected between an Arab mayor under occupation and an Israeli defense minister with an army behind him.

Rahel used to come to my bedside after lights out, when the hospital had closed and my family and other visitors had gone home. I often had to reassure her that I would be as fit as I had been. But my assurances were belied by my bloated face, blue body, spine in a cast, and barely coherent cawing. Nevertheless she clung to my conviction as to a magic charm. "Do you promise?" she would ask, and when I nodded, she would take heart—until the next visit.

My son Udi (Ehud) was also depressed by my appearance. It was he who brought me home when I left the hospital. After managing to get out of the car, I asked him to help me on a short walk round the garden. These were my first steps, and I had to hang onto him with one hand, though I had a cane in the other. I felt a weakness that was total, with no strength in my limbs and only ache and pain within my plaster prison. Udi was watching me, and what he saw was a broken man, blind in one eye, hardly able to shuffle, almost paralyzed, and literally speechless. Was this his father? He told me much later, when I had fully recovered, that in the garden that day he thought that was how I would be for the rest of my life, a permanently crippled, dumb invalid, and he had been hard put to choke back his tears.

Both in the hospital and for some time thereafter, my spine caused me acute pain. When my daughter, Yael, was a child, she would cry when she fell and hurt herself, and I used to ask whether the fall and the pain were not enough and why she had to add to it by crying? Yael would explain that she cried because her knee hurt, and I would insist that the crying itself was a pain, and a needless one at that. It did not convince her, but at least it diverted her attention from the injured knee. Now, with my own pain, I was less successful. Try as I would, I could not take my mind off the torture in my back and find something else to think about. Nor were my friends of much help in steering my thoughts elsewhere. When Ben-Gurion came, he seemed stunned at the sight of me. "Why, you're blue all over! What will become of you?" I had to work hard to make *him* feel better. Even those who came in with forced jocularity and engaged in light banter failed to hide their anxiety. Their expressions gave them away, and they were reluctant to look me in the eye.

The only help was the pain-killing pill or injection. Without it I could not sleep. Six weeks after the accident, Dr. Spiro, the orthopedic surgeon who looked after me and who was an old friend, told me that if I did not stop taking the drug, I would become addicted to it. I asked him when he thought I should stop, and he said as soon as possible. Without a word, I gathered all the pain killers in my possession and gave them to him. I had enough with my back, my eye, and my vocal cord. To add drugs to the list would have been too much.

Tel Hashomer was a remarkable hospital, and Dr. Chaim Sheba

was a remarkable man. I had known him many years and was very attached to him. He was an Israeli edition of Dr. Albert Schweitzer, except that he had not had to wander far from his native land in order to bring succor to impoverished nations. The tribes of Israel from all corners of the world had returned to their land, and Sheba saw himself as personally responsible for their health. When he tended new immigrants from Oriental countries, he understood that it was best not to cut off the patient from his family, or from his habitual way of life. And so whenever you visited his hospital, you could see the patient sitting with his family on the lawn between the bungalow-type wards, formerly military barracks, eating the flat bread and Oriental dishes he was used to at home.

Sheba turned a British army camp into one of the most advanced medical centers in the world in its standards of medical care, treatment and research. With dilapidated huts made into wards, and an annual budget for equipment and pharmaceuticals that covered only six months' expenses, Sheba started this center and trained and nurtured a generation of young physicians. They were drawn to him by his brilliance as a diagnostician and by his personal example of absolute devotion to the patient. He was interested in every aspect of the patient's life and background, and he was equally concerned in furthering research. He had a delicious sense of humor, a quiet contempt for ostentation, and was utterly unassuming. He himself would often wheel a nervous patient into the operating theater and ease his mind with relaxing talk. You did not need an appointment to get to see him in his tiny office. You just called on him, and if he was engaged, you waited until he was free.

Maimonides, the renowned Talmudic scholar, who was also personal physician to the vizier of the sultan in twelfth-century Egypt, once wrote that after completing his day's work in the palace, he would ride home on his horse, grab a piece of bread, attend to the score of patients crowding his courtyard, and then settle down to his prime interest in life—the study of the Torah. Dr. Sheba, after completing his long day in the Tel Hashomer Hospital, would visit other patients in their homes, and after treating them, he would sit and talk with them, and get them to talk about themselves. This, of course, cheered their spirits. But it was not merely a show of interest on Sheba's part. He was really interested. And it was not just his prime interest. It was the entire content of his life. He knew that most people are weak in body or spirit, and even the strong have their weaknesses. All, on occasion, need a healer, someone with an innate primitive strength before whom there are no barriers and with whom one can be completely open. With Sheba's death on June 12, 1971, Israel lost such a healer.

When I was again able to move about freely, I drove out to the Azur quarry to see what chance there might be now of turning up some of the artifacts I had wanted to find. Since my last visit, the dipper shovels had removed almost the entire mound, leaving only a small spur. I scratched around but found nothing. As I returned to my car, I heard a woman's voice behind me exclaiming to a friend: "Gracious me, if it isn't Moshe Dayan, poking around in the quarry again. He must think it's easy to dig him out from under!"

Terror and the border clashes it provoked continued, and they proved unbearable for the local Arab inhabitants in the Jordan Valley east of the river. Their villages and farmlands suffered increasing ruin and were finally abandoned. The unfortunate residents fled what had become the danger zone. Taking their families, their sheep, and their domestic possessions, they left their homes and went to live in the refugee camps near Amman. The lands they had cultivated and made fruitful fell into desolation. These Arabs had become the innocent victims of Arab terrorism. There could have been no clearer, more tragic testimony to the failure of Arab sabotage operations than the difference between the east and west banks of the Jordan River. On the western side, the Jewish farmers, who had been the military, political, and national targets of terrorist attack, continued to work their fields and live in their villages. On the eastern side, the valley had become a desert. The fields had withered, the villages were empty, and their inhabitants had been turned into refugees.

The Jewish farmers in kibbutzim and moshavim adapted their pattern of life to the war situation. With government and army help, they built shelters for their children to sleep in, paved internal roads to prevent mine laying, strengthened their guard, and installed lighting and fencing round the village perimeter. Not a single farm or village was abandoned. Not a single acre of land was left uncultivated. The vineyard of Kibbutz Gesher became symbolic of the mood and pattern in this Jordan Valley border area. It lay within the direct field of fire of the Arab Legion's fortified posts and was often shelled while the kibbutz members were working in it. Yet they never gave it up. They plowed, and pruned, and irrigated the vineyard—and harvested its grapes.

On one of my visits to the adjacent Bet She'an Valley to review our security policy with the representatives of the area, I put forward four guiding principles which should determine our counter-measures against terrorism from Jordan:

• Fatah terrorists could not be excluded from Jordan's obligations under her cease-fire agreement with us.

• If they continued their operations, we would carry the war into their territory. They could not be granted the privilege of conducting their type of warfare on our side of the cease-fire line while enjoying immunity on theirs.

• Our actions should not be conceived as punishment, but as military moves in a campaign, for this was a campaign. It would be long and multi-faceted, and no operation should be considered a one-time action complete in itself. Only by exploiting the total complex of means would the campaign be decisively ended.

• Within this framework—and here I came to the main purpose of the meeting—our border villages had not only to fight, defend themselves, and become part of our security system, but primarily to continue living their social and working lives in full measure. This was the main test both for the state and for the border villages.

During our talk, one of the kibbutzniks had mentioned a grove which had come under frequent shelling and said, "That's one plot where there will be no harvest." I now turned to him. "Ben-Ami, my friend," I said, "we have gathered here for the precise purpose of working out how to ensure that there will be a harvest on *every* plot. On no account can we accept the idea of even a single plot where there will be no harvest. If a particular field or grove or vineyard is vulnerable and exposed to Jordanian fire, then it will be worked only by men. If necessary, we will mobilize people to help, but I refuse to countenance the abandonment of a field under pressure of enemy attack. The chief difference between our side of the river and their side is that on the Arab side tens of thousands of inhabitants have fled and are now in refugee camps at Amman, Irbid, and es-Salt. With us, not only has there been no flight, nor a single vine untended, but we shall increase our border population by calling upon volunteers to come and lend a hand." We did, and they came.

Shortly after this talk to the border kibbutzim, I joined an ambush party. The common ambush was one of the many measures we used to prevent deep infiltration by terrorists. The one I went on was in the Jordan Valley sector, where a paratroop battalion, commanded by Dan Shomron, was deployed. I had a soft spot for this unit, for it was the successor to the 89th Commando Battalion, which I had founded some twenty years earlier.

I reached the unit headquarters at 4:45 P.M. I had not notified them in advance, as I wished to see the officers and men as they went about their normal duties, without spit and polish. I was given camouflage battle fatigues, a steel helmet, and an Uzi sub-machine gun, and I attended the briefing. The men tried to ignore my presence but without much success, and I thought I should explain. I told them that this was not a festive visit, nor an inspection tour. It was simply that I wished to see their operational activity at first hand and to find out what the new soldiers were like, those who had joined the army after the Six Day War.

We reached the edge of the ambush area at dusk, having covered the last stretch of the journey from camp on foot. We were a company strong and now split up into small squads which were dispersed over the length of the Jordan Valley. Mati, my aide, and I joined a squad of four led by a corporal. When we reached our assigned position, I scrambled into an irrigation ditch, cleared away the pebbles, loosened the earth beneath, and lay down, my eyes level with the lip of the ditch. I had perfect observation. The ground stretched away before me to the horizon. But in a few moments, the vestiges of last light vanished, and there was utter darkness. Anyone approaching would be noticed only if he were silhouetted against the sky.

Only a quarter hour after we had begun our vigil, we heard the tread of steps coming toward us. A few minutes later we could make out human forms. When they came within a range of 50 yards, our squad opened fire and promptly followed it up by dashing toward a wadi into which the figures had disappeared. On a track leading from the Jordan River to the West Bank mountains, we found the bodies of three young Arabs. There may have been others who had managed to escape. We returned to our ambush positions and resumed our vigil. The bodies would be examined at first light.

A light rain began to fall, and there was no letup until morning. There was no other incident that night, so shortly before dawn, at 4:25 A.M., I thanked the company commander and the troops, returned to base, and from there went on to Jerusalem.

Driving back, I reflected that I had gotten very little from the professional military side of the episode. There had not been much to learn from the clash with the terrorists, and apart from being satisfied with the performance of the soldiers with whom I had spent a few hours, I was left with no impression of their personalities, for we had necessarily to maintain complete silence. But the real reason for my having profited little militarily from the night's proceedings was that my mind had not really been on the action. Shortly after the shooting, back in my ditch, I ceased to think about the ambush. I gave myself over to the wonders of the night, to the skies now faintly lit by a crescent moon and the clouds scudding before the wind, and to the myriad sounds, each clear and distinguishable—the insistent chirrup of cricket and grasshopper, the strident zoom of mosquitoes cutting across the cries of the night birds, the distant barking of dogs, and the nearby swish of a tail as a lizard or snake slithered by.

As a boy in Nahalal, I loved to sleep out in the open in summer and fall into dreamy slumber with a gentle breeze caressing my face. True, I was no longer a young boy without worry or care who could soar with ease on the wings of imagination. But now, as then, I found nights in the open intoxicating, with the rustling and the whispering, the earthy smells mingling with the perfume of blossom, and the heavens almost within reach. The clash with the three saboteurs seemed remote, a subsidiary episode. And when I curled up in the car going back to Jerusalem, dozing and waking and dozing off again, I carried with me the cozy feel of warm earth, the tender touch of a soft wind, the soothing murmur of nature asleep.

Throughout the next year, 1968, and the beginning of 1969, terrorism continued with varying intensity. Israel strengthened her means of defense and broadened her counter-operations. The frontier line along the Jordan River was fenced, mined, and interspersed with fortified posts. Special paths were laid to pick up the tracks of saboteurs who had crossed the Jordan and penetrated our fence. When such tracks were detected, the infiltrators were pursued on foot and by helicopter, and only a very few managed to get away. But we paid a high price for ensuring the country's safety. Heading the units on these pursuit operations were many of our finest officers, some quite senior, and they were the first to be exposed to enemy fire when the saboteurs found themselves trapped.

In one incident in the Jordan Valley, Col. Arik Regev, commander of the paratroop brigade in charge of the sector, and Capt. Gad Manella, his operations officer, were killed. That same evening I called at Regev's home, and his widow, Ilana, reminded me of my first meeting with her husband—as she had heard it from him. Immediately after the capture of the Old City of Jerusalem, when I had ordered the barriers to be removed so that the Arab and Jewish parts of the city could be reunited, Uzi Narkiss, GOC Central Command, had come to see me together with Arik Regev, who was then the Command operations officer, to appeal the order. Regev had given me to understand that in his view I was out of my mind, to which I had apparently responded: "Young man, it is not important what you said. What is important is that you had the guts to say what you thought."

Since then, I had met Arik frequently at the head of his troops in the field. I regarded him as a magnificent and gifted fighter, one of the "chosen few," like Meir Har-Zion and a handful of others, who stand out in each generation.

Throughout our long history, the Jewish nation coined special terms for those who in times of crisis rose up to defend it and rescue it from danger. In the biblical days of the Judges, they were called "saviours." In the age of the Diaspora, they were "the Righteous"— men, known or unknown, by virtue of whom the nation was preserved in body and spirit. In our own generation, I said at Regev's graveside, it was the young men who stood guard over the nation, dedicating to it their brief lives and paving the path to its resurgence with their blood. Col. Regev was among the most distinguished of our young officers. In a generation noted for courage and fighting skill, he stood out, the most daring among the fearless, first in the assault, a leader in situations of stress, a man of integrity and kindliness, a renowned warrior of the Jewish nation.

In the twenty years since her birth in the midst of war, it had not been given to the State of Israel to abandon the sword: the War of Independence, the reprisal operations, the Sinai Campaign, the border incidents, the Six Day War, and now the campaign against terrorism, war after war, battle after battle. We had been able to sustain our purpose and remain steadfast in our aim thanks to the example of faith and devotion set us by men like Regev.

The attacks from Jordan which had lasted for three years since the 1967 war reached their climactic moment when action by the Israeli army, coupled with the behavior of the terrorists inside Jordan, finally prompted King Hussein to take appropriate measures. The terrorists were now operating as though they were a state within a state, and in February 1970 the government of Jordan issued regulations restricting their freedom of movement. But these edicts were rescinded before they went into effect, under pressure from the governments of Iraq and Egypt, which supported freedom of action for the terrorists.

On July 26 King Hussein announced Jordanian acceptance of the United States' peace initiative as formulated by Secretary of State William Rogers to secure a settlement between Jordan and Israel. The terrorist organizations resolved to torpedo this decision by increasing their operations against Israel, with the expected damaging results for Jordan. Hussein's government could equivocate no longer. Its members had to decide once and for all whether they or the terrorists were to determine Jordanian policy. A clash between the king and terrorist leaders Yasser Arafat and George Habash seemed inevitable. The confrontation came in September.

25

BLACK SEPTEMBER

EARLY IN SEPTEMBER 1970, the terrorists tried to assassinate King Hussein. Clashes followed with a tense Jordanian army. The terrorist organizations then launched their climactic operation. On September 6 they simultaneously hijacked four commercial aircraft over Europe. Only in one attempt were they frustrated, the plane belonging to Israel. The crew of the El Al Israel Airlines Boeing foiled the attempt by mortally wounding one of the hijackers and overpowering his companion, a woman, who was handed over to the London police when the plane landed at Heathrow Airport. She turned out to be Lyla Khaled, who in August 1969 had taken part in the terrorist hijacking to Damascus of a TWA plane on the Rome-Lod flight.

The three planes which the terrorists succeeded in capturing belonged to Pan American, TWA, and Swissair. The Pan American Boeing Jumbo was forced to land in Cairo, where the terrorists blew it up after the passengers were disembarked. The other two planes were forced to land in Jordan, near the town of Zerka, and the passengers were kept on board as hostages.

The Popular Front for the Liberation of Palestine claimed responsibility for the hijackings. It then submitted a series of demands to the governments of Switzerland, West Germany, Britain, the United

States, and Israel as conditions for the release of the passengers. If the demands were not met, or if the Jordanian army tried to intervene and gain control, the terrorists would blow up the two planes together with all the hostages. To back up their threat, they planted numerous sticks of dynamite at vulnerable points of the aircraft.

From Switzerland the terrorists demanded the release of three of their comrades who had been given a twelve-year sentence after they had attacked an El Al plane at the Zurich airport in February 1969. From West Germany they demanded the release of three terrorists who were being held for the attack on El Al passengers in Munich. From Britain they sought the release of Lyla Khaled. From the United States they wanted the release of Sirhan Bishara Sirhan, jailed for the murder of Robert Kennedy. And from Israel they demanded the release of a selected list of terrorists who had been caught and jailed.

Three days later, a third plane was added to the two already grounded on the Zerka tarmac in the blazing sun, their passengers faint from the stifling heat, hunger, and thirst. This was a British BOAC plane which had been hijacked on its way from Bahrein to London. The spokesmen for the Popular Front said the action was intended to hasten the release of Lyla Khaled from a British jail.

The governments of Switzerland, West Germany, and Britain decided to give in to the terrorists' ultimatum. But after the representatives of these countries had met with U.S. Secretary of State Rogers and a representative of Israel, they agreed to refrain from making separate deals and to release the terrorists in their custody only on the condition that all the kidnapped passengers were freed, including the Israelis and other Jews among them.

The U.N. Security Council met in emergency session and unanimously resolved to call on the terrorists to release all the passengers and crews without exception. The Red Cross brought food and medicines to the suffering hostages, who were still confined to their seats in the planes without benefit of air conditioning to ease the effects of the hot desert wind. Gen. Khadissa, commander of the Jordanian army, eventually managed to persuade the terrorists to allow women, children, the aged, and all nationals of India and Pakistan to leave the aircraft and be taken to hotels in Amman. But the terrorists made sixty exceptions. These were Jewish women and children, whom they insisted on keeping aboard "for interrogation." Even the government of Iraq appealed to the Central Committee of the Popular Front to release the planes and passengers, but to no effect.

After six sweltering days, on September 12, at 3 P.M., the terrorists told the passengers to disembark. They then blew up all three planes. Two hundred and eighty of the passengers and the three crews were allowed to proceed to Amman. But the terrorists held back forty hostages, whom they took with them to a refugee camp. They kept them in custody as "prisoners of war." They were freed only when a Jordanian army unit later broke into the camp and gained control.

Bringing the hijacked planes to Jordan and behaving with contempt toward the Jordanian authorities brought the terrorists into direct and open conflict with the Jordanian army. Fighting broke out in the Amman area. Despite several truce announcements from both sides, the battles continued. Certain army units whose commanders favored firm restrictions of terrorist activity extended their operations and attacked terrorist bases near the Syrian border, though this was contrary to the orders of the Jordanian chief of staff. The clashes grew in intensity and soon spread to other districts throughout the kingdom. The terrorists claimed that tank units had shelled their bases in the north and in the Jordan Valley and that scores of their comrades had been killed. Their leaders demanded that King Hussein dismiss his Cabinet, headed by Prime Minister Ziad el-Rifai, and remove those of his army officers who were known to be opposed to the Palestine liberation movement.

In an effort to preserve his crown and his kingdom, Hussein disbanded his civilian government and appointed a temporary military Cabinet of twelve generals, under the premiership of Brigadier Muhmad Da'oud, who had been captured during the Six Day War and spent several weeks in Israel as a prisoner of war before we released him and sent him back to the east bank. The terrorists kept suing for a cease-fire. The government kept agreeing. Yet the civil war went on. The advantage was heavily with the government and the army. In Amman and its surroundings, terrorists who had not taken flight were killed or arrested. The other Arab states sent urgent pleas to King Hussein to stop the actions against the terrorists, but he stood firm. The Syrians thereupon rushed an armored force to aid the terrorists, crossing the Jordanian border on September 18 and seizing a police fort. The next day additional Syrian tank forces, this time accompanied by Iraqi units, moved into Jordan and began advancing toward the capital, Amman. Hussein asked the United States for help. Washington agreed and promptly put her 82nd Airborne Division on full alert, dispatching at the same time a sharp warning to Syria. An Israeli armored unit was also moved to the northern border close to the battle area. The move did not go unnoticed by the Syrians—nor was it meant to.

The Jordanian army attacked the Syrian invasion force, inflicted heavy casualties, and compelled it to retire to Syria. The Egyptian chief of staff flew to Jordan bringing to Hussein and Arafat an appeal from the rulers of Egypt, Libya, and Sudan to cease fire. When it was clear to Hussein that he had the upper hand, he accepted an invitation by Nasser, flew to Cairo on September 27, met Yasser Arafat, and reached an agreement with him—at least on paper. The next day, September 28, Nasser died of a heart attack.

The clashes between the terrorists and the Jordanian army did not cease. At the beginning of January 1971, army units entered the Palestinian refugee camps near Amman and combed out the terrorists. At the same time, other units secured control of the terrorist bases in the area of Jerash and es-Salt. On April 6 Hussein issued an ultimatum to the terrorist leaders, demanding that they surrender their arms. Two days later the army began a thorough search, sealing off the terrorists round Jerash and Ajlun. Supported by tank and artillery units, Jordanian troops went into action, and after a three-day battle not a terrorist remnant was left in Jordan. Those who had not been killed or taken captive fled. Among them was a group of about one hundred who crossed into Israel and gave themselves up, together with their weapons.

The struggle between King Hussein and the terrorist organizations had ended for the moment, and terrorist activity inside Jordan and from Jordanian territory ceased. The terrorists still managed to assassinate Jordan's new prime minister, Wasfi Tel. This murder, however, occurred not in Amman but in Cairo, with Egyptian help. Wasfi Tel had been invited to take part in a meeting of the Arab Defense Council in Cairo on November 27, 1971. He was killed the next day at the entrance to his hotel. The murderers were caught but were released after a short time.

With the liquidation of the terrorist organizations inside Jordan, life there began to return to normal. The families who had fled to the camps near Amman returned to their Jordan Valley homes. With government help, their houses and villages were rehabilitated, and the destroyed aqueduct that brought water from the Yarmuk River was repaired. These farmers could once more plant citrus groves and vegetable plots in this parched region.

The outcome of the Jordanian-terrorist confrontation brought a triple blessing to Israel. The farmers on our side of the Jordan Valley and in Bet She'an were no longer harassed by fire and sabotage and could also return to normal life, with the children sleeping in their homes and not in shelters. Relations between Jordan and Israel improved, with the government, army, and people of Jordan as bitterly opposed to the terror organizations as were the Israelis. This atmosphere was to have a more far-reaching impact of providing a suitable background for cooperation between Jordan, Israel, and the Arabs in the administered territories. All the achievements of peaceful coexistence developed since the Six Day War might have been nullified had it not been for the events of Black September.

Sabotage activity still continued in Israel, but on an insignificant scale. With Jordan no longer available to the terrorist organizations, they operated from bases in the refugee camps of what became known as Fatah-land in Lebanon. But they had little support from the Arabs in Israel and the occupied territories. The system of favor and punishment had its results. Whoever refrained from aiding the terrorists could enjoy a measure of prosperity—and of freedom—they had never known in the past, either under an Arab regime—whether King Abdulla's and King Hussein's in the West Bank or Egypt's in the Gaza Strip—or under the British Mandatory administration. But those who took part in sabotage operations were either killed in clashes with army units or caught, tried, and given jail sentences.

The three main factors which brought about the suppression of terror inside Israel were the policy of the Military Government in the administered territories; the operations of the military and the special measures they adopted—fencing and mining of the border areas, pursuit of infiltrators, and good intelligence; and the developments inside Jordan. This third factor may have reached its climax with the Black September confrontation between Hussein and the terrorists, but its source lay in Israeli policy. If Israel had not reacted so sharply to sabotage operations undertaken from Jordanian territory, the government of Jordan would have reached a *modus vivendi* with the terrorists. Hussein finally resolved to stamp out terrorism because the alternative would have been the destruction of ordered life in Jordan. The Jordan Valley, Karameh, and the other villages which were ruined were just the beginning. The shelling of Irbid and Aqaba, the raid on Zafi south of the Dead Sea, and the air raids on Jordanian army camps added their impact, moving Hussein to curb the terrorists. And when their leaders objected, the question of who wielded real power in Jordan arose in all its gravity. Was it King Hussein or the terror organizations?

Jordan was the sole country of those which had fought us in the Six Day War that in principle did not reject the possibility of solving current problems with Israel by pacific means and of arriving at a peace arrangement. On day-to-day issues, mutual understanding seemed within reach. But not on the issue of permanent peace. There, the gap between the Jordanian and Israeli positions remained. Israel did not reject out of hand Jordan's wish to receive the Gaza Strip under her control. But Jordan was uncompromising in her demand for the return of all the territory that had been in Jordan's possession before the Six Day War. She was ready to make special arrangements concerning Jerusalem, to maintain it as an open city without restriction of movement from one part to another, but it would have to be divided, as it had been before the war, with its eastern part returned to Jordanian control. That was also true of the other borders. She envisaged the possibility of reciprocal "minor changes," but no more.

On other questions relating to the nature of our relationship, the Jordanian approach was liberal. This was also her attitude toward the demilitarization of the West Bank, though not toward major border changes. I do not know what her position would have been about the Etzion bloc of kibbutzim, which had been established before the War of Independence, destroyed by the Jordanians in 1948, and then resettled after 1967. As for the Jewish settlements which had been established in the part of the Jordan Valley formerly under Jordan's control, she demanded their evacuation.

At least Israel and Jordan each knew where the other stood. This led to the avoidance of many misunderstandings which might have arisen in certain tense situations, such as the later Yom Kippur War, and which had arisen in the earlier Six Day War. The Jordanians never threatened to attack us if they failed to secure their demands. And when they sent their units to the aid of Syria during the Yom Kippur War, it had not come as a surprise to us.

The man with his hand on Jordan's tiller is King Hussein. Like his grandfather Abdulla, he would appear to possess considerable personal charm and not a little courage: he can apparently move among a seething mob or visit an army unit without a bodyguard and without fear for his life. Unlike Abdulla, he seems to be an enlightened man of the world. However, despite his education and his familiarity with international developments, he is not very profound or very practical. He undoubtedly recognizes the limitations of his influence in the Arab world. And he must know that certain courses he would wish to follow are barred to him because they are unacceptable to the local and wider Arab public. Still, he permits himself the luxury of viewing reality in fanciful terms when he proposes plans for a settlement of the problems with Israel. He ignores the fact that for almost twenty years Jordan denied Jews access to the Western Wall in Jerusalem, contrary to the stipulation in the

1949 Armistice Agreement; that in 1967 he joined in the war against us even though Nasser had not asked him to and Prime Minister Eshkol had warned him against doing so; that even after that war he permitted the terrorists to use his territory as a base of operations against Israel; and that some of his army units cooperated with them. In spite of all these realities, Hussein still believed that Israel should return to the pre-1967 borders, and rely on Jordan's word that if she did so, it would mark the opening of a new chapter: the Arabs would unreservedly respect the integrity and rights of Israel. He publicly explained away his unfortunate actions in the past as "mistakes" which would not recur. The Arab world would behave toward Israel with kindness and decency if only Israel would return to the old frontiers. The region would be blessed with peace and prosperity, but is denied utopia by Israel's stubbornness. Israel failed to understand that a new era could be opened in the Middle East, and she was missing an historic opportunity by refusing to withdraw to the borders of 1948. I do not know whether the ministers around him, men like Prime Minister Ziad el-Rifai and others, also look out upon the world through rose-tinted glasses. Hussein himself may well be a sincere believer in what he proclaims. His outlook reflects the mixed product of a royal upbringing and the gift of a humanistic soul.

26

DEFENSE MINISTER AT WORK

THERE WAS NO OFFICE for the minister in the Defense Ministry building, for my predecessor, Levi Eshkol, had held both the premiership and the Defense portfolio and he had worked out of the prime minister's Tel Aviv bureau nearby. I was given the office of Moshe Kashti, director-general of the ministry. I found it too elaborate, and had it divided in two, a room for me and a conference room. I also changed some of the interior decoration. A carpenter converted what had been the bar into a bookcase. My visitors drank tea. They also ate fruit, which was always on my table—oranges in winter, apples and grapes in summer, and watermelon on special occasions. I changed the pictures on the wall for the four photographs reflecting Jewish history which had hung in my office when I was minister of agriculture. They were the Gezer Tablet, the Siloam Inscription, Serabit el-Khadem, and an aerial photo of Jerusalem.

Gezer was the biblical city built by Solomon (1 Kings 9:15) in the tenth century B.C. It lies roughly midway between Jaffa and Jerusalem. During archaeological excavations of this site, a three-thousand-year-old tablet was discovered with a Hebrew inscription, believed to be the earliest Hebrew writing known so far. It divided the year into agricultural seasons and listed the farming activities to be performed in each, such as sowing, reaping, and harvesting.

The Siloam Inscription, in classical Hebrew prose, belongs to the end of the eighth century B.C. at the time of King Hezekiah and the prophet Isaiah. It had been written on a prepared surface of the wall of the tunnel which Hezekiah had quarried to bring "water into the city of David." The water came from the Gihon spring outside the city, and it was stored in the reservoir or pool of Siloam, Shiloah in Hebrew (II Kings 20:20 and II Chronicles 32:30). The tunnel was cut to provide the people of Jerusalem with water in time of siege. The inscription gives a vivid account of how the conduit was dug—two teams of miners starting at opposite ends, working toward each other, and meeting in the middle.

Serabit el-Khadem is the site in western Sinai where Semitic slaves were put to work at the turquoise quarries in the latter half of the second millennium B.C. The photograph on my wall showed the ruins of a temple dedicated to the Egyptian goddess Hathor which was built for the Egyptian overseers.

As for the air photo of Jerusalem, well, Jerusalem was Jerusalem.

Though work at the ministry was far from routine, there were certain fixed activities: Cabinet meetings on Sunday mornings; meetings with the General Staff on Mondays; part of Thursday was spent on discussions at the offices of the Labor Party; Fridays I met with the chief of staff, my assistant, and other senior members of the ministry staff. Other days I inspected army units, defense installations, and the administered territories, where I talked to the Arab residents. In addition, I had to take part in Knesset debates and answer members' questions on matters relating to defense, and also participate in meetings with the prime minister whenever necessary.

I would be at my office each morning at 7:30 and leave late in the evening. The hours were long, and I never took a holiday. I had trained myself to sleep, or at least snatch a catnap, in a car or a helicopter on my frequent journeys, and I always had a blanket and pillow with me. Without these naps, I would never have been able to stand the long hours and the tension, for even at home, sleep was often interrupted by the telephone.

The door between my office and that of the secretaries was usually open, and the chief of staff, my assistant, Zvi Zur, or the director-general of the ministry would pop in to clarify a point of current concern which required a decision or to bring an urgent piece of information. These visits were always brief. I suspect that it was not only the pressure of work but something in my own nature which discouraged lengthy chats. I confess that I am rather impatient. I care little for small talk, and I am not the back-slapping hail-fellow-well-met type. Even in my leisure hours I do not like to sit around gossiping with friends. On visits to army units, I had difficulty in exchanging light pleasantries with the soldiers. "What's new, pal?" is not the kind of expression that comes naturally to my lips. I can answer questions and hold a detailed dialogue with a group of soldiers or even with a lone guard in a lookout post where there is a mutual interest in the subjects: what is happening on the enemy side? What are our defects? How can they be rectified? I am also interested in the personal lives of the men. Where do they come from? How do their families live? Do they rest or work when they are on leave? Do they support their parents?

I always found that the troops answered freely and were never afraid to criticize or complain. But these were more in the nature of question and answer than true dialogue. In this respect, I suppose there was no basic difference between my talk with an anonymous private in a Golan Heights outpost and my discussions with the top officials of the Ministry of Defense.

My visits to army units were without pomp or ceremony. I was never greeted with a guard of honor. When I had issued orders abolishing this practice, I was told it would endanger discipline and that it was unthinkable for the army to receive the minister, the chief of staff, the regional commanders, and the air and naval commanders without an honor guard. I did not argue about holding parades for the others. I did not feel disposed to lay down principles of discipline or routine forms which are said to mold the character of the soldier and his combat capability. I had never rejected nor had I been enthusiastic about parade-ground drill and the shouting of sergeant-majors. I therefore said that honor guards would be canceled only as far as I was concerned. When I went to an army camp, it was to visit the unit, to meet with the troops and to consult with the officers, not to force the men into a frantic spit-and-polish scramble for the visiting dignitary. And that became the rule for my visits.

I cannot claim to be well dressed or to wear clothes that are always well pressed, particularly when I emerge after a nap in the back of my car. But my weaknesses were a shaved face and polished boots. The first thing I did in the office after returning from a field trip was shower, shave, and polish my boots. I considered myself something of an expert at polishing, having acquired the skill from my British sergeant when I was a supernumerary policeman in Nahalal forty years ago! He taught me to rub a film of whitewash on my boots before applying the polish, so as to get rid of the grease, and indeed it produced a brilliant shine, with my face reflected twice from my toecaps. Perhaps I enjoyed this pastime because it subconsciously took me back to the world of my youth. The real reason, I think, was that it gave me a few minutes to myself, which I so much needed and so much lacked.

My staff at the Defense Ministry dealt with three branches: the armed services, defense equipment, and the administration of the occupied territories. These, of course, were not equal in importance or scope, nor was the division between them absolute. Heading the army was the chief of staff. It was the practice for chiefs of staff to be appointed by the government upon the recommendation of the minister of defense, but this practice had been established when the defense minister was also the prime minister. When I became defense minister, it was clear to me that I could not propose as chief of staff an officer who was not acceptable to the prime minister and most of the other ministers, for if they objected to my choice, there would be no government majority for his approval. I therefore behaved accordingly when Chaim Bar-Lev completed his term as chief of staff and we had to appoint a successor. I accepted the decision of the prime minister even though I had recommended another candidate.

In the areas of arms supplies and defense installations, I limited myself to the political negotiations and to the determination of policy. I made the basic decisions, but I delegated to my assistant, Zur, the task of carrying them out. I gave him the requisite authority and responsibility—except, of course, for parliamentary responsibility—and I had no reason to regret it. Zvi Zur, the successive directors-general, and the heads of the military industry fulfilled their functions well and with skill.

It was in the six years from 1967 to 1973 that we decided on the development of the army's main weapons systems, and most of these decisions were implemented in a comparatively short time. The *de facto* arms embargo upon Israel by those Western countries which produced the aircraft, weapons systems, and equipment we needed made us realize that we had to produce types of armaments we would not otherwise have tackled. Normally, a small country like Israel cannot get involved in the production of such complicated arms as advanced aircraft and their sophisticated instruments. But we could not afford not to do so. There were times when the effort to establish the necessary industrial basis for the production of weapons systems vital to us seemed as hopeless and frustrating as climbing a greased pole. Yet by 1973 most of these systems had already been absorbed by the fighting services, and some were even exported. Locally produced weapons included the Kfir attack plane, mobile medium artillery and long-range guns, the Shafrir air-to-air missile, air-to-ground missiles, the Reshef missile boat, the Gabriel sea-to-sea missile, as well as most types of ammunition and control systems. I do not think that Israel can attain total independence in armament, but she can reduce her dependence on arms supplies from outside, and the basis for this program was laid by the production of these weapons systems.

To cover armaments, maintenance of the army, fortifications, and the transfer of army bases to the new territories, there was no escaping a formidable increase in the defense budget. It rose sharply, and in 1973 it was almost double what it had been in 1967. However, the defense budget's percentage of the state budget did not increase. It constituted 32.8 percent in 1967 and 31.9 percent in 1973.

The defense budget in those six years changed not only in scope but also in its component parts. We deliberately increased the allotments to the air and armored forces at the expense of the infantry. In the 1973–1974 budget—as approved before the Yom Kippur War— more than 50 percent was allocated to the Air Force and 30 percent to the Armored Corps.

A large part of the budget and no little effort were invested in fortifications, the construction of roads, the installation of water pipelines, and a communications network in Sinai, the Golan Heights, and along the Jordan front. Though the Bar-Lev line did not fulfill its expectations in the Yom Kippur War, nor did the second line, this was due, in my view, more to the manner in which the forces were used than to the initial concept. The fortification lines in these regions are to be seen as elements in an infrastructure serving our ground forces, most of which—tanks and artillery—are mobile. They need logistic arteries, but they cannot be tied down to fortified lines and forward outposts. These lines and outposts should be maintained for as long as it is worth doing so, and abandoned in good time when developments so warrant. There can be various approaches to this problem, but there is no doubt that what ensured Israel's military strength—a strength which stood up to attacking forces three times its size in the Yom Kippur War—were our overall system of fortifications, the advancement of our permanent bases to the fronts, and the massive addition of power to our armored and air forces.

Not all my duties as a minister were directly related to the Defense Ministry. As a member of the Cabinet, and a member of the Labor Party, I also found myself drawn into political activities when the occasion arose. Some six months after the Six Day War, on December 12, 1967, the Rafi convention decided by a 60 percent vote to unite with the Mapai and Ahdut Avodah parties and form the Labor Party. Ben-Gurion had opposed the merger. I fancy that even if Rafi had continued its independent existence, Ben-Gurion would have ceased to be politically active. The party's dissolution marked the end of his political road. During the discussion that preceded this vote, he did not hide his displeasure at members of Rafi who were turning from him to join what he considered the "corrupt" regime of the Mapai Party. The decision of the convention put the seal on his isolation.

A few weeks later, on January 21, 1968, the union of the parties was formally established. Of Rafi's ten members of the Knesset, nine went over to the new united party. The tenth, David Ben-Gurion, refused to join. The man who had been Israel's outstanding prime minister, had headed the powerful Mapai Party and left it, was now, as a member of the Knesset, the head of a one-man party.

With a great artist or a great composer, it is possible to distinguish between the man and his work, but not with Ben-Gurion. He led as a man, and he influenced through the force of his personality no less than through his doctrines. Perhaps in the sphere of religious and ethical principles, an impact can be made through the written word alone. Ben-Gurion's major pronouncements, however, were not abstract principles but decisions on concrete measures to be taken at a specific time and in the context of specific prevailing conditions. They were decisions which not only committed his people but were conditional upon the people's acceptance of them as an expression of their own will. Ben-Gurion's strength lay in the fact that his people did accept them and followed him. They trusted him. The source of his influence and his persuasive powers stemmed not only from the wisdom of his words, but also from the deep and passionate faith with which his entire being was imbued and which he was able to transmit to others with great power.

I recall an address he gave some years ago in which he named the six outstanding Jews who, in his view, had contributed the most to the fulfillment of the Zionist ideal—the rebirth of the Jewish people in their historical homeland. Everyone expected him to lead off with Theodor Herzl, Chaim Weizmann, and other well-known leaders of modern Zionism. Instead he listed three French Jews and three from the Land of Israel. The Frenchmen were Adolphe Crémieux, lawyer and statesman, who abolished slavery in the French colonies, enfranchised Algerian Jews, and went to the Middle East during the notorious "Damascus Affair" to save Jewish prisoners in Damascus from the gallows, and the community from mob violence, following the anti-Semitic blood libel of 1840; Charles Netter, who in 1870 founded and directed the first Jewish agricultural school in Palestine at Mikveh Israel; and Baron Edmond de Rothschild, who invested prodigious efforts and means to establish and develop Jewish farm settlement in Palestine at the end of the nineteenth and beginning of the twentieth century. The three others were Palestinian Jews, Hungarian-born Joshua Stampfer and David Meir Gutman, and Jerusalem-born Joel Moses Solomon, who in 1878 founded Petach Tikvah, the first Jewish farm village in the country in recent times. They were observant Jews from Jerusalem who were determined to redeem not only themselves by living in the Land of Israel but also the land itself, by farming it as had their biblical forebears.

These six Jews impressed Ben-Gurion because, as he used to say, they did not tell other Jews what had to be done. They did it themselves, and thereby did more than any other Jew to lay the foundations for the return of the Jewish nation to its homeland, to work on the soil, and to re-establish the Jewish state.

It required no great flight of imagination to recognize the criteria which Ben-Gurion set himself in determining his way of life in each of its stages and why he considered himself—without saying so explicitly—as belonging to the leading group of "fulfillers of Zionism." Like the six heroes of his address, he understood the Zionist vision in all its implications and recognized that the vision could be translated into reality only through the physical labors of the individual Jew to fulfill it. This is what he did in his early years. Later, when he was at the center of the national leadership, he was called upon to assess the violent changes taking place in the world and to decide on appropriate courses of action: the collapse of the Ottoman Empire, the British Mandatory regime, the rise of Nazism, World War Two, the end of the Mandate, the proclamation of statehood, the War of Independence, and all the challenges that followed. Neither Herzl nor Weizmann could equal Ben-Gurion in his combining of the vision with its realization.

Those who did not know Ben-Gurion may find it hard to understand why he always insisted on retaining the Defense portfolio. He well knew that as prime minister he could have the last word, and the final decision, on all matters of principle—and he never concerned himself with any other kind. Why, then, in all the years that he was in government, did he make sure that he was also his own defense minister? I think there were two reasons. One was objective. He was always aware of the serious potential danger to the State of Israel. He used to say that "only an idiot or a genius among foreign statesmen would support Israel," for no normal person could be expected to understand how Israel could overcome Arab hostility. Even what he said to his own colleagues threw a harsh light on the special complexity of the Israeli situation: "Whoever expects immediate justice from the world cannot be a Zionist"; and "Israel can win a hundred battles yet its problem will not be solved; but if the Arabs are victorious only once, it will mean our end." The inescapable difficulties and paradoxes in Zionism, and the concern and anxieties over what could happen to Israel, led him to regard security and defense as the areas of supreme importance, and the Defense portfolio as carrying the heaviest of all responsibilities.

But there was also a subjective reason. Ben-Gurion was not one of those public figures who derived satisfaction from talk. The greatest of orations was never regarded by him as an achievement. "Only the Lord," he used to say, "could create by uttering a word. He said 'Let there be light,' and there was light. But not mortals." A state and a nation could rise only through deeds, not speeches.

Yet Ben-Gurion was not a man who labored with his hands. I was not with him in Sejera at the beginning of the century when he worked on the land, nor at Rishon le-Zion when he worked in the wine cellars. But I have no doubt that even at that time his principal interest lay in the political field. His main concern was with Zionism, Jewish and world problems, and with the search for and charting of the correct course to be followed at each critical stage in order to advance the "return to Zion," the redemption of Israel and its reestablishment. Ben-Gurion felt an innate reluctance to deal only with general affairs, like a chairman of the board, even if he did so as prime minister. He sought a pattern of life in which decisions—his— were converted into deeds. He wanted a job in which there was tangible creation, the production of something from nothing, the forging of ideas and their incorporation into decisions that gave them muscle and sinew and transformed them into concrete reality. The reality for him was mass immigration, homes for the homeless, conquest of the desert and the creation of new towns and villages and plantations, armed forces with modern weapons to protect the borders, war if attacked, and in war, victory.

I now saw Ben-Gurion only occasionally. I spotted him one morning at the breakfast table of the King David Hotel. He had a newspaper in front of him, his eyes glued on the print. But he was not reading. He was deep in thought. This was the Ben-Gurion of the sculptured face, the firm chin, and the piercing eyes. But it was a dispirited Ben-Gurion, tired and solitary. Was it also the look of defeat? He seemed to lack the joy of life, the alertness. There was a suggestion—not more than that—of sadness in his expression.

I went over to him and sat down. Within a minute he was his old self, as warm and friendly as he had always been with me. I told him what was happening in the area of defense. He listened, asked questions, and then, apparently out of the blue, remarked that our main concern was immigration. We had to do everything possible to strengthen it and to attract immigrants from Western countries, in particular. The strength of the Jewish people, he said, lay in quality not quantity, and only if we raised our quality would we be able to stand up to our numerous enemies. Ben-Gurion had not strayed from our subject. He was still talking about our defense problems, but not in the technical language of tanks and planes. He was using the language of far-sighted vision, the language of Ben-Gurion.

On February 26, 1969, Prime Minister Levi Eshkol died. The Labor Party selected Golda Meir as its nominee for the premiership, and her appointment was approved by the Knesset. At her request, I continued to hold the Defense portfolio. At first I was uncertain as to how we would work together. True, I had had favorable experience in the past when she was foreign minister and I was minister of agriculture. Our ministries were jointly involved in Israel's technical aid program to the underdeveloped countries of Africa and Asia. But much had changed since then. When the party voted for Golda as their nominee to succeed Eshkol, I had abstained. I did not consider her the kind of personality who would open new vistas in the leadership of the state and the party. Yet there was no other candidate with any chance of getting the nomination. Hence my abstention.

After a short time, however, my doubts vanished. The table between us was uncluttered by the wreckage of past contention. Not that we forgot the past, but we both concerned ourselves with the present and thought of the future. In her style of work, she was straightforward and direct and did not resort to evasion. Our discussions always ended in a clear decision or understanding, and not in vague formulas or postponement. Above all, she was not surrounded by house journalists or aides who would arrange special-interest leaks to the press. She had her close friends, and I was not one of them. But on matters within my sphere of work, defense, there was no barrier between us.

27

THE WAR OF ATTRITION

HALF A YEAR after the Six Day War had ended, it became clear that peace was as far off as ever. The United States had notified President Nasser of Egypt that Israel was prepared to withdraw to the international frontiers within the framework of a peace treaty with Egypt and Syria. But the Egyptian president had not changed his stubborn opposition to the existence of Israel. The conclusion he drew from his military defeat was that he now had to rebuild the Egyptian army and unite the Arabs for a political struggle against Israel.

On August 29, 1967, a summit conference was held in Khartoum in which the leaders of eleven Arab states took part: Egypt, Iraq, Jordan, Lebanon, Saudi Arabia, Kuwait, Libya, Sudan, Tunisia, Morocco, and Algeria. Syria was not represented, but Yasser Arafat's Palestine Liberation Organization (PLO) was. Inspired by Egypt's president, the conference adopted "the basic principles to which the Arab states commit themselves." These were the celebrated four noes: no peace with Israel, no recognition of Israel, no negotiations with Israel, no concessions on the question of Palestinian national rights. The oil-producing states also assured Nasser that they would continue to provide financial aid by replacing the revenue Egypt would lose by keeping the Suez Canal closed. Saudi Arabia promised

$120 million a year, Kuwait $132 million, and Libya $72 million. Military aid also increased. The Soviet Union poured equipment and advisers into Egypt and Syria in a massive effort to rebuild their armies. In June 1967 a high-level Soviet military delegation arrived in Egypt. The delegation consisted of ninety-one senior officers and was headed by the Russian chief of staff, Marshal Zakharov. The Russian officers visited every army unit and carried out a thorough investigation of what had happened in the war. At the end of their two-month stay, Zakharov told Nasser that if every one of the Soviet tanks which the Egyptians had deployed in Sinai had fired only ten shells, the Arabs would have won the war. The fact was, he said, that most of the tanks had not fired a shot. The Russians, he added, would show the Egyptians "how to fight."

A week after the end of the war, the Russians started to supply Egypt with arms by both air and sea. Within eighteen months, not only had the Soviet Union restored Egypt's armed might to what it had been on the eve of the Six Day War, but she had strengthened it in armor and warplanes.

The Soviet Union treated Syria in the same way. In August 1967 the Soviet defense minister invited the Syrian defense minister, General Hafez Assad, to Moscow. The Russians asked Assad whether the Syrians preferred to occupy themselves with internal struggles or wished to prepare for renewed action against Israel. He was told that the Soviet Union could not supply the required weapons and equipment if Syrian units were not placed under the supervision of Russian experts. Assad replied that Syria would do what its benefactors asked, and thousands of Russian experts and advisers flowed into Syria to train and direct its army, as others were already doing in Egypt.

On October 21, 1967, four months after the Six Day War, the first grave incident occurred. Out of the blue an Egyptian missile boat of the Soviet Komar type sank the Israeli ship *Eilat* some thirteen and a half miles from Port Said, outside Egyptian territorial waters. Two missiles were fired. The first stopped the ship's engine, and the second hit and sank her. Our losses were forty-seven killed and missing. We reacted by shelling the oil refineries close to the city of Suez and set aflame the adjoining oil storage tanks. The Egyptians returned the fire, and there was an artillery exchange along the entire front. Canal-city residents from Suez, Ismailia, and Kantara had begun leaving their homes during the war. Their departure now turned into panic flight.

I flew down to Suez. The refineries were still burning, and I watched them from the pier on our side of the line. While there I received news that the Egyptians had renewed the shelling in a particular sector. The head of Southern Command was with me, and I told him to keep the action localized.

Following these episodes, there was comparative calm along the front for more than a year. During this period the Egyptians, under the direction of Soviet experts, reorganized their forces and established fortified positions on the west bank of the Canal. In April 1968 Nasser informed his people that "We have reached the consolidation stage." Five months later, the Egyptian defense minister announced that this stage had been completed and the Egyptian army had now moved to "active deterrence." This new stage took the form of raids and artillery and small-arms fire on Israeli forces, causing casualties and damage. But the Egyptians invariably refrained from launching a full-scale attack that would win back the territory we had captured.

The climax occurred in early September, when Egypt opened fire in the northern sector of the Canal, killing 10 of our men and wounding 18. Two weeks later, Egyptian artillery pounded all our positions along the Canal for nine hours, and our casualties were heavy—15 killed and 34 wounded. Under cover of darkness, the Egyptians also sent over commandos who tried to penetrate one of our strongholds. They ran into an Israeli patrol, and the fighting lasted until shortly before dawn, when the commandos withdrew.

I flew south the next day and started my inspection at the "Cobra" stronghold, where most of the enemy shells had landed. The place looked as though it had been hit by a typhoon. A 160 mm. shell with a delayed fuse had penetrated the concrete roof of the central bunker and exploded inside, wounding all the ten soldiers there. Most of the installations above ground had also been badly damaged, but there were no casualties.

The encounter between our patrol and the fifteen-man Egyptian commando unit took place a mile and a half south of this stronghold. When we reached a burned-out half-track hit during the engagement, I got off my command car and continued on foot, following the track which the Egyptians had taken. We had to be careful to step into the fresh footprints left in the sand by the retreating Egyptians, for they had mined the track as they left. Behind a steep, scrub-covered mound of sand, I spotted a dark body. When I got close I saw it was an Egyptian soldier who had apparently died of his wounds during the night. His comrades had taken his Kalatchnikov rifle but had left his belt with its cartridge pouches and a German-made commando knife. I moved to the edge of the Canal, crawling on my belly, and looked across to the Egyptian side. I saw no movement, and no one opened fire on us. A few yards from the water's edge we found two more Kalatchnikov pouches, mines, and bazooka shells. As we returned, we passed two of our tanks which had collided during the darkness and heavy shelling. The first tank had stopped and the one behind had run into it and tipped it over. Blood stains, oil spots, and bits of burned clothing were the grim evidence of the fatal accident.

From our stronghold near the Canal, I could see the city of Suez through field glasses as though it were laid out on the palm of my hand. The first row of houses was in ruins, but behind it I occasionally spotted figures dashing from one point to another. Beyond the city black smoke rose from the burning oil tanks, and at anchor in the port were vessels which had been hit. I turned my field glasses toward the main entrance to the port from the Gulf of Suez. The last time I was here, I had noticed the two huge stone lions which adorned the principal quay of the Canal. I now saw that one of them was shattered. Though they were dark red in color, I fervently hoped they were examples of modern art made out of concrete and not ancient Egyptian statues formed from Nubian sandstone.

Our most urgent need was to strengthen our front-line bunkers. I would also have to find another $5 million to improve the roads, particularly the one through Mitla Pass. I was told about the plan to put up a mined fence along the Canal, like the barrier we had established on the Jordanian sector. I made no comment, though I reflected that even with the most sophisticated devices, it would be impossible for us to seal hermetically our frontiers with the neighboring Arab states. It was more important to devise a policy that would convince them that a peace arrangement, or at least a cease-fire with us, was to their advantage, for war would cost them dearly.

In this situation we decided on a series of counter-strikes. Our Air Force blew up several bridges on the Nile and our paratroops landed deep inside Egypt and destroyed the large power station of Naj Hamadi. Our raids stunned the Egyptians and their Soviet advisers. They realized that the Egyptian hinterland was unprotected. Urgent consultations were held in Cairo, and it was decided to set up civilian and military units to guard likely targets in the Nile Valley.

During the next four months, while the border with Egypt remained quiet, the Israeli army reorganized and fortified the Canal front. Our new chief of staff was now Lt. Gen. Chaim Bar-Lev, who had been appointed on December 3, 1967. I had recommended him as the successor to Lt. Gen. Yitzhak Rabin, who had become Israel's ambassador to Washington, and explained that both Bar-Lev's candidacy and the date for the change of commands had been chosen by the late Levi Eshkol. The government approved the appointment unanimously. There were extensive discussions in the General Staff as to whether to move our forces out of Egyptian artillery range and use mobile patrols backed up by our main armored forces to control the Canal line, or whether to build a series of strongholds or mini-forts that dominated the waterline, backed by good communication routes with the rear. The area between each stronghold would be covered by small mobile tank squads, and some distance behind them would lie the main armored forces ready to rush in quickly and reinforce any spot along the Canal in need of assistance. This second course was the one which Bar-Lev had pressed and which the General Staff finally adopted.

The mini-forts were built along the line of the Canal. Thick layers of fill and stone covered the bunkers. Each fort contained a courtyard big enough to hold a few tanks that was enclosed by a stone wall. The army engineers also paved a road along the length of the stronghold line and erected a sand ramp between the road and the Canal, so that the Egyptians could not see the movement of our soldiers inside the forts. Normally fifteen men manned each stronghold, taking turns in the spotters' nests and emplacements outside the fort. Their main function was to serve as the eyes and ears of the sector. During an emergency they were expected to summon the tanks and artillery stationed in their immediate rear, as well as air support.

Just before we had completed the fortifications, the Egyptians resumed their "war of attrition." While we continued to work under cover of darkness to finish the forts, the fighting escalated, blow and counter-blow following one another. In the four-month period ending July 13, 1969, we suffered 29 killed and some 120 wounded. On that day, I sought and received the approval of the Ministerial Defense Committee to order our Air Force to attack Egyptian forts, gun emplacements, and SAM-2 missile batteries in the northern Canal sector. Four days later our aircraft went into action and bombed and strafed military targets from Kantara to Port Said, at the northern end of the Canal, for five hours. We shot down 5 enemy planes and lost 2 of our own. At the end of July, following two air-to-air encounters in which 12 Egyptian planes were brought down, the commander of the Egyptian Air Force was dismissed.

Shortly thereafter Nasser also had to fire his chief of staff and navy commander following a raid by Israeli forces across the Gulf of Suez in which we destroyed observation and guard posts, army camps, radar installations, and a score of military vehicles along the way.

More than a hundred Egyptian soldiers were killed. The president of Egypt learned about the action only after the mission was over and our forces were already in their landing craft and returning home. He phoned his own chief of staff, who knew nothing about it but who later calmed Nasser by telling him that he had investigated and found that the Egyptian army had repulsed, with heavy losses, what he described as a small Israeli landing attempt. Nor did Nasser know then about the two Egyptian torpedo boats we had sunk the previous night. Eventually, when the full scope and consequences of the actions became known to him, Nasser was shocked both by the success of the raid and by the fact that his commanders did not know what was happening—or, if they did know, kept the information from him.

To put pressure on the Egyptians and compel them to maintain a cease-fire, I proposed to the Ministerial Defense Committee that we carry out air attacks on army bases deep inside Egypt. Altogether, some twenty targets were bombed during the months of January, February, and March 1970, causing Egyptian morale to collapse. Nasser was confronted by a dilemma. He realized that his army lacked the power to prevent our operations, yet at the same time he was not prepared to declare a cease-fire and enter into peace negotiations with us. At the end of January he flew to Moscow and asked the Russians to send him Soviet troops. The Soviet Union agreed, and at the beginning of 1970 Russian missile units, men and equipment, arrived in Egypt. On April 1 they were joined by three squadrons of fighter planes with their Russian crews. Soviet pilots defended the skies of Cairo, Alexandria, and Aswan; Russian troops operated the more sophisticated SAM-3 batteries, and the entire anti-aircraft defense system throughout Egypt was handed over to Soviet command.

The unavoidable was bound to happen. In July, Israeli and Soviet planes clashed in the air. One of our patrols was flying over the northern sector of the Gulf of Suez when it came under attack from eight Soviet MiG-21s flying in two formations. In the course of this dog fight, we shot down five Soviet planes. All our planes returned to base. In the debriefing after the engagement, our pilots said they thought the Soviet fliers lacked experience and flexibility. They behaved in battle as they had been taught in training exercises and stuck to the book. They flew in pairs, close together, and did not break off fast enough. The five pilots bailed out and landed on the Egyptian side of the gulf. Reaching them took the Egyptians a whole day, even though many helicopters took part in the search. All five were finally found. Only one was unhurt; two were wounded, and two were dead.

At the end of the debriefing, I congratulated and thanked our pilots and told them that this engagement had far-reaching political significance. The United States was anxious to prevent an escalation of the war, which might drag the Soviet Union into active combat. We, too, of course, had no interest in such a development. However, I added, Israel was not Czechoslovakia, and our generation was not the generation of Masada, where the defenders of the last Jewish outpost in the war against the Romans in the first century B.C. held out to the end and then committed suicide. We would continue to fight and live.

Apart from the usual technical talk and humorous comments at the debriefing, we were well aware of the gravity of the situation. The question was not whose pilots were better, but how to hold to our vital aims and at the same time avoid clashing with the Russians.

We decided to issue no communiqué on this aerial encounter. Nor did the Egyptians and the Russians mention a word of it in public. But on that very day, July 30, the commander of the Soviet Air Force and the commander of Soviet Air Defenses flew to Cairo. For the Russians, Egyptian air space was now part of their zone.

I recall that it was Tolstoi who said that a book which is not worth reading twice is not worth reading even once. Churchill's letter to President Eisenhower, written immediately after the 1956 Suez Campaign, is certainly worth reading twice. It had an urgent relevance to our situation after the air battle. The United States at the time was exerting the utmost pressure on her allies, Britain and France, to pull their armies out of Egypt, which they quickly did. Churchill was no longer prime minister but he hoped to persuade his wartime friend to relax the pressure. He feared that the United States' demands on Britain and France to retire from Egypt would lead to Soviet penetration into the Middle East and ultimate control of the region. Churchill wrote:

"There is not much left for me to do in this world and I have neither the wish nor the strength to involve myself in the present political stress and turmoil. But I do believe with unfaltering conviction that the theme of the Anglo-American alliance is more important today than at any time since the war. You and I had some part in raising it to the plane on which it has since stood. Whatever the arguments adduced here and in the United States for or against Anthony's [Eden's] action in Egypt, it will now be an act of folly, on which our whole civilization may founder, to let events in the Middle East come between us.

"There seems to be growing misunderstanding and frustration on both sides of the Atlantic. If they be allowed to develop, the skies will darken and it is the Soviet Union that will ride the storm. We should leave it to the historians to argue the rights and wrongs of all that has happened during the past years. What we must face is that at present these events have left a situation in the Middle East in which spite, envy and malice prevail on the one hand and our friends are beset by bewilderment and uncertainty for the future. The Soviet Union is attempting to move into this dangerous vacuum, for you must have no doubt that a triumph for Nasser would be an even greater triumph for them.

"The very survival of all that we believe in may depend on our setting our minds to forestalling them. If we do not take immediate action in harmony, it is no exaggeration to say that we must expect to see the Middle East and the North African coastline under Soviet control and Western Europe placed at the mercy of the Russians. If at this juncture we fail in our responsibility to act positively and fearlessly we shall no longer be worthy of the leadership with which we are entrusted.

"I write this letter because I know where your heart lies. You are now the only one who can so influence events both in U.N.O. and the free world as to ensure that the great essentials are not lost in bickerings and pettiness among the nations. Yours is indeed a heavy responsibility and there is no greater believer in your capacity to bear it or well-wisher in your task than your old friend,

Winston S. Churchill."

As I reread this letter addressed to the president of the United States, I thought that Churchill's fears were even more timely now than when he wrote them.

Finally, after three years of almost continual fighting, Egypt agreed to a cease-fire with Israel on August 8, 1970. It grew out of a peace initiative begun by William Rogers, America's secretary of state, over a month and a half earlier.

It was reasonable to assume that the "Rogers initiative" actually came as a response to a request from Nasser. The president of Egypt had promised his people and the world that "what was taken by force will be recovered by force." During all this time, Egypt conducted an unsuccessful campaign to vanquish Israel, ending with the War of Attrition, which lasted for seventeen months. This war had brought down on Egypt the destruction of her oil refineries. Her cities on the Canal had become ghost towns. Military targets deep inside Egypt had been ravaged by our Air Force and army. As a consequence, Nasser had to dismiss his top military commanders and Egypt's civilian leaders. In addition, he had disappointed his Arab allies, Jordan and Syria, while finding himself ever more dependent on the Soviet Union. All these factors had forced him to turn to Washington for help.

In early December I flew to Washington to meet with President Nixon, Dr. Kissinger, who was then his National Security adviser, Secretary of State Rogers, and Defense Secretary Melvin Laird. The three major topics we discussed were Soviet intervention in the war, the renewal of arms supplies to Israel, and renewal of mediation talks with U.N. emissary Gunnar Jarring. All four American leaders strongly urged us to return to the Jarring talks. They were very worried by what they called the Sovietization of the Egyptian war. I gathered that if the Soviet Union actively intervened, the United States would not be able to stand aside. They were anxious to prevent such a situation from occurring, but they took the view that on no account should they show signs of weakness. Not only the Americans, but we, too, had no choice but to react vigorously to Soviet aggression. On this point we all agreed, and no one criticized us for having shot down the Soviet planes. On the contrary, one of them said, "Shoot the hell out of them!"

When we discussed international affairs, and in particular Soviet intentions and behavior in the Middle East, Nixon, in speech and demeanor, assumed the full stature of the president of a mighty power. He stressed his country's responsibility toward its friends. America would not let them down. As to greater Russian intervention, I gained the clear impression that America's policy would be: "If they come in, we shall not stay out."

My meeting with the president was arranged by Robert Anderson, who had been secretary of the treasury under President Eisenhower. We had known each other ever since his visits to Israel as Eisenhower's secret emissary to try to mediate between Ben-Gurion and Nasser. Tall, lean, white-haired, precise in his speech, Anderson had never been an ebullient character, but he was still as vigorous as ever. Even now, despite his age, he traveled extensively, mostly to the Middle East on oil affairs. He maintained close personal relations with Arab leaders, and when I visited America we would meet. I do not know what his attitude was toward me. But I respected him and looked forward to our meetings, even though, with his customary frankness and sincerity, he would present views that were often not at all pleasing for me to hear. On this occasion, too, what he said caused me no joy. He told me that we should withdraw to the pre–Six Day War borders. That, he said, was in America's interest, and if we failed to do so our situation would be parlous.

In my talk with the president, the main subject concerned our security needs. A curious incident occurred shortly after I began speaking. I complained to Nixon that the United States had promised Egypt that arms supplies to Israel would be stopped for the duration of the negotiations on the Rogers peace initiative. The president said he had not heard of this promise. I then told him that at a press conference given in Washington a few days earlier, Egypt's Foreign Minister Mahmud Riad had announced it, and quoted from an official document. There was an unpleasant moment when the president turned to Melvin Laird and asked him whether it was true. Laird, without dropping his eyes, confirmed what I had said. I then added that, in any case, we—at the non-receiving end—were aware of the unfortunate facts, and the facts were that America had suspended arms sales to us.

The talks on the renewal of aircraft supplies proved very unpleasant. They ended with my feeling that the United States would not renew our supplies and we would not return to the Jarring negotiations. I was wrong. I left Washington and had just returned to New York when there was a telephone call from Joseph Sisco, assistant secretary of state for Middle Eastern and South Asian affairs. He said the U.S. government had given further consideration to the arms problem and had decided to respond favorably to my request. There would be an ongoing supply of aircraft.

When I returned to Israel, I found that the U.S. ambassador had already met with Prime Minister Golda Meir and told her of the policy change. With the renewal of arms supplies, the road was now open for a renewal of the Jarring talks. Foreign Minister Eban notified the secretary-general of the United Nations that we were ready to resume talks with Jarring.

Jarring was no redeemer, and the negotiations he conducted did not bring redemption. After many consultations and clarifications, on February 8, 1971, he presented Israel and Egypt with a document setting out what each side was to concede and asked both sides to commit themselves to it in advance. Egypt was to undertake to enter into a peace agreement with Israel and Israel was to undertake to withdraw her forces from Egypt up to the former international border.

Neither Egypt nor Israel acceded to Jarring's request that they "sign on the dotted line" at the bottom of the form he sent them. Egypt replied that she was prepared to end the state of war but not to sign a peace treaty with Israel. She made the counter-demand that Israel undertake to "settle the refugee problem" and to withdraw not only from Egyptian territory but also from the Gaza Strip and the rest of the Arab lands, retiring to the pre-war borders. Israel, for her part, replied to Jarring that she was ready to enter into peace negotiations with Egypt without prior conditions, but, as stated previously, she would not return to the June 4, 1967, borders.

The replies of the two countries showed that there had been no change in their conflicting positions. Jarring struggled with himself for some time thereafter and eventually wound up his mission. The U.N. secretary-general appointed no other mediator in his place, and the conflict between Egypt and Israel continued.

The most important event of my private life was my meeting with and marriage to Rahel. We were married on June 26, 1973, after we had known each other for more than eighteen years. The marriage service was conducted by Rabbi Mordechai Piron, the chief chaplain of the Israeli army, at a simple ceremony in the rabbi's modest house in Bat Yam, just outside Tel Aviv. Only a few people were present, just enough to make a *minyan,* the Jewish religious quorum of ten men. After the ceremony we went to dinner in a Tel Aviv restaurant, ate well, drank a toast to our wedding, and then telephoned the news to Rahel's two daughters and to my three children.

It was the second marriage for both of us. When I married Ruth Schwartz in 1935, I was a farmer in Nahalal. I was twenty then, and like the birds who fly off and build a nest in the spring, Ruth and I fell in love. We stayed married for thirty-five years. We had three children and lived first in Nahalal, then in Shimron, Hanita, Jerusalem, and Tel Aviv. We traveled a long road together, but our married life was not very successful, particularly the last half. There was no special happening or crisis that left our marriage stranded on a sandbar. It was the absence of the necessary communion of souls and the increasing feeling that we were strangers that fashioned a barrier between us.

In 1971 Ruth asked for a divorce and we parted. It created no complications or difficulties. Our children were married by then, and there were no particular financial problems. I suggested to Ruth that I would leave and she could remain in our house in Zahala, but she refused. She said she wanted to start a new life and build herself another home.

I married Rahel a year and a half later. She had divorced her first husband in 1958. My meeting her was totally unexpected. It was pure chance, and the good Lord who joins couples in heaven had to work hard on earth to arrange it. I was chief of staff at the time and was spending a brief holiday in Europe with my family, when I was suddenly summoned back to Israel by the prime minister. Rahel had been on a trip to Rome and had decided to cut it short and return home sooner than she had planned, making a flight booking at the last moment. The plane was almost full when she boarded, and the last available seat was also the least comfortable one. A Jerusalem lawyer, the late Asher Levitzky, was also on the plane, and since he knew Rahel, and his seat was more comfortable, he offered to change with her. His place happened to be next to mine, and when the change was made, he, of course, introduced us to each other. For the rest, we managed on our own.

I do not know if this was what is called love at first sight. I do know that it is with Rahel that I wish to spend the rest of my life.

PART VII

The Yom kippur War

28

SURPRISE

AT FOUR IN THE MORNING on Saturday, October 6, 1973, I was awakened by the ring of the red telephone next to my bed. This was not unusual. There was hardly a night without two or three such calls. But this time the call was to inform me that according to information just received, before sundown on this very day Egypt and Syria would launch a war. After ensuring that this news had been passed on to Prime Minister Golda Meir, I arranged for the chief of staff to meet me in my office at 6 A.M. There was much for each of us to do in the coming two hours.

I asked my aide-de-camp to alert the senior staff of my ministry, and then I drove to the office. In the east the sky was red and gold. A light sea breeze came in from the west. A silent, tranquil dawn. Even the birds were still quiet. It was Yom Kippur, the most sacred day in the Jewish calendar. There was not a soul on the streets.

The source of the information was reliable. It was not a report on Arab activity in the field but an intelligence message regarding the Arab decision to go to war. We had received similar messages in the past, and later, when no attack followed, came the explanation that President Sadat had changed his mind at the last moment. On this occasion, too, it was indicated that if Sadat discovered that the information was known to us and that he had lost the element of surprise, it was possible that he would cancel the attack, or at least postpone it. On the other hand, both this and other intelligence reports—particularly that the Russians were evacuating their families from Syria and Egypt—seemed sound and realistic, and it was clear that we had to act on the assumption that this time Egypt and Syria really meant to start a war.

The basic decisions had to be made at a meeting with the prime minister. This was set for 8 A.M. In the meantime, I had conferred with the chief of staff and my aides on the steps to be taken. We were faced with four principal issues: mobilization of reserves and reinforcement of the fronts; a possible pre-emptive strike by our Air Force; evacuation of children and women from our frontier settlements in the Golan Heights; and delivery of a warning to Egypt and Syria. There were two aspects to such a warning: it might move the two Arab states to call off their invasion. But if they nevertheless went ahead, the United States would know who was responsible, and this might ensure her support for us. At all events, it would avoid a situation in which America might believe that war could have been prevented but that, even though we had not initiated it, we had not done all in our power to forestall it.

In our preliminary consultation, I told the chief of staff that I agreed to his request for the immediate mobilization of the reserves required for the defense of the two fronts on as full a scale as he found necessary. But I decided to bring before the prime minister the questions of a pre-emptive strike and the immediate mobilization of all the reserves needed under the contingency plan to go over to the counter-attack. (On this latter point, the Agranat Commission of Inquiry into the Yom Kippur War was to establish that "On Saturday morning, October 6, the minister of defense agreed to the mobilization of all that was required for defense, in accordance with the appraisal of the chief of staff.") Both these measures held definite political implications. It was natural for the chief of staff to request them. It is almost a tradition in the Israel Defense Forces for the military chiefs to urge more activity; I speak as a former chief of staff. It is for the political authority to impose limitations when necessary.

The pre-emptive air strike which the chief of staff recommended, after consultation with the Air Force, was to be directed against Syria alone, not at the front, not against the anti-aircraft missile system, but only against air bases deep inside Syria—and even that not before twelve noon. If this pre-emptive strike had been carried out, it would not have had a significant impact on developments in the war.

I rejected the idea of a pre-emptive strike by the Air Force as well as the mobilization of more reserves than were required for immediate defense. I feared that such moves would burden our prospects of securing the full support of the United States. Forces needed for a counter-attack could be mobilized a few hours later, after the Arabs had squeezed the trigger and we had had the opportunity to complete preliminary clarifications with Washington.

These points were thoroughly reviewed at our meeting with the prime minister, and it was finally resolved, at her decision: to order the mobilization of the number of reservists requested by the chief of staff—100,000 to 120,000 men, in addition to the regular army; not to carry out a pre-emptive air strike; to evacuate children and women from the Golan settlements; and to send a warning to Egypt and Syria through the United States. Our request to the United States to perform this goodwill service was to be submitted by both our ambassador in Washington and the prime minister to the U.S. ambassador in Tel Aviv.

Anyone who knows Mrs. Golda Meir will not be surprised by her decisions. She is a courageous, stubborn, and determined woman. She is also blessed by the Lord with the capacity to see the world in bold black and stark white, free from the range of twilight shades. If there were a danger of war, then wide-scale mobilization was the answer. And if American help was to be sought, then the United States had to be given full proof that it was not we who desired war—even if this ruled out pre-emptive action and handicapped us in the military campaign.

The decisions were taken, and I was satisfied with them. The important thing now was not to waste time. If the Arabs were indeed to launch an attack, our foremost task was the immediate issue of appropriate orders and to be prepared for it. We had to see to it that every plane, every tank, and every soldier was in position and that our forces on the fronts were properly deployed and ready for action. After all, we were not starting from scratch. The Air Force was already fully mobilized. On the Syrian front we had a fighting force of some 180 tanks, 11 artillery batteries, and 5,000 men, and on the Egyptian front about 275 tanks, 12 artillery batteries, and 8,500 men. The army was on "C" Alert, as of the day before. And the contingency plans, both for defense and attack, were known and had been rehearsed in maneuvers. True, the warning had come at short notice, but it was not too late.

At 11 A.M. I went down to "Kedem." This is the Hebrew acronym for Operational Consultative Group, but it is also the Hebrew word for "east." In general, I am not a lover of acronyms without meaning or euphony. But Kedem always brought to mind the superb biblical verse of Balaam, who had come to curse and stayed to bless: "Balak the king of Moab hath brought me from Aram, out of the mountains of the east, saying, Come, curse me Jacob, . . . How goodly are thy tents, O Jacob" (Numbers: 23:7).

The Kedem was held in the subterranean war room, popularly known as the pit. It was a long time since I had been there, and I almost got lost. One had to go down long flights of steps to get to the map room. The mood was quiet and serious, but I noticed that officers were smoking rather more than usual—or maybe it just seemed so to me. Before I arrived there had already been a meeting of the group with the chief of staff, so that the subjects which were now presented to me had already been clarified and finalized. The meeting now was thus more a question-and-answer session than a basic discussion, with me asking questions and the chief of staff replying.

Our forces on both fronts would be deployed for containment. The Air Force would maintain air patrols as of noon. The forecast of enemy action in the south was artillery shelling, followed by bridging activity; crossing of the Canal in rafts at certain points along the entire length of the waterway; and operations by heliborne commando units to seize bridgeheads, to raid, and possibly to try to capture Abu Rudeis, site of the oil fields, and Sharm el-Sheikh, the base commanding the entrance to the Gulf of Aqaba.

I was not too worried about Abu Rudeis and Sharm. I was told that by the evening there would be 17 tanks at Abu Rudeis and 40 at Sharm el-Sheikh. The Egyptians might manage to carry out some sabotage at these places, but not capture and control them. The crossing of the Canal posed a more complex problem. Our Air Force would not be able to operate effectively at night, both because of the dark and the enemy anti-aircraft system—batteries of SAM-6s sited close to the line. Firm action against an attempted Canal crossing could be taken at night by ground forces, while our aircraft could go into effective action only the following morning.

On the Syrian front, too, the assumption was that the attack would be launched at night by an artillery bombardment. With it would come an infantry attack, and after that bridging tanks would move to lay paths across our anti-tank ditches for the enemy armored units to traverse at first light. Here, too, our air activity would be very limited at night. In addition to Syria's dense anti-aircraft missile system and to the darkness, the weather in the north was getting worse. Our plan was to deal with the Syrian Air Force the next day and attempt to take it out of the campaign.

Our reservists had been mobilized quickly. While our consultation was in progress, tens of thousands had already been called up. But the armor would reach the fronts only in another twenty-four hours. Thus, in the north, an additional few hundred tanks could be flung into action on Sunday night, October 7, and in the south a few hundred on Sunday and another few hundred on Monday, October 8.

All this, of course, was only a rough estimate of what was in store. The only certainty was that this first night, before the arrival of the reinforcements, would be our toughest. But I hoped that our enemies, too, would require time to apply their full power against us, particularly as the activities of our own forces on the spot would assuredly cause them confusion and delay.

We went on to consider preparations for civilian defense, evacuation of women and children from the Golan settlements, and our own attack plans. I emphasized that our objective in this war would be to destroy the enemy forces, not to conquer territory. In any case, even if we did conquer more land, for political reasons we would not be able to hold on to it for long.

Despite our self-confidence, there was disquiet in our hearts. It was not only that we were not used to a campaign where the initiative was in the hands of the enemy. The entire situation was also out of keeping with our character and with the organic structure of our army, based as it is on reserves and their orderly mobilization. The transition within twenty-four hours from desk, tractor, and lathe to the battlefield is not at all easy. Going to war is not like putting out a fire, where you can rush with blaring sirens and do the dousing in one go.

From the pit I went to a Cabinet meeting which had been called for noon in the prime minister's Tel Aviv office. The government approved what had been decided upon at my earlier meeting with the prime minister, including partial mobilization—of 120,000 reservists. There was a brief discussion on how we might act if Egypt alone opened hostilities, namely, whether to wait until Syria joined in or to make an advance strike on Syria. The Cabinet was also informed that the United States had been in touch with Egypt, directly, and with Syria, through the Soviet Union, telling them of Israel's report that they intended to attack and asking for clarification. The Egyptians had not yet replied, but America warned us not to take any provocative action, adding that news had reached them that we were proposing to attack within six hours. Nor had the United States received any response from the Russians. It later transpired that the Russians had been given prior information by Egypt and Syria of their decision to invade Israel. This had not disturbed them in the slightest. Nor had it deterred them from assuming the role of angel of peace without the flicker of an eyelid.

At 2:05 P.M., I was urgently called to the pit: Syria and Egypt had gone into action. Syrian aircraft had crossed our air space, Egyptian rafts were crossing the Canal, Sharm el-Sheikh and some of our army bases in western Sinai were being bombed. The war had started.

29

THE EVE

THE EGYPTIAN AND SYRIAN ATTACK on Yom Kippur came as a surprise,
though it was not unexpected. Yom Kippur day found the Israel
Defense Forces not yet mobilized and not deployed at their full
strength, but this does not mean that they had not been prepared
for the Arab assault.

I, for one, had never imagined—neither before nor after the Six
Day War in 1967—that the Egyptians would reconcile themselves to
our being entrenched along the Suez Canal, or that the Syrians would
swallow our occupation of the Golan Heights. I felt that our presence
there meant a renewal of war sooner or later. This was not my feeling
about the Gaza Strip, Judea, and Samaria.

I saw the key to the prevention of war in the conclusion of an
agreement with Egypt, even a partial one. If we could reach such
agreement, not only would it lessen Egypt's motivation to renew the
war, but it also offered the possibility that Syria, which would have
to fight alone, would hesitate to do so. I had therefore suggested, as
soon as the War of Attrition had ended, in August 1970, that we pull
back a little way from Suez. (During the Six Day War, I had wanted
the army to stop before reaching the Canal.) The Egyptians could
then resume navigation and rehabilitate their Canal Zone cities, Is-

mailia, Kantara, and Suez. This, I believed, would weaken their desire to make further war upon us.

But the partial agreement was never reached, and it was clear to me that the motivation of Egypt and Syria to renew hostilities had remained as strong as ever. The question was not if, but when.

The answer to when was dependent upon the character and policy of the national leadership in Egypt and upon the fitness of the Egyptian army to go to war. This, in turn, was dependent upon the Soviet Union. There had been ups and downs in the Soviet Union's relations with Egypt and Syria, but Russia had consistently armed, equipped, advised, and trained their armed forces. She had done so with particular vigor throughout 1973. This was very evident in the fields of armor and of anti-aircraft and anti-tank defense.

Fifteen batteries of SA-6 (surface-to-air) missiles were sent to Syria and ten to Egypt. Syria also received Frog-7 surface-to-surface missiles with a range of forty miles. The Russians enabled Egypt and Syria to improve and expand their armored forces and their anti-tank weaponry. Some five hundred T-62 tanks reached these two countries, and with them such anti-tank weapons as Sagger missiles, RPGs (rocket-propelled grenades), and so on. Whatever the Russians' motives, they could not be accused of indifference or neglect toward Egypt and Syria. They were neither laggard in rearming them nor slack in preparing them for war.

Sadat's "Year of Decision," 1971, when Egypt was to attack Israel, passed uneventfully. But in mid-1973, it seemed that Egypt and Syria really intended to mount an invasion. They crystallized plans whereby Syria would capture the Golan Heights and Egypt would conquer western Sinai. Egypt's forces would cross the Canal and advance east to seize the Gidi and Mitla passes and south to capture the Abu Rudeis oil fields and Sharm el-Sheikh. They also set a firm date for launching their attack, but that day passed without incident. Nevertheless, I judged that we were indeed drawing closer to the time when they would renew hostilities. At a meeting of the General Staff on May 21, 1973, in which I asked to participate, I expressed this judgment and ended by issuing orders to the General Staff for the Israel Defense Forces to prepare themselves to meet an all-out attack by Egypt and Syria, without Jordan, by the end of the summer. The Israeli army had to be ready for such a war beginning in June of that year, since the Arab forces were already concentrated in considerable strength along both fronts and had completed their plans.

The master plan, with variations for varied contingencies, prepared by our General Staff to meet the challenge from Egypt and Syria was presented to the prime minister and me in April 1973. It called, among other things, to advance the date of the establishment of additional armored and mechanized infantry units and to speed up the acquisition of tanks and artillery. An extra $17 million was allocated for this purpose. On the basis of this plan, detailed orders were worked out for Northern and Southern commands to deal with several possible situations: reinforcement of the troops holding the line in the south by regular units, without mobilizing the fighting reserves (dubbed "Operation Dovecote"); strengthening the line in the north with limited reserve units (called "Operation Chalk"); and the full deployment of the Israel Defense Forces with all reservists mobilized.

By and large, the deployment of our forces at noon on Yom Kippur on the Egyptian front conformed to the "Operation Dovecote" plan laid down for Southern Command, and, on the Syrian front, was substantially stronger than that called for in the plan for Northern Command. These forces—177 tanks in the Golan and about 300 tanks in the Canal area—were so arrayed as to enable them, with air support, to contain the Syrian and Egyptian attacks until the arrival of additional reserves. However, it must be stressed that the plans were based on the assumption that there would be advance warning of more than twenty-four hours, so that considerable reinforcements of mobilized reservists would already have reached the fronts by the time war broke out. It must also be added that the enemy forces launched their attacks with much greater efficiency than had been estimated when our plans were being devised.

This deployment of our units at noon on Yom Kippur was the result of gradual reinforcements that had been carried out during the previous two weeks. In that fortnight, there had been disturbing signs along both fronts, but both our own military intelligence and that of the United States concluded that Syria and Egypt were not about to start a war. They interpreted the heightened military activity on the Egyptian front as "army maneuvers" and not preparations for an invasion. Nevertheless, we were not at ease, particularly with regard to the Syrian front.

Tension along this front had risen following the air incident that occurred on September 13. That morning, our planes—2 Phantoms with 4 Mirages flying cover—were on a photo-reconnaissance mission. The Syrians sent up two flights of 4 MiGs to deflect them. An aerial battle ensued, with each side sending in more planes. In the first phase of the battle, our aircraft shot down 8 MiGs and we lost 1 Mirage, but the pilot bailed out and landed in the Mediterranean, about three miles from the coast. We rushed a helicopter to rescue him, covered by fighter planes. But the Syrians, seeking an easy kill, sent speed boats to the rescue area protected by 4 MiGs. A second aerial battle followed, and all 4 MiGs were shot down. Our pilot was saved, and our rescue helicopter also saved a Syrian pilot who had ejected from his burning plane and landed in the water not far from our own man. Altogether 12 Syrian MiGs were downed that morning, for the loss to us of one Mirage.

In the past, the Syrians had never failed to react to an incident of even lesser gravity. On this occasion, days passed and they did nothing. I was gnawed by the mounting suspicion that they could be planning a more basic action. Substance was given to my suspicion at a General Staff meeting on September 24, when the GOC Northern Command expressed his strong apprehension that we might fall victim to a surprise attack in the Golan.

It was clear to me that this was indeed a serious possibility. I knew that our situation on both fronts was far from ideal, but on the northern front it was ominous. For almost two years the Arab armies had been deployed at full strength along the fronts, while against them we maintained only very light forces. To reinforce them substantially, we would have had to mobilize our reserves, and we do this only when we are reasonably sure that an invasion is imminent. Otherwise, we would have to call up our reservists for very long periods, and this would be a heavy burden for the state. In normal times, reservists serve more than one month a year—and do this after completing three years of national service. This disproportion of military forces on both sides of all our fronts is one aspect of our principal problem—we are a state of less than three million Jews surrounded by scores of millions of Arabs.

If we were caught by a surprise attack on the southern front, and even if we were forced to retire to a second line, bad as that would be it would not prove catastrophic, for this withdrawal would involve no more than lines of defense in a desert area. This was not the case in the north. There, any withdrawal would probably cause severe damage to our settlements in the Golan and possibly bring the front to the heart of our populated regions of Upper Galilee and the Huleh and Jordan valleys. Moreover, unlike the Suez Canal on the southern front, there was no topographical obstacle in the north. More serious was the Soviet anti-aircraft missile system which had recently been installed on this front. It was so dense and so sophisticated that it covered not only the Syrian side of the border but also most of Israeli territory on the Golan Heights.

I expressed these anxieties to the officers of the General Staff at this September 24 meeting. If the Syrians were preparing for an all-out attack, I said, the situation was most serious, and the General Staff had to put its mind to it immediately. For if the Syrians were to succeed in overrunning our farm settlements in the Golan, it would be an unprecedented disaster. We could not go off to celebrate Rosh Hashanah, the Jewish New Year, in three days' time, leaving things as they were. (Rosh Hashanah occurs ten days before Yom Kippur.) The General Staff had to come up with a solution before then. I asked the chief of staff to meet with me as soon as possible to report on what had been done and what was contemplated.

The meeting took place two days later, September 26, with just the chief of staff, Lt. Gen. David Elazar, and his senior staff generals, together with the GOC Northern Command. The chief of staff informed me that our armored force in the north had been increased from 70 to 100 tanks, additional artillery had been brought up, and all units, including the Air Force, had been put on heightened alert. The task of the Air Force would not be easy. In the Six Day War, Syria possessed not a single surface-to-air missile. She now had 15 batteries of SAM-6s and another 10 batteries of SAM-2s and 3s in the area of the front alone.

Even at the end of this meeting, I was still uneasy, and I decided to go up immediately to Northern Command, visit the front-line positions, and talk to the people in the farm settlements. The chief of staff suggested that I not go, on the ground that my unexpected visit might arouse anxiety among the men and women in the settlements. I did not accept this view, and we flew off, spending the afternoon visiting the front accompanied by the GOC Northern Command. I inspected several advanced outposts and nearby tank units. The deployment seemed satisfactory—but this was no surprise, for the commander of the armored force in this sector was Lt. Col. Yossie, a marvelous young man. I was delighted to see him there that day. I shall never forget my meeting with him some years earlier. It was near the Suez Canal, on a very dark night, in the midst of a battle. Some of his tanks had run onto mines and were ablaze, and those which tried to skirt the mined track got mired in the southern swamp. The scene was one of desperation—I refer to the tanks, not to Yossie. He exuded fighting spirit, persistence, and resourcefulness. How true it is that the real commander shows himself not when the battle goes well but when the going is rough.

Later, together with the chief of staff, I met representatives of the settlements. Since it was the eve of Rosh Hashanah, I explained that I had come to bring them holiday greetings and wish them a Happy New Year. They all raised their glasses and we drank a toast, but none really believed I had come for that. We greeted the New Year Festival with anxious hearts.

We decided to strengthen the front line even more.

I asked to be present at the next meeting of the General Staff, on October 1, and I returned to the subject of the Golan Heights. I said that of the various problems on our three fronts, my chief anxiety was the possibility of a Syrian armored breakthrough to the Golan. I expressed the situation in extreme terms: "On the Jordanian border we have civilian settlements but no enemy. On the Egyptian border we have an enemy but no settlements. On the Syrian border we have both. If the Syrians get to our settlements, it will be calamitous."

On that very day, Operations Branch issued orders aimed at heightening the general preparedness and strengthening the armored force up to 111 tanks and the artillery to 32 field guns in the Golan. Measures were also taken to reinforce Southern Command, bringing up its armored strength to 300 tanks.

The next day, October 2, I again considered with Chief of Staff Elazar the reinforcement of the Golan, and we also discussed the situation on the southern front. The chief of staff informed me that he had again checked with Intelligence the significance of Egyptian activity and had reached the firm conclusion that what was happening there was only an exercise. As for the Syrians, there were no signs of their intention to launch an attack, but information had been received of further preparations. This increased my apprehensions, and I asked the chief of staff to let me have a paper with details of the changes in the deployment of Syria's forces and the information we had on them.

I also decided that the matter was urgent enough to be considered at the government level. The prime minister was on an official visit to Austria at the time but was due back soon, so I telephoned Yisrael Galili, minister without portfolio, and asked him to arrange a meeting with Golda Meir as quickly as possible. I told him that I was not happy about the situation in the Golan Heights and wished to share responsibility on this matter. I would bring with me to the meeting the chief of staff, the chief of Intelligence and the commander of the Air Force. We had received disquieting reports. The Syrians had 650 tanks in the first line and a missile system that also covered our territory, so that our aircraft could be hit even in our own skies. Syria also had 500 pieces of artillery, while we had—well, it was easier to say what we had not got.

Galili promised to arrange the meeting as soon as Golda returned, and it was held the next day, October 3, shortly after her arrival. I explained that I had asked for this meeting because of changes that had taken place particularly on the northern front, but also to a certain extent on the southern one. We had received intelligence of weapons reinforcements on the Syrian and perhaps also on the Egyptian front and of the Syrian-Egyptian intention, or state of readiness, to renew the war. I had therefore thought it proper to bring this matter before the prime minister and any other ministers she wished to invite (two were present at this meeting) for a comprehensive review of the situation and of the steps we were taking to meet it.

The chief of staff, the Air Force commander, and the acting head of Intelligence gave their reports, presenting the activities of the enemy and of our own forces. The Intelligence representative emphasized that the Syrian and Egyptian armies were so deployed along the fronts that they were able at any moment to launch an attack, but he did not think they were about to do so. In his judgment, what was happening on the Egyptian side of the line was annual maneuvers.

The chief of staff reported on the strengthening of our armor on the Syrian front from 70 to 117 tanks and of artillery from 4 to 8 batteries. He recommended that our forces remain at their existing strength, fortified by putting the Air Force on high alert.

The ministers asked about our capacity to bring up additional reserves if necessary. The chief of staff explained that it was possible to add more tanks in the north, up to a maximum of 170, within twenty-four hours. None of the participants at this meeting, neither the Cabinet ministers nor the army representatives, took the problem lightly. But none suggested that further steps should be taken, such as the call-up of reservists.

This consultation at the Prime Minister's Office broadened the shoulders bearing responsibility, but it did not improve the situation, and the next day, October 4, I met again with the chief of staff, his deputy, the GOC Northern Command, and the acting head of Intelligence. We went over the problems to examine what else could be done. Suggestions were put forward to dig a second anti-tank ditch and add to our fortifications. The GOC Northern Command stressed that what we needed was twenty-four hours advance notice of any attack. If that were given us, then our situation would be quite different.

Following the suggestion of strengthening our fortifications and our anti-tank obstacles, I met in the afternoon with the water commissioner, Menahem Kantor, and asked him whether ponds for storing irrigation water might be dug along the Syrian front so that these could also serve as an anti-tank obstacle. From his response I gathered that it was not impossible.

During the night of October 4, we received reports which strengthened the probability that Egypt and Syria were about to launch a war. The most significant item of information was that the Russians had given orders for the families of Soviet advisers to leave Syria. During that night, Soviet passenger planes landed in Syria and Egypt, and it was assumed that they had arrived to evacuate the Russian families.

At the weekly meeting of the General Staff on Friday, October 5, we decided to order "C" Alert, the highest alert, for the army and a full alert for the Air Force. I asked for direct telephone lines to my senior ministry officials, and they were to spend Yom Kippur at home. At 9:45 A.M. on October 5, I met the prime minister. Accompanying me were the chief of staff and the head of Intelligence. We informed her of the night's news and of the additional acts of preparedness which we had ordered. In fact, apart from mobilizing reservists, we had done all that could have been done to strengthen our military position and raise the state of alert. The High Command Post was activated, leaves were canceled, checks were carried out, and instructions were given to prepare for possible mobilization using the public method, which is faster than the secret call-up.

At the end of our discussion with the prime minister, I suggested that she bring the matter before the Cabinet. She agreed and called a meeting for 11:30 A.M., inviting those ministers who were in Tel Aviv that day. Most of the ministers had gone to spend Yom Kippur at their homes in various parts of the country. The fast would begin that evening.

The chief of staff and chief of Intelligence described the situation on the fronts. The Syrians and Egyptians were at emergency stations, which served well for defense and equally well for launching an invasion. But the evaluation of the chief of Intelligence, Maj. Gen. Eli Zeira, which was accepted by Chief of Staff Elazar, was that an attack was not likely. The assumption of the army was that if, indeed, war was imminent, there would be further indications and intelligence reports, and only if and when these appeared would it be necessary to mobilize the reserves and take additional measures. In the judgment of the chief of Intelligence, it was most improbable that the Egyptians would cross the Canal in large forces, though they might open fire and attempt raids. The American evaluation was that neither Syria nor Egypt intended to launch an attack in the near future.

I pointed out that from the point of view of their military deployment, both the Egyptians and the Syrians were in a position to start a war within hours. I therefore requested that the prime minister be given authority to approve the mobilization of reserves if we should ask her to do so next day, Yom Kippur. This was agreed to, and Golda told us she would be spending Yom Kippur in Tel Aviv. If anything unusual happened, she would convene the full Cabinet—if this should still be possible—and not simply the existing, informal, inner Cabinet.

Five ministers apart from the prime minister had taken part in this meeting of the government. It was the last to be held before the Yom Kippur War.

Now, on the eve of the war, Northern Command had 177 tanks and 44 artillery pieces. Southern Command had 276 tanks and 48 field guns, somewhat less than was planned under "Operation Dovecote." Thus, without our having been either complacent or blind to its possible outbreak, the Yom Kippur War broke over us on the very day we did not expect it to.

It happened on the Day of Atonement, the one day in the year when the majority of Jews the world over unite in fast and prayer, in synagogue or at home. In Israel, quiet descends upon the land. All work ceases. Not a bus, truck, or private car can be seen on the streets. It is the religious day of reckoning, the most solemn day for the Jewish people. Henceforth, Yom Kippur would take on an added solemnity.

30

INVASION

THE FIRST DAY of fighting, Yom Kippur itself, was hard. Our losses in men were not light, and we also lost ground and positions of considerable value. Despite this, the chief of staff's report to the government at 10 P.M. was relatively optimistic. It was, of course, clear to all that on this day Egypt and Syria had enjoyed two advantages of the highest importance: the initiative in starting the war, and preponderant superiority of forces. The chief of staff's optimism sprang primarily from the recognition that these two advantages would not remain with the enemy for long. Israeli army reserves would reach both fronts within 24 to 48 hours. Their arrival would tilt back the balance of forces and enable us to retrieve the initiative.

The campaign opened simultaneously on both fronts. At 2 P.M. both armies started with the shelling and aerial bombing of Israeli army camps and installations. In the south, the Egyptians followed up immediately with the crossing of the Canal along its entire length. They set up bridges, used rafts, and some even swam. In the north, under cover of the artillery barrage, Syria's armored forces moved to attack.

Up to midnight on that first day, the Egyptians had brought over to the east bank of the Canal some 300 tanks, out of the 2,200 they had deployed on this front, and they had 1,848 field guns covering the area. They also sited more than 50 anti-tank weapons for each mile of front. Against this force our Southern Command had 276 tanks and 48 field guns.

In the Golan, against our 177 tanks and 44 field guns, the Syrians flung 500 tanks backed by 690 field guns into their first wave of attack. Their full tank deployment on this front was 1,700 tanks and their artillery strength stood at some 1,300 guns.

The enemy offensive opened with our infantry forces outnumbered by roughly 10 to 1. The Egyptian infantry assault units numbered 100,000 men, against 8,500 of ours. In the north, we had 5,000 infantrymen against 45,000 in the Syrian attack force. What was more important, the enemy infantry, unlike in the past, were now equipped with large quantities of very effective anti-tank weapons, and they also carried the Strela, the Soviet personal anti-aircraft missile. We also suffered numerical inferiority in the air, with Egypt's 600 and Syria's 350 warplanes ranged against us.

Despite this grave disparity in armor, artillery, infantry, and aircraft, the GOCs of both Northern and Southern commands estimated toward midnight that they were containing the assaults and advances of the enemy. In his evening report to the government, Chief of Staff David Elazar said that on the Syrian front all enemy attacks had been stopped and the Syrians had registered no significant success. Even when he referred to our fortified position on Mount Hermon, he said that he had just received information that we were still in communication with it, though there had been a report at dusk that communication had been cut and the stronghold was believed to have been captured by the Syrians. The chief of staff said that its men had fortified themselves in its bunker, and he hoped that during the night our forces would succeed in linking up with it.

In the south, the chief of staff reported that the Egyptians had managed to cross the Canal at several points and had apparently captured one of our strongholds. They may have taken some of the defenders prisoner, as we had a report that eight of our men had fallen into Egyptian hands. But considering the circumstances—the initiative being with the Egyptians—in the chief of staff's view we had so far not done badly in holding the enemy. Summing up the first eight hours of fighting, he considered that the situation was under control. We were fighting the battle of containment in the manner in which it had to be fought.

It was clear that the situation at the Canal was less satisfactory than on the Golan. The Egyptians had succeeded in crossing the water obstacle, whereas in the Golan they had not broken through our lines. Moreover, in the Golan, our reinforcements were expected to begin arriving during the night, so that by midday the next day, October 7, we would have more tanks and by evening we would have several hundred. This would not be the case in the south. There was hardly a chance that any substantial number of additional tanks would reach the Egyptian front during the following day. Perhaps Bren (Divisional Commander Maj. Gen. Avraham Adan) might get there about midday with a few score. The main reinforcements would be able to go into action only the day after, on the morning of the 8th, and by then we should have a sizable armored force in the Canal area. In the meantime, we faced another 24 to 30 very difficult hours.

In these circumstances we were changing our original plan and would send our Air Force to the Egyptian, not the Syrian, front in the morning. We had intended striking at Syria's anti-aircraft missile system and airfields in order to neutralize them. Now we were forced to leave them alone and invest all our air strength in helping Southern Command.

I felt heavy of heart, and I did not share the optimism of the chief of staff and GOC Southern Command. The Egyptians had already achieved powerful gains, and we had suffered a heavy blow. They had crossed the Canal, established bridges, and moved armor, infantry, and anti-tank weapons across them. Not only had we failed to prevent this, but we had caused the Egyptians relatively little damage. Their losses in crossing were light—a few hundred casualties and a comparatively small quantity of equipment destroyed.

In addition to my anxiety about our military situation, I was haunted by the question of what had happened. Had we erred in our planning or in its execution? What had happened to the three basic elements in our concept—the armor, the Air Force and the Canal strongpoints, which were supposed to confound any enemy attempt to cross the Canal and inflict heavy damage?

There could be various assessments of what our forces could succeed in doing in the following days to the enemy units that had crossed the Canal. But in the meantime, the crossing was a fact. With the Egyptians on the east bank, surrounding our Canal strongholds, these positions had lost their functions. They would become traps for their occupants, unless we could manage in the shortest possible time to evacuate them or drive the Egyptians back to the west bank. It seemed to me that the GOC Southern Command as well as the chief of staff believed that we could do this. I could not share this assumption.

At the beginning of the 10 P.M. Cabinet meeting on that first night,

I had not thought of expressing my view, since the object of the session was to provide information to the ministers on the military events of that day, and this was the job of the chief of staff. But toward the end of the evening, I saw that the judgments on what was happening, and above all on what we could expect in the immediate future, were so different from my own that I had to say what was in my mind. I believed the government should know what I thought of the situation in all its stark severity, and so I said that I wished to add my evaluation of what had been reported by the chief of staff.

In my view we faced three difficult factors. The first, I said, was the very size of the enemy forces, lavishly equipped with weaponry accumulated during the previous six years. The Egyptians and Syrians were not the Arab armies we had known in 1967. They were good troops using good equipment and fighting with determination. Second was the enemy's anti-aircraft missile system, with the addition of the SAM-6s. This weapon system presented a grave problem to our Air Force, and as long as our planes would not overcome it, they could not provide support for our tanks and help destroy the enemy armor. Third was our need to hold our frontier lines with small forces since we neither wished nor were able to keep our population mobilized all the time. We assumed high risks, for it took time from the moment of call-up for the reserves to reach the fronts.

That was the situation and the danger on the southern front. I doubted whether we could seriously interrupt the Canal crossing for the next 24 to 36 hours, meaning the Egyptians would have two nights during which to put up more bridges and pour additional forces into Sinai. On the northern front, I reckoned that if some tanks would begin reaching the Golan the next morning, followed by a few hundred more during the day, the Syrian momentum would be checked.

The critical battlefield was the Canal Zone. Our Air Force, I said, would face a grim challenge when they went into action the next day. It would have to deal with the Egyptian Air Force as well as the anti-aircraft system, which might prove very costly. We would need a good deal of luck to end the next day's battles in our favor. After that, on the third and fourth days of the war, Monday and Tuesday (October 8 and 9), we should have all the planned armored force in the south, and we would be able to carry out tank warfare. It would not be simple, but the prospects for success were good.

It seemed to me, therefore, that in the south we should retire to a second line, fight the Egyptians within a belt of twelve miles from the Canal, and build up our strength. In the north, I expected that we would succeed in stopping the Syrians at the frontier. At all events, for the moment the war was being fought on the borders, and though it was poor consolation, we could draw a distinction between the historic Land of Israel and Sinai. The situation in the south was difficult, but at least the battle there was taking place in the desert, not inside Israel or close to its centers of population. I concluded with the observation that in Sinai we would ride out the immediate crisis, in the Golan we would face another two days of hardship, and then we would fight a war of armor against the Egyptians.

I had spoken my mind, made known my outlook, and evaluated the current situation. But at the end of the meeting neither I nor the other ministers felt at ease. I was tense and tired and could sense a gulf between me and my Cabinet colleagues. They had not liked what I had said about the Egyptian success, and certainly not my view about retiring to a second line. They wanted the army to push the Egyptians back across the Canal at once. We were not on the same wavelength. They were seized by the optimism in the chief of staff's survey and above all by their own wishful thinking. After midnight, the Cabinet secretariat notified our representative in the United States that in a matter of days we would drive the Egyptians from the east bank of the Canal, and that despite local enemy successes the situation was satisfactory.

The Arab radio stations and the Soviet news agency, Tass, broadcast a version of the day's events in which we had started the war. Radio Cairo reported that at 1:30 P.M. that day, the Israeli Air Force had attacked Zafarana, a small Egyptian port on the Gulf of Suez, and that "Egyptian forces are repulsing the enemy." Tass and Radio Damascus quoted the Syrian military spokesman as saying that Israeli forces had attacked advance positions of the Syrian army and that fighting continued.

The United States' announcement was more worrying. Commenting on the outbreak of hostilities in the Middle East, a White House spokesman said that President Nixon had been "closely following the situation since the early hours of the morning." Morning in Washington was afternoon in the Middle East. The announcement was being made three hours after the Egyptian-Syrian attack without the slightest hint that it was the Arabs who had started the war. When our representative in Washington reported to the U.S. government that the Arabs had launched the invasion, he was told that the Arabs claimed it was we who had attacked them. In Washington, of course, they knew the truth, knew from the beginning that we had not started the war; but perhaps they thought we should have done a bit more than simply "not start"!

31

THE FIGHTING FRONTS

THE SYRIANS LAUNCHED their offensive in the Golan Heights at 2 P.M. on October 6, simultaneously with the Egyptian offensive in Sinai. They attacked in massive force along the entire front, but concentrated their main breakthrough efforts at two points, one north and one south of Kuneitra. They were stubbornly blocked in bloody and skillful fighting by Col. Avigdor's 7th Armored Brigade operating in the northern sector, north of Kuneitra, and by the Barak Armored Brigade under Col. Ben-Shoham fighting in the southern sector. Until they could be reinforced—our reservists would begin to reach the fronts only the next day—these two brigades had to hold back the might of the Syrian invasion force, and they did so successfully all that bitter day.

But late that night the Syrians broke through the southern sector and our situation was serious indeed. Before the war it had been expected that a Syrian offensive would make its main thrust in the northern sector, and the allocation of tanks available to Northern Command had favored Avigdor's brigade. When the enemy directed his principal attack in the southern sector, it had to be contained by the smaller armored force that had been given to Ben-Shoham.

Nevertheless, unlike the situation on the Suez Canal, war in the

Golan found the tanks of Northern Command properly deployed in their assigned stations. The forward armored units were ready on the ramps and met the attackers with effective fire. The advanced strongholds, except for the one on Mount Hermon, had also been reinforced in time, and our artillery was arrayed in accordance with our contingency plan and covered the entire front with well-directed shelling.

Syria sent 500 tanks into the opening assault. Against them were ranged Northern Command's 177 tanks. After midnight, however, Syria brought up an additional 300 tanks, so that altogether she had 800. All the reinforcements that Northern Command could rustle from reservists to meet them was a small unit of 12 tanks!

Late that first night, before the Syrian breakthrough, I left a Cabinet meeting and went down to the pit. The Emergency General Headquarters was like a beehive, but without the honey. From the technical point of view, it was efficient and well organized. They were receiving reports from the battle fronts and marking maps. But from the point of view of control and command—and, more important, of cool and balanced thinking—the war room and the team operating it were far from satisfactory. The conduct of the war was in fact in the hands of the commanders of the fronts, and their sole concern could only be to defend their lines with all their forces, prevent breakthroughs, seal breaches where they occurred, and hold on until reinforcements arrived. In such a situation, the General Staff could make little impact on the conduct of the war. The best thing they could do was to go out to the front commands from time to time and reach decisions after joint consultations with the commander there.

I went to the war room of the Air Force, and the commander told me of his plans for the next day. He intended to attack targets on the southern front in the morning, primarily missile sites and airfields, which would enable him to operate more freely thereafter against Egyptian forces on both banks of the Canal. The chief of staff, too, did not think there was much point in attacking the crossings before silencing the missile batteries. I told them I had a different view. I was skeptical of the chances that the Air Force would be able to destroy the missile sites. At the same time, I foresaw two critical nights and one day during which the Egyptians would move additional large forces of armor to the east bank. My opinion was that the Air Force should shelve for the moment its plans to attack the missiles and do all it could to stop the Egyptians from moving tanks into Sinai, even if it meant losing planes. If the Air Force devoted itself to destroying the missile sites and failed in the attempt, we would lose on both counts: the tanks would cross, and our aircraft would still be limited in their freedom of action.

The minister of defense has political authority. This particular matter was technical, operational. The decision was therefore in the hands of the chief of staff and Air Force commander. The decision to attack the missile sites in the morning remained in force. It was now 2 A.M., twelve hours since the start of the war. I went back to my office for a nap.

I was awakened two hours later. The situation in the north had become serious. A Syrian force had penetrated our lines in the area of Hushniyah, eight miles south of Kuneitra, and was advancing toward routes which offered a descent from the Golan Heights to the Sea of Galilee. Reservist units which had hastily managed to get themselves organized were rushed to hold the slopes and block the enemy. The GOC Northern Command, Maj. Gen. Yitzhak Hofi, gave orders to evacuate all men from the civilian farm settlements. The women and children had been evacuated on Yom Kippur.

I left at once for the northern front. The helicopter flew northward along the coast and then turned east. On other occasions my heart melts when I see the Sharon Plain, this blessed region, rich with orange groves and farm settlements. Now, almost as soon as we had flown over Tel Aviv, it seemed to me that I could already hear the sounds of exploding bombs and shells in the Golan. The depth of the Golan Heights is altogether not more than fifteen miles. If the Syrian forces reached the descent to the Jordan River, it would be very difficult to repel them, particularly when they possessed such powerful quantities of weapons and manpower, and we also had to fight on the Egyptian front. It was evident that we had to stop the Syrians near the point of the breakthrough, even if it meant investing all our strength.

I reached advance headquarters of Northern Command shortly before 6 A.M. to hear from the commanding officer that our defense in the entire southern sector of Golan had collapsed. The Syrians had overcome the forces of Barak Brigade and had moved through the southern part of the Golan Heights to a point almost halfway to the Jordan. Our armored reservist units, which had been mobilized and were on their way with additional tanks, would not be able to meet and challenge the enemy until midday.

I realized that the only force that could hold up the enemy advance at this moment was the Air Force, and not a minute was to be wasted. It had to be flung into action without delay. The head of

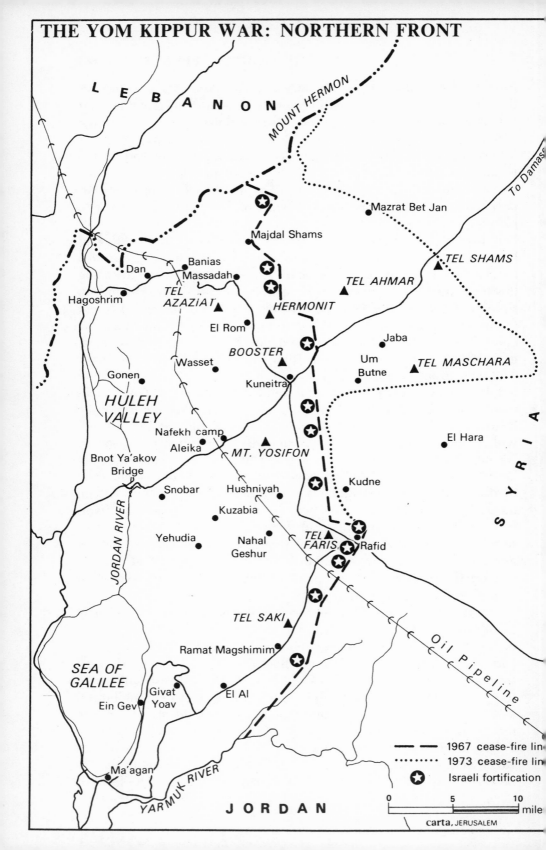

THE YOM KIPPUR WAR: NORTHERN FRONT

L E B A N O N

MOUNT HERMON

To Damas(

Mazrat Bet Jan

Majdal Shams

TEL SHAMS ▲

Banias
Dan
Massadah

TEL AHMAR ▲

Hagoshrim

TEL AZAZIAT ▲

HERMONIT ▲

El Rom

BOOSTER ▲

Jaba

Um Butne

TEL MASCHARA ▲

Wasset

Gonen

Kuneitra

HULEH VALLEY

Nafekh camp
Aleika

MT. YOSIFON ▲

El Hara

Bnot Ya'akov Bridge

Snobar

Hushniyah

Kudne

Kuzabia

Yehudia

Nahal Geshur

TEL FARIS ▲
Rafid

TEL SAKI ▲

Ramat Magshimim

SEA OF GALILEE

Givat Yoav

El Al

Ein Gev

Ma'agan

S Y R I A

Oil Pipeline

JORDAN RIVER

YARMUK RIVER

J O R D A N

— — — 1967 cease-fire lin
· · · · · 1973 cease-fire lin
Ⓢ Israeli fortification

0   5   10
                          mile

carta, JERUSALEM

Northern Command explained that our tanks were mixed up with the enemy armor in close combat and that our pilots might fire on our own troops. I told him to get orders through to the tank crews either to leave their tanks or close their hatches.

Our aircraft had to attack the enemy armor, and not operate according to standard doctrine and attempt first to silence the anti-aircraft missiles. I called Maj. Gen. Benny Peled, the Air Force commander, on the telephone and told him that he had to send his planes into immediate, continuous action against the Syrian tanks that had broken through. His was the only force that could stop them, until additional armor reached us in the afternoon. Otherwise we would lose the southern half of the Golan, and who knew what might happen thereafter with the Jordan Valley settlements. Mottie Hod, the former Air Force commander, was now acting as the Air Force officer attached to Northern Command, and he and his staff there would be directing and controlling the planes assigned for this task. He was standing at my side while I spoke to the Air Force commander and prodding me. "Tell him," he said, "to send up four-somes, so that one group of four after another without stop can swoop down on the Syrian armor and tank crews won't be able to lift their heads." I could not tell whose was the hoarse voice uttering this urgent counsel, the voice of the veteran fighter pilot or of the son of Kibbutz Deganiah in the Jordan Valley—and perhaps, at that moment, there was no difference between them.

This was the first time that I had spoken to the Air Force commander in this way and on such a matter. This was not an order. I had to issue orders through the chief of staff. This was very much more than an order—and so was the positive response. Despite the density of the enemy missile system, the Air Force kept attacking the Syrian tank concentrations without letup, which had a decisive effect on the situation.

During the morning of October 7, Northern Command started consolidating its brigades, which in the previous hours had been flung into action in dribs and drabs, and assigning responsibility for the different sectors to divisional commanders. Maj. Gen. Dan Laner was given responsibility for the southern area of the Golan Heights and Maj. Gen. Raful Eitan for the northern. A third division was due to reach the Golan in the evening hours.

But at 1 P.M. Syrian tanks suddenly appeared at the very fences round our camp at Nafekh, southwest of Kuneitra and only six miles from a bridge across the Jordan which offered access to all our kibbutzim and other farm settlements in northern Galilee. When we spotted the Syrians near the camp, we managed to rush in a few small units who drove the attackers from the camp but not from the area, and they finally found a gap through which they could get to the bridge. Col. Ben-Shoham fought a desperate rearguard action in an effort to hold them back until stronger reinforcements arrived. He and his second in command were killed. But by the evening, the Syrian force was checked and danger was averted in the second grave crisis that had struck this sector of the Golan in twenty-four hours. The two elements which had turned the tide were the Air Force, which bombed and strafed the enemy without pause, and units of a reservist armored brigade who were on their way to the front in small groups from their bases in Galilee. These units, seeing the Syrians advancing toward them heading for the Jordan River, hastily managed to set up barriers and road blocks and create bottle-necks in their path. Northern Command reinforced the newly arrived units, and they blunted the Syrian breakthrough and finally pushed the enemy back. During the night, our forces used the respite to draw breath for a counter-attack.

The third day of the war, October 9, brought its third crisis, this time in the sector held by the 7th Brigade, which was weak and worn by now, after having fought against heavy odds for three days and nights without rest and resisted all enemy attempts to penetrate their lines. The assault on this day was the heaviest ever, concentrated against the approaches to Kuneitra. By midday the plight of the brigade was critical, with no reserves, many tanks knocked out, and ammunition for those tanks still able to fight almost exhausted.

At this point Col. Avigdor of the 7th Armored Brigade notified Divisional Commander Raful Eitan that he could no longer stop the enemy. Raful, too, had almost given up hope of resisting this attack. But at that very moment, he received a message from Lt. Col. Yossie that his unit had just captured a key ridge in the area code-named Booster, just northwest of Kuneitra. The rear of the Syrian forces were turning round and beginning to retreat. This timely news was promptly signaled to Avigdor. "They're breaking," said Raful. "Hold on for another few minutes." The 7th Brigade did so, and shortly afterward the Syrian forward tanks also began withdrawing.

When I reached Northern Command that night, October 9, I found the mood had changed. Despite the bitter fighting and the heavy casualties, particularly among the officers, there was a feeling that on that day they had passed the rock-bottom point and that the

momentum of the Syrian attack had been broken. The enemy forces
had begun to retreat. We had knocked out some nine hundred of
their tanks. I also discovered to my surprise at northern headquarters
that Yossie had taken part in the battles that day. Only two days
earlier I had asked after him and had been told that he was not in
Israel. He was on a delayed honeymoon, spending it in the Hima-
layas. I remembered being at his wedding on Mount Carmel only a
short time before. He had married Eynat, who belonged to one of
the oldest pioneering families in Galilee. It turned out that on the
day the Israel Defense Forces had been put on alert, the young
couple were on a Honda motorbike in the heart of the high mountains. On the following day, the hotel receptionist happened to mention that he had heard on the BBC that there was tension in Israel.
Yossie promptly put a call through to the Israeli embassy in Kat-
mandu and was told, quite simply, that war had broken out on two
fronts. The first plane out of Nepal was leaving the next day. Yossie
and his wife got seats on it and flew homeward via New Delhi and
Bombay, finally arriving in Athens. There they waited for an El Al
plane to get them to Israel.

From the home of Israel's ambassador to Greece, Yossie telephoned his parents, heard news of what was happening, and arranged for them to meet him at Lod Airport and bring his personal
equipment—uniform, sweater, revolver, dust goggles, wind-jacket,
gloves. When he and Eynat reached Israel, he telephoned his unit
and was told that he was posted to the northern front, that the
Syrians had broken through, that his commander, Ben-Shoham, had
been killed and that he was to take over what was left of the unit.
Yossie got into his uniform, said goodbye to his wife, and rushed
north. Two hours later he presented himself in the war room of
Northern Command for a briefing by the GOC, and soon after he
was on his way to the forward armored base. There he found men
working on the repair of the tanks of his unit that had been hit. He
also found Shmulik, his long-time second in command, who had been
wounded on the first day of the war, had bolted from the hospital,
and rejoined the unit. At 8 A.M. on October 9, Yossie and his tanks
were ready to move. He got onto the radio net of the divisional commander, Raful, and was told to rush at once to 7th Brigade's battle
sector and put himself under Avigdor's command. Avigdor was listening on the network and he told Yossie to go at once to the Booster
ridge, which was about to fall to the Syrians. When Yossie arrived
and approached the hill, he met the few remaining tanks of our

force which had held the Booster loaded with many wounded, retreating, and leaving behind flaming tanks.

Then began a race for the hill, and the question was who would get to the top first, the Syrians advancing from the east or Yossie who had come from the west. In the ensuing battle, in which Yossie's 11 tanks engaged more than 60 of the Syrians', with the rival tanks at times almost colliding on the slopes, good Israeli marksmanship paid off. The Syrian tanks were set on fire one after the other, and Booster ridge was soon back in our possession.

When I heard all this at Northern Command, I wanted to get in touch with Yossie and send him greetings. But it was apparently too complicated, and I was able to do so only three days later, in a Haifa hospital. He had been wounded again, badly this time, in an attack the day before on Tel Shams, deep inside Syria.

Our forces by then were very much on the offensive. They had blocked the Syrian breakthrough, thrust the enemy back beyond our lines, and pushed them further into the heart of Syria. There had been a remarkable reversal of fortune on the fronts since the grim opening days of the Yom Kippur War. But the Syrians were still putting up a stubborn fight for key positions in their interior, and when Yossie's unit reached the dominant hill positions of Tel Shams, on the Kuneitra-Damascus road, they found it heavily defended, and came under fire from anti-tank missiles and enemy tank units, as well as Syrian aircraft, which plastered them with rockets.

In a day of fighting, evasive action, and renewed combat, in which the force knocked out the Syrian tanks at the foot of the hill, Yossie decided to exploit this success by storming the top of Tel Shams in a speedy dash, though he had only eight tanks left. He soon discovered his mistake. There were no more tanks at the foot of the hill, but the top contained well-entrenched Syrian infantry armed with anti-tank missiles. Two of them hit Yossie's tank, and the next thing he knew he was lying on the ground beside his burning tank, his left thigh shattered. The bones were sticking through the flesh, and his leg was hanging loose. The tanks which had not been hit had pulled back, and the only person remaining with Yossie was his tank driver, Zvika, who was miraculously unhurt and who pulled Yossie to safety.

Yossie had not lost consciousness, and when the flames had died down and the tank was smoldering, he asked Zvika to retrieve the radio set, which could be worked manually. Fortunately, it was undamaged, and when the driver made contact with headquarters, he put the microphone to his commander's mouth: "This is Yossie. I've lost a leg. I'm near the tank. Come and get me."

Three hours later, the rescue party reached him. Yossie had urged Zvika to leave him and save himself, but he had refused. Instead, he dragged Yossie to an abandoned Syrian trench, brought a jerry can of water from the tank, and obtained radio directions from the army medical officer on how to tie a tourniquet on the arteries of the smashed thigh.

The rescue force was commanded by Yoni. It was dark when they arrived. Syrian artillery shelled the foot of the slopes without interruption, and so Yoni and his men left their vehicles some distance away and approached on foot. It was by the light of the bursting shells that they spotted Yossie's tank and then the shallow trench where Yossie lay. What followed were morphine, stretcher, armored half-tracks, helicopter, and hospital. His wife, Eynat, managed to reach the hospital just as Yossie was being wheeled into surgery. In the spirit of a resumed honeymoon, he told her: "It's nothing. No need to worry. I've checked thoroughly. All I've lost is a leg!"

Some time later I heard how Yoni had come to lead the rescue party. Yoni was second in command of a crack unit that happened to be about seven miles from Tel Shams when he heard the talk on the radio network about rescuing Yossie. He promptly got through to the brigade commander and told him that he and his men would do the job.

From time to time I have had the opportunity to meet the men of Yoni's unit—and not only when they were being briefed before an action or reporting after an operation—and I was always very much impressed. What was particularly impressive was not only their fighting skill, which of course was far beyond that expected of ordinary troops, but the men themselves, the human beings. When you get to know them well—and I have my own private pipeline to this unit, for young relatives of mine serve in it as officers—you discover that each one has his special character and qualities, and all are of a high order. All, of course, are volunteers, all in top physical condition, and most of them are highly educated. But the quality common to all lies more in the human and Zionist spheres, the sphere of Jewish renaissance rather than in the military field. They belong to the band of biblical pioneer-saviors who arose in Israel in ancient days when the nation lived on its own soil, and to the pioneers who began to rebuild the neglected land at the start of our own century, when modern Zionism was taking its first faltering steps. They are young men with a fervent belief in the Jewish destiny and in our strength and will to achieve it, who are ready at all times to carry out the most difficult and dangerous tasks.

Yoni is the eldest of three brothers, all of whom volunteered to serve in this unit. Their parents had left Israel for the United States, where their father is a professor of History at Cornell University. In the Six Day War, Yoni was hit by a bullet which smashed his elbow. He went to the United States and spent a year alternating between hospital clinics and the Mathematics Department at Harvard. When treatment for his arm was completed—though it was still not as it should be—he returned to Israel and to his special unit. Later, he again traveled to the U.S. to continue higher studies in mathematics and also to receive additional treatment for his arm. He returned to Israel one month before the outbreak of the Yom Kippur War. On the first two days of the war, his unit fought on the southern front, and on the third day it was posted to the north. On October 9, Yoni's men stalked and killed more than forty Syrian commandos who had landed behind our lines. They then advanced with the 7th Brigade deep inside Syria. I do not know how many young men there are like Yoni. But I am convinced there are enough to ensure that Israel can meet the grim tests which face her in the future.

Another rescue story I heard from officers of the 7th Brigade on the Syrian front had a sad ending. A brigade reconnaissance detachment had gone to rescue the crew of a tank that had been hit. Their plight was desperate. They were isolated and under attack by a Syrian unit. The detachment reached them in time, beat off the attackers and inflicted heavy casualties, and returned to base with the tank crew. Along the way, however, they had run into a bazooka ambush, which they had successfully negotiated. After safely depositing the crew they had saved, they asked permission to return to deal with the Syrian ambush party. It was granted, and the commander set off at the head of three half-tracks. The Syrians spotted their approach, improved their positions, and in the ensuing engagement twenty-four of the reconnaissance detachment were killed, among them the commander, his second in command, and four other officers. Together with the wounded, it meant that we lost the unit, a heavy price indeed for what was after all a marginal action. With hindsight, it would appear to have been a non-essential operation. But war is not conducted like a grocery store where everything can always be weighed and measured.

At the end of the first week of war on the northern front, it was the Syrians who were on the defensive, and the campaign was being fought on their soil, east of the lines through which they had broken six days earlier.

On the Syrian front, as we have seen, our forces were properly deployed to meet the enemy when the Yom Kippur War broke out. This was not the case on the Egyptian front, and the first to suffer for it were the strongholds along the Suez Canal, the first targets of Egyptian attack. The battles were tough, heroic, and depressing. There were sixteen such strongholds, and together they constituted what had come to be known as the Bar-Lev line. But each fought its individual battle on its own. Each was a solitary, isolated isle, conducting a bitter and desperate struggle, a struggle of life or death, of surrender or breaking free.

These strongholds were small outposts, each manned by 20 to 30 soldiers, spaced out along the water's edge at intervals of roughly five miles. All were subjected to heavy pounding by artillery as Egypt launched its war against Israel. The shelling was followed by massive assaults by Egyptian tanks and infantry, and eventually, except for the one code-named Budapest, which had special topographic features, all these outposts fell: some were evacuated, others were subdued by the Egyptians.

This did not happen immediately. Indeed, although the Egyptians started crossing the Canal soon after firing their first shells, not a single Israeli outpost fell within the first twenty-four hours—not even those which the Egyptians had succeeded in penetrating at the very outset of the battle. On the other hand, not a single stronghold succeeded in stopping the Egyptian advance in its sector. Some managed to sink Egyptian rafts during the crossing. Others effectively directed artillery fire and aerial attacks against Egyptian bridging units and troop concentrations, causing heavy casualties to the invaders. But these actions did not hold up the Canal crossing and the movement of enemy armored and infantry forces to the east bank. When the Egyptians could not capture an outpost, they bypassed it—again, except for Budapest. This fortified position, which was heavily attacked but held its own, did prevent the Egyptian advance along the northern axis of Sinai and forced the enemy to retire to its former positions near Port Said.

The other Israeli strongholds were isolated and cut off from our main forces. Their troops fought with extreme bravery and determination. In most of them, their commanding officers were killed in the opening phase of the battle. Some received the order to evacuate their outposts or surrender and refused to do so. But in the end, surrounded by the enemy, without physical contact with the rest of our troops, they were unable to hold out. The last stronghold to fall and its men taken prisoner was Masrek, which commanded the southern entrance to the Suez Canal.

Some of the strongholds had received the alert shortly before the enemy opened fire, and others only at the very moment of attack. This is not to say that if they had received the warning in time they would have been ready to meet the kind of assault that was launched. The fact is that they were not designed and not built to withstand such attack. The strongest part of each stronghold was the protected part below ground, which held the war room and bunkers. But the firing positions, which were not armored, and the communications trenches leading to them were of necessity above ground. When these open and exposed targets came under very heavy artillery shelling, and soon after under the direct fire from enemy tanks which surrounded them, they collapsed, and the men in them were either killed or forced to abandon them.

Moreover, the technical and organizational arrangements preparatory to an enemy attack had not been carried out. First of all, the tank detachments which should have been stationed between the strongholds, linking them and giving them support, were six miles to the rear, along the artillery line. When the attack started and they tried to reach the strongholds, they found the Egyptians already there waiting for them. They came under heavy anti-tank fire from both banks of the Canal, and most of them were hit, put out of action, and unable to fulfill their designated task.

It must also be said that inside the strongholds, peacetime routine was reflected in the mood of the personnel and the state of the equipment. Such standard items as signals equipment and vehicles were not in proper working order. In some strongholds, weapons and ammunition were below acceptable levels—and in some they were below even the essential minimum. Nowhere in the line were there tanks for evacuation. Above all, the unit manning the strongholds had not been specially selected or even reinforced to enable it to hold the most advanced and difficult of Israel's military lines—the waterline of the Suez Canal! This was an ordinary reservist unit, made up partly of elderly men who had not had any refresher training for more than two years. This was a very different unit indeed from such forces as our paratroopers, who should have been manning the strongholds under the contingency plan. Nevertheless, the unit that was in the line was blessed with first-class commanders. The officers and sergeants were without doubt among the finest in our army.

I do not know if it is possible to determine in precise measure the extent to which the strongholds stood up to the enemy, even for a day or two, and thereby held up the Egyptian forces from advancing further. At all events, it is a fact that the Egyptian army in the first two days did not advance more than a few miles, and in that time the Israel Defense Forces mobilized its reserves, and reinforcements reached Southern Command. Those two days, from the sudden enemy attack on Yom Kippur until the reserves reached the front, were most critical, and the stubborn fight put up by the men in the strongholds was undoubtedly of supreme importance.

As in all our battles, here, too, the first casualties were the officers, most of whom were in the exposed firing and observation posts. With the opening shots of the Egyptians, both Gadi and Ezra, the commander and second in command of stronghold Orkel, were killed. In Lahtzanit, too, the first man to be killed was the commander, Shmuel Malchov, who caught a burst in his chest. Shortly afterward his second in command, Sergeant Aharon, was killed. In Ketuba, the commander, David Sitton, was hit by fire from rafts crossing the Canal toward him. Lieut. Efrati was the first to be wounded in the stronghold he commanded, Mifreket. At Hizayon, the commander, Ahiram Barel, had his arm blown off just beneath the armpit, but he did not lose consciousness, and he handed over the command as though he were on the parade ground: "Itzik, I'm wounded. I've lost an arm. Take command." And he did not forget to add "Good luck."

As the commanders were hit, other men took their places. At Orkel, after the commander and his deputy were killed, Lieut. David Abudarham assumed overall command. Abudarham was born in Turkey and was brought to Israel as a child. If there is such a thing as a nation's gratitude, it should be given in large handfuls to him, not only because he faced danger without fear, rushed from post to exposed post to ensure that men and weapons were properly directed, redeploying his small force whenever his stronghold was badly hit, but primarily because in the grimmest moments he maintained his stronghold as a fighting unit. He showed coolness and a spirit of confidence throughout the tough fighting, gave the right orders, tended the wounded and removed the dead, ensured that each man was in his proper place—and when necessary would slap the face of a soldier seized with fear to get him to his post.

Although the attack on the strongholds opened with the shock of heavy artillery shelling, and as soon as rafts were seen crossing the Canal it was understood that this was war in earnest, the main pressure, military as well as psychological, came later, when thousands of Egyptians accompanied by tanks stormed the strongholds and broke through the gates and minefields into the communications trenches and into the interior of the positions.

The defenders fought their attackers at the shortest possible range with fortitude, flinging back hand grenades before they exploded and destroying enemy tanks with bazookas. When firing posts were abandoned because of casualties or became untenable because of the massive superiority of enemy numbers, the defenders concentrated in other stronghold positions and continued to fight and repulse the attackers.

But as the hours passed, it became clear to the defenders that their situation was becoming increasingly difficult, and that the chances of tanks reaching them to reinforce or rescue them grew fainter. Some who had refused to abandon their strongholds on the first day were beginning, by the second day, to ask that they be brought out. By then it was too late. The approach tracks to them were blocked, and tanks attempting to break through to them went up in flames.

There was a false evaluation of developments at all levels, from stronghold commanders—not all, of course—to brigade, command, General Staff, and even the government level. They hoped on the first day of war that we would be able to dislodge the Egyptians from their hold on the east bank or at least to break through them and link up with the strongholds. On the first night of the war, at the end of the Yom Kippur fast, it was still possible to rescue the men in all the strongholds, but Southern Command preferred not to do so. They assumed that the following days of war would be no more difficult than that first day.

A tank unit managed to evacuate one stronghold, but we lost several tank crews in attempts to rescue others. The men of four strongholds got out alone without loss. There were other cases where our men broke out and tried to make their heroic way through the enemy lines. Some succeeded. Many did not. And one stronghold held out to the end. The rest surrendered, and this was the most depressing part of the battle of the strongholds. Yet in no single case was surrender the product of a psychological crack-up, either of units or of individual soldiers. Nor was it the result of fatigue or loss of fighting spirit. It was an "end of the road" surrender, with the steady hour-by-hour reduction in the number of surviving defenders, ammunition running out, weapons and equipment put out of action, and with no chance of help and reinforcements reaching them in time, while each hour saw an increase in the numbers and strength of the enemy troops which enabled them to penetrate more deeply into the strongholds, overwhelming the defensive positions and reaching the bunkers.

The Bar-Lev line had acquired a certain renown, and because of it, its conquest was a considerable military gain for the Egyptians and greatly boosted their prestige. But the strongholds which constituted this line could not have been expected to provide a capability with which they had never been vested, nor to fulfill functions for which they had not been constructed. They had neither been intended nor designed to prevent—alone, independently, solely with their own fighting and their own fire power—the crossing of the Canal by huge enemy forces. The number of Egyptian troops who crossed outnumbered the defenders in the strongholds by 200 to 1. It was not to be expected that they could hold out many hours if they were cut off, isolated, surrounded, and subjected to onslaughts in massive strength, for they did not constitute an independent military system. The Bar-Lev line and its strongholds were an integral part of the overall military array in Sinai, and they could do their designated job only as long as the other forces, the armor and infantry with whom they were interlinked, were with them or nearby.

Thus, the key to success of the Bar-Lev line on Yom Kippur lay not with the strongholds and their capacity to hold out, but with the proper deployment of the armored units in time, as planned, and the securing of link-up corridors giving access to the strongholds from the rear. If this was not done, it was better to abandon the strongholds, order their men to retire, and mount counter-attacks against the Egyptian forces by armor and infantry based on a line in the rear.

In the first twenty-four hours following the outbreak of war, we were left with only a fraction of our original armored strength on the Egyptian front. With the line of the Canal strongholds broken at several points, Egyptian forces poured through en masse, with an overwhelming weight of armament. The tank brigades of Maj. Gen. Albert Mandler fought desperately to hold them up. They had not been deployed in their positions under the contingency plan when the attack came, and now, as they moved toward the waterline, they encountered murderous fire from the Egyptians already on the east bank. Fierce battles were fought all that afternoon, and the situation worsened during the night and at dawn next morning when fresh waves of Egyptian armor crossed the Canal. Our men fought valiantly, and inflicted grave losses on the enemy. Our troops also suffered heavy casualties in men and armor and emerged after ceaseless battle with only a few tanks still in fighting condition. They had managed to halt the momentum of the Egyptians and hold up their advance. But they failed to drive them back across the Canal.

During the course of the second day, Sunday, October 7, the reservist divisions of Maj. Gen. Avraham (Bren) Adan and Arik Sharon began arriving.

In the morning, before the arrival of the reservists, I flew to Southern Command advance headquarters, having been at Northern Command a few hours earlier. I drank a good deal of black coffee with the GOC in the south, Maj. Gen. Shmuel Gonen, and his officers, but it did nothing to salve my sense of unease as we reviewed the situation on the front. Indeed, as I flew back from Sinai to Tel Aviv, I could recall no moment in the past when I had felt such anxiety. If I had been in physical straits, involved in personal danger, it would have been simpler. I knew this from experience. But now I had quite a different feeling. Israel was in danger, and the results could be fatal if we did not recognize and understand the new situation in time and if we failed to suit our warfare to the new needs.

I told this to Golda Meir when I reached Tel Aviv, after telling the chief of staff, David Elazar, what I proposed to say to the prime minister, so that he could be present and respond with his own views if he disagreed with me. Also present were two other ministers. My main points were that we should abandon the Canal line and organize ourselves at once along a new front some distance from the Canal, hold that line at all costs, and wage the war from there. I also urged that we evacuate the Canal strongholds that night. Our most serious problem was Arab superiority in numbers and arms. The Arabs were fighting with determination and were equipped with excellent Russian weapons, including the sophisticated Soviet personal infantry anti-tank RPG rockets and Sagger missiles. With help from Russia and the Arab States, notably Libya, they were capable of continuing the war even if they suffered heavy losses. We, on the other hand, faced the danger of losing our strength and remaining without a force before we gained the desired military decision. We should now make a supreme effort to secure planes and tanks as quickly as possible from America, and perhaps try to get tanks from Europe too.

The prime minister and the other ministers were shocked, largely I think because I also said I did not believe we could *at this moment* throw the Egyptians back to the other side of the Canal. That very morning, the chief of staff had told the Cabinet that we could. I had missed that Cabinet meeting to go south and had asked the chief of staff to appear instead of me. It was clear from their critical cross-questioning after my realistic remarks that they thought the weakness lay not in our current military situation but in my personal character, that I had lost my confidence, and that my evaluation was incorrect. It was too pessimistic.

The chief of staff said he did not disagree with my estimate, and he agreed to prepare a second line in place of the Canal line. But he also wished to go over to the counter-attack at once. He proposed to fly to Southern Command that evening, study the situation, and decide about a counter-attack to be undertaken by Arik and Bren. He asked me in the presence of the ministers whether he was authorized to make a decision. I said yes, though I expressed doubt that the two formations were yet ready. However, I added, if after consultation in the south he reached a favorable conclusion, he could order an attack against the Egyptian troops on the east bank of the Canal. The ministers breathed a sigh of relief. They could not bear to think that we lacked the power at any moment to throw the enemy back to where they were some thirty hours earlier.

It seemed to me that the root of the difference between other members of the government and myself lay in the degree of readiness to face up to reality and recognize its implications. For example, they were impressed with reports that our Air Force had knocked out the Canal bridges, from which they assumed that the Egyptian forces were now cut off. I had to explain to them that these were not permanent structures but raft or pontoon bridges, which could be repaired during the night. As to our Air Force, of course we had absolute superiority in air-to-air combat. But it was precisely because of this that the Egyptians tried to avoid sending up their planes over the battlefield and relied on their massed batteries of Soviet anti-aircraft missiles. Thus, in the first twenty-four hours of the war, we had shot down 40 Arab planes, but we had lost 35 of our own to the missiles. This was the decisive and unpleasant fact, and what counted in war was how many planes each side could afford to lose.

The implication of this reality was that if we went on suffering heavy losses in incessant frontal attacks, we might be left with an emaciated force in the midst of a campaign, while the Arabs, with their huge forces and arsenals, could hold on. Egypt and Syria had a combined population of eighty million. We had less than three million at the time. Their armies totaled a million troops, and Russia provided them with all the weapons they needed. They could also call on vast financial resources. And other Arab states were swelling their fighting ranks by sending in their own army formations. We had turned to America with urgent requests for planes and tanks, but who knew if and when we would receive them? And we, at all events, had to fight our own battles. No one would do the fighting for us. These were the considerations, together with my judgment of the situation on the ground, which prompted my recommendation that we abandon the Canal line and redeploy along a new line further back, from which we could go forth and resume our war against the Egyptians.

The chief of staff flew to Sinai and telephoned me from Southern Command to say that they had decided on a counter-attack by Bren and Arik to start next morning, Monday, October 8. He returned at midnight, and I went along to the war room in the pit to hear the details at a meeting of the Operations Group. Though we were far from the battlefield, the war room had an eve-of-battle atmosphere. Most of the officers now in staff jobs had served in combat units, and had known that tight feeling, that special tenseness that grips one in the hours immediately preceding an action, when the idea of battle somehow becomes the reality of battle, and the feeling of reality is dominant, driving all else from the mind. One continues to talk, drink coffee, smoke, mark arrows on maps, receive and issue orders. But all this is done on a different level, a strange, external level, as if by someone else. One's real self, all that makes up one's vital being—thought, blood, nerve, muscle, sinew—are already trapped in the web of warfare, seized in a magnetic tension that is unlike any other sensation.

The chief of staff was in good spirits and spoke to the staff officers as though he were addressing a unit about to go into action. If all went well, the counter-attack on the next day would be the turning point in the war. Its purpose was to wipe out the Egyptian armored forces that had crossed the Canal and were now ranged along the east bank, the Egyptian Second Army in the northern sector, and the Third Army in the southern sector. By now, we had sent considerable tank reinforcements to the southern front, and several hundred tanks would be taking part in the attack—not as many as the Egyptians possessed, but still a respectable force. The next day would be the day of clashing armor.

The tanks did clash, there was bitter fighting, and our men fought well. But the day was a total failure. It was not the failure of the counter-attack, for what was fought was not really a counter-attack. The action was not carried out as it should have been. There was confusion at the highest levels about the battle plan, and Southern Command had little idea of what was happening during the course of the day's fighting.

When the chief of staff had reported to us in the pit at midnight, he had come directly from consultations at Southern Command with Maj. Gen. Gonen and the divisional commanders Bren and Albert. Arik had arrived just as the chief of staff was about to take off for Tel Aviv. There was no written summary of the consultations, and the chief of staff left the command post with the conviction that the aim of the action was to attack the Egyptians the next day in phased assaults in the areas of the bridgeheads established at their two main crossing points. Bren's division would attack the Egyptian Second Army starting at Kantara and proceed southward to the Bitter Lake, and Arik's and Albert's divisions would serve as backstops. At the completion of Bren's attack, Arik's division would attack the Egyptian Third Army in the southern sector and Bren and Albert would contain the enemy. The plan did not include a Canal crossing as an objective for this day's action, but the chief of staff did not exclude the possibility that after destroying the enemy forces at the bridgeheads, success might be exploited and our troops would cross the Canal over the Egyptian bridges. The attacks were to be carried out at a distance of about one-and-a-half miles from the waterline so as to avoid the anti-tank missiles of the Egyptian infantry ranged on the banks of the Canal.

It turned out, however, that when Arik Sharon had seen Chief of Staff Elazar for a few moments after the latter had left the meeting, Sharon recommended to Elazar that we should immediately break through to the strongholds and rescue the men. He added that our wisest step would be to seize a foothold on the Canal, cross it, and thereby confound the enemy.

Arik raised the suggestion of breaking through to the strongholds to Gonen, Bren, and Albert when he went into the command post after his brief encounter with the chief of staff. The suggestion was not rejected. As a result, Bren understood that there was the additional possibility that Arik would fight his way to the strongholds at dawn and he, Bren, would stand ready to give him support. Arik understood the same thing.

But at 6:15 A.M. on Monday, October 8, Gonen, the front commander, notified Arik that he would not be attacking in the direction of the strongholds. His division would attack in the southern sector of the Canal, not far from the Gulf of Suez, and if possible seize an Egyptian bridge and cross over. He would attack at noon, depending on the progress of Bren's action and whether he would have to go to Bren's support. A few minutes earlier, Gonen had secured the chief of staff's approval for Bren to start his attack at 8 A.M. and to be given the option of moving a brigade across the Egyptian bridge about midway along the Canal.

Bren's units started moving as planned from north to south, parallel to the Canal but out of range of the infantry missiles, and at 9 A.M. Southern Command gained the impression that all was going well. Gonen talked to Bren and agreed on the first change of plan: to direct units westward to one of our strongholds whose men were under great pressure. This stronghold also happened to be close to an Egyptian bridge. These units turned to the Canal and were promptly assailed by anti-tank missiles and then by RPG rockets from Egyptian troops firing from entrenched positions.

Everything went wrong, but Southern Command was unaware of it. Gonen, thinking that Bren's division was in good condition, got the chief of staff's approval to start Arik's division on its way south so as to reach his target before dark. Arik set off. In the end, this order to move his division before the outcome of Bren's actions became clear was what decided the fate of the counter-attack that day. In the early afternoon, Southern Command got the news that the Egyptians were organizing a counter-assault along the entire length of the Canal. At 2:15 P.M. Gonen halted Arik's southward movement and directed him to come north again. The division did so, but they now had to battle their way through territory which had been clear when they had moved south. The day ended with our line in some cases further to the rear than it had been in the morning.

That night, after a somber Cabinet session, I flew down to Sinai for a meeting I had called with the chief of staff, the GOC, and senior officers of Southern Command and with the divisional commanders, Arik, Bren, and Albert. I got there after midnight, feeling what must have been meant by the biblical "angry, even unto death." After the war had come upon us as it did; after the first day on the southern front when the forces were not deployed in their assigned positions at the proper time; after the strongholds had not been evacuated when there had still been time to do so; now, when we had finally concentrated a suitable force there—three armored divisions and scores of aircraft—which had battled a whole day, that, too, had been wasted, frittered away, all for nothing.

Bren and Arik sat there heavy with fatigue, red-eyed, hoarse, unshaven, and drained. This was their third day of ceaseless physical exertion, flung about inside tanks, without a moment's rest, bearing the full weight of the endless problems of divisions which had been mobilized in a hurry. But above all, the whole of their frenzied dash across the Sinai desert on tank treads had had one purpose—to bring maximum force to the Egyptian front in minimum time, to speed the day when we could go over from desperate defense to devastating attack against the enemy that had crossed the Canal. And now that day had come and gone, leaving in its trail disappointment, casualties, retreat.

Arik was livid. He had studied, analyzed, and understood what was happening in the battle area, and he had also come up with the correct solution—to cross the Canal, destroy the Egyptian missiles, and reach the rear of their Second and Third Armies. But he emphasized that we should not rely on miracles. It was impossible to bank on the chance that we would capture an Egyptian bridge in good repair and could move our forces across it. We needed bridges and rafts, of our own, and these had not yet reached the vicinity of the Canal.

The chief of staff summed up the plans for next day: Arik would make preparations for crossing the Canal. The remaining formations would take up defensive positions, and the fighting men would be given the opportunity to rest, sleep, and get themselves organized.

I had a meeting with the chief of staff in the pit when we returned from Southern Command. The first problem I raised was the replacement of the GOC of that command. In my judgment, the conduct of the campaign in Sinai was beyond the capabilities of Gonen, and we had to appoint another commander for the Egyptian front. I mentioned two candidates: Arik Sharon and Chaim Bar-Lev, a former chief of staff and currently our minister of commerce and industry.

I then went to the central issue—the overall picture of the war. We were in great difficulties. More powerful nations, England, France, Russia, had also found themselves in dire straits in time of war. At such a moment, we had to consider and then decide what were the proper steps for the nation and the army to take. It would come as a severe shock to our people when we told them that for the time being we were unable to throw the Egyptians back across the Canal, and that the strongholds along the Bar-Lev line had fallen. But there was no escaping this fact. We had to tell our nation the truth, so that they would know what the real situation was. We would be short of men. We would need to mobilize older age groups, which we had forgone in the past, and to investigate the possibilities of calling up seventeen-year-olds for preparatory training. We also needed additional weapons, and quickly, and we had to try to get them from the United States.

As to the fronts, in the south, we had to concentrate larger forces and organize ourselves anew before we made another attempt to push the Egyptians back. In the Golan Heights, we should issue a "no retreat" order to Northern Command. There we had to fight to the last man and not withdraw even an inch. If we lost all our tanks in the Golan by our stubborn stand, then we would lose them—but in so doing we would also wipe out the Syrian force. We should give the northern front all-out air support. If we ended the war on that front, we could concentrate all our forces against the Egyptians.

I told the chief of staff that on all these matters I had to receive the approval of the prime minister. I would see her shortly, and I asked him to join me.

I met the prime minister some three hours later, at 7:20 A.M. It was pretty certain that she had not had a moment's sleep—though one could not say the same about cigarettes and coffee—yet I could not imagine anyone with a more attentive ear, open mind, and courageous heart than Golda at this meeting. I told her of the orders I had given about the north—not to retreat, whatever the cost—and that this meant we might have very heavy casualties. Golda nodded her head in agreement. I have known Golda for many years, and I have seen her on more than one occasion with tears in her eyes. But not during war. War is not the time for tears.

I explained my views on the fronts, and then told her that since the Syrians had fired Frog ground-to-ground missiles against our civilian settlements three nights in a row, and this could not be passed over in silence, we wanted to bomb military targets in the Damascus area. She gave her approval. She also gave her agreement and blessing to the appointment of Chaim Bar-Lev to the command of the southern front up to the end of the war.

I raised the question of arms from the United States. Golda made several suggestions, the main one being that she fly to Washington for a secret meeting with the president. She thought it important to explain our situation to the president in a face-to-face talk, tell him about the vast quantities of Soviet arms in the hands of the Arabs, their huge numerical superiority, and what was happening on the fronts. It was not only weapons we needed. She also wanted President Nixon to know what had happened in this war, and why.

I supported her trip wholeheartedly. We needed not only arms from America but also her understanding and support, and there was no one like Golda who could get that.

32

STOCKTAKING

OCTOBER 10TH, the fifth day of the war, was the first day I stopped worrying whether somewhere along the fronts our forces might prove unable to stop the Arabs from breaking through into our territory. Both in Sinai and on the Golan Heights, the enemy had suffered severe setbacks with heavy casualties in men and equipment. Our units had established themselves in strong positions, had become familiar with the new enemy anti-tank weapons, and had learned how to counter them. The Arab armies, on the other hand, after carrying out their pre-arranged plans of crossing the Canal and storming the Golan, were not capable of taking the next step. That next step demanded planning under unexpected conditions, with unforeseen new data, and fighting against forces that were now no longer so sparse and ill prepared. We had reached a stage where we were able to initiate military moves with a choice of alternatives. So far, we had been compelled to block and hold, and our problem had been not what to do, but with what forces to do it. We now commanded options.

But now, too, the judgment of what action to take had to be based largely on operational considerations, so that the final decision was really in the hands of the General Staff and the front commands. If they said there were not enough forces to carry out a particular operation and it would therefore fail, no argument or explanation of its importance would be of any use.

In a democratic country like ours, the military forces come under the overall authority of the civilian government, exercised through the minister of defense. But the minister's powers are limited to policy decisions and do not extend to operational matters. For example, only by the government—in practice, by the minister of defense— could the army be ordered to cross or not to cross, say, the Lebanese border. I could give the order to attack army bases near Damascus and to steer clear of civilian targets, but I could not tell the army how this was to be done, though I might offer my views. This was an operational judgment in which the decisive voice was that of the chief of staff, not mine.

The minister of defense is the political head of the defense establishment. He is not the chief of staff and certainly not a kind of super-chief of staff. Even if he possesses the military competence, he lacks the professional authority and the necessary professional instruments. He has ministry officials but not a military staff. The professional authority is vested in the General Staff of the country's defense forces, headed by the chief of staff, and only with the help of this military staff is it possible to plan, weigh, reject, or approve military ideas and make them operational.

This is not to say that I sat in my office during the fighting and dealt solely with political decisions. I visited at least one of the fronts almost every day. Distances were not great. In one or two hours it was possible to get to any part of any front, and I found this essential to my task. I could not know or understand what was going on at the battlefield, what could or could not be done, simply by hearing reports and explanations from the General Staff. Not even the regional commanders were the most effective means for gathering this information. The best method for becoming absolutely *au courant* with what was happening was to get to the divisional commanders—like Raful and Dan on the northern front, and Arik and Bren on the southern front—spend several hours with them, hear their orders in the midst of action, and talk with them and with their staff officers. Only in this way, and only at these places, could I learn the true situation and understand this 1973 form of war, a war by Arabs equipped with the most modern Soviet weapons. I had grown sufficiently removed from specific military techniques to require a renewed acquaintance with the details of war. But at the same time I was sufficiently well grounded in military affairs to recognize the innovations and changes that had taken place in the weaponry, tactics, and fighting capacity of the Arabs.

And, above all, only on the battlefield can one know about a battle. No report can match first-hand, on-the-spot observation from a nearby hilltop or a patrol along the forward lines. No command headquarters, no map, no reconnaissance photograph can provide as tangible an impression of a battle situation as direct experience.

I drew little satisfaction from my visits to the headquarters of the Northern and Southern commands. The commander of the front was surrounded by his staff officers, there was continuous noise, incessant telephoning, and never a moment for quiet reflection. I did not fit in to any of this activity. I would leave after such visits without feeling any the wiser. All that I had heard could have been gathered from a phone call. I had been told what was happening, but I could not turn this information into a recognizable picture. I understood what the front commander and his staff thought, but what I wanted was to clarify to myself what I thought. The fault may have been with me, but up to the very last day of the war I preferred to skip the command headquarters and meet directly with the fighting forces.

Though my home in Zahala is less than a ten-minute drive from the compound which contains the offices of the General Staff, the Ministry of Defense and the Tel Aviv office of the prime minister, I was almost never there. My three children are married and live in their own homes. All three were mobilized—Yael was serving in the military hospital of Tel Hashomer; my older son, Ehud, was in a naval commando unit; and the younger, Assaf, was a mortarman with a paratroop brigade.

My wife, Rahel, would spend the day at her job in the PX offices, and at night she would wait at home for my telephone calls, which I tried to make whenever I could, and for my lightning visits. On such occasions, while the coffee was being prepared, I would take a turn in the garden and look in on the storeroom where I keep my antiquities. The garden was watered—which Rahel managed to do—but the lawn was not mown, and the weeds had played havoc with the roses. The antiquities remained unchanged, with small lizards and spiders living in and between them, all as it had been. But I could not work up interest in any of this. The garden and the antiquities were part of another world, a distant world, a world in which at some time in the past I had lived, but was now remote and without importance.

On my visits to the front, I wore Israeli army fatigues without any badges of rank, green shirt and trousers, paratroop boots, and a windjacket. The problem was a hat, but I had solved that one before the war. When I returned from my 1966 Vietnam visit, I adopted a somewhat doubtful form of headgear of the kind worn by Vietnamese rear-echelon privates engaged in service duties—cooks, sanitary orderlies, and so on. It laid no claims to elegance, but it could be crumpled and shoved in a pocket when not needed, and it looked no worse when taken out and put on my head. The one article of apparel I was careful about was my dust goggles. I never moved without them, for when the socket of my missing eye gets dry, I suffer severe headaches. I also try to keep my right eye protected. Just as well for an eye accident not to happen more than once.

All these, of course, were minor external matters. The Yom Kippur War wholly engaged my interior life, which was a compound of heavy anxiety, sadness, and a constant effort to concentrate my thoughts. This was my fourth war. In the first, our 1948 War of Independence, I was twenty-five and commanded a commando battalion in battle. It was not sport, and it offered no "joy of creation," but it was easier. There was sorrow, but there was also laughter. The area of responsibility and the psychological pressures were all contained within three companies and the capture of a hill. And when that was successfully accomplished—as it mostly was—I could wrap my *kefieh* round my face and sink into a deep sleep. The Sinai Campaign of 1956 and the Six Day War of 1967 were not difficult wars. The Egyptians were beaten and they fled; the Syrians had no surface-to-air missiles; and the Jordanians had no Air Force.

The Yom Kippur War was different. It was not only a hard war to fight but also a hard atmosphere to fight in. We had to tackle mass forces equipped with large quantities of powerful armor, guns, and surface-to-air missiles, and when we succeeded in knocking out hundreds of tanks, no one made merry. But when one of our front-line strongholds fell, or when we lost thirty tanks in a single action, the nation was plunged into gloom. Some of the best of our young men were officers who led their troops in battle—pilots, tankmen, paratroopers. Each day, each hour, brought news of tragedy—husbands killed, sons killed, sons of relatives, friends, acquaintances, colleagues, neighbors in town and village. Our people did not want to remember what other wars had been like or what had happened in Europe. Nor did they draw consolation from what had *not* happened—that the enemy had failed to break through to our population centers, that destruction was confined solely to the fronts. They saw only our own losses. They had not assimilated the objective fact that we were up against a million Arab soldiers and an abundance of Soviet weapons, yet we were defeating the Egyptian and Syrian armies on the ground and in the air. The people of Israel were wholly given over to grief and anxiety for their men who had fallen, who were captive, or who were wounded. They thought of nothing else.

I, too, lived in this atmosphere. But I was minister of defense, and not for one moment did I stop thinking about the future moves in the war. What should we do now? How would things develop? What was the Soviet Union likely to do? How would the United States behave? Would Jordan open a third front? Would the Arab armies receive additional reinforcements? What were we capable of doing, and what needed to be done, in the north and the south? These were the components of my internal life day and night, without a moment's respite. With all the anxiety and the sorrow, I searched for answers to operational and political questions, hour by hour, day by day.

Basically, as the situation appeared to me, we were faced by three kinds of problems. The first was technical: the latest sophisticated weapons, particularly the anti-aircraft and anti-tank missiles which the Russians had lavishly supplied to the Arabs and our need to find appropriate methods of warfare to overcome them. The second concerned our future relations with the neighboring Arab states. We had to determine the next military moves with a forward look at our postwar relations with Egypt, Jordan, and Syria. Should we or should we not aim at capturing additional territory in Egypt and Syria? The third type of problem related to the attitude of the Great Powers. Was there anything we could do to prevent a deepening of Soviet involvement? Might not the advance of our northern forces and the consequent threat to Damascus bring in its wake the active participation of Soviet troops? And how could we ensure the support of the United States—the supply of arms and, above all, help in neutralizing Soviet military intervention against us.

The principal difference between this war and its predecessors lay in Arab strength. It was much greater and more powerful than anything the Arabs had shown in the past. This increased our casualties and demanded the most determined combat effort from our men. The strength of the Arab armies in men and weapons in the Yom Kippur War was roughly three times what it had been in the Six Day War: 1,000,000 troops against their earlier 300,000; more than 5,000 tanks as compared with 1,700; more than 1,000 planes to 350; and 4,800 field guns as against 1,350 in 1967.

The rise in quantity had been accompanied by a rise in quality. The technological standard of their weapons and equipment had undergone a radical improvement. Apart from their new anti-aircraft missile systems and anti-tank weaponry, they now had the new Soviet T-62 tank, which replaced the old T-34, and a new Russian armored fighting vehicle of quality, the BMD armored personnel carrier. Arab troops equipped with personal missiles and trained to use them in cooperation with the attacking armor were also effective.

There is no doubt that after the Arab defeat in 1967, the Soviet military advisers and experts had learned their lesson and had worked hard to find the formula for strengthening the weak points that had been exposed in the Arab forces. They decided first of all to exploit the quantitative advantage the Arabs had over us. Henceforth, the Arab armies would be even larger and have even more tanks and guns at their disposition. Since the Arab pilots were outmatched by our fliers, the Russians decided to intensify the Arab ground anti-aircraft system in order to deal with our Air Force. This would keep our aircraft out of the skies above the battlefield.

The Soviets also supplied Egypt and Syria with two types of surface-to-surface missiles with conventional warheads: the Frog, with a range of 50 miles and an explosive warhead of 1,100 pounds, and the Scud, with a range of 200–250 miles and a 2,000-pound warhead. In addition, the Arabs received the Russian Kelt, an air-to-surface missile with a 125-mile range and a warhead of 1,100 pounds. These missiles were to be used in place of Arab bombers. In none of the wars had Arab pilots succeeded in overcoming Israeli fighter aircraft and penetrating deep into Israel. With the Soviet missiles operated from the northern and southern fronts, the Arabs could now hit our main towns and industrial centers.

In the absence of immediate technological solutions to the problems posed by these new weapons systems, the answer had to be found in the sphere of battle tactics, the proper direction of the moves of warfare. The key lay with the fighting man, not with an instrument; in human daring and cunning, not in the automatic technology of electronics versus electronics. If, for example, the confrontation were only between aircraft and surface-to-air missiles, the missiles would win. But if the war was so directed that the Air Force was given assignments it was able to carry out, and the armor, artillery, and infantry were used wisely and their qualities fully exploited— skillful use of terrain, deep penetration by the tanks, concentration of forces, and battle initiative—it was possible to overcome both the quantitative advantage and the sophisticated technology which the Egyptians and Syrians currently enjoyed.

In the provisional balance sheet of the first week of war, comparatively few surface-to-surface missiles were fired, and they had no impact on the progress of the war. Several Frog missiles were fired from Syria at the air base of Ramat David and the development town of Kiryat Shmonah in the north. Their effects were poor. Kelt missiles fired from Egyptian Tupolov-16 aircraft were aimed at Tel Aviv and various military targets in Sinai, among them Sharm el-Sheikh. During the first week Scud missiles had not been fired at all (though the Egyptians probably fired one or two Scuds on the area of the Canal bridges on October 22, literally a few moments before the first cease-fire).

The anti-tank weapon of the Arab troops, the RPG rockets, and particularly the Sagger missiles were effective, and at the start of the war we suffered heavy casualties, notably on the southern front. But after a time our soldiers learned how to deal with them. The Arab infantrymen who launched them were vulnerable and revealed themselves through the trail of the missile. The range of these weapons is limited: the RPG up to 325 yards and the Sagger about two miles. They are weapons we had to learn to live with and to hit and neutralize. They operate at the range of other forms of fire power possessed by tanks, and the answer to them is to be found in wise and skillful combat. They do not constitute a revolution, but rather an additional hazard on the battlefield, calling for greater care in the operation of armor. Tanks must resort to sniping and function less like galloping cavalry.

The same, unfortunately, is not true of the SAM batteries. I do not think an Air Force can overcome them completely, and aircraft therefore cannot give close and effective support to ground forces in an area covered by such anti-aircraft missiles. There are, of course, exceptional cases and circumstances, but basically that is a reality one must accept. As a matter of fact, I suspected this as far back as August 1970 at the end of what we call Egypt's War of Attrition, when two of our Phantoms were hit but not destroyed over Abu Suweir, just northwest of the Great Bitter Lake, by Egyptian missiles. Three years had passed since then, but in the contest between planes and missiles, the planes did not come off best. This does not mean that the value of the Air Force has diminished. But it demands changes in methods of operation and in the determination of its function and its role in a campaign.

Six years before, in the Six Day War, the Israeli Air Force had destroyed the bulk of the Egyptian Air Force at the beginning of the war, rendered the Egyptian and Syrian airfields inoperable, and knocked out all the Egyptian anti-aircraft batteries in Sinai. This time, our Air Force was much more restricted in its activities. At this interim stocktaking stage, three principal features of the air record were apparent.

• The Israeli Air Force commanded absolute air mastery and thereby not only prevented enemy bombing of military and civilian targets in Israel, but also enabled all our reinforcement and supply convoys to stream to the fronts without interference. Only those who saw the long lines of vehicles snaking their way undisturbed across the open expanses of Sinai can appreciate this tremendous achievement.

• Apart from Port Said, our Air Force did not clear the area on any front from its protective coverage of enemy anti-aircraft missiles. Even when on one day, October 7, it appeared that our warplanes had neutralized 29 out of 32 missile batteries on the Golan—and paid for it with the loss of several planes—it transpired the next day that all, or almost all, the batteries were back in action.

• The alternatives we faced were either to forgo close air support for ground forces or to pay a heavy price for it. And, indeed, most of the planes we lost in that first week were hit by missiles fired when our aircraft were flying close-support missions.

The tank battles in the first week differed in the north and the south. Even though there are objective basic differences between the two fronts—in the south, desert, the Suez Canal, and a ninety-five-mile front; in the north, a very much shorter front, rocky terrain, and hills that enable observation and command of an area—there is still room for comparison. The difference in the results of the war in the north and south so far lay mainly in three fields:

• In the north, except for the Mount Hermon position, the Syrians were being pushed back from all our territory, whereas in the south the Egyptians occupied the east bank of the Canal.

• The Syrians lost about 900 tanks, while the Egyptians up to then had lost only some 300.

• All except one of our front-line strongholds in the south fell, whereas in the north, this was true only of Mount Hermon.

The principal combat factor was that in the north, most of the fighting took place with Syrian tanks on the attack and on the move, while our tanks were deployed in defensive positions. Thus, not only were conditions favorable for our armor to hit the Syrian tanks, but the Syrian Sagger anti-tank missiles had no special influence on the outcome of the battle.

This was not the case in the south. In the first two days, our tanks were on the attack, hurrying toward the Canal, while the Egyptians— primarily infantry equipped with anti-tank missiles—were in defensive emplacements. And indeed our tank losses in the south were caused by the defensive Egyptian deployment. When the Egyptians crossed the Canal, they first advanced their anti-tank system and their armored forces were deployed under its protective shelter. The Egyptians took only a short step and defended it with anti-aircraft umbrellas and strong anti-tank belts, whereas in the north the Syrian armored forces stormed ahead with the aim of conquering the whole of the Golan Heights.

To my regret, I cannot credit the achievement of the Egyptians and the failures of the Syrians solely to the differences in the character of the fronts and the way their respective armies fought. The fact is that in the north our forces conducted the war well, and in the south they did not. In the few hours available between the warning and the outbreak of war, what should have been done on the southern front was not done. The tanks were not deployed in their assigned positions, and their attacks on the Egyptian units that had crossed the Canal were neither organized nor purposeful. This was the case before the arrival of the reserves, and this was so even when the three divisions under Bren, Arik, and Albert had to carry out their counter-attack on October 8, two days after the outbreak of war.

As for the fighting standard of the Arab soldiers, I can sum it up in one sentence: they did not run away. In the past, flight was a common characteristic of the Arab armies. Not all. Not immediately. But as far as one can generalize, it can be said that when they were hit and badly mauled and their front was broken wide open, they would raise their hands—and their heels. Not this time. Now, in the Yom Kippur War, even when they suffered heavy casualties and recognized that the battle was lost, they did not run, they withdrew. Furthermore, the standard of combat of the Arab soldier had improved. There were units that fought to the bitter end and others that showed good command and skillful operation of the latest technological devices at their disposal. I suspected, therefore, that this time, even though we would gain the upper hand, there would be no general collapse of the Arab forces.

One had also to consider the complex relations between Israel and the United States—the complexity, I might add, being more on the side of the United States than on ours. The American government has helped us a great deal, with the supply of arms, economic assistance, and political support. I hate to think what our situation would have been if the United States had withheld its aid, or what we would do if Washington were to turn its back on Israel one of these days.

Three areas of the American government are involved in decisions that directly concern us—the presidency, the State Department, and the Pentagon. This may suggest room for maneuver, but it does not ease or shorten the process of handling our affairs. When war broke out on Yom Kippur, Washington started asking questions. Who started the war? Was it serious? Perhaps the Israelis were making a fuss over nothing? At the same time, they assumed—and our Washington representatives, on orders from Israel, strengthened this assumption—that we would defeat the Arab armies within a few days.

In this situation, the Americans reacted coolly to our urgent demands for large and speedy supplies of weapons. Even the State Department, which understood our needs, said we could receive immediately only a limited quantity of ammunition and refused to give us additional aircraft as long as the battles continued. We, on our part, could not soften our request for arms. We needed planes, tanks, anti-tank weapons, Hawk anti-aircraft batteries, helicopters, self-propelled guns, and ammunition of various types.

Our highest priorities were ammunition and aircraft. We kept sending urgent personal cables with detailed and painful explanations of our vital and immediate need for Phantom planes. Only on Tuesday, October 9, three days after the war began, did we get a positive response: we would receive two Phantoms, and even these would not be extra but merely part of our normal arms quota! The reluctance to give us anything, even a single screw, arose from Washington's information that Israel had started the war and the formidable oil lobby's demand that Israel should not be supported against the Arabs. We were told that only if and when our situation worsened would we be able to get additional arms. As for tanks, there was no point even in trying to break the ice. In any case, making tanks available would take many weeks, so they would not arrive in time to be used in the war.

On Wednesday, the following day, we were informed that the president had approved most of the electronic equipment we had requested, as well as additional planes. He had also decided on a policy of replacement, namely, whatever we lost in battle would be restored.

It was explained to us privately that many obstacles had to be over-come before this decision was reached and that our friends hoped that various senators would now cease their criticism.

In addition to the difficulties in securing the arms, there was also the problem of how they were to reach us. The Arabs had no such problem. During that very night and morning, October 9 and 10, more than twenty huge Soviet Antonov transport planes landed on Syrian airfields from Russia. The U.S. government was well aware that the Soviet Union had begun massive airlifts of arms to the Arab states. I thought that America would regard this Russian act with real concern and, in response, would decide to speed up and strengthen their arms supplies to us. And, indeed, starting on October 14, the United States began operating a military airlift. It continued for one month, up to November 14. This was a most impressive sup-ply lift, and it solved the ammunition problem.

As for weapons, I suspected that the difficulty sprang not from transport but from American policy. In the end, we did not even receive full replacement for our losses. But the greatest gap remained between our requests and the measure in which they were granted. We got less than half the number of Phantoms we asked for, only about one-fifth of the tanks, and not a single half-track. We wanted a few score field guns and we were given about a third of them; of the TOW anti-tank missile, we received about a quarter of our request.

We were troubled by the shortage of weapons, but we were no less disturbed by our isolation. Could we complain about the Nixon ad-ministration? It was far better to us than the government of Eisen-hower had been during the Sinai Campaign, and better, too, than the administrations of Kennedy and Truman. President Truman was without doubt a sincere friend and supporter of the State of Israel, but he had been unwilling to help us with arms in 1948, even during our grimmest hours when we were fighting for our independence and our very survival. And now, in 1973, was there any other country that was prepared to help Israel with military supplies, even in lesser measure than the United States? Even West Germany, headed by Chancellor Willy Brandt, a socialist and an old friend of our prime minister, put obstacles in the way of using German ports to dispatch weapons to Israel from American military bases in Germany. Great Britain informed us that she was holding up the dispatch of tank ammunition we had already bought. And not a single country in Europe was willing to allow even a transit landing of American planes bringing arms to Israel. During one of my talks with Dr. Kissinger, though I happened to remark that the United States was the only country that was ready to stand by us, my silent reflection was that the United States would really rather support the Arabs.

On the supply of aircraft, our only source would continue to be the United States. For additional tanks, we had two other sources. One was the rehabilitation of our own tanks which had been knocked out in areas under our control. The second was the repairable Soviet armor left behind when the Arab armies retreated. It seemed to me that the replacements we would obtain in this way from the Russians would be much greater than the number of tanks we received from the United States.

At noon on October 10, I visited Shayke (Maj. Gen. Yeshayahu Gavish), who was the commander of southern Sinai and responsible for the area south of the main Sinai theater, which came under Southern Command. Also present with me was the commander of the Air Force. At 2:30 P.M. I called in at Southern Command headquarters. At both posts, after hearing the latest situation reports, I concentrated on two subjects: the possibility that the Egyptians would try to advance southward down the eastern shore of the Gulf of Suez; and the prospect that we would cross the Canal westward.

The first topographic site after Ras Sudar suitable for blocking such an advance was located just north of Abu Rudeis. This is where the mountains of central Sinai almost touch the shore, and this was the obvious place to prepare a defense line, to mine, dig an anti-tank trench, and establish fortified positions for the infantry. But there was to be no withdrawal from our present positions. For as long as we could manage, the Egyptians were to be prevented from making any advance at all, even though the area where our units were currently deployed is flat, with no ground features to help bar the enemy.

On the previous night, a mechanized Egyptian brigade from the 6th Division tried to break through to the south, but before they had even reached Iyun-Mussa, some ten miles south of the city of Suez, they were engaged by one of our paratroop units supported by about twenty tanks and an Air Force flight. The enemy brigade suffered heavy casualties and was forced to withdraw, leaving behind a convoy of more than a hundred shattered and burning tanks, half-tracks, and trucks. Our Air Force could operate freely in this area since it was beyond the range of Egyptian anti-aircraft missile batteries established on the west bank of the Canal. Most of the casualties to the Egyptian formation were inflicted by the Air Force.

After this Egyptian failure and after hearing an appreciation of the situation in their various commands by Shayke Gavish (southern Sinai) and Chaim Bar-Lev (Southern Command), I became increasingly convinced that the Egyptians would not succeed in advancing southward. The paratroopers, the armor, and above all the Air Force would prevent this from happening. And as long as the Egyptians failed to move their SAM batteries eastward, the eastern shore of the Gulf of Suez would be under the control of our Air Force.

This part of Sinai, stretching from the Suez Canal to Sharm el-Sheikh, had been subject to many raids and bombing attacks by the Egyptians, but the night before was the first time they had tried to capture it. Five minutes after the war began on the southern front, Egyptian aircraft bombed military installations in the area and the oil tanks at Abu Rudeis, where three tank farms had gone up in flames and the bombing raids killed seven of our soldiers and wounded seven others. But most of the Egyptian activity in this area had been commando raids. The Egyptians had sent in by boat and helicopter between 700 and 800 men in three commando battalions to the areas of Ras Sudar, Abu Zneima, and Abu Rudeis. Though many of the commandos were still at large, this operation had failed completely. On the second day of the war, our Air Force had shot down eight helicopters in the area of Ras Sudar. During a chase by our troops on October 8, 10 of the enemy commandos were killed and 40 were captured. On the day before, October 9, our aircraft had brought down one helicopter and sunk two missile boats as they approached the shore.

If the surviving Egyptian commandos wanted to hide out, they could do so for quite a time, for southern Sinai is a mountainous region cut by deep wadis that wind between Nubian sandstone rocks and granite cliffs, and there are springs in some of the wadis. But if they attempted to fight, they would be wiped out. Our military installations are concentrated in this southern triangle bounded by the Gulf of Suez in the west and the Gulf of Aqaba in the east. It is a closed and fortified region, and any attempt to penetrate it would be fraught with difficulty. Ever since the Sinai Campaign of 1956, we had regarded Sharm el-Sheikh, at its southern extremity, as the commanding position safeguarding freedom of navigation through the Gulf of Aqaba. When we captured Sharm again in the 1967 war, we built it up and prepared it for defense. I was convinced that the Egyptians could not seize Sharm, and I hoped that the government of Israel would never give it up.

There were other targets on or close to the shore of the Gulf of

Suez which could attract enemy attempts at sabotage or capture. In ancient times one of them would have been Serabit el-Khadem near the turquoise quarries, Sinai's treasure of antiquity. Today's treasure is oil, and a likely target was Abu Rudeis, with its wells. They could be set on fire by bombing and long-range shelling, which is indeed what the Egyptians did immediately upon the outbreak of war and before our forces reached the place. Now, a week into the war, the presence of an Israeli paratroop brigade with armored support had completely changed the situation. The question now, I thought, was not whether the Egyptians would manage to sabotage or seize our installations in southern Sinai, but how many of their remaining commandos would avoid death or capture at our hands.

My younger son, Assaf, was serving as a heavy mortarman with the paratroop unit in this area, and he told me a little about an engagement with the enemy force and the pursuit of the commandos. He also told me something about his officers. His battalion commander, a reservist, was an active member of a right-wing political party known for its uncompromising stand against the demands of the Arab states. The deputy commander was an extreme left-winger who favored maximum territorial concessions to the Arabs. Despite the political gulf between them, they were very close, and both were loved and admired by their men. The right-wing commander was cool and relaxed about the Egyptian commandos. There was no point in hunting down every last one of them. If some were still at large and hiding out, afraid to emerge, who cared? "And if any do come out and attempt sabotage," he said, "well, we'll get them." It was his dovish deputy who was forever badgering him to let the unit scour the wadis day and night. "We must go after them," he kept urging, "and teach them a lesson!"

In Southern Command, too, the question was no longer how to hold back the Egyptians but primarily "What next?" Both at Southern Command and southern Sinai headquarters, I stressed the importance, as I saw it, of capturing Egyptian territory west of the Canal or the Gulf of Suez. We should examine all the possibilities, from Port Said in the north down to Jebel Ataka in the south. The cease-fire was likely to be imposed any moment, and on no account should we be caught in an unfavorable position. On the northern front we had now pushed back the Syrians beyond the 1967 lines and inflicted very heavy damage and casualties. But on the southern front, the Egyptians had captured a strip along the east bank of the Canal, and if we could not drive them out at once, we should try to seize part of their territory west of the Canal. We would then have something with which to bargain, or at least even up the score. Bar-Lev of Southern Command said he agreed with the political considerations which called for the conquest of territory west of the waterline, but at the moment Southern Command was unable to do this. I replied that I thought it would be possible to transfer units from Northern to Southern Command, and Bar-Lev agreed that we should plan an action which would give us a hold west of the 1967 lines. Various places were mentioned. I said that the southern end of the Gulf of Suez did not seem feasible to me, as we would then be dependent on seaborne supplies. What we had to do was capture a piece of territory that could be linked with our rear by a land bridge.

At all events, the guideline of our next step was clear to me. Either in the Golan Heights or in Sinai we had to go over to the attack. And indeed, after midnight, at a meeting with the prime minister, it was resolved that our forces would attack on the Syrian front with the objective of advancing as far as possible in the direction of Damascus. There was no intention of capturing Damascus or even of bombing it. It was our aim to hit the Syrians another hard blow, military and political, so that they would lose forces as well as territory beyond the 1967 lines. They would then come to realize that by launching war upon us, not only would they not gain the Golan Heights or defeat the Israeli army, but their own armies would be routed and their capital, Damascus, endangered. If our military action succeeded, it would also compensate somewhat for our early losses on the Egyptian front.

The attack was to start at eleven in the morning, October 11, and would be preceded by an air strike on SAM batteries and airfields with the aim of clearing the skies. The Air Force would then be able to give close support to the ground units.

The discussion at the Prime Minister's Office was the third that evening on the same subject. Before that I had had a meeting with the chief of staff, and this had been followed by consultations between the chief of staff and the General Staff without me. At the meeting with the prime minister, there were present, at her invitation, two other ministers. The General Staff was represented by the chief of staff; his deputy, Maj. Gen. Tal; the head of Intelligence; and the commander of the Air Force.

These three meetings were not only lengthy—more than six hours, almost without a break—but also comprehensive and basic. We had reached the stage where the initiative could in large measure be in our hands, and we had to know what we wanted to achieve in this war. What was to be done, and how, on each of the two fronts? What if a Security Council resolution called for a cease-fire? How did we envisage the possibility of Jordanian and Iraqi intervention in the war, and were we able to prevent it? Were we capable of a long military haul, and if so for how long? The principal immediate question was in what were we to invest our supreme effort? Was there a chance to deliver a knockout blow to one of our foes?

The Syrian army was now in grave straits. It had lost two-thirds of its attacking force, and its crack formation, the 1st Division, had mutinied. The troops had started running away and the divisional commander had asked for and received artillery fire on his own forces to stop them from jumping out of their tanks and escaping. These methods had had their effect, but they illustrated the magnitude of the debacle the Syrian army had suffered.

The sand in the political clock was also running out. Tension was growing between the United States and Russia, perhaps because both had started to send considerable military aid to the belligerents, and there was now "powerful pressure," according to our representative in Washington, for an unconditional cease-fire. The Soviet Union had approached President Nixon with this suggestion, and the United States, in its anxiety to avoid deterioration in her relations with Russia, was likely to respond positively. This would mean victory for the Arabs, freezing some of the gains of their aggression. We needed another few days to turn the situation on the fronts in our favor. We hoped we would get them. But we had to allow for the possibility that a cease-fire might be reached quickly, now that the Arabs had started to lose. We had to weigh carefully how to use our efforts to ensure the best results by the time the fighting was stopped.

As to how Jordan would behave, she might be wary of entering the war if she saw that Syria was being heavily pounded. But it appeared almost certain that she would take the opposite course. It seemed most unlikely that the Jordanian force which had been assigned to the Syrian front would stand aside when we attacked and began approaching Damascus. I had repeatedly expressed the view that if we attacked in the direction of Damascus, Jordan would join in the war by employing her forces on the Syrian front, rather than opening up a front of her own. From our point of view, this was the lesser of two evils. However, our two principal questions were what could our forces achieve on the Syrian front and what were our plans on the Egyptian front?

On the morning of October 10, while I toured the southern front, the chief of staff was with Northern Command, and he returned from there somewhat depressed. The two divisions under Dan and Raful had tried to advance and failed. The Syrian defense line was as strong as it had been before the war. The enemy attack units that had crossed this line to spearhead their invasion had been badly mauled and driven back by our forces. However, the Syrian infantry brigades had remained in their defense positions, together with their attached tank units. They had not taken part in the fighting, had not advanced, and remained intact. Thus, according to the chief of staff, the Syrian defense line, which had been fortified and strengthened throughout the six years since the Six Day War, not only retained its former power but had now been reinforced by the remnants of the attacking units which had engaged us and withdrawn.

Formally, we had three armored divisions on the northern front, but in fact they were very much below strength. It was possible that during the night more of our damaged tanks would be repaired. Our troops, though, were very tired. Whenever a unit halted, the men fell asleep and had to be awakened to hear the order to move.

We also had to take into account our own defense line in the north. That, too, had been established after the 1967 war, and from the point of view of topography and fortifications it was the most effective defense line in the region. If we advanced a further 5 or 10 miles by the time the fighting ceased, we would be holding a new line which was neither fortified nor based on natural salients.

Despite these negative factors, the prevailing view at the meeting with the prime minister was the need to strike a crippling blow against the Syrian army. It would be possible thereafter to stabilize a cease-fire on the northern front.

The one dissenting view came from the deputy chief of staff. Maj. Gen. Tal argued that the Egyptian front represented an immediate military danger, which was not true of the Syrian front. The Syrians were beaten, worn out, and incapable of going over to a renewed attack, whereas the Egyptians still had this capability. We should therefore concentrate our immediate activities on the Egyptian front and freeze the Syrian one. True, we would not then be able to move forces from front to front. But even with the armed strength we had now in the south, by wise tactical moves it was possible to deliver a shattering blow to the Egyptian army and produce a revolutionary turn in the war.

I was more optimistic than the others about the southern front. I said that I did not think the Egyptians would succeed in advancing either southward or eastward. We had to prepare our forces for attack with the aim of capturing territory west of the Canal, and it was my judgment that we could do this. At all events, the immediate stage called for an attack on the northern front. In the meantime, I felt we should do whatever we could to prevent an immediate cease-fire decision. The war should not be stopped at the present military lines.

33

VICTORY

AT 11 A.M. on October 11, as planned, and preceded by air strikes, our ground forces in the Golan opened their attack against the Syrian armies—which had now been joined by armored formations from Iraq, Jordan, and Morocco. Our troops began advancing, continued to battle their way forward the whole of the next day and part of the day that followed, and spent the rest of October 13 improving their positions. Except for the action on Mount Hermon's military posts, which we would capture almost at the last moment a week and a half later, this ended our operations on the Syrian front and established a new defense line. The northern section of this line was ten miles closer to Damascus than the previous one, the 1967 cease-fire line which had lasted until the Syrian invasion on Yom Kippur. The southern section of the defense line remained unchanged.

During the first two days, when the general attack was in full swing, I kept visiting the forward command posts of divisional commanders Raful Eitan and Dan Laner. I urged upon them the importance of getting as close as possible to Damascus. We had no intention of capturing it, or bombing it—as long as the Syrians refrained from bombing our cities. But it was most desirable that Damascus should be within our artillery range, so that we could hit military targets in the area and its citizens would have a tangible feeling of their true military situation. This would help us achieve our conditions if a cease-fire were reached. At all events, it would demonstrate the Syrians' defeat: they had launched a surprise attack with the object of capturing the Golan Heights and instead the Israeli army stood poised at the gates of Damascus.

Actually, since we did not propose to conquer Damascus, we could be satisfied with the front line we had already gained, particularly since it was suitable for defense against counter-attacks. Moreover, the Russians had harshened their tone as the Syrians kept retreating, and we had to be very careful to prevent the bear from getting out of the forest. We had received reliable information that the Soviet Union was mobilizing three airborne formations to fly to the aid of the Arabs.

At all events, we now had to concentrate on the Egyptian front, and to do this we would be transferring forces from the north to the Canal Zone. We would make this transfer of forces even though our Intelligence Branch reported that there were still nine hundred Syrian tanks—including the reinforcements from Iraq, Morocco, and Jordan—in the area between our front line and Damascus.

On my visits to the north, while sitting in the advance command posts above the front line, I could not help being affected by the dismal landscape, natural and human. The part of Syria stretching northward from Kuneitra, except for the villages at the foot of the Hermon range, was a bare expanse of black basalt rocks, unmarked by tree or bush. In the distance I could see miserable dust-laden hamlets, their houses scrambled together with black unhewn stone. The Sinai desert with its sand dunes and occasional date palms was positively lively in comparison with the melancholy landscape of this part of the Golan. And now, the scene was studded with burned-out tanks, shattered vehicles, and smoking ammunition trucks, while along the side tracks streamed columns of fleeing villagers, their donkeys laden with bedding, their wives carrying large bundles on their heads and infants in their arms. In the fields, between the exploding shells, frightened old men and children led their wretched flocks. War, war, pointless war. This was what the Syrians had gained from their blow against us on Yom Kippur—and brought us reluctantly a few miles closer to Damascus.

After the successful conclusion of our general counter-attack on the northern front on October 13, the center of military gravity shifted to the south. With Egyptian troops on the east bank, it was

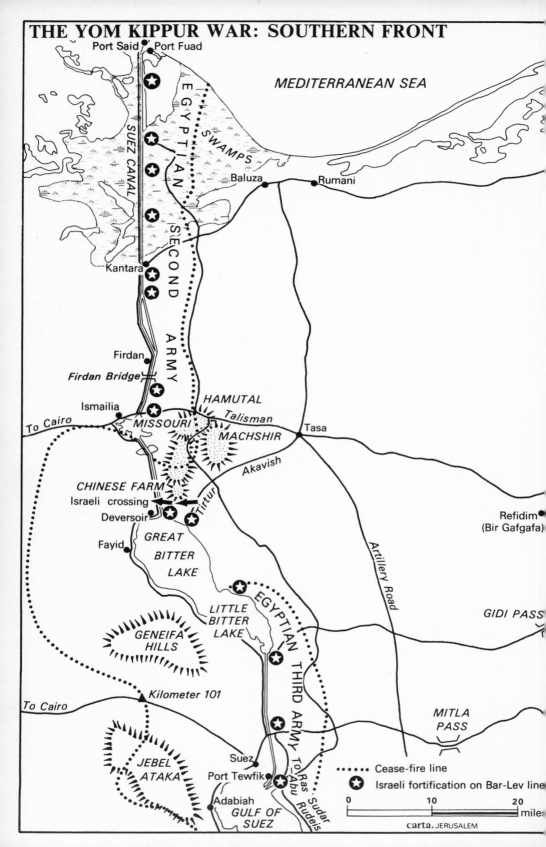

THE YOM KIPPUR WAR: SOUTHERN FRONT

Port Said · Port Fuad

MEDITERRANEAN SEA

EGYPTIAN SWAMPS

Suez Canal

Baluza · Rumani

EGYPTIAN SECOND ARMY

Kantara

Firdan
Firdan Bridge

Ismailia
MISSOURI
To Cairo

HAMUTAL
Talisman
MACHSHIR

Tasa

Akavish

CHINESE FARM
Israeli crossing
Deversoir
Tirtur

Refidim
(Bir Gafgafa)

GREAT BITTER LAKE

Fayid

Artillery Road

LITTLE BITTER LAKE

EGYPTIAN THIRD ARMY

GIDI PASS

GENEIFA HILLS

To Cairo
▲ *Kilometer 101*

MITLA PASS

JEBEL ATAKA

Suez
Port Tewfik

Adabiah
GULF OF SUEZ

To Ras Sudar · To Abu Rudeis

······· Cease-fire line
⭐ Israeli fortification on Bar-Lev line

0   10   20
miles

carta, JERUSALEM

essential to change the situation on the Canal front. We had to ensure that Egypt would not emerge with profit from having made
war on us. And we had to demonstrate that the advantage lay with
our army.

How would we go about it? After a thorough review, we decided
on a Canal crossing and establishing ourselves on the west bank of
the Canal, on the soil of Egypt proper, astride the road to Cairo, and
in the rear of Egypt's armies on the east bank. However, since we
had to expect that the Egyptians would mount a massive attack
against us on the east bank, we considered it wiser to wait a few days,
engage them on this bank first, and cross the Canal later. Combat
conditions would be far more advantageous for us on the east bank.
And, indeed, on October 13 and 14 the Egyptians did attack—and
lost some two hundred tanks.

On October 14, Southern Command issued the warning order for
the crossing. It was set for 7 P.M. on the following night. The crossing
site would be Deversoir, just north of the Great Bitter Lake. Arik's
and Bren's divisions would cross, and two divisions would contain
the enemy on the east bank. Arik's division would secure a corridor
two-and-a-half miles wide by capturing an important road as well
as a stretch of territory known as the Chinese Farm. A paratroop
brigade with armor support under the command of Brig. Gen. Danny
Matt would cross and secure a bridgehead on the west bank. By
morning, two bridges were to be laid. Arik's division would be the
first to cross, clear the area, and protect the bridgeheads on both
banks of the Canal, and then Bren's division would pass through
them and advance on the west bank southward toward the Gulf of
Suez and westward.

With the crossing plan finally decided upon, I was greatly relieved.
I thought it was the correct military move, and though I was aware
of the immense difficulties and hazards, I had complete faith in Arik
that it would be successfully accomplished.

I have known Arik Sharon for twenty-five years, and in military
actions we have marched a long road together. When I was GOC
Northern Command in 1952, he was the command Intelligence officer.
I remember that as soon as I took over command, an order was received from the General Staff to exploit any opportunity to take a
few Jordanian soldiers prisoner, as Jordan was holding some of our
troops and refused to release them. The sun had hardly set on that
day when Arik appeared with several Arab Legionaries. He had
seized them from the Sheikh Hussein Bridge in the Jordan Valley. I've
forgotten all the details—it was long ago—but two I cannot forget:

the reprimand I received from the then chief of staff, General Yigael Yadin, on the illegal manner in which the prisoners had been taken, and how impressed I was with Arik. Prime Minister Ben-Gurion, too, was very tolerant of him, and later, when I became chief of staff, he would respond to all my complaints against Arik—and they were not a few—with "Yes, but . . ."

Ben-Gurion had a specially soft spot for three army generals, Chaim Laskov, Assaf Simhoni, and Arik. He did not just like them. He positively adored them. The three of them were not at all alike. But they had two things in common. All were excellent soldiers; and all—and this I think was the principal reason for Ben-Gurion's special regard for them—embodied the character of the Israeli Jew of his dream: a man of integrity, a daring fighter with confidence in himself, who was unapologetic about his Jewishness, at home in the terrain, knew the Arabs, and knew his profession. Ben-Gurion was impatient with petty arguments and he hated circumlocution. He had no heart for Talmudic disputation, though he had enormous respect for Talmudic scholarship. He despised what two thousand years of Diaspora persecution had done to us. His great love was the nation of Israel of the First Temple period (tenth to sixth century B.C.), the nation living on its own soil, working the land and fighting for its defense, independent, speaking its own language, and creating its own culture. Chaim, Assaf, and Arik were, in his eyes, that kind of Israeli.

I do not know a better field commander than Arik. This is not to say that I never had cause to criticize him. When I appointed him commander of the special paratroop unit, Force 101, I told him that it was not enough to know how to beat the Arabs; one must also know how to live with the Jews. We also had our quarrels. But even when I feel like "murdering" him, at least I know he is somebody worth "murdering."

The Canal crossing would be our third serious confrontation in the war with the Egyptian forces. In the first, when Egypt launched its attack, our units were not deployed in their assigned positions. In the second, on October 8, when we counter-attacked, the operation was not planned and not conducted as it should have been. This time, there was no reason why Bar-Lev, Arik, and Bren should not carry out the action in exemplary fashion. The Egyptians had some 700 tanks on the west bank and 650 on the east bank. In the air, Egypt had some 500 warplanes and the Syrians 250. These figures included 130 aircraft which Egypt and Syria had received as military aid from other Arab states. The balance was heavily weighted on the side of the Arabs, but compared to the balance of forces in the first few days of the war, it was not bad.

I flew south during the day of October 15 to visit units and to be on hand for the start of the battles for the crossing, which were set for 7 P.M. I was at Southern Command headquarters at that hour, as was the chief of staff, when Arik opened his assault to break through the Egyptian lines and capture Deversoir. There had been preparatory aerial bombing and artillery shelling of the crossing area. After the armor reached the Canal, Danny Matt's paratroopers would cross on rubber rafts. Immediately thereafter, tanks would be moved across on rafts. During the night, bridging equipment would arrive. If all went well, two bridges would be in place toward morning.

An hour and a half after the start, I called Arik on the telephone and asked him to send a jeep to take me to him, but he said that the access road was blocked. We agreed that as soon as it was possible for me to get to him, he would arrange it. Arik did not ring off before describing to me the wondrous sight he was beholding at that very moment—moving tanks silhouetted against the brilliant flashes of shells exploding in giant fireworks across the surface of the Great Bitter Lake. I knew Arik, and I knew that his attempt to describe what was happening at the edge of the lake, as though it were a glorious sunset on Mount Carmel, was an effort to hide his tension. However, the point of his remarks was that at last he was once more at the waterline of the Canal, from which we had been pushed back only a week or so earlier. This time we would break through from this line and advance.

Toward midnight came good news and bad news. The good news —Arik reported that he had captured the section of the Canal line prescribed for the crossing. The bad news—the road leading to it was blocked and the bridging equipment could not yet be brought to the water's edge. There had also been a technical mishap with the bridging equipment that would take at least an hour to repair.

The chief of staff, Bar-Lev, and I shared the view that we should proceed with the crossing even if the bridges were delayed. At 1:20 A.M. on October 16, came the signal: "Danny Matt's force on the water." And a few minutes later: "Paratroopers on the west bank of Canal." I cannot claim that my heart did not beat faster.

At 6:15 A.M. the prime minister telephoned. I had wished to speak to her even earlier, but I had pity on her—perhaps she could have snatched a few hours' sleep. I started with the bad news: we had not yet established the bridges. The road was blocked by Egyptian units holding the northern sector of the east bank who had advanced southward, reached the road, and set up a blocking wedge to cut off our bridgehead. We hoped to drive them off, bring the bridges forward to the water, and erect them during the course of the day. But our paratroops were on the west bank of the Canal, and we could rely on Danny Matt. We had no intention of bringing him back, even if the bridges were delayed. The prime minister had been much afraid that the Egyptians would cut off the vanguard force, and there had been much talk of this danger at the Cabinet meetings.

By dawn there were already several rafts in the water and they began ferrying tanks across to the west bank, a few at a time. As against this, it became evident that the Egyptian blocking of the access road was serious. At 8:30 A.M. the chief of staff returned to Tel Aviv. I decided to stay in the south. Since I could not get to the bridgehead, I went to Bren and was pleased to find him looking his old self. I remembered how he had appeared on the night of the unsuccessful counter-attack. This time he was again the confident Bren, quiet, shaven, with the occasional shy smile.

He had three brigades under his command, and if the bridges had been in position during the previous night, as planned, they would already have crossed. But since the road was blocked, they were given the task of opening another route which would enable the bridging equipment to be advanced to the Canal. At this stage, then, three simultaneous battles were in progress. Danny Matt's paratroop battalion together with twenty-eight tanks from Arik's force were fighting on the other side of the Canal, capturing, broadening, and securing the western bridgehead. They were doing relatively well. Other units of Arik's division were battling desperately on the water-line, on the east bank of the Canal. This was the heaviest and most difficult part of the crossing. The Egyptians had not yet understood what our forces were doing on the *west* bank of the Canal. They thought it was just a raid. But they were quite clear about what was happening on the east bank: the Israelis were trying to get them out, had recaptured key strongholds in the early evening, and were now trying to advance along the Canal and open a corridor to the bridge-head in order to pour through additional forces. The Egyptians had to stop this at all cost. And so they had rushed additional units to the area and were fighting hard.

The third battle was being waged by Bren. He put pressure in three directions—thrusting north, to wipe out the Egyptian Second Army's barrier on the Canal access road; south, to prevent the Egyptian Third Army from sending reinforcements to the crossing area; and west, to the Chinese Farm, in order to widen the corridor to the bridgehead and link up with Arik's forces. The battle on this Canal front flared into furious intensity, with heavy fire and lots of bloodshed; a stubborn battle, professional, bitter, cruel. The Egyptians were not the wavering Arab troops of seven years before, and the Israeli forces of Southern Command were not the hastily assembled, insufficiently prepared units rushed into attack of seven days before.

Bren's advance headquarters—two half-tracks and a few jeeps—was located on a sandhill overlooking the Canal area about seven miles away. When I got there, the stretch of ground in front of us was covered with mist. But by the time Natke and Gabi had deployed their brigades, the mist lifted and we could see everything, even without field glasses. The blocked road was laden with Israeli vehicles and they were under incessant Egyptian shelling. Every so often one of them would go up in flames. Tanks that tried to advance toward the Canal were fired on, hit, and, where possible, abandoned by their crews, who moved toward us on foot while seeking folds in the terrain for cover from the enemy artillery.

Bren tried to maneuver and advance his brigades from the flanks, but without success. The Egyptian units were well dug in, particularly in the Chinese Farm, and they laid down very strong and accurate anti-tank fire on any armor attempting to get close to them. The number of knocked-out tanks kept rising. Toward evening, Natke and Gabi informed Bren that their forces were unable to dislodge and drive off the Egyptians and would be unable to open the road. After consultation with the front command, it was decided that the Chinese Farm would be attacked at night by an infantry force. A paratroop brigade under Uzi would be flown up from southern Sinai for this task. I left Bren for advance headquarters of the southern front and from there returned to Tel Aviv.

When I phoned Bar-Lev at 7:20 the next morning, I detected a jovial tone. We had opened the road! Uzi and Bren had done a superb job that night. Bren had pushed his rafts forward, and the first were already in the water. At Southern Command I heard that in its most difficult and bloody operations during the night, Uzi's paratroop formation had suffered heavy casualties and had been extricated in the morning from the Chinese Farm with the help of armor.

When the operation was planned, it was believed that there were several squads of "tank hunters" in the Chinese Farm who would find cover in the many ditches in the area. In fact, it held a dense defensive system, well entrenched, and equipped with anti-tank weapons, machine guns, and mortars. The paratroop battalion reached the battle area at 10 P.M., after a flight from southern Sinai, and went into action after midnight. At about 2:30 A.M. they encountered the Egyptian defenses. Within moments, the area was covered with bursting shells and every attempt to outflank the Egyptian unit was met by very heavy flat-trajectory fire. It was quickly apparent that this came not from a few squads of "hunters" but from a wide, tight, and unbroken defense system of considerable depth which could not be outflanked. Two company commanders were killed and a third was wounded. There were a number of experienced reserve officers in the action, and they took over from the dead and wounded commanders. Enemy fire grew stronger and the number of our casualties rose. Nevertheless, the men went on to storm the Egyptian positions, but the enemy defenses were so dense that when the first line was captured, positions further back continued to direct murderous fire at the paratroops. The Israeli battalion was pinned down and called for artillery fire and rescue tanks. Shortly before dawn, at 4:30 A.M., an armored battalion received the order to get to the paratroops and extricate them. There was no time lost on circuitous routes and complicated maneuvers. The battalion set off immediately, by the shortest route, after asking the paratroops to mark their positions by smoke grenades.

The paratroops were spread along the forward slope of a low dune and pinned in groups of 15 to 20 men to the slight folds in the terrain. Not more than 50 yards away were hundreds of Egyptian soldiers equipped with RPG anti-tank rockets, Kalatchnikov rifles, and night field glasses.

As our tanks approached the paratroops, Egyptian armor came out to meet them. There was a brief exchange of fire, and the enemy tanks withdrew. But the fire from the Egyptian infantry increased. The doctor and two medical orderlies who had come with our armor were killed. The tanks advanced and crushed the enemy infantry posts with their treads. The armored troop carriers went back and forth and evacuated the wounded, while the tanks gave them covering fire. The uninjured paratroops began walking. Five tanks and two carriers were hit and started burning, and the tank battalion commander decided to retire before the rest of his force was knocked out. At about 5:30 A.M. he withdrew. But it was then discovered that not all had escaped. The deputy commander of one company, whose tank had been hit, remained, together with another seven soldiers, and found cover between two knocked-out tanks. Not far from them were three positions, each manned by two Israeli soldiers.

Then began the battle for rescuing the trapped and the wounded. It was conducted by one company from Natke's brigade and one company from Amir's and it lasted several hours. After they had managed to advance and push the Egyptians a little further back, an armored troop carrier went forward under thick smoke cover and picked up the last of the Israeli soldiers.

Although Uzi reported that he had not succeeded in driving off the Egyptians, that indeed he had been forced to withdraw from the battlefield, he and his men had in fact succeeded in their mission. The Egyptians were engaged by this battle, and as soon as it began they stopped interfering with movement along the access road. This enabled Bren to move his rafts forward without delay, and at 6 A.M. he reached the waterline close to the bridgehead.

I contacted Arik and asked him to join me at Bren's headquarters. He arrived at 12:30 P.M. and a half hour later the chief of staff also turned up. We removed ourselves from the soldiers around us and went over to the nearby dunes. There, half sitting, half lying on the hot sand, we held a "Council of War"—Chief of Staff Elazar, Bar-Lev, Arik, Bren, and myself. The tone was relaxed, the style subdued, the mode of address comradely. But tension lay just beneath the surface of the discussion. The heavy casualties, the unceasing pressure, the bombing and the shelling—which even now smothered our voices from time to time—all left their mark. In addition, the personal relationships were not the most harmonious, particularly between Bar-Lev and Elazar on one side and Arik on the other. Arik's judgment of the situation and his views on what should be done almost always differed from those of higher military rank. Worse still, there was an absence of mutual trust. Arik was convinced that they discriminated against him and did not place full confidence in his reports on the battle situation and on his actions. His superior officers, for their part, argued that he did not carry out their orders, that in his activities he was guided by personal motivation—placing himself and the achievements of his unit in the limelight—and that he broke the elementary principles of discipline, telephoning his friends and public figures in the rear from "Africa"—the term which Arik gave to the west bank of the Suez Canal as soon as he had crossed—and involving them, unlawfully, in military affairs.

Arik reached our meeting with a bandaged head—his forehead had been scratched by shell splinters—his silvery forelock awry, his face bearing the marks of days and nights of battle. His division fought with extreme bravery, suffering the most frightful casualties, yet refusing to be diverted from its objective. His men captured the Egyptian bridgehead on the east bank of the Canal in fierce armored battle, with all of them, from Arik and his staff to the humblest of his soldiers, subjected without letup to murderous enemy fire. In this battle more than two hundred men were killed. In Amnon's brigade, all the company commanders were killed—twice: first the original commanders and then their replacements. The present commanders were the third to take over the companies in only a few days. Scores of tanks were knocked out and left burning or destroyed at the strongholds and the Chinese Farm.

The first question raised at our meeting on the dunes was whether Bren was to cross the Canal as soon as the bridge was established. I was in favor of this, despite the apprehensions I expressed that even after the bridge was put up it might be knocked out: in another hour there would be a bridge, but within a day we might again be without it. Bar-Lev, however, thought we should exercise restraint. Part of Bren's forces were still battling on the east bank, and these units now fighting would need to refuel and re-arm after combat.

In the meantime, the enemy began heavily shelling the bridgehead, and our engineers said that the bridge would be ready not at 11 A.M., but only in the afternoon. It thus appeared that by the time the bridge would be in place, Bren's forces would have finished the battle and be ready to cross.

Arik disagreed. According to him, an Egyptian force was being organized about six miles from the crossing, and it was essential that we should advance with the utmost speed and fan out before the Egyptians sealed the ring round our western bridgehead. Of Arik's 30 tanks which had crossed, 3 had been hit. He still had additional tanks on the east bank, and he wanted to bring them over on rafts, but the Southern Command vetoed this idea.

Bar-Lev agreed to the ferrying of additional tanks before the bridge was in place, but just enough to bring the total on the west side of the Canal to brigade strength. All the rest would be moved across only after the establishment of the bridge. The discussion became repetitive. Arik kept arguing that we should immediately move as many tanks as we could on rafts, insisting that it was possible, and essential, to have four brigades on the west side by midnight, two of his and two of Bren's, which would then race ahead. The chief of staff supported Bar-Lev: to ferry across only enough armor to bring the force on the west side up to brigade strength, and to move additional forces only after the bridge was in place.

Bren very much wanted to cross the Canal quickly, and he promised to finish off the current battle with the utmost speed and be on the Egyptian side by evening. It was then 2 P.M., and I left with Arik for the crossing point.

This site, of course, had already been marked by the Egyptians and they laid down a heavy artillery barrage. In spite of this bombardment, between shell bursts the work of our troops continued. Men who were hit were evacuated, and rafts which were damaged were replaced. Bulldozers hacked out breaches in the ramps on both sides of the Canal and smoothed the ground to the projected bridge. Rafts and rubber boats scurried to and fro in the Canal bringing men and equipment from one side to the other. In one corner sat a group of Egyptian POWs. They recognized me and asked me for food and medical aid.

I crossed with Arik to the west bank. Here, unlike the east bank, which is entirely desert, the soil was cultivated and covered with vegetation. Water is brought here from the sweet-water canal, which flows out from the Nile, reaching Ismailia, and extends southward along the length of the west bank of the Canal down to the city of Suez.

In "Africa," Arik wanted us to climb aboard an armored vehicle, but I preferred to walk some of the way. Lying on the earthen ramps were paratroops laden with personal equipment, weary, eyes half-closed—but only half—while further west, deeper in enemy territory, stood several tanks. Arik told me that 7 tanks were left with Danny Matt to defend the bridgehead, while the rest, more than 20, were up front. The day before, operating on the west bank, they had knocked out 20 Egyptian tanks and destroyed two batteries of anti-aircraft missiles.

When I returned to the east bank, the bridge was ready. The rafts had been connected to each other and reached from bank to bank. It was 4 P.M. I returned to Southern Command and from there to Tel Aviv.

Bren was as good as his word. The operation had taken somewhat longer, but was executed perfectly. His armored force knocked out fifty tanks from the enemy's armored brigade and had itself lost none! At 10 P.M. his division started crossing the Canal, and by 6 A.M. it had already penetrated six miles and was advancing in open country. Bren's forces moved along two routes, one westward, deeper into Egypt, and the second parallel to the Canal, southward, to the Fayid air base. I asked Bar-Lev, "Is everything going well?" At first he answered yes, but he then added, with typical Bar-Lev caution, "We'll know in forty-eight hours."

When I crossed back after one of my visits to the west bank, I went to look at the Chinese Farm, which extends east of the Canal between the Great Bitter Lake and Ismailia. This was an estate which had been established to prepare the desert soil for agriculture. It was covered with deep irrigation trenches and scattered buildings, one of them two stories high. In 1967, when our troops had reached this spot during the Six Day War, they noticed markings on the pumps and machine casings which they took to be Chinese characters. They assumed that this was an experimental farm which had been set up by Chinese agricultural experts, and they called it the Chinese Farm. This set off a spate of stories, embellished in the retelling, about the Chinese who were "seen" there. The facts were more prosaic. The farm was established by the Egyptian Agricultural Ministry, and no Chinese had ever been there. The equipment had been bought by the Egyptian government in Japan, and the markings were in Japanese. But this, of course, was no reason not to call it the Chinese Farm ever after!

I could not hide my emotions as I observed it now. Hundreds of mutilated and burned-out war vehicles lay strewn over the fields, some of them still giving off smoke. There were Israeli tanks and Egyptian tanks, only a few yards away from each other; abandoned supply transports, caught in the act of flight and trailing shells and personal equipment; and among them batteries of SAM-2s and SAM-3s. In the center of each battery was a missile launcher dug into the ground, and around it trucks laden with missiles, some of them intact and others hit and dripping with a yellow liquid.

With every tank we approached, I kept hoping that I would not find Israeli army markings beneath the soot-blackened hulls. My heart contracted. There were many of them. I am no novice at war or battle scenes, but I had never seen such a sight, neither in action, nor in paintings nor in the most far-fetched feature film. Here was a vast field of slaughter stretching all round as far as the eye could see. The tanks, the armored personnel carriers, the guns and the ammunition trucks crippled, overturned, burned and smoking were grim evidence of the frightful battle that had been fought here.

In the days immediately following the initial crossing, there was stiff combat on both banks of the Canal, but with each hour our forces on the west bank were being strengthened. Egyptian tanks still outnumbered our own—they had about 1,000 tanks, some 500 on each side of the Canal. But they were now deployed for defense. Their force was also splintered. On the east bank, our bridgehead severed their front, splitting off the Second Army, positioned north of Ismailia, from the Third Army, deployed to the south, opposite the city of Suez. On the west bank, too, the Egyptian units were dispersed over hundreds of miles in the form of a semi-circle sweeping around from

Kantara in the north to the Suez Gulf in the south. But most important of all, beyond such factors as the deployment and array of their forces, and more decisive than their numerical advantage, was the key change: the military initiative had now passed into our hands.

This change in our military fortunes was instantly reflected in the international arena. On October 19 our ambassador in Washington informed us of feverish negotiations between the Americans and the Russians to sponsor an agreed cease-fire resolution by the Security Council, and it was clear that only a few days remained before the end of the war. I called the chief of staff and senior officers to a meeting that morning and decided that before the cease-fire we had to capture the Mount Hermon positions on the Syrian front and reach a favorable line on the Egyptian front. I then called on the prime minister and suggested to her the final line we should try to reach when war ended, which would then become the cease-fire line. I said we should concentrate our attacks on the west bank of the Canal, but not press too far inland toward Cairo.

I then left for the south to see Arik. This was 11:30 A.M. on October 19. The initiative was in our hands, but the Egyptians still had considerable defensive strength. I was supposed to reach Arik's headquarters west of the Canal by helicopter, but the pilot could not find the landing site. We flew back and forth without spotting it, and to avoid ending up in the Egyptian lines, I ordered him to land at an easily identifiable spot, just north of the Great Bitter Lake, east of the Canal. We then continued by vehicle to the bridgehead. As we approached, we were caught in a heavy artillery barrage, and it was impossible to continue. The road was blocked by burning vehicles, whose drivers—those who had survived—had taken cover in foxholes they had dug at the side of the road. We waited some time on the chance that the shelling would be less intense, but Egyptian aircraft joined the guns and bombed the convoy and the bridge. None of this appeared to suit Aryeh, my aide-de-camp, who accompanied me on all my visits to the front. The shelling was getting stronger, and he urged that we return to Tel Aviv. He raced around trying to find a suitable vehicle that would get us out, and after about an hour he found a command car that was free. The driver, a reservist from Ramat Gan, adjoining Tel Aviv, and a typical Israeli, executed a brilliant S-turn between two burning trucks—Aryeh, who was standing in the rear, had to jump off to avoid catching fire—and then came to a halt. He tried to gauge the pattern of the shelling by watching the bursts so as to find a "corridor" between them, explaining, as he started up again on an erratic path to dodge the shells, that "you can always get by—if you know how." Whether or not he was referring to life in general, I do not know. One does not question miracle men. At all events, we got through. Before we parted he asked for my autograph. It was for his two children, he said, and he opened his wallet and drew forth photographs of his family. For a moment, the Canal, the shelling, the enemy aircraft, all were forgotten. The garden-suburb of Ramat Gan, civilian Israel, going about its ordinary life between crisis and crisis and war and war, had taken over, blotting out our immediate surroundings and all that was happening there.

I had more luck the next day, Saturday, October 20, managing to visit the advance headquarters of all three divisions now on the west side of the Canal, Arik's, Bren's, and the division of Maj. Gen. Kalman Magen, who was operating in the southwest sector of the west bank. Magen replaced Maj. Gen. Albert Mandler, who was killed at the front on the eighth day of the war. Mandler was a veteran commander whom I had known well. He was one of the finest of our soldiers, and he was about to be appointed commander of the armored corps when the war broke out. When the Egyptians attacked, Mandler's division was on the Canal line, and it bore the brunt of the bitter containment battles.

On this visit west of the Canal, I urged Arik, Bren, and Magan to secure the essential objectives with the utmost speed as the cease-fire was likely to go into effect in two or three days. I told them of Kissinger's trip to Moscow. The Russians were trying to press America to agree to a cease-fire resolution which would force us to return to the pre-1967 borders! And all this after the Arabs had launched the Yom Kippur War and had been repulsed. Moscow was trying to secure for the Arabs by political means what the Arabs themselves had failed to achieve by war. And at the same time, Russia, Libya, Algeria and Czechoslovakia were pouring into Egypt large quantities of new tanks and missiles for those destroyed in the war.

On another visit west of the Canal on October 21, I asked to see Col. Uzi Ya'iri, commander of the paratroop force that had fought so bitterly in the Chinese Farm. I found him worn out. I knew him well, ever since he had headed the chief of staff's bureau under Bar-Lev. He was a first-class fellow, straightforward, sensible, and very responsible. I knew he had lost a lot of men in combat, but I did not expect to find him so downcast. His face bore an expression of ineffable sadness, and his eyes, swollen from lack of sleep, were—what was worse—without luster. We talked about his battle to open the access road to the Canal. Chaim Bar-Lev, who was with me, said, "Uzi, you suffered heavy casualties, but you opened the road!" Uzi held to his own: "The road was opened not by me but by the armor. I would like to be able to say that my unit did it, but this was not so. We had seventy casualties because we went into action too hastily, without proper intelligence on the enemy's defenses."

At seven in the evening of October 21, I met with the prime minister to give her a progress report and then returned to my office. Two hours later she called and asked me to hurry over. When I entered her office, she opened without any preliminaries. "That's it. Cease-fire. Tonight. At 3 A.M. the U.N. Security Council will meet to adopt a resolution jointly presented by the United States and the Soviet Union, calling on both sides to cease fire not later than twelve hours after its adoption." President Nixon had requested us to accept. The Cabinet convened at midnight and decided to respond to the president's request.

The operation to capture the Hermon range had started at dusk that evening, continued through the night, and ended shortly before noon on October 22. In the early hours of that same day, I urged Bar-Lev to capture Jebel Ataka, the region west of the Gulf of Suez. This would give us an unbroken military hold on the territory running from Ismailia to the Gulf of Suez and cut off and isolate the Egyptian Third Army and the city of Suez. It would also block any possibility of outflanking our forces west of the Canal.

At 2:30 P.M. that day, Radio Cairo announced that President Anwar Sadat had accepted the cease-fire. It was to go into effect at 6:58 P.M. However, both that night and the next day, the Egyptian Air Force maintained its attacks on our troops on the east bank of the Canal, and Egyptian units continued fighting. Apparently this was done because Syria had rejected the cease-fire. The local Egyptian commanders, both senior and junior, ordered their units to advance and seize Israeli positions, and they did indeed try. As for us, if the Syrians, or even the Egyptians alone, had halted the fighting, we would surely have ceased fire and frozen our lines. We would have done so despite our military advantage.

Only on the next day, October 23, at 6:15 A.M. did Syria announce that she accepted the Security Council's cease-fire decision in principle, and even that was on the virtual condition that Israel withdraw to the pre-1967 borders. The Egyptians continued to fight on land and in the air, and their units tried to advance in all sectors.

In this situation, Israel could not consider herself bound by a one-sided cease-fire, and our units also continued to fight. Our planes engaged in air combat with enemy planes, our ground forces repulsed attempts by the enemy to overrun them, the armored forces of Bren and Kalman advanced southward to the city of Suez and the port of Adabiah, on the shore of the Gulf of Suez south of Suez city, and an airborne unit occupied Jebel Ataka.

With Adabiah in our possession, our naval units now joined our ground forces operating from the west bank of the Canal. The naval task was to seal the city of Suez and the Third Army from the south and deny them communications and supplies by sea.

The Israeli Navy was very active in this war. In general, no urgent emphasis was given to our naval force in any of Israel's earlier campaigns. Our borders with all our neighbors are land borders, and as a rule there had been no pressing need to attack Syria or Egypt from the sea—the Mediterranean and the Gulf of Suez—or to take any extraordinary defensive measures against possible seaborne attacks by the enemy. But thanks to the fighting spirit and initiative of the commander of the Navy and his men, our small fleet of fast missile boats carried out a number of dashing operations. They simply thrust themselves into Egyptian and Syrian naval bases, seeking—and finding—opportunities to enter into battle with the enemy vessels, which were armed with Soviet missiles. To overcome the advantage in range of the Soviet missiles, our boats had to approach their targets at speed—to hit them before the enemy could activate his missiles—or shoot down the enemy missile while it was still in the air. The Navy was splendid.

By the evening of October 23, forces from Bren's division had encircled the Third Army and the city of Suez. Damascus and Cairo now recognized that the path they had chosen would yield them no glory, and that their vital and urgent need was an immediate cease-fire. Egypt in particular grasped the grim fact that the city of Suez was about to fall and the Third Army would be cut off.

After midnight of October 23, the commander of the U.N. Observer Force, Gen. Siilasvuo, who was in Cairo, got through to us to say that, on instructions from New York, he would like to send observers to the Egyptian front to supervise the cease-fire. I replied that first there had to be a genuine cease-fire. We, on our part, were ready to accept it, and I suggested the deadline of seven the next morning, October 24, on condition that we received word from the Egyptians that they, too, were ready to halt all fighting at that hour.

By 7 A.M. we had received no reply from the Egyptians, but Gen. Siilasvuo turned up at my office. I gave him a map of the positions held by our forces, including Jebel Ataka and the port of Adabiah on the gulf, and asked him for Egypt's reply to our insistence on a genuine cease-fire. Siilasvuo returned to Cairo, and at 8:45 A.M., his deputy, Col. Hogan, who was stationed in Jerusalem, telephoned me to say that he had just received a radio signal from Cairo with the following Egyptian reply: "Agree, agree, agree."

I asked him whether the Egyptians had really repeated their "agree" three times.

"Four," replied Hogan, who was not a man to waste words.

On the morning of October 22, when I was about to fly south to visit Bren, the prime minister asked me to try to get back by 1:45 P.M. for lunch with Kissinger. When I reached Bren's advance headquarters, we came under heavy shelling, so we got into a half-track, moved to a captured missile site, and reviewed the urgent moves he was to make and the air support he needed. I got back to Tel Aviv in good time for the Kissinger lunch.

We have known each other for many years. I think I first met Kissinger when I was chief of staff, almost twenty years ago. Both before and while I was minister of defense, I would see him on my occasional visits to the United States. I am very much impressed by his wisdom, his broad-ranging knowledge, his prodigious capacity for work, and his ability to set things in perspective. His opening of a new chapter in American-Chinese relations undoubtedly commands enormous admiration. But if he had been secretary of state of a small country—Belgium or Holland, for example—without having at his disposal the power of the United States, he surely would not have accomplished such striking feats. His greatness stems primarily from his knowledge of how to use the powerful lever of the United States to exert pressure and to retaliate, to influence and to promise guarantees. He had at his service the kind of intelligence information which only America, with her advanced technology, is capable of acquiring. Kissinger's unique personal quality lies in the fact that he utilizes not only his own attributes but the full weight of the United States, a method of operation which many of his predecessors failed to employ.

During lunch, the conversation was general, touching on the cease-fire, American-Israeli relations, and above all, continued arms supplies.

As to a cease-fire agreement, we made the categorical demand that there be an exchange of prisoners. We considered this a prime condition: "No prisoner exchange, no cease-fire." Kissinger was unwilling to agree to such an extreme formula. He promised to act and to ask the Russians to help. He cited promises which he had received from Moscow, but he avoided giving us an iron-clad undertaking that there would be a prisoner exchange. His reassurances were bound by such expressions as "We'll work for it." "We'll try." "We'll make a supreme effort." As for getting exit permits for the Jews of Syria, he was even less forthcoming.

The impression created was that we were treading a tightrope which soared above a canyon of monstrous danger but which stretched toward a gleam of light in the distance. We would reach that light only if we learned to tread along the thin cord with wisdom. It appeared that if we had started the war, we would not have received a single solitary nail from the United States. America found herself in a difficult situation at the moment because of the oil embargo, and her leaders would not hesitate to disassociate herself from us if forced to choose between aid to Israel which involved grave suffering for America, and reaching agreement with the Arabs, even at our expense.

Furthermore, the United States supported the cease-fire because a continuation of the war would lead to the radicalization of the Arab world, to the fall of moderate governments, and their replacement by extremist regimes. Not only that, but if the war went on and the Arab armies were utterly routed, the Soviet Union was likely to take extreme measures to save her allies from collapse.

On American-Arab relations, the prevailing view was that if the Arab states failed to renew oil supplies to the United States, Washington would stop dealing with the Arab-Israeli conflict. The Arabs had to recognize that while Russia could indeed supply them with sophisticated weaponry, only America could bring about a political solution.

On the flow of arms to Israel, one had to go on working to secure it, but it was very important for senators and Jewish leaders to express appreciation and not criticism, as they were now doing.

I left the lunch with mixed feelings. I believed that Kissinger would deal energetically and be helpful in the negotiations with the Arabs but I was by no means certain that an improvement in America's relations with the Arab states and the lifting of the oil embargo would not be bought—at least partly—with Israeli currency, namely through pressure exerted on us for Arab benefit.

A Cabinet meeting was held that evening to review the situation along the fronts after the cease-fire. At the end of the discussion the Cabinet decided that if the Egyptians failed to live up to the cease-fire, "the Israel Defense Forces will 'repel the enemy at the gate.'" The quote is from Isaiah 28:6. What a marvelous expression! The classical Hebrew poets would not have been ashamed of such a phrase, though they would have been surprised to hear it used not about the gate of an Israeli city but about Jebel Ataka!

PART VIII

Aftermath

[1973~1975]

34

DIPLOMATIC PERSUASION

A CRISIS FOLLOWED after we cut off and surrounded the Egyptian Third Army. At first it seemed that the two Super Powers alone were involved. But it was soon evident that the United States and the Soviet Union had resolved matters between themselves, and the crisis turned into one between the U.S. and Israel.

The Soviet-American friction had occurred when it appeared to the United States—so we were told—that the Soviet Union intended to send an expeditionary force to liberate the Third Army. I understood that the Russian troops planned to reach Cairo and move on from there to attack our forces west of the Canal. Washington regarded such possible Soviet military intervention with the utmost gravity and on October 25 put her forces on alert.

I, of course, do not know for certain whether the Russians really intended to dispatch their force and desisted only when America reacted or whether the episode was a false alarm. At all events, the "hot line" between Moscow and Washington proved effective, and the Super Power crisis fizzled out. (The episode cropped up again later, when we were asked angrily whether we wanted to precipitate a Soviet-American confrontation over the issue of food for the Third Army!)

The next day, October 26, the ball was back in our court. We were first told by the Americans that they had information that we were attacking the Third Army. This, they said, was a breach of the cease-fire agreement, and we had apparently failed to understand the grave steps the United States was likely to take against us. Half an hour later, following a strong denial from Jerusalem, our Washington embassy received a correction: the Americans had discovered in the meantime that indeed it was not we but the Egyptians who were continuing hostilities! However, they added, this information was not "relevant." The crux of the problem was the situation itself—the isolation of the Third Army, with all the complications that arose therefrom. The Americans could not allow this Egyptian army to be destroyed, or left hungry, or weakened by thirst, or taken prisoner. If the Third Army could not receive supplies in any other way, the Soviet Union would send them, and such a move, they said, would be tantamount to Soviet military intervention. It would be a blow to American prestige. No matter how, the Third Army had to be saved from its plight.

An endless exchange of telephone calls then took place between Washington and Jerusalem—with the Americans occasionally resorting to a tone that could not be described as the acme of civility—while the Israeli Cabinet met for urgent consultation. Finally, the Americans presented their demand more or less in the form of an ultimatum. It had crystallized into the requirement that we grant a one-time permit allowing an Egyptian supply convoy of non-military equipment, food, and water to pass through our lines to the Third Army. If we did not agree to this proposal, we would find ourselves in a crisis situation with the United States. Israel gave approval for one hundred supply trucks to be sent from Cairo.

In effect, this was the end of the blockade of the Third Army, which had lasted for three days (October 23 to 26). Following this one-time convoy came an appeal from President Nixon himself that we allow a further fifty supply trucks through as a goodwill gesture. Then came his further appeal that for as long as Secretary of State Kissinger was negotiating in Egypt, the Third Army be kept regularly supplied. If this failed to happen, the president felt, there would not be an appropriate atmosphere in Cairo for talks on matters infinitely more important than the Third Army. When Abba Eban was Israel's ambassador in Washington, he used to describe Israeli-American relations as "very special." This they certainly were.

The isolation of the helpless Third Army and the friction their plight created served to hasten the procedures for ending the war.

First came the decision of the Security Council on October 26 "to establish a United Nations Emergency Force" forthwith and calling on the U.N. secretary-general "to report within twenty-four hours on the steps taken in this matter." Israel and Egypt agreed, and the Americans informed us that it had been resolved between them and the Russians that the U.N. force would not include American or Soviet troops.

The second step was the agreement between Israel and Egypt for their senior officers to meet. The purpose, as defined by the Egyptians, was "to discuss the military aspects of fulfilling Security Council Resolutions 338 and 339," which had called for a cease-fire. Israel, for her part, envisaged far wider aims for these meetings. At all events, the subjects to be discussed would assuredly be supplies to the Third Army and the city of Suez, exchange of prisoners, and the oil-tanker blockade at Bab el-Mandeb, by the entrance to the Red Sea.

The third step sprang from Israel's understandable reluctance to be forced, by various "requests," into a position of having to live politically from hand to mouth and to determine her purposes on a day-to-day basis. Accordingly, Golda Meir sought a meeting with the U.S. president to review matters with the United States, mainly arms supplies.

The U.N. Emergency Force was under the command of Gen. Siilasvuo, and he came to see me on October 30 to hand me this message: "General Dayan: The secretary-general of the United Nations has instructed me, pursuant to a request of the Security Council in accordance with its Resolutions 338, 339, and 340, to request that Israeli armed forces return their troops to positions occupied by them at 16:50 GMT on October 22, 1973. As instructed by the secretary-general, I therefore, in my capacity of interim force commander of UNEF, make this request to you."

After the Soviet Union and the United States had failed to secure our withdrawal to the lines of October 22, I did not think anyone would seriously think we would do so upon this U.N. request. But apparently, if not on the battlefield, at least in the files of the Security Council, there had to be order. On the whole, I thought one could live with the UNEF. It might not be of much help, but it could do no harm.

The military talks were conducted at Kilometer 101 on the Cairo-Suez road, on the west bank of the Canal, with Maj. Gen. Aharon Yariv heading the Israeli delegation and Maj. Gen. Abdel Gamasi the Egyptian. In the first few days, they dealt with arrangements for non-military supplies to the Third Army and Suez and with the exchange of POWs. The talks were rough going but they fulfilled their immediate function and in the end these two subjects were settled. On the more basic issues, however, such as fixing the cease-fire lines (the Egyptians demanded our withdrawal to the October 22 lines) and lifting the blockade at Bab el-Mandeb, no progress was made. It appeared that the military negotiators were neither authorized nor qualified to raise these weighty issues.

In the meantime, Prime Minister Meir met with President Nixon and Secretary of State Kissinger on November 1. Mrs. Meir's trip to Washington was preceded by feverish consultations among us to determine our position on various questions. It was hoped that in Washington the prime minister would outline a proposal for settling the immediate pressing issues with Egypt and that Kissinger would try to secure Egyptian agreement. He was about to leave on a series of diplomatic calls that would also take in Cairo.

It cannot be said that Washington was enthusiastic over the idea of a visit by the prime minister. Golda's standing was rather special. She was extremely popular in the United States, particularly with the Jews. Moreover, she was known to American leaders as a woman of strong personality, blunt and forthright. When she raised a question, there could be no evasion of it. Yes or no, but there had to be an answer—even from the president of the United States.

On this occasion in particular, Washington was not overjoyed by the prospect. Israel had heavy claims upon the United States. But the State Department was deeply engaged in three political moves associated with the Middle East that were not exactly calculated to stimulate support for Israel. It was attempting to get the Arabs to lift their oil embargo against the United States; to strengthen America's standing and influence in the Arab states, primarily Egypt and Saudi Arabia; and to seek jointly with the Soviet Union a solution to the Israeli-Arab conflict. Only a short time before, when Golda had put out feelers about the possibility of a Washington visit to discuss additional arms supplies, a satirical column in an American paper suggested that President Nixon had no doubt told his aides: "Give her the weapons she wants, but just keep her out of Washington." There is said to be a kernel of truth in every political joke. In this case, I fancy there may have been more truth than joke. The talks with the president and with Kissinger were especially difficult this time. Golda then returned to Israel, and Kissinger flew off to Cairo, carrying with him Israel's conditions for a proposed separation-of-forces arrangement with Egypt.

In Egypt matters apparently proceeded better than had been predicted. President Sadat was in fact anxious to reach an arrangement with us. The main reason was his distressing military predicament. It was unlikely that he would have welcomed either Russian military intervention on Egyptian soil or American Air Force transport planes in Egyptian skies. The one thing of which Sadat was certain was that his armed forces were powerless to break the Israeli siege.

His official spokesmen, and therefore the Egyptian press, kept declaring that it was our forces on the west bank of the Canal who were trapped. But the Egyptian army commanders knew the true situation. They were aware that in order to push us back, or isolate us, their Second and Third Armies would have to link up and thereby sever our bridgehead. But they had not the slightest chance of being able to do that. The Third Army was cut off, with little food and water, and above all without ammunition and weapons. It was also completely exposed to our Air Force, for the SAM batteries which had given it cover had either been destroyed by our troops or withdrawn. As for Egypt's Second Army, it was strong as long as it remained in its entrenched positions, with anti-tank defenses and protection from the air by an umbrella of SAM batteries. But any attempt to move out and proceed southward to link up with the Third Army would have left it open to bombing by our aircraft and ambush by our armor. The Second Army would have been wiped out, as had happened to the Egyptian 25th Brigade earlier in the war when it moved toward our bridgehead in an effort to destroy it and lost fifty tanks in the attempt, without the loss of a single tank by our forces. Sadat understood that his achievements in this war were all behind him, and he had to end it, even at the cost of concession and compromise.

The first agreement that was reached between Israel and Egypt through the mediation of Dr. Kissinger followed the military talks at Kilometer 101 and was signed there on November 11, 1973. It contained six articles and dealt only with Third Army supplies and the exchange of prisoners.

Four days earlier, on November 7, Assistant Secretary of State Joseph Sisco, a member of Kissinger's mediation team, had come to Jerusalem from Cairo with a proposed draft. He met with representatives of our government, and after a discussion of several hours and the introduction of certain changes, we agreed to accept it. The next day the amended draft agreement was brought before the Cabinet and approved. It covered only the immediate topics. The major issues would not be raised at the meetings of the army officers at

Kilometer 101, which were in progress at this time. They would be dealt with at the future peace conference in Geneva under the heading of "Disengagement of Forces"—a new name for an old subject. I must say I was much relieved.

The progress of the Yariv-Gamasi talks at Kilometer 101 had not been to my liking. It had seemed to me that we were about to make vital concessions without receiving anything appropriate in exchange and without a suitable settlement and that I was unable to prevent it. The head of our delegation at the time reported directly to the prime minister. The basic points were brought before the Cabinet for consideration and decision, but I had found little support there for my suggestions. I held the view that we should withdraw from the west bank of the Canal, but we should do so within the framework of a political agreement that would ensure an essential and radical change in the situation—opening of the Suez Canal to shipping, rehabilitation of the cities along the waterway, and a limitation of forces. But it was not possible to secure these objectives in the negotiations between Yariv and Gamasi and without United States mediation and acceptance of responsibility. With all my occasional reservations about Kissinger and his moves, I was not unmindful of his achievements. Egypt was far more anxious for us to quit "Africa" and remove ourselves from the Canal than we were to go, and this was therefore the time to reach a military-political arrangement with her. It might be possible to do so at Geneva, but certainly not at Kilometer 101.

In the midst of our negotiations on a disengagement-of-forces agreement with Egypt, at 10:30 A.M. on Saturday, December 1, 1973, David Ben-Gurion died of a cerebral hemorrhage. I had visited him two days earlier, after his physician had telephoned to tell me of his condition. He had been only partially conscious during his final days and had lost the power of speech. I sat at his bedside. His eyes were closed, his mouth drawn tight, and he looked unworried and lost in deep thought. Indeed, his features were touched by an unusual softness, and he seemed utterly calm. He was leaving a long stormy life in a state of tranquillity.

As I looked at him, I thought he would now be mourned and eulogized even by those who had vilified him in his later years—by the current leaders of the Labor Party which he had led for so long, down to the lowliest writer in the Labor Daily, *Davar*, which had long been known as "Ben-Gurion's newspaper." They would try to distinguish between the man and his leadership; between Ben-Gurion and "Ben-Gurionism"; between the man they would call "the greatest of the Jews, architect of the state, leader of the nation," and the human being who occasionally erred; between his triumphant years and his petty years. The distinction was false. He had taken decisions of genius and vision, and he had also made mistakes, but the historical phenomenon known as Ben-Gurion was a single element. The man and his leadership were one and inseparable.

35

TALKS IN WASHINGTON

AT THE BEGINNING of December 1973, I was scheduled to address several meetings in the United States under the auspices of the United Jewish Appeal. Kissinger was informed of my forthcoming trip, and at his suggestion I advanced my visit by a few days so that I could meet with him and with the secretary of defense. I also had a talk with the then vice-president, Gerald Ford, at his invitation. I had two meetings with Kissinger on December 7. Only one had been planned. But at the end of it he suggested that we resume in the afternoon. With me in the morning were Zvi Zur, my assistant at the Defense Ministry; Motta Gur, our military attaché in Washington; and Simcha Dinitz, our ambassador. Kissinger was accompanied by Joseph Sisco and two aides.

The opening item at our morning talk was arms supplies, and at the first mention of the term, Kissinger broke in with the half-jesting inquiry as to whether the Israeli government would stop paying our ambassador's salary if he failed to raise the subject of arms less than ten times a day!

Zur explained that in assessing the quantities of armaments the Arabs had received, one had to take into account not just airlifts but also the seaborne shipments. The total quantity sent to the Arabs by the Soviet Union amounted to more than 300,000 tons, while we had received less than one-third of this quantity from the United States. I then restated the figures. As against the aircraft we had obtained from America, the Arabs had received more than 350 planes: 200 from Eastern Europe and more than 150 from Arab states. In armor, the Arabs had received 1,550 tanks from Eastern Europe alone, and together with shipments from the Arab states had secured a total of several scores more tanks than the 2,500 they had lost in the war.

At my mention of the help received by the Arabs from other countries, I sensed an atmosphere of discomfort—surprise or disbelief, I could not tell. I said that when it came to combat and one encountered enemy weapons, it made no difference what their source of origin. In Syria we had fought Cuban tank crews, and in Egypt, only the day before, we had shot down a North Korean pilot. We ourselves had limited manpower, and our capacity to absorb planes and tanks was correspondingly restricted. But it was only fair that America should supply us with the quantities that we *were* able to man. We had asked for armored personnel carriers, for example, and had received only about one-eighth of our request. This was also true of other types of weapons and equipment. The number of Hawk surface-to-air missiles we possessed was a small fraction of the quantity of SAMs held by the Arabs.

I asked that we be allowed to order a larger number of aircraft direct from the factories. Before the war we had had to argue about every single Phantom, and when our need was desperate during the war, we had been informed that there were no planes to spare. It was well to prepare in good time.

Kissinger, on his part, set out the position taken by the U.S. administration and the reasoning behind it. In the end I was told that a few of our requests would be granted, and the others would be studied.

The second subject of our discussion concerned arrangements with Egypt and dealt mainly with the Suez Canal. The definitive position of the United States was that she preferred an open Canal within the framework of an Israeli-Egyptian arrangement—even if this meant the waterway would be used by the Russians—rather than a closed Canal and a continuation of the conflict. I told Kissinger that there had been a moment when we had almost lost physical contact with the Canal, but now our control of it was even greater than it had been in the past. The Egyptians were demanding our withdrawal from it, and I wanted him to know my personal view (with the approval of the prime minister) on the subject of an Egyptian-Israeli arrangement.

Removing ourselves from the Canal would be the greatest concession on our part, and it was being demanded of us in the very opening phase of the negotiations. In return we were being offered a very poor exchange—a temporary cease-fire. Any additional withdrawal we might make in the future would be far less important to Egypt, while we would be wanting in return something of far greater significance—a peace agreement. From Egypt's proposals suggested at Kilometer 101, it was evident that we were being asked to give the maximum now and receive the minimum. Therefore, I said, if we were to withdraw 6 to 10 miles east of the Canal, the move should be made within the framework of an agreement that would ensure the termination of hostilities. On this basic issue there should be formal undertakings as well as practical steps—the opening of the Canal to shipping and the rehabilitation and civilian resettlement of the Canal cities. As to the topographical structure of the arrangement, I thought there should be a strip separating the two parties, a buffer zone put under the control of the U.N. forces. To my mind, the United States, too, had an active role to play in the agreement, particularly on the matter of Bab el-Mandeb, which was an international waterway used also by our oil tankers. It was up to the U.S. to guarantee freedom of shipping through these straits, and she was not without the power to meet the possible objection of a couple of Egyptian frigates!

The Straits of Bab el-Mandeb, the Gate of Tears, lie at the southern end of the Red Sea, which narrows at this point to a width of twenty-two miles. The straits are bounded on the east by the People's Democratic Republic of Yemen, at the tip of the Arabian Peninsula, and on the west by the coast of Africa. In the center of the straits lies the island of Perim, controlled by Yemen. The passage between Perim and the Yemen coast is virtually non-navigable, and the main shipping passes through the sixteen-and-a-half-mile channel between Perim and the African coast.

I cannot claim that my ideas fired Kissinger with overwhelming enthusiasm. He disagreed with some and had reservations about others. Curiously enough, there were some areas in which he lacked expert knowledge.

On Bab el-Mandeb, it was clear to me that even though American aircraft carriers in the area might—and, indeed, did—influence the situation, the United States would not be a permanent guarantor of freedom of shipping. She was not the world's policeman. My reading of the position was that America would go to war over U.S. interests but not over an international principle such as freedom of navigation. There was clear evidence of this position in the explanations demanded by Congress after the president placed U.S. forces on alert in October, when the Russians had threatened to send troops to Cairo.

However, I felt there was little chance that Egypt would accede to our demand that she undertake to end belligerency. The Egyptians were insisting that we evacuate most of Sinai even before the phase of peace, and they were unlikely to obligate themselves to non-belligerency at this stage. In addition, in November Yariv had told Gamasi at Kilometer 101 that we were prepared to withdraw from the Canal within the narrow framework of an agreement on the reduction of forces, and he had set no political conditions for the Egyptians.

I told Kissinger that if Egypt failed to accept our political terms, we would remain in our present military positions and Egypt would eventually accept the arrangement she now rejected. I said this even though I knew that it was not only Egypt that was interested in an immediate arrangement. America was too, in order to put an end to the hysteria in Europe over oil. I also knew that if we insisted on staying put for another year, Israel's position vis-à-vis the United States would be far from rosy.

I handed Kissinger the map I had brought, marked with our suggestion for a half-mile withdrawal from the cease-fire lines by both the Egyptian and Israeli forces. This proposal had been devised at the initiative of Gen. Siilasvuo, who considered it a first step in the "disengagement of forces" between the parties. I did not think there was the slightest chance that the Egyptians would accept it.

Despite Kissinger's serious reservations about some of my proposals, it seemed to me that I had managed to get across at least one thing—the recognition that the problem was complex and required meticulous study. We arranged to continue our discussion after he had sounded out the Egyptians. He was flying to Cairo on December 12 and would be in Jerusalem on the 16th.

Two days later, on Sunday, December 9, I met Defense Secretary James Schlesinger. The meeting was unexpected, and in order to keep it I had to rush back to Washington from New York, where I was addressing a meeting on Saturday night. Between my two meetings with Kissinger on Friday, I had lunched with Deputy Defense Secretary William Clements. Schlesinger was out of the country at the time, and I was told that I would therefore be consulting with Clements on arms. And I did. I gathered that the United States, thank heavens, was not short of weapons. The question was purely political. We were not getting arms because it was U.S. policy not to give them to us.

From the luncheon I went to my second meeting with Kissinger, and I gave him a report of my talk at the Pentagon, together with personal regards from Clements. When I returned to my hotel, I was informed that Schlesinger would be returning from Europe the next day, and although it was unusual for him to appear at the Pentagon on a Sunday, he suggested that we meet at ten in the morning in his office.

The discussion with Schlesinger was inconclusive but pleasant. I had not met him before. Tall, relaxed, cultured, he spoke little, but what he had to say was said with clarity and courtliness.

I talked to him about our arms requests, about promises of replacements which had not been fulfilled, and about the huge gap between our arsenal and those of the Arabs. I also told him of my impression the hold-up was political. I asked him to tell me which of the items we had requested would be received and which would not. I then harked back to the question of placing orders directly with the factories. I explained that Israel was the only country in the world that was not permitted to order aircraft or tanks from the plants. Libya could buy all she wanted in France, and every other Arab state could buy arms in the East or the West, with their huge hoards of dollars. We alone, even when we had the money, were unable to buy what we needed. The United States was the only country ready to sell us planes, but even there we were not allowed to order more than two or three a month. We again went over the list of our requests. He listened, but promised nothing.

Toward the end of our talk, he questioned me on the military situation on Israel's northern and southern fronts and on the prospects of peace. I told him that the depth of our bridgehead on the Egyptian front was indeed only a little more than six miles, but there was no fear that it would be cut off. The Egyptians had no chance of doing so, and we could continue to stay on the territory west of the Canal for months and months. There was no other place for which we could get a higher political price. As for a peace arrangement with Egypt, I feared that Egypt would make a final settlement between us conditional upon our reaching an arrangement with Syria and Jordan. It was true that Egypt wanted to end the war and hoped we would first withdraw sixty miles within Sinai. But when it came to negotiating a final settlement, Sadat would insist on a prior solution to the problems of the Palestinian refugees and of Jerusalem.

My meeting with Vice-President Gerald Ford had taken place the previous morning, his first day at work, I was told, in his new position. The atmosphere was very agreeable, with Mr. Ford frank and open. He asked a lot of questions, all of them short, searching, and to the point. I told him briefly about the Soviet weapons we had encountered, about the arms aid we had received from the United States, and what would have happened if these arms had not been sent to us. We would have managed, I said. We would have held firm, but the war would have been tougher and our casualties heavier. I also mentioned my meeting with Clements. Ford was lavish in his praise of Kissinger and said that the Americans believed in him. When he spoke of the prospects of peace, he emphasized that the United States was helping Israel and would go on doing so, but "we want to help you so that you can attain peace." Even when we discussed the $2.2 billion loan and aid for Israel that was being considered, he gave as his judgment that Congress would approve it by a decisive majority. But he indicated without saying it in so many words that this was regarded as an investment in peace, not in a renewal of war. It was clearly his intention to make us understand that American help was given on the assumption that we on our side would do everything to reach a settlement with the Arabs.

As the meeting ended, he again expressed the hope that Kissinger, "who got us out of Vietnam," would succeed in his current efforts to secure a settlement in the Middle East. I told him that we would be seeing Kissinger again on December 16 in Israel. He would be coming to us from Cairo and bringing Egypt's views. I hoped we would find the path to peace and that war would not be renewed.

There was no tangible result to this meeting, nor was one expected. Yet I left the vice-president's office with a pleasant feeling. We had had a straightforward talk, honest and sincere, as befitted the day, Saturday, the Jewish Sabbath.

The next day, straight from my meeting with Schlesinger, I boarded an El Al plane for home. It was carrying equipment and making a direct flight, Washington-Tel Aviv. I went through government dispatches, swallowed a sleeping pill and a double whiskey, and awoke over Europe. A few hours later, on the morning of December 10, I arrived in Israel and went straight to Jerusalem to report to the prime minister.

After adding details to the cabled reports on my talks that had been sent to Golda from Washington, I spoke of our prospects for getting additional arms and of the next stage in our negotiations with Egypt. On the first subject, I told the prime minister that we were likely to face considerable difficulty in securing all the weapons and equipment we needed. On the second, we would hear from Kissinger, who would be coming in a few days and would bring with him Egypt's reaction to our proposals. I told Golda of the popularity of Yariv's suggestion, made to the Egyptians at Kilometer 101 on November 22, and that apparently this had been welcomed by the Russians. But I restated to Golda my objections to the Yariv offer. It spoke only of an arrangement for 3 to 6 months, and what would that give us? There was no need to be hasty. We should exercise patience, remain on the west bank of the Canal, and on no account evacuate the Canal Zone within the framework of a military agreement that lacked political elements. Moreover, it was essential that the United States be involved in the negotiations so that she would share responsibility for its implementation. We would have differences of opinion with the United States, since she wanted to hasten the disengagement-of-forces arrangement in the hope that this would help her get oil from Saudi Arabia.

I also reported both to the Cabinet and to the Foreign Affairs and Security Committee of the Knesset. They wanted my views on the attitude of the U.S. government to Israel. I said that the Americans wished us to make a maximum attempt to reach an arrangement with the Arabs. Their anxiety to see an end to the Middle East conflict, even at the cost to Israel of far-reaching concessions, had been sharpened by the energy crisis, their desire for an understanding with the Soviet Union, and their bitter experience over the Vietnam war. For them, it was better that Kissinger, together with the Russians, should conduct peace talks at Geneva than that we should destroy or subdue the Egyptian Third or Second Army. It was not in our delivery of a further military blow to the Egyptians that they saw the chance for a solution.

I further told the Cabinet that I had not felt any tendency in Washington to press us to concede on issues vital to us. It was explained to me, albeit indirectly, that the Americans did not demand that we surrender our basic interests, but they expected us to advance toward peace. The time might come when they would exercise real pressure, but for the moment I did not think they would try to force us to abandon our position by deliberately keeping us short of weapons. They were spurring us to compromise, but they were not going to sell us out.

At no time did the Americans ask us to withdraw to the lines of October 22; nor did I hear that unless we did so the Arabs would renew hostilities. This was also true of Bab el-Mandeb. The Egyptians had two frigates there. But it was we who had stopped our oil tankers; Kissinger had not requested it. Kissinger, I told the Cabinet, had to be credited not only with intensive and effective efforts at mediation between the Arabs and Israel, but also with realistic vision. On freedom of passage through the Bab el-Mandeb Straits, from the moment agreement was reached with Egypt on disengagement, it was assumed that the Egyptians would not stop our vessels. Moreover, an American aircraft carrier kept moving through the waters near Bab el-Mandeb, while its Phantoms took off from time to time and circled over our ships as well as the two Egyptian frigates at anchor there. The hint was enough.

Four days after my return from Washington, Kissinger arrived in Israel, having visited Algeria, Egypt, Saudi Arabia, Jordan, and Syria. His principal purpose, of course, was to secure the rescinding of the oil boycott against the United States. But this issue, too, was now linked to our negotiations with Egypt and Syria.

He spent several hours on his first day in Jerusalem with the prime minister and the next day he met with Israel's negotiating team—Golda, Allon, Eban, and myself. Also present were the chief of staff, Yariv, and Dinitz. Kissinger was accompanied by Assistant Secretary Joseph Sisco, two other State Department officials and U.S. Ambassador Kenneth Keating. The meeting began in the morning and went on till after midnight. First we took up the perennial subject of American arms, and after that we tackled the problem of negotiations with the Arabs.

Nothing new emerged from our discussion of arms supplies, except for a little more anguish. This was caused less by the practical response to our requests than by the niggling rider attached to the method of their fulfillment. For instance, we had finally managed to buy rifles from the United States, and we now wished to bring them over quickly. The Pentagon, however, insisted that they be brought by ship, not by plane, to avoid the impression that America was rushing weapons to Israel at an emergency pace. Our arguments that the type of transport we used for this purpose was our own concern were brushed aside. The matter was settled in the end, but it left an unpleasant taste—the very idea that we should be forbidden to bring by plane such elementary weapons as rifles simply because the Arabs would not like it!

Our review of negotiations with Syria was devoted wholly to the problem of prisoner exchange. So far the Syrians had refused to give us the list of prisoners they held and had not allowed the Red Cross to visit them. This attitude caused us great anxiety and anger. It was, of course, out of the question to sit with them around the negotiating table at Geneva before this elementary obligation was carried out. It was also the primary demand of the Geneva POW Convention, to which the Syrians were signatories. President Assad of Syria used our prisoners as a lever to try to extract territorial concessions at the negotiations—and what he learned from the press of the Israeli public's deep concern over the prisoner issue must have given him reason to think he would succeed. Our discussion of the matter with Kissinger was inconclusive. He would have to find a way to persuade Assad to transmit the prisoner list and allow visits by the Red Cross before we would begin talks with Syria. Assad was very stubborn, and his real aim, even if he did not say so explicitly, was to destroy Israel.

Egypt was the main topic of our talk with Kissinger. In Washington I had emphasized our need to be sure that the disengagement of forces would bring about the termination of hostilities. I now gathered that upon the signing of the disengagement agreement, Sadat would demobilize part of his army and would also start preparatory work on the opening of the Suez Canal and the rehabilitation of the Canal cities. Sadat wished to regain Egyptian land and restore the honor of his army.

As reported at the time, the proposal Kissinger brought with him from Cairo, and which in principle was based on our suggestions, called for the creation of three zones east of the Canal: Egyptian, U.N., and Israeli. The Egyptian and Israeli forces in their respective zones would be limited both in troop strength and in arms. The three zones together would extend from the Canal to a line twenty miles east of it. The southern limit was not specified. Egypt wanted our forces to be stationed east of the strategic Mitla and Gidi passes, while the western entrance to the passes would be under the control of the UNEF.

On the size of the force in each zone, Sadat was said to have mentioned two divisions, comprising 24,000 men and 200 tanks. He had apparently also agreed not to introduce surface-to-air missile batteries east of the Canal, but he was not prepared to accept any limit to his forces on the west bank.

After various details had been clarified, the discussion narrowed to the knotty issue of our withdrawal and what we would get in exchange. The proposed agreement was for a disengagement of forces, but it was more a unilateral Israeli withdrawal. We alone would be pulling back, both from the west bank of the Canal and from positions we had long occupied on the east bank. Our military situation would be weakened as a result, yet the Arabs would still be dissatisfied, for they wanted us to retire to the pre-1967 lines, and they had much support for this demand beyond the Arab world. What, then, would be gained by our withdrawal? Indeed, once we withdrew, would not the Arabs again threaten an oil boycott? There would be renewed pressure on us to pull back further, and we would be worse off militarily and politically.

The answer to these questions was that we had nothing to lose. Our forces might not be in a military trap, but they were in a political trap. The Egyptians would not reconcile themselves to our presence west of the Canal, and if the war were renewed, the whole world, including the United States, would be against us. The world was interested in oil, not justice, and they wanted the Arab oil-producing states to lift the embargo imposed on the consuming nations to force them into an anti-Israeli position. But even those who agreed with this analysis of the position of Israel vis-à-vis the Arab demands, and the world support they commanded, could not let it rest at that; for the basic question was really "How is it all going to end?" To this there was no satisfactory answer, but the worst that might happen in six months would certainly happen immediately if no agreement were reached. Our strategic political aim should now be to dampen the panic and hysteria that had seized the governments of Europe and countries like Japan, which were under the pressure of the oil boycott. Many of these governments wished to show their own people how active they were in protecting their interests by bringing pressure to bear on Israel.

It cannot be said that these replies were found convincing by all. There were some for whom concepts like gaining time and dampening the oil panic were acceptable political tender. Others wanted things to be clear-cut and tangible. What would be gained by time? Why would anyone expect the world's attitude toward us to change in six months? It was evident that the United States hoped to achieve an end to the oil boycott within the framework of agreements between Israel and the Egyptians and Syrians. Ending the boycott was important to us too, but it was not the key objective. Oil was not the problem between Israel and the Arabs. Each time one mentioned that the world wanted us to return to the pre-1967 borders, there were some who would add the correction: "The world wants oil." The world probably wanted both.

The "How is it all going to end" query called to mind the occasion when I had first heard it. It was in New York, and I was addressing a meeting of Jews on the theme of the call in Isaiah 44:2: "Fear not, O Jacob, my servant." After my speech there were questions from the floor, and the first to rise was an elderly man who asked simply: "Mr. Defense Minister, where will it all end?" He said it in Yiddish, and somehow all the agony of centuries of Jewish suffering was expressed in those five words: *"Vos vet sein der sof?"*

In the talks with Kissinger, I felt that the only solution in keeping with Isaiah's "Fear not, O Jacob" was to return to my old proposal of an interim settlement, a plan which I had been advancing, without success, ever since the Six Day War. I now explained that while Golda was right in saying that what was called disengagement was in fact a unilateral withdrawal of our forces, what we needed in exchange was not a parallel withdrawal by the Egyptians but an agreement. Such an agreement had to contain three essential provisions:

• Disengagement was to be effected within the framework of an Israeli-Egyptian non-belligerency pact.

• Our withdrawal was not to be exploited by the Egyptians to strengthen their front-line forces: their tanks should not be brought in as our tanks were pulled out.

• The area was to be restored to normal. This important proviso meant the rebuilding of the Suez Canal cities; return of the civilian population to the Canal area; renewal of industrial activities, such as the refineries and the operations of the oil pipeline from the Gulf of Suez; and a significant reduction in the size of the Egyptian army. These actions were of greater consequence than a formal guarantee to end the war, for they represented not simply a verbal obligation but the practical implementation of a peaceful pattern of life, a pattern which was incompatible with a continuation of hostilities.

These, then, were the suggestions I had been airing for years, and now, I said, was perhaps the time for them to be put into effect. We had no wish to remain on the territory west of the Canal. As for the east, I, at least, had long thought we should move further back from the waterway—but only as part of an interim settlement.

None of what I said was new to the Israelis present. Nor was it new to Kissinger, for I had mentioned it to him in Washington the previous week. He had then reacted with astonishment. Now he nodded his head in agreement. In the meantime, in good State Department style, he had done his homework and had even tested the proposal with Sadat in Cairo and found it not without possibilities.

I was pleased to hear this news from Kissinger. The path to an agreement would still be long, but it was not blocked. I did not think that Egypt would be ready to reach a final agreement with us on an end to the war—even if we returned to the pre-1967 frontier—without Syria, Jordan, and the Palestinians. But I believed that the key to an arrangement with every Arab state, and particularly Egypt, was the creation of conditions which reduced the Arab motivation for war and promoted the normalization of life. With Egypt, this applied to the Canal Zone. It did not apply in the same measure to the eastern part of Sinai. For one thing, the Egyptians understood its importance to us and its unimportance to them—except for the negative aim of blockading our shipping at Sharm el-Sheikh, at the entrance to the Gulf of Aqaba. For another, since they were unwilling to reach a final agreement with us as long as our conflict with Syria, Jordan, and the Palestinians remained unresolved, our presence in eastern Sinai was not too disturbing; for they could continue, together with the other Arab states, to maintain a position at least of no peace. Sadat, like his predecessors, would echo the slogan from time to time that for him, too, the Palestinian problem was the heart of the matter and that Jerusalem took priority over Sinai. Leaving the eastern portion of Sinai in our hands and continuing the status of belligerency, though not active warfare, solved the practical side of the problem—securing for Egypt what was the most important part of Sinai for her—and paid the required lip service to the symbolic side.

On December 21, there was a ceremonial opening of the Geneva Peace Conference, which then adjourned. Two days later, when our military delegation was to leave for Switzerland, I asked Col. Dov Sion to see me and said that I assumed the chief of staff had already spoken to him about the conference. Maj. Gen. Mordechai (Motta) Gur, who was then our military attaché in Washington, would be heading this delegation to the peace talks and Sion would be his deputy. I handed him the relevant decisions of the government and also my own instructions. Dov Sion had accompanied Aharon Yariv to the talks at Kilometer 101 and was familiar with the subject. Despite my liking for him, my high regard for his intelligence, and our informal relationship—he is my son-in-law, Yael's husband—I was at pains to give him the most explicit definition of the delegation's authority. I had had bitter experience from the talks at Kilometer 101, where our representatives were given vague and general directives, and it was not clear to whom they were directly responsible.

I told Dov Sion that his delegation had authority to present only our official proposals. If they were asked for unofficial suggestions, they were to answer that there was none. (At Kilometer 101 problems had arisen as a result of the unofficial proposals of Yariv.) Kissinger and Soviet Foreign Minister Gromyko had already left Geneva for their respective capitals, and our military delegation had to kill time until after the general elections in Israel on December

31. I stressed that they were answerable to me alone—not to the prime minister or to the chief of staff. They were to send reports to all who required them—to the prime minister, the chief of staff, and the Foreign Ministry—but they would receive instructions only from me.

We would know who would head the new government only after the elections. If Golda continued as prime minister, I did not know whether she would wish me to serve as her minister of defense. But whoever he was, whether I or someone else, the future defense minister would have to hold further talks with the Americans on the proposed disengagement-of-forces agreement. Our ambassador in Washington would find out from Kissinger when he would like to confer with us again.

The meeting with Kissinger was arranged for January 4, 1974, in Washington. To prepare for it, Golda met earlier with a group of five ministers, together with the chief of staff. At her request, I presented my proposal. It contained several provisions. Four were military and dealt with deployment of forces, limitation of forces, timetable for the implementation of the new deployment, and budget required to fortify and provide the necessary services, such as access roads, for the new lines.

Other provisions related to three areas. First, the proposed apparatus for supervising the agreement—U.N. observers and other measures. Second, non-military matters which should be included in the agreement: cessation of hostilities, civilian rehabilitation of the Canal Zone, freedom of passage through the Bab el-Mandeb Straits, reduction of Egyptian and Israeli troop strength, and renewal of passage through the Suez Canal, including Israeli cargoes. Third, an agreement between Israel and the United States which should contain items of bilateral concern, such as arms supplies and economic aid, as well as matters directly affecting Israel and Egypt in which America was involved as a third party. The latter would include guarantees over Bab el-Mandeb and other matters on which Egypt would agree to give undertakings to the United States but not to us. The disadvantage of this procedure was, of course, the absence of direct contact between the Egyptians and us, but it had the advantage of securing the involvement of the United States, if not as actual guarantor at least as a partner to the arrangement.

The chief of staff expanded on the military provisions and displayed the proposed map. Following a discussion, the prime minister summed up and said that the general lines of my proposal would be brought for review and approval before the Cabinet the next day. The Cabinet approved, and I was authorized to present it to Kissinger.

When I saw Kissinger in Washington on January 4, I told him that the proposal I had brought with me, approved by my government, would no doubt be endorsed by the next government to be formed on the basis of the election results. In presenting my disengagement-of-forces proposal, I explained to him that it was devised as a total concept and not as a patchwork quilt. It had a specific logic and would work properly and fulfill its purpose only if it were implemented in its entirety. It could be accepted or rejected, but there was no point in arguing over each of its provisions. It was aimed at creating a new situation and opening a new page in the relations and realities between Israel and Egypt.

I had never believed that Egypt would wish or be able to rehabilitate its Canal cities and operate the waterway while we occupied the east bank, or even if we were further inland but commanded it with our artillery. On the other hand, there was no logic in our removing ourselves from the Canal if the Egyptians had no intention of operating it and restoring civilian life in the zone. We therefore considered our suggestions as being a first step toward peace and not merely a disengagement of forces. We would need assurance from the United States that Egypt intended to open the Canal, guarantee freedom of passage for Israeli cargoes, and demobilize a portion of her armed forces. An appropriate formula would have to be devised to prescribe a cessation of warfare or an end to belligerency. The United States would have to guarantee freedom of shipping through the Straits of Bab el-Mandeb. And we would wish to conclude an arrangement with the United States for long-term arms supplies.

We met again the next day, Saturday. Kissinger had apparently studied the written material and given thought to our previous discussion, and he now raised anew the subject of a reduction of forces, but he dwelled particularly on the Mitla-Gidi line. I knew that for Sadat this was a matter of both practical and symbolic significance. He had gone to war with the aim of reaching the Mitla Pass, and if he could go out to his people with the triumphant announcement that he had driven us from it, he would have achieved a tremendous victory. The practical value to Sadat was also considerable, for if he decided to renew the war, it would be convenient to have the UNEF stationed at the entrance to the passes, since it could be removed with a flick of the hand. It took me an hour to make it clear that I would not move from my position.

After the talks at the State Department, I met with Defense Secretary Schlesinger at the Pentagon. It was difficult to avoid the impression that the American arms policy toward Israel was to give us a little now as a hint that if we reached agreement with the Egyptians, we could expect a long-term agreement on arms deliveries. What such a commitment would be, and in what measure it would be fulfilled, only the future would tell. Our problem was that America was our only friend—with the accent on "only."

36

SHUTTLE TO AGREEMENT

THE NEXT SIX HECTIC DAYS in January carried their own drama, as Henry Kissinger shuttled back and forth between Cairo and Jerusalem. The secretary of state spent January 14 with Sadat and returned to us on the following day. This time he brought the Egyptian proposal. Our differences with the Egyptians focused mainly on two basic points: who would occupy the Mitla and Gidi passes, and a joint reduction of forces. On neither point were we prepared to compromise, even if this meant failure to reach an agreement. Finally, after discussion, definition, erasure, and rewriting, which went on into the small hours of the morning, the work was completed. We had a map and a verbal agreement with the Egyptians and several documents on matters concerning the United States—some linked to our agreement with Egypt and others relating to "understandings" with the United States on bilateral matters. The proposed formula was brought before the Cabinet and it was approved. The session, which had been specially convened for this purpose, was held in the home of the prime minister, who was suffering from a severe cold.

The Cabinet empowered the prime minister to instruct the chief of staff to meet with the Egyptian chief of staff at Kilometer 101 and sign a Disengagement of Forces Agreement and the accompanying maps. Kissinger flew to Cairo and returned on the night of the 16th, bringing with him the final Egyptian text, which contained a few insignificant changes, as well as our withdrawal up to twelve miles from the city of Suez, south of Ras Masala on the east coast of the Gulf of Suez, as well as east of the gulf. I agreed, for there was no special military advantage in our maintaining forces close to Suez. It would not encourage the rehabilitation of the city and would only increase the Egyptian motivation for war.

On the next day, Kissinger left for his last visit to Cairo. From there he would be returning to Washington via Jordan and Syria. Coordinated arrangements were made for the military signing ceremony the following day, and on that day, Friday, January 18, 1974, at Kilometer 101, Chief of Staff David Elazar, on behalf of Israel, and Gen. Abdel Gamasi, on behalf of Egypt, signed the agreement. Gen. Siilasvuo signed as a witness on behalf of the United Nations. The ceremony was held under U.N. auspices, in the presence of American advisers, Russians who were included among the U.N. observers, a crowd of correspondents, and a cluster of television cameras.

The Geneva Peace Conference, which opened with considerable fanfare on December 21, four weeks before the actual signing at Kilometer 101, played no part in the disengagement agreement. The delegations were headed by foreign ministers and included high-ranking officers. The agreements were negotiated elsewhere, in Jerusalem, Cairo, and Washington. Even the festive signatures were affixed not in Geneva's Palace of Nations but in a tent on the Suez-Cairo highway. Some of us referred to Geneva at the time as "the Turkish road." This expression harks back to the period when I was a boy and Palestine was under Ottoman rule. The Turkish authorities, who had little interest in the welfare of the country, used to pave roads so badly that coachmen and wagons—only horse-drawn traffic in those days—would drive to the right or the left of them, anywhere but on the roads themselves. The Geneva Conference, too, was conducted anywhere except Geneva.

January 18, 1974, the day the agreement was signed at Kilometer 101, was the first day that the guns were stilled on the southern front. Throughout the ten and a half weeks since the official cease-fire went into effect on October 24, there had been no end to combat. In the first two months of the cease-fire, there were 452 incidents initiated by the Egyptians, and our casualties were 15 killed and 65 wounded. I do not know the casualty figures for the Egyptians, but I imagine they were higher than ours. Also during this period, 68

Egyptian prisoners of war fell into our hands, 8 of them officers. The intensity of fire was not uniform for each day and in each sector. There were ups and downs. There were some days, in some sectors, when there was absolute silence. There were others when hundreds and even thousands of artillery shells were fired. It depended mainly on the orders issued by Cairo and our reactions to them. These orders specifically instructed the Egyptian troops in the field not to respect the cease-fire. One deliberate order to this effect became more widely known when Egypt's National Assembly was informed of the mobilization of snipers with the special task of harassing Israeli troops stationed west of the Canal. We raised the issue time and again at meetings at Kilometer 101, with Dr. Kissinger, and with the U.N. observers and threatened to stop food supplies to the Third Army if the firing continued.

On January 1, 1974, General Siilasvuo brought us the Egyptian reply. He said that he had met the Egyptian war minister and the chief of staff the day before and they had told him that our fortification works, particularly west of the Canal, had angered the Egyptian troops. It seemed to them that we were digging in with the intention of occupying the territory permanently, and so they had opened fire. The only way to stop them, they said, was for us to stop these works.

It was our policy to reply sharply with counter-fire to every Egyptian shot and also, as a warning, to hold up supplies to the Third Army for a few hours. The Egyptians had to choose between implementing the cease-fire, in all its terms, or scrapping it, which would then leave the Third Army and the city of Suez without supplies.

The heaviest Egyptian fire was in the area of Ismailia, directed against the forces commanded by Arik Sharon, and the toughest replies were given by him. Arik could be relied on not to allow the Egyptians to feel they could do as they wished. Moreover, he knew there was basic approval for the policy of sharp reprisal, and usually did not seek the prior agreement of Southern Command whenever he had to react to Egyptian aggression. The commanders of other sectors would seek prior permission, and the GOC Southern Command, who was now Gen. Tal, would give it with considerable reluctance.

The cease-fire existed on paper, but the continued firing along the front was not the only characteristic of the situation between October 24, 1973, and January 18, 1974. This intermediate period also held the ever-present possibility of a renewal of full-scale war. There were three variations on how it might break out, two Egyptian and one Israeli. One Egyptian plan was to attack our units west of the

Canal from the direction of Cairo. The other was to cut off our Canal bridgehead by a link-up of the Second and Third Armies on the east bank. Both plans were based on massive artillery pounding of our forces, who were not well fortified and who would suffer heavy casualties. It was therefore thought that Israel would withdraw from the west bank, since she was most sensitive on the subject of soldiers' lives.

Egypt, at the time, had a total of 1,700 first-line tanks on both sides of the Canal front, 700 on the east bank and 1,000 on the west bank. Also on the west bank, in the second line, were an additional 600 tanks for the defense of Cairo. She had some 2,000 artillery pieces, about 500 operational aircraft, and at least 130 SAM missile batteries positioned around our forces so as to deny us air support.

In addition to our intelligence information on Egyptian attack plans, there were also indications of differences of opinion, disquiet, and ferment among the top echelons of the Egyptian army. Since the end of the war, many high-ranking officers had been removed—among them generals, brigadiers, and colonels. The most significant dismissal was of course that of the Egyptian chief of staff, Gen. Shazli.

There were various explanations for Shazli's departure. As a former commander of commando units, it was he who had initiated their extensive operational use immediately at the start of the war. The results were disastrous. They suffered the most severe casualties and made no tangible gains. The decision to deploy them came in for particular criticism in Egypt because many of the commandos were well educated and very fit young men who belonged to influential families.

More important, however, was Shazli's basic mistake in failing to discern in time the full significance of the crossing of the Canal by our forces. He just did not understand what was happening. He thought it was simply a raid, did not report it to President Sadat, and failed to take the required radical measures to destroy our bridgehead when it was still in the build-up stage. It was probably because of this misjudgment that Shazli later called for an all-out attack on our forces in "Africa": they were to be destroyed at all cost. Sadat feared the military consequences of such an attack, for by then our forces on the west bank had grown to three divisions, and they had already cleared the area around them of all surface-to-air missile batteries. He accordingly preferred to dismiss Shazli and continue his political negotiations with us through the mediation of Kissinger. However, many of Egypt's top officers still pressed for an attack and chafed at Sadat's decision. They based their view on the opinion of the Soviet advisers, who claimed that from the military point of view the Egyptians were capable of succeeding in this operation, albeit at the cost of very heavy casualties.

We, too, had various ideas about attack operations, in the event that either Egypt or we might renew the war. Arik, who observed with justice that the war with Egypt had not been decisive, felt that we should attack the Egyptian armor positioned between our forces and Cairo. He pointed to places where it would be relatively easy to penetrate between the enemy units, outflank them, and even attack them from the rear. But these were general notions which never reached the concrete planning stage. They did not appeal to me. At the very best, we would destroy another few hundred Egyptian tanks, get closer to Cairo, spread ourselves over an even wider area, and still remain without a clear-cut military-political decision. Even the United States would be reproving, and it was doubtful whether Cairo would raise its hands in surrender. Furthermore, we, too, would suffer casualties, and this was hardly justified for an operation which seemed to me to be of dubious value.

The only feasible possibility was the destruction of the Third Army. It was cut off, exposed to our Air Force, and we could assemble for this operation enough armor to give us superiority. The various possibilities could become realities if the Egyptians were to start a war of attrition against our forces west of the Canal. This condition did not present itself.

On the whole I was satisfied with this agreement with the Egyptians. I did not expect us to attain more, under the circumstances, and I also felt that it had intrinsic merit. It put an end to the war— up to its signature there had been fighting at one point or another along the front—and the essential conditions were included in its articles. From the territorial point of view, the new line—the Mitla and Gidi passes and the hills in front of them—was the best possible, once we had pulled back from the Canal beyond artillery range. And under the reduction-of-forces clause, the military strength which the Egyptians would be maintaining east of the Canal was indeed minimal.

The disengagement agreement also embodied political content of great importance. Certain undertakings were given, and if carried out—and I hoped they would be—they would contribute much toward the normalization of life in the area and serve to defuse war tensions. They would bring about the opening of the Suez Canal to navigation, including the passage of Israeli cargoes; removal of the blockade threat at Bab el-Mandeb; rehabilitation of the Canal cities; demobilization of part of the Egyptian army and of our own reservists; and an improvement in the relations between the United States and Egypt, particularly over the oil problem.

This latter point, on the face of it, was of no direct concern to Israel, but in fact it was important to us. If it was not our function to worry about oil supplies to the United States, it was certainly our duty to foster and safeguard the friendship and help we received from her. In the current situation, I had no doubt that an end to the war with Egypt was what America very much wanted, and it was a positive factor in the fabric of our relations with her. A continuation of the war would have been burdensome for the United States and might have led to a change in her attitude.

The disengagement agreement did not meet the basic problems between Israel and Egypt or the challenge of permanent arrangements. At best, it facilitated discussion of them in due course. The next stage with Egypt would come, I thought, after the implementation of the present agreement, namely, after the opening of the Suez Canal. I imagined this new stage would not occur before the spring or summer of 1975, more than a year after the signing of this agreement. We would then see whether Egypt was in fact carrying out restoration projects in the Canal area. If she was—and was not impeded by inter-Arab and international political circumstances—it might be possible to conduct negotiations on an end to the state of belligerency.

37

THE LAST HURDLE

THE PROBLEM OF DISENGAGEMENT negotiations with Syria was that we were locked in a vicious circle. The Syrians demanded that negotiations begin before they provided us with the list of our prisoners. We said we would negotiate only after we received the list. Not until February 27, 1974, was the impasse broken. On that day, Kissinger, who was on one of his shuttle missions to the Middle East capitals, arrived in Jerusalem from Damascus with the list in his pocket. He handed it to prime minister Golda Meir. It contained sixty-five names. The Syrians had told him that all the prisoners were alive and well and that the stories of murder and torture were untrue.

Kissinger suggested that since this hurdle had been cleared, Israel should now send a representative to Washington to present the government's disengagement plan. The Cabinet decided to accept this suggestion and to send me. Kissinger was leaving for Moscow, and it was arranged that we would meet soon after his return to the United States.

Shortly before my departure, the prime minister called together a ministerial group for a final review of the proposals I would be taking to Washington. By now, after the elections, Golda had formed a new government, and taking part in this meeting were Allon, Bar-Lev,

Galili, Sapir, Yariv, Peres, Rabin, and myself. The chief of staff was also present.

It was decided that in addition to presenting Kissinger with the plan and maps for the separation of forces as approved by the Cabinet, I would insist that the implementation of any agreement with the Syrians would not begin until our prisoners were released. There would also be an article in the agreement banning terrorism. And I was to request of Kissinger that he make determined efforts to secure permission for the persecuted Jews of Syria to leave.

I regretted the necessity of framing our disengagement proposal to take into account not only content but tactics. It became clear that this factor in negotiation could not be avoided. To my mind it was not only the Arabs who forced upon us this bargaining procedure of starting high and ending with compromise. I felt that the Americans, too, favored it, for they could then show the Arabs that it was the United States which had moved us both to give up territory and climb down from our positions. The formula they kept impressing upon the Arabs was that only America could persuade Israel to withdraw. The Arabs could get arms from the Soviet Union, but the key to a political solution lay with the United States.

For us, the difficulty with this kind of bargaining was not simply that we viewed it as undignified, but that it put us in an invidious position vis-à-vis the Israeli public. There are no secrets in Israel. Thus, if we took a particular negotiating stand, it would be widely known. Later, if we dropped our sights, we would be accused of political surrender.

I did not think the content of our proposals would be found acceptable. The Syrians were obdurate, and it seemed to me that they would prefer to continue with the existing situation rather than agree to our plan. Our problem was not simply whether we were ready to continue without a disengagement agreement in the north, but what effect this would have on the Egyptian front. The assumption was that if no arrangement were reached with Syria, Egypt, the only Arab country which had signed an agreement with us, would be unable to carry it out.

I held consultations with the General Staff and particularly with our commanders in the north to ascertain the absolute minimum line beyond which we should not withdraw. I went on repeated survey patrols along the entire length of the lines we had proposed, and I finalized for myself the ultimate line essential to us. In my view, we could give up the town of Kuneitra, or at all events the part lying east of the main road. However, the central problem was not this or that disengagement line but the future of the Golan Heights. This was not the immediate topic on the agenda, but I thought we ourselves should know right from the beginning where we were heading and what positions we would eventually be ready to accept. I did not believe the Syrians would easily reconcile themselves to the loss of the Golan, and our continued presence there might mean a prolonged state of Syrian belligerency. The primary impact would be felt by the civilian settlements in the north. I had expressed these views on several occasions, and I had also spoken with the settlers themselves about what they were likely to experience.

On February 12, 1974, a day after one of the women in the Golan settlement of Ramat Magshimim had been killed by Syrian artillery, several others wounded, and buildings hit, I visited that settlement as well as another in the area, Ein Zivan, and we talked about the future. These two settlements had been established after the Six Day War. The settlers told me that not only had their spirits not been weakened by the Yom Kippur War—even though they had had to abandon their homes during the fighting—but they were now more resolved than ever to stay. They also said that what worried them was not a Syrian attack but the possibility that the government of Israel might decide one day to withdraw.

I met Kissinger in Washington on March 29, 1974, with our full teams. He explained that the Russians were insisting that the Geneva Peace Conference be reconvened at once. They were also complaining about the one-sided manner in which the United States was conducting the negotiations between Israel and Egypt. Kissinger then launched into a long review of the international political situation. The implication seemed to be that if the American efforts at mediation between Israel and Syria should fail, the prestige of the United States in the Middle East would be harmed, and Israel would find herself in a very difficult situation.

I presented my proposals to Kissinger. But, as I reported later, I had not managed to "sell" them, and I was not at all sure that he would even pass them on to the Syrian representative who was due in Washington on April 12 to start negotiations.

We lunched in the State Department dining room. The table, the bowl of soup in the center, the cutlery, the crockery were all familiar. So was the menu, which I remembered from the last visit. We moved on to other subjects—Egypt's violation of the disengagement agreement, exchange of wounded prisoners with Syria, and American arms supplies to Israel that were not being carried out as promised. On the subject of arms, we would go into detail on the following day.

The next day, Saturday, we met at 10 A.M. in Kissinger's office. This time, at his request, without full teams. I expressed my disappointment over the replies we had received concerning arms. I told Kissinger that even a small state like Israel would be able to send a few hundred tanks and carriers to a friendly country at war if the need arose.

We then turned to the future. I told him that if we reached a disengagement agreement with Syria, the basic problem would still remain unsolved, and it was essential to ensure a strong Israel in the coming years. The U.S. secretary of state ' should surely share our thinking on what Israel's situation would be in another 5 or 10 years. We needed the most up-to-date aircraft and other types of sophisticated conventional weapons, which would enable us to defend ourselves now and in the future. It was arranged that I would meet with Defense Secretary Schlesinger on the following Monday.

The talk with Kissinger had been somewhat protracted, and his secretary came in to remind him that he must leave immediately or he would be late for the meeting he had arranged. The "meeting," it transpired later, was his marriage to Nancy.

The Monday morning meeting with Schlesinger at the Pentagon was, as usual, pleasant and friendly, and, typically, not very encouraging. I received no firm commitment on the essential items. Only on the new generation of aircraft did the Pentagon show any readiness to respond positively to our request. I could only hope that when the time came to implement this positive response, my optimism would not prove to have been premature.

In the afternoon I met with the Senate Armed Services Committee. With me was Mottie Hod, former commander of our Air Force, and we had to answer many questions, all relevant and some even technical, such as those posed by Barry Goldwater on the subject of aircraft and anti-aircraft defenses. During the meeting I was called to the telephone and to my surprise was informed that after I had left the Pentagon that morning, my request had again been considered, and despite the difficulties involved it had been decided to give us the tanks and carriers we had asked for. I flew back to Israel a few hours later in somewhat better spirits.

In addition to my talks in Washington, I also addressed United Jewish Appeal meetings in New York and appeared on several TV programs. These brief visits to the United States are no holiday, and there is little rest or relaxation. I did manage to take in two plays. At the first, on the night of my arrival, with the seven-hour time difference, I fell asleep during the first act. I could not enjoy the second, for I was too preoccupied with the urgent matters I had been discussing in Washington. However, what did give me great pleasure were renewed visits to the Metropolitan Museum and the Brooklyn Museum, particularly the Egyptian exhibits. Absolutely marvelous! Prof. Bernard Bothmer was the curator of the Egyptian Department at Brooklyn, and we had become good friends through my repeated visits over the years. His greeting this time was an enthusiastic expression of delight with the air photo I had given him. "Just what I wanted," he said. Some years earlier he had carried out archaeological excavations in Egypt, and when he was about to publish his findings, he needed an air photograph of the mound he had excavated. He had asked the Egyptian government for the picture, but repeated requests had proved fruitless. He then approached the British and U.S. governments, and again drew a blank. At one of our meetings, he asked me casually, more in fun than in earnest, whether the Israel Defense Forces might have an air-reconnaissance photo of this district in Egypt. I asked Benny Peled, the Air Force commander, to look through the files, and he came up with a superb photograph of the very archaeological mound the professor had worked on. It appears in Bothmer's book, with the acknowledgment "Photograph by the Israeli Air Force"!

I had a delightful surprise of a different kind in another setting. At a dinner party in Washington, I was seated between Mrs. Henry Jackson and Mrs. Frank Church and was greatly entertained by their bright, amusing, and witty talk. The surprise came when Mrs. Jackson told me that her father had been a scholarly priest, able to read the Bible in its original Hebrew! He had ensured that his children also studied it thoroughly, and Mrs. Jackson had clearly been an apt pupil.

She revealed a wide knowledge not only of the Bible but also of post-biblical periods. She had visited Israel, had climbed to the top of Masada, and was familiar with all the details of the dramatic story associated with that historic site, where the Jews made their last stand against the Romans in the first century. She questioned me about that military action, and at times I was afraid I might not know the answer. Of course I knew the celebrated oration of the Jewish commander, Eleazar ben Yair, made against the background of the flaming ramparts and a gaping breach in the wall through which the Romans would charge at dawn. But when she asked me to explain how it was that the Romans had failed in their first attempt to break into the fortress, how they had constructed the ramp, and how they had operated such weapons as the battering ram and the ballista, I was hard put to recall the details. But I must say that of all my talks in Washington on the subject of armaments, this was the only one that was pleasant!

On Thursday, May 2, 1974, Kissinger arrived in Israel, together with his team of aides, but this time accompanied by his wife, Nancy. He told us that he proposed to devote intensive efforts to secure an agreement with Syria. The technique was already smooth and polished—flights on the Lod-Damascus-Lod route by day and meetings and discussions at night.

As usual, he first met for a private talk with the prime minister. The teams were to meet at 3 P.M. and continue at a working dinner in the evening at the house of the foreign minister, Abba Eban. Golda's meeting, I heard, had not been satisfactory. The sessions in the afternoon had also been sterile.

At dinner Kissinger turned to me and suggested that we meet privately. I referred him to the prime minister, and at the end of the meal Golda took me aside and asked me to meet with the secretary of state. I told her that I thought I should explain to Kissinger my approach to the problem of Kuneitra. Golda agreed, with the proviso that I present it as my personal view. I asked that Simcha Dinitz, our ambassador to Washington, accompany me, as well as my aide, Aryeh Brown. We met with Kissinger, who had Peter Rodman with him. The time was twenty minutes to midnight, a fine hour to turn in for the night but not to embark on exhaustive consultations.

Kissinger wanted to know the reasoning behind each detailed point in my proposal—why we insisted on retaining certain hills, what was the importance of the road passing through Kuneitra, where exactly was the region of Rafid, and where were our outposts on Mount Hermon. Aryeh went to bring the maps and Rodman the sandwiches. When I left Kissinger's room, it was 1:30 in the morning. I was almost dropping from fatigue, but Kissinger appeared as sprightly as ever.

If anyone had predicted that Kissinger would spend a month shuttling between Damascus and Jerusalem, I would never have believed it. And if Kissinger had known at the outset that this was what he would have to do, he would no doubt have refused. But this, in fact, is just what he did for precisely thirty-two days.

In those days of negotiation in Jerusalem, I saw Kissinger at work at close quarters, and I was amazed. He is what we in Israel call a "Yekke" (jacket), our term of amused endearment for the jacket-and-tie-wearing German Jewish immigrants who managed to flee from Hitler and reach this country in the 1930s. They were neat, precise, sober, quite different from the open-shirted, casual, and easygoing Russian Jewish pioneers who had preceded them. Yet in spite of being a *Yekke,* Kissinger combines a keen wit and highly developed sense of humor with a prodigious capacity for serious work of remarkable thoroughness. After intense study, he registers maps he has never seen before and terrain with which he is unfamiliar and has them fixed in his mind. When proposals couched in generalities and open to more than one interpretation are flung at him, he takes them apart, insisting that they be clearly stated and then written into the record. The late U.N. official Dr. Ralph Bunche, who mediated the Armistice Agreements between Israel and the Arabs in 1949, was different. He would often draft an agreement with deliberately cloudy articles so that each of the parties could give it his own desired interpretations and be prepared to sign. Kissinger did not spare his aides, and he could use harsh words when his instructions were not obeyed or followed quickly enough. Occasionally he would pause in the middle of a conversation, withdraw into silence, stretch his legs, plunge into concentrated thought and seemingly consult with himself. These sudden spells of meditation would be preceded by a warning signal— he would start to chew on his yellow pencil, like a child in kindergarten.

There were moments during that month of Kissinger's Lod-Damascus shuttle when it looked as if we were on a dead-end street and there could be no agreement. There were quite a few harsh exchanges. But what characterized these negotiations was the hard, painstaking work, the slow tortuous bargaining over every point, both over the articles covering the limitation of forces and those dealing with the demarcation of the front lines. Kissinger and his team had little rest.

The first Syrian proposal demanded our withdrawal from half of the Golan Heights, some six miles west of the 1967 cease-fire line. As to Mount Hermon, the Syrians claimed that we had captured it after the 1973 cease-fire decision had been accepted, and therefore we had to evacuate it completely. They also refused to have U.N. forces on their territory. They rejected out of hand the idea of following the Egyptian model, which would create a sandwich of three zones, Syrian, UNEF, and Israeli. In due course, however, they were to give considerable ground on these demands.

We, too, made concessions during the negotiations. At first we said that we would not withdraw beyond the 1967 lines. Later we insisted that only the eastern part of Kuneitra would be given to Syria, while the western portion would be occupied by the U.N. force. Finally we reconciled ourselves to a line which would leave the whole of Kuneitra in Syrian hands. There were also certain additional withdrawals.

The bargaining was tough. In the end, when the details of the only agreement that Syria would be prepared to sign became clear to us, we had to decide whether to accept it or remain without any agreement at all. We had set ourselves two basic principles and we stood firm on them: the first, not to abandon a sound military line, namely, not to withdraw from the hills which dominate Kuneitra and Rafid; the second, not to disturb or leave vulnerable our existing frontier settlements.

We compromised on the size of the U.N. force, agreeing to a far smaller number than we had originally suggested. And even the name of the force had to be changed. On the Syrian front it was to be called UNDOF (United Nations Disengagement Observer Force) and not, as on the Egyptian front, UNEF (United Nations Emergency Force). But the name, of course, was unimportant. In any case, on the Syrian front, apart from the U.N. post on Mount Hermon, the troops would not control but merely observe the implementation of the agreement. In contrast, on the Egyptian front there was a zone occupied solely by the UNEF. However, that was a desert area, while civilians occupied the area along the Syrian front, and it required a civilian Syrian administration.

Parallel with our negotiations with the Syrians, we conducted independent talks with the Americans. It was our task to try to ensure the supply of arms in the coming years, financial aid for the acquisition of these arms, and confirmation that the United States would not demand from us further withdrawals from the Golan Heights.

Along the Syrian front, as along the Egyptian frontier, firing did not cease until the day the agreement was signed. Here, too, the Syrians did not try to capture new positions, with one exception, but maintained steady fire, mostly artillery, across our lines. The exception was the Hermon peak. When we captured the three positions on the Hermon range on the night of October 21, our forces had reached the post on the peak. Later, however, because of the heavy snow and the absence of an access road, we removed our unit from the top position, after making sure that the U.N. observers had confirmed that this post was under our control. After a while, we noticed that Syrian troops were reaching it occasionally and at times even remaining for a while. We thereupon sent up a unit, which found Syrian troops there. Our men attacked and recaptured the post, and thereafter we remained in occupation of this peak site. We fortified it, paved an access road, and brought up tanks.

We encountered problems both in building the road and later in using it. The mountain slopes were very steep and cut by deep fissures, and the only route which could be leveled and paved lay along the shoulder of the ridge. But it was extremely narrow. And it was, of course, accurately targeted by Syrian artillery, which opened fire whenever a vehicle appeared. Our bulldozers, tanks, and armored carriers were hit and turned into obstructions on the narrow track. Several helicopters bringing supplies and troops crashed in accidents. Harsh weather added to our trials. The area was covered by heavy snow, and strong, cold winds blew without letup. Countries in the West have both the equipment and experience to fight under snow conditions. Until then we had trained in the desert and in the hot *khamsin* winds. Our main problem was to dig in and fortify, and both the cold and the stony terrain made this work very difficult. The main protection was afforded by a cave about 100 yards from the highest point on the Hermon.

During the months of April and May, I visited Mount Hermon at least once a week, mostly on the Sabbath. There were signs that the Syrians were preparing to capture our mountain posts. I suspected that such an attack would be attempted, and I wanted to be certain that we held the posts with enough strength and appropriate defense arrangements. Each visit to the top was an experience. The helicopter would thread its way through the ravines and cling to the mountain slopes so as to escape radar detection and avoid exposure to Syrian missiles. My interest in the changes of vegetation as we climbed steadily upward never waned. First came the tree belt. This gave way to bush and scrub. And then came the ridge—bare, exposed, prickly thorns holding firmly to the soil between the boulders and protected from the murderous wind.

There were two features of this outpost called the Hermon peak— the cave and the peak. The cave was a natural cavern which had been deepened and widened by man and had served as a dwelling place in ancient days. In recent years, during the hot summer months, it had served as a base for villagers in the area who came up the mountain to hack chunks of ice, which they sold to wealthy townfolk. It was hard work, and the ice blocks had to be brought by donkey down steep and twisting mountain tracks. But it was apparently profitable, for ice from Mount Hermon was carried by small vessels as far as Egypt!

The second geological feature, the peak itself, was the site of a Hellenistic temple in the third century B.C., and its remains—parts of ruined walls and large hewn stones—can still be seen. This is the highest point on the Hermon range, an excellent observation spot, and this is where the Syrian troops had established a military post.

When we captured the area, though the cave had been targeted by the Syrian artillery, it served as a shelter for our soldiers. It was covered by a thick level of hard rock, which made it safe against even a direct hit by enemy artillery. The outposts we established around the peak were exposed to the most bitter cold, more from the relentless icy winds than from the snow. In a peacetime summer the Hermon may be a paradise for holiday hikers, but it becomes hell for soldiers stationed there in winter.

The final stage of the disengagement negotiations with Syria took place in Geneva. Here, however, the negotiations were not over the substance of the agreement but concerned the timetable of our withdrawal, the exchange of prisoners and the entry of Syrian and U.N. forces into the territory we were evacuating. The discussions were held under U.N. auspices, and the chairman was Gen. Siilasvuo, commander of the U.N. forces. The Israeli team was composed of Maj. Gen. Herzl Shafir and Col. Dov Sion.

At 10:30 on the morning of June 5, 1974, the agreement was signed. It marked the formal end to the Yom Kippur War. The fire at the front died down. The last of the prisoners came home. The Israel Defense Forces could release the reserves. And in Syria the peasants could return to their abandoned villages.

38

MA'ALOT

ONE OF THE most difficult days of my life occurred during the seven and a half months of hectic negotiations that followed the Yom Kippur War. But it had nothing to do with Kissinger. And it had nothing to do with the war. It had to do with another form of violence—perpetrated by the terrorists, operating this time from Lebanon.

Long before Black September of 1970, when King Hussein took command of his own country and cleared the terrorists from his midst, they had begun to turn Lebanon into their central base of operations. After Hussein's action, when they were no longer able to use Jordanian territory, they made increasing use of the Lebanese-Israeli border for their terrorist incursions. They now numbered about five thousand. The Lebanese government proved ineffective in suppressing them. The terrorists directed their attacks at our frontier settlements and development towns, for the most part firing rockets from inside Lebanon. From time to time, however, they would cross the border on a mission of sabotage or murder.

While negotiations were proceeding on agreements to end hostilities and convene a "peace conference" in Geneva after the Yom Kippur War, the terror organizations renewed their activities and even opened a new chapter—seizure of hostages and threats to kill them, and be killed with them, unless their demands were fulfilled: release of their imprisoned colleagues. Two such actions were carried out in Israel within one month, the first at Kiryat Shmonah on April 11, 1974, and the second at Ma'alot on May 15, 1974. Both towns are in Upper Galilee, near our northern border.

At Kiryat Shmonah, at 11:15 A.M. on the day of the action, Radio Damascus announced that early that morning a "suicide squad" belonging to George Habash's Popular Front for the Liberation of Palestine had broken into the town and taken control of the Korcak school, where the terrorists were holding hostages. The announcement warned the Israeli authorities that all attempts to recapture the school would endanger the lives of the children.

When Radio Damascus broadcast this news, the three saboteurs were already dead. They had, in fact, entered the school at seven in the morning, but the youngsters were away on an outing and the building was empty. The terrorists thereupon entered a nearby apartment building, went from dwelling to dwelling flinging hand grenades and firing automatic weapons, and murdered the residents. When they reached the top floor, they barricaded themselves in a room which gave onto the street. As soon as the neighbors realized what had happened, they summoned the security forces. While troops outside the building pinned down the saboteurs, a picked unit entered the building, stormed the barricaded room, and killed the three saboteurs.

The terrorists had murdered 16 civilians—8 of them children. In the exchange of fire with our troops, two of our soldiers were killed.

When I reached Kiryat Shmonah, the battle between the terrorists and our troops had already gone into its final stages. Our soldiers had surrounded the building, and the people living in the neighboring houses had been evacuated. Our troops were firing at the upper story, where the terrorists had barricaded themselves, and when our men burst into the building, they found the terrorists lying on the floor, their bodies riddled, but their faces unmarked. They seemed young, properly shaved, hair neatly cut, and if I had met them in the street, they would have aroused no special curiosity on my part.

I do not know whether they valued their lives dearly, but they had certainly shown no concern for the lives of Jewish women and children. Indeed, they believed—as did their colleagues in the terrorist movements—that killing Jews was an act of heroism, over which they could feel pride and gloat to their friends. One of the bodies was shattered, but I do not know whether or not he blew himself up. He was clearly carrying explosives on his person, but he would naturally have carried them this way to avoid suspicion. I tend to think that the explosives were touched off by a bullet from one of our guns and were not detonated as an act of self-destruction. There is a wide gap between adopting the name "suicide squad" (*fedayun*) and the courage to go through with a commitment to take one's life when a mission fails.

These terrorists did not take hostages. They did not free their comrades. And they themselves were killed. But they did achieve one thing: they generated fear among some of the families in the town, who conjured up visions of horror—a door crashing open, an Arab terrorist appearing with a submachine gun spraying fire, children asleep in their beds, parents frantic, neighbors alarmed. One could understand their panic, but one should never be infected by it. Yet some Cabinet ministers and senior officers handed out ill-conceived and high-sounding promises which were harmful. The very act of promising was damaging, as though one had to be panicked into action by terror. Moreover, some of the promised projects for increased security were half-baked—and some were simply not carried out.

On May 15, 1974, a month after Kiryat Shmonah, came "Ma'alot." The three terrorists committed their first murder even before they reached Ma'alot. Near midnight they attacked a truck taking a group of Arab women home from work. The women worked on a late shift at a textile plant north of Haifa and were returning to their village. The assassins, using Kalatchnikov rifles, killed a woman and wounded ten people, including the bus driver. When the terrorists reached Ma'alot they entered one of the houses nd murdered the Cohen family. Then they went on to the schoolhouse, where 100 children and 4 teachers from a school in Safed were spending the night, and kept them hostage. The youngsters had been on an outing in the Galilee.

The terrorists released one teacher and a few children to carry letters containing their ultimatum, which they repeated through a loud-speaker they had brought with them. We were to release twenty terrorists whom we had caught, tried, and jailed, and have them flown to Damascus. As soon as Radio Damascus reported their arrival, the schoolchildren would be set free. If we rejected their demand, they would blow up the building and all the children in it.

Here, without doubt, there was no question of terrorist suicide. In the end, the terrorists were killed by our troops. It was not clear that the building had actually been set with explosive charges, as the terrorists had claimed. When it was all over, 5 satchels of explosives were found, 2 on the staircase, 2 in the classroom where the children had been held, and 1 in the corridor. They were presumably to have been activated by batteries. Four batteries giving a total power of half a watt were found on the body of one of the terrorists, and near the staircase was a half-watt battery, but it was not clear whether these batteries had been wired to the explosives. What *was* certain was that the explosives were not sufficient to blow up the building and they were not detonated, even though the terrorists had had enough time to do so.

In previous actions the terrorists had had to safeguard their retreat and accordingly had laid mines or sabotage materials with delayed-action fuses, so that they could be well across the border by the time the explosives went off. This new method, however, freed the terrorists from this problem. After murdering whom they wished, they took hostages and made their release conditional upon arrangements for themselves, and their fellow terrorists in Israeli prisons, to be transported peacefully to an Arab country.

This new approach set two problems before Israel. One was basic: should we submit to the terrorists' blackmail? The second was technical and posed a military question: how to fight the terrorists while they were holding hostages?

We had encountered these problems twice in the past. The first occurred in July 1968, when an El Al plane was hijacked and taken to Algiers. (It was the first hijacking of an aircraft by Arab terrorists.) The terrorists demanded that we release a number of captured saboteurs who were in Israeli jails and allow them to leave the country. Only then would they release our plane and its crew. I firmly opposed giving in to their demand. But the Israeli government of the time, headed by Levi Eshkol, consented, and the exchange was made. The problem came up again before the Israeli Cabinet in August 1969, when two Israelis, Muallem and Samuelov, were kidnapped on an American TWA plane hijacked to Damascus and were kept imprisoned in that city. Then, too, the government decided to trade them for two Syrian pilots who were prisoners of war in Israel.

But the episode closest to that of Ma'alot occurred with the Sabena aircraft that was hijacked on its way to Israel and landed at our own Lod Airport. The hijackers made the release of the passengers conditional upon Israel's freeing of 300 jailed terrorists. Our government decided not to give in, and in a military action that took place the next day and lasted a few minutes, 2 male hijackers were killed and the 2 women terrorists who were with them were caught and arrested. Eventually they were brought to trial and imprisoned. During the battle, one woman passenger was killed in the exchange of fire inside the plane.

The penetration of the terrorists into Kiryat Shmonah did not oblige the Israeli government to make any decisions of principle. The terrorists were unable to seize hostages, and there was therefore no negotiation over the conditions of their release. The Israeli army accordingly did what had to be done. Our troops surrounded the building, evacuated the neighboring residents, located the room where the terrorists had taken up position, fought them, and wiped them out.

Developments were to be different at Ma'alot. I flew there with the chief of staff as soon as we got the news. The saboteurs were inside the school with the children as hostages. I telephoned the prime minister and reported on the situation. She had called a Cabinet meeting in Jerusalem to decide what action we were to take.

In Ma'alot, the building was surrounded by our paratroops, and I did a survey of it from all sides. I came as close as I could, while taking care not to be exposed. When I got to the rear of the building, I heard a familiar voice call out: "If you want to get any closer, you'll have to run, for even if you crawl they'll see you."

The voice belonged to Muki, who is married to my niece Nurit. One of the bravest young men I have ever met, he is now an officer in the paratroop reserves. When he heard a news broadcast that morning about Ma'alot, he promptly got in touch with his unit, jumped into his car, and raced to the town. He was now in charge of one of the attack squads.

The Cabinet decided to agree to the exchange of prisoners for the children, but not to the terrorists' plan of how the exchange was to be carried out. The government was prepared to have the children and the prisoners released simultaneously, but not to leave the youngsters in the terrorists' hands and rely on their word of honor that they would free them when their comrades reached Damascus.

At midday I flew to Jerusalem for a hurried meeting with the prime minister. When I left her, I ran to the waiting helicopter which was to take me back to Ma'alot. There I found my nephew Uzi, son of my late brother, Zorik. Uzi, too, belonged to the same reservist unit as Muki. He was now studying mathematics and physics at the Hebrew University. When he heard the sound of a helicopter landing on the pad near the Prime Minister's Office, he figured that someone had come from Ma'alot to report to the government and would be returning there. He reasoned he could get a lift to Ma'alot so that he, too, could join in any action that might take place. He had brought along his army gear and changed during our flight. Though he is quite young, he is already a major.

I explained the Ma'alot situation to him, and I could see his expression grow serious. I know most of the officers of his paratroop unit, but, of course, I would see him and Muki more frequently at family gatherings. After each operation in which these two youngsters would take part, I would talk to them and learn more detailed reports of the action. Above all, I would get the "feel" of their character. I was not at all surprised that as soon as they and their comrades heard about what was happening in Ma'alot, they simply left everything and tried to get there as fast as possible. I doubt whether there is any other place in the world where young men grow up so close to the shadow of death, where, pure of heart, they combine supreme courage with an utter lack of cockiness or arrogance.

Upon returning to Ma'alot, I went over to the side of a house near the school which gave us cover, and peeked out just beyond the corner to get a glimpse of what was happening. One of the terrorists spotted me and apparently wanted to shoot. A girl standing behind him signaled with a wave of her hand that I should get my head behind the house. I watched her through my field glasses, and her features were as clear as if she were standing close to me. She looked sad, and above all tired, as children do when they are dropping with fatigue.

In the meantime, efforts to gain the safe release of the children were complicated by the attempt to use the French and Rumanian ambassadors as mediators. Time passed with agonizing slowness, and as the 6 P.M. deadline approached—when the terrorists warned they would blow up the building with themselves and the children—the government gave permission for our soldiers to break into the school.

I went in after the attacking troops, entering the classroom where the children had been held. The scene was shattering, the floor covered in blood and dozens of wounded children huddled against the walls. Our soldiers had killed the three terrorists but before they were shot the assassins had managed to murder 16 of the school children and wound 68.

Among the wounded was the girl who had signaled to me. The expression on her face was unchanged, only her eyes were closed. As someone placed her on a stretcher, she opened her eyes for a moment, recognized me, and burst into tears. She tried to speak, clearly wishing to describe all that had happened during that long day, but she could only get out between wrenching sobs: "It was dreadful, dreadful."

The attempt to rescue the children was not the most successful military action ever undertaken. One reason can be attributed to delaying the attack until the last minute. During the morning it was still possible to find moments when the terrorists were not alert. However, as the final hour approached they were tense, cautious, and careful not to move about as freely as they had done earlier.

The second error involved the actual execution of the operation. Our men used an inappropriate weapon, the phosphorous grenade. They mistook the floor, went up to the third and had to come down to the second, when they threw a phosphorous grenade and had to wait until its smoke cleared. By that time the terrorists carried out their massacre of the children.

Later in the Knesset, I said that I had opposed the government's decision to accept the conditions set forth by the terrorists. I explained that this decision meant we would not take immediate military action.

Moreover, I thought it was wrong for the chief of staff to continue negotiations up to the last moment, even after the government had already agreed to military action. I repeatedly urged him to advance the time of our attack, and I also pressed my views on the government. But I got nowhere. The only thing left for me to do was to approach the schoolhouse, watch the children through field glasses, see their faces as they stood near one of the terrorists, and grind my teeth. Soldiers had entered the area, waiting for the order to attack. I could see the frightened faces of the youngsters looking through the windows, hoping that at any moment the troops would rescue them. I also saw two of the terrorists. They were young, with mustaches, one wearing a black and the other a red shirt. They walked to and fro, Kalatchnikov rifles in their hands, ready, if attacked, to shoot their young hostages.

I could not act otherwise than in accordance with the government decision. Nor could I take over the Supreme Command and carry out a military operation as I thought it should be performed. But there was something else I could not do. I could not help thinking that in front of my eyes, and with my participation, two serious errors were being committed: surrender to the terrorists and wrong decisions concerning a military operation that required the utmost sagacity.

A week after the murders, I attended a memorial meeting which was held in Ma'alot's communal hall. The mood was very tense. After the meeting I met with the members of the Municipal Council and their chairman, Eli Ben-Ya'akov. Founded in 1957, Ma'alot grew out of two temporary immigrant camps made up mostly of Jews from North Africa. Six years later the town was united with the neighboring and well-to-do Arab village of Tarshiha. A wise and understanding man, Ben-Ya'akov had borne the responsibilities of this town for many years. His demands were constructive, but if they were not met it would not be because they were unjustified, but because it was impossible to fulfill them. There was, for example, the request to double the population as quickly as possible, for doing so would bring about more rapid development of the town and also strengthen its security. Certainly it was necessary to increase Ma'alot's population. However, I did not believe it would be done expeditiously. New immigrants could be directed to Ma'alot, but they could not be compelled to live there permanently if they did not wish to do so. The Municipal Council also proposed that we separate the Arab and the Jewish quarters. This was the only town in the country where two distinct but adjacent population centers—the Arab settlement of Tarshiha and the Jewish settlement of Ma'alot—were joined in a single municipal council.

Of particular interest was not the suggestion itself but the arguments supporting it. I was told no security problem existed and no one criticized the behavior of Arab Tarshiha. What soured the atmosphere was the economic and social prosperity of neighboring Tarshiha as compared with that of Ma'alot. In Tarshiha, every family had its "villa," a car, and property, while in Ma'alot the people were poor and lived in slums. Tarshiha, with a population of 5,000, boasted a secondary school with 500 pupils. The families in the town had sent 32 of their young people to the Hebrew University in Jerusalem and a number of others were studying in the United States. In Ma'alot, with a population of 3,500, no properly organized secondary school existed and only 3 of their young people attended the university.

The reasons for this difference were obvious. The inhabitants of Ma'alot were mostly new immigrants. The inhabitants of Tarshiha were rooted in the soil, worked hard, and had established a stable pattern of life based on hard physical labor. They enjoyed the benefits of high wages—in conformity with the prevailing scale in Israel—and good prices for their farm produce, which they marketed in considerable quantity. They were not profligate with their income. With the money they saved, they built houses and bought vans or trucks, and these in turn provided a fresh source of income, being used for commercial transport. The additional earnings would be invested in tractors, irrigation pipes, terracing and site improvement, thus further enlarging the source of jobs and income for the growing Arab families. The people of Tarshiha received none of the special benefits granted to the new immigrants, but they enjoyed one enormous advantage over their neighbors in Ma'alot. They were farmers tilling their own soil, and not the scattered children of a nation that had assembled them anew in their ancient land and strove to lead them into a different way of life, turning merchants into farmers and shopkeepers into industrial and building workers.

In the old Jewish settlements, where the children were born on the farm and brought up in the cowshed, the cotton fields, and apple orchards—settlements like my own Nahalal—the problem of Ma'alot did not exist. They had no cause to envy their neighboring Arab villagers, for their standard of living was much higher. Since the establishment of Ma'alot, no less than forty thousand people had moved to the town, stayed for a short time, and then left for other parts of Israel. Thus, one solution lay not in separating Ma'alot from Tarshiha, but in getting the people of Ma'alot to strike roots. Ma'alot will yet achieve this goal, if not in this generation of new immigrants, then in the second, the generation of those young people born and brought up there, for whom Ma'alot will always be home.

39

OUT OF OFFICE

PARLIAMENTARY ELECTIONS in the country were to be held on December 31, 1973. They were originally scheduled for October 30, when the Seventh Knesset was to have ended its term, but because of the war the term was extended beyond the statutory four years. These elections would be of special significance on two counts. The results would represent the verdict of the public on the events of the immediate past—there had been sharp criticism of the government for the "mishap" of the Yom Kippur War, and they would determine the path to be taken by Israel in the future. The nation was called on to give its mandate to the party and the personalities on whom it could rely and whose political outlook it shared.

Criticism of the past was not confined to the war. It was also directed against the general policy of the government, one which had failed to bring about peace with the Arabs. There was equal agitation about the future. At issue was choosing the kind of leadership that would be concerned not only with the immediate problems following the end of the war, including the Geneva Conference, but also with Israel's overall political status in the world. Dense clouds had risen over the country's skies. The Arab states carried increasing weight in international affairs, with their virtual monopoly of an essential source of energy. Their oil resources had also vested them with fabulous wealth, which was rapidly turning them into the Croesus of the earth. Israel, on the other hand, had become progressively isolated and, worst of all, its people wallowed in a deep mood of depression.

For me, the elections were of particular importance. In their criticism of the government, the public had given me pride of place, directing their barbs at me both as a minister and as an individual. As minister of defense I bore parliamentary responsibility for the army and for the conduct of the war. On the personal level, because I had enjoyed a certain degree of military and political prestige up to the outbreak of this war, more was expected of me than of another defense minister. "Protest movements," the press, public figures, even army officers demanded my resignation.

There were two aspects to this issue, the formal and the personal. My personal feeling was one of complete confidence that I had not failed in my duties, and I considered myself fully competent to continue in office. But this was primarily a public matter, and it was evident to me that I had to receive a clear and unequivocal reply to the question of whether I deserved to be minister of defense and would be asked to remain. The answer lay with four bodies: the premiership, my political party, the electorate, and the Agranat Commission.

Undoubtedly, the body most competent to pass judgment on the events of the Yom Kippur War, to determine guilt or innocence, was the Agranat Commission. It alone had access to all the material and had studied it with basic thoroughness. Its members were unprejudiced, dispassionate, skilled investigators, and they combined professional qualifications of the highest order in the military and legal fields.

The establishment of this commission followed a number of consultations at various forums. Members of the government generally recognized the need for an appropriate inquiry. The question was to whom to entrust this function. On November 8 the prime minister conferred with several ministers and the chief of staff on this painful subject, one of the most agonizing Israel had ever known. I told those present at the meeting that I felt it essential to ensure that the inquiry would be objective, fearless and professional, impervious to outside influence, and free from party and personal considerations, so that any attempt to stir up charges of bias would be stifled at the outset. I underscored my opinion by sending this note across the table to the prime minister:

"Golda, I am in favor of (1) an inquiry commission; (2) its form —a judicial, public, or internal-army investigation, only as agreed to by the *attorney general*. M.D."

Ten days later the subject was brought before the Cabinet, and after the attorney general had presented the various judicial alternatives, the government decided to establish a commission of inquiry which was to be convened by the president of the Supreme Court. It was to consist of five members.

The commission was to investigate:

"1. The intelligence information for the days preceding the Yom Kippur War on the enemy's moves and intentions to launch the war, the evaluation of this information, and the decisions taken by the responsible military and civil authorities in response thereto.

"2. The general deployment of the IDF (Israel Defense Forces) in case of war, its state of readiness during the days preceding the Yom Kippur War, and its operations up to the containment of the enemy."

These, the Cabinet decision stated, were "today matters of vital public importance which demand clarification."

Following this decision, on November 21, 1973, the president of the Supreme Court, Dr. Shimon Agranat, appointed the chairman and other members of the commission. In view of its great importance, Agranat himself became chairman, and the body therefore soon became known as the Agranat Commission. The other four members were Moshe Landau, justice of the Supreme Court; Dr. Yitzhak Nebenzahl, the state comptroller; Lt. Gen. (Res.) Yigael Yadin, professor of archaeology at the Hebrew University and a former chief of staff; and Lt. Gen. (Res.) Chaim Laskov, the army ombudsman and also a former chief of staff.

While the Agranat Commission conducted its investigation and deliberations, which were to last over a year, the various political parties prepared for the national elections to be held at the end of December. The Labor Party had headed every coalition government since the establishment of the state. As elections approached, it faced two main problems. One concerned personalities. Who would be its candidates? More to the point, who among them would be in the group heading Labor's list, and thus become ministers in the new government if the party polled enough votes? The second lively issue was ideological. On what platform would the Labor Party fight the political contest? What policies would it follow if it were voted into office?

The shock and the sense of helpless frustration which had struck the nation in the wake of the war inevitably found expression in the party. Those members who favored maximum concessions to the Arabs and a rigid limitation on Jewish settlements in the administered territories asserted themselves. The results were quickly seen in the new party program, which replaced the one that had been adopted by the party institutions shortly before the war. Dubbed the "Fourteen Articles," its principal changes related to land settlement and peace efforts.

The previous program had included a call for Israeli settlement in the administered territories—Judea and Samaria, the approaches to Rafah, and the Golan Heights. This was known as "the Galili document," after its sponsor, Minister Without Portfolio Yisrael Galili. This plan was now shelved. Instead, the new platform contained an innocuous paragraph in general terms stating that "all will be done to continue and strengthen land settlement in accordance with decisions which the government of Israel will take from time to time, with priority given to considerations of state security." As a gesture to those who urged withdrawal to the 1967 borders, there was not even a hint of where such settlement would be.

The second change was presumably prompted by the desire to emphasize Israel's striving for peace, and so the word "peace" appeared no less than seventeen times throughout the "Fourteen Articles." The previous party platforms had been just as forceful in calling for peace efforts, and in practice the government and the party had striven desperately for peace in the years before the Yom Kippur War. The tireless repetition of the word could not achieve closer relations with the Arabs. The purpose was to paper over the cracks marking differences within the party.

The compilation of the list of electoral candidates was more dramatic. The original list, like the party platform, had been drawn up before the war. Various groups now challenged it. One such group, styling itself "The Ideological Circle for the Study of the Problems of Society and the State," called for mass demonstrations outside the building where the Central Committee of the party would be meeting to approve the list. Apart from wanting some of the selected candidates disqualified, this group made two further demands: the formulation of peace plans "based on political realism," and a "fresh leadership." Though this was a group of party members, it declared that if its appeals went unheeded, it would urge the electorate not to vote for the party.

The Central Committee, which is the supreme organ of the party, held two crucial sessions, on November 28 and December 5, to determine its electoral program and decide on its candidates. At the first, the new party platform was adopted unanimously and the original pre-war list of candidates was approved by a vote of 256 to 107, with 30 abstentions. But the matter did not end there. At the second session a week later, the candidacy issue was again raised: who would appear at the top of the list as the party's ministers in the new government? This time it was raised by Prime Minister Golda Meir herself.

Golda refused to make the opening speech. Instead, she simply called for a secret vote to decide the committee's choice of candidate for the next premiership. It was a challenge to whoever wanted a different prime minister to display the courage to get up, make the proposal, and put it to the vote. It was also a call for a vote of confidence in her. Even if no other candidate was put forward, Golda was anxious to know what measure of support she commanded in the party. Since the ballot would be secret, anyone could vote as he wished without pressure from any source.

The session lasted all day and far into the night. The hall was crowded, the atmosphere tense. All sat forward in their seats, devouring every word from the rostrum. Only the long-haired cameramen in their working undershirts were continually on the move, unceremoniously turning their powerful lights on the party leaders in the reserved rows. The debate was sharp and uninhibited. The speakers said what was on their minds in plain, hard terms, without embellishment and without reservation.

I sat in the front row, feeling far from calm. When I had approached the entrance to the building, I had been greeted by the demonstrators with prolonged booing, and even inside the hall there were many members of the committee who were by no means my best friends. I recognized that this session was a kind of high court of the party—not, of course, in the Soviet sense. But it was definitely one of those political occasions in a democratic society at which public figures can be brought down. Behind us was the Yom Kippur War. Fire along the fronts had not yet been stilled. Disengagement agreements had not yet been concluded. Most of our young men were still serving in the reserves, still in the line of fire. In Jerusalem the Agranat Commission was absorbed in its agonizing investigation. And ahead of us lay grave problems. There was hardly an area which was not in need of revision—our relations with the Arabs, our relations with the United States, the economy, the patterns of society, the political parties and their leadership. The Central Committee now had to express and record its stand on these matters. Indeed all the speakers, either directly or indirectly, touched on the composition of the next government, responsibility for the shortcomings of the war, settlement in the administered territories, and the problem of permanent frontiers.

Toward evening I requested the floor. I was in no mood for concessions or compromise, either in content or style. I declared at the outset that the party might adopt basic positions which I would be unable to support before the electorate. If, for example, it were decided to recognize an independent Palestinian state, I would leave the party, though not political life. I would not retire quietly to Nahalal and grow flowers. I was not prepared to commit myself in advance to accept the party's verdict on every subject. I belonged, I said, to that political group known as Rafi, the group to which Ben-Gurion had been a member and for which he had been expelled from the party, and I still supported what had been urged in "the Galili document," still believed in the need to establish the city of Yamit on the Mediterranean coast in northern Sinai, and still concurred in the right of the Jews to buy land beyond the pre-1967 frontiers.

I went on to speak of those matters which affected me and which had been the subject of much comment in the debate. The criticism of me personally, I said, was now being investigated by the Agranat Commission, and it would deliver a decision. Quite different was the question of parliamentary responsibility. I bore responsibility for mishaps that had occurred—and I had no doubt that such had occurred—in the army. But parliamentary responsibility obliged me to go to the prime minister, tell her of the mistakes and shortcomings, ask her whether she wished me to resign, and act accordingly. The reply to the question of resignation had to come from the prime minister, and not from the justice minister nor even from the chairman of The Ideological Circle for the Study of the Problems of Society and the State. As for the composition of the next government, I had not requested, nor had I been asked, to be included. After the elections, whoever became prime minister would decide whom he or she wanted in the Cabinet.

Golda Meir was the last speaker, and she, too, touched on all these issues. She did so in her customary basic Hebrew, which all could understand. On the question of parliamentary responsibility, she said that under Israeli law all members of the government were collectively responsible for all its actions, its successes and its failures, and there was no separate parliamentary responsibility for each minister. She told the Central Committee that I had approached her twice on this matter, once during the bitter days of the war and again after Justice Minister Ya'akov Shimshon Shapiro had publicly declared that the defense minister should go. In both instances, she said, I had told her that if she thought I should resign, I would do so immediately, without further ado. She had replied, with the knowledge of other members of the government, that she had full confidence in me. On the subject of the post-election government, she said that the party chose only one person as an office holder in a government. This was the person selected to head its list of candidates, and it was this person who would form and head the new government if the election results made it possible. The party did not choose the other members of the Cabinet. Golda could not have made herself clearer. If the party wanted her as prime minister, it had to leave her the option of selecting her ministers.

Incidentally, when she spoke of the peace efforts made by the government during her years as premier, she mentioned that some years ago I had proposed to her that we should agree to withdraw from Suez so that the Egyptians could open the Canal to shipping and rehabilitate the Canal cities. "I confess," she now told the committee, "that I did not understand what he was talking about. Retire from the Canal? Just like that?"

In the secret ballot which followed, of the 341 members of the Central Committee who participated, 291 voted for Golda to head the party's list of candidates at the forthcoming elections, 33 voted against, and 17 abstained.

While the formal political clarifications were proceeding in the established institutions—government, Knesset, political parties—popular protest movements sprang up in the country and found their various ways to the hearts of the people. Their source was a combination of emotion and politics. They held demonstrations—mostly outside the Prime Minister's Office on days when the Cabinet was meeting—carrying banners with catchy slogans, which came over well on the TV screen. They were given wide coverage by the media, and their leaders were interviewed on television and radio and in the press. Later, there was such a diversified assortment of protesters that some demanded the exact opposite of others. Ultra-nationalist groups demonstrated against Kissinger and against any withdrawal from the Golan Heights, while the extreme left urged the reverse. In time, the value and effectiveness of these movements declined, and in the end, despite their attempts to do so, they failed to unite and develop into a single body with constructive political influence.

Nevertheless, they did have a certain public impact in two specific areas: they demanded "change"—a change in the leadership of the country, above all, me—and they pointed an accusing finger at those they considered responsible for the military and political shortcomings that had occurred on the eve and at the beginning of the Yom Kippur War. The protest movements set off loud reverberations, and the participation of many young men who had themselves taken part in the fighting, as well as young widows and bereaved parents of men who had fallen, gave them a special emotional appeal. One could differ from them over their demands or challenge their slogans, but one could not remain indifferent.

I, at all events, was certainly not indifferent. A minister of defense needs the trust of the public. He is not just an impersonal director of a bureau. He, more than any other political office holder, is responsible for decisions associated with war, with the killed and the wounded, with the prisoners and the missing, and with the bereaved families. The public may not share his views, but it is essential that they have faith in his integrity, dedication, understanding, and responsible approach to security affairs. I had the feeling that the public trust in me was being steadily undermined. On one occasion I passed some demonstrators as I was leaving a Cabinet meeting, and a young woman, probably a widow of a fallen soldier, cried out "Murderer!" It was a dagger in the heart. I knew that never in my life had I ordered a military operation in which I myself was not prepared to take part. And even now, any day and on any front, I was ready to change places with any soldier and go on a patrol in his stead, or join in an attack, or defend a stronghold. But this was my own private truth, and I could never, nor would I ever try to, explain this to the young woman.

Throughout these protest movements, in their coverage by the media and in the exploitation of political opportunities, there ran a hidden strain which was presented as a world outlook, but which in truth was defeatism. It was an undermining of our faith not only in the justice of Israel's cause, but also in its purpose, and a weakening of our power and readiness to fight. I viewed this with extreme gravity. I felt it augured ill for our ability to struggle against the difficulties and pressures which awaited us.

The standard-bearer of the first protest movement, its founder and "copyright owner," as it were, was a young officer, a captain named Mottie Ashkenazi. He had been the commanding officer of Budapest, the northernmost stronghold on the Canal, which did not fall. It was indeed the only strongpoint that was not captured, and this was due more to its geographic location than to Mottie. But the public could not know this. He started his demonstration as the act of an individual. Later he carried the flag for all.

Mottie Ashkenazi was a student at the Hebrew University of Jerusalem, and his teacher, philosophy Professor Natan Rotenstreich, suggested that I meet the young man for a talk. I agreed, and we met at Professor Rotenstreich's home in Jerusalem.

The talk proved to be largely a monologue. Mottie was eager to make himself heard, and I was anxious to listen, to understand, to get an impression of the fellow and what he wanted. He was quite explicit about what he wanted of me. Though he admired and respected me as an individual, he insisted that I had to resign because I bore parliamentary responsibility for a whole series of governmental failures. The army, the war, the policy that preceded the war, and even the previous war, the Six Day War—all were failures, riddled with mistakes and shortcomings. The policy followed by the government had been void of understanding and wisdom, and he demanded a change of leadership. The Cabinet should be replaced, I first and foremost.

Why was the victorious Six Day War of 1967 a failure? Because we should have separated Syria from Jordan, and we should have inflicted a decisive defeat on Egypt. Until that moment with Mottie, I thought we had. In the north, we should have captured the Druze Mountain and remained there permanently, thereby denying territorial contiguity between Jordan and Syria. And in the south, we should have crossed the Suez Canal, brought Egypt to abject surrender, and compelled her to sign a peace treaty with us.

In the Yom Kippur War, everything was bad. Pilots were sent on suicidal missions without need or purpose. He, as commander of Budapest, had seen them fall, and he had urged Southern Command to stop sending our planes to attack the Canal and Port Said —but no one had listened. In the Suez strongpoints nothing went right; the armor had fought poorly; the doctors had not known how to treat shell shock. Israel's military industry had not been properly prepared for a possible war. Its people should have worked day and night to produce the new rifle, the "Galil," for the infantry.

What was needed now was a revolution. Mottie himself wanted change brought about democratically, but there were some who were prepared to use violent means. He had stopped them, he said, but he could not remain silent until there was a basic change in policy, leadership, government, and army personnel. The nation, he said, was with him, and I had to resign.

I listened to him with interest. I, too, thought some of his criticism was justified. But much of the rest was worthless and without substance, and his proposals, for example, on how to reach an agreement with the Arabs seemed to me puerile and confused. He personally gave the impression of sincerity. I did not think he was a "phony." But he was certainly pretentious, over-emphatic, and self-righteous.

There was no chance whatsoever of discussing these important matters with him seriously and soberly—at least not on this occasion. He had clearly come to this meeting as though it were part of his campaign of public demonstrations, with him still on the soapbox, flinging out accusations and charges right and left, making demands, and repeatedly declaring that he would not "turn from his chosen path." I heard him out—till after midnight—thanked my host, and left.

It was not a pleasant meeting. Neither his words nor his manner struck a responsive chord in me. Rather the reverse. They put me off. He kept criticizing and sniping at others without mercy, while heaping encomiums upon his own head. In nothing he said did I find a spark of trust, of faith, of anything constructive. All was nihilistic. It was not by Mottie Ashkenazi and people like him that Israel had been built, and not through them that Israel would grow and prosper. On the face of it, we had been sitting in the same room dealing with subjects known and common to us both. In fact, we were talking of different things and living in two different worlds, separated by something far wider than the generation gap.

The Labor Party entered the elections with a list that was formally united but which contained diverse and even conflicting political trends. It put up its former leadership, but the electorate wanted change, wanted to see new faces. The voters this time were different from those in previous elections. For one thing, there were many more young people on the electoral register. But above all there was the widespread clamor against the mishaps of the war and the policy which had preceded it. Adding to this impact was the effect of the casualties, the many war dead and wounded, the grim descriptions of battle by the troops, particularly the survivors of the beleaguered strongpoints and the POWs returning from Egypt. All this produced a mood of depression, sharpened the criticism, and strengthened the demand for a change of leadership.

The election results reduced the strength of the Labor Party by 5 percent, giving it seven fewer seats in the Knesset (49 out of 120). The opposition parties gained 9 seats. This did not enable the opposition to take office, but it did prevent the Labor Party from forming a government on its own without having to make far-reaching concessions to a few small parties for joining a coalition.

Two days after the meeting of the Central Committee, on December 7, 1973, I invited myself to Golda's house in Jerusalem. After she had served the traditional coffee, I told her I had come to find out if she intended to offer me the Defense Ministry in the next government. But before hearing her answer I wished her to know two things. First, if the Agranat Commission should find even the slightest blemish on my personal record as minister of defense, I would resign immediately. Second, she could, and should, ignore completely any pressure from Rafi or other political groups that might make my appointment the condition of their support of the new government. Under no circumstances would I wish to hold office as a result of such pressure. I would take it upon myself to prevent pressure from Rafi even if she did not wish me to serve as defense minister.

Golda replied that she had not hesitated for one moment over my re-appointment to the Defense portfolio in the next government. This was her firm decision, and if anyone sought to annul it, she was ready to surrender the premiership. She said she had shared responsibility with me. She had been a full partner with me in receiving all the intelligence information and making all the crucial decisions. She added, to the credit of Chaim Bar-Lev, that he had come to her to say that on the eve of Yom Kippur he had met with Chief of Staff Elazar and had asked him his opinion of the situation on the fronts. After hearing that we had 170 tanks in the north and 300 in the south, Bar-Lev, a former chief of staff, had driven home with a quiet heart and without a trace of anxiety—even if the enemy were to launch an attack.

I was pleased that Golda retained her confidence in me and had not submitted to those who had demanded my head. I was doubly pleased by the knowledge that if she had thought the good of the state required my departure, she would have replaced me without compunction, particularly as she was about to form a new government. She had not hesitated to take over the Foreign Ministry from Moshe Sharett in 1956 because she thought it served the good of the state, and she had supported Levi Eshkol without qualm against David Ben-Gurion, who had been her long-time mentor and leader. Our own relationship was one of mutual understanding, and we always worked on what I have called a clean table, clear and open, never doing anything behind the other's back. Whatever I had to say to her or about her, I said in her presence. And since she was prime minister, I acted in accordance with her decisions, even when I considered them mistaken but had failed to change her mind. However, there was never the close personal friendship between us as there was between her and other ministers, like Yisrael Galili or Pinhas Sapir. Thus, if she wanted me as defense minister, it was because she thought it was for the good of the state.

I, too, thought so, but this viewpoint had to be endorsed by the party and the voting public. I would have preferred an electoral system in which I could stand for direct elections. But under the proportional representation system in Israel, the person empowered both in the name of the Labor Party and the electorate to decide whether I was to continue as minister of defense was Golda Meir. It was she who had been chosen by the party to head its list of candidates, and with that choice had come the mandate to form the next government.

But even after the elections, even after the public had had its say, the furor did not die down. The storm winds continued to howl around us. Disgruntled groups, frustrated public figures, and political parties that had failed to swing the electorate to their side gave vent to intemperate attacks and destructive visions of imminent doom, which could serve only to undermine the nation's faith in its strength and its destiny. Since their deeds and utterances were newsworthy, they were widely carried by the media.

It took Golda two months to form the new coalition government. On March 10, 1974, after wearisome efforts and unexpected table-turning, she finally managed to present her new Cabinet to the Knesset.

Her greatest difficulty was the refusal of the National Religious Party to join the government because of its position on the subject of "Who is a Jew." This left only two alternatives—either new elections or the formation of a minority government, that is, a Cabinet that was not backed by a Knesset majority. Golda was not consistent in her stand. At first she announced that if she failed to form a government which commanded at least 61 of the 120 Knesset votes, she would recommend new elections. But she then changed her mind and agreed to head a minority government.

In the meantime, with the continued squabbling and free-for-all within the party, I had little desire to join the new government. There were party members who not only did not support me, but became vociferous in their tirades against me. Even the official organ of the party, Ot, whose editor happened to belong to an anti-Rafi group, poured forth a steady stream of calumny and censure. Knesset members of my own party submitted parliamentary questions designed to embarrass me and undermine my position. Some, handily accompanied by TV reporters, called on leaders of the protest movements, demonstratively shook their hands in front of the cameras, and congratulated them on their anti-Dayan campaign.

I must say that even in the army, discussion occasionally overstepped the bounds of propriety. I was particularly hurt by an incident that occurred at a conference of senior officers held to review the military events of the campaign. I happened to have been away during one of the sessions, and in my absence an officer serving on the liaison team with the U.N. got up on the rostrum and called for my resignation. This was done in the presence of the prime minister and the chief of staff. They sat in the front row, heard what was said, but remained silent. I regarded the incident as most reprehensible, both the meddling by an army officer, at an army conference, in the political issue of who should and who should not be minister of defense, and the silence of the prime minister and the chief of staff, which lent it approbation.

A week later, at a Cabinet meeting, I sent a note to Golda telling her that I would not be joining her next government. Golda read it without shock or surprise—at least so it seemed to me. I reported on this step to my friends in Rafi, and that evening the news was broadcast on the radio. I promptly got an indignant telephone call from Golda asking why I had made my decision public. Then and on several later occasions, she urged me to change my mind. So did the Rafi convention. The members of this wing of the Labor Party called on me and Shimon Peres, my fellow Rafi minister, who refused to enter the next government without me. But I persisted in my refusal to join it. True, I was anxious to secure a fitting end to the war situation, to reach an arrangement with the Syrians, to bring back our POWs, and to release our reservists. But I knew I would be unable to carry out my functions properly unless I had the support of my party, its faction in the Knesset, and my fellow members of the government.

After consulting her closest friends, Golda finally reconciled herself to the situation and decided to go ahead and form a new government without Rafi, which had declined to enter the government without me, and, in the first phase, also without the National Religious Party. It was her reasonable assumption that the National Religious Party, anxious as it was for government portfolios, would in a short time find some excuse to join her.

At 2 P.M. on March 3, 1974, a joint meeting was called to approve the composition of Golda's Cabinet. Participating were the party fac-. tion in the Knesset together with what was called the party's Leadership Bureau. It was suggested that Yitzhak Rabin replace me as Minister of Defense.

The discussion was not lengthy, nor was it very edifying. Most of the speakers were highly critical of the proposed composition of the new government, and those who favored it did so with little enthusiasm. Golda sat through it all, very uneasy. It was understandable. Everything that had happened up to then, beginning with the war and ending with the interparty coalition negotiations, to say nothing of the friendly and not so friendly bargaining within the party, was enough to explain, if not to justify, her impatience. When all the speeches were over and before the proposal on the composition of the new Cabinet was put to the vote—there was no doubt that it would be approved—Golda took the floor. After a brief comment on the criticism that had been voiced, she abruptly announced that she was abandoning the task of forming a new Cabinet and would so inform the president during the course of the evening. And that was that. A great deal of antagonism had indeed been displayed at the meeting. But Golda's reaction, too, was hardly dignified. This was not her finest hour.

What followed was a rather ignominious rushing around of hastily organized delegations to get her to rescind her decision. One called on Golda herself. Another waited upon the president, urging him to persuade her to continue with her efforts to form a government. The crowning touch was a session of the Central Committee of the party specially convened as a supplicatory meeting on behalf of the Labor movement to entreat Golda not to resign.

For me, there was another aspect to all that had transpired at the March 3 meeting. As I listened to Golda's recital of the proposed composition of the new government at the start of that meeting, I thought to myself, Ah, the great day has come at last—a government without Rafi, distrusted partner of the Mapai Party and its close ally, the Ahdut Avodah Party. A government without me, held responsible for the mistakes of the war and the policy which had preceded it. A government even without Yosef Almogi, former minister of labor, who had indeed "repented" and rejoined the Mapai faction, but whose loyalty to Ben-Gurion had never really been forgiven by the present Mapai leadership. And then, lo and behold, at the critical moment, a hurt and angry Golda rises, turns on her lifelong friends, and stalks out. She did not do this because of the National Religious Party's refusal to join the government or because she could not manage a government without Rafi. No, what she did reflected her new assessment of her comrades in Mapai and Ahdut Avodah. At that meeting she had suddenly sensed that when they had finished stoning other scapegoats, they would get to her.

At the meeting of the Central Committee convened two days later to urge Golda to change her mind, most of the speakers played variations on the same theme—that all the party's troubles stemmed from Rafi. Rafi was the culprit, Rafi was to blame, and I most of all.

I also spoke. After observing that I considered it was my last day as minister of defense, I expressed my opposition to the formation of a minority government. I would have supported a national emergency coalition, I said, but since I knew that Golda was not prepared to head such a government, this option did not exist. I was therefore in favor of calling for new general elections.

I did not stay to the end, for a note was brought to me that important intelligence information had just come in and I had to rush back to my office. The decisions of the meeting were sent to me later, in writing, by the party secretariat:

"1. The Central Committee earnestly appeals to Golda to retract and take upon herself the formation of a new government. Approved unanimously. None opposed, four abstentions.

"2. The Central Committee asks Golda to complete her efforts to form a government and present it to the Knesset in accordance with the Central Committee's decision of February 24, 1974. Carried by 238 votes to 7, with 43 abstentions.

"3. The Central Committee appeals to the National Religious Party to help in the establishment of a government under Golda Meir's premiership, urgently needed in view of the pressing political tasks facing Israel. Carried unanimously.

"4. All members, and especially Moshe Dayan and Shimon Peres, who are designated to serve as ministers, are called upon to fulfill their duty as representatives of the Labor Party and to respond to Golda Meir's appeal to them to join the government. Carried unanimously. No opposition and no abstentions."

The urgent intelligence information I found when I reached my office was that Syria had decided to resume the war immediately. Such intelligence would be treated with all seriousness at any time, but especially now, after the Yom Kippur War, when we were all particularly sensitive. I informed the prime minister, and she promptly called a Cabinet meeting for that evening to consider the news. Meanwhile, further reports kept coming in which reinforced the original warning.

The Cabinet met at 8:30 P.M. and sat as the Ministerial Committee for Security Affairs which made its deliberations top secret. The information was digested and analyzed and decisions were reached on the steps to be taken. But the significant feature of the meeting seemed to be the sense of anxiety and dilemma reflected in everyone's expression. Here we were, split and torn from within, with no new government, and with war upon us once again. The external foe was about to attack, and we were still reeling from the internal blows of disunity. What price had Jewish history not paid in the past in precisely such situations? Ministers kept sending each other urgent notes across the Cabinet table. National Religious Party ministers explained that their party would not join a new government unless Rafi did so too.

At the end of the meeting, I called Shimon Peres into another room and told him that in view of the new military situation, with attack from Syria imminent, I thought we should agree to join the new government. The National Religious Party would follow suit, and Golda would receive the confidence of the Knesset. We had to set aside our personal feelings for the moment, forget the bitterness, the charges and counter-charges, and cease persisting in our refusal, which was holding up the establishment of the new government.

Shimon fully agreed, so we went back to Golda and told her that if she still wanted us as ministers, we were prepared to accept. Golda was greatly moved. "I could not have received a nicer present," she said. The next day the National Religious Party also agreed to join, and a week later the new government received the confidence of the Knesset by a vote of 62 to 46, with 9 abstentions.

The expected Syrian attack did not materialize, and naturally this non-event did nothing to heighten the public's trust in the government. But the last straw was provided by two ministers, members of our own party, Chaim Gvati, minister of agriculture, and Shlomo Hillel, minister of police, who gave open expression to the public's feelings. Golda, who was herself aware of her steadily weakening position, decided to resign. If a minister of such integrity as Chaim Gvati, who represented the most idealistic group in the state, the kibbutz movement, said that the nation had lost its confidence in the government, then, she felt, the government had to resign. On April 11, 1974, she announced her resignation to the Knesset, and this time her decision was final. Under Israeli law, the resignation of the prime minister automatically means the resignation of the entire Cabinet. This was the end of the Yom Kippur government.

But not quite—for under the law the old government continues in office until the establishment of the successor government, and this took almost two months. In the meantime, the Agranat Commission issued its first report. It was called a "Partial Report" for it dealt with only two topics: intelligence information on the enemy's moves and intentions, and its evaluation; and the state of preparedness of the Israel Defense Forces. On these matters, its conclusions and recommendations were very clear and most severe. The recommendations dealt with fundamental principles, the conclusions with individual office holders.

The section on individuals was the gravest of all. From the Intelligence Branch of the army, four officers were relieved of their posts. The commission found that Maj. Gen. Eliyahu Zeira, "in view of his grave failure . . . cannot continue in his post as chief of Military Intelligence"; his deputy, Brig. Aryeh Shalev, "cannot continue to work in Intelligence"; Lt. Col. Yona Bendman (who directed the Egyptian desk at the Intelligence Research Department) "should no longer be employed in a position associated with intelligence evaluation"; and Lt. Col. David Gedalia, chief Intelligence officer of Southern Command, "should no longer be employed in any Intelligence post."

At the senior command level, the commission's conclusions dealt with two generals, the GOC Southern Command and the chief of staff. Maj. Gen. Shmuel Gonen (Gorodish) was suspended from active duties pending completion of the commission's investigation into the containment phase of the fighting. Most severe were the commission's findings on Chief of Staff David Elazar. "We have reached the conclusion that the chief of staff bears direct responsibility for what happened on the eve of the war, both with regard to the assessment of the situation and the preparedness of the IDF." In view of this, "we recommend that the term of office of Lt. Gen. David Elazar as chief of staff be terminated."

In dealing with me, the commission reported that it had felt itself free to consider and reach conclusions only about my "direct responsibility. We have not felt called upon to give our views on what can be considered the minister's parliamentary responsibility." Addressing itself to this task, the commission stated, "The question is whether the minister of defense was negligent in carrying out his duties on matters that were within his area of responsibility." Its findings: "We weighed with great seriousness all these matters and reached the conclusion that by standards of reasonable behavior required by the one holding the post of minister of defense, the minister was not required to issue orders for precautionary measures additional to or different from those proposed to him by the General Staff in accordance with joint assessment and consultation between the chief of staff and the chief of Intelligence."

A word about parliamentary responsibility. There are two parts to this question. The first is obvious: any minister is responsible to the legislative body for all the administrative acts emanating from his ministry and must answer to the legislators for such acts. But determining, as the commission put it, "in which cases a minister should resign," was manifestly a political matter, and the commission did not feel obliged to apply itself to this issue.

Thus, the commission did not find exceptionable the way in which I had carried out my ministerial functions, and on the issue of parliamentary responsibility, namely, whether or not I should resign because of the failures of certain military personnel, it was not called upon to lay down the law. Such a decision was in the hands of political forums.

On June 3, 1974, the new government was sworn in with Yitzhak Rabin as prime minister and Shimon Peres as minister of defense.

My last two major acts as defense minister had been the conclusion of the disengagement agreement with Syria and the changing of the army's High Command. Lt. Gen. Mordechai Gur was appointed chief of staff in place of Lt. Gen. Elazar, and Maj. Gen. Shlomo Gazit became the new head of Intelligence. There were also other appointments to the General Staff, the regional commanders, corps, and divisions. Young officers who had distinguished themselves replaced older veterans.

The disengagement agreement with Syria was in itself less satisfactory and less significant than the one with Egypt. But for me it had a special importance. It punctuated the Yom Kippur War with a period. I was leaving my post in the Defense Ministry with that war terminated. Israel could now demobilize her reservists and hopefully enter a more relaxed phase. She could rest a while, breathe, turn over a new page.

Not that this page could in any way be isolated from the one before, but by whatever measure it was at all possible to mark the end of the chapter called the Yom Kippur War, this was done. Moreover, the strength of the Israel Defense Forces, in planes, tanks, artillery, and other essential and sophisticated equipment, was greater than it had been before the war. True, the cease-fire lines involved a degree of withdrawal. In the south, we had withdrawn twelve miles from the Suez Canal, and in the north we had given up the city of Kuneitra. But against these concessions, the front lines were now based on bilateral agreements which were far more stable than the pre-war cease-fire. Most important, we now held lines which reflected the realities of the time—the product of military and political confrontation in the conditions of 1973, and not that of the confrontation six years earlier, when we had fought under totally different conditions. Dreams could be very pleasant, but one had to live with reality.

40

A NEW REALITY

THE YOM KIPPUR WAR grew out of Egypt's and Syria's refusal to reach a peace arrangement with Israel or to leave Sinai and the Golan Heights in Israel's hands. The Arabs wanted to retrieve the territories they had lost in the Six Day War without reconciling themselves to the fact of Israel's existence. This goal could only be achieved through war.

Egypt's position on Israel became fixed shortly after the Six Day War, when the Egyptians showed their confidence in Nasser despite the utter rout of their armies. Tens of thousands of people demonstrated in the streets, appealing to Nasser to withdraw the resignation he had proffered after his country's defeat. These demonstrations were the Egyptian nation's expression that it had not been broken by Israel. Even though Egypt had lost the war, her armies, and the whole of the Sinai Peninsula, the people did not blame their leaders, or each other, and did not descend into a pit of despair. Military defeat did not destroy their faith in themselves or their readiness to continue the struggle against Israel. Egypt's president saw in the people's expression of confidence not only a personal gesture of their belief in him, but a renewed confirmation of his policy of hostility toward Israel. After the war Nasser even added an additional plank to the platform of his country's struggle against Israel: "What was taken by force will be restored by force." Egypt had accounts to settle with Israel not only for the loss of Sinai, but for her military defeat.

Egypt's postwar policy toward Israel was formulated in the decisions at Khartoum: "No peace, no recognition, no negotiations." The military plan for the return of territories she had lost was to be carried out in three stages: "Defense, active deterrence (war of attrition), and victory." The third phase, all-out war for victory, was first set for 1971. President Sadat, Nasser's successor, announced that this would be "the year of decision." All-out war for victory was then postponed to the following year and was finally launched in 1973.

International factors also contributed to the Arab decision to opt for war. The Arabs interpreted the Security Council Resolution 242 of 1967 as requiring total Israeli withdrawal from all the terrritories occupied in the Six Day War. This interpretation was supported without reservation by the Soviet bloc, France, and the nonaligned countries, though not by the United States and Britain, the authors of the resolution.

Immediately after the Six Day War, Soviet leaders promised "to teach [Egypt and Syria] how to fight," to equip their armies with modern weapons, and to plan the coming battle against Israel. Soviet aid was given openly. Egypt and Syria developed close bonds of friendship with the Soviet Union, established radical regimes, and received thousands of Soviet experts and advisers. Egypt's failure in the War of Attrition only heightened Russia's intervention in that conflict and strengthened her influence in both Arab countries. When Egypt could not prevent the deep penetration of our Air Force, Nasser handed over the defense of his country's skies to Soviet forces. As Israel's Air Force improved, Egypt and Syria needed electronic devices and more advanced and sophisticated weapons. Their leaders then turned toward the Soviet Union, which enthusiastically supplied them.

Some years after the Six Day War, there was a growing recognition among Arab leaders and military commanders that their armies had indeed been renewed and rehabilitated and that they had a chance of defeating Israel. In addition to the armies of Egypt and Syria and the expeditionary forces from Iraq, Morocco, Saudi Arabia, and Jordan, Russia stood faithfully at their side, a Super Power eager to build up the Arabs' strength and supply them with sophisticated equipment and arms, a mighty nation which would surely not forsake them when battle came.

Neither the political activity undertaken in those postwar years nor the peace negotiations of Rogers and Jarring gave the Arabs what they wanted. Israel demanded real peace in exchange for the withdrawal of her forces, "a true peace" in the words of Ben-Gurion. Neither Syria nor a more moderate Egypt was prepared to accept such a peace. Their leaders made it a condition that any arrangement with Israel would have to include not only our withdrawal to the 1967 borders but also a solution to the Palestine problem. And the Palestinians insisted on their right to return to their homes, their soil, their land. Israel believed that if she acquiesced in the Palestinians' demand, she would undermine the very foundations of her existence.

During this postwar period, the Arabs became increasingly convinced that only through war could they achieve their goals. After the Khartoum Conference, the Israeli government annulled its decision of June 1967, when it had expressed readiness to withdraw to the international frontiers in exchange for peace with Egypt and Syria. We now took the position that we would not return to the former lines along any of the frontiers. Jerusalem was virtually annexed and new Jewish suburbs were built in the north and west of the capital. At Sharm el-Sheikh on the Straits of Tiran, foundations were laid for the new city of Ophirah. On the West Bank, we established new permanent settlements. And the official spokesmen presented the Golan Heights as an area that would belong to Israel.

Nor was American mediation effective. The Russians, of course, saw in the Middle East conflict fertile ground for extending Soviet influence in the Arab states. But even the United States, which desired settlement by peaceful means, took no forceful measures toward this end for reasons both external—Vietnam—and domestic—Watergate. The pity is that the United States failed to engage in intensive diplomatic activity during the decisive years of 1972–1973, when the Arab military build-up reached its peak.

The basic military preparations had been completed and the internal pressures, particularly in Egypt, began to mount. The enormous cost of maintaining a powerful army proved an extremely heavy economic burden for Egypt, and the cream of her youth, university and high school graduates, had to serve in the army year after year. Sadat reached the conclusion that he could not continue in this fashion and that if no change occurred he would face a severe crisis. Change by political means seemed unattainable after the fruitless attempts by Hafez Ismail, a top adviser to Sadat, to secure Nixon's support. But Sadat believed he had the military capacity to gain his aims through force of arms. On October 6, 1973, Egypt and Syria launched the Yom Kippur War.

Israel was taken by surprise. For two years following Sadat's promise that 1971 would be the year of decision, Egyptian and Syrian announcements of imminent attack were never fulfilled. At the beginning of October 1973, when there were signs of increased activity on the Egyptian and Syrian fronts, our Intelligence Branch reported that the Egyptians were engaging in military exercises and not preparing to launch a war. This was not only the view of Israeli Intelligence but also of the American Intelligence services. On September 12, 1975, *The New York Times* published extracts from a secret report which stated that "the United States Intelligence community acknowledged that it failed to predict the 1973 Arab-Israeli war and that several intelligence agencies even predicted that there would be no war only hours before the hostilities broke out."

According to the *Times,* this report was compiled by the committee charged with advising the National Security Council on war and critical situations. The report disclosed that the committee that met the day the Arab forces attacked Israel said: "We can find no hard evidence of a major, coordinated Egyptian-Syrian offensive across the Canal and in the Golan Heights area."

The *Times* added that the committee report went on to note: "It is possible that the Egyptians or Syrians, particularly the latter, may have been preparing a raid or other small-scale actions." The committee met, its report said, at "9 A.M. on October 6, 1973," which was a few hours before the attack.

According to the *Times,* a CIA bulletin dated the day before the attack said "the exercise and alert activities may be on a somewhat larger scale and more realistic than previous exercises, but they do not appear to be preparing for a military offensive against Israel."

In testimony before the House Select Committee on Intelligence, the paper reported, Dr. Ray Cline, a former director of the State Department's Intelligence Bureau and once a top official of the CIA, declared that the intelligence breakdown was in part a result of Secretary of State Kissinger's unwillingness to accept the conclusions reached by the Intelligence community.

It was our intelligence appraisals that guided the army command and the government and led to the situation whereby too few Israeli forces were in position during the containment or blocking stage, and whereby the reinforcements which were rushed to the front arrived in small numbers with no time to make preparations for a counterattack.

The Arab war aims were more than simply "liberating their conquered lands"—Sinai and the Golan Heights. The Syrians intended to exploit their success and, after their forces had reached the Jordan, to continue their advance toward Nazareth in central Galilee. It was also part of the Egyptian plan to force Israel to withdraw from the Gaza Strip. Sadat estimated that crossing the Canal and capturing the Mitla and Gidi passes would bring about the defeat and collapse of the Israeli army and would enable him to force Israel to give up on his terms. This is the way Sadat saw the situation even at the end of the first week of the war, after the Syrian attack had failed and his own army was in retreat. On October 10, four days after the war began, the Egyptian leader notified the United States that he would accept a cease-fire only after Israel agreed to evacuate the whole of Sinai and the Gaza Strip according to a prearranged timetable. Even a week later, when Israeli forces in the south had already established a bridgehead on the west bank of the Canal and the Syrians in the north were forced to deploy their army for the defense of the capital, Damascus, Sadat again announced in a speech before the National Assembly that Egypt would continue to fight until she conquered "the land seized by Israel and would restore to the Palestinians their legal rights." He added, "Egypt was prepared to accept a cease-fire on the condition that Israel would withdraw immediately from all the conquered territories and retire behind the lines of June 5, 1967."

Another few days had to pass before the president of Egypt recognized that he had suffered a complete defeat. Not only was he powerless to force Israel to evacuate Sinai and Gaza, but he now had to swallow the presence of Israeli forces on the soil of Egypt proper, west of the Canal. Not only was he incapable of continuing the campaign until Israel accepted his terms, but each additional hour of warfare greatly worsened his situation. It took the report of the Egyptian chief of staff, Gen. Saad el-Shazli, together with Soviet air photographs given to him on October 18, to persuade Sadat that the Israeli forces west of the Canal were not in a "pocket" but were in fact a formidable array of hundreds of tanks threatening Cairo and outflanking the Second and Third Armies. On October 20, Sadat cabled Brezhnev that he was prepared to accept a cease-fire with the conditions he himself had rejected on October 16: "Immediate end to the fighting, with each side remaining in its positions." The war ended with Egypt's president continuing to send urgent messages to Nixon and Brezhnev almost every hour on the hour, asking them to halt the Israeli units that continued to advance. Sadat himself, with the Egyptian armed forces, was unable to do so.

On the Syrian front, where the Israeli army had reached to within twenty-five miles of Damascus, President Assad took two steps. He ordered his forces, which had lost half their armored strength, to dig in for the defense of his capital. At the same time he sent angry cables to the president of Egypt, vigorously protesting his acceptance of the cease-fire. Assad demanded that no consideration be given to the situation at the fronts but that the war should be continued "in order to preserve the morale of the soldiers."

The cease-fire conditions, and later even the separation-of-forces agreements, reflected not only the state of the fronts and the policies of the countries at war, but also the interests of the Super Powers. Israel, whose military, political, and economic strength were dependent on American aid, could not ignore Washington's demands. This was also the case of Egypt in relation to the Soviet Union. The two Super Powers wanted an end to the war primarily to avoid the possibility of a confrontation between them. Furthermore, when Egypt faced defeat, with her Third Army surrounded, both Super Powers raced to her aid. The Soviet Union was interested in avoiding the military collapse of her client, and the United States wanted to draw Egypt to her side to ensure for herself the flow of oil from the Arab states.

Nevertheless, the military and political agreements reached after the war were first and foremost an expression of the result of that war. Egypt accepted a cease-fire without a time limit and agreed to free passage through the Straits of Bab el-Mandeb in the Red Sea, limitation of forces, and a buffer zone under the UNEF. All proposals of this nature had been rejected by Egypt before the war. The Security Council, in coordination with the parties, decided to convene a peace conference in Geneva. The Soviet Union, Syria, and Egypt agreed that this peace conference would take place without the participation of the Palestinians and without introducing any changes in Resolution 242, in which the Palestinian item is defined as the refugee problem.

Sadat changed the war policy which he had inherited from Nasser into a peace policy, and he thereby expressed the feelings of his people. This was the principal change brought about by the war. The Yom Kippur War had been preceded by maximum preparations which had continued for six years. These preparations had been made at tremendous cost to Egypt and had absorbed the bulk of her manpower and resources. Yet despite the advantage to Egypt in the element of surprise, the war had ended with the Egyptian Third Army and the city of Suez cut off, her forces and equipment shattered, and the Israeli army closer to Cairo than it had ever been in previous wars.

As a consequence of the war, Sadat decided to concentrate his activities in the political field. His "peace policy" was designed to ensure the reality of peace, though he would not agree to a formal declaration of peace. However, the significance of his policy was in fact a halt to the war with Israel. Within this political framework, Egypt agreed to reopen the Suez Canal, to resettle the Canal cities, and to introduce into the area of the frontier a peacetime pattern of life, even though Israeli forces were stationed twelve-and-a-half miles from the Canal.

The thinking behind the separation-of-forces agreement with Egypt reflects, to my mind, the correct approach in reaching a *modus vivendi* with the neighboring Arab states. It may not be possible to secure peace treaties now, but we should—and I think it would be possible to—secure an end to the state of war. Such arrangements should be based on several principles: a formal agreement annulling the state of war; limitation of forces stationed along the borders; buffer zones with appropriate supervision by the parties themselves and the U.N. forces, which should include American and Russian units to ensure their status and stability; and settlement of the Arab refugees in the countries of their present residence, in the same way that Egypt took out of the camps refugees who had abandoned their settlements during the Six Day War and established them in the cities on the Canal.

It will take a number of years to carry out the constructive articles in the agreements, just as clearance of the Canal took more than two years. The withdrawal of Israel's forces from the border areas should proceed at the same rate. Under these agreements, which are not peace treaties and do not fix permanent frontiers, Israel should make sure that her borders follow the line from Sharm el-Sheikh to El Arish, the length of the Jordan River, and along the Golan Heights.

The Arabs' efficiency in launching their attack was greater than expected. The Six Day War and the various postwar clashes between Israeli and Arab units in the air and on the ground led us to the judgment that if war broke out it would not be difficult for Israel to win. The front lines—the Suez Canal and the Golan frontier—were thought to be well fortified, barriers that would not easily be pierced. The strength of our armor and the superiority of our Air Force over the Arab Air Forces instilled in the army command, and in me, a strong feeling of confidence in our military might and in our political stability.

When the war started, weak points were revealed in our armored strategy and limitations in the operation of our Air Force. In several battles, our tanks used tactics based on the experience of the past. These tactics, which worked well in previous wars, favored the rapid dash of our armored forces, unaccompanied by the infantry and without artillery support, right into the heart of the enemy's positions, on the assumption that this would bring about his collapse. This time the assault units found themselves surrounded by enemy infantry equipped with large quantities of versatile anti-tank weapons—anti-tank grenades, RPG-7s, recoilless guns, anti-tank guns, and Sagger missiles, which were capable of effectively stopping and inflicting heavy casualties on our tank forces.

The fact was that the entire face of war had dramatically changed. Even those who had carefully followed the technical advances that had been made in weaponry in the last few years could not conceive the rate of destruction they commanded. The efficiency of the tanks of both sides in the Yom Kippur War was ten times greater than that of the armor in World War Two and double that of the American forces in Korea. In World War Two, there was only 1 chance out of 20 of a Sherman tank hitting an enemy tank with its first shot at a range of a mile. In Korea, the chances were 1 out of 3. In the Yom Kippur War, the chances were 7 out of 10. The tanks were therefore destroyed at a greater rate and within a shorter time than in any other war. The Arabs lost more tanks than the United States has currently stationed in Europe.

Israel suffered the greatest number of casualties not on October 6, the first day of the war, when we were taken by surprise and few troops at the fronts had to contain hordes of attacking enemy, but after the reserves had been mobilized and the battles were at their height—on October 12 on the northern front and on October 18 in the south.

Our Air Force, which had to operate over areas thick with anti-aircraft defenses, was unable to attack with accuracy and efficiency. The combination of SAM-3 missile batteries and mobile SAM-6s together with anti-aircraft artillery caused heavy casualties to our planes and prevented them from remaining long over the target and from giving significant air support to our ground forces. The expectations of our air operations, particularly during the containment stage, were found to be unrealistic. Even when our planes hit the bridges on the Canal, they had no decisive impact on the Egyptian crossing, since the bridges were quickly repaired. Our Air Force could not attack the hundreds of Egyptian vehicles which stood in long, crowded columns waiting to ford the Canal. Nor could it wipe out well-entrenched enemy units.

There were also operational failures: the lack of adequate preparation in the Hermon outpost above the Golan Heights; the failure of our forces in western Sinai to deploy and advance to the Canal in time; the poorly conducted counter-attack in the south on October 8; and the unsuccessful attempt to capture the city of Suez. These were all the faults of the commanders. The first three failures had an unfortunate impact in the opening stage of the war; the failure to capture the city of Suez affected the end of the war. If Suez had been captured, it would have led to the surrender of the Egyptian Third Army, despite America's intervention. The Egyptian defeat would have been greater, and Egypt's bargaining position weaker.

Israel's extraordinary accomplishment in the Yom Kippur War lay in her capacity to move over to the offensive in so short a time and to achieve victory. And this was done in spite of the initial disadvantage caused by the surprise attack and despite the massive strength of the Arabs—about one million troops, more than 5,000 tanks, more than 1,000 warplanes, and a dense network of anti-aircraft defenses. Three basic factors contributed to Israel's victory: first, the stubborn and daring fighting of the units that withstood the initial onslaught and held on to the lines with incredible courage until the arrival of reinforcements; second, the correct decision to concentrate on blocking the Syrian attack even at the cost of giving the Egyptians time to consolidate their positions east of the Canal; third, the westward crossing of the Canal by our forces and their control of the Ismailia-Jebel Ataka line. In these operations, Israel shed much blood, but that is the law of war.

There are also these startling factors to consider. More weapons were involved and the fire was more intense over short fronts and in a brief period of time in this campaign than in any other campaign, at any time, anywhere in the world. In World War Two, the French had 2,000 tanks in their main defense line, the Maginot line. The Germans attacked with 3,000 tanks. At El Alamein, in the Western Desert, Montgomery had 1,030 tanks and Rommel about 600. In the Yom Kippur War, the Arabs attacked with more than 5,500 tanks. On the Suez front, the Egyptians used double the number of tanks employed by Montgomery, and in the north the Syrians attacked with a force equal to that which Germany sent against France. Both attacks were carried out simultaneously, with the most sophisticated types of tanks, and on extremely short fronts.

The intensity of the fire power, the prodigious quantities, and the lethal quality of the weaponry also have far-reaching political significance. The dependence on outside sources—the Soviet Union and the United States as suppliers of arms—was so great in this war that it would have been impossible for the fighting to continue in defiance of the decisions of Washington and Moscow. The troops of these Super Powers did not take part in the campaign but Israel and the Arabs were dependent on their will. They were not their own masters, either in the opening stage of the war, or in its conduct, or, above all, in determining its end.

After the war, Israel had to make a reappraisal of the military strength required to preserve her capacity to meet a future Arab attack. War creates and exposes new military realities. Even if all the arms markets were open to Israel, she would have to determine with great care the limits of the burden she could bear. How many tanks, planes, and regular troops could we afford to maintain without collapsing under the economic weight of procuring and supporting them? According to the figures published by the Institute of Strategic Studies in London, Israel maintains in *peacetime* an army whose size and cost, in proportion to her population and economy, greatly exceed those in other countries. The Air Force and armor represent 80 percent of Israel's military strength, and if this figure is compared with the situation in other countries, it offers a true reflection of her burden. According to the Institute's figures for 1974–1975, Britain, with a population of 56.4 million, maintained 900 tanks and 500 combat aircraft, and France, with a population of 52.4 million, had 950 tanks and 461 planes. In the same comparative table, Israel, with a population of only 3.3 million, had 2,700 tanks and 461 warplanes. In further contrast, Egypt, Syria, Jordan, and Iraq, with a total population of 58.6 million, maintained 6,600 tanks and 1,189 combat aircraft.

I believe that the extent of Israel's military strength has virtually reached its quantitative limits. It will be difficult for her to go on and on enlarging her army, acquiring many more planes and tanks at vaster cost, with their increasing sophistication, and tying down the young men on military service—while at the same time continuing to meet our constructive civilian goals of social and economic development, integrating the new immigrants, settling the land, creating new industries, and expanding our educational and health services. Therefore, the way in which Israel must secure a balance of forces against the Arab world, which grows in strength with extraordinary speed, lies in improving the quality of her weapons, a quality which should ensure that any Arab attempt to destroy Israel will involve the destruction of the attackers.

Despite Israel's victory, the Yom Kippur War left the country in a profound mood of discontent. The Arab defeat did not add balm to Israel's wounds, and the brilliant resourcefulness that enabled her to overcome the Arab initiative in launching the war did not hide the military and political failures and weaknesses which were exposed by the campaign. The Yom Kippur War was termed "a mishap," and a state inquiry commission headed by the president of the Supreme Court was appointed to investigate who among the political and military authorities was to be held responsible. Even before the Agranat Commission had got down to work, and long before it reported its findings, accusations were flung against those in charge of defense policy, primarily against me. And this chapter in the political and military chronicles of Israel was stigmatized as a failure, a failure which sprang from political short-sightedness, negligence, and shameful complacency.

At a meeting with ex-Rafi members which took place shortly after the war, I expressed the view that the greatest shock to the Israelis would be the discovery that what happened in the Yom Kippur War was not a "mishap" but an expression of present reality. This reality, different from the past, finds expression and is fully exposed in all its starkness only in a comprehensive test—political, military, human, economic, technological: the ultimate test of war. Israel's war was not a mishap, and its result was an absolute victory. It started with mistaken intelligence, errors were made in the course of the fighting— for the most part mistaken judgments and not negligence—and these errors extracted their price. There were failures in combat, and the Bar-Lev line fell. But Dunkirk, the fall of the Maginot line, the retreat of the Soviet army to Moscow, Pearl Harbor, the Philippines, and other chapters in the military history of the Great Powers experienced in the art of warfare should serve as a realistic measure of what can be expected in battle. Two thousand five hundred killed is a very heavy price for Israel. But to fight against an attacking army of one million troops equipped with the most modern weapons, including huge quantities of armor; to destroy 2,500 of their tanks; to shoot down 400 of their planes; to cross the Suez Canal and establish ourselves on the west bank; to capture the strongholds on the peak of Mount Hermon and to reach within a distance of twenty-five miles of Damascus—all this cannot be attained without heavy casualties.

Other nations that were caught in a situation similar to Israel on Yom Kippur regard this war, its progress, and its resolution as a glorious page in our history and a source of faith in our strength and future. Israel lost one-tenth of 1 percent of her population, which is an extremely high and painful price. But no army has ever succeeded, even under the most advantageous conditions, to destroy in combat thousands of enemy tanks and hundreds of warplanes with fewer casualties—one Israeli soldier killed for each enemy tank destroyed.

We must determine from the Yom Kippur War its lessons in political and military administration. Officers who prove ineffective should be replaced, and the sooner the better. This should also be true of ministers, the prime minister, and the parties in power. Military appointments instituted before the Yom Kippur War were made in good faith from among the best senior officers in the Israeli army. Only occasionally does the testing hour for a commander occur in peacetime. It certainly occurs in war, and an army fails to meet its national obligation if it does not remove officers when it becomes obvious that they do not live up to expectation and are not fulfilling the tasks assigned to them. Political leaders and Cabinet ministers did not reach their posts in secret and did not force themselves upon the public. Their personalities, their views, their policies were clearly presented at election time, and standing against them were other leaders from other parties who offered alternative policies.

Nor was the overall military information in the sole possession of a single individual. The chief of staff and the chief of Intelligence appeared before both Cabinet ministers and the Foreign Affairs and Security Committee of the Knesset, which comprises representatives of several parties. In these meetings, representatives of the army reported on the intelligence information in their possession and expressed their view and their assessment of what was happening. As for the responsibility of the public, the government's policies in economics, defense, and foreign affairs were conducted with the knowledge, approval, and according to the choice of its citizens. There is nothing wrong in criticizing members of the government, and the demand that they be changed is not only a right but an obligation on those who are convinced that change is necessary. What is wrong is the attempt to shake off responsibility and turn a nation seeking to ford its way through dire straits into a community of grumblers.

The Yom Kippur War took place in a political and military reality different from that which existed six years earlier during the Six Day War. The military and political might of the Arabs increased, and the countries of the West, including the United States, feared anything that could disturb the smooth flow of oil to them from the Middle East. If the Arabs had succeeded in defeating the Israeli army and capturing the Golan Heights and Sinai, we could have suffered a devastating blow. I do not know what is the military nature of the American commitment to the survival of Israel. But from our national and political point of view, even if we had been saved by American troops, our position would have been extremely grim.

Our military victory did not wipe out the hostile political reality in which we are living and against which we are struggling. But Israel herself and her readiness to persist in the realization of her ideals enabled her to withstand such a reality. Their significance is indefinable and indeterminate. They are bound up with the encouragement and support of other countries, notably the United States, and above all by the powerful bond between the Jewish people and the State of Israel, in their vision of us not simply as a Jewish state but as a community fulfilling the age-old yearning of Israel since its exile. We must learn to live and struggle with the difficult political reality of these times. But our foremost duty is to live up to the vision of ourselves, to fashion a pioneering state, a creative society that flourishes from the fruits of its own labor, a courageous state prepared to fight to the death to defend itself, a people of ideas and ideals striving to achieve their national and historic purpose—the revival of the Jewish nation in its homeland.

EPILOGUE

AFTER SEVEN YEARS in the Defense Ministry, I returned to civilian life. The nights were undisturbed by the telephone, and there was no dashing to the office in the morning. I spent my first free day out of government at Nahal Beersheba, a wadi in the Negev desert. That year we had enjoyed a very wet winter. I remembered the rains pouring down the slopes of the Hebron hills, streaming southward and producing flash floods in the desert wadis. The waters rushing through these normally dry river beds and overflowing their banks soften the sides of the gullies and cause great chunks of earth to crumble. So I went south.

It was now early summer. The water had vanished, but not its impact. I drove along the edge of the winding Beersheba wadi, and at one of the bends I saw what I had hoped to find. Glinting in the sunlight were several white stones embedded in the middle of the north wall of the gully. They were oddly out of place.

Six thousand years ago, this area was inhabited by people who existed by hunting and pasture. They lived in caves burrowed in the hillside, with narrow openings to make them easier to defend. The interior of the cave would be broad and comparatively high. A strip of floor skirting the walls would be paved with stones, usually smooth pebbles taken from the gully, to serve, probably with a covering of animal skins, as sleeping pallets.

Year after year, for thousands of years, the flash floods burst through the wadis, tearing at the slopes in a frenzy of erosion. What had once been the center of a hill, a haven for the cave dwellers of ages past, had now become the wall of a river bed, its stones curiously exposed and out of place—the stones that had caught my eye.

I attached a rope to the bumper of my jeep and clambered over the side, letting myself down the steep cliff toward the white stones. At first I had difficulty finding a hold for my toes, but after swinging and scrambling around I detected a soft stratum, a mixture of earth and ashes. It proved to be part of the floor of a cave. I crawled inside and started exploring. In one corner I noticed a depression in the ground surrounded by small rocks. This was the hearth, its fires used for cooking, for warmth, and for lighting the dwelling. Scattered among the ashes which covered the floor were potsherds, part of a milk churn, a cup, and the bottom section of a soot-laden cooking pot. Beneath the ashes, on the surface of the floor itself, were flint objects, mostly broken blades. I also found an ax head with an oblique edge fashioned from a large pebble. The inhabitants must have taken the rest of their vessels and implements with them when they left the cave, driven out by drought or by enemies, and wandered to another territory.

As I tried to learn more about this ancient cave community and recapture their daily pattern of living, the quiet within was occasionally shattered by the ultra-modern sounds of jet fighters roaring overhead. I examined the animal bones left over from their last meal, saw the fingerprints of the potters on the vessels they had molded. These cave dwellers had lived here some two thousand years before our Patriarch Abraham. They could neither read nor write, but they occasionally drew and painted on rock and stone and decorated their pottery with deep-red stripes. This was their home, the center of their lives. From here they would go out to hunt in the Negev and in the Sinai desert, and they were familiar with every wadi, every hill, every fold in the ground. This was their land, their birthplace, and they must have loved it. When they were attacked, they fought for it. And now here was I, at the end of a rope, having crawled through an opening in a cliffside across their threshold and inside their home. It was an extraordinary sensation. I crouched by the ancient hearth. It was as though the fire had only just died down, and I did not need to close my eyes to conjure up the woman of the house bending over to spark its embers into flame as she prepared the meal for her family. My family.

INDEX

(Page numbers followed by m indicate map references)